For centuries little was known about Nepal. Foreigners were banned so mountaineers and explorers could only gaze longingly at the gleaming Himalaya glimpsed from the distant plains of India. It was considered a secretive mountain kingdom, a Shangri-la grown rich on lucrative trade routes and protected by its ferocious Gurkha soldiers.

When it finally opened its borders in the 1950s, visitors found a country untouched by the outside world, a time-warp back to medieval days. There were no roads and the few cars there were in Kathmandu had been dismantled and carried through the hills by porters. A password was given out daily to the ruling classes, allowing them out after dusk while the rest of the population was under curfew.

Since then Nepal has done its best to catch up with the rest of the world. It's possible to visit its monuments, mountains and jungles with no more hindrance than the cost of an entrance ticket. Those mysterious mountains are now known to contain eight of the world's ten highest peaks, part of the Great Himalayan Range that makes up the breathtaking northern boundary of this stunning mountainous country.

The Kathmandu Valley, with its three ancient rival kingdoms of Kathmandu, Patan and Bhaktapur, contains no fewer than seven UNESCO World Heritage Sites, more than any other place in the world. Once at the heart of Himalayan trade between Tibet and India, the wealth this generated can still be seen in the palaces, shrines and temples of the valley. Modern development and the earthquakes of 1935 and 2015 have taken their toll, but if you know where to look you can still find the medieval cities first glimpsed by the early Western visitors and a way of life little changed by time.

Rob Ferguson

Best of
Nepal

❶ Kathmandu

Nepal's capital city offers gleaming Buddhist stupas, sacred Hindu temples and the opportunity to glimpse a living goddess, all mixed in with the congestion and chaos of a modern Asian city. Its Durbar (or Palace) Square was badly damaged in the 2015 earthquake but is still crammed with shrines, monuments and statues and is as atmospheric as ever. Page 38.

❷ Patan

Constructed around four Buddhist stupas built by the Emperor Ashoka in 250 BC, Patan is famed for the beauty of its Durbar Square, the skill of its craftsmen and its rich Buddhist heritage, with over 1200 statues and monuments dotting the city. Known locally as Lalitpur, meaning 'beautiful city', it's less frenetic than Kathmandu. Page 98.

❸ Bhaktapur

The best preserved of the Kathmandu Valley's three kingdoms, Bhaktapur's brick roads and architecture are reminiscent of how Kathmandu was 30 years ago. Wander its narrow streets and stumble on countless temples and shrines; its three squares contain some of Nepal's most impressive monuments. Despite being damaged in the 2015 earthquake it's still a must-visit destination. Page 124.

❺ Nuwakot

❹ Panauti

Panauti is located at the sacred confluence of three rivers. The Old Town is a warren of alleyways, courtyards and squares untouched by the modern world, its temples and shrines little visited and full of atmosphere. You are as likely to meet a goat as another tourist and can watch life unfold as it has for centuries. Page 161.

Situated on the top of a ridge with spectacular views over two valleys, the tiny village of Nuwakot was the base from which Prithvi Narayan Shah launched his campaign to conquer the Kathmandu Valley in 1768. His fort remains and, although damaged in the 2015 earthquakes, the village still offers great views and walks, historic buildings and an insight into village life. Page 199.

⑥ Bandipur

This small Newari town used to be the centre of a thriving trade route down to the Indian plains, and the wealth this generated throughout the 18th and 19th centuries is evident in the houses of its merchants. The high street is closed to traffic, allowing you to relax and enjoy the atmospheric town. Nearby views north to the Annapurna mountains are spectacular. Page 208.

⑦ Pokhara

Pokhara is regarded as the adventure capital of Nepal and is the gateway to the country's most popular trekking area. It's also a leading world destination for paragliding, with exceptional flying conditions. Throw in a beautiful lake to relax beside and you have a travellers' paradise. Page 220.

❽ The Annapurnas

Over half of all visitors who come to trek in Nepal do so in the Annapurna area and it's easy to understand why. It offers what is considered by many to be the world's greatest trek, the Annapurna Circuit, and has a huge variety of landscapes, peoples and cultures. Whether you want a few day walks from a beautiful lodge or a long, technical trek or climb, the Annapurnas can provide it. Page 236.

❾ Mustang and Dolpo

The high valleys of the Himalaya are home to tiny kingdoms that historically have more in common with Tibet than Nepal. There's a strong Buddhist culture, a hard lifestyle dependant on livestock and trade and a unique high-altitude landscape. Closed for many years to protect fragile cultures, you are still required to acquire special (expensive) permits in order to visit. Pages 245 and 338.

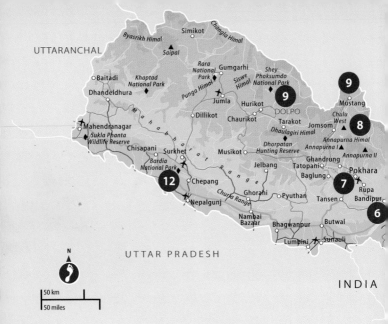

⑩ Chitwan

Nepal is not just about mountains. Its Terai zone, bordering India, is low lying, tropical and offers superb game- and birdwatching. Chitwan is the most famous of the national parks; once a hunting reserve for the country's rulers, it now attracts tourists intent on shooting tigers, elephants and one-horned Asian rhinos with their cameras. Page 250.

⑪ Everest

The trek to Everest Base Camp is an ambition for many trekkers, a high-altitude adventure that takes you through the homeland of the famous Sherpa people, now so synonymous with mountain climbing that their name has come to mean 'guide' to many people. It is a world of glaciers, snow-capped peaks and rocky terrain, dotted with squat stone-built villages under fluttering prayer flags. Page 290.

TIBET
(CHINA)

▲Manaslu
▲Himal Chuli
Syabru
Bensi ◆Langtang
National Park
Gorkha
Nuwakot
Mugling
KATHMANDU
Padriya
Patan
Panauti
Chitwan
National Park
Amlekhganj
Birgunj
Gaur
Jaleshwor
Janakpur

Melamchi
Pul Bazaar
Nagarkot
Bhaktapur
Sinduli
Marhi
Lalbandi
Bardibas
Muksar
Rajbiraj

Kodari
Ghumang
Namche
Bazaar
Jiri
Tumlingtar
Bhojpur
Mahendranagar
Koshi Tappu
Wildlife Reserve
Biratnagar

Everest▲
▲Lhotse
Sagarmatha
National Park
Kanchenjunga▲
SIKKIM
Taplejung
Dhankuta
Dharan
Itahari
Kakarbhitta
Birtamod
WEST
BENGAL

BIHAR

① ② ③ ④ ⑤ ⑩ ⑪

⑫ Bardia

In the west of the country Bardia National Park is a vast tract of indigenous forest that is home to many of Nepal's endangered animals. Reputedly the best place to get a glimpse of a tiger, it's wilder and a lot less visited than Chitwan; a true adventure. Whether you are exploring on foot, by vehicle or boat, the game viewing is excellent. Page 327.

Route planner

Nepal is an incredibly varied country. It's possible to spend months here and still have plenty more to see and do. The most important thing is not to rush your visit and to allow yourself time to experience the country as well as see it. One of the happiest memories for most visitors is the timeless feel and the friendliness of the people. By rushing from one place to the next you risk missing out on these.

All these suggestions start and finish in Kathmandu, by far the most popular arrival and departure point. Fortunately, it is well situated and, while no road journey in Nepal is easy given the mountainous terrain, it is the perfect base to explore from, no matter how long your stay.

One week

cultural highlights and the chance to glimpse the Himalaya

For those who don't have much time, or perhaps are combining their visit with another destination such as Tibet or India, a short stay can still allow a great insight into the country. You start with three nights in Kathmandu. On one day you go to its Durbar Square, hoping to see the living goddess, before visiting Swayambunath, the Monkey Temple, with its great views over the city. The next day you head to the sacred Hindu site at Pashupatinath and the nearby centre of the exiled Tibetan community Buddha, famous for its eyes that gaze out from the towering stupa. You then move to Bhaktapur, one of the valley's three historic cities, en route visiting the stunning Durbar Square of neighbouring Patan. You stay in Bhaktapur for two nights, enjoying the atmosphere of this unspoilt Newari settlement. As well as exploring its three beautiful squares you should also visit the nearby Changu Narayan temple, set in the hills to the north. Your last two days should be spent in the outer valley, visiting the small, unspoilt town of Panauti and the Buddhist shrine at Namobuddha, perched high on a forested ridge. The night is spent on the rim of the Kathmandu Valley, at one

Right: Bandipur
Opposite page: Bhairab Temple, Nuwakot

of the vantage points such as Dhulikhel, from where, in the early morning, you can glimpse the whole Himalayan range, from Annapurna to Everest.

An alternative would be to spend three nights in Kathmandu, as above, before flying to Pokhara to stay on the shores of Phewa Tal for a night or two, getting up early to hire a boat and see the Annapurnas towering above you in the dawn light, reflected in the still water of the lake. You then return to Bhaktapur for the last night or two.

Top: Pokhara countryside
Above: Rafting
Opposite page: Prayer hall

Two weeks

experience Nepal's culture, people, scenery and wildlife

Another week allows you to properly explore the country. After Kathmandu, drive to Nuwakot and spend the afternoon wandering around this quaint and historic village. The next day drive to the mountain town of Gorkha, the ancestral home of the great King Prithvi Narayan Shah, before continuing to the hill town of Bandipur. The next day you arrive in Pokhara for lunch and spend three days walking in the foothills of the Himalaya. The walks can be as easy or hard as you want, day walks or point-to-point trekking. It will give a real insight into the scale and beauty of the Himalaya, with Machapuchare, the 'Fishtail' mountain, towering over you.

From Pokhara head to Chitwan National Park and one of its lovely jungle lodges. Two nights here will allow you to enter the national park in search of tiger, leopard, wild elephant and Asian rhino, exploring by jeep, boat and on foot. The jungle landscape is pure Kipling and a complete contrast to the mountains. From here you can return by road to the Kathmandu Valley and a night or two in Bhaktapur.

Three to four weeks

explore the heart of the Himalaya and enjoy a wilderness safari

A three-week trip will let you explore some of the less-visited areas, getting a real insight into the country and its people. After a few nights in Kathmandu, you can head off on the adventure of your choosing, before returning to finish your trip at Bhaktapur. If you are a trekker, then you have time to enjoy a trek into the heart of the mountains. Gokyo Lake in the Everest region offers stunning high-altitude scenery without the crowds of Base Camp and a better view of Everest. Or perhaps take on the Annapurna Sanctuary, a varied trek that ends with one of the most spectacular mountain views on Earth. If rafting is your passion, then head off on 10-day expedition down the wild Karnali River in the west of the country.

Whichever activity you choose, there is time at the end to fly to Bardia National Park, the largest reserve in Nepal and the best place to see tigers. Much less visited than Chitwan it has a wilder feel to it that makes it a true wilderness adventure. Return by air to Kathmandu or Bhaktapur at the end.

Best
treks

Langtang

Popular with those who have less time but still want to trek in the High Himalaya, the Langtang region is accessed by a scenic drive north from Kathmandu. You may not see any of the famous peaks but you will get stunning scenery varying from forest to high-altitude valleys. The region was very badly affected by the 2015 earthquakes, the main village of Langtang being completely destroyed by a landslip at great cost of life. Trekking is possible once more, and crucial to the local communities, but be aware of the scars that still exist. Page 186.

Manaslu

If you are looking for adventure, the little-visited Manaslu Circuit is similar to the Annapurna Circuit of 30 years ago. You walk through villages unchanged for centuries, the locals getting on with their traditional way of life, from the Gurung-inhabited terraced lowlands to the Tibetan-influenced higher valleys. There is a high pass offering stunning views, forests, fields and high-altitude desert. The teahouses and lodges are more basic and although many were damaged in the 2015 earthquake, they are being repaired and are open for business. A traditional camping trek is a good, if more expensive, option here. It's worth the effort to see such variety and an unchanged Nepal. Page 212.

The Annapurnas

Trekking in the Annapurna area offers the most amazing variety of landscapes, cultures and peoples of almost any area in the world. The Annapurna Circuit is frequently described as one of the world's great treks, taking you to Buddhist monasteries and Hindu shrines, over high passes and through lush rhododendron forest, all under the shadow of the Annapurna Himal, the world's tenth highest mountain. There is also the wonderful Sanctuary trek into the heart of the peaks, as well as an abundance of shorter foothill routes and day walks, all easily accessed from the lake city of Pokhara. Page 236.

Mustang

For many years the Mustang Kingdom was closed to foreigners, its medieval Tibetan culture and desolate high-desert landscape out of the reach of ordinary travellers. This changed in 1992 when special permits started to be issued, but their cost, as well as the remoteness of the area – at the top of the Kali Gandaki Valley – kept visitor numbers down. These days, with a jeep road to Kagbeni and flights to Muktinath, as well as a relaxing of regulations on independent trekkers, 2000-3000 people visit annually to experience this amazing landscape and culture. Go before it changes. Page 245.

Everest and the Khumbu

Perhaps the most famous trekking area in the world, the Base Camp trek is high on many walkers' wish list. Then there is the Gokyo Lakes trek, also offering superb views of the High Himalaya, glaciers and better views of Everest itself. Other options include exploring the lower Khumbu region with the Buddhist monasteries at Thangboche, Pangboche and Thame or trying your hand at one of the trekking peaks in the region, such as Island or Mera peaks. Page 290.

Kanchenjunga and Makalu

In the east of Nepal, the rivers have cut deep valleys heading south to the plains of India. Trekking is challenging with days of ascent and descent. The rewards are vast swathes of the Himalaya little visited and with untouched landscapes and communities. Kanchenjunga is a challenging but rewarding trek, while the foothills of Makalu offer a spectacular but little-used approach to the Khumbu and Everest. Pages 310 and 313.

Below: Manaslu
Opposite top: Langtang
Opposite bottom: Annapurna Circuit

Sadhu, Pashupatinath Temple

When to go

... and when not to

Climate

The wonderful climate as well as the varied geography, vegetation, wildlife, culture, architecture and of course the people, all contribute to making Nepal a year-round destination.

1 October-20 November

Autumn has always been the busiest tourist season in Nepal. As the post-monsoon rains lessen through late September Nepal is left freshly washed, the fields a deep green with mature rice, rivers running full and mountains breaking through the cumulus glisten under their new coat of snow.

The early part of October is still pretty warm on the rivers and humid in the low-lying wildlife national park areas of Chitwan, Sukla Phanta, Bardia and Kosi Tahapu, so, while still worth a visit, it's best to leave these areas until the latter part of your Nepal stay.

20 November-20 December

The oft-neglected shoulder period of late autumn is characterized by clear skies and more settled weather, the ambient and night temperatures drop, but the days are delightful with lots of sunshine and there should be plenty of 'shorts and shirtsleeve' times. Unless there is a spell of bad weather, high-pass crossings and climbing are still possible but the weather forecasts need proper checking.

21 December-28 February

From Christmas onwards (or after the first hint of winter snow in the hills) avoid treks over 3500 m and do not attempt high-pass crossings. Should the weather deteriorate, being caught out at over 4000 m during the winter can be dangerous.

Consider foothill treks between 1000 m and 3000 m. Shorter daylight hours make for cosy time spent indoors around lodge stoves. There is generally still daily sunshine, clear views and fewer trekkers, making it ideal for the Annapurna foothills. Non-trekkers will still find much to do in and around Pokhara and the climate is also ideal for driving trips.

Sometime during this period there can be a three- to six-day period when the grey clouds blow in from the west, the temperature drops and the rains come to all low-lying areas. Snow can dust the Kathmandu Valley rim and settle on the hills at altitudes over 3000 m.

The east–west belt of country bordering India in the south of Nepal lies a bare 200 m above sea level. Being lower, one would expect warmer conditions there, but it can feel very cold when overnight mist fails to burn off and the damp persists through the day. However, it does add atmosphere and excitement to 'rhino hunting' through the high grassland of Chitwan or Bardia national parks.

1 March-15 April

Although this is the other so-called 'high season', tourist numbers never match those of the post-monsoon period, though as far as conditions go they should. Spring is in the air, rhododendron forests are in bloom, birds are singing and wild flowers are bursting through patches of winter snow. It's a beautiful time to visit Nepal and sometime between late March and mid-April those high passes and more remote routes once again become accessible. However, north Mustang, Dolpo and Humla visits are best left until the very end of April and into May and June. That west part of Nepal lies further north than the rest of the country and, on the north-facing slopes, snow is very slow to clear.

This time of year is still good for foothill treks but spring haze, caused by the great variation in temperatures between the Gangetic Plain to the south and the High Himalaya, can diminish mountain views.

With lengthening days and ever warmer temperatures, April and May are the favourite months for climbing expeditions (even though the first ascent of Everest in 1953 did not take place until 29 May). It is also a recommended period for river running, driving trips, Pokhara and wildlife safaris. In the safari parks there is much 'burning off' and grass cutting in the spring. This does not add to the beauty but more open areas improve the chance of wildlife sightings.

20 April-15 June

Late spring is one of the mountains' best-kept secrets. Almost all the trekkers have gone home and, for higher-altitude trekking, the Everest area particularly can be superb; there are few problems with flights and none with accommodation. Temperatures in Kathmandu and Pokhara are pretty warm (28-36°C) and it is hazy and dry with some afternoon thunderstorms. However, it is not the best time of year lower down. The Terai is hot (32-38°C) in this pre-monsoon period, but if you do not mind the heat too much, it can be a good time for wildlife viewing. The animals get lethargic and seek out water holes and rivers to laze by.

The monsoon does not settle in until late June and for many the second half of May and June is considered the finest time for trekking in the rain shadow areas of Mustang, Manang, Dolpo and the far west.

From late March onwards cloud build-up can start early in the day – from 1000 or thereabouts – with the odd thunderstorm in the afternoon. With long daylight hours it is best to start the day's trekking, early and aim to complete your trek by 1400-1500.

16 June to 30 September

Rain dominates the monsoon period but by no means is it all downpour. The rains cool things down and the light can be very beautiful. Often the days dawn bright and dry and rains do not start until the afternoon. The Pokhara area receives 50% more rain than Kathmandu as the water-laden clouds are pushed up the steep south face of the Annapurnas and then it can really pour. The Terai is hot and humid and the leeches come out to play.

But once the rice is planted it is also the greatest time for festivals in the Kathmandu Valley (see below). The countryside grows green and verdant and from mid-September on, the rain clouds start to break up and the freshly washed snow-covered mountains shine through.

Trekking is still possible in most areas, although Ghorepani in the Annapurna foothills has been called 'the leech capital of the world'. Many people cannot abide them, but in reality they do little harm and are no more than an inconvenience on the main trails, as long as you know how to deal with them.

Further north in Manang, Mustang and Dolpo, the rain shadow areas lying to the north of the east–west line of the Himalaya, conditions can be wonderful. The challenge is getting there and back from Kathmandu or Pokhara.

Note The earthquakes that hit Nepal in April and May 2015 caused much damage to a swathe of towns and hill villages running east from the epicentre near the old city of Gorkha. Tragically many thousands of people were killed and injured and the aftershocks rattled on for months. Reconstruction has been slow but the gears are grinding – just.

Naturally it harmed tourist arrivals. Now what Nepal needs most is the return of those visitors from all parts of the world; it still has everything to offer and you will be most welcome.

ON THE ROAD

Trekking seasons

October and November are generally considered the best months. The air is clear and the vegetation still lush after the monsoon. Both day and night temperatures are pleasant at lower elevations, ranging from around 25°C to 3°C. Above 3000 m, meanwhile, temperatures may drop to well below zero at night. These are also the months when the major trails are at their busiest and when flights and guesthouses are often fully booked.

There are two highly recommended treks which suit the period between 20 November and 20 December but are often overlooked. The first is in the east, in the Sherpa country surrounding Junbesi in the 'lower' Solu Khumbu. Most trekkers fly to the Khumbu/Everest area, zooming over the top of this fine country before landing at Lukla. Little do they realize that below them lie wonderful rhododendron and pine forests, apple orchards, bee-keeping hives and fascinating monasteries. The second trek, away in the west in the oft-neglected Lamjung Himal area, a high spine of unspoiled country and villages offering wonderful views of the Fishtail (Machapuchare), the Annapurnas and Manaslu. There are some homestays low down but wonderful tented trek country higher up. This is also an ideal time for those lodge-supported foothill treks between 1000 m and 3000 m in the Annapurna foothills.

December and January are colder, especially at higher altitudes. This is probably the best time of year for completely unobstructed views. High passes, such as Thorong La on the Annapurna Circuit, are closed. Everest looks bare with little snow cover and temperatures at the higher altitudes are very cold. Normally at some stage a winter storm sets in lasting three to seven days and bringing snow to the mountains and rain to the rest of the country.

From **late February** temperatures begin to rise with the steady heating of the Tibetan High Plateau. **March and April** are hazy with views becoming obscured. However, this is the best time of year for seeing both wildlife and the blossoming of the Himalayan flora, notably the rhododendron. **May** is very hot and quite dusty lower down but still good at higher altitudes. Streams are nearly dry and there are regular thunderstorms.

Trekking during the monsoon (**mid-June to mid-September**) can be recommended only for the most ardent and experienced. The climate is hot, humid and uncomfortable at lower elevations. Rivers also rise dramatically and often become unfordable, while many trails become leach infested and treacherously slippery. Cloud obscures mountain views for much of the time. Equipment gets damp and heavier and you will be able to cover shorter distances. It is, however, the time when the vegetation is at its most luxuriant. Weather in late September is unpredictable, but the trails are much less crowded and hence more pleasant. Beware of leeches during the monsoon (see page 451).

Festivals

There are numerous festivals to enjoy, a highlight for many people and worth witnessing if you have the chance.

Every temple has its special festivals. Some, like **Pashupatinath** in the Kathmandu Valley, have festivals that draw Hindus from all over Nepal and India. Others are village and family events. At festival times, you can see villagers walking in small groups, brightly dressed and often highly spirited.

Two solar calendars, the Nepalese and Gregorian, are in common use, but there are three lunar calendars: Nepalese, Newari and Tibetan. (See also Calendars, page 396.) Exact dates of festivals change annually and are calculated by astrologers. The Department of Tourism in Kathmandu publishes an annual brochure. The **Nepali New Year** is in mid-April and the two most important festivals are **Dasain** and **Tihar** in September/October (Nepali months are in brackets).

January-February (Magha)

Magha Sankranti marks the transition from winter to spring. **Tribeni Mela**, on the new moon, is held on the banks of the Narayani river. **Basanta Panchami** celebrates the start of the spring season. Ceremonies at Kathmandu's Hanuman Dhoka Palace, street parades by children and dedications at temples characterize this festival. **Magha Purnima** is celebrated on the last day of Magha, when bathers walk from the Bagmati river ghats to various temples and take a ritual bath in the Salindi river.

February-March (Phalgun)

Rashtriya Prajatantra Divas (or **Democracy Day**) includes parades and processions to celebrate the 1951 overthrow of the autocratic Rana regime. **Holi** is a colourful festival to mark the beginning of spring. People put on new clothes which get ruined when they go round throwing coloured powder, coloured water and just plain water

(often in small balloons), at each other. The **Tibetan New Year** is marked by colourful processions and vigils, especially at Swayambhunath and Bodhnath. **Maha Shiva Ratri** ('Great Shiva's Night') is marked with special celebrations at Pashupatinath which hosts a giant *mela* (fair). There are all-night vigils and music, while many pilgrims take a holy bath every three hours. There is also a gun salute at Kathmandu's Tundikhel and thousands of oil lamps and bonfires at night brighten the festivities.

March-April (Chaitra)

Ghorajatra is celebrated especially in Patan with horse races and displays of gymnastics and horsemanship. Animal sacrifices are offered in the temples of the Ashta Matrikas ('eight mother goddesses'). **Pasa Chare** is a Newar festival, a time of hospitality among Newari people. On the same day as the horse show of the Ghorajatra festival, the demon Gurumpa is carried to the Tundikhel in a midnight procession. **Chaitra Dasain** and the festival of the **Seto Macchendranath** occur simultaneously in Kathmandu. **Ram Navami**, at the magnificent **Janaki Mandir** in Janakpur, celebrates the birthday of Rama.

April-May (Baisakh)

Nepali New Year celebrations of **Bisket** in Bhaktapur, **Balkumari Jatra** in Thimi, and **Rato Macchendranath Jatra** in Patan. **Matatirtha Snan** in late April is highlighted by ritual baths at Matatirtha, near Thankot, for people whose mothers have died in the past year. **Astami** is highlighted in Naxal by ritual sacrifices to ensure a prosperous summer. **Buddha Jayanta** is celebrated throughout Nepal to mark the birthday of the Buddha. There are many pilgrimages to Buddhist shrines, especially to the Swayambhunath and Bodhnath stupas.

May-June (Jyestha)

Sithinakha, throughout the Kathmandu Valley, celebrates the 'divine warrior' by giving domestic offerings. **Mani Rimdu** is a three-day Sherpa religious festival at Namche Bazaar's Thame Monastery. Monks seek to gain merit by performing masked dramas and dances. The festival is repeated six months later at the Thyangboche Monastery.

July-August (Shrawan)

Ghanta Karna is held in all Newar settlements and marks the completion of the paddy planting season in the Kathmandu Valley. The festival is a remnant of demon worship and the decorations are intended to ward off evil spirits. **Naga Panchami**, in the Kathmandu Valley, honours the *nagas*, the divine serpents with control over rain. Celebrations include pinning paintings depicting *nagas* to doors and being blessed by priests. *Lakhe*, mask dancing, also starts in Kathmandu. **Janai Purnima**, or **Rakshya Vandhana**, is celebrated in honour of Shiva Mahadev ('Shiva Great God') with special festivities held at the Kumbeshwar Mandir in Patan and at Gosainkund Lake in the mountains north of the valley. Brahmins and Chhetris renew their *munja* (sacred thread) on this day, while priests distribute yellow threads (*rikhi doro*) to other castes.

August-September (Bhadra)

Indrajatra starts in Bhaktapur with the erection of a tall wooden pole to honour the God of Rain. **Krishnastami** is celebrated in 11 sanctuaries and temples dedicated to Krishna, especially the Krishna Mandir in Patan's Durbar Square which commemorates Krishna's birth with offerings of tulsi plants. **Pancha Dan** (or **Banda Jatra**), the festival of the five summer gifts, is celebrated at the Swayambhunath stupa and throughout the Kathmandu Valley. Women give rice and grains to priests who march through the streets chanting hymns. **Gokarna Aunshi**, Fathers' Day, is highlighted by ritual bathing in the Bagmati river at Gokarna commemorating fathers who have died during the year. **Teej Brata** is marked throughout the Kathmandu Valley with prayers to Shiva and Parvati for a happy married life. Married women traditionally wear their scarlet and gold wedding saris and take ceremonial baths in the Bagmati to honour husbands.

September-October (Ashwin)

The **Ganesh Festival**, on the September full moon, honours Ganesh without whose blessing no religious ceremony or major undertaking begins. **Dasain** (or **Durga Puja**) is the major annual festival. On the first of the 10-day festival, *puja* is marked in homes by planting and nurturing barley seeds in sand and water from the holy river. The devout bathe in holy places over the next nine days. On **Phulpati**, the seventh day, sacred flowers and leaves from the Gorkha palace reach Kathmandu where they are received by crowds accompanied by brass bands at the Hanuman Dhoka gate and the firing of guns in the Tundikhel. On the eighth day, **Mahasthami**, the devout fast and sacrifice animals including buffaloes, sheep and goats on Kalratri ('black night'). This is followed on the ninth day with elaborate mass sacrifices at the magnificent Taleju Mandir in Kathmandu's Durbar Square (open to Hindus on this single day alone) and the sprinkling of the blood blessed by the temple's eponymous goddess on all vehicles and instruments in the hope of preventing accidents. The climax is on the 10th day, **Vijaya Dashami** (the Day of Victory), which marks the triumph of Rama and Durga over evil. Hindus receive a *tikka* of vermillion, curd and rice on the forehead from elders to ensure health and happiness. The fortnight ends with the full moon night when many women start a month-long fast. Dasain has eight days of masked dances in Patan's Durbar Square with kite flying and erection of bamboo swings.

October-November (Kartik)

Tihar (or **Diwali**) is the five-day festival of lights. On the **first day**, small lamps are lit and the first portion of the family meal is given to crows. On the **second day**, dogs are decorated with garlands and a *tikka* on the forehead. The crow and the dog are associated with Yama, the god of death, who is propitiated with offerings and thanks. The **third day** is marked with worshipping and garlanding cows. It is also Lakshmi Puja when thousands of tiny wick lamps and candles are lit on windowsills and in homes throughout the country, to invite the goddess of fortune to enter the home, and fireworks are set off. The **fourth day** is Newari New Year when people worship the divine in one's self (Ma Puja – 'me worship') and families get together. The fifth and **final day** is Bhai Tika, when sisters place multicoloured *tikkas* on their brothers' foreheads to protect them from evil, and brothers make generous gifts in return. **Tihar** marks the end of the harvest, the beginning of the year and the worship of animals. **Haribodhani Ekadasi** is a pilgrimage in honour of Vishnu to Budhanilikantha.

Rato Macindrnath, with its great 60-ft-high chariot being towed around Patan by hundreds of devotees, is to hasten the onset of the pre-monsoon rains; **Ghora Jatra** is the horse festival on the Tudhikel in the middle of Kathmandu; and **Gai Jatra**, the cow festival during the monsoon in Bhaktapur, is when the souls of those who died during the previous years are released to rest in peace. And it is not only the big cities that celebrate the festivals, there are nearly as many in the hill villages and along the length of the Terai as well.

November-December (Marga)

Bala Chaturdasi is celebrated with a pilgrimage to Pashupati and offerings to the deity, Pashupatinath. Lighting of oil lamps on the first night of celebrations is followed by a morning bathe in the Bagmati river. Pilgrims follow the traditional route through the Mrigasthali Forest offering seeds and sweets so that dead relations can benefit in the next world. **Vivaha Panchami** in Janakpur recalls Rama's marriage to Sita with drama, dance and music.

What to do

from temples and tigers to trekking

Birdwatching

Birdwatching in Nepal is outstanding. There have been 876 species recorded to date, including 35 globally threatened species, 19 near-threatened species and 15 restricted-range species. Look out for the spiny babbler, the country's only endemic species. Several of the national parks, especially in the Terai, are popular destinations on birdwatching itineraries.

Climbing

If you like climbing, then where better to visit than the home of eight of the world's 10 highest peaks? If you have the experience (and money) you can attempt to climb Mount Everest with one of the climbing agencies that offer to get you to the summit. There has been talk of tightening up on the permits to the main peaks following a series of accidents over the last few years, but currently they are still available.

If you have less lofty ambitions consider one of the 30+ trekking peaks currently on offer. While many of these are more technical than the name suggests, some have little technical requirement and will allow you to achieve your goal with limited mountaineering experience. As they range in height between 5650 and 6476 m, the peaks are still a major achievement. The highest, Mera Peak (6476 m), is one of the least technical.

Cultural tourism

Kathmandu has more UNESCO World Heritage Sites than any other city on Earth and away from these you'll find small shrines and statues on the corners of many streets. The traditional architecture and hidden courtyards may be vanishing in the modern development of Kathmandu, but it can still easily be found in the outlying towns and villages where life goes on as it has for centuries.

There are festivals every month, celebrated with enthusiasm and colour. Most depend on the lunar calendar so make sure you check with your operator before booking as the dates change year to year. Some only happen every few years, some every decade or so.

Outside the cities Buddhist shrines and Hindu temples still litter the landscape, unchanged by tourism and time; and don't forget that the Buddha himself was born in Nepal, in the small Terai town of Lumbini.

Mountain biking

In the last 25 years, jeep roads and tracks have steadily pushed their way up into the mountains, linking isolated valleys and communities that previously were many days' walk from the outside world. These have in turn opened up myriad opportunities for the mountain biker. The unsurfaced routes offer well-graded ascents and white-knuckles descents, as well as being comparatively free of traffic.

Paragliding

Over the last 15 years the lakeside town of Pokhara has become one of Asia's leading adventure sport destinations. The thermals and currents created by the Annapurna mountains and surrounding lakes make it ideal for sports such as paragliding, and several specialist firms are based in the town. The rewards are obvious. As you soar high above the lake, you get unrivalled views of the whole Himalayan chain stretching away in either direction. It gives you a true feeling of the scale of the landscape as well as the excitement of the flight and landing. Longer flights take you nearer to the mountains themselves – one local pilot has even flown over Machapuchare itself at 6993 m – with the use of oxygen.

Rafting

As you would expect from a country whose northern border comprises the highest mountains on Earth, its rivers channel vast quantities of melting snow and offer some of the finest rafting on the planet. There is a full range of difficulty, from gentle Grade II rapids ideal for beginners and families, right through to white-knuckle Grade Vs for the experienced, thrill-seeker.

Rafting trips

From east to west, Nepal offers an unparalleled diversity in its river layout cutting through the Himalaya and foothills with descents of Grade I-VI. Routes and itineraries depend on the season, water level and local conditions. Also, while new stretches of river are being opened, so old routes may be disrupted by the building of hydroelectric projects.

Suggested tours

Trisuli (1 day) A short drive from Kathmandu, you can do this when heading to Chitwan or Pokhara. Some fun rapids, the chance to swim some rapids if the water level is right, and a few good jumping spots. A good introduction to rafting and for families.

Bhote Kosi (two days) A short drive from Kathmandu, this is a rafting adventure that can be fitted into a longer itinerary. It's got some big rapids – Grade V – so you will get wet and need to do your bit by paddling the boat when instructed. A real adrenalin ride.

Kali Gandaki (three days) Grade III-IV rapids, lovely countryside and some camping nights gives this trip an expedition feel while still experiencing some decent water. Starting near Pokhara it combines well with a trek in the Annapurnas.

Sun Kosi (nine days) This trip provides a real rafting adventure that combines great rapids with amazing mountain scenery, out-of-the-way villages and tropical jungle. Camping on remote sandy beaches under the stars makes it a real adventure.

Karnali (10 days) Remote, big rapids and no way out except down the river, this is a real expedition, travelling through some impressive gorges and untouched scenery. Experienced rafters only.

Recommended companies

Himalayan Encounters, T01-470 0335, www.himalayanencounters.com.
Mountain River Rafting, T01-470 0770, www.mountainriverrafting.com.
Ultimate Descents Nepal, T01-470 0866, www.udnepal.com.

See also Rafting essentials, page 435.

Trekking

From gentle day walks in the Kathmandu Valley or the foothills around Pokhara, to high-altitude treks to the Base Camps of Everest and Kanchenjunga, Nepal is synonymous with trekking.

Other than proper planning and taking informed, sensible care of yourself, your fellow trekkers and surroundings whilst en route, there is no definitive 'way' of trekking nor any speed at which you have to walk; the main thing is to enjoy the experience.

The regions of **Langtang**, **Gosainkund** and **Helambu**, all to the north of Kathmandu, lack the 8000-m-plus giants and therefore are not quite as popular as Annapurna and Everest. But what the area does offer is a combination of High Himalayan scenery with culture and village life, all within driving distance of Kathmandu.

Everest is the magnet of Nepal. Many are attracted by the mountain itself, others by the **Solu Kumbu** region, the home of the Sherpas, and some by both. The **Everest Base Camp** trek remains very popular and most treks involve being at altitude and requires you to retrace your route.

Trekking from Pokhara tends to be into the **Annapurna Conversation Area**. There are three classic treks: the Annapurna Circuit (page 243), Annapurna (or Machapuchure) Base Camp (page 243) and the Ghorepani foothills trek (ideal for those who want to travel light; page 243).

Pokhara is also the gateway for treks into **Mustang**. Geographically part of the Tibetan Plateau it is remote, cold and covered in snow through the winter. At 3000-4000 m it is not particularly high but the dust, cold and unrelenting winds make conditions harsh. You are rewarded, however, by a unique culture and breathtaking landscapes, with natural colours enhanced by incredible architecture.

Far eastern Nepal has a number of long treks up the Arun river towards Everest, to the **Makalu Base Camp** as well as to **Kangchenjunga**. Less developed than the more accessible central Nepal treks, these treks require more planning and preparation.

Western Nepal is the least-developed trekking area. Treks from **Jumla**, **Dunai** and **Simikot** are a logistical challenge and you need to be fully prepared before undertaking them. The treks to **Rara Lake** and the **Dolpo** area also needs planning, with most visitors using the services of a tour operator.

Prominent peaks

Of the world's 10 highest peaks, eight are in Nepal: **Everest** (8848 m), **Kanchenjunga** (8598 m), **Lhotse** (8511 m),

Makalu (8475 m), Dhaulagiri (8167 m), Manaslu (8162 m), Cho Oyu (8153 m) and Annapurna I (8091 m). Of course, climbing expeditions for all the above require experience, detailed planning and mountaineering permits.

But there are currently 33 lesser peaks, euphemistically known as 'trekking peaks'. The somewhat arbitrary distinction effectively means that climbers can bypass the ponderous and costly process of applying for a mountaineering permit. Many of these trekking peaks nevertheless require high standards of climbing skills and should not be attempted lightly. They include: Mera Peak (6654 m), Chulu Peak (6584 m), Singu Chuli (Flute Peak; 6501 m), Hiunchuli (6441 m), Chulu West (6419 m), Kusum Kanguru (6367 m), Parchemuche (6187 m), Imja Tse (Island Peak; 6183 m), Lobuche (6119 m), Pisang (6091 m), Kawande (6011 m), Ramdung (5925 m), Paldor Peak (5896 m), Khongma Tse (Mehra; 5849 m), Kangja Chuli (5844 m), Pokalde (5806 m), Tharpu Chuli (Tent Peak; 5663 m); Mardi Himal (5587 m). Special permits are still required and a qualified guide must accompany each group.

See also Trekking essentials, page 437.

Wildlife watching

With a total of 20 reserves covering a vast range of landscapes and temperate zones, Nepal has some excellent wildlife-viewing opportunities. Chitwan and Bardia national parks in Nepal's Terai provide the chance to see some of the sub-continents rarest animals. The one-horned Asian rhino, wild elephant and tigers all live in the parks, as well as leopards, spotted deer and a host of other animals and birds (see birdwatching, above). In the rivers are gharial and mugger crocodiles, as well as the critically endangered river dolphin.

As you trek in the mountains you may see musk deer or red pandas, while at high altitude there is the elusive snow leopard. And who knows, you too might come across evidence of the yeti, just as Edmund Hillary and Eric Shipton did on their 1951 Everest recce.

Where to stay

from family guesthouses to upmarket lodges

In 1953 Boris Lissanevitch, a White Russian who owned a popular club in Calcutta, opened the **Royal Hotel** in Kathmandu at the invitation of the king. It was Nepal's first hotel for foreigners, an elegant establishment set in an old Rana palace. His restaurant, **The Chimney** still exists (see page 92).

You can stay cheaply by Western standards and most hotels are clean and comfortable. Prices range from US$10-500 per night, for anything from family guesthouses and Airbnb rooms to international-standard hotels in and around Kathmandu. There are also excellent options in other destinations, such as Pokhara and Chitwan.

If staying at the more budget properties, it's best to look at your room before agreeing to stay.

During the peak seasons (March-April and October-November), rooms are often heavily booked in the more popular hotels. Although you may not be able to get a room in your first choice, Kathmandu and Pokhara in particular have a surplus of accommodation so it is never usually a problem to find a decent room close by.

In the cities of Kathmandu, Patan and Bhaktapur some classic old buildings are now being tastefully adapted into Western-standard accommodation. The equivalent in the more remote areas of the mountain foothills are the recently developed 'homestays' offering accommodation with local families.

Most of the accommodation available in Chitwan and Bardia national parks is quite basic. Sauraha, the small town beside Chitwan that has most of the park's

Price codes

Where to stay	Restaurants
$$$$ over US$150	$$$ over US$12
$$$ US$75-150	$$ US$7-12
$$ US$40-75	$ under US$7
$ under US$40	

Price of a double room in high season, including taxes.

Prices for a two-course meal for one person, excluding drinks or service charge.

budget accommodation, has developed and grown over the last 20 years, with a plethora of modern hotels offering rooms equipped with fans or air conditioning.

The lodges and camps that used to be inside the park were all closed in 2011 when the government refused to renew their leases saying they were intrusive to the wildlife. Most moved to locations just outside the park and offer excellent facilities with packages that include food and activities. They can be expensive but are a great way to explore the park away from the crowds.

Thakurdwara, Bardia's accommodation village, is more traditional, with most accommodation still in Tharu-style cottages and with less reliable electricity. There are also one or two upmarket lodges.

Most of the hotels in the Terai towns and cities are basic and functional, aimed at local travellers rather than tourists and their restaurants serve Nepalese and Indian food only. However, prices are inexpensive by Western standards. Top-end accommodation is scarce and there are virtually no luxury hotels.

Bathroom and toilet facilities

Unless you are on a very small budget, most hotels in Kathmandu and Pokhara offer en suite bathrooms. Many, including some of the top-end ones, do not have bathtubs, but they do have good-quality showers. Despite the rivers that cascade from the high mountains to the plains, water is in short supply in the main cities and the hotels are encouraged to conserve it. If a bath is important to you, check with the hotel before booking.

All hotels promise hot water but it may not be available 24 hours a day: many use solar power, so if all the hot water is used in the evening it's unlikely to have warmed up by morning.

Electricity

Nepal suffers from a chronic shortage of electricity, especially during the winter and spring when river levels are low – most of the country's electricity comes from hydroelectric. You may experience 'load-shedding', when areas of town have their electricity turned off for periods of the day or night. All hotels will have a schedule of these power cuts and most have generators they run during the blackouts, although many only use them during the evening and some restrict what the electricity can be used for (for example, lighting and charging but not TV and air-conditioning units. You can check with a hotel before you book to see what their policy is.

Mountain accommodation

The standard of accommodation in the mountains has also greatly improved over the last 20 years. In the 1990s teahouses could be very basic, especially at higher altitudes, with dormitory accommodation and freezing temperatures. Trekkers with better budgets often chose to camp as a more comfortable option.

These days the lodges have improved greatly, with private rooms and much better bathroom facilities, sometimes private. Many use solar power and have hot water and most offer more varied menus cooked on kerosene stoves rather than the traditional fire. There are even chains of small, luxury lodges offering a new level of comfort and the promise of Wi-Fi. But remember that just because you can log on doesn't mean you can download.

Some of the less-frequented areas, such as Manaslu, still have more basic offerings, but popular trekking areas like the Annapurna foothills and Everest Base Camp have many excellent facilities.

Camping

Until the early 1990s, camping was a popular option on most mountain treks. These days it is only used on the most remote itineraries, climbing trips or by special request. The rise of the teahouse and lodge as a cheaper and more comfortable option has taken away the demand.

Nevertheless, there is something wonderful about travelling through remote areas of Nepal, camping beside small villages and communities that rarely see visitors, sitting in mess tents and around campfires. Your bags are carried for you by porters, a cook prepares all your meals and you are guided by local Sherpas. It's certainly worth considering, especially if travelling as a family or group, when the price becomes much more competitive.

Food
& drink

from momo and dal to rakshi and chang

Food

One dish more than any other characterizes the food of Nepal: *dal bhat*. *Dal* is a lentil sauce that is eaten with the *bhat* (rice). It is usually served with *tarkari*, a generic name for a vegetable curry that can be prepared in different ways according to seasonal availability of vegetables and local preferences, and *achar* (pickles). Typically, you will be given a plateful of *dal bhat* with refills periodically served until you have eaten enough, making it the Nepalese equivalent of an all-you-can-eat buffet.

Meat curry is also popular, but as meat is expensive many households only have it on special occasions. Tibetan influences increase the further north you go, although perennial favourites, such as the *momo* (a stuffed dumpling, fried or steamed), are widely available in the lower regions too.

There are plenty of restaurants in Kathmandu and Pokhara serving 'typical Nepali food'. This generally consists of rice, *dal* and two or more types of *tarkari* (with or without meat), sometimes accompanied by *rakshi* (local alcoholic brew), and followed by a Nepali sweet and tea.

In Kathmandu there are also many excellent restaurants offering Western, along with Indian and Tibetan, dishes at reasonable prices. The city has acquired a justifiable reputation for its steaks: served with garlic sauce, cheese, rum, brandy, mushroom, pepper, onion or any other variety of sauce, or the plain fillet steak, sometimes called *mignon, classic* or *à la française*. Steaks are sometimes buffalo meat, because of the sacredness of the cow to Hindus. Often in Kathmandu, however, it will be genuine beef that is served, imported from India.

Nepali eating habits and customs

A cup of tea usually starts the day, followed by a substantial brunch late in the morning and a second main meal in the evening. This reflects the rural lifestyle of most of Nepal's population, ensuring that the daylight hours are fully exploited and work done before the heat of the day builds and after it wanes. In

Kathmandu and the other big cities this has changed as workers fit around more Western office hours.

If you are invited to a meal, socializing takes place before dinner (which may be served late by Western standards), with guests leaving soon after finishing the meal. Remember that only the right hand should be used for eating, handling and passing food or drink. It is customary in many rural households for women to remain in the background during the meal and to eat only after the men have finished their food. In Kathmandu and the main cities everybody eats together. As the kitchen in a Hindu home is sacred, non-Hindus should ask before entering.

Drink

International brands of beer made in Nepal include San Miguel, Guinness, Carlsberg and Tuborg. Nepali beers include Gorkha, Everest and Khumbu which are similar to continental lagers.

Nepal also produces spirits, including rum, whisky, vodka and gin. They are inexpensive, but most are really awful and are best consumed with a large quantity of mixer, although the Kookri Rum tastes good, especially on a cold night on the trail when mixed with coffee or hot chocolate.

Himalayan country liquor includes *chang*, a type of beer usually made of millet. This is said to be a particular favourite of the Yeti and a common cause for them raiding villages.

In the middle and lower reaches of the country, *rakshi* is more common. This rice-based concoction can be highly intoxicating, though there are many varieties. It is often served at wedding receptions or other special occasions in some communities.

Arak, produced from potatoes and *tongba*, is the Tibetan drink. Though they are interesting to sample, the taste can be an acquired one.

The role of alcoholic drinks varies between different communities. In the higher, colder regions of the Himalaya, it is often as normal for women to drink as it is for men, while in some Terai communities, alcohol is rarely consumed by men and never by women. The ill-effects of alcohol are widely recognized by women in particular throughout Nepal and experience has led some to regard it as the 'demon drink'. A women's pressure group has succeeded in prohibiting the sale of alcohol in the Kanchanpur district of southwest Nepal (the Bhimdatta [Mahendranagar] area), though this has led to an increase in the clandestine production of *rakshi* and to the 'smuggling' of alcohol from neighbouring districts.

All the usual soft drinks are available in Nepal and sometimes it is a good, safe option if you are unsure of the water. Mineral water is widely available but, as always, check the seal before buying. A popular and refreshing option is lemon/lime soda, cheaper than other soft drinks and very refreshing.

You may see green coconuts being sold on the street and their coconut water is tasty and refreshing and is said to be good if you have a stomach upset. *Lassi* is another popular drink made of yoghurt (*curd*) with crushed ice and sugar. You can also get fruit lassi, salt lassi and, in some places, *bhang lassi*, whose special ingredient is illegal and usually smoked.

Eating out

In Kathmandu and Pokhara there is a huge selection of restaurants and styles of cuisine. There are restaurants offering Nepali food, as well as those specializing in specific ethnic groups such as Newari dishes. Tibetan restaurants are common, often run by Tibetan families who fled the Chinese invasion in the 1950s.

There are also plenty of Western menus, from steaks and burgers to some excellent pizza and pasta offerings. Mexican, Chinese, Korean and Japanese food can all be found. Vegetarians too are well catered for as many local and Indian dishes are meat-free.

Since the days of the hippies in the 1960s there has been a tradition of bakeries serving fresh breads and cakes. In the last 10 years many cafés have opened to complement these, most serving excellent local and imported coffees and teas, together with sandwiches and cakes. Most have tables to sit at and free Wi-Fi.

Menu reader

Snacks
achar pickles
aloo wo potato fritters
chop fritters of spiced chopped meat or vegetables, may be covered with mashed potato and breadcrumbs
dal bhat rice with lentil sauce
kothe *momo*, but fried
momo steamed dumpling stuffed with meat or vegetables
pakora deep-fried meat or vegetables in soft batter, usually spherical or circular
samosa triangles of deep-fried meat or vegetables in thin, crispy batter
tarkari vegetable curry

Meat
bangur komasu pork
gai komasu beef
hansa komasu duck
khasi komasu the meat of a castrated male goat
kukhura komasu chicken
machha fish
masu meat
puka masu fried meat
rango komasu buffalo
thupka a Tibetan meat soup or stew
tsampa a variety of unleavened bread

Vegetables
aloo potato
bandarkobi cabbage
bhanta aubergine
chyaau mushroom
chukandar beetroot
gajar carrot
gholbeda tomato
kauli cauliflower
maatar peas
piaj onion
saag spinach or greens
simi beans
tarkaria vegetable dish

Fruits and nuts
aam mango
amba guava
angur grape
bhogate grapefruit
bhuin katahar pineapple
chaksi sweet lime
kera banana
kagati lemon
kaju cashew nut
mewa papaya
nariwal coconut
painyu cherry
rukha katahaa jackfruit
suntala orange
syau apple
tarbuj water melon

Drinks
arak liquor fermented from potatoes, grain or fruit sap
chai tea (chiya)
chhang strong mountain beer of fermented barley, maize, rye or millet
lassi yoghurt drink
thukba thick Tibetan soup

Dairy
curd yoghurt
ghee clarified butter, used as a cooking medium
makhan butter

Improve your travel photography

Taking pictures is a highlight for many travellers, yet too often the results turn out to be disappointing. Steve Davey, author of Footprint's *Travel Photography*, sets out his top rules for coming home with pictures you can be proud of.

Before you go
Don't waste precious travelling time and do your research before you leave. Find out what festivals or events might be happening or which day the weekly market takes place, and search online image sites such as Flickr to see whether places are best shot at the beginning or end of the day, and what vantage points you should consider.

Get up early
The quality of the light will be better in the few hours after sunrise and again before sunset – especially in the tropics when the sun will be harsh and unforgiving in the middle of the day. Sometimes seeing the sunrise is a part of the whole travel experience: sleep in and you will miss more than just photographs.

Stop and think
Don't just click away without any thought. Pause for a few seconds before raising the camera and ask yourself what you are trying to show with your photograph. Think about what things you need to include in the frame to convey this meaning. Be prepared to move around your subject to get the best angle. Knowing the point of your picture is the first step to making sure that the person looking at the picture will know it too.

Compose your picture
Avoid simply dumping your subject in the centre of the frame every time you take a picture. If you compose with it to one side, then your picture can look more balanced. This will also allow you to show a significant background and make the picture more meaningful. A good rule of thumb is to place your subject or any significant detail a third of the way into the frame; facing into the frame not out of it.

This rule also works for landscapes. Compose with the horizon two-thirds of the way up the frame if the foreground is the most interesting part of the picture; one-third of the way up if the sky is more striking.

Don't get hung up with this so-called Rule of Thirds, though. Exaggerate it by pushing your subject out to the edge of the frame if it makes a more interesting picture; or if the sky is dull in a landscape, try cropping with the horizon near the very top of the frame.

Fill the frame
If you are going to focus on a detail or even a person's face in a close-up portrait, then be bold and make sure that you fill the frame. This is often a case of physically getting in close. You can use a telephoto setting on a zoom lens but this can lead to pictures looking quite flat; moving in close is a lot more fun!

Interact with people

If you want to shoot evocative portraits then it is vital to approach people and seek permission in some way, even if it is just by smiling at someone. Spend a little time with them and they are likely to relax and look less stiff and formal. Action portraits where people are doing something, or environmental portraits, where they are set against a significant background, are a good way to achieve relaxed portraits. Interacting is a good way to find out more about people and their lives, creating memories as well as photographs.

Focus carefully

Your camera can focus quicker than you, but it doesn't know which part of the picture you want to be in focus. If your camera is using the centre focus sensor then move the camera so it is over the subject and half press the button, then, holding it down, recompose the picture. This will lock the focus. Take the now correctly focused picture when you are ready.

Another technique for accurate focusing is to move the active sensor over your subject. Some cameras with touch-sensitive screens allow you to do this by simply clicking on the subject.

Leave light in the sky

Most good night photography is actually taken at dusk when there is some light and colour left in the sky; any lit portions of the picture will balance with the sky and any ambient lighting. There is only a very small window when this will happen, so get into position early, be prepared and keep shooting and reviewing the results. You can take pictures after this time, but avoid shots of tall towers in an inky black sky; crop in close on lit areas to fill the frame.

Bring it home safely

Digital images are inherently ephemeral: they can be deleted or corrupted in a heartbeat. The good news though is they can be copied just as easily. Wherever you travel, you should have a backup strategy. Cloud backups are popular, but make sure that you will have access to fast enough Wi-Fi. If you use RAW format, then you will need some sort of physical back-up. If you don't travel with a laptop or tablet, then you can buy a backup drive that will copy directly from memory cards.

Recently updated and available in both digital and print formats, Footprint's Travel Photography by Steve Davey covers everything you need to know about travelling with a camera, including simple post-processing. More information is available at www.footprinttravelguides.com

Kathmandu

a bustling mix of medieval and modern

The name Kathmandu has always conjured mystery and excitement in the minds of travellers. It doesn't disappoint. Its Old Town is a maze of narrow streets, littered with small shrines and statues of gods worn smooth from centuries of devotion.

Towering Buddhist stupas and vibrant Hindu temples exist alongside bustling bazaars and chaotic traffic to create the everyday, fascinating life of the city. It's a place to explore on foot, with many small alleyways and hidden courtyards making you feel you've slipped back in time, allowing you to enjoy the friendliness of its inhabitants and experience its sounds, sights and smells.

It's also a city in transition, its population having grown from 100,000 to nearly two million in less than 50 years. Sprawling suburbs seem to have been thrown up with scant regard for planning or tradition. The fumes from its gridlocked streets obscure the snow-capped peaks that used to be its backdrop, and at times its bustle and vibrancy can almost overwhelm.

Best for
Culture ▪ Shopping ▪ Temples

Kathmandu

Footprint picks

★ **Durbar Square**, page 45

The heart of the Old Town, still
recovering from the 2015 earthquake.

★ **Thamel**, page 65

The backpacker quarter full of restaurants, bars, shops and souvenir sellers.

★ **Pashupatinath**, page 72

The cremation *ghats* at one of Hinduisms most famous sites.

★ **Swayambhunath**, page 79

Visit the Monkey Temple perched high above the city.

★ **Bodhnath**, page 85

Asia's largest stupa and the heart of the Tibetan community.

Essential Kathmandu

Finding your feet

All international flights land at Tribhuvan International Airport, 5 km east of the centre. Few people stay near the airport as it is so close to the city. There is a taxi desk in the Arrivals hall from where you can pay a set price (currently Rs 800/US$7.30) for a taxi to central areas. Unofficial taxi drivers also tout for business, charging about half this rate but inspect their vehicles first as some can be very old and decrepit.

Getting around

The central areas and Old Town can all be explored on foot both during the day and in the evening. The distances are not great and,

other than avoiding the chaotic traffic and ubiquitous motor bikes, it is safe.

There are plenty of local minibuses that ply their trade throughout Kathmandu but they are usually packed and, as they have no signs stating where they are going, other than a conductor shouting, it's hard to use them without ending up on the wrong side of town.

Taxis are inexpensive and the best way to visit the outlying temples and shrines, but don't forget to haggle over the price. Many drivers speak enough English to let you be understood and know where the main attractions, hotels and restaurants are located.

Footprint picks

1 **Durbar Square**, page 45
2 **Thamel**, page 65
3 **Pashupatinath**, page 72
4 **Swayambhunath**, page 79
5 **Bodhnath**, page 85

January	February	March	April	May	June
☀	☀	☀	☀	🌦	🌦
15°C	17°C	21°C	25°C	26°C	26°C
4°C	6°C	10°C	13°C	17°C	20°C
10mm	10mm	30mm	30mm	100mm	200mm

July	August	September	October	November	December
🌧	🌧	🌦	🌦	☀	☀
26°C	26°C	25°C	23°C	20°C	16°C
21°C	21°C	19°C	15°C	9°C	5°C
370mm	320mm	180mm	50mm	0mm	10mm

When to go

During the monsoon of June to early September Kathmandu is humid and wet although the rain keeps the pollution down and everywhere is very lush. The autumn months of October and November are a great time to visit, with pleasantly hot days, warm evenings and, being post monsoon, less dust in the air. During December and January it cools and although there is rarely a frost temperatures drop to only 1-2°C at night. It can be cloudy and some rain falls but visibility and views of the distant Himalaya are good during the sunny periods. The spring months of February to May are also a pleasant time, although the heat and humidity do build once more as the monsoon approaches.

Time required

A couple of days to see the highlights; a full week will allow more in-depth exploration of the whole Kathmandu Valley.

Tip...

Kathmandu's museums are under resourced and rather antiquated. So it's worth considering a visit to those located in the nearby cities of Bhaktapur and Patan. If you only have time to visit one museum during your stay, then go to the superb Patan Museum (see page 107). This atmospheric museum covers many aspects of Nepali life, from religion to local craft. It also has a great garden café.

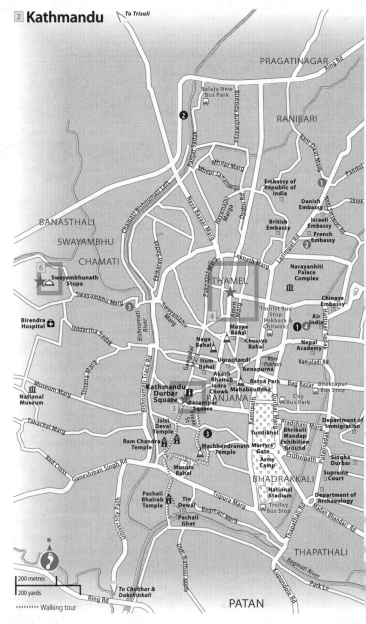

To Trisuli

PRAGATINAGAR

Ring Rd

Balaju New
Bus Park

❷

RANIBARI

Birendra Aishwarya

Manohara Sadak

Mhepi Marg

❶

Rani Devi Marg

Mhepi Janamarga

Chamati Bishnumati Link

Naya Baxar Marg

Narayanhiti Marg

Divan Marg

Pandol

Embassy of
Republic of
India

Shree

BANASTHALI

Iktharan Sadak

Danish
Embassy

SWAYAMBHU

British
Embassy

Israeli
Embassy

❷

Lamptart Rd

French
Embassy

CHAMATI

Leknath Marg

Narayanhiti
Palace
Complex

Paknajol Marg

THAMEL

🏛

❻

Swayambhu Marg

★

Swayambhunath
Stupa

Swayambhu Marg

❸

Amrit Marg

❹

Tourist Bus
Stop
(Pokhara &
Chitwan)

Chinese
Embassy

Air
India

Hattisar Sadak

Siddartha Sadak

Bishnumati River

Musya
Bahal

🏛

❶

❹

Birendra
Hospital ✚

Naga
Bahal

Ugrachandi

Chussya
Bahal

Nepal
Academy

Simana Marg

Gangahal Marg

Itum
Bahal

Rani
Pokhari

Annapurna

Kamaladi Rd

Bishnumati Track Rd

Akash
Bhairab

Indra
Chowk

Ratna Park

Mahabouddha

Bag Bazar

Bhaktapur
Bus Stop

Museum Marg

🏛

Kathmandu
Durbar
Square

RANJANA

Basantpur
Square

🏛

City
Bus Park

Dharma Path

Kantipath

Pradhani Marg

Department of
Immigration

National
Museum

❸

Freak St

Jaisi Deval
Temple

❸

Tundikhel

Bhrikuti
Mandap
Exhibition
Ground

Putali Sadak

Singha
Durbar

Tahachal Marg

Ram Chandra
Temple

Machhendranath
Temple

Martyrs'
Gate

Prithvipath

Supreme
Court

Ganeshman Singh Rd

Musum
Bahal

Army
Camp

BHADRAKKALI

Department of
Archaeology

Red Cross

Pachali
Bhairab
Temple

Tin
Dewal

Tripura Marg

National
Stadium

Trolley
Bus Stop

Madan Bhandari Rd

University Path

Pachali
Ghat

Bagmati Marg

Thapathali Rd

THAPATHALI

Didi Bahini Marg

★ N

Bagmati River

Kupondole Rd

Park Ln

200 metres

200 yards

▽ *To Chobhar &
Dakshinkali*

Ring Rd

PATAN

••••••• Walking tour

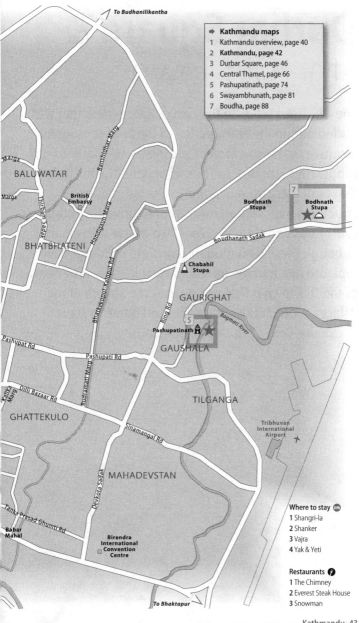

To Budhanilikantha

Marga

BALUWATAR

Banshidhar Marg

Handigaun Marg

Maharajgunj Marg

Marga

Thirbam Sadak

British Embassy

BHATBHATENI

7

Bodhnath Stupa ★ ⌂ △

Bodhnath Stupa

Boudhanath Sadak

Bhrikutimandap/Rani Road

Chabahil Stupa △

GAURIGHAT

Ring Rd

Bagmati River

5 Pashupatinath ★

GAUSHALA

Pashupat Rd

Pashupati Rd

Rudramati Marg

Pashupati Rd

Kanti Path

Dilli Bazaar Rd

Sinamangal Rd

TILGANGA

GHATTEKULO

Tribhuvan International Airport ✈

Devkota Sadak

MAHADEVSTAN

Tanka Prasad Ghumti Rd

Babar Mahal

Birendra International Convention Centre

To Bhaktapur

Where to stay 🛏
1 Shangri-la
2 Shanker
3 Vajra
4 Yak & Yeti

Restaurants 🍴
1 The Chimney
2 Everest Steak House
3 Snowman

Kathmandu•43

Durbar Square &
the Old Town

The Old Town refers to the part of Kathmandu that was walled during the Malla period of the 16th century AD. It consists of narrow streets and alleyways, packed with shops, stalls, shrines, traffic and people. The tall buildings that hem them in were *bahal's* – Newari-designed structures that focused inwards onto private, central courtyards and shrines. Over 100 of these still remain although these days modern, concrete buildings have replaced much of the traditional architecture. The heart of the Old Town is Durbar Square – the Square of the Palaces, a UNESCO Heritage Site and home to some of the city's most impressive buildings.

This astonishing area of religious and regal architecture and monuments is the spiritual and cultural heart of Kathmandu, as well as being home to Nepal's most famous inhabitant, the living goddess. It grew up at the crossroads of important trading routes. The Old Royal Palace was at the centre of the city, surrounded by temples and other important buildings. The Durbar Square area in fact comprises three large open squares and contains more than 50 monuments, the oldest dating back over 800 years. Many of the old buildings were rebuilt after the 1934 earthquake, but not always to the original design.

Kasthamandap (1)

In the southwest corner, straddling the crossroads of the ancient trade routes, was one of Kathmandu's grandest temples, the Kasthamandap (*kastha* = wood; *mandap* = platform or pavilion). This famous building, the central point around which the whole city

Fact...
The temples often have several different names and a variety of spellings. The most common alternatives are added in brackets.

Essential Durbar Square

Entrance pass

Durbar Square is open to the public dawn-dusk, Rs 750 (US$6.90). You pay at booths at any of the entrances and once paid you have access to everywhere in it. The ticket is valid for one day. If you are in Kathmandu for longer than this it's worth going to the Site Office, situated on the south side of Basantapur Square, and getting it converted to a pass that is valid for the duration of your visa. It is free to do but you will need your passport and one passport-sized photo. Even if only walking through the square over the next few days you would be expected to buy a new ticket if you don't have one.

Walking tours

Numbers in brackets beside the headings correspond to the map on page 46 and have been arranged so that they form a logical walking tour if you start in the southwest corner. See also the south of Durbar Square walking tour on page 62.

The 2015 earthquakes

Many temples and monuments were either destroyed or seriously damaged in the 2015 earthquakes, more than any other of the historical attractions in Nepal. The south of the square bore the brunt of the quake. However, it is still certainly worth visiting the square, with well over half of the shrines undamaged and open for worship.

Work has started on restoration but will take many years to complete. The destroyed monuments have been cleared so that the rubble can be sorted for reconstruction. Other monuments are propped as they await structural strengthening. The various shrines are marked with red or green signs to tell you of their condition, red means do not enter and stay behind barriers, green means OK.

Temples, shrines and buildings destroyed in the 2015 earthquake have been left in the guide as there are plans to rebuild them all. We have highlighted their current condition.

developed, was almost completely destroyed in the 2015 earthquake, with only its original plinth remaining, and will take several years to rebuild.

It was widely believed to have been built in 1596 by King Lakshmina Narasimha Malla from the wood of one enormous sal tree (*Shorea robusta*); it is now known to have a much earlier origin, as references to the temple have been found in a manuscript dating from

3 Durbar Square

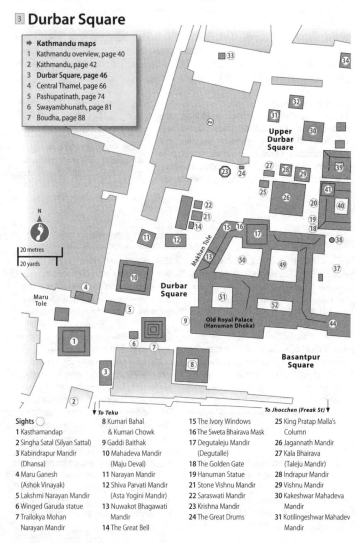

⇒ **Kathmandu maps**

Upper Durbar Square

Durbar Square

Maru Tole

Old Royal Palace (Hanuman Dhoka)

Basantpur Square

To Teku

To Jhocchen (Freak St)

Sights ○
1 Kasthamandap
2 Singha Satal (Silyan Sattal)
3 Kabindrapur Mandir (Dhansa)
4 Maru Ganesh (Ashok Vinayak)
5 Lakshmi Narayan Mandir
6 Winged Garuda statue
7 Trailokya Mohan Narayan Mandir

8 Kumari Bahal & Kumari Chowk
9 Gaddi Baithak
10 Mahadeva Mandir (Maju Deval)
11 Narayan Mandir
12 Shiva Parvati Mandir (Asta Yogini Mandir)
13 Nuwakot Bhagawati Mandir
14 The Great Bell

15 The Ivory Windows
16 The Sweta Bhairava Mask
17 Degutaleju Mandir (Degutalle)
18 The Golden Gate
19 Hanuman Statue
21 Stone Vishnu Mandir
22 Saraswati Mandir
23 Krishna Mandir
24 The Great Drums

25 King Pratap Malla's Column
26 Jagannath Mandir
27 Kala Bhairava (Taleju Mandir)
28 Indrapur Mandir
29 Vishnu Mandir
30 Kakeshwar Mahadeva Mandir
31 Kotilingeshwar Mahadev Mandir

the 12th century. It was originally a rest house or community centre for merchants trading with Tibet and so had an open ground floor.

In those days merchants would cross the malaria-ridden Terai in winter to escape the mosquitoes before resting in Kathmandu until spring melted snow on the high passes to Tibet and let them proceed. This was instrumental in Kathmandu's prosperity and rise to dominance.

Later it was made more ornate and converted into a temple dedicated to Gorakhnath. His shrine was at the centre of a small enclosure, although the temple also housed a few smaller shrines to other deities. For some years tantric devotees lived here using the temple for tantric *chakra puja*. The Malla kings greatly embellished it. Two bronze lions guarded the entrance, scenes from Hindu epics were portrayed along the cornices of the first floor, and at the four corners there were figures of Ganesh. Because of these it was said to represent the four main temples to Ganesh in the valley and that by worshipping here you covered all four at once.

Singha Satal (Silyan Sattal) (2)
Immediately to the south of the Kasthamandap, the Singha Satal is said to have been built from wood remaining after the construction of the Kasthamandap. It was badly damaged in the 2015 quake with only the lower storey surviving. It had already been reconstructed after the 1934 earthquake. *Singha*, or *singh*, means 'lion', and the temple takes its name from the four lions guarding it at each corner. Inside, the four-handed image of Vishnu in his incarnation as Hari Krishna is considered to be among the finest in Nepal. Vishnu is riding Garuda, the half-

To Makan Tole & Indra Chowk

- Lion Statue
- Pratap Malla Statue
- Parthivendra Malla Statue

To New Rd

Ganga Path

32 Mahavishnu Mandir
33 Kot Square
34 Mahendreshwar Mandir
35 Taleju Mandir
36 Tanu Deval Mandir
37 Nasal Chowk
38 Narasimha
39 Sundari Chowk
40 Mohan Chowk
41 Mohan Tower
42 Panch Mukhi Hanuman
43 Mul Chowk
44 Basantpur Tower
45 Kirtipur tower
46 Lalitpur tower
47 Bhadgaon tower
48 Lohan Chowk
49 Dahk Chowk
50 Masan Chowk
51 Nhuche Chowk
52 Lam Chowk

Tip...
Visit early in the morning to see men praying before work and women arriving to make offerings of flowers to the gods. After dark, candles, small electric lights, shadows and wisps of incense give the temples an altogether different atmosphere.

BACKGROUND

Kathmandu

Kathmandu was founded in 723 AD by the Licchavi king Gunakamadeva at the confluence of the Bagmati and Vishnumati rivers. The hub of the city was its oldest building, the Kasthamandap (destroyed in the 2015 earthquake but scheduled for reconstruction), which stood at the crossroads of two important trade routes between India and Tibet. The name Kathmandu, itself derived from this temple, did not enter customary usage until after Prithvi Narayan Shah's conquest in 1768; previously it was known as Nepala or Nepal Mandala.

The valley remained a patchwork of small kingdoms until the 14th century when King Jayasthiti Malla successfully united them, including Kathmandu, Patan and Bhaktapur, and made Kathmandu the main administrative centre. It managed to keep this historic pre-eminence in the minds of outsiders even when the three cities became separate kingdoms under later Malla successors. Then, in the late 18th century, following on the Gorkha unification of the kingdom by King Prithvi Narayan Shah, it naturally became the capital of the newly formed country. This sparked off a long period of expansion.

In the 19th century, the ruling Rana family travelled frequently overseas, as a result of which new European building styles were introduced. The palaces that Jung Bahadur built from 1850 onwards were European in concept and contrasted sharply with the indigenous Newari style. Singha Durbar, a palace with 17 courtyards and over 1500 rooms, was built within a year (1901). Reputed to have been the largest contemporary building in Asia, it was severely damaged by fire in 1974. Other palaces were built at Patan and Kathmandu, but with the eclipse of the Rana family's power in 1951 and the strengthening of the monarchy, these became neglected. Many are now used as offices.

man half-bird god, on his way to slaying Bhaumasur, the demon king of Assam, and releasing 1600 captive girls.

Kabindrapur Mandir (Dhansa) (3)

Opposite the Kasthamandap to the east, this temple is dedicated to Shiva in his dancing form (Natyeshwar) and is a temple favoured by Kathmandu's dancers. The broad, three-storeyed structure was renovated in the mid-1980s. The ground floor is enclosed by wooden lattice screening through which you can see various images of the dancing Shiva which constitute the temple's focal point. The second floor in particular has some finely carved wooden struts supporting a protruding veranda whose seven windows testify to equally skilled and intricate craftsmanship. The smaller top storey is surmounted by three white vase-type pinnacles.

Maru Ganesh (Ashok Vinayak) (4)

This small but important golden temple is dedicated to Ganesh (Vinayaka/Ganapati). As the god of wisdom, success and good fortune, Ganesh is prayed to by departing travellers asking for safety on their trip. Pilgrims also ring the bell here before starting their worship anywhere in the square so there's a continual flow of people throughout the day; stalls beside it sell butter lamps and other offerings. The gilded roof was added in 1874 by King

Surendra Bikram Shah Dev, and each new King of Nepal used to come here to worship Ganesh immediately after his coronation.

Lakshmi Narayan Mandir (5)

Offset to the north between the Kasthamandap and Maju Deval, the Lakshmi Narayan Mandir was a two-storeyed temple conspicuous by its decorative banality in Durbar Square's concentration of artistic and architectural masterpieces. After the 2015 earthquake only the base remains. Like the Kasthamandap, it was built as a rest house for pilgrims and travellers and only later did it assume religious significance. Inside there were two shrines which could be seen from the northern-facing entrance: one appropriately dedicated to Lakshmi Narayan riding his vehicle, Garuda, while an image of Avalokiteshwara (Tib Chengrisek) representing the infinitely compassionate aspect of God occupies the other. Today, souvenir vendors have established themselves on the temple plinth.

Winged Garuda statue (6)

On the Kasthamandap side of the Trilokya Mohan Narayan Mandir is a statue of the winged Garuda, exquisitely sculptured in stone. The faithful vehicle of Vishnu is kneeling with hands folded in prayerful homage of Vishnu. The statue was erected in about 1689 either by Queen Riddhi Lakshmi, widow of Parthibendra Malla, or by her son Bhupalendra.

Trailokya Mohan Narayan Mandir (7)

This temple directly to the east of the Kasthamandap is dedicted to Vishnu but was destroyed in the 2015 earthquake. Just the plinth remains. It was built in the 1680s by King Parthibendra Malla as a memorial to his elder brother, Nripendra. The five-stepped platform supported a three-tiered building which had finely carved roofs, struts and window screens. Carvings illustrated the 10 incarnations of Vishnu – fish (Matsya), tortoise (Kurma), boar (Baraha), man-lion (Narasingha), dwarf (Vaman), Brahmin (Parasuram), Rama and Krishna (respectively the central protagonists of the *Ramayana* and *Mahabharata*), Buddha, and destroyer of sinners (Kalaki). These gave the temple its other name, Das Avtar Dekhaune Mandir ('Ten Incarnation Views Temple').

Kumari Bahal and Kumari Chowk (8)

To the southeast of the Trailokya Mohan Narayan Mandir is the Kumari Bahal and Kumari Chowk. This is where the 'living goddess' (Kumari) resides for up to a dozen years until reaching the age of puberty (see box, page 50). The stucco façade has a number of intricately carved windows on its three floors. This 18th-century building and monastic courtyard is guarded by two large painted lions, one on either side of the entrance. Note how the lintels are carved with laughing skulls, while deities, doves and peacocks decorate the balcony windows. The building is in the style of the Buddhist monasteries of the valley, and was constructed by King Jaya Prakash Malla who instituted this tradition of virgin worship, reputedly as an act of penance.

Inside, four large and beautifully carved windows look over the quadrangular courtyard where there is also a small stupa that marks the Buddhist worship of the Kumari as Vajra Yogini. Hindus come here to receive *darshan*, a glimpse considered to be propitious, from the Kumari. If you look through the yellow gate you may glimpse the ceremonial chariot that the Kumari rides on through the streets during the Indra Jatra festival.

Non-Hindus are allowed into the courtyard, but not upstairs. You may not photograph the Kumari who usually appears at the middle window whenever there is a small crowd, dressed in her finery. It is respectful to make a donation in the box provided at the centre of the square.

ON THE ROAD

The living goddess

Not many cities in the world have their own living goddess you can actually go and see. Pop along to the Kumari Bahal in Durbar Square and with a bit of luck you too will be able to glimpse her and receive a blessing. Known as the Kumari, she is worshipped by Hindus as the living reincarnation of Shiva's consort Parvati. There has been a Kumari in residence here for over 200 years.

The goddesses are selected from the Newar Shakya, the gold and silversmith class, according to strict criteria. They normally commence their duties aged about four or five and need to possess certain set physical features: blue or black eyes, curls in their hair turning to the right, eye lashes "like those of a cow," a voice "of a sparrow," thighs "like a deer" and a body "like a Banyan tree" are a few of the 32 signs of perfection they have to match.

The potential Kumari not only needs to be in excellent health but also to undergo a test of courage: she will be taken to the Taleju Temple at Kalrati where she has to remain calm when confronted in the dark by buffalo and goats' heads. The final test is for her to identify clothes of her predecessor from a pile of garments.

Once chosen the Kumari lives in the Kumari Bahal, only leaving to perform religious ceremonies elsewhere, but always carried in a palanquin, as to touch the ground would make her impure. For short distances she has to walk on cloth spread before her. On such occasions she has a third eye painted on her forehead.

Her time as Kumari ends when she starts menstruating or loses her perfection. It's believed that the spirit of the goddess enters her when she becomes the Kumari and to bleed means to lose this power. Her reign might end early if she becomes ill and needs an operation, cuts herself or just loses a tooth.

Being a retired Kumari is not easy. Although they now receive a good education while in the Kumari Bahar and a good dowry upon departure, it's still thought of as unlucky for a man to be married to an ex-goddess and some never marry.

For a fascinating insight into the life of a Kumari read *From Goddess to Mortal*, by Rashmila Shakya and Scott Berry (2005), the former having been Kumari between 1984 and 1991.

Gaddi Baithak (9)

To the north of the Kumari Bahal is this palatial annex of the Hanuman Dhoka complex that was built in 1908 by Chandra Sham Sher, a Rana prime minister under King Prithvi Bir Bikram Shah Dev. This was severely damaged in the 2015 earthquake and, although still standing, requires extensive restoration and reconstruction.

This section of the palace was a product of the influence of European travels on the Nepali aristocracy of the time, it is a large white colonnaded building in the European neoclassical style said to be based on the National Gallery in London. Although magnificent in its own right, it does sit rather uncomfortably amidst the area's indigenous Nepalese architecture.

It houses a royal throne together with life-sized portraits of all the Shah kings, and large chandeliers complete the opulence. It is normally used for state functions and for dignitaries and officials to pay their respects to the Kumari although is currently closed due to the ongoing work. Beneath its foundations lie the remains of a Lichhavi-era temple that was discovered during its construction, hinting at the importance of the site of Durbar Square as a religious centre for the city.

Mahadeva Mandir (10) (Maju Deval)

To the west of the Gaddi Baithak, on the western edge of the square, was the smaller shikhara-style Mahadeva Temple that is considered to be especially auspicious for singers and dancers who came to worship here. It was destroyed in the 2015 earthquake. Built around 1690 by Queen Riddhi Laxmi, the terracotta edifice contained an image of the linga, symbolizing the creative male force of Shiva, in its usual combination with yoni, symbol of the female genitalia. Local lore has it that a golden image of Natyeshwar was stolen from the temple. Natyeshwar is the name given to the many-armed dancing Shiva enclosed in a circle of fire, and is particularly revered by Newars as patron of music and dance. Its many steps were always a great spot to while away some time watching the crowds and its plinth still remains for those needing a sit down.

Narayan Mandir (11)

To the north of the Mahadeva Mandir, the much smaller Narayan Mandir was three storeyed and built on a three-stepped platform. Each roof was tiled and small bells dangle from the top roof, ringing gently in a breeze. This was destroyed in the 2015 earthquake.

Shiva Parvati Mandir (Asta Yogini Mandir) (12)

Next to the Narayan Mandir, the wooden images of Shiva and Parvati observing life from an upper window have given this temple its alternative nomenclature. Asta Yogini refers to the eight mother goddesses whose images are contained within the rectangular building; two large, painted, stone lions guard it from the bottom of the steps. Built in 1750 by the grandson of the great King Prithvi Narayan Shah, its architecture is similar in style to a traditional Newari house. Wonderfully carved ornamental doors and latticed windows allow a glimpse of the interior, while Shiva and Parvati look out arm in arm from the shade of the temple's overhanging tiled roof adorned by three decorative pinnacles. The eminent Nepali scholar, Prof TC Majupuria, considers the temple "one of the finest examples of Nepalese architecture".

Nuwakot Bhagawati Mandir (13)

Directly to the north of the Shiva Parvati Mandir, this small temple has some of Durbar Square's most beautiful wooden window and balcony carvings – if you can ignore the gaggle of souvenir sellers beneath. The upper two roofs are gilded while the first floor is tiled. Wooden figures of various female deities lavishly decorate the struts supporting each roof. The temple was built during the first half of the 18th century by King Jagatjaya Malla in honour of his grandfather Mahapatindra whose image it contained. But the image was stolen in 1766 and the shrine remained empty for many years until it was again occupied, this time by a small image of the goddess Bhagawati installed at the behest of King Prithvi Narayan Shah. Every year the image is taken to the village of Nuwakot, 57 km north, for an annual festival. A ceremony takes place each morning in which sweet cooked rice is offered to the deity.

The Great Bell (14)

Installed by Bahadur Shah in 1797 the bell is rung whenever ceremonies are held at the adjacent Degutaleju Mandir. It is popularly believed that the ringing of the bell wards off evil spirits, and in its early days it was also used as a general alarm. Suspended by metal chains from its decorative pagoda-style roof shade, it arrived in Kathmandu some 50 years later than similar bells in the Durbar Squares of Bhaktapur and Patan.

The Ivory Windows (15)
Opposite the Great Bell, the beautifully carved windows giving onto the corner balcony are another example of the fine craftsmanship concentrated in this area. The middle window is of polished copper while those flanking it are carved from ivory. The six wooden struts supporting the balcony are embellished with figures of Shiva and other deities. It is said that this was a perch from which early Malla rulers of Kathmandu would watch as processions passed through Durbar Square.

The Sweta Bhairava Mask (16)
Adjacent to the balcony and behind a large wooden grille is a huge and fiercely grimacing mask of Shiva in the form of Bhairava. Although also depicted in black or dark blue, Bhairab is most often portrayed in white (hence *sweta*, *seto* or *seti*) as is the case here, allowing for the addition of golden hues. Wearing an elaborate crown of skulls and jewels, Bhairab is associated with tantric worship, has fanged teeth, a red tongue, wild eyes and the all-seeing middle eye. His purpose is to ward off devils and evil spirits, a task for which he has been well endowed by the artist's skill.

The mask was commissioned by Rana Bahadur Shah in 1796. The wooden grille is removed only during the Indra Jata festival each September (approximately), though at other times you can see the mask through the grille. During the festival, *jand*, a rice-based liquor, is offered to the deity and having thereby become blessed, the consecrated liquor flows through the image's mouth to be eagerly consumed by worshippers.

Degutaleju Mandir (Degutalle) (17)
Beside the Bhairab Mask to the east, this three-tiered pagoda-style temple is a smaller and visually less impressive version of the huge Taleju Temple dominating the northeast corner of the square. Standing some 15 m high, it is built on top of a house that is part of the palace and the wooden struts below its gilded roofs are once again decorated with elaborate carvings. Taleju was the Malla kings' personal goddess, which helps explain the number of temples dedicated to her around the city.

The Golden Gate (18)
The main entrance to the Hanuman Dhoka, or Old Royal Palace, is brightly painted in green, blue and gold and is flanked by two stone lions, one carrying Shiva, the other his consort Parvati. The door itself is thought to have been installed by King Girvana Yuddha Bikram Shah in 1810, while the entrance dates back to the Mallas. In the niche above the gate is Krishna in his ferocious tantric aspect, flanked by the more gentle, amorous Krishna surrounded by the *gopi* (cowgirls), and by King Pratap Malla (believed to be an incarnation of Vishnu) playing a lute, and his queen.

Hanuman Statue (19)
To the left of the Golden Gate is the popular Hanuman Statue, installed by Pratap Malla in 1672. The monkey god is wrapped in a red cloak, his face smeared with red vermilion powder and mustard oil, and has a golden umbrella above. In fact, there is so much paint on his face, left by devotees, that it's now impossible to see any features. Hanuman, a hero of the Hindu epic *Ramayana*, is worshipped to bring success in war.

Stone inscription (20)

Further to the left, outside the palace wall, is a stone inscription in 15 languages, including French and English, in praise of the goddess Kalika. It was carved on 14 January 1664 during the reign of Pratap Malla, a talented poet and linguist.

Stone Vishnu Mandir (21)

Next to the Great Bell (14) stands the Stone Vishnu Mandir, a square red-columned structure supporting a grey stone and bell-shaped upper portion, and standing on a three-tiered platform. The temple was badly damaged in the 1934 earthquake and has only recently been fully restored. Its origins are unknown. An image of Vishnu atop Garuda stands in the earth-floored interior.

Saraswati Mandir (22)

Also recently renovated after earthquake damage, this small single-storeyed temple has an image of Sarawati, goddess of knowledge and learning, flanked by four-armed Lakshmi, goddess of wealth, and Ganesh, the elephant-headed god of wisdom and success.

Krishna Mandir (23)

Destroyed in the 2015 earthquake, this was one of only a few eight-sided temples and was built by King Pratap Malla in 1648, either in response to the impressive Krishna Mandir in Patan, or as a religious consolation for his earlier failure to conquer the city, or else in memory of his two wives; it may have been a combination of all three. The three-tiered traditional Newari building was supported by stone columns around the circumference of the base. The image of Krishna inside the temple was accompanied by his two wives, Satyabhama and Rukmani, all of which, according to a Sanskrit inscription, bear deliberate resemblance to Pratap Malla and his own two queens. Its platform remains and makes a good spot to climb and look out over the northern end of the square.

The Great Drums (24)

Beside the temple a pair of Great Drums mark worship at the temple. Added by King Girbana Yuddha Bikram Shah in 1800, they were formally used in combination with the Great Bell (see above) to sound alarm or as a call for people to congregate, but are now used only twice a year and accompany the sacrifice of a goat and a buffalo.

King Pratap Malla's Column (25)

Opposite the Krishna Mandir to the east, this beautifully decorated column with statues of Pratap Malla, his two wives and four sons, was modestly erected by Pratap Malla himself in 1670. The column still remains but the statue fell during the 2015 earthquake and is currently being renovated. It shares a platform with several smaller religious objects, while the figures on top of the column were seated and used to look directly into the prayer room used by Pratap on the third floor of the Degutaleju Mandir.

Jagannath Mandir (26)

This two-storeyed temple is the oldest in Durbar Square. Built on a three-tiered platform in 1563 by King Mahendra Malla, it contains images of Vishnu and Jagannath. A total of 48 wooden struts support the tiled roofs and are decorated with an amazing variety of sexually explicit carvings. Eight miniature shrines are affixed to the ground-floor walls, but the deities they once contained are missing. Why the erotic carving is there is a source of debate. While some think it is to highlight the tantric path to enlightenment, others believe it is to stop the goddess of lightning, a bashful maiden, from striking the temple through embarrassment.

Kala Bhairava (Taleju Mandir) (27)

Opposite the Jagannath Mandir and immediately to the north of the Pratap Malla Column, the Kala Bhairava (Black Bhairava) is a fearful image of Shiva the Destroyer, carved out of a single stone. The large, colourful portrait has a constant flow of worshippers coming to appease this fearsome deity.

Indrapur Mandir (28)

Standing to the northeast of the Kala Bhairava, this temple is recognizable by the small but typically Newari open balcony of its first floor where an image of Indra was traditionally shown during Indrajata. A Shiva lingam stands inside the temple, but the image of Garuda is conspicuously positioned outside to the south, suggesting that it may once have been a Vishnu temple that was subsequently rededicated to Shiva.

Vishnu Mandir (29)

Immediately adjacent to the Indrapur Mandir to the east, this Vishnu temple is constructed on a four-tiered plinth and its three storeys rise attractively above its neighbour. Its exact origins are also unclear, although it is believed to have existed during Pratap Malla's reign. Its black and gold image of Vishnu as Narayan is seated. Its posture suggests that that it was originally playing a flute.

Kakeshwar Mahadeva Mandir (30)

This small temple was built in 1681 by Queen Bhubhan Lakshmi and destroyed in the 2015 earthquake. It is scheduled for reconstruction and rightly so as it was an interesting combination of Newari and Indian architectural styles. On a two-tiered platform, the ground floor had wooden columns supporting the sloping red-tiled roof, while the upper portion contrasted totally with its bright white shikhara-style edifice. The whole was surmounted by the *kalasa*, a vase traditionally held by Hindus to contain the primeval water of Brahma the Creator, while Buddhists believe it holds *amrit*, the elixir of immortality.

Kotilingeshwar Mahadev Mandir (31)

In the northwest corner of the Durbar Square, this temple was built by Mahendra Malla in the 16th century and is one of the square's oldest temples. It is dedicated to Shiva and, with a Nandi bull, it differs from the surrounding temples. It is a cube with a bulbous dome in the Gumbhaj style, similar to early Muslim tombs in India. Attractively built of stone brick on a three-tiered platform, it also has a smaller adjoining dome above a square, columned porch.

Mahavishnu Mandir (32)

Heading up from the Kotilingeshwar Temple, the Mahavishnu Mandir nearby was built by Jaya Jagat Malla in the first half of the 18th century. The eponymous golden image of Mahavishnu was moved to the Royal Palace following the damage caused by the 1934 earthquake to the temple. It has remained there ever since, and the Mahavishnu Mandir has no replacement image. The temple has a miniature shikhara-type spire topped by a golden umbrella, a royal insignia.

Kot Square (33)

Just off the northwest corner of Durbar Square is the Kot Square. In 1846 Jung Bahadur Rana, the founder of the Rana Dynasty, murdered all his potential opponents from the local nobility before seizing power. As if commemorating that event, during Durga Puja each year, at this spot, young soldiers attempt to cut off a buffalo head with a single stroke of their *khukuri*.

Mahendreshwar Mandir (34)

Just to the east of the Mahavishnu Mandir, this two-storeyed temple was built by Mahendra Malla in 1561. Steps lead beneath a simple metal arch to its main entrance from where the Shiva image can be seen. The stone deity (Kamadeva) is standing, clearly demonstrating the procreative aspect for which this image of Shiva is worshipped.

Taleju Mandir (35)

This is the tallest and the most magnificent of all the temples in the Durbar Square area, and stands in Trishul Chowk, a courtyard named after Shiva's trident which is stationed at its entrance. It is 36 m high, soaring above the Hanuman Durbar complex. The Taleju Mandir is closed to the public

> **Tip...**
> Look out for the small shrine to the west that has been completely squashed by a large tree.

except on the ninth day of the annual Dasain festival in autumn when Hindus may enter. It was built in 1564 and only important priests are allowed regular access. Taleju was a patron goddess of the Malla kings, from the time of Jayasthiti Malla in the late 14th century.

The image is said to have come from Ayodhya, an ancient city in northern India believed to be the birthplace of Ram and therefore one of Hinduisms most sacred places. One story recounts how it was damaged by an unnamed king in his fury at not being allowed to marry the wife of his choice, because she was not of his caste. The rulers of Bhaktapur and Patan followed suit and established their own Taleju temples beside their palaces, though neither could match this original for beauty and grandeur.

The entrance on the east side, on Indra Chowk, has a large peepul tree (often found by Hindu temples and religious sites) which gives shade to an image of Vishnu accompanied by his vehicle, Garuda. The main entrance (Singha Dhoka) on the south side of the temple has two stone lions guarding it and its arched frame is decorated with numerous brightly painted terracotta carvings some of which were apparently pillaged from Bhaktapur by Pratap Malla in 1663. On the broad eighth stage of the elaborate 12-stage plinth a wall providing additional protection has 12 miniature two-storeyed temples outside it, while another four are placed at each of the four corners within.

At the top of the platform are two large bells, one installed by Pratap Malla in 1564, the other by Bhaskar Malla in 1714, which are rung during temple worship. Smaller bells hang from the edges of all three roofs and ring gently in the breeze. Metal flags engraved with portraits of various deities are suspended from the corners of the first two roofs, while four *kalasas* hang from the corners of the top roof. It has ornately carved wooden beams, brackets and lattices, and superb wood and engraved bronze window decoration on each side.

The extensive use of copper gilt makes it an even more attractive sight at sunset. The peak decoration, in keeping with the lavishness of the rest of the temple, has four small bell-shaped spires surrounding a larger central spire of gold which is topped by a golden umbrella.

Tanu Deval Mandir (36)

In the northeast extremity of the square, this small temple comprises two shrines, one dedicated to Vishnu, the other a Newari-style house complete with brightly coloured carved window struts and a five-point spire, which was formerly used for tantric worship.

Hanuman Dhoka (The Old Royal Palace)

The palace was badly damaged during the 2015 earthquake, especially the southwest wing which houses the museums. While the vast majority is still standing, visitors are not currently permitted into any of the buildings as work is ongoing to repair them.

You can, however, still visit two of its best courtyards, or chowks. The entrance is on the Ganga Path, where the palace wall ends and a gateway is guarded by a military checkpoint. Walk through here and turn left, passing a huge tank on your right to enter Lohan Chowk. You continue through the main Nasal Chowk before leaving the Palace by the Golden Gate, what is actually the palace entrance and into Durbar Square. This is included in the price of your Durbar Square ticket; just show it as you reach the entrance to Lohan Chowk.

The plan is to restore the palace entrance to the Golden Gate as soon as it is repaired so we have left this as the starting point for a visit.

The Old Royal Palace is a collection of buildings which takes its name from the **Hanuman Statue (19)** at the entrance. It was originally built around more than 30 courtyards (chowks), but the constant building of new structures over the centuries have left just 10. The site is believed to date back to the late Licchavi era. Mahendra Malla started the present buildings in the 16th century, and during the 17th century Pratap Malla added many temples. The south wing was added by Prithvi Narayan Shah in 1771, and the southwest wing by King Prithvi Bikram Shah in 1908.

The **Golden Gate (18)** leads to **Nasal Chowk (37)**, meaning the 'courtyard of the dancing one', after the small figure of the dancing Shiva in a white temple on the east side of the courtyard; it is the largest of the 10 palace courtyards and is where coronations used to take place. Malla rulers used Nasal Chowk as both a theatre and a forum where the king would meet his subjects. Immediately on the left as you enter, a wooden door with exquisitely carved panelling leads to the former Malla living quarters. Images of the Mallas' protecting deities, Jaya and Vijaya, stand on either side. An interesting story lies behind the framed, dark and animated statue of the half-man/half-lion god **Narasimha (38)** in the act of destroying the demon Hiranyakashipu – the silver-inlaid stone image was placed there by King Pratap Malla in 1673 as penance for publicly dancing while dressed in Narasimha costume. Just beyond the image, there is a line of portraits of all Shah kings, the Sisa Baithak, beneath which is a ceremonial throne that was used by the king at official functions – a sword would take the monarch's place in his absence. The image of Indra which is usually kept in the Degutaleju Mandir is brought here during the Indra Jata festival and stood on the large central platform that used also to be used as the Coronation Platform.

Nasal Chowk, along with the **Sundari Chowk (39)**, **Mohan Chowk (40)** and **Mohan Tower (41)**, was originally built by Pratap Malla in the 17th century. Mohan Chowk, to the northwest of Nasal Chowk, was renovated by Rajendra Bikram Shah in the early 19th century and was used exclusively by the king to entertain visiting royalty. Tradition also stated that heirs to the throne had to be born here for their claim to be legitimate, an issue that caused the last Malla King, Jaya Prakash, quite a few problems as his mother was unable to make it there when she went into labour.

Carved wooden verandas illustrating the exploits of Krishna look down on the chowk on three sides. Intriguingly, there are also some depictions of figures in Western costume along the north wall. The decorated golden waterspout named Sundhara was also built by Pratap Malla, who brought cool clear water from Budhanilakantha to a bath 3.5 m below ground level. Sculpted portrayals of the mythical Indian king, Bhagirath, who is credited with bringing the Ganges river from Heaven to its earthly course, adorn the waterspout, while various deities decorate the surrounding walls. Thus Pratap Malla was able to combine bathing with daily worship, cleansing both body and spirit simultaneously.

In the northeast corner of the complex is the **Panch Mukhi Hanuman (42)**, a round five-storeyed building which only the temple priests may enter for worship. The five faces (the monkey, winged Garuda, boar, ass and man-lion) of Hanuman are portrayed on the mid-17th-century structure.

Mul Chowk (43), beside this round tower and at the northeast of the complex, is unfortunately not open to visitors, but contains numerous statues, images and carvings, and was used for coronations by the Mallas. Mass animal sacrifices apparently take place here during Dasain.

You used to be able to climb to the top of the 18th-century **Basantpur Tower (44)**, or **Kathmandu Tower**, that overlooks the square but it was badly damaged in the 2015 earthquake, losing the top two of its nine storeys. Situated in the southwest corner of Nasal Chowk with beautiful wooden windows and superb carvings on the roof struts it offered great views out over the square.

Prithvi Narayan Shah renovated many of the earlier buildings and from 1768 onwards extended the palace to the east. He introduced the fortified tower to Durbar Square, adding the smaller towers which are named after the ancient cities of **Kirtipur (45)** to the northwest with its superb copper roof, **Lalitpur (46)** to the southeast, and **Bhadgaon (47)** to the northeast. It once overlooked beautiful gardens with a clear view of the Taleju Temple, all set around **Lohan Chowk (48)**.

The area west of Nasal Chowk was built in the latter half of the 19th century. This includes **Dahk Chowk (49)**, **Masan Chowk (50)**, **Nhuche Chowk (51)** and **Lam Chowk (52)**. The **Degutaleju Temple (17)**, dedicated to the Mallas' personal goddess, was erected by Shiva Singh Malla who reigned from 1578-1620.

Tribhuvan Museum
This museum is dedicated to the lives of the last kings of Nepal. Due to the damage to the palace during the 2015 earthquake, and damage to the exhibits, it is not expected to open again for several years.

The museum housed a small but interesting collection of the chattels of **King Tribhuvan** (1911-1955), who was responsible for overthrowing the Rana's and wresting back control of the country. It featured a dramatic account of how he escaped their clutches by swerving into the Indian Embassy in his car as he headed off on a supposed hunting trip. It also included thrones, bicycles, clothes and ceremonial dress, hunting trophies and guns, a display of jewels, and a reconstruction of Tribhuvan's study and bedroom. Among the more bizarre objects it contained was his favourite stuffed bird.

Smaller displays were dedicated to King Mahendra (1955-1972) and King Birendra (1972-2001).

From the northeast corner of Durbar Square, you can walk along Makhan Tole towards Indra Chowk, Asan Tole and the Rani Pokhari tank. This thoroughfare is the old artery of the city, the start of the ancient trade route to Tibet. You will pass an enclosed old stone image of the Shiva linga and yoni that is supposed to be a smaller replica of the one at Pashupatinath. It is referred to as a five-faced image, but only four are visible. On your left in the corner of the square is a statue of Garuda.

After the 1934 earthquake, much of Makham Tole's traffic was diverted along New Road, although these days with Kathmandu's congested and clogged streets it's hard to believe. It retains much of its character, however, with colourful shops and stalls and thriving markets. Much of the old architecture may have been replaced with modern buildings but dive up side alleys and through doorways to hidden *bahars* and the old Kathmandu is still there.

Indra Chowk

Indra Chowk, the first crossroads, is at the intersection of Makhan Tole and Shukra Path. The southwest corner has a popular small, brass **Ganesh shrine**. The **Akash Bhairava Mandir**, to the west, has a silver image of the rain god which is displayed outside for a week during the Indrajata festival. Two large lions flank the entrance and the walls are decorated with red and white chequered tiles, while the balcony is of attractive gold and black with four more fierce lions looking out. Two roof vents allow incense smoke to escape. This Bhairav is used by the State carrier **Nepal Airlines** as their logo. Non-Hindus are not allowed in. The square used to be an open textile market and many shops still specialize in blankets, shawls and cloth. In the northeast corner is a **Shiva Mandir**, usually buried under the stalls of textile sellers, as well as a second smaller temple.

Off to the west is the **Itum Bahal**, the largest remaining *bahal* in Kathmandu. Follow the alley that heads west from the northwest corner of the square. After a couple of hundred metres it kinks to the left and the entrance is here, a low door on the right beside three small shrines painted red. It used to be a Buddhist monastery and there is a small, white stupa in the middle of its central courtyard. On its west side is **Kichantra Bahal**, originally dating to 1387 and currently being renovated in a joint project between the Nepalese and the French. Outside stands an ancient tree that has crushed the small stupa it has grown out of. All around the courtyard are shrines, statues and plaques mixed in with the modern signs of the schools and businesses that currently occupy it. To the south of the square look out for the dilapidated shrine guarded by two lions. The large window overhanging the door displays extraordinary skill typical of Newari craftsmen.

Back in Indra Chowk continue up Makham Tole until you come to the small square called **Kel Tol**. Set back on the west side of the square is the **Sweta Matsyendranath Mandir** (or Jana Bahal), one of the most venerated Buddhist shrines in Kathmandu but one that is equally popular with Hindus. It has a two-tiered bronze roof and two brass lions guard the entrance. The courtyard is filled with small shrines, carved pillars and statues.

Tip...
Watch out for the pigeons if you decide to sit down in a shady spot, they are excellent shots.

The white-faced image inside the elaborately carved shrine is **Padmapani Avalokiteshwara**, a form of the compassionate and benevolent divinity Matsyendra. There are an astonishing 108 paintings of Avalokiteshwara throughout the temple.

A colourful procession of the main image around town takes place during the Rath Yatra, or chariot festival, in March/April. The complex is surrounded by small shops selling *thankas* and various offerings and gifts.

The pagoda Hindu temple next door to its north is the **Lunchun Lumbun Ajima**, a shakti temple with erotic carvings. Dedicated to Ajima, protecting goddess of children, it also contains an image of Ganesh and has numerous faces staring out at you from the ridges of its metal roof.

Directly opposite the Jana Bahal is an alleyway heading east. It is lined with dress shops, the dazzling colours of the fabrics making it quite a spectacle. Keep looking through doors and down side alleys as you follow it. This is the heart of the old city with *bahals* and house courtyards still very much in evidence, a maze in which traditional life still goes on.

At the end of the alley turn right and you arrive at **Mahaboudda**, dominated by the large white stupa in a compound at its centre. It is surrounded by other shrines and monuments. It is particularly colourful as this part of town seems to specialize in selling toys, with large teddies hanging up outside several shops.

Asan Tole

Leave the square by the same way you entered but continue straight rather than turning left at the first junction. You will soon arrive at Asan Tole, an area that is the ancestral home to some of the wealthiest Newari families in the valley and used to be the Old Town's fruit and vegetable market. It is still regarded as the commercial heart of the area with the main rice market and has three temples dedicated to Annapurna, Ganesh and Narayan in it.

The **Annapurna Mandir**, also known as **Yoganvara**, is an attractive three-storeyed temple with copper-gilt roofs whose rounded up-turning corners give a distinctly oriental impression and have copper birds attached to the end of each. Lions once again stand guard at the entrance and the divinity (an abstract silver form of *pathi*, a unit of weight) is worshipped by local traders for success and prosperity. They walk around the temple, touching a coin to their head before throwing it to the goddess as an offering and ringing the bell.

On the opposite side of the square to the east, the **Ganesh Mandir** is a two-storeyed temple with a fine golden bell-shaped spire topped by an elaborately carved umbrella. It is also a shrine popular with Buddhists.

The smaller **Narayan Mandir** is slightly offset from the centre of the square and is considered less significant locally than the above two. Its main image of Vishnu as Narayan is accompanied by those of Uma Maheshwara and Lakshmi Narayan.

A tiny temple or shrine dedicated to **Uma Maheshwara** stands beside the Ganesh temple, while on the east side of the square a small water tank contains a statue of a fish. The fish is one incarnation of Vishnu and is venerated accordingly. Various legends compete with one other to explain its origin. One of the most mind-boggling has it that the tank was placed here after a fish fell from Heaven, the exact place where it landed having been foretold by a father and son, both tantrics, though the son's prophecy turned out to be the more accurate as he remembered to allow for the bounce as the fish crashed to the ground.

Bangemudha

Exit Asan Chowk to the west along Bangemudha and you leave the old trade route which continues to Kantipath, Boudhnarth and ultimately Tibet. On the south side of the road you will see the **Ugratara Mandir**, a three-tiered pagoda dedicated to Ugratara, a goddess associated with curing eyesight problems.

Continue west and you come to the junction between Bangemudha and Shukra Path. Here you will see the **Vaisya Dev**, dedicated to the Newari toothache god. Embedded in the temple is an ancient log, known as the **Toothache Tree**, where people hammer in coins as an offering to cure dental problems. Needless to say there are plenty of dentists in this area in case the offering doesn't work, their business signs resplendent with images of dazzling white teeth.

While in the square, look out for the beautiful carved Buddha on the north side of Bangemudha, set in the wall between a dentist's and an electrical shop. It dates from the fifth century and is a great example of why you need to keep your eyes open as you wander around Kathmandu, with ancient statues and shrines hidden behind parked cars, bicycles and stalls. Similarly, on the southern wall of the square, behind a protective grille, is a beautifully carved lintel depicting, once more, the Buddha.

If you head south at this junction you will return to Indra Chowk and Durbar Square. Heading north you will come to the **Kathesinbhu**, its entrance flanked by large lions set on red pillars. Walking through these you will find yourself in a large courtyard with the Kathesinbhu stupa at its heart. It was supposedly built from leftovers when Swayambhunath was built – its name derives from the words 'Kathmandu' and 'Swayambhunath', and the presence of Lichhavi-period (fifth to sixth centuries) statues attest to the age of the site. More likely the present stupa dates from somewhere around the 17th century and is meant for those pilgrims too old or unwell to climb the steps at the main Swayambhunath complex. While in the courtyard, look out for the small shrine to Harati in the northwest corner.

Take the small alley that heads north just to the left of the impressive **Brubgon Jangchup Choeling Monastery**, watching out for the ducks that are sometimes let out to roam from the poultry sellers. When you reach the road at the end, turn left if you wish to visit the small Ganesh temple you can see, otherwise turn right and then left at the next junction.

You will arrive at Thahiti junction, centred on the 15th-century Thahiti stupa. Legend has it that it was built to protect (and hide) a spout that dispensed gold to the virtuous who visited it. Sadly, the stupa does a good job in protecting this and there is no opportunity to give it a try.

The road running west to east is **Jyatha** which marks the end of the Old Town. Follow it east a short distance and you will see the **Musya Bahal**, again with a carved door and lions outside. This is a monastery, dating from the 12th century, although the Chaitra in the centre probably dates all the way back to the seventh century. The carvings around this, although covered in devotional paint and offerings, are of great quality.

A little further on is the freestanding **Chusya Bahal**, identifiable by the two stone lions around its entrance and the carved shield above. If its ornately carved doors are locked, you can gain access through a small door at the back that leads to an archway into the central courtyard. If it's closed, give it a gentle push. It is worth the effort as the *bahal* has a lovely, unspoilt feel as if you are stepping back in time. Built around 1640, it was renovated in the 1980s. The carved balcony over the main entrance, and the small temple opposite with its elaborate lintel and guarded by elephants, shows how *bahals* would have looked in their Malla-era prime.

ON THE ROAD
Pollution

The phenomenal growth of Kathmandu, especially over the last 30 years, has brought with it the new problem of pollution. The whole valley sits in a bowl surrounded by mountains, once a vast lake. Pollution cannot escape and hangs over the city, exacerbated by the city's narrow streets which retain the fumes of daytime traffic congestion.

In 1951 there were 100 cars in the valley, all carried here in pieces through the foothills from India by porters. By 2014 there were over 700,000 motor vehicles on less than 1000 km of roads in the valley, most concentrated in the capital itself; it was ranked 177th out of 178 countries in the Yale's Environmental Performance index.

Since the early 1990s, more and more pedestrians and cyclists have taken to wearing protective masks. While anti-pollution laws do exist, they are often ambiguously applied. A vehicle's maximum permitted carbon monoxide emission is 3%. In June 1996, even the prime minister's Mercedes failed a routine, though high-profile test. The penalty is to fix it within two months or be banned from driving in the valley, but nobody takes any notice as a small bribe negates the need to have it mended and buses, lorries and battered cars continue to belch fumes into the atmosphere.

The pollution has also worsened as a result of the building boom, with brick factories in the southeast of the valley taking advantage of the local clay to churn out millions of bricks. The Himalayan views from the city are no longer the constant backdrop of 30 years ago and are now only occasionally glimpsed on winter days and in early morning.

Kathmandu is particularly difficult for asthma sufferers. If you are going to be in the city for more than a few days then get a mask, available locally.

South of Durbar Square

the chaos and colour of everyday Kathmandu

The area to the south of Durbar Square may well have been the centre of the city during the Licchari period as inscriptions and carvings that hint to its origins have been unearthed. These days it's predominantly an untouristy area, where Hindu traditions thrive. This was not always the case. In the 1960s it became famous as part of the hippy trail, an annual circuit between Goa and Kathmandu where hippies came in search of cheap (and legal) hashish. This ended in 1974 when drugs were made illegal.

New Road, extending southeast from Durbar Square, was constructed in the aftermath of the devastating 1934 earthquake, and is now the city's main commercial thoroughfare. Here are supermarkets, textile and clothing stores, jewellers, the **Nepal Bank** and **Nepal Airlines** on its intersection with Kantipath. It is a mass of congestion, pollution and humanity and assails the senses as you leave the comparative calm of Durbar Square itself.

Freak Street

Running south of Durbar Square is Freak Street, so-called because of the many hippies who stayed here during the 1960s and 70s, their shaggy, dishevelled appearance earning

WALKING TOUR

South of Durbar Square *See map, page 43.*

There are some interesting temples in the Old Town area, although not as many as north of Durbar Square as this is the southern edge of the old perimeter. Many more of the older, historical Newari buildings survive as shops, houses and offices and you will glimpse traditional homes and courtyards down small alleys. There are no concessions to tourism, no signs in English; it is certainly a world away from Thamel.

An easy circuit can be followed to visit the best of these sights. You start at the site of **Kasthamandap** in the south corner of Durbar Square, taking the left fork of the two streets that head south, called **Chikanmungal**. It's a bustling thoroughfare lined with traders selling fresh fruit and vegetables from their bicycles. You soon pass the **Adko Narayan Temple**, one of the four most important Vishnu temples in the valley, and its associated pilgrim shelter. Soon after is a second Vishnu temple, followed on the other side of the street by the **Hari Shankar Temple** dating from 1637.

A small detour can be made here to the **Bhimsen Temple** by following the small lane that turns off by the Hari Shankar Temple. After 100 m or so you emerge directly opposite the Bhimsen Mandir, which is dedicated to the Newari deity of that name who looks after traders and originally dates from the 12th century. It's appropriate then that the lower story of the temple is packed full of small shops while the upstairs is closed to non-Hindus. Next door to it is a large sunken water tank, still used by the local residents to fill water containers for drinking water and as a place to do washing.

Return to the Hari Shankar Temple and turning right, continue down Chikanmungal until you reach the site of the **Jaisi Deval**. Dating back to the Licchavi period, this was an impressive three-roofed temple dedicated to Shiva that stood on a seven-stepped platform. The temple was completely destroyed in the 2015 earthquake and only the platform remains. Look out for the impressive stone phallus opposite, a place visited by those who want children.

Turn right and, as you are leaving the square, there is the entrance to the **Ram Chandra Temple**, mainly famous for the erotic scenes carved onto its roof struts. There are 16 positions illustrated in total, a testament to the carpenter's flexibility as well as his craft. It has some damage but is still standing.

This area has some of the least spoilt *bahals* in Kathmandu. After 100 m or so, **Tukan Bahal**, opposite another small temple complex, centres on a 14th-century stupa even as everyday life goes on around it as it has done for over 600 years. Its size is impressive, with its base taking up nearly all the floor space.

Keep following the road as it swings to the left and you will arrive at **Musum Bahal**, a great example of how everyday life exists side by side with sacred places. Here there are a couple of shrines, a beautiful covered well as well as several phallic-shaped *chaityas*.

Bagmati Ghats

You can extend the walk by heading south to the Bagmati Ghats. Take the road that heads south directly opposite the Musum Bahal. You soon arrive at the ring road, which you must cross. Take care, it's always busy. Once across take the road slightly to your left which drops down towards the river and take the first left off this. You can see the entrance to the **Pachauli Bhairava** as you turn off.

It stands on the northern bank of the Bagmati river, albeit set back about 150 m. According to local tradition, it was built in the ninth century by King Gunakamadev to protect the cities southern gate. A small, golden statue of Bhairab stands in a sunken area, shaded by an impressive pipal tree. There is also a life-size human figure, reclining as if on a medieval tomb. This represents a *betal*, Bhairab's vehicle as well as a representation of death, and worshipping here is believed to protect you from death. According to legend, this shrine was so sacred that all important treaties were signed here, as to break the tradition would bring Bhairab's wrath and ultimately death to the offender.

Leave the temple compound by its southern gate and there are two pathways leading off towards the river. Take the right-hand one and this will lead you to the **Pachauli Ghat**, one of the more impressive, even if it now only exists in a state of faded glory. Hundreds of statues, inscriptions and small temples line these old embankments, so look out for Newari gods, like Hanuman and Saraswati, as well as Vishnu, Buddha and Ganesh.

Nearby are a whole series of old ghats, although these are not used for cremations any more due to the receding waters of the Bagmati river leaving them high and dry. Many of the old ghat platforms are now tumbling away down the river bank towards a modern concrete ghat recently constructed with steps down to the water for the devout, and new cremation platforms on the edge of the river.

If you turn left when you reach the river you can return to the Pachali Bhairab up the other path that leads from its southern gate. To the right of this was the **Tin Dewal**, more Indian in character, with three tapering brick towers, or Shikra, each containing a small Shiva shrine with phallus. It was built in 1850 by Bom Bahadur Kunwar after a successful but bloody coup, but it was destroyed in the 2015 earthquake.

From the temple you retrace your steps across the ring road and back to the shikhara temple. Continuing to the right follow the road until you come to the Musum Bahal (see above).

Return to the road and continue until it turns sharply to the left. Keep your eyes open and you will see a small alley, past a small Ganesh shrine, that takes you into the **Ta Bahal**. This large courtyard with central *chorten* is completely surrounded by houses packed tightly on all four sides and is a popular place for celebrations and wedding festivities.

Continue on to Lagan Square where the **Machhendranath Temple** stands, as well as several other shrines and monuments. This large (by Kathmandu standards) open space is a popular gathering space for the local community, as well as for children playing with makeshift balls and skateboards.

Leave the square by the road in the northeast corner, bearing left at the junction soon after. Keep right and, when the road splits, you'll see a sacred stone embedded in the middle of the junction with worshippers dodging in and out of the traffic to ring the small bell hanging beside it.

On the right you pass **Om Bahal**, containing three white stupas as well as several other smaller shrines, inscriptions and a covered well. Continue straight on and after a couple of smaller junctions you find yourself back on **Freak Street** – the signage changing from Nepalese to English – and the promise of hot water, Wi-Fi and excellent fresh cakes.

the area this name. In its heyday the street was packed with cheap guesthouses, bars, restaurants and hash houses. Walking down Freak Street today there is only the echo of its colourful past, with some small bakeries and cafés reflecting that period in their names and appearance. The tourist centre of the city has now shifted north to Thamel.

Bhimsen Tower (Dharahara)

This 60-m-tall column was completely destroyed in the 2015 earthquake. It was built as a watchtower, one of two erected by Bhimsen Tappa in 1832. The other collapsed soon after construction and the surviving one had previously been badly damaged in both the 1834 and 1934 earthquakes.

When the tower collapsed, 180 people lost their lives, although amazingly a couple of people who'd been at the very top when the earthquake struck managed to survive. Reconstruction work started on 24 April 2016 when Prime Minister Oli laid a new foundation stone, with him and many senior politicians donating one month's salary towards the cost of the work. It is being rebuilt with earthquake-proof technology incorporated in its structure.

The tower resembled a Muslim minaret and the design seems to have been strongly influenced by Kolkata's Ochterlony Monument (now renamed Shahid Minar), which was constructed in 1828 as a memorial to Sir David Ochterlony who led East India Company troops against the Nepalese in the war of 1814-1816. You had to climb 213 steps to get to its top, where an outside balcony gave great views out over the city.

At its base is the revered **Sundhara** or 'golden water tap', a below ground level quadrangle with spring water flowing from the mouth of a gilded crocodile statue. It's said that Bhimsen Tappa once rode his horse off the top of the tower and survived when he landed in this tank. Why he rode off the top is not explained.

Thamel

★ Thamel is a district of central Kathmandu located north of Durbar Square and the Old Town. It takes its name from a former Buddhist monastery and rest house, the Tham Bahal, but these days is famous for being the undisputed focal point of travellers, trekkers and tourists. Its crowded streets are packed with small hotels, guesthouses, restaurants, cafés and bars. There are tour and trek agencies, rafting specialists, bike hire, bus and coach agents and plenty of shops renting and selling trekking equipment. The streets are full of touts trying to persuade you that theirs is the best offer in town. There is fresh bread and pastries in the morning and happy hours in the evening. Whether you want a steak, pizza, curry, Mexican or most other world cuisines then Thamel is the place to go.

Where the Old Town is packed with temples, shrines and palaces, Thamel has little to offer in way of historical highlights. It's a place to stay and play rather that explore, so if you need to relax after a few weeks in the mountains it's the perfect place to head.

Garden of Dreams

The Garden of Dreams may not be very old but is worth a visit nonetheless. The Keshar Mahal was the residence of a leading official Keshar Shamsher Rana (1891-1964). It is now used as a government building but contains the Keshar Library (see below).

It's said that Keshar planned the garden to ensure each of the six seasons were represented, meaning that whatever the date of your visit, some fruits and flowers will always be in bloom. It is a tranquil oasis which boasts a decent restaurant and café, run by the excellent **Dwarika's Hotel**, offering a good selection of Nepalese teas and coffees as well as light lunches.

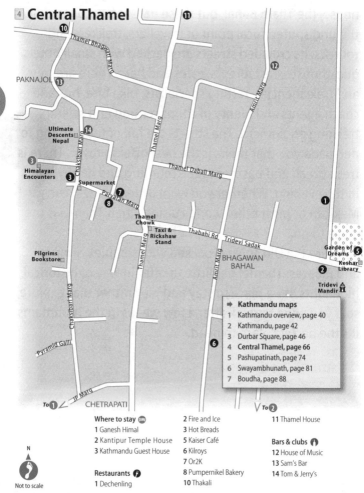

4 Central Thamel

Kathmandu maps
1 Kathmandu overview, page 40
2 Kathmandu, page 42
3 Durbar Square, page 46
4 Central Thamel, page 66
5 Pashupatinath, page 74
6 Swayambhunath, page 81
7 Boudha, page 88

N

Not to scale

Where to stay
1 Ganesh Himal
2 Kantipur Temple House
3 Kathmandu Guest House

Restaurants
1 Dechenling
2 Fire and Ice
3 Hot Breads
5 Kaiser Café
6 Kilroys
7 Or2K
8 Pumpernikel Bakery
10 Thakali
11 Thamel House

Bars & clubs
12 House of Music
13 Sam's Bar
14 Tom & Jerry's

Keshar Library

Corner of Kantipath and Tridevi Marg, www.klib.gob.np, Sun–Thu 1000-1600, Fri 1000-1500, Rs 200 (US$1.80).

Located within the grounds of the Ministry of Education, the Keshar (or Kaiser) Library occupies a wing of the former palace of Field Marshal Keshar Shamsher.

A small newspaper reading room leads to the library proper which is guarded by a huge stuffed tiger of menacing disposition, a trophy from one of Keshar's hunting expeditions. Shelves on two floors are dominated by books on military strategy and the Second World War, but there are also volumes on European history, philosophy and religion, some League of Nations and early UN year books, as well as several finely bound collections of Hardy, Tolstoy, Chesterton and Dickens. There is even a large, white leather-bound *David Copperfield* illustrated in colour by Frank Reynolds and signed by the artist, which was published in London then sold by a Bombay bookseller in 1915. Keshar also collected books on Nepal, India and China, but many of these are kept in closed metal cupboards on the first floor.

The field marshal was as eclectic in his collection of portraits which now hang alongside a couple of suits of armour and trophy heads of antelope, wild buffalo and more tigers as well as the skull of a rhinoceros. Among them are those of Nelson and Napoleon, Gandhi and Churchill, Tolstoy and Lenin, Shakespeare and Mao, and George V and Kaiser Wilhelm. There is also a large photograph of the Delhi Durbar of 1902, and a smaller, signed photograph of a young Lord Mountbatten, later to be India's last viceroy, presented in 1921 when he visited Nepal during his ill-fated tour of the subcontinent with the future King Edward VIII, then Prince of Wales. On the ground floor, a silver frame encloses a mysterious photograph of one Mrs Smith, but sadly without accompanying elaboration.

Truly fascinating for its reflection on the priorities, pursuits and interests of a bygone age, it is the kind of library a well-read (and well connected) colonial colonel might have kept.

Tridevi Mandir (or Thamel Bahal)

Near to the famous **Fire and Ice** restaurant on Tridevi Marg is a cluster of three small but attractive temples that give the road its name (*tri* is three, and *devi* refers to feminine divinity) and are dedicated to the goddesses Dakshinkali, Jawalamai and Mankamna. It is focused on a pagoda whose front wall is covered in pans and other cooking utensils left as offerings.

An almost biblical legend is associated with the site's origins. A rich man named Bhagawan Bal (who, in the way of things, has reached demi-god status in the minds of many) was on a pilgrimage to Tibet when he had a dream. The dream warned him to leave the place where he and his travelling companions were staying at once and not to look back, for there were demons there. A white horse was sent to spirit them away. After some time, they reached a river and were about to cross it when a group of beautiful women appeared. They begged the men to stay, but their horse continued through the water. The women continued to urge them back and so appealing were their cries that all but Bhagawan Bal turned to see them one last time. To their horror, they saw not women but demons who consumed the men. After many adventures, the good Bhagawan Bal eventually returned to Kathmandu and stayed in the house of a peasant in Thamel. But even here the demons would not leave him. After killing the poor peasant, they entered battle with Bhagawan Bal. Our hero fought valiantly and killed many of the demons before those remaining, now resigned to defeat, promised to leave and never to return to Thamel.

East of
Kantipath

Kantipath is the main north–south road that divides Kathmandu. To its west lies the Old Town, with its narrow streets and alleys, temples and shrines. To the east is the more modern city, the wider boulevards laid out during the Rana period of the mid- to late 1800s when this area was still countryside in which they built their sprawling palaces, the largest with over 1000 rooms.

There are still some temples and shrines but these belonged to the small villages that have now been engulfed by the urban sprawl or were on the old trade route to Tibet.

Durbar Marg

boutiques, bakeries and fine dining

Durbar Marg runs parallel to Kantipath, extending southwards from the Royal Palace as far as the Army Camp at the southeast corner of the Tundikhel. At its northern end, the road forms a T-junction with Tridevi Marg heading towards Thamel to the west, and towards Nag Pokhari and Bodhnath to the east. Heading southwards along Durbar Marg takes you past some of the most prestigious hotels in Kathmandu, as well as exclusive boutiques, shopping malls, jewellers and one of the best bakeries in Kathmandu outside the Annapurna Hotel. At the crossroads with Jamal Road you can cut down Rani Pokhari. To the south are the government areas, parade ground and national stadiums.

Royal Palace
Open Thu-Mon 1100-1500, Rs 500 (US$4.60).

At the northern end of Durbar Marg is the southern gate of the Royal Palace. Its official name is **Narayanhiti Durbar**, after a Vishnu (in the form of Narayan) temple to the east and the adjacent waterspout (*hiti*). The original palace buildings were constructed in 1915 for Rana Bahadur Shah and are situated behind the ultra-modern pagoda extension seen from Durbar Marg which was completed for the wedding of King Birendra Bir Bikram Shah (then heir to the throne) in 1970; the angular design and pink tinge of this façade are recognizable from that era. In total the grounds cover more than 30 ha.

You start in the **State rooms**, where the king greeted foreign heads of state and dignitaries as they entered the huge front door. The first thing that they would have seen as their eyes adjusted would have been, rather bizarrely, a huge polar bear rug. The king would have been seated at the far end of the hallway, two stuffed tigers rearing up on their back legs behind. This sets the tone for the palace, the royal family's passion for hunting being evident from the number of trophies on display. Most impressive is the **Gorkha Baithak**, the home of the ceremonial throne and where most of the important ceremonies were held. Look up to see the four extraordinary columns that snake to the high ceiling, adorned with paintings from Hinduism.

It was in the palace that in 2001 the Crown Prince Dipendra shot and killed nine members of the royal family, including his father, King Birendra, and his mother, Queen Aishwarya. His parents did not want him to marry his girlfriend, Devyani Rana, and it was this opposition combined with his known volatile temper and penchant for alcohol and drugs that led him to go on the rampage. Dressed in combat fatigues and armed with automatic weapons he stalked the palace, killing his father in the billiards room and his mother in the garden. He then shot himself.

The late king's brother Gyanendra succeeded to the throne, albeit two days later when the crown prince finally succumbed to his self-inflicted wounds. Gyanendra was an unpopular figure who imposed a pseudo-dictatorship as he tried to reassert royal dominancy on the country. He failed. In 2006 he lost control and a year later was given just two weeks to vacate the palace forever. In 2008 Nepal became a republic and in 2009 the palace was opened to the public as a museum.

The massacre took place in the **Tribhuvan Sudan**, a building where the royals lived when not entertaining state guests. It has since been dismantled, with just rough walls left and signs telling you who was shot where. A few bullet holes can still be seen, and are labelled on adjoining walls. The neglected pond and gardens, complete with a rusting children's climbing frame, are a sad reminder of the human tragedy that occurred.

Nag Pokhari

At the southeast corner of the Royal Palace grounds is Nag Pokhari, a water temple where people have traditionally prayed to Naga, the serpent deities, for rainfall. A fine gold serpent image stands atop a tall, narrow plinth in the centre of the tank.

Rani Pokhari

Back on Kantipath, Rani Pokhari (Queen's Pond) is a huge tank with a white temple dedicated to Shiva in the middle. The Rani in question was Pratap Malla's queen who in 1667 commissioned its construction in memory of their son, Chakravartendra, who, following his father's abdication in favour of his four sons each of whom would rule for one year, died on the second day of his reign, apparently having been trampled by an elephant. The pagoda temple originally installed by the Mallas fell into disrepair and was replaced with the current edifice in 1908 by Jung Bahadur Rana. The water with which the pond was originally filled was taken from 51 sacred rivers throughout Nepal, thus ensuring its sanctity.

Access to the temple is along a white stone walkway from Kantipath, but the area is kept locked except for one day during the Tihar festival (October-November). The temple has a domed roof reminiscent of classical Indian Mughal architecture and is surmounted by a copper spire. The main image is of the Shiva lingam, but other deities also feature.

Four small shrines at each corner contain images of Bhairava, Harishankar, Shakti and Tarkeshwari. On the southern embankment is a statue of an elephant carrying three passengers on its back, thought to be three of the male members of the Pratap Malla family, while a fourth person is held in its trunk.

Not surprisingly, various myths and legends have come to be associated with Rani Pokhari over the years. It is said to be haunted by ghosts, including one especially seductive female spectre, which managed to unnerve even the great Pratap Malla. The pond was also used for a time for 'ducking': suspected criminals were immersed and if they drowned they were guilty, but their innocence was proven if they survived. Fortunately, it seems that most suspects were innocent.

If you can ignore the fumes, the hooting, beeping, buzzing and other vehicular distractions (these are reduced if viewed from the east side), Rani Pokhari can be magical in the sunset, while a moonlit night gently illuminates the temple to contrast beautifully and mysteriously with the calm water.

The large clock tower (**Ghantaghar**) to the east of Rani Pokhari stands in the grounds of a college and serves as a useful local landmark. The tank contains fish whose numbers are said to be increasing following their serious depletion in the 1960s when toxic chemicals were emptied into the water. The pond also attracts small numbers of ducks, herons and the occasional migratory waterfowl, as well as snakes and frogs.

Tundikhel and around

the footprint of Rana Kathmandu

The Tundikhel, meaning literally 'open grassy field', is immediately to the south of Ratna Park and about 1 km south of Rani Pokhari. To its north, the Royal Pavilion has statues of six Gurkha recipients of the Victoria Cross, awarded for outstanding bravery during the two World Wars. The Tundikhel has traditionally been used for army parades and major ceremonies (eg National Day in February, and Dosain in October/November), overseen by the prime minister, military leaders and other senior civil servants. Many thousands of people throng the Tundikhel on such occasions, but if you can find a strategic viewing place (standing on a wall has been recommended) the colour and pageantry is well worth the effort. Army drill sessions take place here early most mornings, when much of the Tundikhel is off limits.

After the 2015 earthquakes many of Kathmandu's inhabitants fled here as the nearest open, safe space. It became a tent village for all those who had either lost their homes or were too scared to return to theirs and was a focal point where people came to give out clothes, blankets and food to those in need. The tents have now gone but piles of rubble do still remain in certain areas. Debris from the destruction was allowed to be dumped here for the city to dispose of so that people could get on with the job of rebuilding.

Mahakal Mandir

On the west side of the Tundikhel, this attractive three-storeyed pagoda temple is venerated by Hindus and Buddhists alike. Hindus worship the image as Bhairava while Buddhists consider it as Amitabha ('endless light'). Gilded copper covers all three roofs which have divine images carved on the beams. The main entrance is an arched gate topped by a *kalasa*.

Shahid Smarak (Martyrs' Gate)

On Prithvi Path just east of the GPO, this memorial arch encloses a statue of King Tribhuvan and is dedicated to those who fell or were executed during the struggle for democracy and against the Ranas in 1940. Black marble statues portray four eminent martyrs: Dharma Bhakta, Dasarath Chand, Ganga Lal and Shukra Raj Shastri. Wreaths are customarily placed here by visiting foreign dignitaries. Just to the east is the **Bhadrakali Mandir**, a small temple dedicated to the goddess Kali. Its alternative name, **Lunmari Mandir**, is derived from a popular legend which tells of how bread (*mari*) baked by a local baker turned into gold (*lun*).

Singha Durbar

Heading east from the Shahid Smarak, you reach this magnificent former Rana residence set in a 30-ha complex which, since 1951, has been used as the central government's bureaucratic headquarters. When it was built by Chandra Shamsher Rana in 1901 it was the largest building in Asia, its splendid neoclassical façade reflecting the influence of the Ranas' newly found taste for European sojourns. It's said that during its construction the entire population of Kathmandu had to stop eating *dal*, a staple of their diet, as it was used in the mortar and the builders' needs were such that there was none spare.

The palace contains over 1000 rooms and a similar number of servants were retained for its upkeep. Inside, the huge marble-floored Durbar Hall was used to host lavish receptions: illuminated by giant crystal chandeliers, its walls were hung with ornate mirrors and portraits of previous Rana rulers, while stuffed tigers stood in each corner and richly embroidered carpets were rolled out for the guests. In July 1973 much of the eastern part of the building was destroyed by fire and has since been only partially restored. The complex also includes the Supreme Court.

Chabahil

Heading east from the city centre towards Bodhnath, you reach Goshala (where there is a road leading south towards Pashupati and the airport). Continue eastwards from this crossroads, and you pass through Chabahil where there is a small but elegant stupa known as **Dhanju Chaitya**. Believed to pre-date the Bodhnath stupa, it is widely thought to have been built by King Dharmadeva who also contributed to the early growth of the Pashupati complex. During Licchavi times, Chabahil was a village at the crossroads of a major trade route between India and Tibet. Ashoka's daughter, Charamuti, is said to have lived here and, with her husband Devapala, founded two monasteries. Some sources also credit her with construction of the stupa itself, which is occasionally still known locally as Charamuti. Tantric Buddhist monks were based here during the early ninth century. The stupa, which stands over 12 m high, was rebuilt during the seventh century and again renovated during the 17th century. There are even now some old *chaityas*, their form possibly influenced by that of the Shiva linga, and statuary at the site, including a ninth-century free-standing Bodhisattva. Unusually, the stupa has no prayer wheels. Images of Dhyani Buddhas are found on each of the four sides around the stupa. On the northern side of the stupa is a 3.5-m statue of Buddha in *bhumiparsha mudra* pose. It is said that the copper gilt in which the stupa was originally plated was removed and sold by the Mallas to raise funds for their ultimately futile defence of the valley against the invading forces from Gorkha.

The Chabahil area is also well known for its **Ganesh Temple**, which is one of the four Ganesh temples protecting the Kathmandu Valley. For the local people, this temple has the reputation of curing sores and pimples. The Ganesh image is reputed to date from the eighth-ninth centuries and once a year is taken around locally in a chariot. Tuesdays are the most popular days for devotees.

Pashupatinath

★ Some 4 km northeast of central Kathmandu, Nepal's most important Hindu pilgrimage site is located on the banks of the Bagmati river, in the dry season no more than a trickle of badly polluted water. It survived the 2015 earthquake with virtually no damage.

To enter it you must pass the chaos of stalls outside with vendors selling souvenirs to visitors and pilgrims alike. It covers an area of more than 260 ha with almost as many temples and religious monuments. Pashupatinath has been designated a World Heritage Site by UNESCO and it's a bustle of religious fervour and activity, making it one of the most evocative places in Kathmandu. The early morning or the evening are the most atmospheric times to visit.

The site of the burial ghats and the endless flow of cremations, the smells of incense and sandlewood and the devout demeanour of the pilgrims, mourners and worshippers make it a truly unique place in Nepal and one not to be missed. To be cremated at such a sacred place is the goal of most Hindus as it breaks the cycle of rebirths, ending the spiritual journey.

For other pilgrims the rite of bathing is considered to give great blessings, although anyone who sees the fetid trickle of water in the winter and spring would think it a blessing simply to survive. It's believed that if you bathe in these waters with your husband or wife you will ensure that you will be married again in your next life. Festivals are the most popular time for ritual bathing.

Pashupatinath Temple
Free.

The original temple was reputedly built by a Licchavi king, Supuspadeva, 39 generations before Mandadeva (AD 464-505), but later underwent considerable repair and reconstruction. The main temple was renovated by Queen Gangadevi during the period 1578-1620, turning it into a pagoda of brass and gilt with silver-plated gateways. Upon her death the Pashupati linga is said to have emitted a cry of lamentation so loud that local residents were deafened.

Non-Hindus, which usually includes Western converts to Hinduism, are not allowed into this 17th-century temple, but from the southern entrance you may get a glimpse of the gilt Nandi bull, Shiva's vehicle. It is thought to be around 300 years old, though was not placed here until 1879. The black, four-headed image of Pashupati inside the temple is older, and it replaced one destroyed by Muslim invaders in the 14th century.

The temple courtyard
For non-Hindus the best views of the main Pashupatinath Temple are from the steps rising above the east bank of the Bagmati which overlook the eastern gate. Cross the footbridge and climb until you see the fence of the deer park on your left, walk beside this and after a small café you will see a row of benches running north overlooking the Arya Ghat. This is a great place for viewing the complex and ceremonies that are in progress. Looking through the main temple entrance you can see the back of the gilded bull facing the main shrine. This is a two-storeyed pagoda temple that dominates the complex, its gold- and silver-bedecked roofs rising majestically from the centre and supported by wooden struts carved with portraits of various deities. Adorning the pinnacle are Shiva's trident (*trishul*), axe and drum.

The Pashupatinath Temple and inner courtyard has been administered by a *guthi* or a trust of priests from the Bhattas order from South India since the 1650s. This almost ended in 2009 when the new Marxist Government carried out a review and the then chief priest was forced to resign due to corruption. He and his assistants were taking most of the money offerings, paying themselves with it and sending much of the rest to Karnataka in southern India. He was replaced with Nepalese priests.

The government imposed a new pay system, meaning that the senior priest now receives a salary and expenses package of Rs 156,000 per month while his four assistants receive Rs 125,000. All offerings go towards the Pashupati Area Development Trust, created in 1987 to manage the whole complex and the changes are noticeable. Much of the land has been cleared of shanties and a new electric crematorium has been opened, something not yet embraced by the local population.

Essential Pashupatinath

Getting there

Located about 4 km from the centre of Kathmandu, the easiest way is to get there is to take a taxi (US$3.50-4). You might consider negotiating a rate that takes in both Pashupatinath and Bodhnath which is nearby and can easily be visited together in a day. The cost of this trip should be about US$7-8 post haggle.

It's possible to walk from the town centre but the roads are congested and polluted and there are few things of note to see along the way. The walk takes just under an hour.

Vasuki Temple

In the northeast of the courtyard is the Vasuki Temple, dedicated to the image of the Naga king Vasuki, whose lower body appears as an intricate tangled body of snakes. Devotees generally circumambulate the Vasuki Temple before worshipping Pashupatinath, as Vasuki is considered the main temple's protector. It was constructed by King Pratap Malla during the Malla period. In the northwest corner, images of Shiva's consort Parvati decorate the Tandav Shiva Temple, while to the southeast, the Kotilinga Temple is a three-storey circular building surrounded at its base by a large number of linga-yonis.

Just to the west of the main temple, a large building with a sloping grey roof (visible from the east bank of the Bagmati) houses a collection of religious images. Elsewhere in the courtyard numerous statues stand freely, including those of Hanuman, Unmatta Bhairab, Vishnu and Garuda, King Mahendra, and a large Shiva trident.

Surrounding the main Pashupatinath temple complex are numerous structures and temples which are open to non-Hindus.

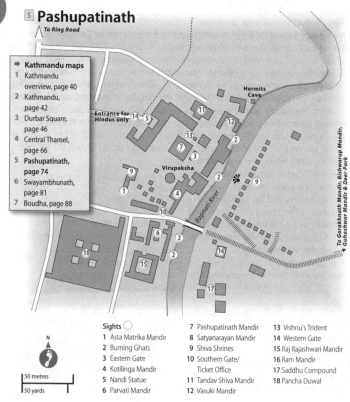

⑤ Pashupatinath

↑ To Ring Road

→ **Kathmandu maps**
1 Kathmandu overview, page 40
2 Kathmandu, page 42
3 Durbar Square, page 46
4 Central Thamel, page 66
5 Pashupatinath, page 74
6 Swayambhunath, page 81
7 Boudha, page 88

Hermits Cave

Entrance for Hindus only

Virupaksha

Bagmati River

To Gorakhnath Mandir, Bishwarup Mandir, Guheshwar Mandir & Deer Park

N

50 metres
50 yards

Sights ○
1 Asta Matrika Mandir
2 Burning Ghats
3 Eastern Gate
4 Kotilinga Mandir
5 Nandi Statue
6 Parvati Mandir
7 Pashupatinath Mandir
8 Satyanarayan Mandir
9 Shiva Shrines
10 Southern Gate/ Ticket Office
11 Tandav Shiva Mandir
12 Vasuki Mandir
13 Vishnu's Trident
14 Western Gate
15 Raj Rajashwari Mandir
16 Ram Mandir
17 Saddhu Compound
18 Pancha Duwal

Panchadeval
Just west of Pashupatinath complex is a cluster of white temples called Panchadeval ('five temples'). Built in 1870, the central temple and the four surrounding it all have Shiva lingas as their central shrines. The pilgrim rest houses around the temple are used for homeless old people, and outside vendors sell an array of *puja* accessories including a colourful selection of powdered dyes which entrepreneurial traders push as paint dyes to tourists.

Parvati Temple
To the south and near the river is the sixth-century Parvati (or Bacchereshwari) Temple, another two-storeyed pagoda with a crescent moon unusually forming part of the pinnacle. This contains a number of erotic Hindu tantric carvings and it is thought that in the past human sacrifices were made here during the Shivaratri festival. The adjoining **Narayan Temple** is said to have been constructed in the course of a single night in 1929, a memorial to the late prime minister Chandra Shamsher Rana. Nearby is a fine but neglected seventh-century Buddha statue while a little further down the river is the **Raj Rajashwari Temple**, notable for its carved windows and roof struts, and where many congregate during the Shivaratri celebration. It contains life-sized images of Rama, his consort and three brothers, and at the entrance is a huge Shiva linga image. The upper floor has five dome-like structures with gilt finials and commands a very good view of Kathmandu.

The Cremation Ghats
Along the western riverbank are the Cremation Ghats, four on either side of the footbridge by the Parvati Temple. Cremations follow prescribed rituals and are presided over by a *pandit*, or Hindu priest, with family members also playing an active role in the ceremony. You can observe ceremonies from the opposite bank or from the rooftop above the southern ghats. Although conducted in the open air, a funeral is, as in the West, a profoundly emotional occasion, so sensitivity to the grief of the mourners is recommended. Conspicuous photography of a cremation is intrusive and is considered, at best, impolite.

Arya Ghat Located north of the footbridge is the Arya Ghat. The further upstream the ghat, the more important the person being cremated, as here the water is purest and the positioning immediately outside the temple. The furthest used to be reserved for members of the royal family (after the Royal Massacre of 2001 the army had to build additional temporary ghats to cope with the number of cremations). The next one downstream was for VIPs, such as high-caste families and important dignitaries. Now the royal family has lost its status, they are all used for high-status ceremonies.

You will also notice people on stretchers, laid out on the stone steps of the ghats with their feet in the water. These are pilgrims, often staying in the temple's guesthouses, who are dying and want to die in the river to ensure they escape reincarnation. A drink of the sacred waters is also believed to help (and judging by its putrid state it might well help speed up the end at least!)

Between the footbridges is the **Vatsala Mandir**, a two-tiered temple dedicated to an incarnation of Parvati. The roof struts, depicting dancing skeletons, give an indication as to the nature of the temples goddess. According to tradition, human sacrifice used to be practiced here but has been replaced by an annual festival during which the idol is worshipped with beer. In front of the temple is a row of small carved *nandis* (Shiva's bull mount), as well as a couple of lions. Nearby is a small enclosure dedicated to Ganesh with some ancient but undated statues.

Slightly further upstream is the **Ananta Narayan**, an elegant terracotta figure standing in a small brick archway. It dates from the 18th century, made by a local craftsman who, when refused permission to erect it in the main courtyard, put it up here.

Ram Ghat To the south of the footbridge is Ram Ghat, open for the cremation of all castes and as a consequence always busy. To its southern end you can see a Buddha statue, said to date to the fifth century, set in a brick arch and standing against a white shrine. You are not allowed onto the ghat itself. To its south stands the **Raj Rajeshwari**, an oval shrine named after a 19th-century queen forced to commit *suti* on the cremation fire of her husband. To its south, in the same group of buildings, lies the **Nawa Durga**, a guilded pagoda dedicated to the nine manifestations of the goddess Durga.

Pashupatinath: east bank

sadhus, monkeys and the best viewpoints

The east bank of Pashupatinath covers a larger area, much of which is still wooded in memory of where Vishnu lived as a stag before he was captured. Deer are still kept here, although they are fenced into certain areas.

As you cross the footbridge from the west bank you see the stepped ghats stretching away in both directions. To the north they are backed by a long row of shrines (built in the mid-18th century and each containing a stone linga) that was erected to commemorate widows who had committed sati and are dedicated to Shiva.

At the northern end of the stepped ghats, across the river on the west bank is the **Hermit's Cave**, one of several caves that have been cut into the rock on both banks of the river which are used by sadhus for meditation.

To the south the ghat stretches away and there are three temples to Vishnu. You reach the first one by climbing the first few steps of the stone stairway in front of you and turning right into the compound, the second opening. This is dedicated to Ram, his mortal incarnation, and contains a large black stone statue of King Vishnugupta dating to the seventh century. Standing opposite its entrance are three lovely statues, each covered in paint offerings. They are of Ganesh, Hanuman and Garuda.

Behind these, beside the low compound wall, is a large metal plate in the ground. This was put in to cover the entrance to the **Satis' Gate**, a flight of steps that led directly down to the ghat itself and was a popular route for satis to take before throwing themselves on the cremation pyres of their dead husbands. When the practice was outlawed in 1920, the gateway was blocked.

Walking south, past a large building used for yoga, you come to the entrance to a second compound in which the other two Vishnu temples lie. They are dedicated to Lakshmi Narayan and Ram Janaki. They are smaller and surrounded by other shrines and sacred stones. The highlight of this compound is the sadhus who sleep around its edge, some in small cells, others in open-fronted spaces. There is often someone reciting sacred texts with a small group of listeners as you enter the compound.

Looking over its wall is also a good spot for watching the ceremonies unfolding on Ram Ghat from a discreet vantage point.

Gorakhnath Temple
Behind the ghats, at the top of the steep stone staircase that climbs from the footbridge before swinging left through the forest on a shrine-lined path, is a tall brick shikhara structure with a brass trident in front, surrounded by lingas. This is one of the oldest temples dedicated to Gorakhnath, a semi-mythical figure who is considered a guardian deity of the Nath sect. He is said to have arrived in Kathmandu around about the 11th century. The temple was built by Jayasthiti Malla in the late 14th century on a site dating several hundred years further back and is believed to contain the footprints of Gorakhnath.

There are several recently renovated guesthouses around the temple for pilgrims, including many sadhus, to stay in. You will see plenty in this area, many sitting in particularly photographic spots for a reason. A small offering will be expected if you take their photo. The whole area from the top of the steps to the temple is an atmospheric place, away from the noise of the city and with shrines everywhere, some tumbling peacefully into disrepair.

Bishwarup Temple
When you reach the top of the stairs, with a Ganesh statue on your left, the stone path swings left. If you continue straight, along a broken-surfaced path, you will soon come to the Bishwarup or Vishvarupa Temple. (Non-Hindus are not allowed inside.) It is a Mogul-style building with an onion-domed edifice in which there is a huge image of Shiva in union with his Shakti, almost 6 m high. It was damaged in the 2015 earthquake, with half the dome destroyed. Repairs are planned.

Guheshwari Temple
Beyond the Gorakhnath Temple the stone trail descends towards the Bagmati river and in front of you is the Guheshwari Temple, built in the 17th century and dedicated to Kali, the goddess of destruction and re-birth. It is closely identified with the original sati. This goddess is said to have exploded with grief when her husband Shiva was not invited to a feast by her father. Shiva carried her dead body with him as he travelled the world and, according to the legend, the remains of her reproductive organ, or yoni, fell to the earth here.

The arched tubular metal construction covers the main temple. Near the top, four gilded snakes support the roof apex illustrating the yantra diagram (geometric triangle).

In the centre of the temple is a pool covered at the base in gold and silver. At the head of the pool is a jar which is worshipped as the goddess Guheshwari and the water from the pool is accepted as her offering. Again, only Hindus are allowed inside to see the gilded shrine room. Thousands of devotees visit Guheshwari daily.

Just to its east lies the **Kirateshwar Mahadev Mandir**, a burial ground for the Rai and Limbu people. Their burial customs differ from the usual cremation.

Warning The many monkeys living in the area should be treated with caution. These wooded parts are popular spots for picnics and the monkeys know all about food kept in bags. Keep a tight hold of bags and avoid tempting them with food, as they will not hesitate to assert their perceived right to your packed lunch. In the late afternoon they are fed inside the temple courtyard – the sight of the advancing monkey mob is memorable indeed.

Swayambhunath

★ About 2 km west of Durbar Square is one of the most sacred sites of Nepal. The Swayambhunath Stupa is revered as the oldest and one of the two most important sites of Buddhist worship in Kathmandu. It is a major landmark, towering above Padmachala Hill and 175 m above the valley, offering great views especially in the cool of early morning.

Swayambhunath Stupa

the atmospheric monkey temple

According to legend, the hill and stupa occupy the site where the Buddha of the previous aeon, Vipashyin, is said to have thrown a lotus seed into the lake which then filled the valley, causing it to bloom and radiate with a 'self-arising' luminosity, identified with that of the primordial Buddha, Vajradhara. This 'self-arising' or 'Swayambhu' is what gave the site its name, making the hill appear magically above the lake waters. The bodhisatva Manjushri is believed to have made this lotus light accessible to worshippers by using his sword to cleave a watercourse for the rivers of the valley, and thereby draining the lake. Newar Buddhists hold that the primordial Buddha Vajradhara is even now embodied in the timber axis of the stupa.

Another legend tells that the site was visited by the Great Emperor Askoka over 2000 years ago but the earliest historical associations of the site are linked to Vrishadeva, the patriarch of the Licchavi Dynasty, who is said to have built the first shrine, perhaps using

Essential Swayambhunath

Getting there

A taxi from Thamel or Durbar Square will cost about US$2.75.

Swayambhunath is a comfortable 45-minute walk from Durbar Square, along Maruhiti Tole to the river which you cross by a footbridge. There are cremation ghats on the riverbank. The path then leads through a built-up area with a sizeable Tibetan carpet weaving community. If you get lost keep looking up as the temple is often visible between the buildings and will guide you in. The locals are always happy to point you the right way. As everywhere in Kathmandu the traffic is chaotic and motorbikes proliferate so take care.

Opening times

Dawn until dusk.

Entry fee

US$1.80.

a pre-existing projecting stone. Later inscriptions attribute the stupa's construction to his great-grandson King Mandeva I (c AD 450) and its reconstruction to the Indian master Shantikara, a contemporary of King Amshuvarman. It became a focal point for Indian pilgrims and was frequented by Padmasambhava, Atisha and others. By 1234 it had become an important centre of Buddhist learning, with close ties to Tibet.

In 1349 Muslim troops from Bengal sacked the shrine, but it was soon rebuilt with its now familiar tall spire. In 1614 additions and renovations were made by Zhamarpa VI during the reign of Pratap Malla. Access from Kathmandu was improved with the construction of a long stairway and a bridge across the Vishnumati. Pratap Malla also added two new temple spires and a large *vajra* placed in front of the stupa. Later repairs were carried out by Katok Tsewang Norbu (1750), Pawo Rinpoche VII (1758), and the Shah kings (1825 and 1983).

The famous stupa is the centre and focal point of the complex which also includes numerous *chaityas*, shrines and decorative religious art. The stupa was renovated between 2008 and 2010 when 20 kg of gold was used to re-gild it and it survived to 2015 earthquakes without serious damage, although a couple of the smaller shrines were damaged.

Eastern stairway (1)

As you climb the eastern stairway (keep to the left as the right side is for descending), it soon becomes apparent why the complex is also known as the 'Monkey Temple'. Numerous monkeys live around the stupa and are not afraid of people. Indeed, they view them as a source of food and are not shy in coming to find it: treat with caution and take care of bags.

The climb up the 360+ stone steps is more impressive than the modern road you can take up to the western side. At their foot are three painted images symbolizing the Three Precious Jewels of Buddhism, which were erected in 1637 by Pratap Malla and his son, Lakshmandra Singh Malla. A large footprint in the stone is said to be that of either the Buddha or Manjushri. At regular intervals are pairs of eagles, lions, horses and peacocks, the vehicles of the peaceful meditational Buddhas. There are also a few places to sit down if you need a rest, including an area halfway up where it opens up a little bit and you will find three more Golden Buddhas. The steps after this are very steep so take care.

When you reach the top there is the ticket office on your left and you then enter the compound. If you need to recover from the climb before looking around the complex, there is a viewpoint around to the left with views out over Kathmandu. Arrive early if you want the best view otherwise they disappear into a cloud of smog.

As well as the main monuments listed below the whole hill top is covered in smaller stupas, bells, prayer flags, sacred stones and shrines. In places you have to squeeze between them to get through but they are all worshipped, daubed with offerings and paint, and give the complex a wonderful feel.

Great Vajra (2)

The first thing you see is the Great Vajra set upon its drum base, symbolizing firmness of spirit, and a huge bell to one side. It is flanked by two lions, with bronze flags behind. A *vajra* is a ritual weapon with the properties of diamond for indestructibility and a thunderbolt for irresistible force. Around the pedestal are the 12 animals from the Tibetan calendar: hare, dragon, snake, horse, sheep, monkey, bird, dog, pig, mouse, ox and tiger. Legend has it that it was built on the site of an old well that reflected images of the dead. People would see the reflection of loved ones, jump in and drown so it was covered up.

Pratapur (3) and Anantapur (4)

These two shrines flank the Great Vajra to its north and south. They were both bullet-shaped *shikari*, Indian in style. They were built by Pratap Malla in 1646 to house the protector deities Bhairava and Bhairavi. Sadly, the Pratapur was damaged after a storm in 2011 although it still stands to its full height. The Anantapur was destroyed down to ground-floor level in the 2015 earthquake. There are plans to repair and rebuild.

6 Swayambhunath

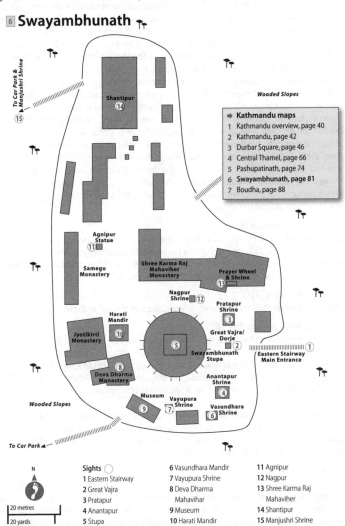

➡ **Kathmandu maps**
1 Kathmandu overview, page 40
2 Kathmandu, page 42
3 Durbar Square, page 46
4 Central Thamel, page 66
5 Pashupatinath, page 74
6 **Swayambhunath, page 81**
7 Boudha, page 88

Wooded Slopes

To Car Park & Manjushri Shrine

Shantipur (14)

(15)

Agnipur Statue (11)

Samegu Monastery

Shree Karma Raj Mahaviher Monastery

Prayer Wheel & Shrine (13)

Nagpur Shrine (12)

Pratapur Shrine (3)

Harati Mandir (10)

Jyotikirti Monastery

Great Vajra/ Dorje (2)

Swayambhunath Stupa (5)

Deva Dharma Monastery (8)

Anantapur Shrine (4)

Eastern Stairway Main Entrance (1)

Museum (9)

Vayupura Shrine (7)

Vasundhara Shrine (6)

Wooded Slopes

To Car Park ◄

N

20 metres
20 yards

Sights ○
1 Eastern Stairway
2 Great Vajra
3 Pratapur
4 Anantapur
5 Stupa

6 Vasundhara Mandir
7 Vayupura Shrine
8 Deva Dharma Mahavihar
9 Museum
10 Harati Mandir

11 Agnipur
12 Nagpur
13 Shree Karma Raj Mahaviher
14 Shantipur
15 Manjushri Shrine

Stupa (5)

With a diameter of 20 m and standing 10 m high, the stupa has been a model for subsequent stupas constructed throughout Nepal. It was seriously damaged by a storm in the summer of 1816, coinciding with the arrival of the first official British Resident in Kathmandu, an association not lost on the suspicious Nepalese. Repairs were carried out a decade later.

The various tiers of its base and dome respectively symbolize the elements: earth, water, fire, air, and space. Above the dome is the square, golden *harmika*, each side of which has the eyes of the Buddha, added during the 16th century, gazing compassionately from beneath heavy black eyebrows. This is fringed by a curtain of golden ornaments, including chimes and bells that move in the wind. The shape of the nose is considered by some to represent the number '1' in Nepali script, symbolizing unity.

The 13 steps of the spire surmounting the *harmika* represent the successive bodhisatva and Buddha levels and the crowning canopy represents the goal of buddhahood. Some believe that this canopy, which looks like a small umbrella, is full of precious jewels.

On each of the four sides of the domed white stupa, at the cardinal points, there are golden shrines dedicated to one of the meditational Buddhas, each with its distinct posture and gesture, but barely visible through the metal curtains and security grilles that cover them. Aksobhya is in the east, Ratnasambhava in the south, Amitabha in the west, and Amoghasiddhi in the north. Vairocana, the deity in the centre, is actually depicted on the east side, along with Aksobhya. The female counterparts of these Buddhas are located within the niches of the intermediate directions. The faithful turn the prayer wheel as they walk clockwise around the shrine.

Vasundhara Mandir (6)

Circumambulating the stupa clockwise, as you always should, you will pass the Newar shrine dedicated to Vasundhara. This is a traditional brick building, with ornately carved figures on it roof struts and tile cobras on the side of the door. Vasundhara is actually the same being as Annapurna and Lakshmi, the Earth Goddess.

Vayupura shrine (7)

This small, marble shrine is dedicated to Vedic, the god of wind and storms.

Deva Dharma Mahavihar (8)

Climb up the stairs and on your left is this small monastery, damaged during the 2015 earthquake but still in use for prayer. Look out for the two bronze statues of the White and Green Taras, the deified Nepali wives of an eighth-century Tibetan king called Sondtsen Gampo, who are credited with introducing Buddhism to their adopted country. They stand between the monastery and the stupa behind glass panels.

Museum (9) This small museum, tucked in behind the Deva Dharma Mahavihar, contains a collection of both Buddhist and Hindu carvings and statues, mostly behind security grilles and glass but with some beautiful examples on display. There is also a small reclining Buddha to whom you can make a cash offering.

Harati Mandir (10)

This completely gilded temple is dedicated to Harati, the goddess of smallpox and children's illnesses, and looks dazzling if you see it in the midday sun. As she is the goddess of both the diseases and the cures there are often mothers with their children making offerings. The original idol was destroyed by Rana Bahedir Shah in a fit of rage when his wife died of smallpox. The temple is too small to enter and photography of its interior is banned.

Agnipur (11)
Dedicated to the Vedic fire god Agni, this shrine is identifiable by the two lions in front of it. It consists of a large white boulder with a red face painted on it, with two small bells hanging to the sides to ring when you make an offering.

Nagpur (12)
This small water tank is dedicated to appease all the snake spirits in the valley. If it has been drained when you visit look out for the idol carved on its floor. It is surrounded by railings to stop people falling in and also to allow butter lamps to be lit and left as offerings.

Shree Karma Raj Mahaviher (13)
This monastery contains a large Buddha and has plenty of character, usually with many butter lamps flickering away, prayer wheels spinning and pilgrims worshipping. In the late afternoon there is often a ceremony, a good chance to listen to the extraordinary Buddhist chanting.

Shantipur (14)
Situated at the northern end of the courtyard, the Shantipur, also known as the Akashpur or 'sky palace', was damaged in the 2015 earthquake and, while it is still standing, has structural issues that prevent you from entering. It is a shrine to the fifth-century holy man Shanti Shri. Legend has it that towards the end of his life he sealed himself in a chamber beneath this shrine, saying that he would meditate and only reappear when the valley needed him. In 1658, during a terrible drought, King Pratab Malla is said to have entered the chamber to ask for help. After surviving bats, ghosts, evil spirits and snakes he's said to have found the holy man and returned, somewhat shaken, with a rain-making symbol.

Your chances of seeing the holy man are slim but when the Shantipur reopens you can admire the frescoes inside the shrine, said to depict scenes from various creation myths of the valley.

A flight of stone steps goes down to the left of the Shandipur and drops to the saddle between the two summits of Swayambhunath. This is where the access road finishes, with two stupas and a large bell constructed in 2009, as well as a Golden Buddha standing in a large pool of water with an offering vessel in front of her. It is a popular pastime for Nepali visitors and pilgrims to buy coins from the numerous old ladies with coin stalls and attempt to throw them into this pot.

Manjushri Shrine (15)

Situated on the second small hilltop to the west, this canopied Chaitra is believed to be over 1500 years old. Manjushri is the Buddhist God of Wisdom and believed to be the founder of all civilization in the valley. Normally he would be represented by an empty niche, but in a piece of cultural merging typical of Nepal, a statue of the Hindu Goddess of Learning, Sarawati, now fills the space. This statue is itself believed to be over 300 years old and is a place of pilgrimage for Hindus.

A pleasant walkway circumnavigates this hilltop, offering great views the whole way round of both the sprawling city and the foothills beyond. There are monasteries, temples and stupas dotted all around and their rooftops and the trees are festooned with prayer flags, some strings hundreds of metres long. It makes for an enjoyable stroll to escape the bustle of the city.

National Museum

South of the Swayambhunath complex, www.nationalmuseum.gov.np, open Wed-Sun 1030-1630, Mon 1030-1430, US$1.40.

This small museum houses an eclectic collection of antiquities of national importance, most dating from the early 18th century onwards. On display are vestments of previous rulers and prime ministers, including the personal drinking pot of Bhimsen Thappa, Nepal's first prime minister, military uniforms, coins from the 14th century, khukri knives, pistols, rifles and other weapons, many associated with the Gurkhas.

The **Judda Art Gallery**, immediately on the left as you enter, has a collection with some wonderful *thankas*. Especially memorable are those featuring a series of scenes from the *Ramayana* and *Mahabharata* epics. The museum also has a collection of sculptures going back over 2000 years, some exquisite wood carvings, a poorly maintained display of taxonomy and even a Hudson car imported from the US.

Rather than being run-down, the museum gives the impression of never seriously having been run-up, but it is worth a visit if passing as part of a day at Swayambhunath.

Bodhnath
Stupa

★ Bodhnath Stupa, about 5 km east of central Kathmandu, is the centre of the Tibetan community, many arriving after fleeing the Chinese invasion of their homeland in the 1950s. It's also one of the most sacred and atmospheric places in Nepal. It was damaged in the 2015 earthquake when the central tower crowning the stupa became unstable. It was dismantled to stop a collapse damaging the lower structures. Reconstruction work has started and it is due to be completed in early 2017.

When complete it is 38 m high, 100 m in circumference, and looms above the road dominating the ancient trade route between Kathmandu and Lhasa. Travellers and traders used to stop to either pray for a safe journey or to give thanks for their arrival and it is revered by both Tibetan and Newar Buddhists.

Monks chant in the many monasteries near the stupa, the smell of incense and butter lamps pungent in the air, while Tibetan exiles and pilgrims circle the stupa, praying and spinning the prayer wheels. One spin of a prayer wheel at this sacred site is said to be the equivalent of saying the Buddhist mantra 11,000 times. It is especially atmospheric at full moon when it is lit by thousands of small lamps.

Stupa

By its sheer size, the Bodhnath Stupa may seem even more impressive than the one at Swayambhunath. It too has a hemispherical dome symbolizing the emptiness from which everything emanates, topped by a square *harmika* painted on each side with the eyes of the Buddha symbolizing awareness, above which rises the spire with its 13 steps or stages to the canopy which symbolizes the goal of buddhahood.

However, it is now almost hidden from distant view by the surrounding buildings, which create an attractive courtyard effect for the stupa itself. One of the best places to see the stupa in its full glory is by visiting one of the rooftop cafés and restaurants that surround it.

Around the octagonal three-tiered base of the stupa there is a brick wall with 147 niches and 108 images of the meditational Buddhas, inset behind copper prayer wheels. Each section of the wall holds four to five such prayer wheels.

The main entrance to the stupa area is on the south side, and the principal shrine dedicated to the female protectress Ajima or Hariti is to the northwest. Ajima is shown sucking the intestines out of a corpse and in legend stole children to feed her own. It was only when Buddha took one of her children and she realized the suffering she was inflicting did she stop; she is now worshipped as the protector of children.

Around the stupa there is a pilgrims' circuit which is densely thronged in the early mornings and evenings by local Tibetan residents and by pilgrims from far-flung parts of the Himalayan region and beyond. You occasionally see devout pilgrims prostrating themselves one body length at a time as they circle the stupa. Some are said to have done this all the way from Lhasa.

Numerous shrines, bookstores and handicraft shops surround the circuit, the speciality being Newar silverware cast by the cire perdue (lost wax) process. There are also plenty of places to eat or grab a drink.

Boudha *See map, page 88.*

In recent decades Boudha, once a remote village, has become a densely populated suburb of Kathmandu. There is a particularly high concentration of Tibetans here, alongside the older Newar and Tamang communities, and this is reflected in the prolific temple building in which the various Tibetan traditions have engaged since the late 1960s.

If you wish to visit one, try the **Tamang Gompa** ① *free entry but it is polite to leave an offering*, directly opposite the Ajima shrine. Look out for the enormous prayer wheel which you can spin. If the main doors are open, you are allowed into the main prayer hall (remove your shoes as you enter and if worship is in progress sit quietly at

BACKGROUND
Bodhnath Stupa

Tibetans believe the stupa to contain the bone relics of either the past Buddha Kashyapa or a fingerbone of Siddhartha himself but, since the inside is sealed, no one knows for sure. There are two main legends as to its origins. Tibetan texts say that it was built by a lowly poultry keeper and widow four times over named Jadzimo, who was originally the daughter of Indra but who'd been exiled to Earth for selling flowers. Wishing to utilize her meagre resources in an offering to the Buddha, Jadzimo sought permission from the king to build a shrine. She was granted permission to build something in the area that a buffalo skin could cover; so she cut the hide into strips, tied them together and marked out a huge plot.

When construction started, the local nobility became jealous and resentful that such a great stupa was being constructed by one of such humble social standing. They demanded that the king order its immediate destruction, but the good-hearted monarch refused with the words *'Jarung Kashor'* ('The permission given shall not be revoked') from which comes the stupa's Tibetan name, Chorten Jarung Kashor. Jadzimo's sons are said to have been subsequently reborn as King Trisong Dtesen, Shantaraksita and Padmasambhava, who together established Buddhism in eighth-century Tibet, while the widow herself is said to have attained buddhahood and is known as the Protectress Pramoha Devi. Today the stupa is known as Chorten Chempo or simply as the Great Stupa.

Newar chronicles, in contrast, hold the stupa to have been constructed by the Licchavi King Manadeva in the latter half of the fifth century AD in order to atone for his crime of patricide. His father, Vrisadev, was advised by his astrologers that only the sacrifice of a virtuous man would end a terrible drought. He therefore told his son Manadev to go a certain place and behead the man he found there. This his son did and was distraught when he drew back the shroud on his victim to find his father. To atone he was told to build the stupa on the site where a freed bird landed.

The stupa's Newari name, Khasti Chaitya (Dewdrop Stupa), comes from a story that a terrible drought coincided with its construction when workers put out cloths at night to be able to drink the dewdrops which accumulated. Other versions maintain that the name comes from the Khas Mallas, a dominant ruling house of the time of the stupa's construction, or from the relics contained within Khasa, the name both of a village on the Tibet-Nepal border and a Tibetan lama, or from Kasyapa, a previous Buddha.

The structure was subsequently restored (some sources say re-constructed) by the Nyingmapa lama Shakya Zangbo in the early 16th century, perhaps after damage inflicted by the Mughal invasion. Later, following the 1852 treaty between Nepal and the Manchus, which ended the Tibeto-Nepalese border wars, the abbotship of Boudha was granted in 1859 to a Chinese delegate whose descendants, known as Chini Lamas, continued until recently to hold a privileged position in local affairs.

the back). Back near the entrance area there are steps up to the first floor which has a lovely balcony overlooking the shrine and stupa. You can continue up the stairs to the roof where there are more great views. It is free to enter but polite to leave an offering.

The other monastery directly on the square is the **Maitreya** ⓘ *open 1500-1800*, situated on the west side of the stupa.

It's worth exploring the area if you have time; an hour will let you see some of the impressive monasteries that crowd around this important Buddhist site. Getting into some of the back streets and alleys lets you see everyday life going on around the stupa and shows how strong the Tibetan influence is.

Leave the square in the northeast, passing the temple of 1000 Buddhas and following the road north. The first turn on the right brings you to the **Shakya Tharig Monastery**. This was damaged in the 2015 earthquake and is currently being rebuilt. When it reopens it can be visited at between 1000 and 1100. Continue further along the road until you come to the **Pal Dilyag Monastery** ⓘ *you can visit the courtyard at any time but the main*

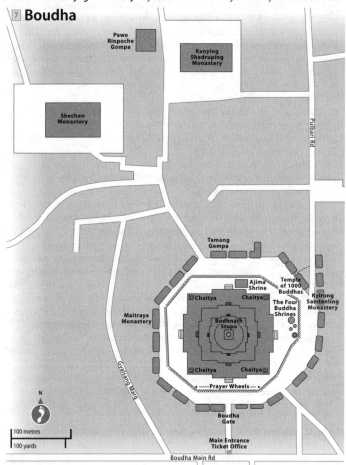

7 **Boudha**

Pawo Rinpoche Gompa

Kanying Shedruping Monastery

Shechen Monastery

Pulbari Rd

Tamang Gompa

Ajima Shrine

Temple of 1000 Buddhas

Chaitya   Chaitya

Kyirong Samtenling Monastery

The Four Buddha Shrines

Maitraya Monastery

Bodhnath Stupa

Gyalrang Marg

Chaitya   Chaitya

◀——— Prayer Wheels ——▶

N

100 metres
100 yards

Boudha Gate

Main Entrance Ticket Office

Boudha Main Rd

gompa is only open 1430-1530, free entry but usual to leave an offering, on your left. You enter a large courtyard with the monastery in front of you and the accommodation blocks for the monks on either side. The monastery is adorned with huge, colourful paintings. Look out for the Wheel of Life on the right.

Retrace your steps to the main road and continue north. You will soon come to a colourful archway on your right denoting the entrance to the **Tharlam Monastery** ⓘ *open 1000-1100*. Follow the road for a couple of hundred metres and you will enter the monastery complex with its guesthouse and restaurant on your left. Inside the courtyard you will see the gompa on your left with the monk accommodation on the other sides. Remove your shoes in the small entrance hall on the left. Look out for the intricate Wheel of Life drawn on a table in coloured sand. Don't sneeze! This is one of the most important monasteries in the area, with over 80 senior monks and 100 novices. They are very friendly and the younger monks often approach you to practice their English.

Return to the main road and head south until you see a right turn. Follow this and the **Kanying Shedupling Monastery** ⓘ *open 1400-1500*, is on your right. It is known locally as the White Monastery as its exterior is much less decorative than the other establishments. This is a favourite teaching monastery with Westerners who come for stays from a few weeks to a few years to receive meditational and spiritual guidance.

Continue along the road turning left and first right to arrive at the **Shechen Monastery**, one of the largest in the Boudha area. You can see it as you approach, rising up on your right-hand side. Enter the courtyard and climb the steps to approach the impressive gompa although it's not possible to enter at present due to repair work being carried out after the 2015 earthquake. The monks' quarters are arranged either side (it is currently home to over 100 monks). To the left is their guesthouse and small café, a lovely, peaceful spot to relax and take refreshments.

Retrace your steps to the main alley and turning right you will soon re-emerge in the Boudha square, opposite the Ajima shrine.

Tharlam
Monastery

Shakya
Tharig
Monastery

Pal Oilyag
Monastery

Tip...
If you want to see some of the many monasteries in the area, hire a local guide from outside the ticket office for a couple of hours. The fee should be no more than US$7-7.50.

ON THE ROAD

Boris of Kathmandu

Boris of Kathmandu is a near legendary figure in Nepal, seen as the man who opened up this small Himalayan country to tourism. Born in Odessa, Ukraine in 1905, the son of a wealthy horse trader, Boris Lissanevitch's life changed forever in the Russian Revolution of 1917. Until then he had been destined for a military career. Instead, to avoid the attentions of the Communists, his parents enrolled him in a ballet school and he worked at the Odessa Opera House.

When the opportunity presented itself, Boris fled to Paris and claimed asylum. He managed to get a position with the Ballets Russes and was invited to tour Asia. He visited India, China, Singapore and Indo-China and discovered wildlife tourism, which in the 1930s meant shooting. On his three-month tour of Cambodia, Boris found time to shoot 13 bantengs (a type of wild cattle), 12 gaur (bison), six leopards, two clouded leopards and six tigers.

Boris realized that Asia offered him opportunities he wouldn't get in a Europe where war was once more looming. He arrived in Calcutta and opened the exclusive 300 Club. It brought him into contact with the cream of Indian society, including Maharajas, the ruling British elite and King Tribhuvan of Nepal with whom, it is said, he secretly plotted the downfall of the Rana regime.

The successful restoration of the monarchy in 1950 and the king's new policy of opening the country to the outside world gave Boris the chance he needed. He successfully negotiated a monopoly of alcohol in the Kathmandu Valley, hoping to control its production and trade in return for an annual payment. The venture failed and he was jailed for failure to pay; locals came in to look at him in prison as if he were an attraction at the zoo.

Boris was released after a few weeks and asked if he would be willing to provide the catering for the new King Mahendra's coronation and help look after the foreign dignitaries and guests. So Boris opened the Royal Hotel in an old Rana palace on Kantipath, the very first hotel in Kathmandu suitable for Western tourists.

As climbing permits for mountaineering expeditions started to be issued in the 1950s, the Yak and Yeti Bar at the Royal Hotel (see page 91) became a second home for many of the mountaineers. Boris was charged with organizing Queen Elizabeth II's visit to Chitwan in 1961, and facilitated several big-game hunting trips for other rulers and VIPs.

He became good friends with one of the regulars, Jimmy Roberts, an experienced climber and explorer, who set up a guiding agency in 1964 called Mountain Travel Nepal, and helped to establish the trekking industry.

Boris Lissanevitch died in Kathmandu in 1985 and is buried in the cemetery of the British Embassy. His extraordinary life can be read about in the biography *Tiger for Breakfast*, by M Peissel, available in most Kathmandu bookshops.

Orgyen Dongak Choling

The only temple of importance on the south side of the main road is Orgyen Dongak Choling, the seat of the late Dudjom Rinpoche, a charismatic meditation master and scholarly head of the Nyingmapa school, whose mortal remains are interred here in a stupa.

Tourist information

There are ticket kiosks around
Durbar Square that will provide maps
of the square and offer assistance.

Nepal Tourism Board
Brikuti Mandap, T01-425 6909, www.
welcomenepal.com. Mon-Thu 0900-1700
(0900-1600 in winter), Fri 0900-1500.
Provides a few brochures, maps and
free posters.

Where to stay

Thamel *map page 66.*

$$$-$$ Kantipur Temple House
T01-425 0131, www.kantipur
templehouse.com.
Located in the south of Thamel the Kantipur
Temple is well placed to explore the Old
Town and reach the restaurants of Thamel.
A modern hotel built to reflect traditional
Newari architecture, it has a small garden,
a good restaurant and very friendly staff.

$$$-$ Kathmandu Guest House
T01-470 0632, www.ktmgh.com.
Opened in the 1960s this Kathmandu
institution is a converted Rana palace
located at the heart of Thamel. It offers
a wide range of rooms and is arranged
around a pleasant garden. The modern
wing offers excellent rooms overlooking
the garden, while those in the original
building are basic and inexpensive.

$$-$ Ganesh Himal
T01-424 3819, www.ganeshhimal.com.
A great-value establishment with a good
selection of 30 or so rooms, all with en suite.
There is a nice garden, plus a rooftop and
plenty of balconies to find a sunny spot.
Decent restaurant, relaxed feel and well
positioned for both the bustle of Thamel
and the sights of the Old Town.

Durbar Marg *map page 42.*

$$$$ Hotel Shangri-la
Lazimpath, T01-441 2999,
www.hotelshangrila.com.
Situated to the north of the Royal Palace, this
luxurious hotel has stylish rooms, wonderful
gardens and a host of other amenities.

$$$$ Yak & Yeti
Durbar Marg, T01-248 8999,
www.yakandyeti.com.
Based in an old Rana palace, this is one of the
most famous hotels in town. Situated just off
Durbar Marg it has lovely gardens with a pool
and an excellent restaurant.

$$$-$$ Hotel Shanker
Lazimpath, T01-441 0151,
www.shankerhotel.com.np.
Inserted into an old Rana palace, this
atmospheric property offers great value
in a fairly epic setting, although it has
an air of faded glory.

Further afield *map page 42.*

$$$$ Dwarika's Hotel
Battisputali, T01-447 9488,
www.dwarikas.com.
The best place to stay in town, so long as
your pockets are deep enough. Built using
reclaimed carved wood and stonework,
it's like living inside a wonderful, luxury
museum. Beautiful gardens and great
restaurants complete it.

$$$ Gokhana Forest Resort
Gokarna, T01-445 1212, www.gokarna.com.
If you need to get away from the city then
this is a good option, located in indigenous
forest only 15 km from Kathmandu. It has
a country club feel, pleasant rooms, a pool,
golf course and walking trails.

$$-$ Hotel Vajra
Bijeshwari, T01-427 1545,
www.hotelvajra.com.

Located near Swayambunath, this friendly hotel offers traditional architecture, a lovely garden and good-sized rooms. It's an easy walk to see dawn and/or dusk from the monkey temple.

Restaurants

Thamel *map page 66.*

$$$ Dechenling
Keshar Mahal Marg, off Trivdi Marg, T01-441 2158. Open 0900-2200.
Some of the best Tibetan food in Kathmandu, try the house speciality *momos*. There is a lovely garden for summer lunches and wood-burning stoves to keep you warm inside in winter.

$$ Fire and Ice
Tridevi Marg, T01-425 0210, www. fireandicepizzeria.com. Open 0830-2230.
Popular with locals and expats, this is the place to go for a great pizza cooked in a proper wood-burning oven.

$$ Kaiser Café
Garden of Dreams, T01-442 5341, www.kaisercafe.com. Open 0900-2200.
One of the best places in Kathmandu to dine al fresco. Set in the corner of these lovely gardens, the café serves snacks as well as main courses and is a great place to while away some time reading your favourite guide book.

$$ Kilroys
Jyatha, T01-425 0440, www.kilroygroup.com. Open 1000-2200.
If you need a steak or some European home-cooking after weeks of *dal bhat* on trek then this is the place to go. Great Irish stew, plenty of beers and some delicious deserts.

$$ Or2k
Thamel, T01-0442 2097, www.or2k.org. Open 0900-2300.
Popular with serious, batik-wearing travellers, this vegetarian restaurant offers delicious Middle Eastern food. Choose between a table or cushions and rugs around low tables. The takeaway snacks from the street counter are excellent.

$ Thakali
North Thamel, T01-441 0388, 1000-2200.
If you fancy an authentic local meal this is a good option, serving Nepali food as well as Tibetan favourites such as *momo*.

$ Thamel House
Thamel Marg, T01-441 0388, www. thamelhouse.com. Open 1100-2200.
Excellent choice if you want to try some of the local Newari food, served in a lovely, traditional location.

Cafés

Pumpernikel Bakery
Thamel, T01-425 9185, see facebook.
Part of a chain with several branches in the valley, this is a great place to stop for a sandwich or cake in the small, peaceful garden behind the store.

Durbar Marg *map page 42.*

$$$ The Chimney
Yak and Yeti Hotel, T01-424 8999, www.yakandyeti.com. Open 1830-2130.
Excellent fine dining in a restaurant founded by Boris Lissanevitch, the man who opened the first hotel in Kathmandu in the 1950s (see box, page 90).

Cafés

Hot Breads
Daily 1000-2200.
Nowhere to eat-in but if you fancy a pastry or cake on the hoof then this is a great place, with a good selection of savoury and sweet. Also found in Patan if you get addicted to their doughnuts.

Further afield

$$$ Bhanchha Ghar
Kamaladi, T01-422 5172, www.nepali bhanchha.com. Open 1000-2200
Located in a traditional Newari house and specializing in Nepali food served in a contemporary style. They also offer culture shows at 1830 and 1930.

$$$ Krishnarpan
Dwarika's Hotel, Battisputali, T01-424 8999, www.dwarikas.com. Open 1800-2130.
If you want to fine dine a traditional Nepali meal, then this is the finest place to go. Wonderful traditional surroundings and furniture and great food.

$$$-$$ 1905
Kantipath, T01-422 5272.
Set in a beautiful old colonial building, there is a varied menu with an emphasis on Asian cuisines.

$$ Bhojan Griha
Near Dilli Bazaar, T01-441 1603, www.bhojan griha.com. Open 1200-1500, 1800-2230.
Excellent traditional culture shows and good Nepali food in an old Rana palace.

$$ Everest Steak House
Naya Bazar, near Balaju New Bus Park bus station, T01-438 7091. Open 1000-2200.
A Kathmandu institution, doing what it says on the tin by serving excellent steaks and burgers at reasonable prices.

Cafés

Snowman
Freak St, T01-424 6606.
A survivor from the hippy era. This café has been producing excellent pies and cakes since the 1960s and visiting it feels like part of the cultural tour of Kathmandu.

Bars and clubs

Thamel *map page 66.*

House of Music
T01-441 8209, 1500-2400.
Good place to catch live music. Nice bar and rooftop restaurant.

Sam's Bar
Open 1600-2400.
Popular place both with travellers and residents, especially with its terrace seating for balmy summer evenings.

Tom and Jerry's
Open 1600/1700-2400.
Perfect for a relaxing beer and with big screens for sporting events. The bar is surrounded by signed shirts from hundreds of expeditions and treks. Open fire for the colder months.

Entertainment

Cinema
Kathmandu International Mountain Film Festival, *www.kimff.org.* Held at the **Russian Centre of Science and Culture** (Kamal Pokhari, T01-441 5453), every Dec.
QFX, *317 Narayanhiti Marg, T01-444 2220, www.qgxcinemas.com.* If you fancy catching the latest Bollywood blockbuster then this modern cinema shows them all, as well as dubbed Western films.

Theatre
There are no permanent theatres in Kathmandu. Some hotels organize events and plays, as does the **British Council, Lainchaur** (T01-441 0789, www.britishcouncil.org/Nepal.htm).

Festivals

All the major festivals are fixed according to lunar patterns.

Pashupatinath *map page 74.*
In addition to the other major Hindu festivals, the following are celebrated with special ardour at Pashupatinath. The dates of each vary according to the lunar calendar, and all attract large numbers of pilgrims and visitors.
Jan/Feb Chhaya Darshan, meaning literally 'sacred sight of the shadow', is marked by the laying of a cloth crown on the head of one of the Pashupatinath images.
Feb/Mar Pashupati, the focus for Maha Shiva Ratri, is a festival celebrating the birth night of Shiva. The Pashupatinath temple remains open all night, packed with pilgrims and sadhus and lit by thousands of candles and butter lamps. The next day up to 750,000 people cram into the temple area, packed so tight it's impossible to go

anywhere but where they are going. Entry to the temple can be 'fast-tracked' with a Rs 1000 ticket (US$9), a controversial new policy unpopular with most of the pilgrims who cannot afford the price.

Aug/Sep Teej is celebrated in honour of women. Traditionally, unmarried women have prayed for good husbands and married women for a happy conjugal life. In theory, women are supposed to maintain a total fast on this day and it has been customary for women to bathe and wash 365 times in the Bagmati river, but today a symbolic contact with the water is often considered to suffice for many.

Nov/Dec Balachaturdashi honours those who have died during the preceding year and their families. A 24-hr vigil is kept with worshippers taking a dip in the Bagmati and distributing a number of propitious seeds in the forest.

Swayambhunath *map page 81.*
Both these festivals are very crowded, but colourful and worth a visit.

Feb/Mar Tibetan New Year (Losar), a time of joyous revelry.

Apr/May Buddha Jayanta, which commemorates the Buddha's birthday.

Bodhnath Stupa
Jan/Feb A lively procession carrying the goddess Mamla around the Bodhnath area is the main attraction of the **Mamla Jatra** festival.

Feb Tibetan New Year, or Losar, is celebrated here on the 3rd day of the new moon with special prayers, processions, masked dances and a feast.

Apr/May Buddha Jayanti commemorate Buddha's life and is particularly picturesque. Thousands of butter lamps are lit during the evening and a procession carries an image of Buddha around the stupa.

Shopping

Books and maps
Kathmandu has plenty of English-language bookshops where you can buy a new novel and part-exchange your old one. Most also sell trekking maps for all the main routes and new/second-hand guide books. There are also works by local authors, printed in Nepal or India, often focusing on one area or topic. The quality of the books can be a bit dubious but the content is often very good.

The Map Shop, *Ganeshman Singh Rd, Thamel, www.himalayan-maphouse.com. Open 1030-2000.* If you need a map you will find the most comprehensive selection here, as well as most trekking guides and books of local interest. **Himalayan Maphouse** actually have 5 shops in Kathmandu, 3 in Bhaktapur, 3 in Pokhara and 2 on Namche Bazaar. Full details on their website, including a list of international distributors, should you want to get copies before you arrive.

Pilgrims Book House, *JP School Rd, Thamel, T01-422 1546. Open 0900-2100.* One of the oldest bookshops located in the heart of Thamel, Pilgrims offers a wide range of maps, guides, coffee table books, novels and mountaineering memoirs. If you want a book on religion or local philosophy, this is where you'll probably find it.

Camping equipment
It's hard to walk far in Thamel without passing an outdoor equipment shop. Nearly all the merchandise, despite the supposed branding, is fake, made locally, albeit often to a reasonable standard. While fine for general wear and lower-altitude treks, it is not suitable for more extreme conditions. This, as well as boots, should be brought with you. Most high-quality, original footwear and equipment is no cheaper in Nepal and there is less choice.

Black Yak, *Tridevi Marg, T01-441 6483. Open 0930-1800.* An official manufacturer outlet. The equipment is of a good standard and its performance claims can be believed.

Shona, *Jyatha Thamel, T01-426 5120. Open 0900-1900.* Large range of clothing and equipment that can be bought or rented.

Carpets and rugs

The manufacture of handmade carpets has become one of Nepal's most important industries and one of its largest exports. The sector has boomed since the influx of Tibetan refugees since the 1950s. Many shops and showrooms sell the carpets in Kathmandu but you'll need to haggle hard. A good place to start is the **Jawalakhel Handicraft Centre** (page 121) in Patan.

If you do decide to make a purchase, ensure the item is certificated by **Goodweave** (www.goodweave.org) who are working to eradicate child labour from the industry.

Clothing

If your idea of high fashion is a yak wool hat with earflaps supporting pompoms then Kathmandu is the place for you. Wool items, such as hats and gloves, are great value. You can also get good prices on pashminas and sweaters. In Thamel there are plenty of clothing shops, often with tailors who are skilled and inexpensive in making up shirts and other clothes once you've chosen a design and material.

Handicrafts and souvenirs

There is a huge range of handicrafts produced in Nepal, ranging from prayer flags and prayer wheels to singing bowls and *thankas*. There are plenty of shops selling these in Thamel and many other areas of Kathmandu that tourists visit. Most of these souvenirs are produced in other parts of the valley, where they can be bought slightly cheaper and from places offering a wider choice. There are also workers' co-operatives that offer direct sales that cut out the middlemen.

If you do shop in Thamel, just remember to negotiate hard and with a smile on your face. Go low in the first shop. You can always move on to the shop next door where they will have the same or very similar item. If you are haggling over a small item with a street vendor remember that a few rupees to you is just a few pence but to them it is their livelihood.

Thankas

If you are interested in a *thanka* or *poubha*, painted scenes depicting the Buddha's life or aspects of Buddhist doctrine, there are several painting schools in the northern part of Durbar Square. Here you can watch the painters work and have some of the symbolism and technique explained to you. It's a fascinating process at the end of which they will be keen for you to buy one of their works. Prices vary enormously depending on the numbers of hours worked on each piece; it's usually fairly easy to see which of the works is the finest and most detailed.

What to do

There are numerous travel agencies, tour operators and specialist operators in Kathmandu, based in Thamel or in one of the many hotels. For a commission, the travel agencies will book you onto a tour with one of the operators.

They are useful for booking excursions and bus tickets, but for activities, it's probably better to go directly to the operator so you can ask detailed questions about safety, guiding experience, skills and equipment.

Getting recommendations from fellow travellers is an excellent way of choosing an operator. The internet provides a plethora of feedback to trawl through.

For trekking you can look at the **Trekking Agencies Association of Nepal (TAAN)**, www.taan.org.np.

Mountain biking

Annapurna Mountain Bikes, *T01-691 2195*, *www.annapurnabiking.com*.
Biking First, *T01-470 1771, www.bikingfirst.com*.
Himalayan Single Track, *T01-470 0909*, *www.himalayansingletrack.com*.

Rafting and kayaking

Drift Nepal, *T01-470 0797, www.driftnepal.com*.
Footloose in the Himalaya, *T985-105 2795 (mob), www.footlooseinthehimalaya.com*.
Mountain River Rafting, *T01-470 0770*, *www.mountainriverrafting.com*.

Ultimate Descents Nepal, *T01-438 1214, www.udnepal.com.*
Ultimate Rivers, *T01-470 0526, www.ultimaterivers.com.np.*

Trekking and tour operators
Ace the Himalaya, *T980-200 2225, www.acethehimalaya.com.*
Himalayan Encounters, *T01-470 0335, www.himalayanencounters.com.*
Summit Trekking, *T01-552 5408, www.summit-trekking.com.*

Transport

Air *See also Getting there, page 421.*
All International and domestic flights land at Tribhuvan International Airport, 5 km east of the city centre. Few people stay near the airport as it is so close to the city. The international terminal is small but copes OK unless several flights arrive at the same time. Facilities are limited but there are banks for currency exchange once you've passed through Immigration. There is also a taxi desk.

The domestic terminal can be chaotic in the morning when most flights depart. Leave plenty of time to check-in, as you have to pass through security to get to the check-in desks. A new domestic terminal has been built but is currently empty. Baggage reclaim entails the luggage train being parked outside and everybody taking their bag off it.

Transport from the airport
Most people arrive on organized tours and treks and will be met. You will need to pass through Immigration and, as you leave the terminal, you will be met by your driver/guide holding up a sign. It is possible to be met airside and escorted through. Ask your operator for details.

If you are travelling independently it's worth reserving your hotel for the 1st night or 2 as many establishments offer free transfers to/from the airport. This saves you time and money and wandering around Thamel after

a long flight, carrying all your bags and being hassled by touts after a quick commission.

There is a taxi desk in the Arrivals hall from where you can pay a set price for a taxi to central areas, the cost currently being Rs 800/US$7.30. Unofficial taxi drivers also tout for business, charging about half this rate; but inspect their vehicles first as some can be very old and decrepit.

Bike hire
There are several places that rent out bikes and in certain places it's a good way to explore the city and valley. It's not what it was, however. Traffic is heavy, including lots of buses and trucks and most roads are narrow and bumpy. Much of the valley is now built-up, leaving very few areas of open countryside to explore. Your best bet is to get mountain bikes which can take you away from the main roads and towards the rim of the valley. Here the tracks are quieter and give some great views. **Pathfinder Cycling**, T01-470 0468, www.tibetbiking.com, and **Annapurna Mountain bikes**, T01-691 2195 both rent out good bikes and can advise on routes.

Bus
Kathmandu is the centre of the transport network for the whole of Nepal. Every day buses leave for all the main cities, as well as border crossings and towns and villages in the mountains. There are different types of bus: local, long distance and tourist.

Local
Local buses ply routes not only in Kathmandu and the Kathmandu Valley but also across the country. They are the cheapest way to travel – a few US$ can get you a long way – but also the most crowded and uncomfortable. Local Nepalis use them as their main way of getting around and, since there is no rail network in Nepal, for many they are the only way of getting around. They are therefore almost always packed.

On city services, expect to be wedged in and for the bus to stop constantly to pick up or disgorge passengers. They very rarely have signs in English so you will need to ask the conductor – usually the one hanging out of the door shouting, or somebody at the bus stop who looks like they are going your way.

Most local buses leave from the **Ratna Park Bus Station**, on the east side of Ratna Park. Rather confusingly it's also known as the **City Bus Stand**. It can be rather chaotic, with few English signs and a lot of buses, so ask a local to point you in the right direction.

For some destinations, buses leave from elsewhere – Bhaktapur is served from Bagh Bazaar, for example – so if you are going to use the buses to explore the city or valley, check with your hotel first as to where to catch it. For destinations in the southeast of the valley you may well have to change in either Patan or Bhaktapur.

Long distance

Buses to destinations outside the Kathmandu valley leave from **Gongabu Bus Station**, also known as the **Kathmandu Bus Station**. This too can be a bit confusing but they are used to lost-looking tourists and the conductors will normally point you in the right direction if you ask. A taxi here from Thamel is about US$2.30.

Tickets on these services should be reserved a day or two in advance, something that the travel agents in Thamel or your hotel will be able to do, saving you the cost and time of going there yourself. Turn up in good time for your service to ensure your seat is not in the back row.

Tourist

There are several tourist services that ply the most popular routes, namely to/from Pokhara and Chitwan. These services are more expensive (although still good value by Western standards), give you a reserved seat and the more expensive ones include a meal/snack at a break point halfway through the journey. They also leave from Thamel, making them much more convenient to catch. They can be booked direct or through

local travel agents or hotels. They include **Greenline** (www.greenline.com.np) and **Golden Travels** (T01-422 0036).

Car hire

Driving in Nepal is chaotic. It's nothing short of miraculous that Kathmandu keeps moving. Cars squeeze past each other, fighting to move forward centimetres at a time. Motorbikes fill non-existent gaps and clog junctions and the road. Starting at about US$40 per day, it isn't expensive to hire a car, especially if it's split between a few people. It will also save you a lot of time as you will be able to see a lot more in a day than if you were travelling by bus. You can hire cars from travel agencies or from hotels where affiliated drivers wait for you. Tell them your destination/s and then haggle hard. After that, sit back and watch in wonder as you somehow reach your destination.

Rickshaws

Cycle rickshaws still ply their trade, mostly in Thamel where they shuttle between the hotels, restaurants and Durbar Square. They are not expensive – about US$0.90 for a typical hop – and are skilfully manoeuvred through the traffic and pedestrians with the air of old-fashioned hooters.

Taxi

Kathmandu is full of taxis, small Indian or Japanese cars, usually painted yellow, that congregate outside main attractions or sights, or who drive past blowing their horn in the hope you will flag them down. The price is always negotiable; they are inexpensive and if you are going to visit one of the outlying sights you will save long, hot walks through crowded and polluted streets. As an example, a taxi to Pashupatinath will cost about Rs 400 (US$3.60).

You can also charter a taxi for the day if you want to visit several sites or places. Tell them the route and then haggle. Normally you can get a good price. Some taxis only have permits for the city or the valley, so if they are not interested that will be why.

Patan

Patan lies south of the Bagmati river and is now almost a southern suburb of its burgeoning neighbour Kathmandu.

During its heyday of the 16th-century Malla period it was one of the three great cities of the valley, known as Lalitpur, the 'beautiful city'. You can still see why. Its Durbar Square is the most impressive in the valley, a large open space packed with temples and shrines and flanked by the magnificent palace.

Around the square are side roads and alleys where more temples lie hidden in the everyday life of the city's inhabitants. It is a lot less chaotic than Kathmandu, with fewer crowds and a gentler pace of life.

According to legend, Emperor Ashoka visited in the fifth century BC, building the four stupa that delineated the city boundaries and marking the city's eminence at this time. The legacy of Buddhism has run through the city ever since, and over 1200 Buddhist monuments and shrines are still in existence today.

Patan's craftsmen are famed throughout the country for the quality of their work, and the influx of Tibetan refugees since the 1950s has led to a booming carpet industry. More recently it has become a popular place for expats to live, escaping the chaos of the capital while enjoying the excellent local cafés and restaurants.

Best for
Buddhism ▪ Culture ▪ Handicrafts ▪ Museum ▪ Shopping

Kathmandu
• Patan

Footprint picks

★ **Durbar Square**, page 103
The most compact and impressive of the valley's Durbar Squares.

★ **Patan Museum**, page 107
The best museum in Nepal located in the beautiful Royal Palace.

★ **Golden Temple**, page 114
Twelfth-century Buddhist monastery packed with statues and images and capped with a golden roof.

★ **Mahabouddha**, page 116
Small temple covered in images of Buddha, crammed into a tiny, hidden courtyard.

★ **Ashoka Stupa**, page 117
Four 2000-year-old stupa that turn the old city limits into the Buddhist Wheel of Life.

Essential Patan

Finding your feet

All international flights land at **Tribhuvan International Airport**, 4 km northeast of Patan, and few people stay near the airport as it is so close to Patan. There is a taxi desk in the Arrivals hall from where you can pay a set price for a taxi to central areas, the cost currently being Rs 800 (US$7.30). Unofficial taxi drivers also tout for business, charging about half this rate but inspect their vehicles first as some can be very old and decrepit. Most people visit Patan from Kathmandu. A taxi will cost about US$4.60 from central Kathmandu to Patan's Durbar Square. See also Transport, page 123.

Getting around

Walking is the best way to experience Patan. The distances are not great and you can explore the smaller streets and courtyards. Taxis are inexpensive and the best way to visit the outlying temples and shrines, but don't forget to haggle over the price. Many drivers speak enough English to let you be understood and know where the main attractions, hotels and restaurants are located. See page 110 for a suggested walking tour of Patan.

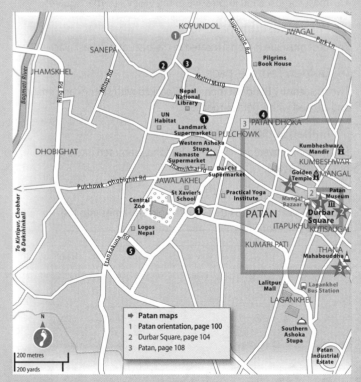

⇒ **Patan maps**
1 Patan orientation, page 100
2 Durbar Square, page 104
3 Patan, page 108

200 metres
200 yards

Walking tour

Numbers in brackets beside the headings correspond to the map on page 104. For a walking tour of Patan, see page 110.

When to go

The autumn months of October and November are a great time to visit, with pleasantly hot days, warm evenings and, being post monsoon, less dust and pollution in the air. In December and January it cools and although there is rarely a frost it gets down to only 1-2°C at night. It can be cloudy and some rain falls. The spring months of February to May are also a pleasant time, although the heat and humidity do build once more as the monsoon approaches. During the monsoon of June to early September Patan is humid and wet.

Time required

A full day is enough to see the main square with its museums, as well as the main outlying temples and stupas. It's also worth visiting the artisan and the Tibetan areas to look at the carpets. Haggle hard but there are some great deals available as this is where the rugs are made.

Where to stay
1 Summit

Restaurants
1 Bakery Café
2 Black Pepper
3 Bu Keba
4 Dhokaima Café
5 Higher Ground Bakery

Footprint picks

Sights

Bounded to the north by the Bagmati river, the Ring Road effectively encloses the city on all other sides. It is easily reached from Kathmandu with three bridges spanning the Bagmati to Teku, Tripureshwar and New Baneshwar, while the Ring Road crosses the Bagmati to the west and to the east into Koteshwar and on to the airport. The city is easily navigable on foot: it is about 3 km from the Teku bridge in the northwest to the Patan Industrial Estate to the southeast.

Although it has fewer options for accommodation than its northern neighbour, there are hotels catering for most budgets and the number of travellers choosing to spend at least one night in Patan has increased over recent years. There are views over Kathmandu and the mountains on clear days from the Kopundol area.

Several of the large non-governmental aid organizations have their offices in Patan and many Westerners working in Kathmandu have chosen to live here for what they consider to be its more peaceful and attractive environment.

More compact, more concentrated and more the city's focal point than either of its namesakes in Kathmandu and Bhaktapur, Patan's Durbar Square is a celebration of Newari architecture. Its distinct character is a product of the traditionally pivotal role of religion in society combined with the rivalry that existed between 17th- and 18th-century Malla rulers of the valley's three city states. It ranks between Kathmandu and Bhaktapur in both size and number of monuments, although there are similarities in conception insofar as most temples and structures are built facing the Royal Palace complex which completely dominates one side of the square, separated by an avenue or tangible open space. Further temples and Buddhist monuments are located to the north and south of Durbar Square.

Krishna Mandir (or Chyasim Deval) (1)
At the southern corner of the main thoroughfare, this, the only octagonal temple in Durbar Square, was built by Yogamati, daughter of King Yoganarendra, in 1723. Made completely of stone with some fine sculpting, it stands on a three-stage base and is considered the lesser of the square's two Krishna temples. The columns of the ground floor are topped by small minaret-like structures from which the shikhara spire emerges.

Bhai Dega Mandir (2)
This was a small Shiva temple, in the west corner of the square, that collapsed in the earthquake. It contained an image of the linga and stood topped with a Mughal-style dome sitting on a cube-like main structure. The platform still remains and reconstruction is planned.

Taleju Bell (3)
This large bell, hanging between two thick pillars, was cast by King Vishnu Malla and his wife Rani Chandra Lakshmi in 1736. It was the first of the great bells to be installed in all three of the valley's Durbar Squares. Although now largely ceremonial, it was rung during worship at the temples and could also be used to sound an alarm. Some accounts assert that by ringing the bell, citizens could draw the king's attention to injustices suffered by them. Behind it is a small fountain.

Hari Shankar Mandir (4)
The three-storeyed Hari Shankar Mandir was destroyed in the 2015 earthquake, leaving just its platform and a tiny temporary shrine on its top. As it awaits reconstruction, it makes a good vantage point from which to view the rest of the

Essential Durbar Square

Admission
Open 0700-1900, Rs 500 (US$4.60), the ticket kiosk is at the south end of the square.

Walking tour
Numbers in brackets beside the headings correspond to the map on page 104. See page 110 for a suggested walking tour of Patan.

The 2015 earthquakes
The square suffered some damage in the 2015 earthquakes, and a few of the smaller buildings were destroyed, but most survived intact to maintain the beauty of the square.

square. It was built by Yogamati, King Yoganarendra Malla's daughter, and was completed in 1705. The temple was notable for its roof struts whose carvings recall Dante-esque images of the inferno, which local wits suggest are a warning to mere mortals against the overindulgence depicted in some of the scenes on the struts of the nearby Vishvanath Shiva Mandir (see below).

Yoganarendra Pillar and Statue (5)

To the north of the Hari Shankar Mandir stood a bronze statue of King Yoganarendra Malla, complete with headgear, sitting in a gilded basket on top of a 6-m-tall stone pillar gazing into the Taleju Mandir, opposite. This toppled in the earthquake and the statue has

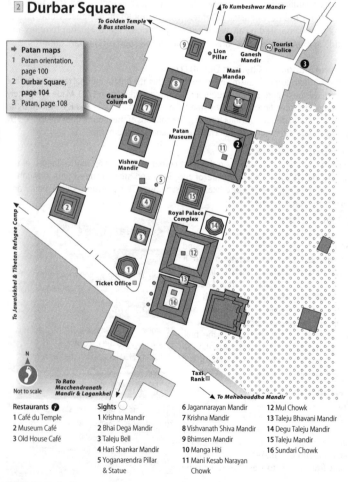

② Durbar Square

Patan maps
1 Patan orientation, page 100
2 Durbar Square, page 104
3 Patan, page 108

To Kumbeshwar Mandir
To Golden Temple & Bus station

Lion Pillar
Ganesh Mandir
Tourist Police

Mani Mandap

Garuda Column

Patan Museum

Vishnu Mandir

Royal Palace Complex

Ticket Office

To Jawalakhel & Tibetan Refugee Camp

N
Not to scale

To Rato Macchendranath Mandir & Lagankhel

Taxi Rank

To Mahabouddha Mandir

Restaurants
1 Café du Temple
2 Museum Café
3 Old House Café

Sights
1 Krishna Mandir
2 Bhai Dega Mandir
3 Taleju Bell
4 Hari Shankar Mandir
5 Yoganarendra Pillar & Statue

6 Jagannarayan Mandir
7 Krishna Mandir
8 Vishvanath Shiva Mandir
9 Bhimsen Mandir
10 Manga Hiti
11 Mani Kesab Narayan Chowk

12 Mul Chowk
13 Taleju Bhavani Mandir
14 Degu Taleju Mandir
15 Taleju Mandir
16 Sundari Chowk

been removed for restoration, with plans for it to be rebuilt in the near future. Pieces of the toppled column are still lying where they fell. A bronze naga, or cobra, rose behind him, its head forming a protective umbrella for the king, on which stood a small bird. A local legend recounts how the god-fearing Yoganarendra left his palace one night for the ascetic life and that as long as the bird remains, the king may return to his palace. A window was kept open for his return, and a hookah (pipe) ready for his use.

Jagannarayan Mandir (or Charnarayan Mandir) (6)

Also dedicated to Vishnu (as Narayan), this was said to be the oldest temple in the square dating from about 1566, although some scholars date it from the late 17th century. It collapsed during the earthquake. Two stone lions used to stand proudly on either side of the entrance but they now stand side by side awaiting its reconstruction. The red brick edifice contrasted attractively with the beautifully carved wooden doors, windows and roof struts. The latter were abundantly illustrated with erotic carvings.

Krishna Mandir (7)

Standing beside the Vishvanath Shiva Mandir and set further back from the main thoroughfare, this is one of two temples in the square dedicated to Krishna and is sometimes referred to as the Krishna-Radha Mandir. This impressive shikhara-design structure, built by King Siddhi Naransingha Malla and completed in 1637, is unlike the other Malla temples in that it uses stone in a combination of early Mughal and Nagara architecture.

It is one of the best known temples in Nepal, noted for the high quality of its stonework. The first three floors have chattri pavilions and open colonnaded sides reminiscent of the great Emperor Akbar's Panch Mahal at Fatehpur Sikri in India. On the second floor is a Shiva linga. Capping it is the curvilinear Hindu shikhara which contrasts with the traditional pagoda temples dominating most of the square and is similar to those in the Kangra Valley of Himachal Pradesh. A golden Garuda, the faithful bird-headed vehicle of Vishnu, faces the temple from atop a pillar on the east and was erected on completion of the temple by King Narendra Malla.

Inside are superb stone bas relief carvings of scenes from the Hindu epics with fine details, and stories from the *Mahabharata* depicted on the first floor and from the *Ramayana* on the second. A popular festival is held on Krishna Janmastami in August/September when devotees gather to pay homage to Krishna on his birthday. Only Hindus may enter.

Vishvanath Shiva Mandir (8)

Standing on a three-stage plinth, this two-storeyed temple is dedicated to Shiva and was built in 1627 by King Siddhi Narasingha Malla. It has a large linga-yoni throne and the beams and brackets are profusely carved with erotic motifs. Two stone elephants guard the entrance to the east, the right-hand one crushing an enemy underfoot, while a statue of the Nandi bull stands to the west.

Bhimsen Mandir (9)

This three-storeyed gilt-faced building at the north end of Durbar Square has twice been restored: once by King Sri Nivas Malla in 1682 after a fire and again in the late 1960s following the damage it suffered in the 1934 earthquake. It once again received partial damage in the 2015 earthquakes but is standing and open for business. Look out for the beautiful gilded balcony on the first floor. In front of the temple stands a pillar surmounted by a lion (currently being restored). In the *Mahabharata*, an ancient Sanskrit epic from India, Bhimsen, the god of traders, is seen as an exceptionally strong god, able

BACKGROUND

Patan

Although disputed by a number of historians, it is popularly held that Patan owes its origins to the visit of Emperor Ashoka to the Kathmandu Valley during the third century BC. Regardless of its accuracy, it has been convenient to believe that such a pilgrimage did indeed take place and this has served to promote the city's worthiness as a historical Buddhist centre, a perception which assumes added significance in the context of the cultural heritage of the valley's other two cities.

Several stone monoliths, situated by the road to the north of the Golden Temple, hint at an early Stone Age settlement but the city itself was probably founded during the early Licchavi period, from the fifth century AD, when it was known as Yupagrama Dranga. Amongst the earliest written records, there are allusions to a fifth-century 'palace' belonging to one of the Mangaladhipati kings, after which Mangal Bazaar, to the south of Durbar Square, may have been named. There is, however, little or no archaeological evidence to confirm either its existence or exact location, though there is a natural spring (Manga Hiti) in Durbar Square which may have provided drinking water to early residents.

Inscriptions dating from the seventh century refer to changes made by the Licchavi king Narendra Deva to the taxation system, which suggests that the town was fully established by then and had a sophisticated administration.

The medieval period brought political changes with the Mallas assuming a hegemony in the valley in about 1200, while the town's old name was replaced by Lalitpur. During the rule of Yaksha Malla in the mid-15th century, the valley was divided into three city states, with Patan ruled by Yaksha Malla's son and daughter, respectively named Dharmavati and Ratna. There followed a period of unprecedented growth for the city, by now the valley's largest. Many of Durbar Square's magnificent temples, monuments and other buildings were constructed during the reigns of three generations of Malla kings: Siddhi Narasingha Malla (1618-1658), Sri Nivas Malla (1658-1685) and Yoganarendra Malla (1685-1706).

Patan remained one of the valley's three independent kingdoms until discord and rivalry between the ruling Mallas of Kathmandu, Patan and Bhaktapur allowed their eventual conquest and the unification of Nepal by the King of Gorkha, Prithvi Narayan Shah, in 1768. Patan's political importance slowly decreased with the choice of Kathmandu as the Shah capital; today it is seen by some as little more than a proud southern suburb of its sprawling neighbour.

to lift horses. Not surprising therefore that this is a popular temple, always busy with local businessmen. Non-Hindus are allowed to climb to the upper level, which gives an interesting insight into the temple and also offers a great view.

Manga Hiti (10)

Directly to the north of the Royal Palace complex is the Manga Hiti, the conduit of spring water which may have existed at the time of the founding of Patan from the fifth century. Steps lead down to the pool shaped as a lotus and water comes from three stone spouts carved in the shape of crocodiles. Still in use today, there is often a queue of water containers waiting to be filled. The Mani Mandap, or Royal Pavilion, built in 1700, stands beside it that was originally used for Royal Coronations.

The Royal Palace and the Patan Museum

US$3.70. There are 2 entrances to the palace. The first is into Mani Keshab Chowk and the Patan Museum. The 2nd entrance, south of this, is into Mul Chowk. The same ticket gets you into both.

Occupying the entire area to the east of the main thoroughfare is the Royal Palace which gives the square its name. The exact origins of this magnificent complex are unclear, but it dates back to at least the 14th century, which makes it the first of the valley's Durbar Square palaces to be built. The bulk of its construction occurred during the 17th century, in the latter Malla period, when the palace complex is said to have comprised at least seven chowks, or courtyards: Agan Chowk, Dafoshan Chowk, Kisi Chowk, Kumari Chowk, Nasal Chowk, Nuche Agan Chowk and Sahapau Chowk. The complex was badly damaged during Prithvi Narayan Shah's conquest of the Kathmandu Valley in 1768 and again in the 1934 earthquake. Some renovations were made by the early Shah occupants, but today there are three main chowks (Sundari Chowk, Mul Chowk and Mani Keshar Chowk) each enclosed by a palace building. There was some light damage in the 2015 earthquake but all areas are open to visit.

Mani Kesab Narayan Chowk (11) The most northerly chowk is, according to some sources, the most recent, though its exact dates are not known. Records show that a structure of some sort on this site was used for a gathering of the Kathmandu Valley's religious leaders in 1631 (which could actually make it the oldest of the three chowks) and that the chowk was renovated or rebuilt in the mid-1670s. Substantial alterations were carried out again in 1733 and much of the building dates from then. Following the conquest of Patan, this chowk became the residence of Dalmardan Shah, Patan's first Shah king and brother of Prithvi Narayan Shah.

The main entrance to the chowk is through the splendid golden gate from Durbar Square's main north–south thoroughfare. It was originally built in 1734 but an inscription on the gate chronicles its restoration under Jung Bahadur Rana in 1854 at a cost of Rs 321, less than the cost of your entry ticket today! Above the gate is a fine golden *torana* engraved with images of Shiva and Parvati, while a golden window shows Avalokateshvar. A small shrine dedicated to Kesab Narayan stands in the courtyard and gives the chowk its name.

★ **Patan Museum** ① *T01-552 1492, www.patanmuseum.cov.np, open 1030-1730, last admission 1600, US$3.70. Refurbishment of the museum was completed in the mid-1990s.* The museum, which houses a total of almost 900 exhibits, offers an excellent insight into the culture and art of the valley, with galleries on religion, imagery, architecture and the art of the Kathmandu Valley, and explanations of the sculptures, techniques and artwork you'll see in the many shrines and temples you visit across the country. Beautifully lit and labelled, it is the best museum in the country and well worth a visit.

Most of the exhibits are religious ornaments and statues of national importance. The oldest are believed to date back to the Licchavi era and, although precise dating is virtually impossible due to the absence of either written records or inscriptions indicating the maker's name or the origin of the commission, some are certainly seventh-century masterpieces of Patan's celebrated Sakhya community of metalsmiths. Images of Avalokiteshwar, the Buddha, Shiva and Vishnu dominate in a collection, which also includes many other representations of images from Nepal's Hindu-Buddhist pantheon.

The museum is beautifully displayed over three floors of the old palace, linked with steep wooden stairs. You can stop in places and look out of the intricately carved windows at life going on in Durbar Square, just as the royal family would have done centuries ago. Take care on the stairs between the floors, they more resemble ladders in places. While on the top floor, you can walk out onto the narrow balcony that runs around the whole of the chowk.

When you are finished there is a great café in the gardens, run by the excellent **Summit Hotel** (see page 119), where you can sit in the sun and enjoy a cool drink or hot meal. You can visit the café even if you don't want to visit the palace or museum – just ask at the ticket counter where to go and they will direct you through.

Mul Chowk (12) The construction of this building and chowk was started in 1627 by King Siddhi Narasimha Malla. A major fire destroyed much of the building and it was left to Siddhi Narasimha's son, King Sri Nivas Malla, to complete his father's work in 1666. The chowk forms the core of the Royal Palace complex and has a small gilded Vidhya Mandir at the centre dedicated to the family deity and placed there to commemorate the completion of construction. There is also a post where animals awaiting sacrifice used to be tied to. The cloister is a two-storeyed building, comprising the Patan royal family's

3 **Patan**

⇒ **Patan maps**
1 Patan orientation, page 100
2 Durbar Square, page 104
3 Patan, page 108

Where to stay 🛏
1 Café de Patan
2 The Inn
3 Newa Chen
4 Traditional Homes Swotha

Restaurants 🍴
1 Kwalkhu Café
2 Museum Café

200 metres
200 yards

⋯▶⋯ Walking tour

erstwhile residence, with three Taleju temples around the courtyard. The smallest of these, the three-storeyed Bhutanese-style **Taleju Bhavani Mandir (13)** on the south side of the chowk, is considered to be the most important. It was built at around the same time as the rest of this section

Tip...
The three temples are closed to non-Hindus.

of the palace and the main entrance is flanked by two brass images of the shakti Ganga on Kurma, a tortoise, and Yamuna on the mythical Makara, a crocodile.

The main courtyard was used by the Mallas for the performance of religious ceremonies and is still used today when, during the Dasain festival, the image of the goddess of the Taleju Bhavani Mandir is carried into the chowk to be worshipped and offered sacrifices of buffaloes and goats. There are, once again, many examples of fine Patan craftsmanship throughout, including statues of various deities, metalwork and roof struts carved with images of Bhairav.

To the east of the chowk is the **Bhandarkhal Garden**, dedicated to the family deity and containing a pond of lotuses and a number of images. On the northern side, meanwhile, the original structure of the **Degu Taleju Mandir (14)** was built in 1640, then destroyed by the great fire of 1662 before being renovated four years later. Just to the north of that, the five-storeyed **Taleju Mandir (15)** soars majestically above Durbar Square and is the largest and most spectacular of the palace's temples. A late addition to the main palace buildings, it was constructed in 1736 and rebuilt following its destruction by the 1934 earthquake.

Sundari Chowk (16) The name means 'beautiful courtyard' and it is the smallest and southernmost of the three chowks. Its eastern wall was partially destroyed in the 2015 earthquakes but you can still visit as it is being reconstructed. The entrance is guarded by stone statues of Narasimha, Ganesh and Hanuman. The fine three-storey palace has carved roof struts and windows. The central window above the entrance was originally gold plated, while those on either side are of ivory. The ground-floor *dalans*, or open areas, surrounding the courtyard were used by the Malla kings for official functions. The numerous pillars here are ornately carved. Seventeen images of Hindu deities carved from wood are set in niches around the courtyard.

The centre of the chowk is occupied by the magnificent **Tusha Hiti**, a sunken royal bath decorated with fine stone and bronze carvings. There is an incomplete set of carved stone Ashta Matrika deities, eight divine mother goddesses who attend Shiva and the god of war, Skanda; the eight Bhairabs, incarnations of Vishnu; and the eight Nagas, serpent gods. The bath is shaped as a yoni. The bronze-plated water tap is formed in the shape of a conch shell and bears a small figure of Lakshmi Narayan. Beside it are stone statues of Hanuman and Krishna. Sadly, the source that supplied water to the bath dried up in the 1970s. The stone block by the steps leading down into the bath was used by King Siddhi Narasimha Malla (who is credited with the construction of this part of the palace and chowk in 1670) and his descendants for meditation and prayer following ritual bathing.

A walk around Patan *See map, page 108.*

Start the walk at the southern end of **Durbar Square** (see page 103) and work your way northwards. When you have looked at the **Bhimsen Mandir** (page 105) leave the square by the road in the northwest corner, heading west. It's a normal Patan thoroughfare, with small shops and traders going about their everyday business, traditional architecture vying with more modern buildings and small shrines dotted along its way. Keep looking left and right for the small *bahars* that are tucked away.

You will soon come to the **market**, Sasto Bazaar, on your right. It's an everyday place, full of fruit and vegetables as well as fish and some rather unappetizing cuts of meat.

Continue along the road until you come to the **Pim Bahal Pokhari**, a large water tank with a platform in the middle that is home to some geese. Walk around this is a clockwise direction. On its west side you will pass a white stupa, believed to date from the 15th century, and on the north side you will see the **Chandeswari Temple**. This has three tiers (although after the 2015 earthquakes the top tier is at a bit of an angle) and dates from 1663.

Return to the southeast corner and leave the square, taking the alley that heads northeast, to the left of the way you arrived. This will take you through an older suburb of town with some beautiful carving, but also collapsed buildings from the earthquake.

You emerge into a small square and, to your right, on the south side, is the **Lokakirti Mahavihar**. This old Buddhist monastery contains parts of the chariot used in the Rato Machhendranath festival and is a pleasant, peaceful spot. An old man is often here, on the platform just inside the door, selling papier-mâché masks he makes himself for Rs 50-75 each.

Cross the square and go through a doorway marked Bhaskar Varna Mahavihar and you will emerge into the **Nyakhuchchowk Bahal**, one of the larger courtyards in the city. There is an assortment of *chaitra* and stupas here, alongside parked motorbikes.

You leave by another small doorway, this time in the east side, with a 'Mind your head' sign over it. They are not kidding. Both the doorways and corridor are very low. You emerge into the **Naga Bahal**, another large, lived-in *bahal*. You will see a bull surrounded by prayer wheels and, behind a grille, a painting of a snake that is repainted every few years at the Samyak festival. There are also *chaitras* and a popular concrete table tennis table.

Head for the eastern exit once more, again a small doorway, and you emerge into a much smaller yard, with the Harayana Library on your right. Walk to the entrance of the **Golden Temple** (see page 114), which is in the southeast corner.

When you have completed your visit, leave by the eastern, and main, entrance and turn left onto the street outside. You will see on your left, on a slightly raised platform and with telegraph wires hanging around them, a series of ancient monoliths. These are believed to be the oldest religious objects in the whole Kathmandu Valley, although little is known of their origins.

Continue up the street until you emerge onto a colourful square and right in front of you is the **Kumbeshwar Mandir** (see page 112).

Leaving the temple, walk east along the south side of the square and continue until you come to a T-junction. Turn left and follow the street as it turns first right, then left and you come on your left to the **Northern Ashoka Stupa**, the best preserved of the four (see page 117).

Retrace your steps past the Kumbeshwar Temple turn and, just after this, on your left, is the **Uma Maheshwar Temple** (see page 112).

Continue south and you come to a small square that used to have three monuments. Sadly, the three-tiered **Radha Krishna Mandir** (see page 112) was destroyed in the 2015 earthquakes, but a smaller onion-domed temple remains, as does a pretty two-tiered pagoda-style shrine on the other side of the road.

Keep heading south until you reach Durbar Square. Visit the **Royal Palace** with its excellent **Patan Museum** (see page 107), as well as stopping for some refreshment in its peaceful café (see page 120).

Once both parts of the palace have been visited, walk to the south of Durbar Square, past the ticket kiosk, cross Hakha Tole and continue down the road directly opposite. This is one of the Old Town's main shopping streets, with stalls and traders displaying their wares. As you pass a small square with some shrines and a sunken stone, look to the right up an alley that specializes in copperware, pans and saucepans hanging up outside all the shops.

Continue until you come to a *hiti*, or water tank, on your left with modern water stands on a small platform behind it. Turn right opposite them, up a small alley and through the doorway to find yourself in a large courtyard with the impressive **Rato Machhendranath** in its centre (see page 115). Retrace your steps to the water tank and behind it you will see the Minanath Temple.

Come out of the temple and turn left, then left again up the alley that runs east to the south of the **Minanath Temple** (see page 115). Keep going past the small shrine on your right and up a short flight of steps until you come to a T-junction. Turn left, drop down to another T-junction and turn right. This area of the Old Town still has many old *bahals* so keep your eyes open for their small doors and by glancing down small alleys. As you walk eastwards you will pass **Dinbara Baha** and **Rupbarna Baha** (both on your right) and see several others that can all be visited.

You soon arrive at the **Rudravarna Mahavihar** (see page 116), again on your right. This is one of the oldest and most beautiful monasteries in Patan.

Retrace your steps and take the first turn to the right (northwards) looking for the sign on the left of the road 'Mahabuddha' for the **Mahabouddha Mandir** (see page 116). Go in the entrance, lined with metalwork shops, and at the end is the ticket kiosk on the left. Entrance costs US$0.45.

Head north again, crossing the main road, and immediately on your right is the **Lipi Thapu Cuthi**, a two-tiered Buddhist shrine with prayer wheels.

Continue north up the alley until you come to a small *hiti*, covered with duck weed, with a blue Krishna in the middle. Turn left up the alley opposite this. You come to a T-junction, with a dry *hiti* on your left and a well opposite. Turn right and at the road 150 m later turn left. This will bring you back to the northern end of Durbar Square, near to the **Manga Hiti** (see page 106) and a couple of lovely rooftop cafés to recover in.

Radha Krishna Mandir

Just to the north of Durbar Square, this three-tiered temple was renovated in the 1990s by a trust concerned with the conservation and restoration of the valley's architectural heritage. Sadly, it was destroyed in the 2015 earthquake, leaving just the platform. The attractive entrance had led to the shrine dedicated to that most popular of Vishnu's incarnations, Krishna, and his lover Radha, an incarnation of Lakshmi. There are two smaller shrines still standing, seemingly unscathed, in the same square.

Uma Maheshwar Mandir

Continuing north from Durbar Square, about 300 m beyond the site of the Radha Krishna Mandir, you reach this two-storeyed temple on your right. It is unusual in that it is made entirely of stone and is topped by an onion dome. A black stone frieze inside the shrine depicts the Uma Maheshwar, the name popularly given to this peaceful representation of Shiva and Parvati sitting closely together on Mount Kailash. Strictly speaking, Uma is one of 108 names used for the wife of Shiva – in this case, Parvati – while Maheshwar (Maha and Ishwar) means 'Great God'.

Kumbeshwar Mandir

Some 300 m along the road which leads north from Durbar Square stands this imposing five-storey temple. It is easily identified by the colourful stalls outside selling marigolds and other offerings for worshippers to buy and bring in with them. Dedicated to Shiva, it is the oldest existing temple in the city and, with Bhaktapur's Nyatapola Mandir, is the other of the two detached five-storeyed temples in the valley. Construction of the original temple on this site is credited to Bhaskar Deva in 1392.

A small tank on the northern side of the temple is said to be fed by an underground stream whose source is the sacred Lake Gosainkund in the Himalaya (about a week's walk from Patan): immersion is believed to confer great merit upon the bather. This is the *kumbha*, literally a pot carrying holy water for use during temple worship, which gives the temple its name. *Ishwar* is a Sanskrit word for God. During the Janai Purnima festival in July/August, large crowds of pilgrims take a ritual bath and worship a silver and gold linga, placed in the tank. Brahmins and Chhetris replace their sacred threads at the festival amidst frenetic dancing by strikingly dressed *jhankri*, witch doctors.

A Shiva linga is enshrined in the temple and some people believe that the temple is Shiva's dwelling place during the six months of the year that he is away from Mount Kailash. There are also different forms of Shiva carved in wood around the temple, as well as statues of Shitaladevi, Suriya and even Vishnu. Some are said to date from the late Licchavi period. The whole structure is acclaimed for its dimensional equivalence, an asset which doubtless helped it survive the earthquake which destroyed many other older buildings throughout the valley and beyond in 1934 and again in 2015.

Non-Hindus are allowed in the courtyard but not in the main shrine. The courtyard, though, is well worth a visit. Holy men sit on colourful cloths, waiting for customers to come and ask for blessings, either for themselves or some venture they are embarking on. They chant from sacred texts, an array of paints, petals and other devotional materials in pots in front of them to use in their work.

To the south of the temple is the **Baglamukhi Mandir**, a Newari house in which devotees implore the eponymous crane-headed goddess for succour in times of adversity.

The two-family craftsmen

At the height of the Malla era the artisans of Patan were so valued for their craftsmanship that many were enticed away throughout Asia by kings and nobles who wanted the very best workers for their temples and palaces. The Newari styles are seen in the Imperial Court of China, as well as the cultures of Southeast Asia.

Nowhere is this cultural interchange more apparent than in Tibet where the craftsmen's work was prized highly. To make the most of this profitable trade, many of Patan's best artisan families sent their sons to open workshops in Lhasa and other prominent Tibetan cities; they would often be away from Kathmandu for three to four years at a time.

Many of these craftsmen had families in both Kathmandu and Tibet. After their term in Lhasa they would return to Kathmandu for a few years, before returning once more to Lhasa. When they finally retired back to Kathmandu they would often bring their Tibetan family with them and set them up in a separate house, the two households kept completely apart.

Vishvakarma Mandir

Leaving Durbar Square to the south, this three-tiered temple is situated on the first road on the right after about 200 m. Vishvakarma means 'Creator of the World' and is the patron deity of this locality's artisans whose own creations on and in the temple pay seemly homage to the god. The temple's frontage is lavishly screened with embossed copper plate, while suspended bells flank the entrance and a large stone lion stands guard just outside.

National Library

www.nnl.gov.np, Mon-Fri 0900-1700, winter 0900-1600, free. To get there, follow the main Mangal Bazaar road west from Durbar Square for about 1 km until you reach a T-junction at Pulchowk. Turn right (north), then left (west). The library is situated inside the Harihar Bhavan building a short walk along this lane.

Nepal's National Library contains a total of approximately 84,000 volumes. The core of the collection was the personal library of Rajguru Hem Raj Pandey, which was purchased for the nation in 1956. Most titles are in English, but there are also a few Nepali and Hindi titles as well as some in Nepal's regional languages. There also exists a small and scholarly collection of books in Sanskrit, the ancient language of the northern areas of South Asia. The library's oldest books (in English and Sanskrit) date from the 17th century.

Patan is steeped in Buddhist history, tradition and legend, stretching back as far as the disputed visit of the great Emperor Ashoka in the third century BC. More than half of the city's population is Buddhist. Shrines and temples were often built to become the geographical focus of the local community. Many of the temples and *bahals* are open to visitors, their monks happy to explain their traditions and to show the exquisite craftsmanship that decorates some of the buildings. A number of other Buddhist monasteries located throughout the city have sadly fallen into disrepair and now lie as defunct relics of a former age. With the exception of the Ashokan Stupas and the Golden Temple, all of the following are situated south of Durbar Square.

★ Golden Temple (or Hiranyavarna Mahivihara)
US$0.45. Leather items, including belts and watch straps, are not allowed inside the temple.

Also known as Kwa Bahal and Suvarna Mahavihara, this Buddhist temple and monastery is two minutes' walk north of Durbar Square and its fabulous craftsmanship and lavish decoration should not be missed. Though first documented in 1409, it was renovated by the 11th-century King Bhaskaradeva. It was presumably constructed some time before then – some sources say by a local trader in gratitude for the wealth he had accumulated in Tibet.

Behind the inconspicuous entrance (look for the street sign) guarded by a pair of decorative stone lions, the complex is surprisingly compact. The central courtyard contains a small but spectacular shrine dedicated to Swayambhunath. Mythical, griffin-like creatures stand on pillars at its four corners, and each side has wooden lattice windows. The golden pagoda roof is brightly polished and four nagas combine to support the *kalasa* at its pinnacle. On one side is a rack of prayer wheels. This shrine is a late addition and, because it is no longer possible to view the fine façade of the main temple from across the courtyard, is considered by some purists to have diminished the earlier aesthetic appeal of the complex.

The courtyard, circumambulated in a clockwise direction, is surrounded on three sides by lines of prayer wheels which form the inner enclosure of a continuous veranda. Several shrine rooms used by Buddhist monks for prayer are located off this veranda, their dim candlelit interiors, wisps of incense and murmured venerations exuding the essence of devotion. The second floor is similarly arranged.

A large bell hangs beneath a gilded canopy near the entrance to the main temple, while above the entrance is a series of 12 carved images of the Buddha. On either side, the eyes of the Buddha are engraved into the bronze border and two richly decorated elephants stand guard. The temple itself is a marvellous three-storeyed pagoda building with each roof covered in copper, whose colour gives the temple its popular name. Small statues of birds in flight are attached to the four corners of each roof,

> **Tip...**
> You might see a tortoise or two wandering around so try not to step on one. They are considered to be the temple's guardians. The main priest is a boy under the age of 12 who holds the position for a term of 30 days before passing the role on.

while bells hang along the length of their rims. Latticed window screens and carved roof struts are found on the first two floors. The 13 steps forming the pinnacle represent the Buddhist stages on the path to enlightenment. Two bronze lions shown carrying the goddess Tara flank the entrance to the sanctum. Tara, it is said, was created from a teardrop of Avalokiteshwar, the Bodhisatva of compassion, and provides protection in the journey through the ocean of existence.

Directly in front of the sanctum are a number of broad oil lamps, some hanging from the ceiling, which help to illuminate the many engravings and rich golden hues of the interior. The shrine has a frieze depicting the life of Shakyamuni Buddha where the strong Hindu component in some images illustrate the extent of religious cross-fertilization in the valley.

Rato Macchendranath

Heading southwest from Durbar Square, you reach the Rato Macchendranath temple, another major religious site revered by both Hindus and Buddhists. It also known as Taha Bahal and Bungadhya, the latter name linking it with Bungamati, regarded as the 'home village' of Macchendranath.

The construction of the original temple is attributed to Narendra Deva in 1408, though the present temple dates from 1673. It is venerated as an abode of the Bungamati Macchendranath, also called Karunamaya Avalokiteshwar or, in Tibetan, Bukham Lokeshwar. Legend has it that when Gorakhnath, a disciple of Karunamaya, visited Kathmandu, he was not shown due respect. In his anger he cursed the people and consequently they suffered drought and famine lasting 12 years. When Karunamaya learnt of this, he told Gorakhnath to pardon the people and lift the curse; this was done and rain poured down. In honour of Karunamaya's kindness, King Narendra Deva built this temple. He also instigated the annual chariot race.

A number of pillars supporting statues of various creatures related to the Tibetan calendar stand in front of the elaborately decorated main north entrance, and a large bell hanging from a Tibetan-style shaft is to the left. The revered image, made of sandalwood and clay, is repainted in red (hence *rato*) before each annual chariot race, and is further embellished with jewellery and garlands. It is worshipped as a god of rain and Hindus also believe that simply seeing the chariot festival of Rato Macchendranath is enough to attain salvation. The courtyard is filled with sculptures of animals including horses, lions and bulls.

For several weeks from April onwards (in the month of Baisakh), the deity is trundled through the streets of Patan in an enormous chariot. This culminates in the **Boro Jatra** festival, strategically timed prior to the onset of the monsoon, when the chariot reaches Jawalakhel. The lower roof of the temple is tiled, while the upper two are overlaid with copper. Carvings on the struts of each roof depict various deities with lesser beings placed deferentially at their feet.

Minanath Mandir

On the main road leading south from Durbar Square, behind a water tank, lies the entrance to the Minanath Mandir. It's smaller than the Rato Macchendranath Mandir, opposite, but both are dedicated to forms of Avalokiteshwar, and the bronze image of its deity, Bodhisattva Lokeshwar, also has a place in the annual Boro Jatra festival.

Various legends explain the personage of Minanath, including this almost biblical account: Minanath was a fisherman who plied his trade in southern Bengal where the Ganges meets the open sea. One day he hooked a whale, but was swallowed by it. He remained in its stomach for 12 years until the whale happened to overhear a sermon preached by Mahadeva which prompted it to release Mininath who then built the temple in thanksgiving.

A temple was first built on this site during the Licchavi era. Two bronze lions stand guard on either side of the entrance and a large prayer wheel stands beneath a canopy to one side. Like its neighbour, the lower roof is tiled while the upper is overlaid with copper.

Mayurvarna Mahavihara

Dedicated to Maya Devi, the revered mother of the Buddha Gautama Siddhartha, this temple and monastery is located at Bhimcche Bahal, near the Rato Macchendranath Mandir. Feline guardians at the entrance are flanked by two suspended bells and the bronze *torana* above the main entrance depicts scenes from the lives of Maya Devi and the Buddha. Inside are three stupas. Both roofs are tiled. Legend has it that the group of *chaityas* here were commissioned by the Emperor Ashoka.

★ Mahabouddha Mandir
US$0.45.

To the southeast of Durbar Square, and along a southwest-leading alleyway, is the 16th-century shikhara-style Mahabouddha Mandir, dedicated to the thousand Buddhas of the auspicious aeon (Tib Sangye Tongsta) whose names are enumerated in the Bhadrakalpikasutra. Among these, Shakyamuna Buddha was the fourth, and the next to appear in the world will be Maitreya. Tightly hemmed in by surrounding buildings, the terracotta and tile building is difficult to locate but signs have been erected to help you find it. Following the 2015 earthquakes the temple is covered with scaffolding as a precaution while a full survey takes place.

The temple is somewhat reminiscent of the great Mahabodhi Temple at Bodhgaya in India. This is a masterpiece of terracotta and each of the 9000 or so bricks is said to carry an image of the Buddha, and the face of Buddha is portrayed on blocks of the shikhara structure. In the centre is a gold image of the Buddha, which, some sources maintain, was brought here from Bodhgaya in northern India. Surrounding the shrine are numerous friezes depicting scenes from the Buddha's life, while the many oil lamps here are lit also in honour of Maya Devi. A narrow staircase leads to the upper part.

Although it was completely destroyed in the 1934 earthquake, it has been rebuilt true to the original. The small shrine standing behind the main temple is said to have been built with bricks remaining from the post-earthquake reconstruction. The temple is surrounded by Newar Buddhist craft shops, most of them selling images of Buddhist deities fashioned in the renowned *cire perdue* (lost wax) process. The temple, whose name means 'Great Bouddha' (sometimes translated as 'One Thousand Buddhas') was completed by 1585 by Pandit Abhaya Raja in the reign of Mahendra Malla.

Rudravarna Mahavihara (or Oku Bahal, or Bankali Rudravarna Mahavihara)
US$0.45.

About 100 m south of the Mahabouddha Mandir, this temple and former monastery is one of, if not the oldest in Patan. The use of the site for religious purposes probably dates back to the early Malla period and some of the fixtures of the present building are said to be from the 13th century. The main temple rises from the centre of the monastery buildings. The tiled lower roof of the two-storeyed pagoda temple is topped by five decorative stupas and small statues of peacocks, and the copper upper roof has beams trimmed with images of demi-gods. Above the richly adorned entrance are bronze friezes with various Buddhist representations, including Maya Devi. Inside the rectangular complex are courtyards alive with reflections of the culture of Patan, with bronze and stone statues of elephants, peacocks, Garudas and, remarkably, many lions, as well as mirrors, woodcarvings, bells, *vajras*, minor deities and a statue of the Rana prime minister responsible for rebuilding much of Kathmandu after the earthquake, Juddha Shamsher. The courtyard also contains a central statue of the Buddha and a line of oil lamps.

Ratnakar Mahavihara

Southwest of Durbar Square, this attractive three-storeyed temple and monastery, also known as Ga Bahal, is home to Patan's own 'living goddess', the Kumari. The role here does not have the profile of Kathmandu's Kumari, nor does it come with palatial accommodation. The Bahal is notable for the double row of Buddha images above the main entrance and, either side, the guardian lions which carry statues of the Buddha. Patan's Kumari is chosen from amongst the daughters of the priests of the Ga Bahal and lives with her family. Her major duty of the year is to take part in the Boro Jatra festival of Rato Macchendranath.

★ Ashokan Stupas

The remains of four stupas, their construction attributed to the Mauryan Emperor Ashoka in the third century BC, are located approximately at the cardinal points delineating the ancient boundaries of Patan. All but the northern stupa are now mostly grassed over, though still recognizable. Every August full moon many Tibetans and other Buddhists walk around all four stupas in a day as an act of worship.

Northern Stupa (Bahai Thura) Located north of Durbar Square, beyond the Uma Maheshwar Mandir on the road towards the bridge to southeast Kathmandu, this is the best preserved of the four stupas. A lotus-shaped adornment supports the *kalasa* pinnacle above the spire's 13 steps, and a group of *chaityas* form part of the circumference wall at the base of the stupa. A natural spring, active only during the monsoon, is said to exist on one side. A small shrine dedicated to Saraswati, the Hindu goddess of knowledge, stands on the northern side. The exterior of the stupa has recently been renovated.

Eastern Stupa (Bhate Thura) This is the most out of the way of the four stupas and lies beyond the Ring Road to the southeast of Durbar Square at Imadole. Four *chaityas* are fitted into the brick perimeter wall at the cardinal points and a small stone structure, the remains of the pinnacle, projects from the top of the grassy hillock. The stupa is a landmark of sorts, but outwardly is otherwise undistinguished and attracts few visitors.

Southern Stupa (Lagan Thura) This, the largest of the four, is situated by a lotus pond just to the east of the main road leading south from Durbar Square and gives this area of Patan (Lagankhel) its name. Protruding from the top of the stupa is a small hemispherical stone edifice painted with the eyes of Buddha, replacing an earlier wooden structure, and supporting a compact spire representing the 13 stages on the path to enlightenment. The circumference wall is interesting for its inset hewn images of Buddha.

A stone *mandala*, representing the 'palace' of the meditational deity, stands beside the eastern *chaitya*, while the western *chaitya* has a shrine containing images of Amitabha (Tib Opame), one of the five peaceful meditational Buddhas forming the Buddha-body

ON THE ROAD
Emperor Ashoka

Ashoka, the greatest of the Indian dynasty of Mauryan emperors, took power in 272 BC. He inherited a full-blown empire based in Patna in modern-day Bihar, but extended it further by defeating the Kalingas in what is now Orissa, before turning his back on war and preaching the virtues of Buddhist pacifism. Ashoka's Empire stretched from Afghanistan to Assam, and from the Himalaya to Mysore. He inherited a structure of government set out by Chandragupta Maurya's prime minister, Kautilya, in a book on the principles of government, the *Arthashastra*. The state maintained itself by raising revenue from taxation on everything from agriculture to gambling and prostitution. He decreed that "no wasteland should be occupied and no tree cut down" without permission, not out of a modern 'green' concern for protecting the forests, but because all were potential sources of income for the state.

Described on the edicts as "Beloved of the Gods, of Gracious Countenance", Ashoka left a series of inscriptions on pillars and rocks across the subcontinent. Apart from that at Lumbini, two of the most accessible for modern visitors to South Asia are in the Indraprastha Fort in Delhi, where Feroz Shah Tughluq had it taken in the 14th century, and in the Asiatic Society's small museum in Kolkata. Over most of India, these inscriptions were written in Prakrit using the Brahmi script, although in the northwest they were in Greek using the Kharoshti script. They remained unintelligible for over 2000 years after the decline of the Mauryan Empire until James Prinsep, one in a line of distinguished amateur Oriental scholars attached to the Asiatic Society, deciphered the Brahmi script in 1837.

Through all the edicts, Ashoka urged all people to follow the code of Dharma, or Dhamma, translated by the Indian historian Romila Thapar as "morality, piety, virtue and social order". He established a special force of Dharma officers to try and enforce the code which encouraged tolerance, non-violence, respect for priests and those in authority and for human dignity. In addition to exercising a liberal domestic policy, Ashoka had good relations with his neighbours. However, Romila Thapar suggests that the failure to develop any sense of national consciousness, coupled with the massive demands of a highly paid bureaucracy and army, proved beyond the ability of Ashoka's successors to sustain. Within 50 years of Ashoka's death in 232 BC, the Mauryan Empire had disintegrated and with it the whole structure and spirit of its government.

of perfect resource. Amitabha is red in colour, symbolizing the purity of perception and the discerning aspect of Buddha-mind. He holds a lotus to symbolize the purification of attachment and the altruistic intention.

Western Stupa (Pulchowk Thura) Situated in Pulchowk, about 1 km along the main Mangal Bazaar road heading west from Durbar Square, this is a large mound topped by a stone structure painted with the eyes of Buddha and with four *chaityas* in the base. This is where the annual **Boro Jatra** festival of Rato Macchendranath begins its procession.

This area of southeast Patan, pronounced Jowl-a-kel, is renowned for its large Tibetan community and the Tibetan Refugee Camp, now occupied by only the poorest of the exiles. Nepal's only zoo is also located here.

The refugee camp, with those in Pokhara and at Bodhnath, is one of three major camps established by the Red Cross to accommodate the influx of Tibetans from the early 1950s, developed from a transit camp into a focal point for the manufacture of handicrafts and carpets. With further help from the Swiss Association for Technical Assistance, the production of Tibetan carpets blossomed, growing so rapidly that by the early 1990s carpet export accounted for more than half of Nepal's total export earnings. You can watch all stages of their production, from the dyeing and spinning of yarns to the weaving and final trimming. There are fixed-price shops where you can buy the carpets made here along with blankets, jackets and pullovers.

From Durbar Square, you can get here by following the road south of the square, then turn right (west) onto the main road just past the Rato Macchendranath Mandir. Continue along here for about 1 km until you reach a major crossroads with a roundabout, just beyond the Haka Bahal. Turn left and follow this road south and past the zoo for less than 1 km and the Tibetan Refugee Camp and handicraft centre are on your left, just inside the Ring Road. A taxi will cost a couple of hundred rupees.

Listings Patan maps pages 100, 104 and 108.

Tourist information

Tourist Information Office
Northern end of Durbar Square.

Tourist Police
Durbar Square, to the right of Café du Temple.
The ticket kiosk at the south end of Durbar Square gives out a map when you buy your ticket which covers the Old Town.

Where to stay

The Kopundol area has some excellent hotels and some beautifully renovated Newari houses converted into small inns in the heart of the Old Town.

$$$$ Summit Hotel
Kupondol, T01-552 1810,
www.summit-nepal.com.
Set around delightful gardens in Kupondol, the older wings have lovely traditional architecture. On (rare) clear days there are views of the mountains and Kathmandu. There's a good restaurant with excellent weekend barbeque and a large pool.

$$$ The Inn
Swotha, north of Durbar Square,
T01-554 7834, www.theinnpatan.com.
Another brick and timber Newari house beautifully restored to offer 10 individually designed rooms. Their restaurant serves good food and looks out over the small peaceful courtyard, making it an atmospheric spot.

$$$ Traditional Homes Swotha
A block north of Durbar Square, T01-555 1184,
www.traditionalhomes.com.np.
This beautifully restored Newari House is in the heart of Patan's Old Town, within easy walking distance of most of the main attractions and temples. Its 6 rooms ooze character and the owners are charming.

$ Café de Patan
Mangal Bazaar, T01-553 7599,
www.cafedepatan.com.
A Patan travellers' institution, offering simple,
clean rooms in a great location. There is a
courtyard and roof terrace but only a few
rooms have en suites, so remember to ask
for one.

$ Newa Chen
Kobahal Tole, north of Durbar Square,
T01-553 3532, www.newachen.com.
This old Newari house, dating from the Malla
period, was restored as part of a UNESCO
project and offers comfortable stays in the
heart of the Old Town. There is a charming
garden. Watch out for low ceilings if you
are tall.

Restaurants

$$ Black Pepper
Kupondol, T01-552 1897, http://blackpepper.
com.np. Open 1200-2000.
Newari-style building with indoor and
outdoor seating, there is a wide range on
the menu from steak to North Indian dishes.
Popular with the large expat community
that lives in this area.

$$ Bu Keba
Kupondol, T01-552 4368. Open 1100-2200.
Another restaurant with inside and outside
seating, the mainly organic menu offers
lighter snacks, such as hummus and pitta,
through to larger meals. Also popular with
the expats.

$$ Dhokaima Café
Patan Dhoka, T01-552 2113, www.
dhokaimacafe.com. Open 0800-2100.
This lovely restaurant café has a secluded
courtyard garden and offers a great range
of organic, healthy meals. The salads are
excellent, as are the cakes.

$$ Kwalkhu Café
Golden Temple, T01-621 2154.
Open 1000-2000.

Set in a traditional house, with small garden
at the back to sit in, this is a pleasant spot
to have lunch or a drink when sightseeing
in the town.

$$ Museum Café
Patan Museum, T01-552 6271.
Open 1030-1730.
Situated in a peaceful, sunny spot in the
back courtyard of the Patan Museum, this is
a great place to escape the bustle and enjoy
either a drink or an excellent meal. It is run by
the **Summit Hotel** (see above). You do not
need to buy a ticket to the museum to visit
the café. Just ask as you enter and they will
direct you through.

$ Café du Temple
Durbar Square, T01-552 7127, www.
cafedutemple.com. Open 0900-2100.
Worth visiting for the great view from its
roof terrace; you can get a good-value
Nepali meal here while looking down
on the world. Get there early at meal
times as the best tables get taken quickly.

Cafés

Bakery Café
Jawalakhel Chowk and Pulchowk, T01-
522 2949, www.thebakerycafe.com.np.
Open 1030-2130.
Part of a chain of Nepali cafés that provides
training and employment for the deaf.
Perfect for a drink and quick bite.

Higher Ground
Jawalakhel and Ekantakuna, www.
higherground.com.np. Open 0730-2000.
Good place to stop for a drink and bite,
offering hot and cold drinks plus cakes,
wraps and light meals. Its aim is to train
women as bakers to give them a trade
and income.

Old House Café
Durbar Square. Daily 0800-2000.
Good rooftop terrace to look out over
the square, serving drinks and snacks
as well as meals.

Bars and clubs

Moksh
Jhamsikhel. Tue-Sun 1100-2300, closed Mon.
Live music at the weekends ranging from traditional folk to rock. Also do great pizzas served in the garden, bar or roof terrace. Popular with local expats.

Entertainment

Theatre and art
There is no theatre in Patan but there are occasional outdoor productions in Durbar Square, which makes for a spectacular backdrop under the floodlights. Ask at tourist information office at the north of the square for information on any upcoming productions.
Sattya Media Arts Collective, *Jawalakhel, T01-552 3486, www.sattya.org.* This interesting place hosts performance art events, as well as art displays and lessons.

Festivals

Feb **Ilhan Samyek**, is held every 4 years in Patan (next in 2020), every 12 years in Kathmandu and annually in Bhaktapur. It celebrates the role of alms-giving in Buddhism and is marked by devotees offering rice and coins to images of the Buddha, especially at Naga Bahal.
Apr-May **Rato Macchendranath** is the month-long festival when the red-faced image of the patron deity of the valley, the god of rain and harvest, is taken around the city. His chariot moves by daily stages and may not return for some months. The image is prepared for the event in Pulchowk, when it is washed and repainted awaiting the assembly of the remarkably tall chariot. The procession through the streets is accompanied by musicians and soldiers and the nightly halts are marked by worship and feasting. The arrival in Jawalakhel several weeks later is witnessed not only by the royal family but also by Patan's Kumari, the 'living goddess'. Every 12 years the procession continues on to Bungamati,

a village 5 km south of Patan, where the image is ensconced in a second home for 6 months. This next occurs in 2027.
Jul **Janai Purnima** celebrates the Hindus' annual changing of their sacred thread, the *janai*. At the Kumbeshwar Mandir the occasion is marked by the placing of a linga on the platform in the centre of its holy tank. Rice is also offered symbolically to frogs here following the monsoon rains.
Aug/Sep **Krishna Janmastami** (or **Krishnastami**) celebrates the birth of Krishna, the 8th incarnation of Vishnu. It centres around the Krishna Mandir in Durbar Square, where, on the '8th day of the dark moon', an all-night candlelit vigil is held by devotees from throughout the valley and prayers are recited. Much of Durbar Square is beautifully illuminated.
Mat Ya is a Buddhist festival in which processions carrying candles and incense tour the city's Buddhist sites, accompanied by musicians. Patan residents are expected to partake at least once during their life.

Shopping

Patan is regarded as the best place for handicrafts in the valley. Many of the handicrafts you buy in Thamel and throughout Kathmandu will have been made here, so there is more choice and it is usually cheaper to purchase them here.

The area around Kupondol has become the centre of ethical shopping in the valley, with a growing number of outlets that let artisans and cooperatives sell their wares directly to the public. These often make them great value for money and it is reassuring to know that the craftsmen get a fair price for their work.

Carpets and rugs
The centre for carpet manufacture is the Tibetan area of **Jawalakhel** where you can watch the entire production process.
Jawalakhel Handicraft Centre, *Jawalakhel, T01-552 1305. Sun-Fri 0900-1200, 1300-1700.*

ON THE ROAD

Metalwork

The art of metal-casting in the Kathmandu Valley stretches back to at least the second century AD and possibly further, to pre-Buddhist times. Earliest references to the craft are traced to the community of Sakhya artisans in Boku Bahal, in southeast Patan, where the Rudravarna Mahavihara now stands and which remains an important centre for the manufacture of fine metal images, intricate designs from the pantheon of Nepali deities being their speciality.

The reign of King Amshuvarman in the seventh century witnessed the acme of metal-casting in Patan: the Minanath Mandir's image of Lokeshwar is said by some to date from that time. Others maintain that the dissemination of Buddhism to Tibet was advanced by the huge number of statues and images brought by Amshuvarman's daughter, Bhrikuti, as part of her dowry for her marriage to Prince Songtsen Gampo. So beautiful were the statues that Songtsen, together with Bhrikuti, constructed the Jokhang Temple in Lhasa, now Tibet's most sacred shrine, to house them. The main temple gate faces Nepal, its design is based on a Newar model and the images Bhrikuti brought (including those of Amitabha, Akshobhya, Maitreya, Mahakarunika and Shakyamuni Achalavajra) were installed in the building according to a strictly geomantic system.

The casting process begins with the shaping of the figure in beeswax. A combination of cow dung and clay (chira) is then applied to the figure with another layer added when the chira is dry. Then a mixture of damp rice husks and yellow mud is applied and left to dry. The wax is removed and the mould is ready. The metal is heated to about 1200°C and poured into the mould. It is crucial that this is done in completely still conditions, as any breeze can disfigure the image. Once cooled, features are painstakingly chiselled into the figure. The figure is then coated with a mixture of mercury and gold dust to which a strong flame is applied which leaves a golden complexion. Finally it is polished.

The tradition of excellence has endured and Patan's accomplished community of Sakhya artisans continues to produce skilled works of art, statues and images of deities with both local and worldwide commissions.

This vast enterprise allows you to watch the carpet-making process, a vital part of Nepal's annual exports that has mushroomed with the arrival of Tibetans since the 1950s. Having toured the centre you can look at its fixed-price showroom where any purchases can be shipped home for you. The prices are worked out per sq m, depending on the density of knots. Prices start from around US$100 per sq m, with a typical small rug being about 2 sq m.

Handicrafts

Dhukuti, *Kupondol, T01-553 5107. Sun-Fri 0900-1900*. Large selection of handicrafts and clothes, including pashminas, leather items and copperwork.

Kumbeshwar Technical School, *Kumbeshwar Mandir, T01-553 7484. Daily 1000-1700*. A school that trains disadvantaged people with a profession. Their shop raises funds and sells their own produce, including carpets and other woollen products.

Mahaguthi, *Kupondol, www.mahaguthi.org. Sun-Fri 1000-1830, Sat 1000-1700*. The produce of craftsmen of Janakpur, Dang and Thimi, with a wide selection including jewellery, ceramics and home furnishings.

Jewellery

The skill of the gold- and silversmiths of Patan has international renown and fine pieces of their work can be bought in the jewellery shops near Durbar Square. Trinkets are available in and around Durbar Square as well as Jawalakhel.

Metalwork

Patan has a long metal-working tradition and produces fine statues of the Buddha, various *bodhisattvas* and the Buddhist tantric deities. Its metalworkers were so well regarded that they worked on the Potala Palace and Jokhung Temples in Lhasa, as well as many other places throughout the region.

Prices for gold-plated bronze figurines start from about US$25 and can run to well over US$450.

The **Mahabaudha** (**Oku Bahal**) area, south and southeast of Durbar Square, has a tradition of high-quality metallurgy. Here you can get some of the best bronze, brass, copper and other metallic images and idols available in the valley and also

high-quality goods not usually available from Thamel's itinerant handicraft *wallahs*. There are numerous shops, many with their own speciality, so look in several before you decide what you want to buy. It's not unusual to see Buddhist monks shopping for their monasteries here.

Transport

See also Essential Patan, page 100.

Bus

There are frequent bus services between Patan and Kathmandu, leaving/arriving at either the Patan Dhoka or Lagankhel bus stations. It takes about 30 mins, depending on the time of day and costs Rs 15.

Buses for **Bungamati**, **Bhaktapur** and other villages and towns in the south of the valley leave from Lagankhel at regular intervals, costing just a few 10s of rupees.

Taxi

A taxi to/from Kathmandu will cost about US$3.70. There is a taxi rank, normally quite chaotic, to the left as you leave the southern end of Durbar Square. Taxis also wait near the tourist office at the northern end. Remember to negotiate.

Bhaktapur

one of the best-preserved medieval towns in Asia

Walking around Bhaktapur is like walking back in time. It is how Kathmandu was when visited by the mountaineers and adventurers of the 1950s, a city where the modern world hasn't yet imposed its clogging traffic and concrete buildings.

The great joy of Bhaktapur is that its streets are as much part of the heritage as its monuments and squares. Its buildings are still predominantly of the traditional brick and timber Newari style, its streets and alleyways too narrow for the modern traffic. You can wander the brick-lined streets, discovering small tanks and corner shrines daubed with paint and offerings. Its potters are famous for their skill, and areas of town are carpeted with thrown pots drying in the sun.

As one of the three great Malla kingdoms in the Kathmandu Valley, its many temples and shrines were renowned for their intricate carving and the beauty of their design. Today these monuments and squares still give an insight into the skill of those craftsmen and into life in Kathmandu before the country opened itself to foreigners.

Although very badly affected in the 1934 earthquake, its historic buildings survived the 2015 quakes with comparatively little damage. Some of the residential areas were, however, badly hit, with many old houses destroyed and a heavy death toll.

Best for
Atmosphere ▪ Culture ▪ Pottery ▪ Temples

Kathmandu
Bhaktapur

Footprint picks

★ **Durbar Square**, page 129
Home to some of the finest carving and craftsmanship in Nepal.

★ **Taumadhi Square**, page 135
The vibrant centre of modern-day worship and everyday life.

★ **Dattatreya Square**, page 140
A tranquil oasis with the Peacock Window and other fine woodcarvings.

★ **Potters' Square**, page 143
Watch potters throw pot after pot and leave them to dry in the sun.

Essential Bhaktapur

Finding your feet

A taxi from central Kathmandu costs around US$7-7.50 one way. You will normally be dropped at the tourist car park to the northwest of town. This is where private tour minibuses and coaches park as well. Buses from Kathmandu, a journey of between 45 minutes and one hour, US$0.30,

Fact...
There is much less traffic in Bhaktapur than the other valley cities.

stop at Guhya Pokhari to the west of town and a short walk from Durbar Square.

To enter Bhaktapur you must pay US$15 for a ticket, available from numerous kiosks at all the main entry points to the town. Your ticket is inspected when you enter Durbar Square. If you are staying for more than one day, bring your passport and they will validate the back of your ticket for as long as you request.

Footprint
picks
1 **Durbar Square**, page 129
2 **Taumadhi Square**, page 135
3 **Dattatreya Square**, page 140
4 **Potters' Square**, page 143

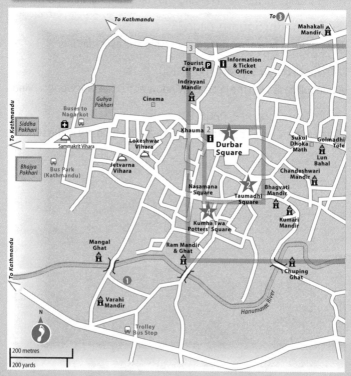

Getting around

Bhaktapur can easily be explored on foot. It is a small place and the three main squares are within easy walking distance of each other. As most vehicles are banned from the centre there are few other options. The great joy of Bhaktapur is to wander and explore. It's hard to get lost and a friendly inhabitant will always point you to the direction if necessary.

In Bhaktapur, there are three main squares that together form the point from which all other areas have developed and are connected by a newly paved main road, the city's central artery. Either side is a network of narrow, occasionally cobbled but mostly earthen lanes proceeding through the main residential areas down to the river to the south and to the Old Town limits to the north.

For a walking tour of Bhaktapur, see page 136.

For a walking tour of Bhaktapur, see page 136.

Museums...

One ticket costing US$1.40 gives entry to all three of Bhaktapur's museums. They are open Wednesday-Sunday 1000-1700 (mid-October to mid-June 1000-1600), Mondays 1000-1430, closed Tuesdays. The ticket office closes 30 minutes before they close.

When to go

During the monsoon of June to early September Bhaktapur is humid and wet. The autumn months of October and November are a great time to visit, with pleasantly hot days, warm evenings and, being post monsoon, less dust and pollution in the air. In December and January it cools and, although there is rarely a frost, temperatures drop to only 1-2°C at night. It can be cloudy and some rain falls. The spring months of February to May are also a pleasant time, although the heat and humidity do build once more as the monsoon approaches.

Time required

A half day is enough to see the highlights; a full day will let you explore the backstreets and alleys. Staying overnight will give you time to enjoy the town when the day trippers have all gone and to explore the squares and temples as the locals come out to worship and socialize.

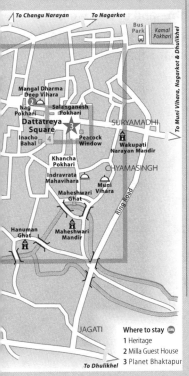

To Changu Narayan   To Nagarkot
Bus Park
Kamal Pokhari
To Muni Vihara, Nagarkot & Dhulikhel
Mangal Dharma Deep Vihara
Nag Pokhari   Salanganesh Pokhari
Dattatreya Square
SURYAMADHI
Inacho Bahal   Peacock Window
Wakupati Narayan Mandir
Khancha Pokhari
CHYAMASINGH
Indravrata Mahavihara
Muni Vihara
Maheshwari Ghat
Ring Road
Hanuman Ghat
Maheshwari Mandir
JAGATI
To Dhulikhel

Where to stay
1 Heritage
2 Milla Guest House
3 Planet Bhaktapur

> ⇒ **Bhaktapur maps**
> 1 Bhaktapur orientation, page 126
> 2 Durbar & Taumadhi Squares, page 130
> 3 Bhaktapur walking tour, page 138
> 4 Dattatreya Square, page 141

Sights

Bhaktapur is approached from Kathmandu via the Ring Road, passing to the south of the airport on the wide dual-carriageway that marks the start of the Arniko Highway to Tibet. You pass the walled city of Thimi, not that you notice as it is now engulfed in the modern sprawl of Kathmandu.

Most people arrive at the northeast of town, near the tourist vehicle park and ticket office. Here you can buy your ticket (you get given a town map with it) and start exploring on foot. Take the right hand of the two lanes, heading south. This will climb up into town and bring you out just to the west of Durbar Square.

The 1934 earthquake caused considerable damage to buildings in the square which consequently appears more spacious than its two namesakes in Kathmandu and Patan. It is still an architectural showpiece, exhibiting numerous superb examples of the skills of Newari artists and craftsmen over several centuries. It was extensively repaired, much of the work paid for by the German government, in the 1980s and 90s. Although there was damage inflicted by the 2015 earthquakes, with a few of the monuments destroyed and one wing of the palace damaged, the majority was unaffected and it remains an evocative place to visit. Numbers in brackets below refer to the map on page 130.

Shiva/Parvati Mandir

As you approach Durbar Square from the west, in front of you is this small, two-roofed temple dedicated to Shiva who is depicted with his consort, Parvati. The main gate to the square is just beyond. Erected by King Bhupatindra Malla in the early 18th century, it is elaborately decorated with various auspicious symbols, images of Kartikkaya, a son of Shiva and god of war, as well as large carved images of Bhairab on the left and Hanuman on the right.

Statues of Ugrachandi Durga and Bhairab (1)

On your left after entering the square a pair of large stone lions stand either side of the entrance to a school. Just beyond them stand these two fine stone statues representing the 18-armed goddess Ugrachandi Durga and the 12-armed Bhairab. Durga is the furious form of Parvati, Shiva's consort, and is shown plunging her trident into the prostrate body of the demon Mahishasur whilst maintaining an air of remarkable serenity. Bhairab is a tantric deity, a terrible form of Shiva. Both are garlanded with human heads and were commissioned in 1707 by Bhupatindra Malla. So pleased was the king with these sculptures, and so concerned that neither Kathmandu nor Patan should acquire their equal, that he ordered the hands of the unfortunate sculptor to be cut off.

Rameshwar (2), Bhadri (3) and Krishna Mandirs (4)

Opposite the two statues are three temples of lesser importance, dedicated respectively to incarnations of Shiva (Rameshwar), Vishnu/Narayan (Bhadri) and again Vishnu as Krishna. The Krishna Mandir is the largest of the three, a two-storeyed simple pagoda design with a statue of Garuda, Vishnu's faithful vehicle, placed on a column facing the main entrance. The Rameshwar was damaged in the 2015 earthquake.

Shiva Mandir or Kedarnath (5)

Heading on towards the middle of the square, this shikhara-style temple was constructed in 1674 by King Jita Mitra Malla. Images of various deities adorn the exterior on all sides. It lost its tip in the 2015 earthquake but is scheduled for repair.

Royal Palace (6)

The original Royal Palace, built in 1427 by King Yaksha Malla, was situated in Dattatreya Square but was reconstructed in Durbar Square during the reign of Bhupatindra Malla (1696-1722). It

Fact...
Bhaktapur's population is dominated by Newars who constitute more than 90% of its people.

was completed by King Jaya Ranjit Malla in 1754 and the result bore little resemblance to the original structure. The original complex is said to have consisted of no fewer than 99 chowks, or courtyards, and although this is almost certainly an exaggeration it was certainly larger than it is today.

The palace was badly damaged in the 1934 earthquake and, despite extensive renovations, much of the artwork was lost and only six chowks remain (Bhairab Chowk, Igta Chowk, Kumari Chowk, Malagti Chowk, Mul Chowk and Siddhi Chowk). The palace is renowned for 55 fabulously carved windows (after which it is sometimes known) as well as its Golden Gate (Sun Dhoka), Taleju Mandir and the National Art Gallery. (Currently only half is open due to one wing of the palace being structurally unsafe.)

② Durbar & Taumadhi Squares

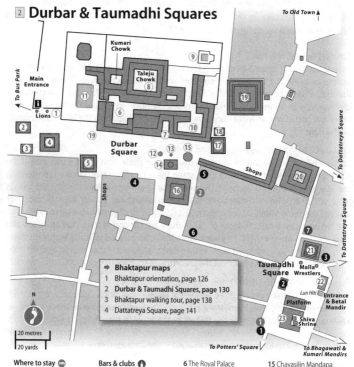

➡ **Bhaktapur maps**
1 Bhaktapur orientation, page 126
2 **Durbar & Taumadhi Squares, page 130**
3 Bhaktapur walking tour, page 138
4 Dattatreya Square, page 141

Where to stay 🛏
1 Bhadgaon Guest House
2 Shiva Guest House

Restaurants 🍴
1 Bhadgaon Café
2 Café Nyatapola
3 Namaste Café
4 Palace
5 Shivas Café Corner
6 Watshala

Bars & clubs 🍸
7 Black Olive

Sights ○
1 Statues of Ugrachandi Durga & Bhairab
2 Rameshwar Mandir
3 Bhadri Mandir
4 Krishna Mandir
5 Shiva Mandir or Kedarnath

6 The Royal Palace
7 The Golden Gate
8 Taleju Mandir
9 Naga Pokhari
10 The Palace of Fifty Five Windows
11 Sundari Chowk
12 King Bhupatindra Malla's Column
13 Taleju Bell
14 Vatsala Durga Mandir

15 Chayasilin Mandapa
16 Pashupatinath Mandir
17 Siddhi Lakshmi Mandir
18 Vatsala Mandir
19 Fasidega Shiva Mandir
20 Tadhunchen Bahal
21 Nyatapola Mandir
22 Bhairabnath Mandir
23 Til Mahadev Mandir

Golden Gate (7) (Sun Dhoka) Widely regarded as one of the most important artefacts in the valley's heritage, this stunning portal to the middle section of the palace complex and the Taleju Mandir was commissioned by Ranjit Malla in 1745. Actually made of brass, it is set into and contrasts attractively with the main brick

edifice. A pair of small gilded lions stand on their own miniature plinths either side of the remarkably small door, which is surrounded by images of six deities engraved in each side of the vertical brasswork. The large tilting *torana* above the door has a central image of a multiple-limbed Taleju, above which it is crowned by a dynamic image of Garuda, vehicle of Vishnu. The surrounding masonry is framed with brass, with the upper portion having small finials of elephants and lions, flags, three central *kalasas* and a larger *kalasa* rising to form the pinnacle.

Go through the Golden Gate, cross the small courtyard and through a second door into the palace. A large drum sits on either side behind screens as you enter. Follow the path around the building and you will see the entrance to the Taleju Mandir.

Taleju Mandir (8) Completing the trio of major temples dedicated to the Malla patron deity, Taleju, in the valley's three Durbar Squares, this temple has its origins in the early 14th century, which makes it the oldest of the three. The temple and the courtyard in which it stands (Mul Chowk) are not open to visitors, although the guard may allow you to look from the open entrance. The temple is only open to Hindus.

The temple itself is a lavishly decorated, one-storey structure, and is considered to be Bhaktapur's holiest religious site. It is believed to have some of the valley's finest artwork. There are statues of various deities. One window of the temple is said to have been carved by Bhupatindra Malla himself. Squeezed between Taleju Chowk and Sundari Chowk is the tiny Kumari Chowk, again richly decorated.

Naga Pokhari (9) Go through the small door on the north wall of the courtyard and you see the Palace Pokhari, overlooked by a pavilion on its northern side. It is surrounded by two carved snakes, their tails entwined at the western end, their heads facing each other in the east. Two more snakes rear up and face each other, one in the centre of the tank and the other at its northern end.

Palace of Fifty-Five Windows (10) This is the eastern section of the complex and is named after the superbly carved balcony of windows in the red and black outer wall of the large Durbar Hall, the centre of what remains of the original Royal Palace after the 1934 earthquake. They are widely considered to be the finest examples of decorative woodcarving in the valley and were commissioned in the early 18th century by Bhupatindra Malla.

Sundari Chowk (11) This is the westernmost chowk of the palace complex. The name means 'beautiful courtyard'. Like its namesake in Patan, it contains a bathing tank used by the ruling Malla family, but is bigger than the one in Patan. An upright brass naga, or serpent deity, is situated on your right as you enter, with another fixed to the base of the tank. The sides of the stone tank are elaborately adorned with carvings of various deities. It is now in the compound of the local police station, but you can look through the entrance at it or see it from the upper storey of the museum.

National Art Gallery ① *Open Wed-Sun 1000-1700 (mid-Oct to mid-Jun 1000-1600), Mon 1000-1430, closed Tue. 1 ticket costing US$1.40 gives entry to all 3 of Bhaktapur's museums.* Located on the first floor of the old part of the Royal Palace and opened in 1961, half of the museum is currently closed due to one wing of the palace being structurally unsound. Its collections include some especially fine displays of *thangkas* and *paubhas*, palm-leaf manuscripts and examples of Bhaktapur's craft heritage.

> **Tip...**
> When reopened, the collection of strange, colourful 17th-century Newari animal paintings on the second floor should not be missed.

The entrance is flanked by statues of Hanuman in the tantric form of Bhairab, and Vishnu as Narasimha. These were commissioned in c 1698 by King Bhupatindra Malla, who purportedly wanted to combine the deities' respective powers in an effort to maintain law and order in the city. On either side of the entrance are inscriptions in stone: one dates from the Licchavi king, Shiva Deva, the other is more recent and was carved during the reign of one of the first Malla rulers, King Yaksha Malla (1428-1482). Many of the *paubhas* are strongly influenced by Tantrism and have depictions of various shaktis.

At the top of the stairs look out for the portraits of all the Shah kings, from Prithvi Narayan Shah, who unified the country in 1769, to the King Gyanendra, who was reigning when the monarchy was abolished in 2008. There is even one of Crown Prince Dipendra who was king for three days after he massacred his family (including King Birendra) in 2001, surviving on life-support after he turned the gun on himself.

Stunningly painted manuscripts include an opus of Buddhist Prajnaparamita (a class of Mahayana literature focusing on the bodhisattva paths which cultivate the perfection of discriminative awareness) penned in golden ink and lavishly illustrated throughout. There is also a hand-painted/written 'biography' of the much-revered King Pratap Malla (reigned in Kathmandu 1640-1674) who was responsible for the construction of many of the temples and monuments in Kathmandu's Durbar Square. It is thought to be Nepal's oldest existing biographical manuscript.

King Bhupatindra Malla's Column (12)
The mastermind behind the major development and beautification of Durbar Square is immortalized in brass opposite the Golden Gate. Reverentially seated atop a stone pillar, the life-size statue of the king wears a turban-like headpiece, while a shield and sword lie at his side. His gaze is directed towards the Taleju Mandir within.

Taleju Bell (13)
This large bell, like those in Patan and Kathmandu's Durbar Squares, was used during temple worship and could double as an alarm. It was installed in 1737 by King Jaya Ranjit Malla, apparently in an attempt to thwart the nightmares that plagued him. It is also known as the 'Barking Dogs Bell', because its ring seems to incites the local canine population to collective howling.

Vatsala Durga Mandir (14)
Beside the Taleju Bell was this shikhara-style temple, one of two dedicated to Vatsala in Durbar Square, but it fell in the 2015 earthquake. The plinth is still there, its steps

BACKGROUND

Bhaktapur

The early history of Bhaktapur is vague. Its origins lie in the Licchavi period, but credit for its founding is widely attributed to King Ananda Malla in the late ninth century AD. The city began as a trading centre known as Khopring and was renamed Bhaktagram ('village of devotees') in the early Malla period. Its steady growth led to the replacement of the suffix *gram* with *pur* ('city').

The city is said to have been laid out in the shape of a conch shell and the main road, which still winds its way through the centre of the city, may (with a little imagination) be thought to resemble the outline of a conch shell (although the road also approximately parallels the course contours of the Hanumante river to the south).

The peak of the city's influence was between the 14th and 16th centuries when it became the valley's de facto capital. It was fortified in the 15th century. Many sources suggest that the Royal Palace was originally situated in Dattatreya Square before being relocated subsequently to its present Durbar Square location.

Rivalry among the valley's 17th-century Malla rulers was also expressed in the arts, with each city striving to exalt itself and endorse the authority of its rulers through the character and splendour of its architecture. Many of the temples and monuments adorning the three squares date from the late 17th and early 18th centuries, during the rule of King Bhupatindra Malla.

With the Gorkha unification of Nepal and the selection of Kathmandu as the national capital by Prithvi Narayan Shah in 1768, Bhaktapur's influence declined dramatically. In many ways it was this decline that led to its preservation as a medieval city. As Kathmandu has developed into a modern city, Bhaktapur has existed as a forgotten town that has maintained its ancient feel and streets of Newari-style architecture and shrines.

The city's architectural heritage was significantly damaged by the 1934 earthquake with many temples and buildings destroyed. A major development project was initiated with German funding in 1974, which resulted in the further restoration and renovation of many of Bhaktapur's buildings as well as road construction and improvement and the establishment of sewerage and drinking water systems. It received more damage in the 2015 earthquakes but most of the main structures survived intact. It was the old housing in the east and south of the city's Old Town that suffered the most, with over 100 houses destroyed and many damaged.

flanked on either side by five stone animals; they used to lead to the shrine that was attractively surrounded by a pillared porch or veranda. Towards the top of the shikhara were further stone representations of minor deities. The temple was built in 1737 by King Jaya Ranjit Malla.

Chayasilin Mandapa (15)

Standing in front of the Palace of Fifty-Five Windows and beside a small tank is Durbar Square's only octagonal structure. The original pavilion was probably used by members of the ruling Malla family to sit and watch Durbar Square life, but it was destroyed in the 1934 earthquake. The present pavilion, an attractive double-storeyed pagoda, was a gift from Germany in the 1990s. It was copied from a 19th-century photograph and is an exact replica of the original. It is one of the few structures to contain steel in its structure rather than brass or copper. In survived the 2015 earthquake intact.

Pashupatinath Mandir (16)

The exact origins of this temple are disputed: some say it dates from the late 15th century, a posthumous tribute to King Yaksha by his widow and son, while others maintain it was built much later, in 1682 by King Jita Mitra Malla. The design of the two-storeyed pagoda is based on the central shrine of the more famous Pashupatinath on the banks of the Bagmati river in Kathmandu. The roof struts have carvings depicting scenes from the *Ramayana* as well as some erotic themes. The shrine contains a Shiva linga.

Siddhi Lakshmi Mandir (17)

Returning to the eastern corner of the Royal Palace, this stone temple has statues of various animals as well as of men, women and children either side of the steps leading up to the entrance, another small shrine standing before it. The eponymous deity is the same as that to whom the shrine of the magnificent Nyatapola Mandir in Taumadhi Square is dedicated. Its construction was started by King Jita Mitra Malla and completed by Bhupatindra Malla after the death of the former in 1696.

Vatsala Mandir (18)

The second Vatsala temple in Durbar Square stands on a three-stage plinth beside the Siddhi Lakshmi Mandir. It is again of shikhara design and was built by King Jaya Ranjit Malla in 1737, an especially productive year in the history of Durbar Square. The central shikhara is surrounded by three smaller shrines. Southeast of the temple is a pair of stone lions.

Tadhunchen Bahal (19)

From the Fasidega temple, the square narrows to become an alley leading southeast to the neighbouring Taumadhi Tole. On your right (south) after the line of shops is this large 15th-century monastery, the only Buddhist building in the vicinity. The shops occupy what were *dharamsalas*, pilgrims' rest houses. Its design is classical Newari, and has some finely carved supports. If you continue west from the *bahal*, this paved road, the city's central artery, leads to Dattatreya Square after about 1 km.

Fasidega Shiva Mandir (20)

To the north of the Vatsala Mandir, this temple stood prominently on a six-stage plinth, which, after the 2015 earthquakes, is all that remains. The steps led up to the main entrance and were flanked by elephants and other animals. In contrast to the surrounding monuments, the shrine itself was plain, a cuboid structure topped by a small dome. It contained an image of the linga and yoni, which apparently replaced the originally intended deity, Macchendranath.

From Durbar Square's Pashupatinath Mandir, follow the alleyway round to the south of the Tadhunchen Bahal and after 100 m you arrive in Taumadhi Square. It is effectively an extension of Durbar Square to the southeast and, though much smaller, it contains Bhaktapur's finest and most impressive temple, the Nyatapola Mandir. From here you can head south to the city's famous pottery area, or east to join the road leading to Dattatreya Square. Around the Nyatapola Mandir is a small bazaar, or market area, where various handicrafts as well as local produce are sold. It was in this square that David Beckham brought the town to a standstill when he played soccer here with some local children in 2015. Numbers in brackets below refer to the map on page 130.

Nyatapola Mandir (21)

With a height of 30 m, this is the tallest free-standing pagoda temple in Nepal, and is unquestionably the city's most superb example of temple architecture. It stands in the northern part of the square and completely dominates the area. The five-storeyed temple was constructed by King Bhupatindra Malla in 1708 and, remarkably, emerged almost unscathed from the 1934 and 2015 earthquakes, the only damage being experienced by a small section of the uppermost roof. Some say that Bhupatindra built the temple as a foil to the terror of Bhairab, to whom a neighbouring temple is dedicated. It makes a great place to climb and look out at the views, or to sit and gaze out over the square.

The successive tiled roofs are supported by fabulously carved and painted beams and struts, with equally decorative windows. Five pairs of stone carved figures line the steps of the five plinths. Each figure is considered to be 10 times stronger than the one below. The images of the fabled Bhaktapur wrestlers, Jaya Malla and Phatta Malla, who are reputed to have had the strength of 10 men, kneel at the base and are followed in ascending order of strength by elephants, lions, griffins and finally the goddesses Baghini and Singhini respectively depicted in the form of tiger and lion. The metaphor of strength serves to underline the power of the temple deity. Some people also come here to worship the goddess Bhairabhi, in a belief which has tantric origins.

The interior, accessible only to priests, is Sino-Thai in character. It contains a shrine (but no idol) dedicated to the Hindu tantric goddess Siddhi Lakshmi who is also carved into the 180 roof struts. The temple has a well-planned geometry, with the size of each roof smaller than the one beneath by a constant proportion. Similarly, extrapolations of lines drawn to connect the corners of the supporting plinths will meet at the top of the entrance doors on each side.

Bhairabnath Mandir (22)

To the southeast of the Nyatapola Mandir and contrasting markedly with it, this three-storeyed temple owes its rather stocky appearance to its unusual rectangular base and to its originally intended design as a single-storeyed place of worship. It was built during the reign of King Jagat Jyoti Malla (1613-1637). The second and third roofs were added by King Bhupatindra Malla in 1718. The whole building collapsed in the 1934 earthquake; the present structure is a replica which used those pieces of masonry and wood that could be salvaged from the remains of the original. A large prayer bell is suspended in front of the main entrance.

ON THE ROAD
A walk around Bhaktapur

Bhaktapur is a great place to explore on foot, especially the atmospheric Old Town, with its narrow streets and alleys.

From the northeast corner of Durbar Square, take the alley that heads north to the right of the old Fasidega Shiva Mandir, towards a small shrine to Ganesh. Turn right and walk until the road opens into a larger square with buildings in the centre. Turn left, then right to walk around the north side of this square. The central buildings include a Vishnu shrine with a winged Garuda facing its entrance on a column outside. You also pass a small *hiti*, a water tank, and two small shrines. In the northeast corner stands the **Tripurasundari Temple**, dedicated to one of the nine Navadurgas, the fearsome incarnations of Shiva's consort.

Continue past this down to the main road linking Taumadhi and Tachupal squares, and pass the **Bhimson Temple**, built on the spot of a 16th-century Buddhist monastery, the Lun Bahal.

Walk east up the street until the first turning on the left, taking you north into some of the smaller backstreets and alleys. It curves to the right and you will come to a small Ganesh shrine also on the right.

Keep following the road as it curves back to the left and you emerge at the **Naga Pokhari**, a large water tank with a snake's head rearing from the centre. Walk along the northern side of the Pokhari. If it's a sunny day you may see dyed wool drying in the sun, stained a vivid yellow with saffron.

Leave the square in the northeast corner, following the road north. You will see a small red shrine in front of you. You are looking for a small door into a *bahal* just before this. When you get to the last stone steps before the shrine, on the right-hand side, climb them and go through the door. It may look like someone's house but it's a public thoroughfare. Walk through the *bahal* with its central *chaitya* and continue through to the next one. Take the exit to your left and follow the passage around to the right. On your left is the entrance to the **Mul Dipankar Bihar**, which has an image of Dipankar, the Buddha of light. It is undergoing renovations after earthquake damage.

Return to the lane you were on, turning left, and continue until its end. Turn left again, by a small lotus-roofed Vishnu temple and you will soon emerge at the southwest corner of the **Kwathandau Pokhari**, another of the large reservoirs within the old city walls. Turn right and walk east along its southern side. In the southeast corner there is a small shrine and *hiti*, and behind these on the street heading south is the **Nava Durga Temple**. This is a Tantric Shaivite temple and only Hindus can enter. Look out for its fine golden pediment above the door.

Follow this road south and it gently swings to the left and opens into a long, thin square. At the far end you pass a house on the left that has been restored in memory of the Swiss Geologist Toni Hagen, who surveyed Nepal in the 1950s.

Continue along this alley which winds southeast, before turning south and coming to the main east–west road through town. This area was badly hit by the 2015 earthquakes.

Turn right onto the main road. Very soon, on the left, you come to the **Wakupati Narayan Temple**, dating from 1667. This two-tiered golden temple is always busy with people making offerings and prayers to Vishnu.

Continue along the main thoroughfare until **Dattatreya Square**. Here you can follow the route described on page 140. The Peacock Café, overlooking the square, is a great place for a cold drink or meal.

You leave the square in its southwest corner, continuing along the main street. As the road swings to the right there is a small open area on the left with a two-tiered shrine in its centre and a platform along its rear. Turn left here, taking the alley that runs to the left of this platform, past the small *hiti* on your right.

Directly opposite this *hiti* is the **Sri Indravarta Mahavihar**, a 17th-century Buddhist temple. Enter through the small door and you will see it directly in front of you.

Continue down the lane and you will come to a modern Buddhist monastery, the **Munivihar**. When you reach it, turn right for the entrance a few metres away. Return to the lane and walk around the monastery on its left, swinging right to walk down towards the river. The south of town was the worst affected by the 2015 earthquake and some collapsed houses can be seen here on the right.

At the bottom of the hill you come to **Hanuman Ghat**, with a large collection of shrines, *chaitras* and shiva statues. There are also two enormous lingams as well as many more lined up against the wall of the ghat complex. You can walk inside; some of the carvings within the complex are excellent. You can get a view of the ghat by walking onto the bridge and looking back at the complex.

Do not cross the bridge but take the road heading west, passing a small *hiti* and platform with large *pokhari* behind. Take the first left, then right, towards the large tree built into a porters' resting platform. Turn right up the hill and soon, on your left you come to the **Bagwati Temple**, its entrance guarded by two lions. This has a small lingham in a tiled shrine.

Continue up the hill, the road lined with stalls and shops selling clothes and shoes. At the top of the hill, at the T-junction, turn right and you will find yourself in **Taumadhi Square**. Here you can follow the description of the square on page 135. Café Nyatapola is a great place for watching the world pass by.

Leave the southwest of the square, following the main road and soon turn left, down the hill, on a smaller alleyway. After 100 m or so turn right where it opens up and you will find yourself in **Potters' Square**, on sunny days full of freshly thrown pots, cups and plates drying.

Leave the square by the alley to the northwest which brings you back to the main road. You have two options. If you go straight over and head north, you will pop out on the south side of Durbar Square. Alternatively, turn left and walk along this busy shopping street. After 200 m you come to a crossroads, with a beautiful old building on the northwest corner. Walk on a little further and just after this building is the tiny entrance to the Buddhist **Jetvarna Vihara** (see page 142).

Return to the crossroads and head north, past the small black shrine. The alley kinks slightly to the left but keep climbing. Just before the alley seems to stop you turn right, opposite a small flight of stone steps on the left that lead to a small courtyard with Buddhist monuments. Just follow this alley as it winds its way past the Shiva Guest House and you find yourself back at the western end of Durbar Square.

Dawn and dusk are the most interesting time to visit. At dawn the devout go about their morning prayers, leaving offerings of rice and flowers, lighting butter lamps and ringing the prayer bell. In the evening, prayers are offered by an endless stream of worshippers, some in groups that sit on the nearby platform with candles, chanting from sacred texts.

The image of Bhairab is surprisingly small, standing just 30 cm high, and is the focus of worship during the chariot processions of the annual Bisket festival. Parts of the chariot used during the festival can usually be seen stacked up against the temple's northern wall. The main entrance is through the small Betal Mandir, located behind the temple, although only priests are allowed inside. The main door does, however, have a small hole through which you can push offerings. Betal is a protecting deity. There is a raised platform in front of the temple covering most of the southern part of the square which was used for performances of dance and drama, and shrines dedicated to Shiva and Narayan behind. Immediately south of the Bhairabnath Mandir is a small spring and tank, the **Lun Hiti**.

Til Mahadev Narayan Mandir (23)

Inconspicuously situated in the southeast corner of the square, this two-storeyed temple is one of the oldest in Bhaktapur. Its curious name ('til' means sesame) is attributed to a travelling salesman who, upon setting up his stall on this spot, found an image of Narayan in his sack of sesame seeds. A stone inscription refers to this as a site of religious importance since 1080. The image of Narayan in the shrine is said to date from the 12th century.

A statue of Garuda, vehicle of Vishnu (Narayan), stands on a pillar in front of the entrance, as does a *chakra* (wheel) and a delicately poised representation of a conch shell, both images associated with Vaishnavism. Next to it is a shrine dedicated to Shiva which includes a linga and yoni, the

▶ Bhaktapur maps
1 Bhaktapur orientation, page 126
2 Durbar & Taumadhi Squares, page 130
3 Bhaktapur walking tour, page 138
4 Dattatreya Square, page 141

③ Bhaktapur walking tour

········ Walking tour

former being carved with four faces while the 'fifth' is 'invisible'. To get here, go through the small doorway that leads off the square to the south of the Bhairabnath Mandir, or follow the lane towards the Potters' Square and turn left as soon as you can.

Café Nyatapola (24)

This popular restaurant occupies a former pagoda temple. Renovated in the late 1970s as part of the Bhaktapur Development Project, it has some fine carved wooden beams and lattices. The roof strut carvings are dominated by erotic imagery.

East of Taumadhi Square

shops, banks and everyday bustle

Leaving Taumadhi Square by a lane at the northeast end of the square, you join the main road through Bhaktapur which leads to Dattatreya Square after barely 1 km. The road is unusually and attractively paved with red brick, again a result of the Bhaktapur Development Project.

Although many buildings along here have also been restored, you nevertheless get a reasonable impression of the city's life, with activity around traditional Newari houses, men and women sitting on the pavement selling rice and vegetables, and groups of men engrossed in board games. You will also see tiny workshops where artisans chip away at a wooden or metallic sculpture, or are busy counting the beads onto a necklace. This is also the city's main commercial thoroughfare lined with shops and ATMs.

As the road bends to the right after Taumadhi Square, there is the **Sukul Dhoka** on your right. This math is home to some of the local temple priests, and was built as a monastery in the mid-18th century by King Jaya Ranjit Malla, Bhaktapur's last Malla king before Prithvi Narayan Shah led the Gorkhas to victory over the valley's cities. It was renovated in the late 1980s and the first floor in particular is decorated with some accomplished woodcarving.

The **Lun Bahal** just beyond was built as a Buddhist monastery in the 16th century, but in 1592 was transformed into a Hindu temple dedicated to Bhimsen, a deity of exceptional strength and courage. A little further on you arrive at **Golmadhi Tole**, a minor square with a small three-storeyed temple dedicated jointly to Ganesh and Bhairab who feature on the carved roof struts. There is also a *chaitya*, or small Buddhist shrine, small Shiva and Vishnu shrines, and a sacred water tank. Continuing along the main road and just before it veers north, the road widens with a small shrine and platform to your right, a place where religious plays and dancing takes place.

You then pass the small and variously decorated **Inacho Bahal** on your left. From here it is a short stroll into Dattatreya Square. The road continues on through Bhaktapur's eastern suburbs and Nagarkot before it eventually arrives at Kodari on the Nepal–Tibet border.

peaceful oasis with some excellent carving

The easternmost of Bhaktapur's three main squares is also the oldest. It is widely thought that the original Royal Palace was built here by King Yaksha Malla in 1427 and later relocated to its present location in Durbar Square. The square is dominated by the large Dattatreya Mandir and has a good restaurant with excellent views across the square. In an alley southeast of the square is the remarkable and justifiably celebrated Peacock Window, a masterpiece of woodcarving. It also has two interesting museums (see below) with exhibitions of bronze and woodcarving. Numbers in brackets below refer to the map on page 141.

Bhimsen Mandir (1)
This 17th-century rectangular temple sits at the western end of the square in front of a small spring and tank. The ground floor is open while lattice windows enclose most of the middle floor. The much smaller second roof appears like an afterthought and is copper covered. In front of the temple to the east is a raised brick platform which was used, like that in Taumadhi Square, for performances of drama and dance.

Salan Ganesh Mandir (2)
Behind a large, old house on the northern side of the square, this small temple has roof struts carved with images of Ganesh and Bhairab as well as representations of the Ashta Matrika, or eight 'mother-goddesses'. It also dates from the 17th century. Its main image is a rock said to be a likeness of the elephant-headed Ganesh.

> **Fact...**
> There are many sacred stones, often carved into the shape of a lotus flower, embedded in the ground outside houses on which small offerings are left by the household every morning.

Dattatreya Mandir (3)
Dominating Dattatreya Square from the eastern side, the construction of this temple was started by King Yaksha Malla in 1427 and completed in 1458. The temple is dedicated to Dattatreya, a syncretistic deity believed to be either an incarnation of Vishnu, a teacher of Shiva or a cousin of the Buddha. The presence of the winged Garuda standing on a tall pillar opposite the main entrance and, beside it, of a conch shell atop a smaller column, indicate that in this case the deity worshipped is Vishnu.

The structure of the temple is reminiscent of the Kasthamandap in Kathmandu's Durbar Square and, similarly, the Dattatreya Mandir is said to have been built from the wood of a single tree. Its original purpose is unclear, but a further parallel with the Kasthamandap is suggested by those who argue that it was built as a pilgrim's rest house and was only later developed into a temple by the addition of the second and third floors. Its unique and somewhat ungainly second floor protrusion seems to serve only as embellishment. A large bell hangs suspended at the southwest corner of the temple and two huge painted statues of Jaya Malla and Phatta Malla, Bhaktapur's legendary wrestlers, stand guard at the main entrance.

Pujari Math (4) and the Peacock Window (5)

Forming the southeast corner of the square is a complex of former maths. Maths are religious houses where prayers and other religious activities take place, usually according to a set schedule, and which can provide accommodation for celibate men at various traditional stages of Hindu life; the term is also used in the Jain religion. Pujari means those who perform *puja*, so the establishment therefore served as a semi-monastic residence for local priests.

The original math dates from the 15th century. It was renovated and further buildings were added by King Jaya Ranjit Malla in 1763, five years before the Mallas were ousted from power by Prithvi Narayan Shah. The complex now houses the Woodcarving Museum (see below). It was once more renovated in the 1980s as part of the German-funded Bhaktapur Development Project. When you go inside, watch your head. The ceilings are low and the doorways even lower.

Of the many examples of magnificent woodcarving in Bhaktapur, the Peacock Window is the best known. It is situated on the first floor of the east-facing façade, a few metres along the narrow street leading off from the southeast corner of the square. The small window depicts a peacock displaying its fan of 19 feathers in a circular arrangement, surrounded by foliation and cherubic figures in the top corners. Thirty-five smaller birds form a border on three sides while deities are carved into the base. Three delicately carved eaves form the vertex. The (live) chickens belonging to the neighbouring household provide a humorous diversion by regularly parading along their own windowsill.

On the north side of the square, opposite the Woodcarving Museum, is the Bronze and Brass Museum (see below). It is also set in a lovely old renovated building with low ceilings.

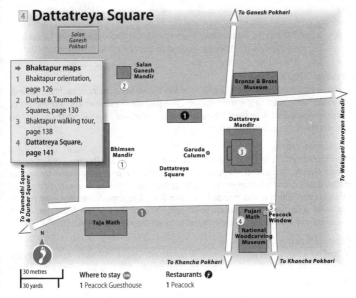

4 Dattatreya Square

To Ganesh Pokhari

Salan Ganesh Pokhari

Salan Ganesh Mandir

Bronze & Brass Museum

➡ **Bhaktapur maps**
1 Bhaktapur orientation, page 126
2 Durbar & Taumadhi Squares, page 130
3 Bhaktapur walking tour, page 138
4 Dattatreya Square, page 141

Dattatreya Mandir

Bhimsen Mandir

Garuda Column

Dattatreya Square

To Wakupati Narayan Mandir

To Taumadhi Square & Durbar Square

N

Taja Math

Pujari Math

Peacock Window

National Woodcarving Museum

To Khancha Pokhari

To Khancha Pokhari

30 metres
30 yards

Where to stay 🛏
1 Peacock Guesthouse

Restaurants 🍴
1 Peacock

National Woodcarving Museum
Open Wed-Sun 1000-1700 (mid-Oct to mid-Jun 1000-1600), Mon 1000-1430, closed Tue. One ticket costing US$1.40 gives entry to all 3 of Bhaktapur's museums.

This small museum is in the restored Pujari Math in the southeast corner of Dattatreya Square. It has some fine examples of Newari arched windows, roof struts, statues and ornamental carvings from throughout the valley. Most date from the 17th century onwards. The small courtyard is enclosed by fabulously carved windows. On the ground floor is a mask of Jaya Malla, one of the pair of Bhaktapur's legendary wrestlers. The recently renovated main staircase faces north in accordance with local geomantic practices which prescribe that a staircase must never face south. The Peacock Window is actually an exhibit, but is viewed from the outside (see above).

Bronze and Brass Museum
See National Woodcarving Museum for entry details.

Located in the 15th-century Chikamfa math on the northern side of Dattatreya Square, opposite the Pujari Math and the Woodcarving Museum, this offers a collection of domestic and religious metalware. Exhibits include *kalasas* (the vase-like pots often used as temple finials), hookahs (or 'hubble-bubble', a smoking vase in which the smoke is drawn through water by sucking on a long flexible pipe), and spittoons.

Buddhist Bhaktapur

a hidden and near forgotten legacy

Although Bhaktapur has a predominantly Hindu tradition, a Buddhist presence is maintained in the city's shrines and monasteries (*viharas*). Unfortunately, many show the effect of years of neglect and the Bhaktapur Development Project has largely passed them by. Some have been converted and others have fallen into disuse. They are minor attractions compared to the ones in Kathmandu and Patan.

Jetvarna Vihara
The Jetvarna Vihara has a raised platform on which two small *chaityas*, or shrines, stand. Two *vyalas* are placed at the front corners. The pagoda-like shrines contain images of Shakyamuni and Avalokiteshwar. Squeezed between the two is a small white *chaitya* and behind it stands an ornamental pillar.

Lokeshwar Vihara
This is probably the city's most attractive Buddhist structure and its only three-storeyed pagoda temple. In front of the entrance, a Buddha statue is surrounded by several smaller *chaityas* and other objects. Two large bells are installed on either side of the main doorway which is also guarded by stone lions. The temple is noteworthy for the *jangha*-like arrangement of household utensils between the first two floors, which are symbolically offered to the temple deity with the petitions of the faithful.

Mangal Dharma Deep Vihara
Located on a side street just southwest of Dattatreya Square, the name means 'holy (or blessed) religious flame', but this small *vihara* is memorable only for its ornately attired image of Dipankar.

Indravrata Mahavihara

South of Dattatreya Square and on the northeast side of Khancha Pokhari, is this uniquely designed *vihara*. Below the small upper pagoda roof, the square building has three floors. The middle one is compressed, giving the whole an almost sandwich-like appearance. The decorative main entrance has the ubiquitous lion guardians which in turn are flanked by racks of prayer wheels. A beautifully carved window frame above the architrave is the centrepiece of the stunted second floor.

Muni Vihara

Following the main road as it leaves Dattatreya Square to the east on its way to Dhulikhel and eventually Tibet, you arrive at this active monastery after about 700 m. It has an attractively columned veranda. Inside, the shrine has a large statue of the meditating Buddha accompanied by two smaller Buddha statues in different poses.

The ghats

a jumble of tumbling shrines and monuments

There is no actual footpath that follows the slender Hanumante River, but you can reach its ghats along streets leading south from the centre of town. For much of the year the river is little more than a polluted trickle so weak that the ashes from the cremations can hardly be washed away.

Mangal Ghat, the westernmost of the main ghats, is surrounded by a number of small buildings and religious monuments. You can cross the river here and after 200 m there is the small Vaishnavite Varahi Mandir. **Ram Ghat** is about 200 m downstream. It is used for cremations and bathing and has a temple, the Ram Mandir.

If you leave Taumadhi Square heading east (near the entrance to the Til Mahadev Narayan Mandir) the road passes two temples (**Bhagvati Mandir** and **Kumari Mandir**) as it loops south and crosses the river to **Chuping Ghat**, a melange of small monuments and a cremation site.

You can reach the largest and busiest ghat, **Hanuman Ghat**, from either Taumadhi Square or Dattatreya Square. The ghat is used for bathing, washing and burning. It is surrounded by numerous small monuments and lingas, and there is an image of Hanuman beside a Rama shrine. On one side is a *dharamsala*, a pilgrims' rest house. The site also marks the junction of two channels of the Hanumante river and is thus considered to be endowed with greater holiness.

★ Kumha Twa – Potters' Square

thousands of pots drying in the sun

Bhaktapur has earned a reputation for its pottery and produces much of the valley's terracotta pots, vases and souvenirs. The main pottery area (Kumha Twa, or Potters' Square) is south of Durbar Square and you can go there to watch the wheels go round in its open courtyards and verandas. A visit is well worthwhile and you can buy souvenirs – anything from an ornamental candlestick to the traditional round water containers used by women in villages throughout the subcontinent – both in the square and from small stalls lining the street from Taumadhi Square.

ON THE ROAD

Bhaktapur pottery

The art of pottery is almost as old as civilization itself and traditional methods have been maintained by Bhaktapur's Kumha potter community. Like the Sakhya community of metalsmiths in Patan, the trade is largely hereditary, its skills handed down through generations of the same families, with workshops and studios remaining in one locality. A major factor behind Bhaktapur's terracotta success has been the quality of clay found particularly in areas to the south of the city. The village of Sipadol, some 3 km south by a small river whose clay soil, known as *dyo cha* or 'black clay', is highly valued by Kumha Twa potters who barter their earthenware products for clay from the village farmers.

Follow the street leading downhill from the southwest corner of Taumadhi Square and take the first turning on your left (southwest). After about 100 m the square opens to your right. You can continue along this street for a further 400 m and arrive at the small Ram Mandir and Ram Ghat (bathing and cremation) by the Hanumante river (see above).

As you enter Potters' Square from the north, there is a shrine dedicated to Ganesh, the patron deity of the local potters. Built by a Kumha Twa potter, the two-storeyed **Jeth Ganesh Mandir** dates from 1646 and tradition has it that its priest comes from this potter community.

Other areas

wander back in time

While the splendour of Bhaktapur lies most conspicuously in its three major squares, its rustic charms extend both north and south of the city's central artery. Turn off up small alleys and lanes and you will discover ornate tanks and taps, often with water vessels lined up to be filled and women washing their clothes in a lather of soap. Small shrines and statues appear around corners, daubed with paint and garlanded with flowers and the ground is dotted with sacred stones, usually covered in offerings. Traditional houses line the way, open doorways leading to hidden courtyards and *bahals*. The best way of seeing Bhaktapur is to wander around it. You cannot get too lost and if you do there is always a friendly local to point you in the right direction.

Tourist information

Tourist office
At the west end of Durbar Square.
Open 0600-1930.
Maps in various language and 30 mins of free internet. When you buy your entrance ticket you get a city map with information about the main sites.

Where to stay

$$$ Hotel Heritage
Barahipith, T01-661 1628,
www.hotelheritage.com.np.
Situated 4 mins to the south of the Old Town, the Heritage is the best hotel in town. Built in the Newari style using old reclaimed carvings and brick, it has lovely rooms, gardens and restaurant. Some rooms overlook Ram Ghat.

$$ Bhadgaon Guest House
Taumadhi Square, T01-661 0481,
www.bhadgaon.com.np.
Beautifully located on the southwest corner of Taumadhi Square, this Newari-style property offers comfortable rooms, a decent restaurant and café and great views of the square from its terrace. Ask for the rooms on the upper floors which have great views over the square but bring ear-plugs as worshippers start ringing the prayer bells early.

$$ Milla Guest House
Northwest of Dattatreya Square, T98510 24137, www.millaguesthousebhaktapur.com.
Designed by Götz Hagmüller, the architect of the Patan Museum and the Garden of Dreams in Kathmandu, you stay in a traditional home located a couple of mins' walk northwest of Dattatreya Square in the heart of the Old Town. With only 2 rooms, it's great for families and small groups.

$$ Planet Bhaktapur
10 mins' walk to the north of the Old Town, T01-661 6038, www.nepalplanet.com.

This great modern property is run by an Italian and offers a good base for trips to this part of the valley.

$ Shiva Guest House
Durbar Square, T01-661 9154,
www.shivaguesthouse.com.
Offering a range of rooms, its big attraction is the location: you are in the heart of the town and many rooms have views over Durbar Square. The rooms are simple but clean and there's a decent restaurant.

$ Peacock Guest House
Dattatreya Square, T01-661 1829,
www.peacockguesthousenepal.com.
Located in a wonderful World Heritage-listed building, this small guesthouse on Dattatreya Square is focused around a small courtyard and has a great café and bakery. Full of atmosphere and popular so best to ring ahead. Doorways and roofs are low.

$ Vajra Guest House
Balakhu, T01-661 0782,
www.vajraguesthouse.com.
Newari-style modern hotel with comfortable rooms, good views from the roof terrace and well placed in the heart of the Old Town.

Restaurants

$$ Palace Restaurant
Durbar Square. Open 1000-2100.
This atmospheric building is set on the 1st floor of the building on the south side of Durbar Square, with the tables all looking out through traditional wooden windows. The menu covers some Newari and Nepali dishes, as well as continental favourites.

$$ Peacock Restaurant
Dattatreya Square. Daily 1000-1800.
Probably the best place for lunch in Bhaktapur, a popular restaurant on the 1st floor of a well-maintained Newari wooden building with commanding views of the

Dattatreya Mandir and Square. Good menu including continental and Nepali food.

$$ Shivas Café Corner
Durbar Square, T01-661 3912. Open 0800-2030.
This guesthouse restaurant offers a range of dishes from Nepali to Italian, served in a pleasant wood-lined room with great views over the square. Some outside seating during the warmer months.

$$ Watshala Restaurant
Off Durbar Sq. Daily 0700-2100.
If you want to escape the bustle then this restaurant, set in a pleasant courtyard, is the place to head to. Local and international cuisine.

$ Namaste Café
Taumadhi Tol, T01-661 6094. Open 0800-2100.
A great roof terrace gives super views of the square and the adjacent Nyatata Temple. Varied menu includes local dishes.

Cafés

Café Nyatapola
Taumadhi Square.
This large pagoda building (sometimes confused with a temple) in the middle of Taumadhi Square is said to have been built using materials remaining from the reconstruction of the Bhairab Mandir, opposite. Popular for snacks and meals.

Bhadgaon Guest House café
Taumadhi Square, T01-661 0488.
Great coffee either on the terrace outside, watching the traders sell their vegetables and other produce, or high up on their 2nd-floor balcony with fine views of the city.

Bars and clubs

Black Olive
Open 1000-2200.
Bhaktapur is not renowned for its nightlife, most locals being tucked up early. This is a good place for a drink, however, with a pleasant bar for the winter and roof terrace for the hotter months. There is also live music at the weekend.

Festivals

Jan Basant Panchami. Marks the coming of spring and is dedicated to Saraswati, the goddess of knowledge. In Bhaktapur it is celebrated particularly by craftsmen.
Apr Bisket (Snake Slaughter). Special celebrations to commemorate the great battle in the Hindu epic *Mahabharata*. Chariots carrying Bhairab and Bhadrakali are drawn through the narrow streets. A tug-of-war between the upper and lower parts of town decides who will be fortunate for the coming year. A tall wooden pole (sometimes up to 20 m high) is erected near the riverside at Chuping Ghat with cross beams from which two banners, signifying snake demons, are hung. On the following day (New Year) it is brought crashing down after another tug-of-war. There is dancing and singing in the streets over four days.
May Sithi Nakha. Celebrates the victory of Kumar, god of war, over the demons, as well as marking the onset of the monsoon rains. A palanquin carrying an image of the goddess Bhagawati is the focus of a procession through Taumadhi Square.
Aug Gathan Muga (or Ghantakarna or Gathe Mangal). This festival derives from Tantrism and marks the completion of the season's rice planting by a sort of mass celebratory 'exorcism' of evil spirits which may affect the crops' growth. Effigies of the demon, Gathan Muga, are made of straw or dried rice stalks and in the evening are immersed in the river. Offerings of cooked rice are placed along the streets to placate the demons and iron nails (the Newari equivalent of 'Transylvanian' garlic) are driven into the horizontal beam above the doorway of each house.
Aug/Sep Gai Jatra. A folk dance unique to Bhaktapur is performed during this festival. Families who have been bereaved during the past year are supposed to send a cow to join the procession, in the belief that the sacred cow will assist the departed soul in its onward journey. Alternatively, they will wear fancy dress resembling a cow. The

procession is jovial and accompanied by music and dancing. Evening feasts centre around *kwati*, a type of bean soup.

Sep   Panja Dan. A Buddhist festival of charity when rice and other consumables are ritually offered to Buddhist monks. Uniquely in the valley, Bhaktapur celebrates the day with colourful processions carrying 5 images of the Dipanker Buddha. The festival is also marked at Swayambhunath and Bodhnath.

Shopping

Most of the handicraft shops in Bhaktapur are concentrated around the 3 main squares. If you wander along the side streets leading off the main road that runs through the centre of the city, you will come across numerous small shops where artisans demonstrate remarkable dexterity by simultaneously using hands, feet and tools to fashion metal statues, pieces of jewellery and other souvenir handicrafts; follow the gentle tapping noises.

Handicrafts
The beautiful Nawa Durga puppets made in Bhaktapur often show tribal people with tools of their trade or armed deities clutching little wooden weapons in each hand. You can also buy Nawa Durga masks made of papier mâché, better than the clay ones for transporting home.

Other quality handicrafts include pashmina shawls, rice paper prints and other local textiles made with traditional patterns and designs.

You can get good *thangkas/paubhas* in Durbar Square, and *topis* (traditional Nepali caps worn by men) from shops near the Bhairabnath Mandir in Taumadhi Square.

Pottery
For terracotta and earthenware products, the best place to go is the pottery area, south of Durbar Square where you can buy direct from the potter. Although the mainstay of the area's output has traditionally been water pots and other household containers

for local sale, attractive ornamental items are increasingly being produced. You can get anything from decorative candlesticks and piggy banks to masks of various deities. As always, expect to bargain hard. Try also the various streetside vendors between Dattatreya Square and Hanuman Ghat, and along the main road heading east from Dattatreya Square.

Woodwork and carving
You can find the wonderful woodcarvings for which Bhaktapur is acclaimed sold on the street below and near the Peacock Window, off Dattatreya Square. Please note that all genuine antiques require certified permission from the Dept of Archaeology, Singha Durbar, Kathmandu, in order to be exported. Miniature reproductions of the window are popular, but if you want a full-size replica carved to order by a skilled craftsman, this can be done within a month for US$230.

Transport

Bus
The terminus for buses to and from Kathmandu (Bagh Bazaar, City Bus Park and Martyrs' Gate bus stops) is at **Guhya Pokhari**, about 800 m west of Durbar Square. There are frequent departures throughout the day at approximately 15-min intervals or when the bus is full, US$0.30, journey time approximately 50 mins.

Taxi
The rate for a taxi from central Kathmandu to Bhaktapur is about US$7.50 each way, but this can usually be reduced a little with some good-natured negotiation. Hiring a taxi for the day is generally cheaper than going to a car rental firm. It allows flexibility and you can easily combine Bhaktapur with Dhulikhel or Nagarkot on a whistlestop tour of the eastern valley. Make sure that you fix the price with the taxi driver before setting off and pay him at the end.

Kathmandu Valley

hidden temples, unspoilt villages and Himalayan views

The Kathmandu Valley is largely overlooked by visitors who tend to explore the three cities but ignore the surrounding countryside and villages. If you do have time, it's well worth the effort to explore for a day or two.

Amongst its many pagodas, temples, villages and towns, there is a little-visited UNESCO World Heritage Site in a beautiful, evocative location.

Kathmandu's remorseless sprawl is certainly taking its toll. Areas that used to be fields and villages are now just an extension of the city, but know where to look and you can still find the rural valley of old. In the north of the valley lies the Shivapura National Park, an accessible alternative for those who wish to walk but don't have time to trek. The rim of the valley also offers several villages and towns with breath-taking views north of the main Himalayan chain from the comfort of some lovely lodges.

The 2015 earthquake devastated several of the outlying towns, reducing many old houses and several famous temples to rubble. Rebuilding is planned but it will take years to replicate the craftsmanship of old. Plenty, however, survived and it is worth escaping the bustle of Kathmandu to visit some.

Best for
Day walks ▪ Temples ▪ Views ▪ Villages

Footprint picks

★ **Changu Narayan**,
   page 152
Stunning UNESCO heritage temple.

★ **Vajra Jogini**, page 156
Ancient temples in lovely forest;
worth the climb.

★ **Nagarkot**, page 157
A tiny village on the valley rim
with fine Himalayan views.

★ **Panauti**, page 161
This ancient town resembles the Kathmandu of old.

★ **Namobuddha**, page 168
One of the most sacred Buddhist sites in Nepal, with fabulous views.

★ **Dakshinkali**, page 178
Worship of Kali at its most fervent and raw (and bloody).

★ **Kirtipur**, page 179
The much smaller, often overlooked fourth city of the valley.

Essential Kathmandu Valley

Finding your feet

All these sites can be visited in a day from Kathmandu. There are buses to most of them from the main bus stations. For some of the more remote places, such as Namobuddha, it is worth taking a taxi or car as they have no direct bus services.

Getting around

The distance to many of these places is not great so it is possible to visit them on bike. But the traffic within the valley is heavy, so it doesn't always make for the most restful and relaxing of rides. The actual sites and attractions are small and can be easily explored on foot.

Best experiences

Watching sunrise from one of the valley rim resorts, page 159

Getting lost in the backstreets of Panauti, page 161

Chatting to Buddhist monks and Tibetans at Pharping, page 177

Watching the sacrifices at the Dakshinkali Mandir, page 178

Time required

Most of these places can be visited in an hour or two so you can easily combine several of them. A visit to Changu Narayan,

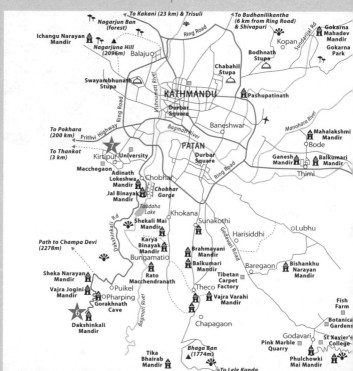

for example, can be combined with a visit to Bhaktapur. Namobuddha and Panauti combine well as a day trip or as a great overnight excursion with a night at Dhilikiel. The town of Kirtipur can be visited en route to the Kali temple at Dajshinkali. In the north of the valley, a walk in the Shivapura National Park can be combined with a visit to the reclining Buddha at Budhanilikantha and the forest temple of Vajra Jogini.

Best views
Nagarkot, page 157
Dhulikiel, page 165
Namobuddha, page 168

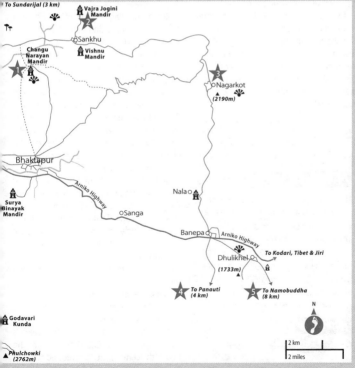

To Sundarijal (3 km)

Vajra Jogini Mandir

Sankhu

Changu Narayan Mandir

Vishnu Mandir

Nagarkot (2190m)

Bhaktapur

Arniko Highway

Nala

Surya Binayak Mandir

Sanga

Banepa   Arniko Highway

To Kodari, Tibet & Jiri

Dhulikhel (1733m)

To Panauti (4 km)

To Namobuddha (8 km)

N

Godavari Kunda

Phulchowki (2762m)

2 km
2 miles

beautiful temple in stunning location

The ancient Hindu temple of Changu Narayan ranks as one of the finest and most dramatic of all sites in the valley and is a UNESCO-designated World Heritage Site. Perched on the Dolagiri hill some 125 m above the valley floor, 6 km north of Bhaktapur and 13 km east of Kathmandu, it has superb views across the valley.

It survived the 2015 earthquakes more or less intact, although it currently has wooden supports while minor structural repairs are undertaken. A section of the courtyard gallery collapsed and there is damage to a couple of the minor shrines. You can still see the old ceremonial chariots within the courtyard gallery at the northeast of the site, but other areas have been cordoned off due to the damage.

Its origins are widely believed to date back to the fifth century AD. Some sources suggest an earlier beginning and that it was built by King Hari Dutta Varma in AD 325, while others say the temple was built on an ancient animist place of worship. Before the 18th century unification of Nepal, it was part of the independent Malla kingdom of Bhaktapur. The temple is acknowledged to be the oldest extant example of the Nepalese style of pagoda architecture, though much of the present structure dates from 1702 when it was rebuilt following a fire.

The **main temple (1)** is a two-storeyed building standing slightly off centre in a rectangular courtyard which also contains two smaller temples and numerous statues. The shrine contains a gold image of Vishnu as Narayan which is said to date from the seventh century, but is not open to visitors. Each of the four entrance doors is ornately decorated. The north door is guarded by a pair of winged lions; the east door by griffins; the south door by elephants; and the west door by lions. The torana and lavishly engraved brasswork surrounding the main west door is particularly memorable for its intricacy and detail. Each of the roof struts of both floors is a masterpiece of Newari woodcarving.

Caryatid-like figurines of the various incarnations of Vishnu, characteristically painted with blue skin, form the centrepiece of each below which are depictions of other deities all in seated posture.

Standing just in front of the west door are statues of **Garuda (2)** and of Bhaktapur's **King Bhupatindra Malla (3)** with his queen in a gilded cage. That of Garuda, Vishnu's winged vehicle shown here in reverential pose, is believed to have been sculpted in the fifth or sixth century and is one of the valley's most important works of art. Two **pillars (4)** stand at the temple's western corners, supporting a *sankha*, Vishnu's conch shell, on your right, and the *chakra*, Vishnu's discus, to your left.

Near the *chakra* pillar is the valley's oldest **inscription (5)**. Dating from the mid-fifth century, it is credited to the

Licchavi king, Manadeva, and chronicles how he successfully deterred his mother from committing *sati* by going to battle. **Garuda (6)** appears again in more dynamic form in the northwest corner of the courtyard. He is shown carrying Vishnu in a representation which is reproduced on the back of the Nepali Rs 10 note.

In the northeast corner is a **Shiva linga (7)** and between it and the temple are more images of **Vishnu (8)**. The eastern gateway leads to the small village of Changu Narayan. Moving to the southeast corner, there is a statue of **Ganesh (9)**, standing next to a rough-hewn statue of an elephant. Alongside this is a golden-roofed shrine to Kali decorated with an array of **floral tiles (10)**. Continuing clockwise, you next come to the **Vishwarup (11)**, which portrays Vishnu in his full, multi-limbed and multi-headed splendour as protector of the universe set upon the naga.

Behind this lies the **Sri Kileshwar Shiva Temple (12)**, immediately to the west of the main temple. It is currently being restored by the German Government.

Beyond was the two-storeyed **Lakshmi Narayan (13)** temple/shrine which was destroyed in the 2015 earthquakes, leaving only the platform. You can still see two important eighth-century arch-shaped stones containing bas-relief images of Vishnu. One shows the god in his fifth incarnation as the dwarf Vikrantha (or Vamana) who, in order to save the world, appeared in this form before the demon Bali and asked him for as much land as he could cover in three strides. Once granted, Vishnu became a giant,

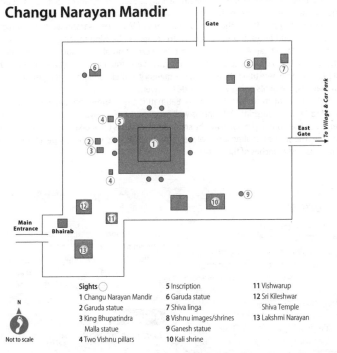

Changu Narayan Mandir

Sights ○
1 Changu Narayan Mandir
2 Garuda statue
3 King Bhupatindra Malla statue
4 Two Vishnu pillars
5 Inscription
6 Garuda statue
7 Shiva linga
8 Vishnu images/shrines
9 Ganesh statue
10 Kali shrine
11 Vishwarup
12 Sri Kileshwar Shiva Temple
13 Lakshmi Narayan

N
Not to scale

covering the earth in three strides and leaving only hell to the demon. The other is of the half-man half-lion god Narasimha, Vishnu's fourth incarnation, who came to destroy another demon, Hiranyakasipu, who could not be killed either by day or night, nor by god, man or beast. Reminiscent of the denouement in Shakespeare's *Macbeth*, the demon's riddle of immortality was summarily solved by Vishnu as neither man nor beast, at sunset when it was neither night nor day.

Gokarna

striking temple with statues of the Hindu trinity

Some 7 km northeast of Kathmandu, Gokarna is a former royal game reserve used for hunting trips and now home to a luxury hotel and golf course. The park's forested hills are inhabited by deer, antelope and boar, as well as numerous species of bird and butterfly.

To the north of the park, standing on the west bank of the Bagmati river in its early stages, is the **Gokarna Mahadev Mandir**. This three-storeyed pagoda temple dates from the late 16th century and is built on an ancient sacred site. It is dedicated to Shiva and the shrine contains a linga. Above the main eastern entrance is a *torana*, or metal plaque, depicting Shiva with his consort, Parvati.

Leading to the temple and surrounding it is an unusual collection of religious statuary, the extent of which is possibly unique in Nepal. In addition to several representations of Shiva plus appendages, there are also images of Vishnu as Narasingha the man-lion incarnation, and in the form of Narayan. To complete the Hindu trinity, Brahma is also portrayed – as a bearded figure – in a rare representation of the Hindu god of creation. The open space by the complex is used In August/September each year, when thousands of people come here to pay homage to the memory of their forefathers. It is also used for cremations, the ghats being visible beside the river.

Behind the main temple, beside the Bagmati is the **Vishnu Paduka**, a low pavilion that stands by a footprint of Vishnu as well as an image of Narayan reclining on a bed of serpents. Look out to the north for the small shrine that has been taken over by an ancient fig tree. The shrine has almost completely crumbled away to leave its shape imprinted in the roots and branches of the huge tree.

Essential Gokarna

Finding your feet

Gokarna is situated on the road that goes out of Kathmandu past the Bodhnath Stupa (page 85). Buses leave Ratna Park and take about 45 minutes, US$0.30. A taxi costs about US$7 one way and the trip could be combined with a visit to Bodhnath.

It is possible to cycle but the road is busy and built up the whole way. After Bodhnath continue a further 1 km and the road forks. Take the left-hand fork (northeast) which becomes the Sundarijal Road. Climb for about 2 km until you arrive at the temple. On your right is the small Bagmati river valley.

Admission

Open dawn to dusk, US$0.90.

Essential Sankhu

Finding your feet

Sankhu is 15 km from Kathmandu on the main road heading east from Chabahil past Bodhnath. There are bus services from Kathmandu's Ratna Park taking about one hour and costing US$0.50.

If you hire a car or taxi, it is possible to combine a visit to Vajra Jogini and other attractions in the valley such as Nagarkot. Negotiate the rate in advance. A taxi will cost about US$14 one way. A private car and driver should be US$40-60, depending on where else you wish to visit.

Alternatively, you can hire a mountain bike although there is heavy traffic for the initial journey and it is a long and steep climb if you continue on to Nagarkot.

Sankhu

old village badly damaged in the 2015 earthquake

Sankhu, 15 km east of Kathmandu, emerged as a result of its position on the ancient trade route that linked India and Tibet. A permanent settlement was first established here during Licchavi times. Today, Sankhu is a village which in many ways typifies how the old way of life is disappearing as urbanization creeps to most corners of the Kathmandu Valley. Old Newari houses, their structural woodwork often dilapidated whilst simultaneously displaying the fine carvings, which seem to have been taken so much for granted in traditional Newari architecture, are being replaced by modern concrete buildings. Cheaper to build and maintain and offering more living space, they must seem an obvious choice to the local inhabitants. The 2015 earthquake took a heavy toll here, with a lot of damage to the older structures that hadn't been maintained.

The village is surrounded by fertile agricultural land, particularly to the east and northeast. This is arranged in a series of gentle terraces which enables farmers to make the most of natural water run-off from the hills to irrigate their paddies. This makes for a spectacular lush green landscape as the crops begin to mature. Harvesting and planting, when everyone who is physically fit enough joins in, are particularly worth watching.

Large and colourfully decorated arched gateways mark the village limits. There are several shops in the village selling cold drinks and snacks, but only one restaurant, situated on the left-hand side as you approach from Kathmandu, the Sankhu Resort. From Sankhu, you can head north to the temple of Vajra Jogini, or continue east towards Nagarkot.

atmospheric temple in lovely forest setting

This delightful three-storeyed pagoda temple, built by King Prakash Malla who was responsible for many of the buildings and monuments standing in Kathmandu's Durbar Square, is situated some 2 km north of Sankhu on a forested ridge.

You climb to the temple from the road along a long stone staircase through the forest, with small shrines and drinking spouts at regular intervals. As you reach the final flight, with the temple ahead of you, look out on the left for the large shrine with yoni that has tumbled from the top and now rests upside down, held in place by trees that have grown over it.

The uppermost roof is said to be of gold, while the two lower roofs are copper gilded. The struts of all three roofs are lavishly carved with depictions of various deities and mythical animal figures. The main entrance of richly engraved copper is guarded by two large and brightly coloured stone lions. Just below and on plinths on either side of the steps are two smaller metallic lions.

The site has long been associated with religion and, although the current temple structure dates from the 17th century, it is widely believed that the location was used as a place of worship even during Licchavi times. This can still be seen in the nearby building with the stone dome that may well date back to the seventh century, although the dome itself was damaged in the 2015 earthquake. Its deity, a fearsome shakti aspect which normally remains out of sight, derives from tantric traditions and, as part of a local festival, is carried in an annual journey to Sankhu every April.

Around this main temple is a variety of statuary and religious icons and to the east another smaller temple with some fine woodcarvings that is dedicated to one of the Buddhist Taras. There are two meditation caves at the back of the compound. If you can squeeze through the entrance into the Dharma Pap Gupha you can prove your virtue but beware, fail and you display your vice.

Basic *dharamsala* accommodation is available for devotees in the nearby pilgrims' guesthouse situated at the top of a flight of steps, although some of it was damaged in the 2015 earthquake. It centres on a courtyard with lovely sunken oval tank complete with water spout. Look out for the huge overturned frying pan on the ground floor, used, according to legend, by an ancient king to offer parts of his body as a sacrifice to the goddess.

Essential Vajra Jogini Mandir

Finding your feet

From Sankhu it is a 30-minute (2-km) uphill walk. Go through the arch at the north of the village, follow the road until you come to a cobbled path heading off on the left which turns into a stone staircase as the incline increases. It is a steep climb, especially towards the end.

If you have hired a car or taxi it can drop you at the bottom of the stone staircase.

Admission

Open dawn-dusk, free.

Tip...
Beware of the numerous monkeys always interested in a quick snack of any food you may be carrying.

At the far east of the valley, 32 km from Kathmandu and at an altitude of 2190 m, Nagarkot is widely considered to have the best views of the Himalaya from the Kathmandu Valley. On a clear day, there are panoramas extending from the Annapurnas – Annapurna S (7273 m), Annapurna III (7557 m), Annapurna I (8090 m) and Annapurna II (7937 m) – in the west, to Everest (8848 m) and Kanchenjunga (8597 m) in the east. The best months for viewing are from November to February. In October and March views may be obscured, while at other times the mountains remain concealed for most of the time by clouds. The views can be exceptional at sunrise and sunset when the mountains are bathed in perceptibly changing hues of pink, red and crimson. To the east, the Indrawati and Chok rivers are visible far below the village.

Nagarkot itself is barely a village, though it has an army camp, a shrine and an increasing number of small hotels of varying standards. The army camp is a legacy of history: Nagarkot's strategic location allowing clear lines of vision through almost 360° led to a military presence being established here several centuries ago, a fact to which the small *kot* (fort) is attributed. Its recent growth – especially in the number of hotels – is almost entirely the result of tourism. A visit is highly recommended and the place is particularly relaxing after Kathmandu. Due to the altitude, temperatures are invariably lower than in Kathmandu (by as much as 10°C) and warm clothing is advised outside the hot summer months. It can also be windy and is popular with kite flyers. The spring flowers and unusual rock formations make short and undemanding treks from Nagarkot particularly attractive.

Walks from Nagarkot

To the Observation Platform This is the easiest of the walks, following a small tarmac road that winds its way along the top of the ridge. From the village continue past the **Club Himalaya Resort** (on your left). The road passes an army camp – first the officers' quarters and then, a bit higher, the general barracks. (No photos in this area.)

Keep climbing and after an hour or so you arrive at a cluster of refreshment stalls with the path to the platform heading off to the left. It's a five-minute climb to the small open space with platform. Be careful if you climb the tower, the metal ladder can be slippery. There are superb views on a clear morning from the area around it.

When you return to the refreshment stalls, there is a path that runs off opposite (not the track, which is a secondary route to Bhaktapur). This path heads through forest for a few minutes before emerging at a small glade with a Shiva shrine and pool. Just after it is the Bhaktapur track you can join and climb back up to the refreshment stalls.

To Sankhu and Vajra Jogini Leave Nagarkot on the track that heads initially east through the village, passing the **Nagarkot Farmhouse Resort** after a couple of kilometres. An alternative route is to follow the **Nature Ecotrek Route 3**, set up by the local tourism group. It is coloured purple on the large map outside their office in the village centre. This heads off to the left after the school and contours around the hill through the **Kusum Community Forest**. It emerges on a track just below the Nagarkot Farmhouse Resort. Follow the switchbacks down to the village of **Kattike**. Take the left turn – you can always ask in the small teahouses in the village. Continuing downhill, it is a 6-km walk to **Sankhu**. The road twists and turns,

Essential Nagarkot and around

see page 159

Finding your feet

Bus There are no direct buses from Kathmandu; you need to change in Bhaktapur. Buses from Bhaktapur to Nagarkot are irregular, leaving the bus park when full, US$0.50. A tourist minibus service leaving **Hotel Malla** at 1300 and returning from Nagarkot at 1000 can be booked through travel agents in Kathmandu. The two- to 2½-hour journey costs US$3.50.

Taxi/car The taxi fare from Kathmandu is around US$18, about 1½ hours. You can usually find a taxi to take you back to Kathmandu just below the **Club Himalaya Resort**, see page 159, or a private car in their car park. Hiring a private car for an overnight stay will be not much more expensive and will give you the option of visiting other attractions as well.

Tip...
Always make sure that you take enough water and food with you. A compass could also be useful occasionally.

Helicopter A helicopter service from Kathmandu is operated by the **Club Himalaya Nagarkot Resort**, see page 159, as part of their one- or two-night package deals. Book through the **Kathmandu Guest House** (see page 91).

Getting around

There are several excellent walking opportunities from Nagarkot. You can even walk back to Kathmandu, an all-day hike, although the last sections involve main roads with their heavy traffic. Trekking through the valley is an agreeable substitute for the more demanding mountain routes – especially for those who do not have time for longer treks – and does not require trekking permits.

If you are going to walk, get yourself a good map – Nepa 1:25,000 scale maps are ideal. There are also some good local guidebooks available from the bookshops in Kathmandu.

Nagarkot Naldum Tourist Development Committee office in the village (see page 159) are very helpful and provide good information and advice on the walks.

---

you cross a few small streams and walk through the villages of **Bishambhara** and **Palubari**. Just before you reach Sankhu, the road crosses the small Sanadi river and on your right is a temple dedicated to Vishnu. Turn right (north) at Sankhu and continue through the village; the **Vajra Jogini** temple complex is a 30-minute (2 km) climb from here.

There are irregular bus services from Sankhu back to Kathmandu, but there is one reasonable hotel if you get stuck. Ask locally for directions and a local guide if you so wish.

To Changu Narayan Follow the **Nagarkot Tamang Village** walk, marked purple and white on the map in the village. This leaves the Bhaktapur road just after the police post, dropping to the right. The trail is tricky in places, so a guide is a good idea. It passes through several villages, including **Bakhrigaum** and **Gairigaun**, before eventually arriving at **Telkot**. (Telkot is on the road, so you can considerably shorten the walk by getting a lift/ bus to here.) The whole walk takes about five hours; from Telkot about 1½ hours.

To Dhulikhel This, the longest of these three walks, covers about 16 km. It is well signposted, although the signs are easy to miss, so keep a keen look out. If you do think you've gone wrong, there are several places to ask for directions.

Leave Nagarkot along the ridge road heading south towards the viewing platform. After a gentle climb of a couple of kilometres a track drops off the road to the left after the army camp. It is signposted. For the first section, you contour through forest, passing several new lodges in various stages of construction. At a clearing soon after, marked with a map, you continue straight through the forest, listening to the amazing birdlife. Turn right at a junction (not left which is the mountain-bike route) and then look out for the trail dropping down the side of the ridge on a long stone staircase descent. You hit a track and follow it to the village on the small col. Keep straight on, climbing the small ridge that continues on the other side of the village. Quite quickly you go left off the main track and climb through terraces to a Buddhist chortern with prayer flags on the top. It's a good place for a rest and if the skies are clear there are great views.

Walk through the village, keeping left, and follow the signs as you drop down through **Opi** and then **Panchakanya** towards **Dhulikhel**. Only the last section, approximately 500 m, is along the main road.

Listings Nagarkot and around

Tourist information

Your hotel will also be able to organize guides.

Nagarkot Naldum Tourist Development Committee
In the middle of the village, T01-668 0122. Sun-Fri 1000-1750.
Small, helpful office providing good information on the walks and can arrange a guide if you want one (about US$28 per day). They have a large map outside their office giving you an idea of the routes, distances and timings.

Where to stay

Nagarkot has a range of accommodation to fit in with most budgets. Most hotels are within a 30-min walk of the village, though rooms are also available in private residences on both the approach from Bhaktapur and from the northern route. Most visitors come for an overnight stay, arriving in the afternoon. All hotels are accustomed to catering for early risers. Although there is usually more than enough capacity to cope with demand, in peak season it is advisable either to book in advance or to find a room immediately upon arrival.

$$$ Club Himalaya Resort
A 5-min walk from the village, T01-668 0080, www.nepalshotel.com.
Perhaps the most upmarket of the options, with a large round building housing a good restaurant, swimming pool and bar. The view from the rooms is excellent, especially the new wing, and there is a huge roof terrace with skyline photos to help identify the peaks. There's a helipad if you want to book a transfer that misses the windy road.

$$ The Fort Resort
T01-668 0149, www.mountain-retreats.com.
Set in over 4 ha of grounds, the resort sits on the site of the old fort that gave Nagarkot its name and which protected this old mountain pass into the valley. An extensive modern building of traditional design and traditionally decorated offers a comfortable stay, with good rooms in the building or in small cottages in the grounds. Peaceful and with great views and a good restaurant.

$$ Hotel Country Villa
T01-668 0128, www.hotelcountryvilla.com.
Rooms and suites at reasonable prices, the latter particularly with excellent mountain views. It is light with a modern feel and a restaurant and activities.

$$ Nagarkot Farmhouse Resort
A few kilometres away from the village,
down the Sangkhu road, T01-620 2022,
www.nagarkotfarmhouseresort.com.
This lovely resort offers tranquillity as well
as great views. With a traditional Newari
feel and set in fabulous gardens, much of
the excellent food is home grown. There are
walks from the resort as well as plenty of
easy chairs from which to enjoy the views. It
is owned by the same people who own the
Hotel Vajra in Kathmandu (see page 91)
and has the same relaxed, authentic feel.

$ Hotel at the End of the Universe
Up the ridge from the village, T01-668 0011,
www.endoftheuniverse.com.np.
A range of accommodation to suit all
budgets, from cottages or huts to doubles
with en suite facilities and great views,
all set in lovely gardens. It also has suites
with several bedrooms that are perfect for
families. A short walk up the ridge from the
village, so either the universe is smaller than
believed or Nagarkot is on the edge of it. It
also has a decent restaurant.

Restaurants

All hotels and guesthouses have some
dining facilities (see above), but Nagarkot
is by no means known for its culinary
excellence. As most visitors are on
overnight half-board packages, there is
not much business for restaurants to
target. If you do eat out, remember to
take a torch as there is no street lighting.

$ Berg House café
On the main road in the village, T01-668 0061.
This pleasant restaurant has views from
the small terrace back over the Kathmandu
Valley and an eclectic selection of in-house
decorations. A decent and well-priced
traveller menu ranges from excellent fried
rice to pizza. Perfect for a lunch.

What to do

Tour operators
Package tours are widely available at travel
agents in Kathmandu and include transport
and overnight accommodation. Prices start
at around US$50, but as always there is
room for negotiation. Many hotels in the
valley's three cities run their own half-day
tours to catch the sunrise from Nagarkot,
but these usually involve a horribly early
start and are subject to cancellation if there
are not enough bookings to make it worth
their while.

Thimi

Thimi is the first town you come to after leaving Kathmandu, some 3 km before
Bhaktapur, and almost impossible to identify in the modern sprawl of Kathmandu.
It is renowned for its craftsmanship, especially pottery and papier mâché masks.
Indeed, its name is a derivation of the Newari for 'capable people'. The majority of
the masks sold in Kathmandu are produced here, and some are also used during
local festivals.

The surrounding land is a rich source of clay and, as in Bhaktapur, it is fascinating to watch
as potters throughout the town prepare then turn the clay on large manually operated
wheels. You can buy their wares – anything from practical water pots to ornamental
candlesticks – direct from the potters or from the shops scattered throughout the town.
With a little bargaining, prices are amongst the cheapest that you will find.

Thimi used to be the fourth largest town in the valley and the architecture of the old town is very much Newari in character, but it is rather run down and there are few buildings of real interest. The Balkumari Mandir in the square at the southern end of town is a 16th-century structure and is dedicated to the *kumari* in her child form, but the temple has no 'living goddess'. The three-storeyed Ganesh Mandir can be reached via a stone stairway. Less than 1 km further north towards the Manohara Khola is the village of Bode with its 16th-century Mahalakshmi Mandir.

All Bhaktapur buses will drop you at Thimi, Rs 20. Taxis cost about Rs 600 (US$5.50) one way.

★ Panauti   *See map, page 162.*

an unspoilt, little-visited and picturesque town

The old town of Panauti lies some 32 km southeast of Kathmandu, at the confluence of the Roshi and Punyamati rivers. A third river, the Rudrawati, is also believed to join, making it a tri-junction in the shape of Lord Shiva's trident and a very sacred place. Sadly, only seers and holy men can see this third river but it became a site of pilgrimage as a result.

Much of the attraction of Panauti is to wander its small streets and alleys, losing yourself in a Newari town little changed over the centuries. There are plenty of small temples, shrines and monuments to look out for, as well as traditional houses, water fountains and squares.

The town is said to be built on one vast single rock that protects it from the effects of earthquakes. It certainly survived the huge 1934 earthquake almost unscathed but was damaged by a tremor in the Terai the 1988. The 2015 earthquake did some damage but the main monuments all survived intact. Mythology also gives a clue as to this immunity, saying that the town is built on the coiled body of the serpent king Basuki. The fact that these myths and legends have had time to grow does indicate a certain good fortune when it comes to earthquakes. It is also protected by serpent idols built at the three corners of the triangular-shaped peninsula.

You arrive in the small, modern town – a congestion of concrete, shops and traffic. Drop to the suspension bridge over the river to enter the old town and a different era. Newari architecture still predominates; chickens and goats roam the streets dotted by temples and shrines. It has been designated by the Department of Archaeology of Nepal as a 'Protected Monument Zone' and has been submitted to UNESCO for classification as a World Heritage Site.

Panauti's recorded history stretches back to the Lichhavi era with surviving carvings from that time, but it was undoubtedly a thriving settlement before then because of its position in a fertile side valley. Like the rest of the valley, Panauti fell under the influence of the Malla dynasties in the 13th century and remained so until 1355 AD when a local ruler, Jayasingh Ram Vardhana, declared himself sovereign and managed to remain independent until his death in c 1400. The area then reverted to the Mallas, mentioned in the Gopalrajvansavali chronicle as under the control of King Rama Malla until his death when it came under the control of Bhaktapur.

Situated near the trade route to Tibet, its position gave it strategic importance, as well as being an important commercial centre famed for its production of metal items. The Kingdom of Kathmandu tried to gain control of this trade network throughout the Malla era, until the conquest and unification of the valley by Prithivi Narayan Shah. It remained an important trading centre into the last century and some impressive Rana-period mansions illustrate the wealth that still existed at that time.

These days it is a small market town, a backwater known for the potatoes that are grown in the surrounding fields. Being forgotten by the outside world has protected the brick-paved streets and winding alleys of the old town. The two (or three) rivers may be little more than polluted streams in the dry season but they have preserved it from later development by shifting the site of the town to the north and in so doing saving the old buildings and architecture.

Indreshwor Mahadev Temple (1)
Open daily 0730-1700, Rs 300 (US$2.75) includes the museum.

The Indreshwor Mahadev Temple is situated at the eastern end of the old town, near the **Tribenighat** (three river confluence). It is one of the oldest and best examples of the traditional multi-roofed pagoda style of temple building in Nepal, boasting three tiers. The roof of the top tier and its pinnacle are made of gilded, hand-beaten copper.

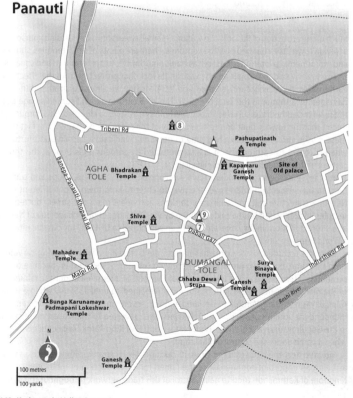

Panauti

Its origins are unknown but it is believed that the first temple was built on the spot in 1294, making it the oldest in Nepal. Records show that the Golden Pinnacle was given by King Jayasingh Ram Vardham in 1383 when he ruled the area. The gold-plated copper roof was added in 1816 by King Sundra Bikram Shah. Its most recent facelift was in the 1990s in a joint renovation project with the French Government.

The wood carving on the temple is particularly fine, much of it dating back to the Malla era, with the biggest roof struts in Nepal. Each side has carving depicting a different theme. The north side has images of the Matrikas, the mother goddesses. The east side shows the Salabhanjikas and the cult of Fertility, while the south and west sides depict scenes from two great Hindu epics the *Mahabharata* and *Ramayana* respectively.

The Lingam in the inner sanctum is the object of worship. During the Makar Mella, a Hindu festival held in January/February every 12 years, huge crowds gather to wash in the sacred rivers and worship the Lingam. It is next held in 2022.

Unmatta Bhairab Temple (2)

This traditional 16th-century temple has two storeys with a terracotta, or Jhingati, roof. Its most famous feature is the large and elaborate wooden doors that lead into the shrine, dedicated to Shiva in his Unmatta form, that of peace and passion.

Its other famous features are the carvings of the gods that appear at the three main upstairs windows, apparently gazing out at the devotees below.

Tulanarayan Temple (3)

This small temple, situated in the courtyard of the Indreshwor Mahadev Temple complex was damaged in the 2015 earthquake, despite Panauti's supposed immunity to such tremors. Rebuilding is already underway. The temple houses a black stone image of Vishnu, known as a Tulanarayan and famed for its artistic skill and beauty, that was installed in 1382.

Although its origins are unknown, there is a reference to the temple in an inscription dating from 1400, in which the King Jayasingh Ran Vardham is said to have donated his weight in gold to the shrine. A stone column outside, complete with notch on its top, is where the scales were supposedly set up for this transaction to take place.

Panauti Museum (4)

Situated in the courtyard of the Indreshwor Mahadev Temple, the museum was opened in 2011 by the local community. Set in a lovely large L-shaped room it brings

Sights ○
1 Indreshwar Mandir
2 Unmatta Bhairab
3 Tulanarayan Temple
4 Panauti Museum
5 Tribeni Ghat
6 Ghat Sattal
7 Sorhakhutte Pati
8 Lam Pati
9 Dhamadhatu Stupa
10 Nhubaba Bihar

together artefacts from the craftsmen of the town and the community in general. As well as items from the main temples, there are displays on stone craft, wood carving, masks and weaving, laid out on tables and in cabinets.

Tribeni Ghat (Khware) (5)

Located at the very tip of the peninsula, at the sacred point where the three rivers supposedly meet, this complex of shrines – dedicated to a pantheon of Hindu deities – and cremation ghats is flanked by the Ghat Sattal, a three-storey 19th-century building that offered

> **Fact...**
> Every year, normally about the 14 January, hundreds of worshippers come to this sacred spot to bathe.

shelter to those who had come here to die. It is decorated with beautiful paintings, scenes from the many lives of Vishnu as well as the occasional Buddha for good measure.

On the steps down to the river there are small body-sized ramps. This is where the stretchers of the dying can be laid with their feet in the water and the dead prepared for cremation. The cremations are held on the platforms at the very tip if the peninsula, where the waters of the streams join. Newari inhabitants are cremated on the far shore, to stop their spirits haunting the town.

Amongst the other monuments are a small, three-tiered Krishna temple and the Dhananjaya Basuki Nag statue. On the opposite bank lies the Brahmayani Temple, dating to the 17th century and built for Brahmayani, the main goddess of the village. It contains a statue of her which is pulled around the village in a chariot to celebrate the end of monsoon every year.

Patis and sattals

These are traditional resting places available to those either visiting the town for trading or on pilgrimage. Some, like the **Ghat Sattal (6)**, have accommodation, while others are just shaded places to sit and rest. Many of Panauti's were renovated to their original condition in the 1990s, the sheer number of them illustrating what an important trading centre it used to be.

Perhaps the most elegant is the **Sorhakhutte Pati (7)**, a square, single-storey structure with open sides and 16 wooden columns supporting the roof. Another of interest is **Lam Pati (8)**, a two-storey building with an open platform on the ground floor and intricately carved wooden balcony and windows above. Dating from the 18th century it is unusually long and thin.

Stupas and bihars

In total, there are nine stupas still existing, the largest and oldest of which is the **Dharmadhatu Chaitra (9)** located at Wolachhen Tole. They all follow the same basic design and symbolism of such stupa, with the square plinth representing the earth; the dome, water; the pinnacle, air; and the (usually) golden tip, fire.

There are two bihars in Panauti, both situated in the Aghatol area. The most important is the **Nhubaba Bihar (10)**, also known at the **Dyochhen**. This is reputedly the birthplace of the prince who donated his body to the hungry tigress at Namobuddha. Every August there is a festival held here to commemorate that event.

Sculptures and shrines

The whole town is littered with statues and shrines. The earliest are estimated to date from the eighth and ninth centuries AD, to be found on stone pillars near Yalachhen Tol.

Another piece, depicting the theme of Umamaneshwor, is found on the northeast corner of the Layaku Square.

Other later carvings from the Malla era are dotted around town, set in walls and shrines, daubed with coloured paints and offerings from the inhabitants. These include the **Laxmi Narayan**, the **Krishna Narayan** and the **Navagraha panel**. There are also the water fountains, many carved into the shape of crocodiles, the oldest of which is located near the Layaku Durbar and dates from the 1600s.

Tourist information

There is a small tourist information office in the courtyard of the Indreshwor Mahadev Temple, where you buy your ticket. It is located at the entrance to the museum. They have a map, a useful guide to the temples and the town.

Where to stay

Most people visit Panauti on a day trip from Kathmandu so the accommodation options are very basic and limited.

$ Hotel Panauti
Dalinchok Rd, T01 166 1055.
Clean and basic, some rooms with private bathrooms. It also has a roof-terrace restaurant serving local dishes.

Festivals

Jan/Feb **Makar Mella** is held every 12 years at the Indreshwor Mahadev Temple. It next happens in 2022.

Feb **Mahhav Narayan Jatra**.
Apr **Bel Biwah** and **Nava Durga Jatra**.
Jun **Punhi Jatra**, the main festival, falls on the full moon in June and is celebrated in the main temples.
Aug **Namobuddha Jatra** is celebrated in honour the prince who sacrificed himself to the hungry tigress.

Transport

Bus
Frequent buses leave **Kathmandu**'s **Ratna Park Bus Station** for Panauti, 45 mins-1 hr, US$0.50. There are also minibuses from the **City Bus Park**.

Car
Kathmandu to Panauti takes 40 mins by car. A day's car hire costs approximately US$40-60, depending on how long you wish to go for and whether you want to combine it with other places.

Dhulikhel and around

great views and a good base for an overnight stay

Dhulikhel is the last major town in the Kathmandu Valley through which the Arniko Highway passes on its way to Kodari on the Nepal/Tibet border. About 30 km from Kathmandu, it stands on the southeast slopes of the valley at an altitude of 1585 m and is a popular day trip or overnight destination with good mountain views. On either side of the highway it feels like a transit town, with repair shops, snack bars and stalls servicing the hundreds of buses that pass through every day.

In contrast to Nagarkot, with which it is often compared, Dhulikhel has a history of settlement that goes back to its days as a stopover on the India–Tibet trade route. Its

There are regular bus services leaving from the Ratna Park in Kathmandu from early morning. The journey goes via Bhaktapur and takes two hours or more, US$0.50. The bus stop is on the main road east of the village. To get into the old village either turn right just after the bus stop or walk 200 m and turn right as the road bends.

You can make the journey in less than half the time by taxi or private car. Once again, negotiation is essential; expect to pay around Rs 1500 (US$14) one way.

people are predominantly Newari. The main part of the old village lies to the west of the Arniko Highway, where the winding street leads up through the laid-back, old and rustic residential areas before descending towards Banepa.

Views of the valley from here, though, can be magnificent, particularly if your visit coincides with the expanse of fields below appearing as a glorious patchwork of lush green or golden crops. To the east you can see the Indrawati river meandering down from the Himalaya towards the Terai. As elsewhere, mountain views are dependent on the weather. The best months to visit are from October to March. During and around the monsoon time you will be lucky to get a glimpse of the mountains, although the otherwise entirely occlusive cloud cover is most likely to break in the early morning and late afternoon. The views stretch from Langtang along to the east, with Everest a distant speck.

Entering the village from the east, you come to a junction and square where roads branch off to the southeast and northwest. A small *pokhari*, or tank, of rather forlorn appearance lies beside a statue of King Mahendra and the square is used as something of a local meeting point and bus station.

Old Town

The Old Town is tucked behind to the southwest of Dhulikhel. A small main square has a **Hari Siddhi Temple** and a **Vishnu Temple**, both with three-tiered roofs and Garuda statues in front of them. Nearby you will find a traditional **Newari Bhagwati Shiva Temple**. The 2015 earthquake did little damage to these structures although some of the houses in the old town developed cracks and are propped. Repair work has started.

Kali Temple

If you want to combine your mountain views with a temple or two, then head off on the **Namobuddha Trail** for a steep 30- to 40-minute climb to the Kali Temple. From the lower end of the Old Town square, follow the road heading southeast for a couple of kilometres until you reach a turn-off after some playing fields. It's a good trail and the views from this modern temple are great, further improved if you use the nearby viewing platform. It can get very busy with local tourists at weekends and on holidays. As you climb you will pass a large Golden Buddha called the **Shanti Ban**.

Shiva Temple

Just after the turn-off for the Kali Temple is a small Ganesh shrine and the route down to the Shiva Temple. It's an atmospheric spot, a simple lingam shrine topped with a metal roof and with statues of the old Malla kings dotted around.

Walks from Dhulikhel

There are numerous interesting walks around Dhulikhel. For the more adventurous, there are trails leading all the way to **Budhanilikantha** via **Nagarkot**, **Sankhu** and the **Vajra**

Jogini Temple (see page 156), or eastwards beyond the Kathmandu Valley. The walking trail to Nagarkot is fairly well signed, just ask locally to find the starting point a few hundred metres down the Arniko Highway towards Kathmandu.

The most popular walk is to **Namobuddha**. The trail starts by climbing past the Kali Temple and is well signposted. You walk through the villages of **Kavre** and **Phulbari** and can see the monastery a good way before you arrive. The Namobuddha stupa is below the monastery, on the right-hand fork in the track. The walk takes three to 3½ hours.

You can also continue this walk to the lovely, traditional town of **Panauti** (see page 161), some two hours or so further down the track that passes the stupa. There is a bus station here to get you back to **Banepa** on the main highway.

Listings Dhulikhel and around

Where to stay

There are plenty of good guesthouses and hotels in Dhulikhel and along the northeast-facing ridge.

$$$$ Dwarika's Resort Dhulikhel
T011-490612, www.dwarikas-dhulikhel.com.
Best place in town and one of the best in the country. As you'd expect from the owners of the superb Dwarika's in Kathmandu, this beautiful resort is all about traditional brick and carved wood buildings set in nearly 9 ha of grounds. Infinity pools, pottery workshops and meditation make it a real mountain retreat. Price is for full board.

$$$-$$ Himalayan Horizon
T011-490296, www.himalayanhorizon.com.
Excellent mountain views from all rooms and good food. Built using local materials it has a pleasant atmosphere and sits in lovely grounds; the restaurant and its terrace are particularly nice for relaxing and gazing out at the peaks.

$$ Dhulikhel Lodge Resort
T011-490114, www.dhulikhellodgeresort.com.
Great views, nicely designed rooms and a lovely fireplace to relax around on the chilly mountain evening. Higher rooms have less obstructed views.

$ Snow View Guest House
T98-4148 2487.
A small, pleasant homestay offering views from some rooms and a rooftop from which everybody can enjoy the superb vista. 6 rooms all common bath, food available.

Restaurants

Nearly all of Dhulikhel's best eating places are attached to the hotels and most of their packages are at least half-board. Even if you're on a day trip it's worth eating at one of the hotel restaurants as they are better than small stalls around the bus park. The **Himalayan Horizon Hotel** offers a range of Nepali, Indian and continental dishes that can be eaten on their large terrace with great views.

Namobuddha is one of Nepal's holiest Buddhist sites and a popular place of pilgrimage for many Tibetans. It commemorates the supreme compassion of the Buddha when he sacrificed his body to a starving tigress. According to the legend, the Buddha, in a previous life as a local prince from Panauti, came across a starving tigress while walking in the hills. When he saw that the tigress had three cubs all about to die because their mother could not produce milk for them, he allowed her to eat him instead so that they could all survive. This selflessness transported him to a higher realm of existence (see page 170).

The Tibetan name for the site is Takmo Lujin which translates as Tiger Body Gift and it is believed that the bones of the prince are buried under the chortern. Namobuddha is a more recent name from the 16th century that came into common use when pilgrims started believing it unlucky to say the real sacred name. Most buses and taxis stop at a small saddle in the ridge where the road forks. Follow the track down to the right to get to it. This road continues on to Panauti. The paved road that leads off right slightly further along the saddle climbs to the monastery and its excellent views.

The origins of the hilltop site are unknown, though some sources suggest that the architectural style is indicative of construction in the 17th or 18th centuries. It is dominated by a large stupa (**Dharma Dhatu**) to which many prayer flags and banners are attached. It is surrounded by numerous *chaityas*, bells, prayer wheels and other Buddhist accoutrements.

On the top of the hill is the **Thrangu Tashi Yangtse Monastery**, a large new complex of Tibetan Buddhist monastery buildings and temples, officially opened in 2008 and almost unscathed in the 2015 earthquake. You can go inside the main prayer hall as well as visit a giant Golden Buddha in the upper hall. Other smaller monasteries and gompas dot the area.

Follow the path along the ridgeline to the west and you come to a small cave with a tablet and picture of the tiger. A nearby tree at the end of the ridge is festooned with so many prayer flags you can no longer see it. There is another small cave on an adjacent hill. No one knows which cave is the one that the sacrifice was made to the tigress but in true Buddhist spirit no one is that concerned.

Tip...
There are several small restaurants on the saddle of the hill below the hill perfect for a cold drink and bite to eat.

Listings Namobuddha

Where to stay

$$ Namobuddha Resort
T985-110 6802, www.namobuddharesort.com.
An eco-resort of small cottages set in lovely grounds. It is located on a small hill top about a 25-min walk from the main complex, offers home-grown vegetarian food and great views of the Himalaya.

$ Thrangu Tashi Yangtse Monastery
T984-901 4446.
It's possible to stay in the monastery's guesthouse, sleeping in clean but basic rooms and eating what the monks eat. It's certainly a real insight into Tibetan monastic life and is in a picturesque location. You need to book ahead as they get full, especially during the main festival times.

Festivals

Mar The main festival of the year takes place in Mar when pilgrims, especially Mahayana Buddhists, come to offer prayers.

Transport

It's possible to walk to/from Dhulikiel and Paunati, on pleasant trails through decent countryside. If you start at Namobuddha there is less climbing and more descent.

Bus
Once the road leaves the Koirala Highway it soon becomes a jeep track. Buses run to the small hamlet of cafés at the bottom of the hill, departing from **Banepa** and **Dhulikiel** but they are not very frequent.

Car and taxi
Taxis and private cars will bring you to the same point, expect to pay about US$60 from Kathmandu for the vehicle and make sure they don't try to kick you out when the asphalt stops.

Kodari and the Arniko Highway

the spectacular but unreliable Tibet road

The Arniko Highway, linking Kathmandu to the Tibetan border, is an engineering marvel, albeit one under constant repair due to the terrain it weaves through. Landslides are common, especially during monsoon. This spectacular drive takes you to the village of Kodari, that clings to one side of the deep gorge that separates Nepal from Tibet. However, the border crossing here has been closed since the 2015 earthquake and, although it is due to reopen, the date keeps slipping. It's believed that the Chinese want to keep this route closed and use the Trisuli crossing, to the west of Kathmandu, as the main access point due to its comparative proximity to the railway they are building across the Tibetan plateau. The Chinese side of the Kodari border crossing – a village called Khasa – has been evacuated as the Chinese authorities attempt to stamp out the smuggling that has become endemic there.

> **Tip...**
> If you want some adventure comparatively near to Kathmandu then the adventure resorts on the Arniko Highway are a great choice. Ring ahead as they are very busy during the main seasons but close during the off-season. Check online or by phone before travelling (see page 169).

Although the views from here are wonderful, Kodari itself is an uninspiring assortment of huts and houses and its interest lies mainly in its strategic location. Please note that even if the border crossing does reopen you can only enter Tibet as part of an organized group.

Listings Kodari and the Arniko Highway

Where to stay

These resorts offer exciting activities in lovely settings. They are destinations in their own right and if you fancy a day or 2 of adrenalin-fuelled excitement then they are well worth the trip. They are both about 2½-3 hrs from Kathmandu.

LEGEND
The tigress of Namobuddha

There once lived a king named Great Charioteer (Shingta Chenpo) who ruled over the small kingdom of Panauti. Due to the king's sensible rule all his subjects enjoyed happiness and wellbeing with rains coming at the right time and crops and livestock that flourished. He had three sons: the oldest was named Great Sound (Dra Chenpo), the middle Great Deity (Lha Chenpo), and the youngest Great Being (Semchen Chenpo). Skilled in the martial arts and self-assured, the two elder sons helped the king in governing the kingdom. The youngest son, Great Being, was very bright and renowned for his kindness and compassion. He gave freely and generously to others.

One fine day the king, queen, his sons and ministers left the town for a picnic in the countryside. The king and queen rode upon an elephant while the rest were mounted on beautiful horses. After half a day's ride they arrived at a forest full of birds and flowers and the king ordered the servants to stop and prepare the feast. They immediately unpacked everything. They erected tents, built a hearth and were soon preparing food and drinks. The younger people began to sing, dance and play, as the king, queen and ministers watched the entertainment while enjoying an 18-course meal accompanied by wine and sake.

Once they'd finished, the three princes picked up their bows and arrows and headed off. As they walked deeper into the forest, they noticed a den in the densest part. They crept up to it and discovered a tigress sleeping beside her cubs. The two older sons notched arrows and prepared to shoot but the youngest stopped them saying that killing them was wrong. Glancing into the cave again, Great Being noticed that the tigress could not move as she'd just given birth; she feared that if she left to hunt, another animal might harm her cubs. Tormented by hunger, she lay on the ground unable even to lift her head.

Great Being was moved to tears and asked his brothers, "What food can we give them to save them?"

They responded, "This kind of red Indian tiger eats only the warm flesh and blood of a recent kill. If you want to help them, you must find flesh and blood that is fresh."

He thought for a moment and nodded. "You are right warm flesh and blood is needed. But then I'd have to kill another living thing and that would mean killing one to save another. What else can I do?" He thought for a long while but couldn't think of a solution.

Then his brothers said, "We've come hunting to have a good time. It's pointless worrying about this tigress and her cubs. It's time to return to our parents." And so they left.

As he followed his brothers back to the encampment, Great Being thought, "For a long time, I have been reincarnated, wasting my countless lives, sometimes due to excessive desire, sometimes aversion, and sometimes ignorance. I have rarely met such an opportunity. What real use is this body?" Finally he decided, "This time I must be truly generous."

He yelled ahead to his brothers, "You two go on ahead. I have something to take care of and will catch up with you."

He returned quickly to the tigress's den and found the stricken animal still collapsed through exhaustion, unable even to open her mouth. He gently reached out his hand to touch her face, but she was so weak that she couldn't even bare her fangs. He fetched a splinter from a nearby tree and cut his hand with it, blood running down his hand which he allowed the tigress to lick. As her energy returned she leapt to her feet and with a huge roar pounced on the prince and ate him.

The two brothers had decided to wait for their brother but the youngest prince did not come, so they set out to find him. When they arrived at the den they cautiously looked inside. All that was left of their brother was some blood, bones, nails, and bits of clothing. They collapsed in shock and when they were finally able to move again quickly collected some pieces of their brother's clothing and, sobbing with sadness, raced back to their parents' encampment.

The queen had been taking a nap and in a dream had seen three doves flying high in the sky. As they fluttered around, a hawk swooped down and carried off the smallest one. Waking in terror, the queen immediately related her dream to the king. He replied solemnly, "I believe the three doves are our three sons. The youngest of them, carried off by the hawk, is my most beloved son. Something dreadful has happened to him." He immediately sent out his servants to search for the sons.

Soon the two princes arrived back and the king asked, "What has happened to my youngest son?" Crying with grief they told their parents about the tigress and what Great Being had done. The queen fainted and the king was overwhelmed by sorrow. When the queen came round the two princes took the king and queen to the den, so they could see for themselves the bones and rivulets of blood left behind by the tigress.

Meanwhile, Great Being had been reborn as Great Courage (Nyingtob Chenpo). He wondered, "What did I do to be reborn here in the celestial realm of Tushita?" Through his divine eye, he searched the five realms and saw, gathered around the bone fragments he had left behind, his parents and two brothers crying together.

He thought, "My family are experiencing such unhappiness, I must talk to them." He descended from space to the lofty sky and appeared before them: "I'm the prince Great Being. I gave my body freely to the starving tigress and I have now been rewarded by being reborn in the celestial realm of Tushita." With tears in their eyes, the king and queen said, "Offering your body to the tigress was most praiseworthy but whom can we tell of our suffering? We miss you".

Great Courage replied, "Please don't be unhappy. The end of birth is disintegration, and the end of gathering is separation. No one can transcend this for it is the nature of things. It is the same for everyone. If you perform evil actions, you will fall into the realms of hell; if you perform virtuous actions, you will be reborn in the higher realms. Therefore, pursue virtue. Make prayers of aspiration, and in the next life we will definitely meet again in this wonderful place." With this, he smiled and disappeared.

The king and queen felt happier and agreed they would follow a virtuous life from then on so they could see their son again in a future life. They had made a small casket covered with seven kinds of jewels in which they laid the bones of their son and built a stupa over the place that it was buried. This is Namobuddha.

$$ Borderlands Resort
T01-470 0894, www.borderlandsresorts.com.
A few kilometres from Kodari, this great resort, with safari-style tents dotted around lovely gardens, occupies a picturesque spot by the Bhote Kosi river. There is a thatched bar and restaurant to relax in after enjoying the activities on offer – trekking, rafting and canyoning. There is an office in Kathmandu to book through (T01-438 1214).

$$ The Last Resort
T01-470 1247, www.thelastresort.com.np.
Sitting on a ridge this resort is reached over a high suspension bridge from where, should you wish to, you can throw yourself off on the end of a bungee. Its comfortable safari tents are located around the grounds and

there is a large bar and restaurant. It also offers a full range of activities, normally included in an all-inclusive price, as well as a small pool and spa.

Transport

The journey from **Kathmandu** to Kodari takes 4-5 hrs, although it is very prone to landslides and slips and is currently taking longer. It's not unusual to have to walk around a blockage and join a different vehicle on the other side. There are several private buses bookable via local agents and also local services. Last buses leave late afternoon so (if the border reopens) don't leave crossing too late or you will be stuck in Kodari for the night.

Godavari and around

wonderful springtime gardens

This small town, 10 km southeast of Patan's ring road, is notable principally for its National Botanical Gardens and as a stop-off on the way up to Pulchowki.

National Botanical Gardens
Feb-Oct 1000-1700, Nov-Jan 1000-1600, US$2.

The gardens lie to the northeast of Godavari. An inexpensive map together with a guide to the gardens are sold at the main entrance. Since almost all the plants are unlabelled, these will be useful if you intend to do more than just enjoy the colour and variety. Though not enormous, the gardens are both interesting and appealing with numerous endemic and exotic species. There are several small ponds and streams, a Japanese garden, a rockery and the **National Herbarium** where research into the medicinal use of plants is carried out. A number of tropical species are on display in the greenhouses, including various cacti and orchids. It is also a popular picnic spot so be warned that Friday and Saturdays are not the most tranquil. The best months to visit are March-April and September-November when the gardens are at their most colourful.

The **Godavari Kunda**, a sacred water tank, is located on the main road just beyond the turning to the National Botanical Gardens. Fed by natural spring water, whose source some believe to be spiritually if not physically associated with the Godavari river in India, it is regarded as an important holy bathing place. A special

Essential Godavari

Finding your feet

Minibuses leave Patan's Lagankhal bus station every 15-20 minutes, taking around 50 minutes.

A private car for the day from Kathmandu costs about US$40, allowing you to visit several sites in a quicker time.

festival is held every 12 years (next in 2027), when pilgrims attain merit by bathing in its waters. Next to it is a large Tibetan Monastery, the **O Sal Choling Godavari**.

Opposite the tank is the **Godavari Community Forest**, 31 ha of woodland with over 300 bird species, a small oasis in the increasingly developed and crowded valley.

Phulchowki Mai Mandir (Naudhara Kunde)
Entry is free although a donation is expected.

This is one of two similarly named temples dedicated to the local female deity, Phulchowki Mai. The other is situated at the summit of Phulchowki. It is a three-tiered pagoda with two large tanks before it, fed by the Naudhara Kunda or nine water spouts. It was damaged in the 2015 earthquake but is still standing.

Naudara Community Forest
Open 0700-1600, US$0.90.

Adjacent to the temple is the Naudara Community Forest, nearly 150 ha of managed woodland set up with the assistance of the **Bird Conservation Nepal organization** ⓘ *www.birdlifenepal.org*. As you would expect, it's excellent for birdlife and local guides can be arranged at the gate. Request one who speaks English but if not available it's not the end of the world as the guides are still great spotters and, with the aid of a reference book, can enhance your walk (US$5-6 for a couple of hours).

Bishanku Narayan
About 3 km north of the Bus Park in Godavari. Take the dirt road that forks off to the left and continue for 1 km to the village of Godamchaur. Continue straight over the minor 'crossroads' (northeast) and up the hill. The temple is on your right after another 1 km.

This temple marks the place where Vishnu is said to have delivered Shiva of the malevolent intentions of the demon Bhamasur. The temple, amongst the most revered by the valley's Vaishnavites, is a natural cave set into the hillside.

The entrance is reached down a set of steep stairs, where you'll find a statue of Hanuman and of Vishnu, the images curtained off by chain mail in a small cave. To go further you must squeeze through a narrow fissure in the rock. The inhabitants believe it to be a sign of faith, and a successful passing means getting rid of all your previous sins.

Phulchowki Peak
At a height of 2762 m (1200 m higher than Godavari) it's a climb, but the rewards are awesome. Phulchowki, the highest of the peaks around the valley, commands breathtaking views over the valley with a Himalayan panorama beyond; on a clear day, you can see as far as Dhaulagiri in the west to Everest and Kanchenjunga in the east.

Forest covers much of the mountain slopes and provides a habitat for deer and other wild animals. It remains relatively unspoilt by human settlement. The area is renowned for its flowers – indeed, *phul chowki* means 'flower place' – and you pass through wide tracts of rhododendron on your way up as well as orchids and a host of other wild flowers, most of which bloom from March to April. At the top is

Warning...
Robberies of lone hikers have occurred in this area so always go as a group. It is also advisable to stay on the trails. The area was mined during the Maoist uprising and, although the mines have been officially cleared, some still remain.

a telecommunications tower, which serves the Kathmandu Valley, and the area's other Pulchowki Mai shrine. During winter, the summit can be snow-capped.

The trail starts behind the Phulchowki Mai Mandir (see above), before joining a track that takes you to the summit. The car journey takes about 45 minutes. There are also a couple of footpaths which can take about four hours up and three hours down. These need a map and ideally a guide, and should be done as a group (see warning).

This is a steep ascent. If you do walk up, ensure that you start the day early enough and calculate your return to Godavari within daylight hours. Bring water and snacks.

South of Patan

rural villages of the southern valley

Khokana
US$0.90 is paid at the small tourist office, if open.

Leaving the Patan ring road south of Jawalakhel, you reach, after about 5 km, the village of Khokana, although in reality you never truly leave the urban sprawl of Patan. This is a traditional agricultural community. It has not featured prominently on tourist

> **Fact...**
> A local tradition dictates that chickens are not reared in the village.

itineraries, but during harvest it really comes alive as the sheaves of crops are winnowed and the grain spread across the cobbled streets to dry in broad, though neatly defined, rectangles. The rest of the year, goats and ducks wander the streets as women spin wool on traditional wheels.

The surrounding fields are also used to grow mustard and the village is a traditional centre for the production of mustard oil, a pungent and distinctively flavoured ingredient used in much of the subcontinent's cuisine.

The village suffered badly in the 2015 earthquake, with lots of damage to the older houses. Much of this has been cleared and rebuilding has started.

When you enter the village, you cannot really get lost. The main streets take you to the main square and the **Shekali Mai Mandir**, a three-storeyed temple dedicated to a local female deity. It is currently propped up after the earthquake as a precaution but is believed to be structurally sound. Also in the square are a couple of smaller shrines, a stupa and a large tank, popular with the ducks. If you continue down the street past the temple it takes you to a second small square with a covered yoni, other shrines and a well.

> **Tip...**
> October is a good time to visit to coincide with its masked festival, the five-day Khokana Jatra.

It's an atmospheric place, with plenty of traditional buildings, small alleys and *bahals*, perfect for a brief wander. It may seem sleepy, but don't be fooled. The sign outside a tiny museum (that never seems to be open) states that its building was the first in all of Nepal to be lit with electricity.

Bungamati
There is a good bus service from Patan's Lagankhel bus station to Bungamati, US$0.20, 45 mins. Kathmandu buses go from the Ratna Park Bus Station, US$30. A taxi from Patan costs US$3.70 one way.

Bungamati is 1 km from Khokana. Just before you get there you can visit another temple, the **Karya Binayak Mandir**, about 200 m to the west of the road. The small temple is one of the four most important Ganesh shrines in the Kathmandu Valley.

Some 6 km from Patan, the village of Bungamati stands on a plateau just above the valley floor, surrounded by gently terraced slopes. These days, houses have been built in the surrounding fields, taking away the feeling of a compact settlement. But walk into the village and you soon find its traditional heart. It used to be simply a farming village but now it is noted for its weaving and for its numerous woodcarving workshops which supply Kathmandu's shops with many of their souvenirs.

Bungamati has long been known, however, as the residence of Rato Macchendranath for the six months over winter when this deity's image is not installed in its Patan temple. The practice, which originated in the 16th century, is believed to have derived from a legend that relates how the Guru Macchendranath delivered the valley from years of drought by making Gorakhnath rescind his curse. Much celebration surrounds the annual procession of the image to and from Patan. Every 12 years (the last was in 2015) the whole village takes part as the god is carried on a huge chariot in a journey which can take weeks. The enormous wheels and axles can be seen just outside the square, pushed up against a wall.

Sadly, the **Rato Macchendranath Mandir** was completely destroyed in the 2015 earthquake. The Government of Sri Lanka have pledged the money to rebuild it and the process of tendering contracts is currently underway. Villagers believe it will take five or six years to rebuild as, being expert wood carvers, they want the very best work done using properly seasoned wood.

The square in which the temple stood is still the focal point of the village. There are information boards showing plans of the temple – a large shikhara structure painted white. The courtyard also contains a number of smaller shrines and has several souvenir shops in it.

Chapagaon

There is a good bus service from Patan's Lagankhel Bus Station, US$0.20, 45 mins. A taxi from Patan costs about US$3.70 one way.

Chapagaon lies due south of Patan on the opposite, east bank of the Nakhkhu Khola river to Bungamati. The village has three temples of note. The first you come to is a Vishnu shrine, while just to the south is a small shrine dedicated to Bhairab. As you enter the village, a road leads off to your left (east) for some 600 m to the **Vajra Varahi Mandir**. The mid-17th century structure is situated in a wooded park that is a popular picnic spot, on a site which has traditionally been used for religious worship.

The eponymous goddess is a wrathful tantric shakti deity portrayed in the *nrityamurti asana* position, a posture typical of Tantrism in which the left leg stands slightly bent (in this case, on a prostrate Bhairab) while the right leg is bent in towards the thigh. The temple also contains images of the eight mother goddesses, the Ashta Matrika. Two lions guard the gate and a large bull stands on a plinth, covered by a suspended brass umbrella and covered in fat, especially his private parts.

A new Tibetan monastery is being built just outside the park area.

Tip...
There are monkeys about, as at all popular picnic spots, so watch out for any snacks you may have brought.

Chobhar

There is no direct bus service but any service for Pharping can drop you off a few mins from the village, US$0.20-25. A taxi from Kathmandu costs Rs 600 (US$5.50) one way.

The small village of Chobhar stands on a hill on the west side of the Bagmati river, about 6 km from central Kathmandu. The village is dominated by a three-tiered **Adinath Lokeshwar Mandir** (also known as Chu Vihara or Karuna Maya), an unusual Buddhist temple adorned by an extraordinary number of metal pots, pans, mirrors and other household items nailed to wooden boards. These utensils are supposed to have been offered to the temple deity by recently married couples and others in a prayer for domestic contentment. The temple was built in the 15th century and renovated in 1640.

Its origins as a religious site, however, are said to date further back to an earlier Hindu temple dedicated to Macchendranath and only later converted to a Buddhist shrine. This may explain the appearance of the deity in current occupation, a red-faced image closely resembling the Rato Macchendranath image of Bungamati and Patan. The top roof of the temple is of gilded copper and the copper *torana* above the entrance to the shrine has six engraved images of the Buddha.

Chobhar Gorge

At the Chobhar Gorge the Bagmati river narrows to cut its way through the rocky hills. The gorge has an important place in Newari Buddhist lore. Legend recounts how the bodhisatva Manjushri came from the mountains of Tibet and drained the huge lake that was the Kathmandu Valley of its waters by slashing the hills to the south with his mighty sword during an earthquake. He thus created the Chobhar Gorge and a fertile valley fit for human habitation. Spanning the gorge is an old iron suspension bridge, built in Aberdeen and installed here in 1903. Sadly, the gorge has been mined over the decades and was the site of a now-abandoned cement factory, which does nothing to enhance its beauty.

Jal Binayak Mandir

Just to the south and standing majestically on the bank of the Bagmati is the beautiful Jal Binayak Mandir. Built in 1602, this is one of the valley's four most important Ganesh shrines (Binayak is another name for Ganesh). The main three-storeyed temple is incorporated into the western flank of the complex edifice and has a copper upper roof. In the centre of the courtyard facing the shrine is a rare bronze image of Mushika, the divine vehicle of Ganesh in the form of a shrew. The main image of Ganesh, meanwhile, is a large rock which is believed to resemble the shape of an elephant. There is also an image of Uma Maheshwar, a depiction of Shiva and Parvati, which is thought to have been made in the early 12th century. The pagoda roof struts are carved with images of the eight mother goddesses, the Ashta Matrika, and of Ganesh. Steps lead from the main entrance of the complex to the river ghat, and on its southern side is the old cement factory.

Sadly, the Bagmati river carries the pollution of Kathmandu – sewage and other urban waste – for much of its course south. A further 2 km south of Chobhar, between the Dakshinkali Road and the river, is the small **Taudaha Lake**. This is the only residue of the valley's original lake and was the mythical repository of the nagas released during Manjushri's draining of the valley.

LEGEND

Sacrifices to Kali

The goddess Kali (literally 'black'), described in the *Mahabharata* as "born of anger ... the cruel daughter of the ocean of blood, the drinker of blood", is the terrifying form of Durga, the consort of Shiva, one of the trinity of 'all powerful' Hindu gods. Kali is perhaps the best known of all the tantric shakti divinities and is seen as representing, or controlling, destruction and death in the unending cycle of life.

Often known affectionately as Ma ('Mother') Kali by devotees for her other, protective qualities, her worship in the past occasionally involved human sacrifice; in the modern era it continues to include, inter alia, animal sacrifice. This practice, which emerged as a prominent feature of Hindu worship during the late Vedic period (c 900-500 BC), is seen as continuing the process of creation by repeating the first great sacrifice in which the world was created. There are specific rites and rituals associated with it and the value of the sacrifice depends upon their correct performance by a priest. Kali is usually portrayed with multiple arms, a protruding tongue, wearing a garland of skulls and treading on the prostrate figure of Shiva.

Pharping

There is a good bus service from Kathmandu's Ratna Park Bus Station to Pharping, US$0.30, 1 hr 20 mins. A taxi from Kathmandu costs about Rs 2500 (US$23). An alternative is to hire a car and driver for the day and do a circuit of several of the southern valley's highlights.

After Chobhar, the road climbs steadily for 11 km to the village of **Pikhel** and a number of scattered settlements collectively known as Pharping. Before the 18th-century unification of Nepal this was an independent kingdom.

In recent years, it has become a place of importance to the Tibetan community, with several new, large monasteries opening and drawing Buddhist pilgrims from all over the region. It's hard to get lost and a great place to wander around and explore. In town, there are some good shops from which to buy religious art and *thankas*.

The **Shekha Narayan Mandir** stands below a steep limestone cliff at the first of Pharping's settlements. This Vaishnavite temple, dedicated to the fifth incarnation of Vishnu as the dwarf Vamana, contains statues said to date from the seventh century. Beneath it, at road level, it has several water tanks well stocked with fish. The colourful main temple building, situated under a large stalactite hanging from the cliff, dates from the 17th century, though the site itself is believed to have been used as a place of worship for considerably longer.

The place is also sacred to Buddhists to whom it is known as **Yanglesho**. The cave alongside the temple is revered as the place where Padmasambhava attained his realization of the Mahamudra teachings. Legend relates how snakes came to disrupt Padmasambhava during meditation. The guru reached up and turned them all to stone, an act commemorated by the stone images of snakes hanging here today.

Adjacent to the Shekha Narayan Mandir and approached via a flight of steps, is the **Buddhist Monastery** which maintains the Katok and Longchen Nyintig traditions.

On a ridge a few hundred metres beyond, there is an ancient Newari pagoda site dedicated to **Vajra Jogini**. This 17th-century temple is one of the four main Vajra Jogini sites of the valley with an inner sanctum that is home to a couple of images of the bloodthirsty Bajra Yogini holding skulls and knives.

Higher up the hillside, there is the **Astura Cave**, where Padma Sambhava attained enlightenment. The cave is venerated by Hindus as an abode of Goraknath. It is also a popular place for Tibetan pilgrims to visit, many in traditional dress and chanting holy mantras. There is a handprint in the rock just above the cave entrance they hold their prayer beads to as well as their hands, created as cosmic power surged through the Rinpoche at the moment of enlightenment.

There are several other Tibetan Buddhist temples and monasteries which have been constructed on the hillside around and below this cave in recent decades and which principally represent the Nyingma and Kagyu traditions. Monks are everywhere in town, and when walking near the monasteries you can hear the novices yelling as they play football or other games.

An exquisite 'self-arising' rock image of the tantric deity, the **Green Tara**, which was not so long ago exposed to the elements, has now been incorporated within a large temple complex. A monk is on constant duty reciting sacred texts 24 hours a day.

★ Dakshinkali Mandir
Entry US$0.30. Frequent buses run from Kathmandu's Ratna Park Bus Station, 2 hrs, US$0.50. By taxi, the journey from Kathmandu takes a little under 1 hr. Expect to pay around Rs 2500-3000 (US$23-27) for the return trip; it can be combined with Pharping. You can also make your way by mountain bike, but it is uphill all the way to Pharping and much of the road is in poor condition and busy with local traffic and pilgrim coaches. Allow 2½-3 hrs with time to take in the scenery.

As you leave Pharping, you go under an archway and pay an entrance fee. The road then snakes down the hill for 3 km until you come to the parking area for the Dakshinkali Mandir (*dakshin* means 'southern'). You get to the temple by walking along the road lined by vendors of red *sindur* and other coloured powder dyes, fruits, vegetables, chickens and souvenir carvings and paintings. Uncastrated black male goats, the most common sacrifice for those who can afford it, are brought by the worshippers, though chickens are a popular alternative.

From here there are two stone staircases down to the temple complex; a row of seven waterspouts line the west bank pathway for pilgrims to wash themselves at. The temple complex straddles the banks of a small river in a ravine surrounded on three sides by steep, densely wooded slopes. The combination of the location's natural grandeur with the devout, though oft seemingly brutal, worship of a demanding goddess imbues the whole area with a remarkably intense atmosphere.

The temple was built by a Malla king in the 14th century to appease Kali with a great sacrifice of buffaloes when the country was in the grip of a cholera epidemic. The path down from the car park crosses a bridge guarded by a pair of stone lions that leads to the temple. Its gilded canopy roof is supported by four bronze nagas, while the shrine beneath contains the image of the goddess formed of black stone. In front of it hang three large bells as well as two long rows of butter lamps that the devout can fill and light. All around the edge of the precinct are smaller bells left as offerings and now so tightly packed in that they are hard to ring.

Tuesday and Saturday are the busiest days, when pilgrims and visitors come by the busload and when the sacrificial knife is at its most active. Worshippers ritually wash in the river before and after *puja*. The sacrifices take place on a mosaic stone floor beside the shrine. They are mercifully quick: a single swing of the knife is usually enough. The streams of blood flow along drains and into the river below where they mingle with huge quantities of chicken feathers before disappearing with the drift of the besmirched, ruby waters. Although visitors are not allowed into the shrine, there are walkways on both sides of the river from where you can view proceedings.

Follow the covered walkway that climbs up the left side of the stream and the stone stairway will bring you to the Mala Temple, perched high on a small outcrop. A triangular fire pit in the small shrine produces prodigious amounts of smoke from the incense burnt here, smoking out an adjacent pigeon coup if the wind is in the wrong direction. At the bottom the path is lined with refreshment stalls should you require a drink or sit down.

Chandragiri Hill Cable Car
www.chandragirihills.com. Mon-Fri 0800-1700, Sat-Sun 0700-1800, US$22 return, US$13 one way.

If you haven't got time for a night in Nagarkot or Dhulikhel then this is a quick option to get a look at the mountains from a base in the valley.

Situated in the village of Godam near Thankot, where the Prithvi Highway leaves the Kathmandu Valley, this new cable car takes you on a nine-minute ride to the top of Chandragiri Hill. Here there is a viewing platform, as well as the Bhaleshwor Mandir, a Shiva temple that, according to local legend, was worshipped in by Prithvi Narayan Shah before he started his campaign to conquer the valley.

Located at an altitude of 2251 m it's worth getting to the top early as, on clear winter mornings, the view is incredible, taking in both Annapurna and Everest, and running along the northern horizon. It also shows how the sprawl of modern Kathmandu has now covered most of the valley.

★ Kirtipur

the valley's fourth historic city

Formerly classed as one of the four cities of the Kathmandu Valley, and with a predominantly Newar Buddhist population, Kirtipur has a proud though bittersweet place in the history of the valley and its name means 'glorious city'.

Essential Kirtipur

Finding your feet

From Kalimati in the western suburbs of Kathmandu, the main Prithvi Highway to Pokhara heads westwards. Turning southwest from this highway, a side road leads from Kalimati 1.5 km west of the confluence of the Bagmati and Vishnumati rivers to the medieval hilltop town of Kirtipur (1400 m).

Buses leave from Kathmandu's Ratna Park, US$0.20, and take about 30 minutes, depending on the time of day. A taxi from Kathmandu costs about US$4.60 one way.

You can combine Kirtipur with some of the valley's other southern attractions, such as Dakshinkali. To do so it's easiest to hire a car with driver (about US$40 for the day), or charter a taxi.

Admission

Kirtipur Guides Association Office, T01-433 4817, is where you buy your ticket and get given a basic but adequate map, open 0900-1700, US$1; a two-hour tour costs US$4.50.

These days Kirtipur has been engulfed into the Kathmandu urban sprawl but its position on a hilltop has protected it from the rampant, unsightly development seen elsewhere and kept the roads and traffic away, giving it a calmer feel than its neighbouring suburbs.

Kirtipur is often considered to be among the most quintessentially Newari of the valley's towns. In some ways, it bears comparison with old Bhaktapur: an undulating maze of narrow cobbled streets typically hemmed in by terraces of three-storeyed earthy-red houses often with fabulously carved windows and doors. Unlike Bhaktapur it is a mixture of the old and new, with modern building alongside the old and the nitty gritty of everyday life all around. It feels like a real Nepalese town, perhaps like Kathmandu did 20 years ago. It is also much quieter, with little through traffic meaning you can wander the brick and stone paved streets in comparative safety and peace.

The town's people had traditionally been involved in agriculture but the manufacture of handicrafts, particularly carpets and textiles under the auspices of the Kirtipur Cottage Industry Centre, now occupy many of its inhabitants.

The town offers some fine views of Kathmandu, especially if you arrive in the cool of early morning before the smog rises.

Uma Maheshwar Mandir (1)

This temple stands on a high point on the western side of the town from where you have marvellous views of Kathmandu. You can also look out over the town and understand just what a great strategic position it held when its walls were encircling it.

Two elephants stand guard on either side of the impressive stone stairway that leads up from the east. The three-storeyed temple was built in the 17th century. The smaller Vaishnavite shrine nearby is dedicated to Vishnu as Narayan together with his consort Lakshmi in an interesting complement to the Uma Maheshwar image of Shiva and Parvati.

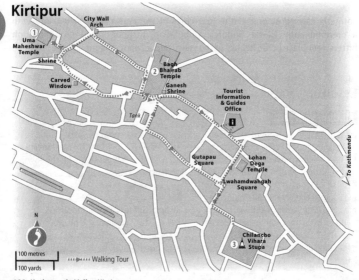

Kirtipur

ON THE ROAD
A walk around Kirtipur

Kirtipur is the kind of place that is worth a wander, to explore small alleys and streets and see everyday life going on as it has unchanged for centuries. See also the map, opposite, with the following walking trail on it.

As you leave the **Kirtipur Guides Association Office** (see page 179) turn left and take the road to the right of the one you arrived on, looking like a switchback. You can see a small white stupa in front of you. Turn right up the hill before you reach this stupa and climb to the Indian-style shrine in **Lwahamdwahgah Square**. Leave the square by the far-left (southwest) corner and pass the **Jiuadharma Vihar** building dating from 1647.

The first alley on your left takes you to the **Chilancho Vihar Stupa** (3, page 182). Retrace your steps to Lwahamdwahgah and turn left, past two large standing golden buddhas and then through **Gutapau Square**, with its small white stupa and shrine. You soon arrive at the southern end of the main square. To your right is a large, recently restored water tank and beyond this stands the **Bagh Bhairab Mandir** (2, page 181). Leave the temple and turn right, soon entering a square with a building standing in the middle and then follow the wide road that opens up afterwards. Look out on the left for the amazing **carved window** above the door of a small shop and on the right for a small Newa Cultural Museum that always seems to be closed.

At the end of the square turn right beside the shrine and after a few metres you will see a stone staircase climbing to the **Uma Maheshwar Mandir** (1, page 180). Return down the steps and turn left, following the alley as it drops to a brick arch that marks the location of the old city walls. Turn right here beside the white stupa and small black shrine covered in red paint. You will see the Bagh Bhairab Mandir in front of you. When you reach it, turn right and you will find yourself back in the main square. Take the road that leaves the square on the far side of the temple, past a small **Ganesh shrine** and this brings you back to the Guide Association Office.

Take time to look at the bell that hangs to the right of the shrine, on top of the platform. It was made by Gillett and Johnson Foundry, Croydon in 1895. Sadly for the reputation of British craftsmanship, it has a large crack in it but you do wonder how it ended up in the Kathmandu Valley having been made 57 years before the valley opened to the outside world.

Bagh Bhairab Mandir (2)

In the centre of town, just north of the main square, is Kirtipur's best-known temple. *Bagh* means 'tiger' and the clay image of Bhairab is shown with the mask of a tiger, which underlines the deity's ferocious character. This image has no tongue, a deliberate absence derived from the story of a Kirtipur boy who once made a clay model of a tiger and, upon returning from the wood to fetch a leaf for the tongue, discovered that his model had come to life. The site has been used as a place of worship for as long as Kirtipur has existed, though the three-storeyed temple was built much later. Its principal attractions are the swords and shields which adorn the temple, fascinating vestiges of the battle in which Kirtipur fell to Prithvi Narayan Shah, and a selection of sacrificed animals' horns on the west side.

BACKGROUND
Kirtipur

Kirtipur's origins are traced back to the 12th century when it belonged to the kingdom of Patan. By the 15th century it had broken these links and was established as an independent Malla kingdom. Its hilltop location gave Kirtipur a strategic advantage over attackers and its defence was increased by the building of a fortified wall around the town, the remains of which can still be seen today. The wall had 12 gates which opened to each of the town's precincts. It was the last of the valley's towns to fall to the invading and ultimately unifying armies of Gorkha under Prithvi Narayan Shah. So fierce was the town's resistance, aided by its strategically high location, that it withstood the Gorkhas three times before eventually falling in 1769, a year after the submission of Kathmandu, Patan and Bhaktapur. Retribution for the town's opposition came swiftly, however, as Prithvi Narayan Shah famously ordered the noses of all men to be cut off, save those who could play wind instruments. It was reported that the severed noses filled two baskets with a combined weight of 40 kg! An erroneous, though amusing piece of hearsay has it that the noses of Kirtipur's men are still shorter than average.

The Bagh Bhairab festival takes place in autumn when the image is carried on a palanquin through the village and down to the river. Sacrifices are offered to Bhairab on Tuesday and Saturday. From the back of the compound you get some good views north over the valley.

Chilancho Vihara (3)

Also known as Chilandev Bahal and Jagatpal Mahavihara, this stupa stands in a square on Kirtipur's southern hilltop. Like those of Patan, its construction is widely attributed to the Emperor Ashoka, though it is strongly disputed whether Ashoka ever actually visited the Kathmandu Valley. The oldest known reference to the stupa, pertaining to its enlargement and renovation, dates to 1509.

The central stupa is 11 m high and above the dome 13 circular brass steps lead to the *chhatra*. An iron frame, once made of bamboo, supports an additional umbrella above the stupa. At the cardinal points around the base are smaller *chaityas* and between these are other shrines, some containing images of Dhyani Buddhas and various depictions of Tara. The entrance is guarded by two trunkless elephants and a bell, installed here in 1755, is suspended on one side. Typical of the idiosyncratic nature of religion in Nepal, images of various Hindu deities, including those of Ganesh and Sita, are placed as you enter the site. Around the stupa are a number of *dharamsalas* as well as the buildings of a disused monastery.

Leaving the stupa, a path leads south towards the market area of Naya Bazaar. Just beyond is the new Nagara Mandapa Kirtivihara, a temple gifted to Kirtipur by the Thai government in the 1980s and built in the Thai style. At the extreme western end of town is the **Kirtipur Cottage Industry Centre**.

Situated some 8 km north of Kathmandu is an impressive 5-m-long sleeping statue, the largest in the valley. Revered as an emanation of Avalokiteshwara by Newar Buddhists, and by Hindus as Narayana, an incarnation of Vishnu lying on a bed of Naga spirits or snakes, this remarkable image is one of three fashioned by King Vishnugupta in the seventh century. Another lies at Balaju, while the third was installed in the old Royal Palace for King Pratap Malla. In his four hands the deity holds the four attributes: a discus (symbol of the mind), a mace (primeval knowledge), a conch shell (the five elements) and a lotus seed (the universe).

The statue lies in a small tank at the foot of the Shivapuri Hills and is thought to have come from beyond the valley. The basalt rock it's carved from comes from the southern hills many miles away and it must have been dragged here overland, quite a feat when you study the terrain they had to cover. Local legend has it that it was lost for many centuries and only rediscovered by a local farmer ploughing his land.

The outer courtyard is ringed by brick walls and shrines, with small shrines and sacred stones surrounding the central shrine. This is enclosed by railings with a large yellow cloth suspended over it as a roof. Most daily worship is done at a large rectangular platform, surrounded in butter lamp stands and with a linga in the centre. It is covered in paint and flower offerings.

Only Hindus may enter the inner sanctum by descending to the tank on a stone causeway. A priest washes the god's face each morning at around 0900. Jayasthiti Malla revived the Vishnu cult at the end of the 14th century, pronouncing himself to be an incarnation of Vishnu, a belief held by successive rulers to the present day. You can get a great view of the sanctum through the railings that surround it.

Since the time of King Pratap Malla (17th century), who dreamt that his successors would die if they were to visit the image, no King of Nepal ever entered the precinct again.

Essential Budhanilikantha

Finding your feet

Buses run from Kathmandu's Ratna Park Bus Station or minibuses from Kantipath, taking 40 minutes or so and costing US$0.30.

To hire a car or taxi is a quick option that allows you to combine the statue with a visit to Shivapuri National Park (see below). A taxi costs about Rs 600 (US$5.50) each way, a car and driver costs about US$40 for the day.

It's also possible to cycle but the traffic can be heavy for much of the journey.

Admission

Dawn to dusk, free.

Fact...

According to legend, Vishnu sleeps for four months of the year and the festival of Haribondhini Ekadashi, held in late October or November, celebrates him waking after his monsoon nap.

The Shivapuri Nagarjun National Park was created to the north of Kathmandu as a way of securing the city's water source. In the 20 or so years since the reserve was created it has been a great success, now the most-visited park in Nepal. It is home to a wide range of flora and fauna, from musk deer and leopard to a dazzling array of birds. Admittedly most visits are only for the day, but as an option to trek in some beautiful mountain landscapes, it is a convenient and worthwhile destination. At the weekends it gets very busy with day trippers and their picnics.

Most visitors head for Shirapuri peak which, at 2732 m, is the second highest point on the valley rim and offers great views north to the main Himalayan chain. There are two main routes to the summit. The first is a stone staircase that climbs steeply to a small col near to the summit, from where you follow the ridge to the top. Just beyond is **Baghwar**, the place where the sacred Bagmati river emerges from the rock and the site of a small Hindu shrine. It is also a small Buddhist site, revered as the place where the Buddha Krakuchhanda preached and effected the origin of the Bagmati river. The word *bagmati* means 'stream of words'. The second route is further, contouring its way up the hill, initially on a track and then on footpaths.

Essential Shivapuri National Park

Finding your feet

The main gate is situated just north of Budhanilikantha, so a taxi or car could be used to combine both attractions. You can also take the bus to Budhanilikantha, then walk or get a taxi to the park gate.

Admission

T01-437 0355, open 0800-1630 (tickets sold until 1400).

It's a fair climb and, with the gates only opening at 0800 and closing late afternoon, you are not able to get to the summit for sunrise or sunset when the views tend to be at their clearest. It's a great place just to go to and walk through beautiful forest with mountain streams cutting over the trail. These days, houses run right up to the park gates but there are few other places in the valley you can reach so easily to escape the noise of bustle of the city.

Vehicles are allowed on a limited network of tracks that run through the park (4WD required). You can also mountain bikes in the park, either independently or on guided tours from specialist operators in Kathmandu.

Walks & treks
from the
Kathmandu Valley

The days of walking through unspoilt countryside in the main Kathmandu Valley have gone. As the city continues its relentless growth, few areas are without the modern, concrete buildings that are replacing the traditional Newari brick architecture.

However, day walks are possible in the reserves and parks and up on the valley rim. Shivapura National Park offers some beautiful trails and there are good options to the south of the valley where the urban creep has been slower. The sections on Nagarkot (page 157), Dhulikhel (page 165) and Phulchowki (page 173) provide walking options.

For those who want to go trekking without having to fly up to the mountains, there are some excellent options to the north of the Kathmandu Valley. The Helambu Valley area immediately north of Kathmandu offers some great three- to six-day treks, with homestay and lodge accommodation available. Further north, Langtang has always been overshadowed by the Annapurna and Everest regions but it is still a popular and established trekking area.

Holy waters of Gosainkund

Hindu myth tells how Shiva came down from his sacred home on Mount Kailash to meditate while other gods were churning the world's oceans to create amrit, the legendary elixir of immortality. Their churning, however, produced a burning poison and they turned to Shiva for help. He immediately drank the poison and thereby saved the world. But the poison burned his throat and he ran to the Himalaya, flinging his trident into the mountains. Water began to flow from three springs created by its three prongs and created three lakes. Shiva threw himself into the largest of these, Gosainkund, and cooled his throat in its icy waters.

Shaivite pilgrims come from far and wide to worship here and some even say that they can see Shiva in the form of a rock at the bottom of the lake. Some believe that Gosainkund is linked by underground channels to the Kumbeshwar Mahadev Mandir in Patan, where those that cannot make the journey to the lake congregate and worship during the August full moon festival.

Langtang National Park

diverse and accessible trekking region

Situated in the Central Himalaya, Langtang National Park is the nearest park to Kathmandu. It starts 32 km north of the capital and runs all the way north to the Tibetan border. Within the park are two major river catchment areas, the west side of the park for the Trisuli and the east for the Sun Kosi. Langtang offers some of the best examples of graded climatic conditions in the Central Himalaya.

The complex topography and geology, together with the varied climatic patterns, have enabled a wide spectrum of vegetation types. These include small areas of subtropical forest (below 1000 m) while oaks, maple, fir, blue pine, hemlock spruce and various species of rhododendron make up the main forest species. Above these are areas of alpine scrub and high pasture that give way to rock and snow.

Culturally the area is mixed but the main population is Tamang, traditionally arable and livestock farmers, who have Buddhist and Bon beliefs and are famed for their weaving skills. Although they remain in the park they are still allowed to live their traditional lifestyle, grazing their animals and collecting firewood. This adds greatly to the attraction of the area, as the beautiful landscapes and mountain views of Langtang Lirung (7246 m) and Himal Chuli (7864 m) are complemented with this social insight. There are also Sherpas living in some of the higher valleys.

The region is famous for the **Gosainkunda**, an area of high-altitude lakes reached either from Dhunche or from Sundarijal. Thousands of Hindu pilgrims visit these lakes during Janai Purnima festivals in August as Gosainkunda lake is believed to have been created by Lord Shiva.

The Tamang Heritage Trail covers a comparatively new trekking area located between Langtang and the Ganesh Himal. A culturally rich region steeped in Tibetan tradition, the local Tamang people are some of the warmest and most welcoming people in Nepal.

The trail offers the opportunity for homestays, living in village houses. The duration of your trek can vary from a couple of nights to a week or so, depending on how much walking you want to do.

Visiting the villages and settlements gives an insight into their Tibetan-based culture. Predominantly Buddhists, their lifestyle is based on agriculture – potatoes, barley, corn and millet – and trade. Local dress is colourful and they live in houses adorned with beautiful woodcarvings.

Trekking Langtang

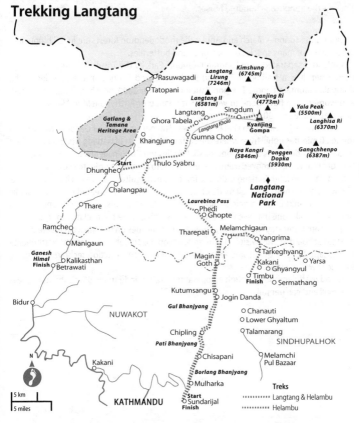

ON THE ROAD
The Tibetan Lama of Tarke Ghayang

Kathmandu was once in the grip of a great plague. It claimed countless lives and the king was deeply disturbed. So he sent some of his men to ask the help of a well-known holy man who lived in a small village high in the mountains of Tibet. Upon hearing of their plight, the lama took pity and accompanied the king's men to Kathmandu. Within seven days of his arrival, the plague was contained.

So grateful was the king that he asked the lama what gift he could give in return. A horse, thought the lama, would be useful for getting around his village in Tibet. The king then presented him with 100 horses. But before long, the horses became a burden to the lama, so the king instead gave him a plot of land in the mountains near Kathmandu on which he could build a *ghayang*. The temple the lama built was soon known as Tarke Ghayang, situated in the Langtang area, which in Tibetan means the temple of a hundred horses.

During the spring – March and April – the rhododendron forests are in full bloom and are a haven for many species of flora, birds and butterflies.

Gatlang is separated from Langtang National Park by the Trisuli river cutting through from Tibet. It is a traditional Tamang settlement, and is built on the hillsides of the Pumpala Mountain Range. The population is just over 2000, which includes those men and women who have gone to work in Kathmandu or further afield in Malaysia or the Emirates. There are 300 homes in the village.

There are technically two Gatlang villages. The old, abandoned Gatlang (Khe Dho) is found 20 minutes uphill from where the current settlement of Gatlang sits. Every resident of Gatlang is descended from one of six families who originally lived in Khe Dho. It is thought that villagers moved from one settlement to another in order to live closer to their plots of farming land. Gatlang is unique for its Tamang culture, as well as its architecture. The walls of the houses are all made of stone. The rooftops are created in the split shake style, with planks of wood held in place by rocks. Rows of houses are built connected to one another, like one may see with town houses. This is done for insulation purposes.

There are homestays in Gatlang as well as other villages on the small circuit created by the tourist board to bring visitors to the area. It reopened in July 2015 after the earthquakes and escaped better than some areas due to the local construction techniques – using timber as well as stone.

It's advisable to book through an operator in Kathmandu (page 95) as the homestays are small and can get full.

TREKKING ITINERARIES

Langtang trek

A varied and picturesque trek linking Langtang with Helambu can be made by crossing the Lauribina Pass and finishing back in the Kathmandu Valley. Allow 12-15 days. The village of Langtang itself was severely damaged by the 2015 earthquake and there was a high death toll of both local inhabitants and trekkers. Lodges are being rebuilt and reopened. There is disruption, however, so check locally as to the current situation before setting off.

Days 14 days   **Highest point** 4984 m (Tserko Ri)   **Trek type** Camping/lodge

Days	Itinerary	Altitude	Duration
Day 01	Drive to Barku (6-7 hours) and camp	1900 m	6 hours
Day 02	Barku to Thulo Syabru	2250 m	5 hours
Day 03	Thulo Syabru to Lama Hotel	2470 m	6 hours
Day 04	Lama Hotel to above Langtang	3410 m	6 hours
Day 05	Langtang to Kyanjingompa	3870 m	3 hours
Day 06	Free day in Kyangjin (climb Tserko Ri 4984)	3870 m	5 hours
Day 07	Kyangji to Lama Hotel	2470 m	7 hours
Day 08	Lama Hotel to Thulosyhyabru	2250 m	6 hours
Day 09	Thulosyabru to Chandanbari	3330 m	6 hours
Day 10	Chandanbri to Gosaikunda	4380 m	4 hours
Day 11	Gosaikunda to Ghopte (cross Lauribina pass 4610 m)	3430 m	6 hours
Day 12	Ghopte to Kutumsang	2470 m	6 hours
Day 13	Kutumsang to Chisapani	2165 m	7 hours
Day 14	Chisapani to Sundarijal and drive to Kathmandu	1350	4½ hours' walking 1½ hours' driving

Helambu trek

Helambu is a lush region to the north of Kathmandu inhabited by both Sherpas and Tamang peoples. Trails pass through beautiful forests and interesting villages where customs practiced for centuries are still in evidence today.

Days 6 days   **Highest point** 3960 m   **Trek type** Camping/lodge

Days	Itinerary	Altitude	Duration
Day 01	Drive to Sundarijal. Start trek to Chisapani	2165 m	7 hours
Day 02	Chisapani to Gulbhanjyang	2130 m	6 hours
Day 03	Gulbhanjyang to Magenkoth	3220 m	6 hours
Day 04	Magenkoth to Tharepati to Melamchi Gaon	2640 m	7 hours
Day 05	Tarke Ghayang	2640 m	7 hours
Day 06	End trek in Timbu, drive to Kathmandu	870 m	8 hours

Ganesh Himal

To the immediate north and west of Gatlang lies Ganesh Himal and the Tirudanda ridge. If you want to visit somewhere off the usual trekking routes, then this is a great option. Unspoilt scenery, traditional villages and little visited by trekkers. You will need to camp as there are fewer facilities.

Days 14 days **Highest point** 4045 m **Trek type** Full camping

Days	Itinerary	Altitude	Duration
Day 01	6-7 hours' drive to Arughat and trek to Laxmi bazaar	620 m	1 hour
Day 02	Laxmi bazaar to Manbu	1335 m	7 hours
Day 03	Manbu to Maje Kharka	2345 m	8 hours
Day 04	Myangal Bhanjyang	2975 m	5 hours
Day 05	Lapagaon	1850 m	5 hours
Day 06	Borang	1730 m	8 hours
Day 07	Serthung	1920 m	7 hours
Day 08	Serthung to Phokthang	2850 m	7 hours
Day 09	Phokthang to Pansang Bhanjyang	3850 m	7 hours
Day 10	Rest day	3850 m	
Day 11	Pansang to Shingla Phedi	3900 m	7 hours
Day 12	Shingla to Gongang (through Singla Pass 4045 m)	2800 m	6 hours
Day 13	Gongang to Pokhari	700 m	7 hours
Day 14	Pokhari to Betrawati and drive to Kathmandu.	1400 m	5 hours

Kathmandu
to Pokhara

traditional villages and stunning mountain scenery

The area that stretches between the western edge of the Kathmandu Valley and Pokhara is known as the Middle Hills.

The journey between the two cities takes six or seven hours along a spectacular road called the Privithi Highway. This 200-km adventure winds its way along the valley of the Trisuli river, sometimes down by its rushing waters, at others high up the mountainside.

The Middle Hills consist of the Mahabharat Range that lie between the road and the Terai to the south and the foothills of the Himalaya to the north. In any other country they would be called mountains. Hidden in their valleys and perched on their ridges are small towns, temples and villages where some of the most important historical and religious sites in the country can be found.

This is the Nepal of old, with traditional architecture and a way of life that exists unaffected by the modernization and sprawl of the cities. Farmers tend their precipitous terracing, women fetch water from stone taps and wells while chickens and goats wander in and out of houses and yards.

Best for
Countryside ▪ Traditional towns ▪ Unspoilt villages

Footprint picks

★ **Nuwakot**, page 199
The mountain fortress of Privi Narayan Shah, now a sleepy village.

★ **Daman**, page 202
Situated on the Raj Path and offering some of the best mountain views.

★ **Manakamana Temple**, page 204
Perched high on a ridge and reached by a soaring cable car.

★ **Gorkha**, page 205
The ancestral home of the Shah kings, with their palaces and temples.

★ **Bandipur**, page 208
A Newari trading town offering traditional architecture and great views.

Essential Middle Hills: Kathmandu to Pokhara

Finding your feet

The Middle Hills are bisected by the Prithivi Highway that runs through them from east to west. Roads branch off it north and south to all the main attractions, as well as to the Terai at Mugling. Tourist and local buses from Kathmandu or Pokhara serve most places, although a change may be required for some of the most out-of-the-way destinations.

Getting around

The towns and villages of the Middle Hills are small and compact, meaning they can be explored on foot. There are trails and tracks around them that offer some great short walks. At the Manakanama Temple there is a cable car.

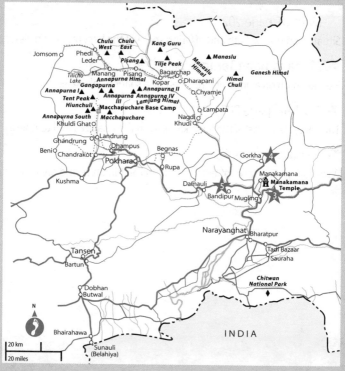

When to go

During the monsoon of June to early September it is humid and wet. The autumn months of October and November are a great time to visit, with pleasantly hot days, warm evenings and, being post-monsoon, less dust and pollution in the air. In December and January temperatures drop and although there is rarely a frost it gets down to only 1-2°C at night. It can be cloudy and some rain falls. The spring months of February to May are also a pleasant time, with the spring flowers coming out and the paddy fields turning green, although the heat and humidity do build once more as the monsoon approaches.

Time required

Many people drive straight from Kathmandu to Pokhara or vice versa without stopping, which is a great shame. Nepal is developing fast and these towns and villages give you a chance to experience something of the older, traditional Nepal while breaking up an otherwise long and slow journey. One overnight stay is recommended as a minimum.

Footprint picks

Prithvi
Highway

Probably the stretch of road most travelled by tourists in Nepal, the Prithvi Highway links the country's two main centres of tourism. This is Gurkha country. Once out of the Kathmandu Valley, the journey enters the attractive Middle Hills. Precarious at times but also graceful, the road winds its way across hills and valleys, passing grassy, rocky countryside dotted with small springs and picturesque villages. For much of the time, the spectacular snow-capped peaks of the Annapurnas can be glimpsed on the northern horizon.

The 206-km-long road was built from Kathmandu to Dumre with help from the Indian Government, and from Dumre to Pokhara with help from the Chinese. It is a slower journey than the distance suggests, particularly because landslides during the monsoon have damaged the carriageway in places and due to the winding nature of the road. Add to this the sheer volume of traffic and the fact that if you get stuck behind an old truck carrying a heavy load you can be there a while. The journey should take five to six hours, but don't be surprised if it takes eight.

ON THE ROAD
Nepalese driving

Driving in Nepal is a competitive sport. In Kathmandu the chaos somehow manages to work, with six rows of traffic wedged into two or three marked lanes, police frantically blasting whistles as they struggle to manage junctions and sacred cows sitting unconcerned in the middle of busy roads. It's almost balletic at times, as endless vehicles merge, swerve, move as one, millimetres between them, but rarely touching. Any small gap is filled by a car trying to gain a few metres or with two or three motorcyclists oblivious of the concept of traffic flow and letting someone through. All this to a constant chorus of horns.

Nepal is not a country designed for roads. On the narrow highways, deep potholes and vertiginous drops do little to dampen the enthusiasm to overtake. Horns blare on blind corners as cars tiptoe around buses and lorries, sometimes sliding to a halt as they come nose to nose with oncoming traffic. Microbuses weave in and out of the traffic, relying on other drivers to swerve or slow down to allow them to complete their overtake. Traffic jams form quickly as break downs and blow-outs occur and there is nowhere but the highway to stop.

Drivers of tourist vehicles drive with more reserve, overtaking in places where overtaking is possible, driving fast enough to not be overtaken by buses and lorries but slow enough to allow enjoyment of the amazing scenery and to wonder at the whole crazy process of driving in Nepal.

West from Kathmandu

The suburbs of Kathmandu sprawl right up to the rim of the valley at Thankot where the road starts its drop down to the River Trisuli, winding its way through a series of switchbacks, one of the slowest sections of the journey. Once out of the Kathmandu Valley, you'll enter the attractive Middle Hills, dotted with villages and farms set high on ridges, perching beside patches of steep terracing.

The road follows the River Trisuli to Mugling (110 km from Kathmandu), the confluence of the Trisuli and Marshyangdi rivers, which together form the Narayani or Sapt Gandaki, which flows south to the plains. The point of confluence is attractive and unmistakable, joining the brown water of the Trisuli with the milky-white and green of the Marshyangdi. For 2 km or so, these two streams of water flow side by side in one river before gradually merging. If you turn south at Mugling, the road brings you to Narayanghat and the Chitwan National Park (see page 250).

Mugling to Pokhara

The small town of Mugling (pronounced Moogling) is situated at an important junction linking the Prithvi Highway with the main road heading south to Narayanghat, where it joins with the Mahendra Highway that extends east–west across the entire Terai. Almost all buses running between Kathmandu and Pokhara stop at Mugling for a tea and toilet

Tip...
From Kathmandu, the best views of the high mountains and rivers are from seats on the right-hand side of the vehicle, and on the left-hand side from Pokhara. If you don't like long drops then don't sit on those sides, as sometimes the fall from the road is precipitous.

ON THE ROAD

The Gurkhas

The Gurkha soldiers of the British Army take their name from the hill town of Gorkha, the original home of Prithvi Narayan Shah. In their 200 years of service, the Brigade of Gurkhas have won 26 Victoria Crosses, the highest award for valour in the UK. The first was to a British officer John Tytler in 1878 for his actions during the Indian Mutiny, a conflict in which the Gurkhas remained loyal to the British. The first Nepalese recipient was Kulbir Tharpa in 1915 in France. It's worth noting that Gurkha soldiers, as opposed to officers, only became eligible for the award in 1911 and since then they have won 13 of the 16 awarded.

You can read many of the stories at the Gurkha Museum in Pokhara, often scarcely believable tales of selfless courage. The citation for the award to Kulbir Tharpa explains how he saved three wounded soldiers in no-man's land when trapped there after an attack. Under fire he carried the men away from the German lines to a safe spot, sheltered from German snipers. On the third occasion the Germans, so impressed by his courage, are said to have stopped shooting and started cheering him. Being pragmatic as well as brave he took this opportunity to get himself and the man he was carrying all the way back to his own lines.

stop. Mugling has little to recommend it as a destination in its own right. It is a purely functional town with houses, shops, eating places and a few small hotels flanking the main road. The junction is on the western edge of the main road, marked by a lopsided sign pointing in the direction of Narayanghat. It marks the lowest and warmest point along the highway, and is the start point for one of the country's most popular rafting trips along the lower Trisuli river, as well as the finishing point for trips rafting down the Marshyangdi and Seti rivers.

The highway continues attractively alongside the Marshyangdi for 42 km, as far as Dumre, passing the huge concrete Marshyangdi Hydroelectric Project Control Centre. Completed with World Bank assistance in 1990 at a cost of over US$200 million, it is responsible for generating a large proportion of Nepal's electric energy. Another 20 km brings you to Damauli and soon after you enter the Pokhara Valley, the road straightening and widening as it approaches the town. Soon after is the turning to Rupkot and Begnas Tal, two lakes that are undeveloped and little visited.

Trisuli Road

winding road rumoured to be the new Tibet road

From the small village of Kakani on the northwest rim of the Kathmandu Valley, the Trisuli road follows the route taken by Prithvi Narayan Shah when he invaded the valley and unified the country in 1768.

The road was built in the 1970s to link a large hydroelectric scheme on the River Trisuli with the valley and is a spectacular, if slow, drive. It starts by descending steeply into the Tadi Khola river valley. The Tadi and the road then run southwest to join the River Trisuli. Veering north for an hour or so it reaches Trisuli Bazaar, following the east of the Trisuli river. The distance is only 42 km but the winding, twisting road takes several hours to complete.

Trisuli Bazaar was previously a popular starting point for treks into Langtang but most of these itineraries now start at Dhunche, 50 km further north. A more recent road follows the Trisuli river down to the Prithvi Highway at Gulcchi. Although further, this is often used by drivers as the quickest route from Kathmandu.

★ Nuwakot

a secret gem of untouched Nepal

To the west of the Kathmandu Valley, situated high in the Middle Hills, lies the small village of Nuwakot, perched on a ridge above the small town of Trisuli Bazaar. For the final six or so kilometres you climb steeply up a narrow tarmac road that winds its way initially through sal and then pine forests and back in time. It may be a backwater now, but for several years in the late 18th century it was the most important place in Nepal. Its history, stunning location and unspoilt charm makes it one of Nepal's greatest treasures, despite its small size.

Nuwakot's tiny kingdom was conquered by Prithvi Narayan Shah in the 1760s and it was here that he planned his successful campaigns against the Malla Kings of the Kathmandu Valley, culminating in his triumphant sweeping to power in 1769. In 1762 he built himself a magnificent palace on the ridge, with commanding views down the main valleys and it was here the great king died in 1775.

The village today lies along the ridge, a line of small shops and houses on either side of the narrow road, and is centred on a small square on the western slope. To the south of the village lies the Durbar Square, dominated by the seven-storey palace which still stands at its heart. It was badly hit by the earthquake and, although most buildings are still standing, restoration work is due to start in late 2016, reputedly to be undertaken as a gift to Nepal from the Chinese Government.

What has survived is the feeling of authenticity. Walk through the village at dawn, heading to the palace in time for sunrise, and you get a feel for rural Nepal. The women are gathered around the communal spouts and taps chatting as they fetch water. People on their way to work in the fields stop to offer quick prayers at small shrines, lighting candles and ringing bells. Chickens wander about the deserted main street while goats squabble for fodder that is hung out for them.

ON THE ROAD
The curse on Prithvi Narayan Shah

According to the legend, Prithvi Narayan Shah, the founder of the kingdom of Nepal, once came across the holy man called Gorakhnath in the forest. He offered the yogi some curd so he could continue meditating. Gorakhnath drank it and then promptly regurgitated it and offered it back to the king. A repulsed Prithvi Narayan shook his head and as he poured it out on the ground some of it splattered across his 10 toes. The enraged holy man cursed him, saying that, because of his pride, his dynasty would fall after 10 generations.

Fast forward over 200 years to 2001, when the popular King Birendra was present at the midnight massacre along with the rest of the family. Nepal remembered the old tale and the fact that the murdered king was the ninth descendant. After the massacre its perpetrator the Crown Prince Dipendra became the tenth generation. Having shot himself after committing the killings, he was crowned king but died without regaining consciousness.

Prithvi Narayan Shahs' unbroken line was dead. The late king's brother Gyanendra ascended the throne in 2001 amidst fearful prophecies that Gorakhnath's curse had come true and the new successor would not be able to wield the sceptre for long. So it proved to be as Gyanendra was forced from power in 2007.

Durbar Square
Despite its tiny size, Nuwakot has an impressive Durbar Square, set on top of the ridge and with great views on both sides. Maintained by the army, with their usual zeal for whitewashing stones bordering paths, it is an atmospheric place to wander around. It may not have as many buildings as the larger squares of the valley, but it makes up for this by its location and pleasant backwater feel.

Taleju Temple ① *Closed to non-Hindu's and open to Hindus only during Dasain. It is currently closed to everybody as it sustained structural damage in the 2015 earthquake.* This is the largest temple in Nuwakot. It predates the occupation of Prithvi Narayan Shah, having been built in 1564 by Mahendra Malla. Standing 35 m high and entered through a door reached by a flight of brick steps, it has four storeys, the top one with a wooden balcony running around the entire building.

Saat Tale Durbar ① *Currently closed for restoration. Normally Feb-Oct Tue-Sat 1030-1600, Sun 1030-1500, Nov-Jan 1030-1500, US$1.40.* Prithvi Narayan Shah's Palace was built by him in 1762 when he had conquered the town. He recognized the strategic importance of the site and this seven-storey fortress was intended to ensure he kept control of it. It's said that he built the palace so high, complete with a small tower on top, so that he could have the same view of Ganesh Himal as he had back at his ancestral home, the main palace in Gorkha. It was a favourite place for the great king and he died here in 1775.

Despite the village's tiny size, it was an important centre and was actually the capital of Prithvi Narayan Shah's empire until he overran the Kathmandu Valley six years later, perhaps one of the smallest capital cities ever. The first emissary ever sent to Nepal by the British was received in the palace, probably to prevent him from seeing the fertile Kathmandu Valley and to stress the impregnability of Nepalese defences.

The building contains some information about the king and the area and boasts some excellent views from the upper storeys.

Ranga Mahal This Malla-era entertaining hall came through the earthquake with only minor damage. Four storeys high, its main door is crowned by increasingly large windows on the storeys above, all beautifully carved.

Garad Ghar Another flanking building dating to the Malla period, this lovely building was badly damaged and is in need of complete renovation.

Bhairab Temple Situated at the end of the ridge beyond the fortress complex and down a second small street is the Bhairab Temple, dedicated to Shiva in his wrathful manifestation. Guarded by lions it is easily identifiable by its golden roofs.

Its main claim to fame is that during the Bhairabi festival in March-April, the priest drinks the blood direct from the severed vein of a sacrificed buffalo's neck. Traditionally he would have drunk every drop before vomiting it back up. The faithful would then drink this from the ground to receive blessings. Happily, the practice has been stopped.

The temple is flanked by an unusually designed pilgrims' guesthouse.

Walks around Nuwakot

A network of trails and tracks run off along the ridge, offering some good walks through the forest, with stunning views down over the valleys far below or up at Peak 29 and Ganesh Himal. Terraces open up, clinging to the steep slopes, and you pass small farmsteads and field shelters. There is a lovely walk to the **Malika Temple**, situated on a nearby hilltop and with excellent views. The temple was damaged by the 2015 earthquake. Another walk takes you to a viewing tower. Ask for directions from your hotel or in the village.

Listings Nuwakot

Where to stay

$$$ The Famous Farm
T01-470 0426, www.rural-heritage.com.
Situated a few hundred yards up the ridge to the north, this is the best place to stay, with terraced gardens offering lovely views down the Trisuli river valley. It comprises 2 traditional buildings, now converted to offer 14 rooms and which stand around a lovely courtyard overlooked by the open kitchen. It suffered some damage in the earthquakes but this has now been repaired and it is back to its full glory.

A stay here is an experience in itself. The rooms are full of traditional furniture with floors of plaster, ornately carved windows and the top-floor rooms have ceilings

of exposed slate. There is no glass in the windows, just shutters and panels to close and lock and the ceilings are low. Some have tiny traditional wooden balconies.

When you arrive you are asked about any allergies and dislikes and then the fixed menu is prepared using vegetables from the garden, usually served on tables dotted around the courtyard and gardens. It's a wonderfully atmospheric place to stay, an understandably popular escape from Kathmandu for expats.

Transport

There are 3 direct buses a day from **Kathmandu**, taking 4 hrs and costing US$1.80.

If you wanted to do an overnight stay, then hiring a car and driver from Kathmandu would cost about US$50 per day, including the driver's overnight expenses. Having your own car allows you to stop and enjoy some of the superb scenery en route, as well as try out one of the long suspension bridges that span the Trisuli.

The Raj Path (Tribhuvan Highway)

Nepal's first road to the outside world

About 25 km along the Prithvi Highway from Kathmandu lies the small town of Naubise and the junction with the Raj Path ('Royal Way'). This was the first road to be built through the mountains and the first link between Kathmandu and the outside world. It is a twisting affair, climbing switchbacks up the steep mountainsides.

It was built in the late 1950s by India and it's said that the Indians chose this steep, winding route as at the time they were concerned about Chinese influence in Nepal. They didn't want too good a road in case the Chinese seized power and used it as a highway to invade the plains of India. It is 32 km as the crow flies from **Naubise** to **Hetauda**, the town on the Terai where is emerges, but the Tribhuvan Highway makes it an astonishing 107 km.

These days the road is largely ignored, with nearly all commercial traffic routing via Mugling. It has left the villages along its path less developed and offers some wonderful scenery and mountain walks. Initially you climb through areas of steep terracing and mountainside, the road winding its way into the hills. After 35 km you arrive at **Tistung**, situated at just over 2000 m, and drop into the small **Palung Valley**. Daman lies a further 9 km away, at the end of a steep climb to an altitude of 2322 m.

The highway sits in some wonderful scenery and offers the longest mountain panoramas in Nepal. On a clear morning you can get an uninterrupted view from Dhaulagiri in the west to Everest in the east. That's nearly 400 km of Himalayan peaks.

The highway is to be recommended as a mountain-biking route, but you have to be both adventurous and extremely fit to do it. At least after the punishing climb on Day 1 you can look forward to a 2000-m+ descent spread along nearly 60 km of road.

★ Daman

Standing at 2322 m, Daman offers stunning (some say, Nepal's best) views across the Himalaya. However, early mornings offer the best chance of clear skies at most times of the year, which usually means staying overnight.

The village is dominated by the enclosed viewing tower (Rs 50), situated in the grounds of the **Daman Mountain Resort**. From here you have superb views of the mountains including seven 8000-m peaks. There are two telescopes to give close-up views of the mountains, including Everest which is otherwise a tiny dot. You also get great views of a large section of the Kathmandu Valley and, to the south, across the Terai plains and into India. To the immediate north is the Palung Valley, while the highest point along the Tribhuvan Highway is a few kilometres to the south at **Simbhanjyang** (2840 m).

Mountain Botanical Gardens ① *Open 1000-1700*. These botanical gardens comprise 78 ha of indigenous forest and are famous particularly for their rhododendrons. To see them in flower you have to visit between February and March.

Shree Rikheshwar Mahadev Mandir One kilometre south of the village you can take a trail for just under 2 km to this small Shiva shrine, and a Buddhist gompa, the Rimburje, adorned with prayer flags.

Walks around Daman

As well as the shrine walk there are other trails going off into the hills. These are not signposted and a local guide is recommended, especially for longer walks. The resorts can arrange local guides. In the spring the rhododendron forests are stunning.

Listings The Raj Path

Where to stay

Daman is cold, especially in winter, so bring warm clothing. Both these options can be booked from Kathmandu as part of a package, including transport to/from the capital. There is a limited choice for budget travellers.

$$$ Everest Panorama Resort
T01-442 8500.
The most comfortable place to stay is found a couple of hundred metres from the Raj Path, set in lovely grounds with unsurpassed views towards the Himalaya. The rooms are all heated, have good hot showers and excellent mountain views. The restaurant is of a good standard and offers the option of Western-style food. There is even a steam room to warm up in. The resort can organize local guides if you wish to walk.

$ Daman Mountain Resort
T984-717 5577, www.damanresort.com.
A small resort of bungalows and the deluxe rooms are comfortable and have hot water. This little bit of faded glory is convenient for early-morning forays to the viewing platform, found in its grounds.

Transport

To get there you need to take buses from Kathmandu heading to **Hetauda** in the Terai, 4 hrs, US$2.30. There are 3 buses to **Kathmandu** daily, US$2, and a microbus service, US$2.30. There are more bus services to **Palung** located just a few kilometres away. To continue to the Terai there are 4 buses a day to **Hetauda**, US$2.30.

Manakamana

temple packed with pilgrims and devotees

The Manakamana temple, located 6 km north of Mugling and 12 km south of Gorkha, is the most important Hindu site in western central Nepal. Situated on a conspicuous ridge, the temple overlooks the Trisuli and Marshyangdi rivers, with views of the mountains as far as Manaslu and Annapurna. Badly damaged in the 2015 earthquake, reconstruction work is underway. It stands in a small square, shaded by a huge champ tree, and is approached through a tangle of souvenir and snack stalls.

One of its main claims to fame is the cable car that was installed in 1998 to carry pilgrims up the steep hill from the Prithvi Highway at Cheres. Look out at the bottom for the price list. All categories get a return tariff, except for goats who are ominously quoted just one way as their journey will end at the temple in sacrifice.

Finding your feet

The **Cable Car** (T064-460044, www. chitawoncoe.com.np, US$20 return, 0900-1200, 1300-1700) is a spectacular way to arrive at the temple. This Austrian-built cable car was constructed in 1998 at a cost of over US$7 million. It rises over 1000 m in the 2.8 km it covers and takes just under 10 minutes.

The alternative is to walk the old pilgrim trail to the temple. This starts at the village of **Abu Khaireni**, situated to the west of Mugling and takes four to five hours.

Opening hours

Dawn to dusk.

★ The temple

The temple attracts around 500,000 visitors every year – almost all of them pilgrims – and is renowned for being Nepal's premier wish-granting temple. The name is taken from the words *mana* 'heart' and *kamana* 'wish'. It is dedicated to Bhagwati, an incarnation of Parvati. Saturdays is the most popular day for locals to visit, making it very busy and a bit gory – the goat sacrifices are in full swing and a lot of blood is flowing.

The first shrine was built on this site in the 17th century by one Lakhan Thappa. When the Gorkha king Rama Shah died in 1636, his queen committed sati on his funeral pyre on the Manakamana river. Sometime later, a farmer discovered blood and milk pouring from a stone in a nearby field.

When Lakhan Thappa heard about this, he was convinced it was a sign from the dead queen, and constructed a temple in her honour.

The present temple is a 19th-century replacement, a two-tiered pagoda with numerous carved roof struts. Tradition has it that the temple priest must be a descendant of Lakhan Thappa. Goats and chickens are regularly sacrificed to the deity queen, Manakamana Devi, in the sacrifice pavilion beside the temple itself.

Listings Manakamana

Where to stay

Manakamana has plenty of small and basic guesthouses catering to the local pilgrim market but most tourists visit for a few hours en route to another destination.

$$$ River Side Springs Resort
Located in Kurintar about 3 km from the lower cable car station, T056-540129, www.rsr.com.np.
Pleasant resort on the banks of the River Trisuli with cabins, tents and a swimming pool.

Transport

Buses run from Kathmandu and Pokhara to **Mugling** from early morning, around US$2.30 each way. If you are on an ordinary bus, just get it to stop at Cheres. If it is an express go to Mugling and then take a local bus to **Cheres** (6 km).

If you are travelling in your own vehicle you drive past the cable station on the main highway. It's hard to miss, not only because of the cables and pylons, but also because of the large signage on the mountain opposite advertising one of its mobile phone sponsors.

the birthplace of King Prithvi Narayan Shah

Despite being at the epicentre of the first of the 2015 earthquakes, Gorkha survived with surprisingly little damage, underlining the arbitrary and unfathomable nature of these tremors. What damage there was is being quickly repaired.

Gorkha is 24 km north of the village of Abu Khaireni on the Prithvi Highway, along a good all-weather road, 136 km west of Kathmandu and 106 km east of Pokhara. It is the ancestral home of the Shah dynasty, the birthplace in c 1723 of King Prithvi Narayan Shah, after whom the Prithvi Highway is named, and lies at the heart of the recruiting area for Gurkha regiments. Despite the ruling dynasty losing power in 2008, it remains an important place for the Newar people, many of whom consider them to have been living incarnations of Vishnu himself.

The modern town lies to the south of Prithvi Narayan's Gorkha Durbar headquarters and, considering its role in the history of Nepal, is surprisingly small. It clings to a hillside, clearly visible as you climb your way up to it on the far side of the valley. There is a bus terminus, a bank, post office and *tundhikel* (parade ground), but only a few hotels and restaurants, mainly catering for the local market and NGO workers, as most visitors come here en route to somewhere else.

Gorkha

Where to stay ⊜
1 Gorkha Gaun
2 Gurkha Inn

Gorkha Durbar
US$0.50. Photography is permitted for a fee: camera US$2, video US$2.70.

It's a steep 1-km walk from the town to Gorkha Durbar. Leave Tallo Durbar Square by the far-left corner as you stand in front of the Tallo Durbar Museum. After 100 m turn right up the stone stairs labelled 'Gorkha Durbar'. At the road, turn right for 50 m, then left up the stone steps past a large school. Keep climbing. You come to a large tree with a stone rest place where the trail splits. Keep right, climbing past small souvenir and refreshment stalls until you reach the complex.

Strategically located to overlook the village and beyond, thereby allowing early warning of any approaching aggressors, this impressive complex comprising fort, temple and palace was built by Prithvi Narayan Shah to celebrate his conquest of the Kathmandu Valley. Views from the Durbar are quite spectacular: to the south is the lush Trisuli Valley, while a 200-km stretch of the Himalaya forms a majestic northern horizon.

Despite being close to the epicentre of the first 2015 earthquake, the Durbar complex escaped with comparatively little damage. Repair work is expected to conclude shortly.

Access to most areas used to be barred to all but the king and certain appointed Brahmin priests, but since the abolition of the monarchy you are free to explore. It is a very sacred site so all leather, including belts and shoes, should be removed. There are many fine examples of Newari woodcarving and craftsmanship on view.

Kalika Mandir The first building you come to is the 17th-century Kalika Mandir, one of the most important Hindu temples in the region. Only Brahmin priests can enter the inner sanctum as it is said that anyone else would die upon glimpsing the shrine's terrible image. Dedicated to the goddess Kali, wrathful consort of Shiva, the temple is the focus of Gorkha's principal festivals of Dasain in October and Chaitra Dasain in April when sacrifices of goats and chickens are made near the entrance. The exterior of the temple has some intricately carved window frames, including one beautifully decorated with peacocks.

Dhuni Pat Beside the temple and central to the complex is Prithvi Narayan's birthplace, the Dhunipati Durbar, again with examples of window decoration exquisitely carved by Newari craftsmen originating from the Kathmandu Valley. This is regarded as the ancestral home of the Shah dynasty and, although not open to the public, contains the eternal flame commemorating King Prithvi and the throne on which he was crowned.

Just beyond the Dhunipati are stairs leading down to a shrine that marks the cave where **Gorakhnath**, the village's patron saint and traditionally spiritual mentor to a young Prithvi Narayan, lived. You are not allowed to photograph this; look out at the priest who sits outside. Often he will have a stick pushed through his ear lopes to show him as an initiated follower of the seer.

Elsewhere are numerous Hindu deities and small shrines where attendant priests and devotees lend a sense of added authenticity to the role of the complex as a historical and spiritual centre of the old ruling dynasty. Look out for the paint-encrusted hanuman statue on the col in the ridge to the east of the palace complex and a set of stone footsteps attributed to Gorakhnath, set further along the ridge line to the east.

Fact...
The path from the village approaches the complex from the west from where you can see the impressive set of steps leading to the entrance.

Upallakot Continue from the footprints to the highest point of the ridge, about 40 minutes' walk to the east of Gorkha Durbar. This is the site of an old upper fort, really little more than a hut used as a warning station, but there are stunning 360° views from the Annapurnas to the Ganesh Himal. Sadly, a TV/communication tower also takes advantage of the site.

Tallokot An indirect route back to the village heading west along the ridge from Gorkha Durbar takes you past a Shah monument before reaching the small disused fort-watchtower of Tallokot. From here a path leads south through terraced fields to Gorkha.

Gorkha town
Near the tourist office (see below) is a small, fortified **Ratna Temple** that used to be the Gorkha dwelling of the last of the Shah kings, Gyanendra.

About 100 m north of the bus stand, itself situated at the top of the new town, is the **Rani Pokhari**, a large tank. In this square are a number of locally important buildings, including a two-tiered **Vishnu Temple** as well as a white *shikhara* dedicated to **Ganesh**. Veering right, you reach the Tallo Durbar on your right.

Tallo Durbar ⓘ *Open Wed-Mon 1030-1430, US$0.90.* This later Newari-style palace was built in the main village of Gorkha in 1835, designed to be the administrative centre of the kingdom. It is set in pleasant gardens and has been renovated and opened as a museum. Some of its displays are somewhat unusual – the dioramas are not the most convincing – but there are some interesting exhibits. Look out for the ferocious-looking weapons that were used at the time of the Prithvi Narayan Shah. The best thing is just to enjoy looking around a traditionally designed *durbar* or palace.

Gorkha is an optional starting point for treks in the Annapurna region and along the Buri Gandaki in the Manaslu region. These trails are a lot less used that the main Annapurna trails and offer a good alternative for a foothills walk. See Trekking in the Middle Hills, page 211.

Listings Gorkha *map page 205.*

Tourist information

There is a tourist office just above the main bus station, at the bottom of the grounds of the Tallo Durbar. It mainly consists of rows of empty shelves and a few leaflets on other places in Nepal, but the staff are very friendly, speak good English and, for a small donation, will provide you with a decent map of the town.

Where to stay

Most visitors don't stay but visit on a day trip or en route to somewhere else. This is reflected in the meagre choice of hotels. There is a selection of small guesthouses but the quality is sparse.

$$ Gorkha Gaun
T09801-010557, www.gorkagaun.com.
A small resort of bungalows a few kilometres south of Gorkha makes for a rustic and peaceful stay. Comfortable rooms and good local food. Views from most rooms of Manaslu. Just refurbished after the earthquake.

$ Gurkha Inn
T064-420206.
It's not luxury but it is a pleasant enough place to stay, with bright and airy rooms. It sits in lovely grounds and has a good restaurant looking out over the valley. Earthquake damage is being repaired.

Restaurants

There are Nepali and Tibetan food outlets near the bus stand and in the small square outside the Tallo Durbar.

Transport

Gorkha is well connected by local buses and microbuses which go regularly throughout the day to and from **Abu Khaireni** and on to **Mugling**. A number of buses link the village with key tourist centres, including **Kathmandu**, US$2.70, **Pokhara**, US$2.30, and **Tadi Bazaar** (for Sauraha and the Chitwan National Park). Frequency varies with season. Most departures to and from Gorkha, especially on the longer routes, leave in the morning. Tickets are available from the bus stand.

★ Bandipur

peaceful, characterful town with superb views

Twenty years ago, Bandipur didn't featured in any guidebook. Situated 8 km above the Prithvi Highway, up a narrow road that climbs through forest along the top of a ridge, it is an old Newari trading centre that got forgotten as roads were built along the valley floors. Colonized by traders from Bhaktapur to exploit its strategic position on the main trade route, its heyday came in the 1800s when commerce was at its height. Its sudden fall from grace become its salvation, as its centre is unblighted by the modern development that has ruined so many other Nepali towns.

It is not possible to drive into the town, so vehicles drop you just outside the pedestrian area and you walk from here to your accommodation – hotels and guesthouses are on the central Marg. This paved area has the feel of an Italian piazza. The buildings, many dating from the late 19th century, are three or four storeys high, with wooden shutters and are painted in various pastel shades. The tables from the cafés and restaurants spill onto the wide paving, making it a lovely place to relax and watch the world go by.

The village

The big attraction of Bandipur is Bandipur itself. The main bazaar is a wide street, paved with stone slabs and lined with traditional and unchanged Newari dwellings. At the east end of the street is a small square, with the Padma library, a lovely rest shelter and the

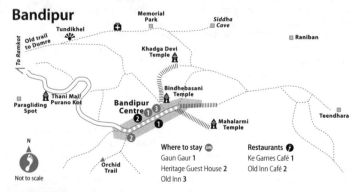

Bandipur

Where to stay 🛏
Gaun Gaur 1
Heritage Guest House 2
Old Inn 3

Restaurants 🍴
Ke Garnes Café 1
Old Inn Café 2

Bhindebasini Mandir. This two-tiered temple is dedicated to Durga; it's worth looking inside at the ancient paintings when the doors are opened each evening. The street is lined with everyday shops selling meat, fruit and vegetables, mixed in with small cafés, restaurants and guesthouses. It makes for a relaxing place to spend a night or two, enjoying the peaceful atmosphere, walking in the surrounding hills and taking in the superb views.

The Tudikhel

The old trading area, once full of merchants buying and selling loads to take to Tibet or India, was also used as a parade ground for British Army Gurkhas. It is now a sports ground used by villagers. Situated to the north of the village, well signposted and easily walkable, is the best place to go to enjoy the view. The ground to its north and east falls steeply away, in cliffs in some places, to give exceptional views over the Marsyangdi river valley, the Annapurnas and the Manaslu Himal. It's a pleasant spot, with tall trees giving shade, to relax.

Khadga Devi Mandir

Located up the steps that leave the north side of the High Street, this temple, a rectangular design, houses a sacred sword believed to have been given by Shiva to a local king in the 1600s. Although taken out once a year to be viewed, the blade is kept hidden in cloth as to see the metal would, it is believed, lead to the viewer's death as if struck by the sword itself.

Thani Mai Temple

This small, fairly uninspiring temple sits on top of Gurungche Hill but it's the location that makes the steep, 30- to 40-minute climb worthwhile. Get there for sunrise (bring a torch) and on clear mornings you get a stunning view of the main Himalayan chain as well as 360° views in all directions.

Siddha Gupha

Open 0800-1700, US$1.80, compulsory guide US$4.60.

Only discovered in 1987, the Siddha Gupha is the largest subterrainean chamber known in Nepal. It is approximately 10 m wide, over 400 m long, 50 m high and is packed full of stalactites. There are no handrails and you need to bring your own torch unless you are happy to hire a local one.

It is signposted from the square but the signs are easy to miss. Your guesthouse will be able to provide a guide which also helps you find its entrance. It takes about 90 minutes to walk down from town, and longer for the return climb. There are lots of bats inside the cave so don't expect the sound of silence inside.

Walks around Bandipur

Other than the short walks mentioned above, there are some lovely day hikes available. The most popular is to the Magar village of Ramkot, about four or five hours away. The countryside is very scenic, and by hiring a local guide from either the tourist office or your guesthouse, you can explore some unchanged villages and their tranquil way of life. A guide costs around US$6.50-9 per day.

Fact...
Its not only the beautifully preserved buildings and unchanged atmosphere that make Bandipur so popular; to its north, across the valley, is the most wonderful vista of the Annapurna range.

Tourist information

At the east end of the high street is a small office of the Bandipur Development Committee. Its hours are somewhat erratic but when open it does provide maps and leaflets.

Where to stay

$$$ Gaun Gaur
T065-520129, www.gaungaur.com.
Another converted Newari house, it also offers comfortable and atmospheric stays. Situated next door to The Old Inn, its terrace offers great views and an accomplished restaurant.

$$$ The Old Inn
T065-520110, www.theoldinnbandipur.com.
The original guesthouse in town, this lovely old converted house offers very comfortable, traditional rooms with en suite facilities. Rooms at the back look at the mountains and there is a great terrace on which to sit and enjoy a drink or meal while admiring the view.

$ Heritage Guest House
T065-520015.
This comfortable guesthouse offers fine, clean rooms, some with small bathrooms at the western end of the main street. It has a good menu and seating outside on the paved bazaar.

Restaurants

Most people eat at their guesthouses but there are some nice cafés to wander into while out sightseeing.

$ Old House Café
Opposite Gaun Gaur guesthouse.
Outside seating, excellent snacks such as the ever-popular *momo*, as well as a full choice of hot and cold drinks.

$ Ke Garnes Café
Near Gaun Gaur guesthouse,
on the same side of the road.
Great café downstairs, fun bar upstairs for later in the evening.

Transport

To get to Bandipur you turn south off the Prithvi Highway 2 km west of Dumre, about 2 hrs from Pokhara and ¾ hr from Mugling. The small road climbs up a tree-covered ridge until it arrives in the village. It takes about 20-30 mins. Buses from here cost about US$0.30, while a taxi will be US$1.80.

Trekking in the
Middle Hills

Most people hurry though the Middle Hills on their way to Pokhara and the Annapurnas, but there are some great walks and trekking on offer. As well as day walks from both Nuwakot and Bandipur there is the Manaslu range to the north.

The region was near the epicentre of the first of the 2015 earthquakes and many of the villages sustained damage. Much has been repaired, including the lodges, and the circuit is open for business but you're advised to check locally about accommodation a day or two in advance as you proceed.

Much of the trekking is in the Manaslu Conservation Area, a large tract of mountains that adjoins Annapurna to its west and Tibet to its north. It contains a vast range of terrains, rising in altitude from 600 m to 8163 m as it sweeps northwards. Over 7000 people live in the conservation area, mainly Gurungs with their Tibetan and Buddhist origins.

TREKKING ITINERARIES
Manaslu Circuit

This challenging circuit climbs the Budi Gandaki river valley before reaching the Larke Pass (5106 m) and crossing over into the Manang District of the Annapurna Conservation Area. It offers a diverse range of terrain and cultures and traverses regions much less geared to trekkers, revealing an unchanged Nepal.

Days 20   **Highest point** 5160 m (Larkya Pass)   **Trek type** Camping/lodge

Days	Itinerary	Altitude	Duration
Day 01	Drive to Arughat; overnight Arughat	608 m	7 hours
Day 02	Liding	860 m	6 hours
Day 03	Machakhola	869 m	6 hours
Day 04	Jagat	1340 m	8 hours
Day 05	Philim	1570 m	4 hours
Day 06	Deng	1860 m	5 hours
Day 07	Namrung	2630 m	7 hours
Day 08	Lho	3180 m	5 hours
Day 09	Samagaon	3520 m	4 hours
Day 10	Rest day at Samagaon	3520 m	
Day 11	Samdo	3875 m	4 hours
Day 12	Rest day at Samdo	3875 m	
Day 13	Dharmashala	4460 m	5 hours
Day 14	Bimthang (Cross Larkye la)	3590 m	12 hours
Day 15	Rest day in Bimthang	3590 m	
Day 16	Gho	2515 m	6 hours
Day 17	Tal	1700 m	6 hours
Day 18	Syange	1100 m	5 hours
Day 19	Bulbule	840 m	5 hours
Day 20	Drive to Kathmandu	1400 m	

If you want a shorter trek, you can travel from Tal to Besisahar on local jeeps/vehicles and then onto Kathmandu.

If you have time it's possible to spend a few nights exploring the remote and very beautiful **Tsum Valley**, located near the Tibetan border. The area was only opened to trekkers in 2008 and retains a strong Buddhist culture, Tibetan in origin. There are several monasteries to visit, such as the **Rachen Gumba** and **Gumba Lungdang**. A huge number of *mani* stones litter the trails, surrounded by some beautiful mountain scenery as rivers drain glacier water from the slopes of Ganesh Himal.

Note A separate permit is required that must be obtained before arrival.

Trekking Manaslu

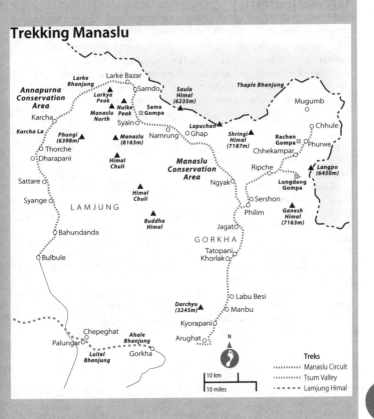

Annapurna Conservation Area

Karcha

Larke Bhanjung

Larke Bazar

Samdo

Larkya Peak

Nulke Peak

Manaslu North

Sama Gompa

Syain

Saula Himal (6235m)

Thaple Bhanjung

Mugumb

Karcha La

Phungi (6398m)

Thorche

Dharapani

Manaslu (8163m)

Namrung

Ghap

Lapuchan

Shringi Himal (7187m)

Rachen Gompa

Chhekampar

Chhule

Phurwe

Langpo (6450m)

Himal Chuli

Manaslu Conservation Area

Ripche

Ngyak

Lungdang Gompa

Sattare

Syange

LAMJUNG

Himal Chuli

Sershon

Philim

Ganesh Himal (7163m)

Bahundanda

Buddha Himal

Jagat

GORKHA

Bulbule

Tatopani

Khorlak

Labu Besi

Darchyu (3245m)

Manbu

Kyorapani

Chepeghat

Ahale Bhanjung

Arughat

Palungar

Luitel Bhanjung

Gorkha

N

Treks

.... Manaslu Circuit

.... Tsum Valley

– – – Lamjung Himal

10 km

10 miles

TREKKING ITINERARIES

Lamjung Himal

This trek allows you to walk from Gorkha (or the Marsyangdi Valley) westwards to Pokhara, visiting an area that is little visited by other trekkers. Lamjung Himal is within the Annapurna Conservation Area but bypassed by the vast majority of visitors. Because of this it is much less commercialized and yet still gets you close to the mountains. Facilities are more basic than in other areas.

Days 13 days   **Highest point** 3353 m   **Trek type** Full camping

Days	Itinerary	Altitude	Duration
Day 01	Gorkha and trek to Darongdi river	800 m	2 hours
Day 02	Palungar	1200 m	6 hours
Day 03	Paudi	1300 m	7 hours
Day 04	Chisapani	1700 m	6 hours
Day 05	Baglung Pani	2000 m	6 hours
Day 06	Ghanpokhara	2400 m	6 hours
Day 07	Forest Camp	2591 m	6 hours
Day 08	Telbrung Danda	3100 m	5 hours
Day 09	Lamjung Base Camp	3353 m	6 hours
Day 10	Rest at Lamjung Base Camp		
Day 11	Taprang Danda	3100 m	6 hours
Day 12	Tangting	1900 m	6 hours
Day 13	Tangting to Lama Khet and drive to Pokhara	820 m	

Pokhara & the Annapurnas

Nepal's trekking and adventure capital

Nestled in a valley in the shadow of the Annapurna mountains and on the shore of Phewa Lake, Pokhara is Nepal's most popular tourist destination after Kathmandu.

There are two Pokharas. One is the bustling Nepali town of traffic, bazaars and noise. The other is the relaxed, laid-back area of hotels and restaurants in a lovely setting along the shore of Nepal's second largest lake and with stunning views of the breathtaking Annapurna mountains.

Pokhara sits on the Seti Khola river which runs through town in a deep gorge, hardly noticed by the visitor. It is overshadowed by the towering Machapuchare (6997 m), the Fishtail Mountain. Reflected in the still waters of the Phewa Lake it is one of the most beautiful mountains in the world, from Pokhara appearing as an almost perfect pyramid.

Annapurna, just 30 km to the north of Pokhara, towers more than 7000 m above the valley. The sheer majesty and enormity of the Himalaya is especially apparent when viewed from the lake, and you can often see people downing oars to gaze in wonder at the snow-capped peaks.

Pokhara has always been the main centre for trekking in Nepal, with foothill walks and high-altitude treks all starting from here. The scenery of the Annapurnas, from lush terraces to high peaks combined with the irresistible mix of Hindu and Buddhist cultures, make it a fascinating and compelling destination.

Best for
Adventure ▪ Relaxing ▪ Trekking ▪ Views

Footprint picks

★ **Lakeside**, page 221

Relax on the shores of Lake Phewa in one of its many cafés or bars.

★ **Paragliding**, page 229

If you only do it once, do it here. A tandem flight offers views you will never forget.

★ **Sarangkot**, page 234

Combine superb mountain views with an adrenalin-fuelled descent.

★ **Annapurna Circuit**, page 243

Perhaps the world's most famous trek, now rerouted to avoid the encroaching roads.

★ **Poon Hill**, page 244

The most famous viewpoint in the range, with sweeping panoramas of Dhaulagiri and Annapurna.

★ **Mustang**, page 245

Remote ex-Buddhist kingdom feeling more like Tibet than Nepal.

Essential Pokhara and the Annapurnas

Finding your feet

Most people arrive in Pokhara either by road or air from Kathmandu. The flight takes just under an hour and lands at the old airport, a short 10-minute drive to Lakeside. Construction of a new airport is due to start shortly. Contracts have been signed with the Chinese to build a longer runway that runs east–west rather than north–south. This will allow larger planes to land and opens up the possibility of international flights direct to Pokhara.

Buses arrive at the bus station near the airport, also a short transfer to the Lakeside hotels. There are also services to/from Chitwan and the Terai and to the towns of the Middle Hills.

Fact...
Pokhara gets at least 250 days of good weather a year.

Getting around

The Lakeside area is small enough to wander around on foot. You can hire boats on Phewa lake by the hour, either with or without a boatman. There are always taxis available on the main Lakeside thoroughfare if you wish to travel further afield, as well as rickshaws. For trips into the mountains there are local

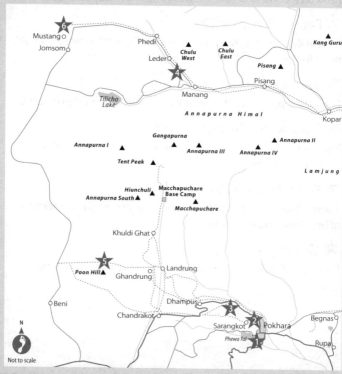

buses, taxis and plenty of local trekking agencies (see page 456) who can provide transport to/from the required trailhead.

When to go

During the monsoon of June to early September, Pokhara is humid and wet. The autumn months of October and November are a great time to visit, lovely hot days, warm evenings and, being post-monsoon, less dust in the air. The trails are busy, however, and the best hotels and lodges are all booked. In December and January it cools down and temperatures can drop to a few degrees at night. It can be cloudy and some rain falls. The spring months of February to

Tip...
Pokhara has three very interesting museums which are well worth a visit: the British Gurkha Museum, situated at the north end of the city; the Natural History Museum, located not far from Lakeside; and the International Mountaineering Museum.

May are also a pleasant time, although the heat and humidity do build once more as the monsoon approaches.

Winter daytime temperature never falls below 10°C and reaches 20°C. Summer temperatures rise to 36°C or higher.

The mountain walks and treks all have different climates, depending on their location in relation to the Himalaya. For more details, see page 19.

Time required

This depends on the length of your trek. You can easily spend anything from one day to one month in the Annapurnas, depending on your priorities and time restraints. It's a good idea to plan a night in Pokhara before your trek and a couple of nights at the end.

Footprint picks

Pokhara
& around

It was Pokhara's beautiful setting that first attracted tourists in numbers during the late 1960s and early 1970s, when it became particularly popular with hippies. Since then much of the town has been transformed into a travellers' retreat of hotels, small family-run guesthouses, cafés, bars and restaurants. Despite this development, its Lakeside area has maintained a chilled atmosphere as a great place to relax pre- and post-trek.

It's a place people come to for adventure and excitement, being the starting point for some of the finest walking and trekking in the world. Over the last decade it has also developed into a world-leading destination for activity sports. Updrafts, created as hot air is pushed up before the Annapurnas, make it perfect for paragliding and the experience of looking down on the lake as the snow-capped Himalaya fill the northern horizon is unforgettable. Also on offer are zip-wires, rafting and a host of other pursuits.

Pokhara is a place where you come to do rather than see. Its historical and cultural attractions are limited as it has grown over the last 50 years from a tiny trading outpost of a few thousand people to a modern city of over 300,000. For the traveller, however, it's a great place to relax after the exertions of your trek, while admiring one of the world's greatest views.

beautiful lake reflecting the Himalaya

The Phewa Tal is the focus of visitors to Pokhara and around it has grown the town's principal concentration of hotels and restaurants, known as Lakeside. A second area – Damside – used to rival it as a popular place to stay, offering the widest views of the mountains, but the laid-back charm of Lakeside has gradually taken over.

Phewa Tal is Nepal's second largest lake after Rara in the west. It is fed from the west by the small Harpan Khola while to the southeast it narrows to become the Pardi Khola for 2 km which in turn feeds into the Fusre Khola. The hydroelectric dam was built with Indian aid in 1968.

Seen from Lakeside, the lake reflects the richly wooded hills to the south, capped by the World Peace Pagoda, appearing emerald green across a crystal surface disturbed only by the ripples of boats and swimmers. But more magnificent still is the sight from its western and southern banks. Take a boat from Lakeside and row diagonally across to the other side. From here you can see the mighty Annapurnas, geological enormities whose lofty, snow-capped elegance shimmers on the blue water.

The lake has traditionally been a rich source of fish for local communities, but over-exploitation has led to a serious depletion of reserves, so that the fish that are widely advertised on menus as coming 'fresh from the lake' now usually come fresh from the Begnas and Rupa lakes to the east of Pokhara or from fish farms elsewhere in the valley.

Boat hire You can hire a wooden *doonas* for US$3 per hour or US$7.50 for the day. The boats are stable and easy to paddle on the lake's still waters. If you don't want to row yourself, it will cost US$3.50 per hour for a boatman and boat. Lifejackets are available for hire. It's also possible to hire pedalos and small sailing boats, the latter coming with or without a guide. As motorboats are banned from the lake it is a peaceful and fun way to explore, especially at dawn and dusk when the mountains can be perfectly reflected in the calm waters.

Swimming If you decide to swim in the lake (some people do) make sure you keep well away from the dam as currents can be strong and also from inhabited areas where the pollution is at its worst. Poisonous snakes, including cobra and green mamba, as well as other non-poisonous varieties, are known to inhabit the lake, especially the areas where trees and undergrowth extend down to the shore. Leeches can also be a problem in summer and often attach themselves to the side of the boat.

Varahi Mandir

This two-tiered pagoda-style shrine is situated on a small island in Phewa Lake, a short distance from the shore. It is easily reached by boat and makes a great focal point for a boat journey on the lake. It is dedicated to Varahi, the Hindu god Vishnu's third incarnation in the form of a boar. Originally built in the 18th century, it has since been renovated and enlarged, but it is an atmospheric spot and worth the paddle.

Fact...
Pokhara is situated in the centre of Nepal at an altitude of 884 m, some 400 m lower than Kathmandu.

Shanti Stupa/World Peace Pagoda

From Lakeside, the temple is clearly visible by its solitary twinkling lights at night. It has an idyllic location on the high ridge, from where the views of Phewa Lake, Pokhara city and the mountains to the north, and over the Fusre and Seti rivers to the south, are simply unsurpassed. (A dawn view is especially recommended.)

Monks from the Nipponzan Myohoji organization began construction of the World Peace Stupa in 1994 and it was finished in 2000. The stupa itself is 40 m high, set in a long

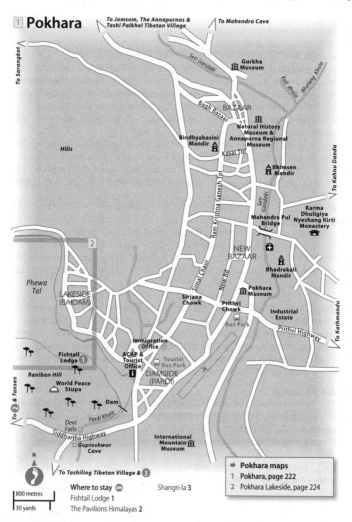

Pokhara

To Jomsom, The Annapurnas &
Tashi Palkhel Tibetan Village

To Mahendra Cave

To Sarangkot

Seti Gandaki

Gurkha
Museum

Kali Khola

Bhalang Khola

Bagh Bazaar

BAZAAR

Natural History
Museum &
Annapurna Regional
Museum

Bindhyabasini
Mandir

Kasai Tol

Bhimsen
Mandir

Hills

Ram Krishna Ganesh Tol

Seti Gandaki

Karma
Dhuligiya
Nyeshang Kirti
Monastery

Mahendra Pul
Bridge

To Kahnu Danda

NEW
BAZAAR

Simal Chaur

New Rd

Bhadrakali
Mandir

Phewa
Tal

LAKESIDE
(BAIDAM)

Sirjana
Chowk

Pokhara
Museum

Prithvi
Chowk

Industrial
Estate

To Kathmandu

Bus Park

Prithvi Highway

Immigration
Office

ACAP &
Tourist
Office

Tourist
Bus Park

Fishtail
Lodge

DAMSIDE
(PARDI)

Raniban Hill

World Peace
Stupa

Dam

To 2 & Tansen

Devi
Falls

Pardi Khola

Siddhartha Highway

Gupteshwor
Cave

International
Mountain
Museum

N

To Tashiling Tibetan Village & 3

800 metres

30 yards

Where to stay
Fishtail Lodge 1
The Pavilions Himalayas 2

Shangri-la 3

➡ **Pokhara maps**
1 Pokhara, page 222
2 Pokhara Lakeside, page 224

BACKGROUND

Pokhara

The origins of Pokhara can be traced back to its time as a stopover for travelling merchants plying ancient trading routes from the plains to the Himalaya. During the Middle Ages the Pokhara Valley was known as Kaski and ruled by a king from Kaskikot, or Kaski fort, built in the 15th century on a high ridge north of the town near the present-day village of Sarangkot.

During the 17th century, the region's traditional Gurung and Magar communities were joined by Newars from the Kathmandu Valley who came at the invitation of this king as traders and the modern site of Pokhara was adopted.

The bazaar, to the north of the Phewa Lake, is the oldest established part of Pokhara and in small, ever-decreasing areas its architecture reflects the influence of these Newars. Although 'endless street' (as Giuseppe Tucci called it in 1950) still forms the main north–south thoroughfare, the area has expanded greatly since then.

The population has grown from a few thousand in the 1950s, to 47,000 in 1981 to 265,000 in the last census in 2011. British Gurkha officers remember in the early 1970s freewheeling from their camp in the north of town all the way to the airport in the south without having to stop or turn on the engine.

A seemingly haphazard maze of smaller lanes now backs off the main road to the east and west; in character, the area is considerably further removed than the actual 5 km separating it from the tranquil settings of Lakeside, the tourist quarter on the shores of Phewa Tal.

courtyard garden it's a peaceful spot to relax after your climb. There are a few small cafés nearby where you can enjoy a cool drink.

To get to the stupa you can either take a boat to the shore directly opposite Lakeside for a steepish 45-minute climb to the top, or you can take a taxi and drive around to near the monument itself on the south side. The row/climb to the temple makes an excellent half-day excursion, with several peaceful places to stop for a drink or meal on the way up, but wear good trainers or boots as the rocks can be very slippery. The **Rani Ban forest** is home to numerous species of exotic birds and an ornithologist's delight.

Pokhara town

a tale of two towns

Bindhyabasini Mandir and Bhimsen Mandir

Sitting on a small rise and resting on a shady platform, **Bindhyabasini Mandir** is a shikhara-style temple dedicated to the goddess Durga in her Bhagwati manifestation. Bhagwati is Pokhara's guardian deity, also known as the destroyer Kali. This was illustrated when the temple was destroyed by fire in 1949. The shrine is a saligram (marine fossil) of local black ammonite, providing a link to an earlier and warmer geological age when the valley was submerged by water. Being a Kali shrine, sacrifices are fairly common, especially on Saturdays.

To the east, in the Bazaar area on the northern part of town, **Bhimsen Mandir** is a small Newari-style temple dedicated to Bhimsen.

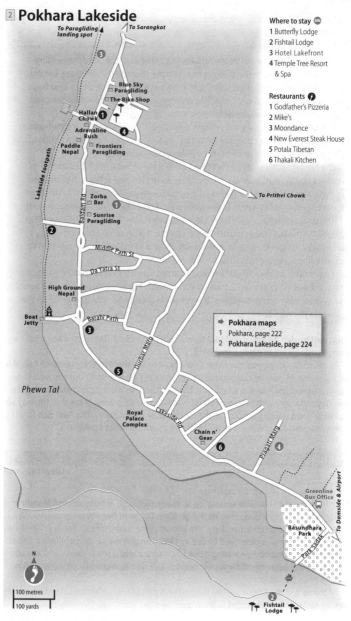

② Pokhara Lakeside

To Paragliding landing spot

To Sarangkot

Blue Sky Paragliding
The Bike Shop
Hallan Chowk
Adrenaline Rush
Paddle Nepal
Frontiers Paragliding

Lakeside footpath

Zorba Bar
Baidam Rd
Sunrise Paragliding

Middle Path St
Da Yatra St

High Ground Nepal

Boat Jetty
Barahi Path

To Prithvi Chowk

Durbal Marg

Lakeside Rd

Phewa Tal

Royal Palace Complex

Chain n' Gear

Pragati Marg

Greenline Bus Office

To Damside & Airport

Basundhara Park

Park Srnok

Fishtail Lodge

→ Pokhara maps
1 Pokhara, page 222
2 Pokhara Lakeside, page 224

Where to stay
1 Butterfly Lodge
2 Fishtail Lodge
3 Hotel Lakefront
4 Temple Tree Resort & Spa

Restaurants
1 Godfather's Pizzeria
2 Mike's
3 Moondance
4 New Everest Steak House
5 Potala Tibetan
6 Thakali Kitchen

N

100 metres
100 yards

Natural History Museum and Annapurna Regional Museum
Open Sun-Fri 0900-1300, 1400-1700, closed Sat, free.

Nearby, on the Prithvi Narayan University campus, this small, eclectic museum has some very uninspiring displays of dead animals and birds but there are two excellent redeeming features. First is its collection of butterflies, that gives real insight into the amazing variety of species found throughout Nepal. Displayed in a series of cases and drawers, you can poke around and explore the collection at your leisure. The curator is on hand to answer questions and show you the best of the collection.

Second is its interesting displays on the ecology of the Annapurnas, past and present, as well as on the work of the Annapurna Conservation Area Project (ACAP) and on the contemporary challenges facing the area's environment.

Tip...
If you are going trekking in the Annapurnas this museum will show you what to look out for.

Gurkha Museum
http://gurkhamuseum.org.np. Daily 0800-1630, US$1.80.

Just north of the Natural History Museum is the Gurkha Museum, identifiable by the monument outside and two large bronze cannons on either side of its entrance. This museum tells the history of the British Army Gurkhas and the many acts of heroism performed by these Nepalese fighters.

The museum tells the story of all those who were awarded the Victoria Cross, most with photographs and many for heroic acts that defy belief. There are plenty of exhibits, from old uniforms to the ferocious kukri knives they are so famous for carrying, as well as explanations of the campaigns they have fought in over the last 200 years. Prince Harry spent time here on his visit in March 2016 to honour this anniversary and to celebrate the long relationship between the British Army and the Gurkhas.

Bhadrakali Mandir
About 20 minutes' walk to the northeast of the main bus stop, the small Bhadrakali Mandir sits attractively atop a green hillock with pleasant views to the east. Legend states that the Goddess Bhadrakali told a priest to dig at a certain place in the hills and here he found a statue of the deity. The temple was established and worshippers come to make offerings in exchange for wishes being fulfilled. It's also popular for weddings and picnics at weekends.

Pokhara Museum
Open Wed-Mon 1000-1430, closed Tue, US$0.30.

Just to the southwest of Bhadrakali Mandir, this government-sponsored museum has mediocre displays of costumes, artefacts and cultures of various ethnic groups living in central/western Nepal and the Pokhara area (including Gurungs, Magars, Thakalis and Tharus). There is also a display of an 8000-year-old settlement from Mustang and a Gurung roundhouse.

International Mountain Museum
South of the airport, www.internationalmountainmuseum.org, open daily 0900-1700, US$3.70.

This large, spacious modern museum is divided into sections relating to the various mountain peoples of Nepal. You can tell that the project had Japanese funding as the first display you come to describes, rather incongruously, the mountain people of Japan.

There are displays of everyday tools and utensils, as well as equipment and clothing from several Everest and other 8000-m mountain expeditions. An excellent model of Everest shows the main climbing routes. Other displays demonstrating the effects of climate change and of increasing urbanization make it an interesting hour or so. There is also a reconstruction of a Tibetan monastery and a life-size model Yeti you wouldn't want to meet on a dark night.

The museum is set in large grounds where you can be photographed sitting on top of a model mountain, reputably based on Manaslu.

Devi Falls
Daily 0600-1800, US$0.30.

A few kilometres to the southwest of town, Devi Falls is a sink hole (waterfall) where the **Pardi Khola** disappears from view, emerging 200 m further south just in time to join the Fusre Khola. Known locally as Patale Chhango, the 'waterfall to the underworld', it is best visited during or soon after the monsoon; at other times, the Pardi Khola may be no more spectacular than a trickle of water.

A popular local legend ascribes the name Devi Falls to an unfortunate tourist named David or Devi who, whilst peering down, unwittingly obeyed the laws of gravity with devastating consequences. Another cites a Swiss woman who died skinny dipping in the carefree 1960s. Most likely the name is derived from the word *devi*, meaning goddess.

Gupteshwor Mahadev Cave
Open 0600-1900, US$0.90.

Opposite Devi Falls is a cave famous for its huge stalagmite that is worshipped as a Shiva lingam. The cave was allegedly discovered in the 1600s by locals cutting grass for their livestock. On looking inside they found old shrines to Shiva, Parvati, Mahadev and several others.

It is thought to be Nepal's longest cave system, at nearly 3000 m, and comprises two main chambers. The first contains the shrines, the second, lower one is closed when water levels are high as the subterranean river from Devi Falls occasionally floods it. Bring a torch and good footwear as it can be rough, slippery and dark inside.

Listings Pokhara town *maps pages 222 and 224.*

Tourist information

Annapurna Conservation Project (ACAP)
T061-463376. Sun-Fri 1000-1700, Sat and winter 1000-1600.
You need a permit to trek in the Annapurnas and this is where you get it from. It costs US$18.50 and is issued on the spot but you will need 2 passport-sized photos. If you try to enter the ACAP area without a permit you will be charged US$36.50 at the gates.

Immigration Office
T062-465167. Sun-Thu 1000-1600, Fri 1000-1500.
Convenient for visa extensions, you must first apply online at www.nepalimmigration.gov.np, following the links to 'Tourist Visa' and uploading a photo into the application. Make a note of the Submission ID number and take this, plus your fee, to the office within 15 days. Costs are US$30 for an additional 15 days, US$2 per day for additional days up to 30 and then US$20

extra if you want a multi-entry visa. Nepali rupees are the preferred currency.

Nepal Tourism Office
T061-465292. Sun-Fri 1000-1700.
Nepal Tourism has an office at the very south of Lakeside which is friendly enough and conveniently in the same building as **ACAP** (see above). If you are trekking independently you have to register here on the TIMS – Trekkers Information Management System (www.timsnepal.com). This is a safety system aimed at keeping records of where trekkers are, so that, should they go missing, there is a better chance of locating them. 2 passport-sized photos are required and there is a charge of US$10 if travelling on an organized trek or US$20 if you are trekking independently. You can also register at the **Trekking Agencies Association of Nepal** (T01-442 7473, open daily 1000-1700).

Tourist Police
Beside the Tourism Office, T100.
They also have a small booth opposite the Moondance Restaurant at the southern end of the main north–south road on Lakeside.

Where to stay

2- and 3-storey concrete hotels, often remarkably similar in design and offering comfortable rooms and Western bathrooms, are increasingly replacing more basic, traditional guesthouses that offer a valuable insight into the Nepali way of life. As competition gets fiercer, there are often good deals to be had.

Lakeside extends along almost the entire eastern shore of the Phewa Lake. The main north–south road runs alongside the lake and, together with the 5 roads leading off it to the east, is the centre of Lakeside's activity.

$$$$ Fishtail Lodge
T061-465071, www.fishtail-lodge.com.
Situated on Phewa Tal and accessed by a pontoon, Fishtail was the 1st lodge in

Pokhara. Originally built in the 1960s, it occupies the best position and the views along the lake to the Annapurnas are superb. Its 60 rooms are in 5 circular buildings, set in lovely gardens with the forests behind. It's peaceful and, while the rooms might be a little small, the location makes up for it.

$$$$ Tiger Mountain Pokhara Lodge
T061-691887, www.tigermountain pokhara.com.
Undoubtedly the most atmospheric place to stay around Pokhara, this is the perfect place to either recover from a long trek or to escape to for a few days of relaxation, day walks and birdwatching. Sitting on top of a ridge about 10 km east of the town, it lies on the old Royal Trek Route. The accommodation is in small traditional beautifully decorated cottages and the main dining terrace and pool have superb views of the mountains. Recommended.

$$$ The Pavilions Himalayas
T061-694379, www.thepavilionshimalayas.com.
This stunning boutique resort must be the most eco hotel in Nepal. Everything is self-generated or home-grown and it is built using local materials. The villas are gorgeous and are set in a lovely rural valley only a few kilometres west of Phewa Lake. It's a peaceful escape and ploughs much of its profits back into the community.

$$$ Temple Tree Resort and Spa
T061-465819, www.templetreenepal.com.
Built using local materials Temple Tree has a relaxing feel and has been well designed around its small grounds; it has one of the best swimming pools in town, making it a good choice for families. The rooms and bathrooms are nicely fitted and it has the atmosphere of a high-class establishment. Popular with expats escaping to Pokhara for the weekend so gets booked up.

$$ Shangri-la
T061-462222, www.hotelshangrila.com.
Situated away from Lakeside, to the south of Damside and the airport, this is a good

choice if you want to relax post trek and do nothing. It's close enough to get a taxi to the restaurants and bars of Lakeside but away from the bustle. Its rooms are arranged in wings that run along the side of lovely lawns and gardens, with plenty of places to relax and a decent pool for cooling off in.

$$-$ Hotel Lake Front
T061-463908, www.hotellakefront.com.
One of the few mid-range hotels with direct lake views, this place is situated just north of Hallen Chowk. The rooms are all modern and comfortable, with Wi-Fi, TVs and a pleasant garden to sit in and watch the world walk by on the Lakeside path while paragliders land nearby. There are 2 small cottages in the grounds which are the pick.

$ Butterfly Lodge
T061-462129, www.butterfly-lodge.org.
This friendly lodge has been going for over 35 years and offers spacious, clean rooms at a good price. Their newer block offers good views from the top floors and there is a pleasant garden to relax in. They offer free pick-ups from the airport.

Restaurants

The quality and range of food available in Pokhara has improved dramatically over the last few years and the standards are now very good. As well as excellent Nepali food, most other types of international cuisine are also available.

Lakeside
There are plenty of restaurants and cafés that open onto the lake, providing a relaxed atmosphere that Kathmandu struggles to match. Those with thatched seating in gardens sloping down to the lakeshore rank among some of the country's most pleasant places to enjoy a meal. Fish, fresh from one of the valley's lakes, is a speciality while the influence of Pokhara's Tibetan communities is represented by several excellent eating

places. Good pizzas and Mexican dishes are also widely available.

$$$ Moondance Restaurant
T061-461835, www.moondancepokhara.com. Open 0700-2230.
This popular restaurant with excellent food is almost an attraction in its own right, feeding trekkers and visitors for a quarter of a century. Friendly service, pleasant ambiance and a large central fireplace for cooler evenings. Many of the vegetables come from their own organic farm.

$$$ New Everest Steak House
T061-466828. Open 0900-2200
Steakhouses are synonymous with eating in Nepal, a bit strange as the cow is sacred to Hindus. This is a particularly good one, perfect for that post-trek blow-out, with the meat flown in from India and a vast array of sauces to choose from. Not surprisingly (given its clientele) the 'trekkers steak' is a perennial favourite.

$$ Godfather's Pizzeria
Open 0800-2300.
If you fancy a pizza then this is a good option. Wood-fired oven, varied selection and a good atmosphere make this a firm favourite with tourists and locals alike.

$$ Mike's Restaurant
Open 0700-2100.
Great location with tables on the lakeshore under a large pipal tree. Varied menu from Nepali to continental and good Mexican options. In keeping with its roots at **Mike's Breakfast** in Kathmandu (which was taken over and is not what it used to be), the breakfasts are hearty.

$ Potala Tibetan Restaurant
Open 0800-2100.
Everybody should try a *momo* – Tibetan dumpling – while in Nepal and this is an excellent place to do it. Run by a Tibetan family, you can sample the various different types while washing them down with a Tibetan *tungba* beer.

$ Thakali Kitchen
Open 1100-2100
This small eatery to the south of Lakeside
serves local Thakali cuisine in the form
of thalis, as well as some interesting side
dishes and snacks.

What to do

Pokhara is not only the best outdoor activitiy
destination in Nepal but also one of the
finest in the world. Its walks and treks offer
the greatest variety of scenery and culture
anywhere on earth, with options ranging
from day walks to snow ascents of Himalayan
peaks. For options and details, please see
page 243. For general information see
Trekking essentials, page 437.

Cycle hire

This is a popular option and a good way of
getting around Pokhara and further afield
without being restricted to set itineraries.
There are plenty of cycle hire places in
Lakeside renting anything from an old-
style 2-wheeler with panniers to the
latest-generation mountain bikes.

Once out of the fairly busy streets of
Pokhara there is plenty to explore. Several
places hire out bikes, with cost for a decent
Indian mountain bike starting from around
US$9 per hr or US2.75-4.50 for the day.
Premium bikes are from US$10 upwards.

If you want to explore with a guide, there
are a number of day rides, ranging from
exploring the Pokhara Valley to an ascent
of Sarangkot. Overnight trips in the valley
and longer itineraries into the Annapurnas
are also available.

The Bike Shop, *T061-465587, www.thebikeshop
nepal.com*. Agency with good equipment
and experienced guides, offering a full
range of guided day and overnight trips.

Chain n Gear, *T061-463696, www.pokhara
mountainbiking.com*. Another operator
offering good equipment and plenty
of guided options of the city, valley
and mountains.

★ Paragliding

The potential of Pokhara as a wind sport
destination was first recognized back in
the 1980s by the Himalayan pioneer Jimmy
Roberts, the man attributed with turning
trekking into an industry. While exploring
the southern Annapurnas he realized that
the huge updrafts created as the hot air
from the plains hit the Annapurna massif
would be perfect for gliders, the then
most popular aerial pastime. He imported
2 gliders but sadly the government refused
to issue permits, suspicious of why people
would want to pursue the activity unless it
was to spy.

Aerial activities were only permitted in
the early 2000s and since then they have
boomed. Paragliding is particularly popular
as Pokhara is one of the best launch spots
in the world, with a longest recorded flight
reaching Nuwakot on the edge of the
Kathmandu Valley some 140 km away. One
of the professional local guides, with the use
of oxygen, has also flown over the summit of
Machapuchare at 6993 m.

The launch site is located at Sarangkot, a
village high on a ridge to the north of Lake
Phewa (see page 234) and there are now
numerous agencies that will take you on a
tandem flight. A 20- to 30-min flight to see
the amazing view of the Annapurnas costs
US$78. A longer flight, to travel towards the
mountains, of up to 1 hr is US$106. Most
centres also offer paragliding courses to
get you your basic licence and paratrekking
when you fly to different landing and launch
sites over a period of days.

One unique experience available in
Pokhara is **parahawking** – a tandem
paragliding flight in the presence of Egyptian
vultures. The birds will fly with you, guiding
the pilot to thermals and even land on your
outstretched hand mid-flight for a deserved
rest. These flights can be arranged through
Blue Sky Paragliding (see below) and a
donation is made from each fee to vulture
conservation projects in Nepal.

As well as those listed here, there are several other agencies to choose from. Check the experience of the pilots, standard of equipment and their safety records when enquiring about a flight.

Blue Sky Paragliding, *T061-464737, www.blue-sky-paragliding.com*. An older, established agency, they offer the usual range of flying options as well as parahawking (see above). They also operate out of Bandipur.

Frontiers Paragliding, *T061-466044, www.nepal-paragliding.com*. Tandem flights and courses from one of the Pokhara pioneer agencies.

Sunrise Paragliding, *T061-463174, www.sunrise-paragliding.com*. One of the pioneers in the area and with the 1st fully qualified Nepali guide, now their MD. They offer tandem flights, as well as paratrekking and courses.

Microlight flights

If you want to get up in the air and close to the mountains then the microlight option is a good one. You buzz over Pokhara town, Phewa Lake, Sarangkot, along the Seti Valley and seemingly to within touching distance of Machapuchare. It's windy and chilly up there, so wear warm clothes and keep your camera well secured. The best times are early morning and late afternoon. Flights do not operate during the monsoon. Recommended, but not an experience for the faint-hearted. Both the listed operators have offices in Lakeside but the flights leave from the airport.

Avia Club Nepal, *T061-463338, www.avia clubnepal.com*. The most established operator in Pokhara you can choose flights from 15 mins up to 1½ hrs. You'll need the longer option to get close to the mountains, reaching an altitude of nearly 5000 m. Prices start from US$100.

Pokhara Ultralight, *T061-466880, www.fly pokhara.com*. A similar range of options and prices to Avia Club, the 15-min flight lets you fly around the lake and over the World Peace Stupa.

Rafting and whitewater

If you have 1-2 days free and fancy the thrill of some water activities, there are plenty to choose from. You can enjoy 1-day whitewater rafting trips on the Seti or Trisuli, right through to 10 days on the raging Karnali. There are also daily canyoning trips, as well as kayaking and tubing.

The water conditions vary greatly throughout the year, dependent on the level of the rivers. Post-monsoon they are at their fullest and fastest, the levels slowly dropping into the spring.

Adrenaline Rush Nepal, *T061-466663, www.adrenalinenepal.com*. Established and experienced agency with offices in Pokhara and Kathmandu, offering a full range of activities with qualified guides.

Paddle Nepal, *T061-465736, www.paddle nepal.com*. Another reputable operator with good equipment and guides, offering lots of options from half days on the Seti to major rafting expeditions and kayak clinics.

Zip-wiring

Pokhara is home to what they describe at the tallest, longest and steepest zip-wire in the world. It also offers perhaps the best views. It starts near the top of the ridge at Sarangkot and runs for 1800 m, has a drop of some 600 m and takes about 2 mins to complete. You can reach speeds of 120 kph. As it's a dual line you can experience it with a friend and discover who screams the loudest.

High Ground Nepal, *T061-466349, www.high groundnepal.com*. As well as operating the zip-wire, they also have a bungee platform in case you have some adrenalin left. The zip-wire and bungee each cost US$60, or a combined ticket is yours for US$100.

Transport

Air

The airport is located more or less in the centre of town at the end of the Prithvi Highway, very close to the lake. It takes about 15 mins to get to Lakeside, a taxi costs US$3.70. See also page 218.

There are approximately 12-15 flights a day to/from **Kathmandu**, taking 50 mins. Try to get seats on the right-hand side of the plane when arriving and on the left when leaving for stunning views of the Himalaya. There are 3-4 flights to **Jomsom** (25-30 mins) but these are very dependent on the weather at the destination airport and in the Kali Gandaki Valley. There are also 1-2 scheduled flights to **Manang** per week, again weather dependent.

Bus
Public buses

All public buses run from the main bus park east of Prithvi Chowk. There are about 6 buses nightly to **Kathmandu**, as well as numerous departures throughout the day, US$4.50-5.50. There are also microbuses for the same price. These buses all stop at **Dumre** (for **Bandipur**) 2 hrs, US$1.50.

Buses also leave here for all other national destinations, including the **Terai**. **Tansen** is 5 hrs away, US$5, **Nepalgang** (for **Bardia**) is 12 hrs, US$10, and **Gorkha** is 5 hrs, US$3.

For the trail heads for trekking in the Annapurnas you need to go to the **Baglung Bus Park** in the north of town.

Tourist buses

Several premium bus services offer a guaranteed seat, no crowding, no stopping and a meal during a midway break.
Kathmandu to Pokhara, 6-7 hrs. Booking can be made direct or through Lakeside or Thamel travel agents. Most leave from the **Tourist Bus Park**.

Greenline, T061-464472, www.greenline.com.np. Perhaps the best of the a/c services, running to a stop located in south Lakeside. **Kathmandu** is US$23, **Sauraha** (**Chitwan**) is US$17.

Golden Travels, T01-422 0036, and **Blue Sky** (see What to do, above) are 2 other operators offering at least 1 daily departure. Other tourist buses are more basic but much more comfortable than public services; they cost US$7.50-11 depending on a/c etc.

Taxi

Most areas of Lakeside Pokhara are within walking distance of each other, often a pleasant stroll along the lakeside path. Taxis are readily available between Barahi and Hallen Chowks in the heart of Lakeside to take you to other parts of town and are not expensive if you barter. US3-4 should get you to most places in the town.

If you are trekking independently it's possible to hire taxis to get you to the trailheads. For example, the fare to **Phedi**, the start of the Poon Hill trek (see page 244) will cost about US$12 one way.

ON THE ROAD

Pokhara's Tibetans

Following the Chinese invasion of Tibet in 1950, refugees flooded into Nepal. Many settled in the Kathmandu Valley, but some who'd crossed into Mustang and descended the Kali Gandaki found their way to Pokhara. While not as conspicuous a population here as in Kathmandu, there are nonetheless several prominent Tibetan-owned and run hotels and restaurants where portraits of the Dalai Lama hang proudly indoors and prayer flags flutter optimistically in the breeze outside. Few Tibetans are directly involved in retail, but groups of women are often to be found wandering the Lakeside streets offering their varied handicrafts for sale to tourists.

Pokhara Valley

ridges, lakes and forests

Sarangkot

High above the northern end of Phewa Lake lies the small village of Sarangkot. Situated at an elevation of just under 1600 m, it is perched on a ridge and offers panoramic mountain views from Dhaulagiri across the Annapurnas to Manaslu, as well as south over the Pokhara Valley. There is a viewing platform near the village and many other places along the ridge with equally good views. An old fort sits just above the village, on the crest of the ridge, and makes an atmospheric spot to gaze out at the mountains.

In the last decade Sarangkot has become one of the world's foremost places to paraglide. On a clear day you can see up to 100 paragliders, many circling together as they use the thermals to gain altitude and enjoy breathtaking views of the Himalayan chain. A road from Pokhara now winds its way up the ridge to the village. It's also the start of a zip-wire that will rocket you back down to the valley should you be tired of walking.

Some people walk to Sarangkot as preparation for a longer trek, but the village makes a decent destination in its own right, either as a day excursion to watch the paragliders launch themselves off the hillside or for an overnight stay (a selection of accommodation is available), especially as the views are often at their best at dawn.

Kaski

The region's former capital is now a small village about 45 minutes' walk along the southern side of the ridge due west of Sarangkot, passing the village of Kaule on the way. A couple of small shrines either side of the path mark your arrival into Kaski where the ruins of its 200-year-old fort, **Kaskikot**, can also be seen. If you climb to the top of the ridge (there are no set paths), you can get a fine view over its steeply wooded northern slope and across to the villages that dot the confluence and valleys of the Mardi and Seti rivers. About 1 km east of Kaski, a 1788-m hillock is the highest point along the ridge between Sarangkot and Kaski.

Kahnu Danda

Situated on a ridge to the northeast of the town, Kahnu Danda is an alternative to Sarangkot, with views from a slightly lower elevation over the valley and – although more obstructed than those from Sarangkot – to the Annapurnas. You can get a clear view of Machapuchare from here and a good view of the Seti river as it comes out of the Annapurna Sanctuary.

ON THE ROAD

Tibetan villages

Several Tibetan settlements are dotted around the Pokhara area. The Tashiling Tibetan Village, just to the south of the Devi Falls, is probably the best known, as it is the most accessible. North of the town, at Hyangja on the Pokhara–Baglung Highway some 5 km from the lake, is the village of Tashi Palkhel with over 1000 inhabitants and a monastery (*gompa*) of about 70 monks. The village also has some excellent views of the Annapurnas and was the first established, set up by the Swiss geologist Toni Hagan with support from the Swiss Government.

These villages originated as refugee camps and are now bustling centres for the manufacture of woollen carpets and handicrafts for export; you can watch the carpets being woven. Not surprisingly, local sales of carpets and handicrafts are enthusiastically promoted by residents; each village also has a small shop selling the locally produced wares. Both villages can be reached by taxi.

About 2 km north of Mahendrapul is a Buddhist monastery called the **Manang Gompa** or **Karma Dhubgyu Chokhorling**. A trail climbs through the small hamlets of **Phulbari** from here, rather indistinct in places. Head for the lookout tower from where you get the best views of the mountains and across the valley. There are also the remains of a 250-year-old-fort, **Kahnukot**. Allow two hours for the walk up.

Rupa Tal and Begnas Tal

At about 15 km these two picturesque lakes are a world away from the tourist hub of Phewa Lake and Lakeside. In places, indigenous forest still tumbles down to the water's edge; in others terraced paddy fields climb steeply up from them. The lakes used to be an integral part of the old Royal Trek's final days, an itinerary put together for Prince Charles's visit in 1986.

Begnas, the larger of the two, has rowing boats for hire. Commercial fishing takes place on both lakes and their fish are acknowledged to be the ones described simply as 'fresh from the lake' on Pokhara restaurant menus. There are many fine and picturesque walking opportunities in the area around the lakes and it is an especially good place for birdwatching, with varieties of waterfowl always in evidence.

Listings Pokhara Valley

Where to stay

Sarangkot

Most people stay in Pokhara. Sarangkot's guesthouses are fairly basic but comfortable. A new large hotel is currently being constructed in the village, with Japanese financial backing. It will no doubt offer a higher standard at a higher cost.

$$$ Himalayan Front Resort
T061-412398, www.ktmgh.com.
Situated about halfway along the ridge from Pokhara to Sarangkot, the Himalayan Front is the latest addition to the **Kathmandu Guest House** group. It's large and modern, but rooms are very comfortable and have superb mountain views. An enclosed roof bar and open terrace ensure excellent views whatever the temperature and the ground floor has a decent restaurant. Pool.

$ Sherpa Resort
T061-691171, www.sherparesort.com.
Set in nice gardens on top of the ridge the Sherpa Resort is located a couple of hundred metres west of the viewing tower. Rooms are clean, comfortable and have en suite bathrooms. Get one with a stunning view of the Annapurnas.

Rupa Tal and Begnas Tal

$$$ Begnas Lake Resort and Villas
T061-560030, www.begnaslakeresort.com.
A lovely retreat on the slopes above Begnas Lake, its small cottages are set in gardens with views of the lake and mountains beyond. A good restaurant, pool and spa make it a relaxing place to stay.

$ Begnas Coffee House
T061-692775, www.neplaiorganiccoffee.com.
This tiny guesthouse may only have 6 basic rooms but it is very comfortable and in a great location. The family that own it make their own coffee from locally grown beans under the superb name of **Machapuchare Flying Bird Coffee**. Their hospitality is warming and you can also sample their various flavours of home-made honey.

$$$$ Rupakot Resort
T061-622660, www.rupakotresort.com.
This large, modern resort sits on top of the ridge to the south of the lakes, reached by a 40-min drive up from the main highway, much of it unsurfaced. The luxury rooms are in 10 cottage-style buildings made of local stone and wood. The views are exceptional, both down over the lakes and north to the Himalaya. A pool and spa are being built. There are some lovely walks nearby, including to a nearby shrine.

Walks around Pokhara

The real charm of Nepal lies outside its tourist areas. If you don't have the time, inclination or energy for a long trek there are a number of shorter, one-day walks that can be undertaken from Pokhara.

★ To Sarangkot
Two main routes lead from Pokhara to Sarangkot. Some people take the gentler path along the ridge up and descend via the steeper route to Lakeside.

From Lakeside, follow the road north for about 2 km past Hallan Chowk in Lakeside before turning right by a painted stone and beginning the steep climb up a long stone stairway. The steps ascend through cultivated land and rocky scree. Blue painted arrows point towards the top. This is a steep walk and can be tiring and although there are shortcuts they are just as strenuous. Views are mainly to the south with the full range of mountains not visible until you have almost reached Sarangkot. Allow three hours.

You used to be able to walk up from town along the top of the ridge. The lower part of this walk has been seriously developed and a new road now runs to Sarangkot along this route. A good compromise is to take a taxi to 1 km after the **Himalayan Front Resort**. Just after the hairpins you can start walking up the old trail, passing through some hamlets offering refreshment, and be rewarded for much of the climb with great mountain views.

> **Tip...**
> Never walk alone. It is dangerous should you fall and injure yourself and also there have been robberies on this trail.

Phewa Tal Circuit

This walk takes you around the Phewa Tal and over the ridge towering above its southern bank. It's an all-day outing (leave early) that involves a fair amount of ascent and descent. It also crosses two small rivers and passes through some muddy land; it is best avoided during and after the monsoon. In spring water levels are at their lowest. Alternatively, the circuit can be done as two semi-circular walks, to the north and south of the lake respectively.

A final and shorter option is to row across the lake and follow the trail up to the World Peace Pagoda. This is a steep climb of just under an hour, but contours through the forest and is very picturesque. After a look at the pagoda and some refreshment you descend to your boat the same way. The path is slippery so wear good walking shoes.

The circuit trail can be hard to follow so don't be afraid to ask directions. Get a map of the lake before leaving. Head off on the road north from Lakeside as it becomes a track and swings westwards around the north of the lake, passing the **Waterfront Resort** near the primary paragliding landing area. After about 1 km, a path to the right leads up towards Sarangkot. After a further 2 km, the trail hits a 'crossroad'. The right-hand path follows a steep ascent again to Sarangkot, while the left-hand turning veers southwest.

An option here is to follow the path straight ahead towards the west. After 2 km this brings you to the small village of **Pame** set amid cultivated fields at the base of the northern ridge, where there are some tea shops. From Lakeside, allow two to 2½ hours to walk to Pame. From here cross the suspension bridge and path to **Margi** village, then the trail to **Pumdi**, **Lukunswara** and finally the **World Peace Pagoda**.

Alternatively, returning to the 'crossroad' of paths, the trail veers southwest and goes across two small rivers (cross with care) and continues at some distance from the lake. These are crossings on log bridges and it can be very marshy so be careful. **Note** This is not recommended during or after the rainy season.

After 1 km the path begins its ascent up the southern ridge, passing through attractive and at times dense woodland, home to wild deer and a variety of birdlife, including pheasants and parakeets. This is a steep climb of almost 2 km and has worn out even those alleged to be in full fitness. The climb ends at the village of **Pumdi** where you can stop for tea. The path then follows along the ridge. From here you get outstanding views of the mountains from Dhaulagiri right across the Annapurnas, and of much of the Pokhara Valley.

From the Peace Pagoda a wooded descent to the east brings you to **Damside** about 100 m south of the dam. Turn left when you meet the road to bring you onto the main road through Damside and back to Lakeside.

Alternatively you can get rowed across the lake and climb to the pagoda for dawn, and walk back along one of the two above options.

Trekking in the
Annapurnas

The Annapurna region, situated to the north of Pokhara, is the most popular trekking area in Nepal. Originally protected in 1986 through the Annapurna Conservation Area Project (ACAP), it has grown to 7629 sq km and offers a huge variety of landscape, flora, fauna and culture. As well as containing over 100 types of mammal, it is home to 475 bird species and 1226 flowering plants, including 40 species of orchid and nine rhododendrons.

It is centred on the Annapurna Himal, a horseshoe of peaks including Annapurna I (8061 m) and, standing forward of the other peaks, is the beautiful Machapuchare (6997 m), Fishtail Mountain. The region contains the deepest gorge in the world, the highest freshwater lake in the world and the largest rhododendron forest in the world.

The area is also home to over 100,000 people drawn from several different ethnic groups with varying cultures and religions. Its northern areas, populated by the Thakali and Manange, are Tibetan in origin, Buddhist and traditionally traders by profession. The south is dominated by Gurung, Magars, Chettri and Bahuns (Hill Brahmins) who are Hindu and farm the more fertile terraced foothills.

Trekking options range from gentle foothill walks to viewpoints with excellent views of the high mountains from Dhaulagiri to Manaslu, to high-altitude passes and trekking peaks. It includes the once-forbidden high-altitude Kingdom of Mustang and the sacred Hindu shrine at Muktinath.

ON THE ROAD

The Thakalis

Traditionally subsistence farmers, the Thakalis have cashed in on the trekking boom since the 1980s by establishing many of the small lodges and shops that line the main trails of the Annapurna region.

They have had a virtual monopoly on this lucrative trade. The secret of their success lies in a system of communal investment (*dighur*) where family members and friends pool a fixed amount of money per person and give the total to one among them. The recipient can use it at his own discretion and his only obligation is to contribute to the *dighur*. When everyone has received their lump sum, the group is dissolved. The system is based on trust and encourages individualism, giving the person enough capital to achieve their ambition.

Thakalis are related to the Magars, Tamangs and Gurungs, and their religion is a mixture of Hinduism, Buddhism, shamanism and animism. In this they differ from their Tibetan-related neighbours in Mustang.

Their sturdy houses are built with flat stones cemented together with clay. They cultivate barley and potatoes, an indication of the severity of the climate and their flat roofs are used for drying grain and hay. Yaks are good grazing livestock and the milk is drunk and made into cheese, while yak hides and coarse wool are also used for clothing. Juniper is often used for tea.

The road to Jomsom

one of the world's most incredible roads

Over the last few years a road has been completed all the way to Jomsom, at the top of the Kali Gandaki river valley. This route used to be the second half of the Annapurna Circuit trek but the trail has now been rerouted to the east side of the Kali Gandaki river to avoid the traffic. On the plus side the road has opened up many trekking possibilities as you can now drive to trailheads that previously were many days' walk away. The road is still prone to landslides but it is generally reliable. You do sometimes need to walk across sections of damaged road and then pick up another vehicle on the other side, especially during or after monsoon.

You still need to get your ACAP permit and TIMS cards. It's best (and cheaper) to get these in Kathmandu or Pokhara before settling out. There are checkpoints for both: TIMS in Tatopani, the ACAP in Ghasa, Jomsom and the Manang Valley.

The road north from Pokhara passes through numerous villages and settlements. The road is in good(ish) repair until **Beni**, about 80 km from Pokhara, three to four hours by car. Above this the road deteriorates, with the 25 km to **Tatopani** taking at least two hours. One good thing is that you won't be bored as the scenery is stunning.

Between Tatopani and **Marpha** the road cuts through the deepest gorge in the world, some 6500 m deep when measured from the summits of Dhauligiri I and Annapurna I (set 38 km apart) to the valley floor. The scenery slowly becomes more arid, the lush forests of the lower valley turning into a wide, stark riverbed and zones of high-altitude desert as you cut through the Himalaya and enter the rainshadow area of Marpha, Tukache and Jomsom.

Tatopani

In the 1980s Tatopani was a popular stop on the Annapurna Circuit. 'Tato' means hot and 'pani' water. For most trekkers it was the first water they'd seen for two weeks. The **hot springs** ⓘ *US$0.90 entry fee*, from which the village takes its name emerge beside the Kali Gandaki river in two stone enclosures. Before the tanks were built bathers had to stand in the river where the hot spring water and icy river water mixed to a pleasant temperature, a balancing act that usually led to one scalded leg and one numb one.

Tatopani is where trekkers on the Annapurna Circuit prepare for the climb to **Ghorepani** (meaning 'horse water' – a stopping point for traders on the old trade route); at 1800 m it's the longest climb on the whole route. For visitors from Pokhara it is a weekend break to enjoy the mountain scenery and hot springs.

Marpha

You know you are approaching the small town of Marpha when you see orchards of fruit trees appearing by the road. These are the result of a 1960s project to discover cash crops

Trekking the Annapurnas

Treks		
	Poon Hill & Gandruk	
·········· Circuit	▪ ▪ ▪ ▪ Khopra	
▪ ▪ ▪ ▪ Sanctuary	·········· Jomsom	

that the inhabitants could grow. Such was its success that you can now buy apple brandy in supermarkets in Kathmandu. They also produce peach and apricot varieties.

The town itself is centred on an atmospheric cobbled high street, the squat stone houses squeezed around it to keep the strong prevailing winds at bay. This is a traditional style used in the area, very different from the lowland architecture but making use of local materials to deal with the harsh conditions. There are small lanes and alleys darting off, piles of stacked firewood and chickens wandering around.

If you break your journey here, and in many ways it's a more interesting and traditional place than Jomsom, there are several walks to do. The **Samtenling Gompa**, renovated in 1996, is worth visiting especially during the **Mani Rimbu festival** held every autumn. You can also visit the site of the old village or just climb the valley edge for views of the town.

Jomsom

Daily flights from Pokhara to Jomsom, landing at the small airstrip to the southwest of town, offer a quicker way of getting to the area's main town than driving or walking.

The town itself is the administrative centre of the area and really a gateway to other places rather than an attraction in itself. Most of the hotels and restaurants are near the airport, as well as the bus station.

If you have a little spare time then visit the **Mustang Eco Museum** ⓘ *Tue-Sun 1000-1700, Fri 1000-1500, winter 1000-1600, US$0.90*. Also take a look at the old **wooden bridge** across the Kali Gandaki, damaged in the 2015 earthquake but now restored.

Muktinath

Muktinath's shrines are some of the holiest places in the Hindu world. They include the **Jwalamai Temple**, home to the eternal flames – small, natural escapes of gas that burn constantly. There is also a **Vishnu Temple** and a **Buddhist Gompa**, leading to a happy mix of Buddhist and Hindu pilgrims wandering around. For more details, see www.muktinath.org.

You can get to Muktinath from Jomsom in under two hours in a 4WD (US$7) along a bumpy road. You are dropped at the small town of **Ranipauwa** and walk from

> **Tip...**
> Be careful with altitude: Jomsom is at 2765 m and Muktinath at 3800 m. It makes an excellent acclimatization day trip there and back if you plan to go higher.

ON THE ROAD

The first ascent of Annapurna

Annapurna was the first of the 14 8000-m peaks to be climbed. A French expedition, led by Maurice Herzog, arrived in Nepal in April 1950. As the country was still officially closed to foreigners – they had received special permission from the Rana rulers – the Europeans knew nothing about either Dhaulagiri or Annapurna. They spent the better part of a month reconnoitring the Dhaulagiri massif before giving up. "Dhaulagiri – one of the team wrote later – isn't just difficult, it's impassable. I never want to set foot on that mountain again."

They settled on Annapurna which proved almost as challenging. Herzog and his companion Lachenal opted for light boots to make a quick dash for the summit of Annapurna I. The two summiteers suffered appalling frostbite – Hertzog lost all his toes and most of his fingers. It then took two weeks to descend and they only made it thanks to the help of their Sherpa porters and team. It was still a stunning achievement with no oxygen used and was the only 8000-m peak successfully climbed at the first attempt. No one else got to the summit until 1970.

there. There is nowhere to stay in Muktinath itself, unless you are a sadhu, but there are a number of hotels around the bus stop.

Kagbeni

The atmospheric village of Kagbeni is on the trail to Mustang, as far as you are allowed to go without a special permit. It has a medieval feel with narrow streets, small alleys, tightly packed houses and small chorterns, all protected by little clay effigies of the village protectors that dot the village. Looming above the village is the **Kagchode Thubten Sampheling Gompa** ① *0600-1800, US$1.80*, founded in 1429 and worth a visit to see some of the old artifacts on display, including some centuries-old religious texts.

To get there you can either walk the 10 km upstream from Jomson, or pay for a ride in one of the 4WD taxis. Leave early as an afternoon wind blows up the valley from late morning.

Listings The road to Jomsom

Where to stay

Tatopani
There are many lodges to stay at, most comfortable and with varied and tasty menus.

$ Dhaulagiri Lodge
T974-1194872.
Near to the springs, with lovely gardens, comfortable rooms and a great restaurant, this is the pick of the lodges.

Marpha

$ Neeru Guest House
T985-765 0489, www.hrikamala@yahoo.com.
Set in the old town, this is one of several inexpensive places to stay, with the rooms arranged around a nice garden. The food is excellent and the hospitality of the owners second to none.

Jomsom
There are plenty of places to stay.

ON THE ROAD
Annapurna Conservation Area Project

Due to the number of visitors, the standard of lodges is excellent on many of the routes, all hopefully abiding by the policies of ACAP about the use of kerosene to cook, solar power to heat and hygienic waste management. Some are obviously better that others so check the lodge facilities before booking in and, if necessary, vote with your feet.

The ACAP project has been a success and a pioneer in the conservation of inhabited areas. It is not directly government managed or funded but is authorized to charge an entrance fee. This is used to develop both conservation projects within the area as well as development initiatives for the local communities. What makes the area so different is that local people are still allowed to live and own property, maintaining their traditional rights to natural resources and lifestyle. They are governed by rules as to how they look after visitors and dispose of rubbish. In effect, the residents are responsible for policing the area and as they benefit from the money that tourism brings into their remote communities, it is they who have the greatest interest in protecting both the environment and the creatures that live within it.

To allow this to be achieved more effectively, ACAP is divided into seven conservation offices so that each can focus on specific issues affecting one small area, rather than be governed by one 'cover all' approach. To the north are **Jomsom**, **Manang** and **Lo-Manthang** located in the Trans-Himalayan region, and to the south are **Bhujing**, **Sikles**, **Ghandruk** and **Lwang**.

The focus of Jomsom, Manang and Ghandruk, the most popular trekking areas, is integrated tourism management and development activities to benefit the local communities and environment. In Bhujing, Sikles and Lwang the focus is on eradicating poverty through agriculture development and agro-forestry.

There are also issues that can be highlighted in just one or two areas. Upper Mustang, which came under the jurisdiction of ACAP in 1992, works on controlled tourism on a sustainable basis, and heritage conservation in an area that is culturally fragile. This is done by charging a high fee and thus limiting access. Some policies are implemented uniformly throughout the area, especially education on the benefits and practical policies for conservation of the environment. It is a model that has been used elsewhere in Nepal and studied by many countries around the world.

Om's Home
T069-440042, www.omshomejomsom.com.
One of the nicest options in Jomsom, Om's Home has clean, comfortable en suite rooms, a great restaurant and is well located around a pleasant courtyard with excellent café.

Kagbeni

$ Red House Lodge
T993-691011.

This basic lodge is set in an atmospheric 350-year-old house, complete with its own Buddha statue and prayer wheels. There's also a good roof terrace.

$ Shangri-la
T984-1163727.
A more comfortable option.

ON THE ROAD

Mustang's last mountain monarch

Logyalpo Jigme Palbar, the last Rajah of Mustang, is far removed from most people's image of royalty. He was born in 1932, the 25th in a line of kings of the Palbar dynasty which ruled Mustang from the 14th century. He became king in 1964 when his father died, shortly after the death of his elder brother. He remained king until the monarchy was abolished in 2008, ruling with his nephew for the last few years. When approached by the government to step down he agreed immediately to become a private citizen. Although his duties were mainly ceremonial, he remained the highest authority in this remote region and was regularly called upon by his subjects to offer royal counsel or to arbitrate in disputes.

Mustang's historical isolation has given this tiny ex-kingdom a unique character, one in which the monarch is still strongly identified with and respected by many of his people. He lived in the four-storeyed palace dominating Lomanthang, the main settlement of just over 1000 people. Following a breakfast of Tibetan bread and *sojapurja* (tea churned with butter and salt), the king busied himself with daily administrative tasks until lunch at noon, which usually consisted of *dal-bhad-tarkari*, eaten from low, ornately carved tables brought by his ancestors from Tibet.

Having married Sahiba Sidol Palbar Bista, a Tibetan royal, in 1950, he opposed the Chinese occupation of Tibet. In the 1960s he allowed Tibetan Khampa warriors, trained by the CIA, to use Mustang as a base for attacks on Chinese troops in Tibet. Afterwards he spent much of his reign fighting to preserve the unique culture of his tiny kingdom. It was he who imposed a limit of 1000 visitors per year, a limit that still applies.

Luxury trekking

comfy beds and en suites

These days it's possible to trek in the Annapurnas in a degree of luxury that early explorers such as Maurice Hertzog (see box, page 240) could only dream off. Luxury lodges and hotels are dotted along the main routes, with warm, comfortable en suite rooms, lovely gardens and public areas such as lounges and dining rooms warmed by roaring fires. They may not be true luxury, when compared to the standard of properties elsewhere in the world, but they are a huge improvement on the shared facilities of the old teahouses.

Ker & Downey ($$$, T01-4435686, www.keranddowneynepal.com, with offices in Kathmandu and Pokhara) is the oldest chain. They have six lodges in the southern Annapurna foothills, as well as one beside the Seti river and one at Bandipur. You can either stay at one of their lodges for a few nights, doing day walks, or trek from lodge to lodge guided by one of their Sherpas and with local porters carrying your luggage. All the lodges are built in lovely locations, it's a great option for those who want to get into the mountains proper but don't want to rough it.

Lodge Thasang Village ($$$, T019-446514, www.lodgethasangvillage.com), is another similar property that sits on a ridge above the village of Thasang, on the way to Martha. Offering great views of, amongst others, Dhaulagiri, it is somewhere to stay and explore the local area on foot or by 4WD.

TREKKING ITINERARIES

★ Annapurna Circuit

You have to be fit to undertake this arduous but popular trip. The circuit is best done anti-clockwise so as to be better acclimatized for the crossing of the **Thorung La Pass** (5410 m). The trek used to take three weeks, but with road development up the Manang and Kali Gandaki valleys, the heart of the trek can now be done in 12 days. It can always be extended by adding days at the end if you trek out via Ghorepani and Ghankdruk.

Days 12 days   **Highest point** Thorung La (5416 m)   **Trek type** Lodge

Days	Itinerary	Altitude	Duration
Day 01	Drive to Besisahar. Local jeep to Jagat.	1300 m	7 hours
Day 02	Tal	1700 m	6 hours
Day 03	Timang	2270 m	7 hours
Day 04	Chame	2670 m	5 hours
Day 05	Pisang	3200 m	4 hours
Day 06	Braga	3360 m	3 hours
Day 07	Rest day in Braga	3360 m	
Day 08	Yak Kharka	4018 m	4 hours
Day 09	Phedi	4450 m	4 hours
Day 10	Cross Thorung La (5416 m) to Muktinath	3760 m	8 hours
Day 11	Jomsom	2720 m	3 hours
Day 12	Fly Jomsom–Pokhara (or trek back down the Kali Gandaki Valley)	1400 m	

Annapurna Sanctuary/Base Camp

You can trek into the heart of the horseshoe-shaped Annapurna massif by following the narrow valley of the **Modi Khola**. Machapuchare towers to the east and you must be careful of the conditions as avalanches are not infrequent during the spring. In the sanctuary you can visit the Machapuchare and Annapurna I base camps.

Days 12 days   **Highest point** 4130 m   **Trek type** Lodge or camping

Days	Itinerary	Altitude	Duration
Day 01	Drive to Nayapul and trek to Tikhedunga	1540 m	4 hours
Day 02	Tikhedunga to Ghorepani	2860 m	7 hours
Day 03	Ghorepani to Tadapani	2630 m	6 hours
Day 04	Tadapani to Chomrung	2170 m	6 hours
Day 05	Chomrung to Dovan	2600 m	6 hours
Day 06	Dovan to Deurali	3200 m	5 hours
Day 07	Deurali to MBC	3700 m	4 hours
Day 08	Hike to ABC and camp at MBC	3700 m	3 hours
Day 09	MBC to Bamboo	2310 m	6 hours
Day 10	Bamboo to Sinuwa	1784 m	5 hours
Day 11	Sinuwa to Tolka	1700 m	5 hours
Day 12	Tolka to Kande and drive to Pokhara	900 m	4 hours

TREKKING ITINERARIES

★ Poon Hill and Ghandruk

One of the most popular short treks, visiting the most famous Himalaya viewpoint. The start and finish points are easily accessible from Pokhara. It gets very busy during the peak seasons. From Poon Hill at dawn/dusk you can enjoy uninterrupted views of Dhauligiri and Annapurna. The rhododendrons are magnificent in spring.

Days 5 days **Highest point** 3210 m **Trek type** Lodge

Days	Itinerary	Altitude	Duration
Day 01	Drive to Nayapul. Trek to Tikhedunga	1570 m	3 hours
Day 02	Ghorepani	2840 m	5 hours
Day 03	Hike up to Poon Hill (3210 m). Trek to Tadapani	2610 m	6 hours
Day 04	Ghandruk	1940 m	4 hours
Day 05	Trek to Nayapul (1010 m). Drive to Pokhara.		

Khopra Trek

There are plenty of trekking options in this area that has been largely overlooked in the past. Pretty villages, great viewpoints and stunning scenery as you trek through the Annapurna foothills with big peaks towering overhead. It's a good area for community homestays and there are several schemes running in the area (http://nepaltrek.wix.com/nepalcommunitytrek). Book in advance.

Days 9 days **Highest point** 3670 m **Trek type** Camping, lodge or community

Days	Itinerary	Altitude	Duration
Day 01	Drive to Dimuwa and camp at Thulo Chaur	1785 m	5 hours
Day 02	Jogikuti	2900 m	6 hours
Day 03	Tin Pokhari	3000 m	5 hours
Day 04	Swanta (hike to Punhill, 3210 m)	2650 m	7 hours
Day 05	Dhankharka (Shistibang)	3050 m	5 hours
Day 06	Khopra	3670 m	4 hours
Day 07	Rest day (hike to lake, 3935 m)		
Day 08	Narchaeng Lake	2100 m	6 hours
Day 09	Narcheng Besi (Tatopani). Drive to Pokhara.	900 m	2 hours

TREKKING ITINERARIES

★ Mustang Conservation Area

The 'forbidden' kingdom of Mustang was opened to the outside world in 1992, allowing visitors for the first time in recent history to visit it and La Manthang, its capital dating back to the 15th century. It became a dependent territory of the Shah kings in the 18th century and its last King Jigme Dorje Palbar Bista only lost his title when Nepal became a republic in 2008.

Known as the former Kingdom of La, it is situated along the north central border of Nepal, north of the main range of the Himalaya in the upper reaches of Mustang District. Lo and Baragaon, the area directly to its south, both fall within Upper Mustang and are one of the most dramatic and stunning areas of the Himalaya.

The people of Upper Mustang are called Bhotias, while those from Lo are called Lobas. They speak various Tibetan dialects. Historically, their art and culture flourished due to contact with traders, monks and religious masters passing between Tibet and India, Ladakh and Bhutan.

The climate and geography of Upper Mustang are almost identical to those of Western Tibet and, as such, are dramatically different from the temperate and tropical areas of Nepal on the south side of the Himalaya. The dry, windswept ecology of this Trans-Himalayan region is extremely fragile. With very few trees, wood is virtually non-existent and water is scarce. The infertile land doesn't produce enough food while the grasslands support only limited livestock.

Mustang Trek

Days 13 days   **Highest point** Charang (3960 m)   **Trek type** Camping

Days	Itinerary	Altitude	Duration
Day 01	Fly Pokhara–Jomsom. Kagbeni	2810 m	3 hours
Day 02	Samar	3660 m	6 hours
Day 03	Ghiling	3570 m	5 hours
Day 04	Ghami	3520 m	5 hours
Day 05	Charang	3960 m	5 hours
Day 06	Lo Manthang	3810 m	4 hours
Day 07	Lo Chosar-Lo Manthang	3810 m	
Day 08	Dhakmar via Ghar gumba (3950 m)	3820 m	7 hours
Day 09	Shyangmochen	3800 m	6 hours
Day 10	Chusang (visit caves on the way)	2980 m	7 hours
Day 11	Muktinath (high route)	3760 m	8 hours
Day 12	Jomsom	2720 m	3 hours
Day 13	Fly Jomsom–Pokhara		

It's best to leave a spare day in your itinerary in case of flight delays which are not uncommon. If the cloud comes down, the flights don't fly.

Chitwan & Central Terai

land of the tiger and birthplace of the Buddha

Forty years ago the Terai area of Nepal was a jungle wilderness, home only to the Tharu people who had a natural resistance to the endemic malaria that ravaged the area.

The discovery and widespread use of DDT meant that malaria was eradicated and led to the migration of people from the mountains to the fertile land and easier terrain. What used to be forests roamed by tigers, elephants and rhino has now become wide expanses of paddy fields, dotted by small villages and homesteads.

Happily the king recognized the threat to the region's wildlife and in 1973 created Chitwan National Park, the most famous tiger reserve in Nepal. It was based around his old hunting reserve, and his jungle palace and hunting lodge can still be seen on the northern fringe of the park. Visitors have a great chance of seeing the endangered Asian rhino, as well as sloth bears and, for the lucky few, a glimpse of a leopard or tiger.

The other big draw of the Central Terai is Lumbini, located close to the Indian border. It was here that Siddhartha or the Buddha was born and it is a place that attracts hundreds of thousands of pilgrims every year.

Get away from the main east–west highway and the few other surfaced roads and you can explore the rural way of life that permeates this picturesque and sleepy backwater.

Best for
Birdwatching ▪ Buddha ▪ Rural life ▪ Wildlife

Footprint
picks

★ **Chitwan National Park**, page 250
Your chance to go in search of tigers, rhinos and wild elephants.

★ **Tansen**, page 266
Traditional hill town with great mountain views.

★ **Lumbini**, page 271
The birthplace of Buddha and fascinating place of worship for
Buddhists worldwide.

Essential Chitwan and Central Terai

Finding your feet

Most people arrive in the Central Terai by road, coming from either Kathmandu or Pokhara on the Mugling road. This clings to the side of the Trisuli river valley as it cuts its way through the hills to the plains. It's twisting and narrow although currently being upgraded to widen and straighten it as much as possible in a project financed by the World Bank. You can also fly to Bharatpur, about 45 minutes from the national park.

From Pokhara it's also possible to follow the Siddhartha Highway which heads south, via the small mountain town of Tansen to the plains. This is a good option if you wish to visit Lumbini.

Getting around

There are plenty of local buses regularly plying the routes between all the main towns and attractions. You can also hire taxis and, for shorter journeys, rickshaws, at cheaper rates than in Kathmandu and Pokhara.

This area is a great place to hire bikes and head off into the countryside. It's flat, but the roads are unsurfaced meaning that what little traffic there is goes (comparatively) slowly.

In Chitwan you can travel by safari vehicle, canoe, on foot or by elephant.

Pokhara

Tansen ⭐2

Butwal

Tilottama ○

Lumbini ⭐3 ○

Ramgram ○

Devachuli ○ Gaindakot ○

Kawasoti ○ ○Narayangkhar

Piple ○

Kudiya ○

⭐◆ *Chitwan National Park*

Birgunj ○

Raxaul ○ Bazaar

INDIA

N

20 km
20 miles

Footprint picks
1 **Chitwan National Park**, page 250
2 **Tansen**, page 266
3 **Lumbini**, page 271

Weather Chitwan National Park

January	February	March	April	May	June
22°C	25°C	31°C	33°C	35°C	33°C
8°C	10°C	15°C	20°C	23°C	26°C
20mm	10mm	20mm	40mm	70mm	200mm

July	August	September	October	November	December
32°C	32°C	31°C	30°C	26°C	23°C
26°C	26°C	25°C	20°C	13°C	8°C
430mm	270mm	250mm	100mm	0mm	0mm

When to go

Year-round temperatures are hotter in the Terai than the hills, affected by the same weather patterns but without the cooling altitude. During the monsoon of June to early September it is very hot and humid with frequent heavy rain. It is also very green, with the main rice crop coming through in the fields and a real jungle lushness everywhere. The autumn months of October and November are a great time to visit, pleasantly hot days, warm evenings and, being post-monsoon, less dust and pollution in the air. December and January are slightly cooler and it can be cloudy with some rainfall. The spring months of February to May are also a pleasant time, although the heat and humidity do build once more as the monsoon approaches.

Time required

To visit Chitwan you need at least two nights. Game viewing is best in the early morning and late afternoon when the animals are at their most active and therefore visible, so two nights will allow you to do four activities. If you want to see a tiger then stay longer as they are very hard to spot. It takes patience. The best way is to sit and wait at a place where they like to cross a river. It is also advisable to spend a night at Lumbini.

Chitwan
National Park

★ At the heart of the Terai region, Chitwan is the oldest and best known of Nepal's jungle reserves. The park itself covers 932 sq km and consists of swamp, tall elephant grass and dense forest. It is a natural habitat for the tiger, great one-horned Indian rhinoceros, leopard, gaur, sloth and wild bear, sambar, hog and barking deer, civet, mongoose and otter.

Formerly, the Chitwan Valley was renowned for big game hunting and was, until 1950, exclusively managed as a private reserve for the Rana prime ministers and their guests. In 1963, the area south of Rapti was demarcated as a rhinoceros sanctuary and then in 1970 King Mahendra approved, in principle, the creation of the national park. It was finally established in 1973 to preserve a unique ecosystem and help save the Bengal tiger and the one-horned rhino from extinction. It was made a UNESCO World Heritage Site in 1986.

Essential Chitwan National Park

Finding your feet

Chitwan lies 120 km southwest of Kathmandu and a similar distance to the southeast of Pokhara. There are flights from Kathmandu to Bharatpur, near Narayanghat and a short drive to the park. There are bus services from both Kathmandu and Pokhara, mostly on surfaced roads; tourist services are direct; local buses involve a change at Narayanghat.

Visitors tend to stay either in the small town of Sauraha, with its plentiful small hotels and guides, or at one of the resort hotels dotted along the park fringe. Since 2011 there are no lodges in the park itself, the government refusing to renew their leases saying that their presence disturbed the wildlife. The situation may change again in the next few years and several of the properties, including the iconic **Tiger Tops Lodge**, are being maintained in the meantime and make excellent picnic spots.

Getting around

Trips into the park have to be organized with an authorized guide or tour operator. The most popular ways to visit are by jeep, canoe or on a walking safari. The walking safaris can be up to five days long, and involve staying in overnight shelters. Most of the private lodges include activities, permits and fees within their prices. In Sauraha there are plenty of guides and travel agents offering a whole array of activities.

When to go

The months between October and March when it is pleasantly warm and there is little rainfall have the best weather. However, elephant grass which covers significant areas of the park, grows high from the onset of the monsoon and provides cover for many of the park's animals. In late January, a fortnight is given over to local people to cut the grass inside the park – this is used for thatching and fodder. Your best chance of sighting rhinos, tigers, leopards and other animals is therefore from mid-February onwards. The spring begins in March and it steadily warms until summer days are typically an average 30°C. Monsoon starts in July when it is hot and humid. The rising river levels make it all but impossible to tour the park by jeep and again the tall grass reduces the chances of seeing a rhino.

Park information

Entry fee is US$16 per day. Valid for one day plus two days' access to adjacent community forests.

The **National Park Headquarters** (T056-521 9320) are inside the park, over a bridge from Kasara. There is a small visitor centre. See also www.chitwannationalpark.gov.np.

ON THE ROAD
Jungle talk

Evocative, immortalized by Kipling and now widely used to describe realms as diverse as urban morass and legal double-talk (as well as tracts of dense forest vegetation) the word 'jungle' first entered the English language between 1770 and 1780. Anglicized by early European colonists in India, the word is a derivation of the Hindi word *jangal* or the Prakit word *jangala*, meaning a rough, waterless place.

Flora and environment

The park's vegetation is characterized by tropical to subtropical forest, dominated by sal (*Shorea robusta*). Nearly a quarter of its area is tall grassland and, in the lower wetter areas, riverine forest with flowering species including the sissoo (*Dalburghia sissoo*), silk cotton tree (*Bombax ceiba*) and flame of the forest (*Butea monosperma*). These beautiful trees bloom from January until the early spring, the large, bright red blossoms of the silk cotton tree (or simal) being especially conspicuous.

The grasslands form a diverse and complex community with about 60 species. The *Sacchrum* species, often called elephant grass, can reach 8 m in height. The shorter grasses such as *Imperata* are useful for thatching.

Wildlife

Chitwan is home to the tiger, leopard, one-horned rhino, sloth bear, gaur buffalo and Asian elephant. The most common sightings for most visitors to the park are rhino and deer – including the swamp deer (*Cervus davaucels*), spotted deer or chital (*Axis axis*), barking deer (*Muntiacus mutiak*) and hog deer. They are often found in herds of up to 100 or more. These elegant animals are important prey species of both the tiger and leopard and usually feed around the forest margins.

Chitwan National Park

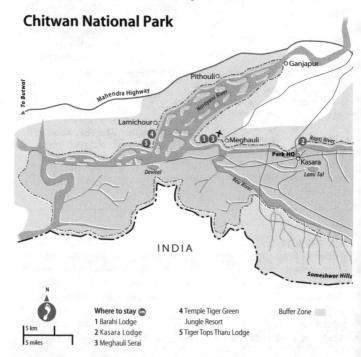

Where to stay
1 Barahi Lodge
2 Kasara Lodge
3 Meghauli Serai
4 Temple Tiger Green Jungle Resort
5 Tiger Tops Tharu Lodge

Buffer Zone

The park's rivers and swampy areas are home to various reptiles including two important species of crocodile: the marsh mugger (*Crocodilus palustris*) and the gharial (*Gavialis gangeticus*). The gharial, which can grow up to 5 m in length, is a fish eater and the destruction of its riverside habitat and of the Terai forest from the 1950s seriously threatened its eradication from Nepal. Their numbers have increased in Chitwan since the establishment of a conservation project in the late 1970s.

Chitwan provides a natural habitat for over 450 species of bird. There are many seasonal migrants including waterfowl attracted by the rivers and wetlands as well as larger storks, colourful parakeets and kingfishers, various singing and laughing species, and birds of prey. Among the endangered birds found in the park are Bengal florican, giant hornbill, lesser florican, black stork and white stork. A few of the more common birds seen are peafowl, red jungle fowl and different species of egrets, herons, kingfishers, flycatchers and woodpeckers. The best months for birdwatching are March and December.

Community forests

Along the length of Chitwan's western and northern borders lie large tracts of protected jungle called community forests. These were created in 1996 and enclose over 750 sq km of land. Local villagers are allowed to access and use these areas for certain tasks such as collecting firewood (so long as saplings are planted), and cutting tall grasses for both thatching and fodder.

To Mugling, Kathmandu & Pokhara

rayanghat *haratpur*

Tadi Bazaar

Bhandara

Sauraha

To Hetauda

Parsa Wildlife Reserve ◆

Churia Hills

The community forests are designed to create a buffer between the park and the villagers' fields, stopping wild animals from destroying crops and villagers from entering the park and destroying its virgin habitat. They have been very successful and tiger and rhino sightings are not at all unusual. Many lodges offer activities in these forests, including elephant rides, and make a contribution to the community in exchange for this access.

Some community forests enclose areas worthy of national park status. The **Bis Hajaar Tal** (Twenty Thousand Lake) community forest, for example, offers unrivalled birdwatching and covers the country's second largest wetland zone.

ON THE ROAD
The Chitwan Big Five

These are the animals that visitors to Chitwan come to see and it's safe to say that they are generally more elusive than their African Big Five counterparts. They are more secretive, live in a forest and many are active only at night. With patience, time and a good guide you should see some of them.

Bengal tiger The Royal Bengal tiger (*Panthera tigris*) is perhaps the most glamorous – and elusive – of Chitwan's animals. Hunted almost out of existence in their traditional habitat in the forests of the Gangetic plain, the Chitwan tigers are now estimated to number just over 100. Tigers have excellent eyesight and usually feed at night, preying largely on the park's deer. Depending on the terrain and available prey, males command an area of about 50 sq km and females 35 sq km.

Indian elephant The elephants seen by most Chitwan visitors are trained, owned and operated by either the government Elephant Breeding Centre (page 259) or by one of the lodges. A small number of wild Indian elephants (*Elephantus maximus*), however, can sometimes be seen in the eastern part of the park and are occasionally spotted on game drives. They tend to be migratory so at certain times of year they cross the border back into India.

Leopard You have a marginally better chance of seeing a leopard than a tiger, as leopards hunt by day, also preying on deer as well as other smaller mammals. The **common leopard** is mainly seen around the edges of the park, where its territory does not completely overlap with that of the tiger. The rarest sighting is of a **clouded leopard**. Recognizable by the patchwork pattern on its pelt, it was believed to have become extinct in Nepal in the 1850s, but has been back in Chitwan since the 1980s. It is the best climber of all the big cats and sleeps high in trees during the day.

One-horned Indian rhino The great one-horned Indian rhinoceros (*Rhinoceros palustris*) is the world's third largest land mammal and it is estimated that between one-third and a half of Asia's total population is found in Chitwan. During the hot summer months especially, you can see them wading or soaking in the rivers to keep cool. They also enjoy feeding on the weed that grows from the riverbeds and spend quite a lot of time grazing when water levels are low enough.

Sloth bear The sloth bear (*Melursus ursinus*) is probably named after its diet rather than its disposition. It can grow up to 2 m in height, weigh 200 kg and feeds largely on termites and insects, for which it has developed a hooked claw on its front paws to rip into insect nests. There are an estimated 200-250 sloth bears in the park. Mainly nocturnal, they are good climbers and often sleep in the trees where it is safer. They have a shaggy coat and are good swimmers. When they walk they look rather ungainly but don't be fooled as they can run faster than a human.

Jeep safaris

A 4-hr jeep safari costs about US$20, for a seat in a shared jeep. A full-day excursion costs about US$230 for the vehicle, with a maximum of 8-10 passengers.

Jeep safaris are the most popular way of exploring Chitwan and they are available from most lodges and tour operators. Depending on where you are staying, the jeeps are either kept in the park with you getting a boat across the river at the start and finish of the trip, or you are picked up from your lodge and driven into the park. Either way it is an adventure.

The excursions usually start at dawn as this is the best time to see the animals, before it gets too hot and they find shelter from the heat of the day. It is a beautiful time, with mist hanging over water and the light slowly growing to reveal the jungle. When you stop the engine at a viewpoint the sound of the jungle waking up is memorable, straight out of Kipling's *Jungle Book*.

There is a network of tracks through the park that the vehicles must keep to and various viewing platforms where you can get out and climb. These give a bird's eye view over open grassland areas and river courses and sometimes you'll meet rangers and soldiers on anti-poaching watch. They do a great job – 2015 was a zero-poaching year.

Some jeep trips just have a driver guide, others have a driver and a guide. The latter is preferable as the thick vegetation within the park means that a guide who is just concerned with spotting is much more likely to see the animals and birds.

You can book a morning trip, which last about three or four hours or a full-day trip with packed lunch. The full day gives you a better chance of seeing a tiger, as the best way of achieving this is to park near a known river crossing and wait for the tiger to come to you.

Boat trips

A canoe safari of 8-10 km costs about US$7 for a seat in a shared canoe. You don't have to paddle.

Canoeing along the Rapti or Narayani rivers is a popular way of seeing the wildlife and birds of Chitwan. The canoes are made from the hollowed trunk of the silk cotton tree, normally paddled by two boatmen, one in the bow and one in the stern. You sit on small folding chairs with no legs so are close to the water.

The great joy is the tranquillity. With no engine chugging away you are able to hear the sounds of the park, a constant backdrop of insects and birds. Because you move so silently you get to see wildlife that otherwise would have heard you coming and hidden. It's not unusual to get great sightings of rhinos, in the river to feed on the weed, and if you are very lucky a tiger or leopard coming to drink. You can also get good, and very close, sightings of the gharial and marsh mugger crocodiles.

An excellent time to enjoy a boat trip is late afternoon as the animals start to stir after the heat of the day and come to the water to drink. Some trips finish with a sundowner drink on the banks of the river. It is not considered safe to canoe during the monsoon when river levels are high; and in spring, when levels are at their lowest, you may have to get out and push part of the way.

Walking safaris

A half-day jungle walk costs about US$10, a full-day trip is about US$20. If you want to go with a private guide you will need to negotiate, but prices are not that much more and you'll get a quieter experience, escaping the sound of other people's camera shutters blasting away.

Walking in Chitwan National Park will undoubtedly enable you to get up close to the forest and its life. Walkers should always be accompanied by a qualified and experienced guide, preferably two. All guides are required by law to be insured. Use only officially licensed guides.

It is important to take your guide's advice as to where to go and where not to go, especially when the vegetation is sufficiently high to hide a rhino or any other animal which may not appreciate your presence in its vicinity. There are obviously risks involved and although incidents are relatively rare, they do happen and occasionally end in fatalities. See Tiger attack, page 330.

Elephant rides
An elephant safari costs about US$15.

There is debate about whether these captive animals should be used for giving rides. One lodge – **Tiger Tops** (see page 260) – has ceased giving rides on their elephants, one of the largest private herds, and instead have opened a dedicated elephant camp at which you feed and help look after the animals for the duration of your stay. Many Western operators no longer offer the rides as part of their programmes, acknowledging that it is not a practice to be encouraged.

Fact...
The World Elephant Polo Championships take place every year, although it's uncertain how long this will continue.

The government owns a large herd of elephants. These are not currently used to give rides but to do maintenance work and carry out anti-poaching duties within the park. Private herds owned by some of the lodges still offer rides – check before you book. There are also elephants in Sauraha (see page 258); you see them chained in their camps as you walk through town.

Elephant rides used to be a popular and in many ways are the best method of game-viewing in Chitwan. High on the back of an elephant you can see over the tall grasses and have a good chance of getting close to the wild animals. But elephants were banned from entering the national park itself in 2011, the government citing the presence of tuberculosis in some domesticated elephants as a possible source of infection for the wildlife. However, they are still allowed in the adjoining community forests.

Sitting in a *hauda*, a box-like cushioned platform seating about four people, the *phanit*, or driver, has a number of commands which the elephant understands, but he also controls and disciplines the animal by striking its head with a metal bar, a seemingly barbaric action which, so the *phanit* maintains, is more painful to the eyes of the onlooker than to the elephant. In total there are just over 100 domesticated elephants around Chitwan, compared to a wild elephant population of somewhere around 150.

Tip...
If you want to get up close to an elephant but don't want to ride one, then the elephant bath time and breeding centre, both in Sauraha are great opportunities (see pages 258 and 259).

ON THE ROAD
Hunting in Chitwan

Chitwan's wildlife has always been a big draw although previously it was for very different reasons than today. From the late 19th century, the Rana prime ministers held Chitwan as their private hunting reserve.

Groups would leave Kathmandu en masse to spend weeks stalking and shooting for leisure, and newly stuffed trophies from the expeditions would adorn Kathmandu's palace walls within weeks of their return to the capital, sometimes in an aggressive pose designed to underline the animal's ferocity and reflect the skill and bravery of the hunter.

Although it is easy to condemn from the perspective of contemporary morality, 19th-century hunters were not faced with the dilemma of endangered species and would presumably have justified the pastime as a combination of sport and social responsibility; Chitwan's villagers would have welcomed any effort to combat the menace of large animals who regularly destroyed crops or attacked people.

In a country still suspicious of outside influence, few foreigners were permitted entry. Exceptions were made, however, usually for visiting dignitaries such as European royalty and viceroys of India, but even then they rarely ventured beyond Chitwan. Massive hunting parties were organized, aided by a continuous line of beaters driving the game to wholesale slaughter.

In his first year as monarch, King George V led a party to Chitwan in 1911, the second British royal to visit Nepal after his father who had hunted in the western Terai 35 years earlier. Accorded sumptuous hospitality, while Queen Mary toured the more appropriately genteel attractions of western India and the Taj Mahal, the king's party is said to have shot 37 tigers and eight rhinos.

During his ill-fated tour of the subcontinent in 1921, Edward, Prince of Wales (later Edward VIII) escaped the hostility he faced in India with a trip to Chitwan where his group shot 18 tigers and eight rhinos. The Maharajah of Nepal and his guests, meanwhile, shot a staggering 433 tigers and 53 rhino in the period 1933-1940.

The biggest trip of them all, however, was in 1961 when Queen Elizabeth II and Prince Philip were given a guard of honour of over 400 elephants, trained to raise their trunks as she passed, when they arrived by small plane at Chitwan and were driven to the reserve. An area of 5 ha had been cleared for their Royal Tent, which offered 11 rooms, including a bathroom. Acutely aware of his role in the embryonic World Wildlife Fund, Prince Philip emerged on the day of the hunt with a large bandage around his trigger finger saying he was unable to shoot. The British Foreign Secretary took his place and face was saved all round.

Amaltari

Amaltari is a small Tharu village on the western boundary of the park. It lies on the banks of the Narayani river, about 6 km from the main east–west highway. It is also a base from which to visit the park. You can stay in one of the several luxury lodges here, including some that had to relocate when their leases inside the park were not renewed. Alternatively, there is the successful Tharu homestay project, allowing you to live within the local community, experiencing first hand their traditional lifestyle.

> **Tip...**
> There are far fewer visitors to the western end of the park, and few of the game activities penetrate this far. It is a peaceful and unspoilt experience, worth paying a little extra for.

Kasara

Situated on the northern bank of the Rapti river to the west of Sauraha lies the village of Kasara. It is linked by a bridge to the park's headquarters, as well as the **Gharial Breeding and Conservation Centre** and is the base for the Nepalese army in Chitwan. This was the site of the Old Rana hunting lodge that housed George V plus entourage during their hunting expedition of 1911 (see box, page 257).

The park's headquarters contain a small and rather uninspiring display of Chitwan wildlife. The **Gharial Breeding Centre** ⓘ *open 0600-1800, US$0.90*, is more interesting and you can see the crocodiles at all stages of life. It is reached over a high bridge into the park, offering great views down to the Rapta river and the surrounding grassland. This is a favourite place for rhinos and the sight of them grazing in the mists of early morning is quite wonderful.

Only a handful of lodges and their vehicles use this entrance, which is much quieter than the Sauraha area. Mostly of the lodges are top-end and their prices include all activities. Check when you book.

Sauraha

The majority of visitors stay at Sauraha. This was once a traditional Tharu village, but with the promotion of Chitwan as a major tourist destination it has been rapidly developed into an agglomeration of budget and mid-range hotels and lodges. Electricity was introduced to Sauraha in 1996, but supply can be erratic.

You can see why it has become so popular. Its location on the northern bank of the Rapti river, at a confluence with the smaller Dhungre river, gives great views across into the park and along the river to the west. The river bank has been developed into a lovely spot to sit and relax. There are bars and restaurants with their tables set up on the sandy shore where you can get a pizza, steak or ice cold beer. It's an atmospheric place to watch the sunset, often with animals coming to drink opposite. There are even deckchairs to give it a beach vibe if you fancy a quick sunbathe.

Every morning at 1100 elephants are brought for a bath just east of the main bar area. It's great watching these lovely animals enjoying themselves as they cool off. If you want to get involved and give them a brush you can for US$1.80.

Elephant Breeding Centre
T056-580154, 0600-1800, US$0.50.

This government-run centre is situated at Khorshor, about 32 km to the west of Sauraha. It not only breeds elephants for Chitwan but trains them to work in the national park. As the gestation period lasts for about 23 months, the centre is hardly packed, but there are always a few youngsters there. The best times to go are before 1000 and after 1600 as during the day many of the elephants are out working in the park or community forest areas.

When they are not working, the elephants are kept chained to a central pole. There is pressure from various groups to improve the elephant's conditions, and have them living in stockades rather than being chained. There are just over 100 domesticated elephants in

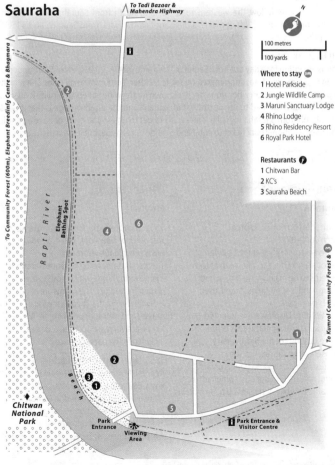

Sauraha

To Tadi Bazaar &
Mahendra Highway

N

100 metres
100 yards

Where to stay 🛏
1 Hotel Parkside
2 Jungle Wildlife Camp
3 Maruni Sanctuary Lodge
4 Rhino Lodge
5 Rhino Residency Resort
6 Royal Park Hotel

Restaurants 🍴
1 Chitwan Bar
2 KC's
3 Sauraha Beach

To Community Forest (600m), Elephant Breeding Centre & Bhagmara

Rapti River

Elephant Bathing Spot

Beach

Chitwan National Park

Park Entrance

Viewing Area

Park Entrance & Visitor Centre

To Kumrol Community Forest & 3

Nepal, compared to a wild population of between 100 and 150 depending on the season and migration habits. It's now illegal to import elephants from India so the breeding centre is important for maintaining the population. The elephants are used in anti-poaching work and play a key role in getting rangers deep into the park.

Baghmara Community Forest

Successfully developed over the last few years as an area promoting environmental regeneration, the Baghmara Community Forest now covers 400 ha to the northwest of Sauraha. It shares its wildlife with Chitwan and is known to have rhinos, leopards, deer, sloth bears, monkeys, wild boar, crocodiles and possibly a few tigers. Some lodges offer elephant rides in the forest. There are a number of pleasant walking opportunities and it takes about five hours to walk around the circumference; but again it is advisable to take a guide.

To get there, follow the western road heading north from Sauraha, then take the second turning on the left. It makes a pleasant half-day walk from Sauraha and a lovely bike ride.

Bij Hazaar Lakes

This is an option for a day out from Sauraha. The name means '20,000 lakes'. Surrounded by an ever-decreasing forest dominated by sal, it is either a group of small lakes or a marshy expanse, depending on when you visit. It is known for the wide variety of birdlife it attracts.

Bij Hazaar is situated to the northwest of Sauraha and the disadvantage is that it is just far enough from Sauraha to make it awkward to get to unless you cycle or have a vehicle. You need a national park ticket to enter and a guide once inside, but it's worth the expense.

Listings Around Chitwan National Park *maps pages 252 and 259.*

Tourist information

Sauraha

Tourist Information Office
Open 0600-1600.
There is a small office at the Chitwan National Park Office to the south of town. It seems to be mainly visited by school groups and is sometimes locked, used as a bicycle park.

A **Wildlife Display**, a few hundred metres to the east of the park office, in the grounds of the **Biodiversity Conservation Centre** has some interesting displays and panels giving useful information but also some rather macabre exhibits of preserved baby animals.

Where to stay

Amaltari

$$$$ Temple Tiger Green Jungle Resort
Just north of Tiger Tops, T01-426 3480,
www.greenjungleresort.com
This comfortable resort is centred around a large roundhouse which houses the restaurant and bar. The rooms are all individual villas, thatched in the local grasses and well appointed inside. All jungle activities are on offer, usually included in the package price.

$$$$ Tiger Tops Tharu Lodge
Near the Narayani river, T01-4411225,
www.tigertops.com.
Chitwan's most famous lodge comprises 2 traditional Tharu-style buildings with rooms as well as a number of safari tents. A lovely garden, with pool, overlooks paddy

fields and is shaded by tall trees. Its nearby elephant camp, with just 6 tents, provides the opportunity to live with and look after elephants, feeding and washing them, and accompanying them as they go out to graze and collect fodder. Superb guides and a lovely atmosphere, it remains one of the places to stay.

$$-$ Homestay

If you want something completely different then it might be worth considering a homestay. There are about 40 houses providing this, under the control of the local Buffer Zone Committee. The idea is that you stay with a local family, eating and living with them in their house. Conditions are very basic but you get the ultimate insight into local culture and discover what a lovely people the Tharu are. It is best to book this through a travel agent in Kathmandu (see page 95) as communication can be difficult. There are plenty who offer it, as do specialist overseas operators.

Kasara

$$$$ Barahi Lodge
On the banks of the Rapti river, T01-441 1113, www.barahijunglelodge.com.
All the cottages have great views out over the river and the park beyond. A super pool sits in front of the dining room and the open terrace also has views to the river. It lies right next to the community forest in one of the best locations of any lodge at Chitwan.

$$$$ Kasara Lodge
A short drive from park headquarters, T01-443757, www.kasararesort.com.
This luxury lodge offers Balinese-style villas, with lots of privacy and great comfort. The restaurant and bar are open-sided, offer great food and have views out over the community forest. There are larger villas with 2 bedrooms and a decent pool. All activities are offered.

$$$$ Meghauli Serai
www.tajhotels.com.
This top-end property is the most luxurious in Chitwan, as you would expect from a Taj group property. Superb villas, breathtaking public areas and perhaps the best infinity pool in Nepal. It even has its own Tharu village where you can eat in the evenings. The Presidential suite will not disappoint.

Sauraha

There is a wide selection of accommodation in Sauraha, from homestays to large, modern resorts. Most of the accommodation is budget but the standards are high. Most of the luxury resorts are not in Sauraha but around the periphery of the park where they have more space and fewer visitors.

$$$ Maruni Sanctuary Lodge
T01-470 0632, www.ktmgh.com.
This comfortable lodge has 31 well-appointed rooms set in pleasant grounds a couple of kilometres east of Sauraha, on the edge of the community forest. Its standards are good and it offers all wildlife activities and good food.

$$ Rhino Residency Resort
Across the road from the National Park Office, T01-442 0431, www.rhino-residency.com.
The Rhino Residency Resort is well located for exploring the park but a couple of minutes' walk away from the bustle of town. The rooms are in 3 circular buildings in a large garden, with pool. Above reception is a decent restaurant.

$$ Rhino Lodge
T056-580065, www.rhinolodge.com.np.
A large, modern hotel in the centre of town, with a lovely garden opening onto a small meadow and the banks of the Rapti river. There's a choice of rooms, all well appointed and comfortable. It's near the elephant bathtime spot so beware of elephants taking a shortcut through the hotel garden in the late morning!

$$ Royal Park Hotel
In the middle of Sauraha, T056-580270, www.royalparkhotel.com.np.
Set in nice grounds, the Royal Park has good comfortable rooms and a very pleasant bar and restaurant. There is a small pool and the property has a nice outdoor feel, with balconies and terraces.

$ Hotel Parkside
A few hundred metres to the east of the National Park Office, T056-580159, www.hotelparkside.com.
The Parkside is a popular resort, with basic but comfortable rooms, a great garden and excellent restaurant. The main building has a great roof terrace with view of the national park (and a distant Annapurna if you get a clear day). Bike hire available.

$ Jungle Wildlife Camp
T056-580093, www.nepaljunglesafari.com.
Modern hotel in the middle of town, situated on the banks of the Rapti. The upper rooms of the new wing have great views over the river and park opposite, as well as the elephant bath-time area. They offer some good-value packages which include activities.

Restaurants

Sauraha
Tours often set off early or get back late so most people find it convenient to eat in their lodges or hotels. If you do want to eat out in Sauraha there are a few options.

$$$ KC's
T985-505 6483, www.kcsrestaurant.com.
This is the best place to eat in town, a branch of the famous Kathmandu restaurant. Set in lovely gardens that run down to the river, you can eat on the terrace or inside the traditional stone and thatch main building. The menu is basically European, and steak is a popular option. It's also a great place for a coffee or cold drink.

$ Chitwan Bar & Restaurant and the **Sauraha Beach Restaurant** both have tables and chairs on the wide sandy bank, the perfect place to enjoy sundowners or an evening meal under the stars.

What to do

Sauraha
Cycle
Sauraha has several cycle hire places, including the lodges themselves. Cycling is not permitted inside the park, but Bij Hazaar Lakes are within cycling distance or you can explore some of the Terai landscape and culture. This is a far better way to see a typical Tharu village than on an organized tour.

Rafting
Several rafting companies operate a package that combines rafting down the Trisuli river with a visit to Chitwan. Most trips start at **Mugling** and finish at **Narayanghat**, and last 2-3 days. Prices vary enormously depending on what is and what is not included. Go with an established and reputable company.

Transport

Kasara
Air
A small private airstrip in the village of **Meghauli**, just north of the Rapti river, is the nearest access but there are currently no scheduled flights; there are rumours they might start soon.

The nearest airport is at **Bharatpur** (see Sauraha, below), from where your lodge will transfer you if you are on a package. If you are in your own vehicle make sure you have good directions, the last few kilometres can get confusing in the maze of local tracks.

Sauraha
Air
There is an airport at **Bharatpur**, near Narayanghat and about 20 km from Sauraha,

which has regular scheduled flights to/from **Kathmandu** with **Yeti** and **Buddha Air**. The flight takes about 30 mins, US$110.

Bus

There are several dedicated **tourist buses** that serve Sauraha. This includes **Greenline**, T01-560126, www.greenline.com.np, which provides services to/from **Pokhara** and **Kathmandu**. The cost is US$20.

Sauraha is well served by public buses that stop at **Tandi Bazaar**, a few kilometres north of town. The journey to **Kathmandu** costs US$4.50, to **Pokhara** US$4, with both journeys taking 5-7 hrs. There are also services to all the main Terai towns. Many hotels will transfer you to/from the bus stand as part of your rate. Otherwise a shared taxi is a few hundred rupees; a shared *tonga* (pony cart) is a bit less.

Parsa Wildlife Reserve

little-visited and remote

This reserve, in an area covering about 500 sq km and bordering Chitwan National Park to the east, is designed to be an uncommercialized and protected sanctuary for the region's wildlife. Not many visitors come here as game-viewing in Chitwan is considered easier and better. In 2015 the reserve was extended by 128 sq km to include the Bara forests, a move that the Zoological Society of London had been campaigning for, and allow prime habitat for up to 40 more tigers.

The rugged Churia hills, with their numerous gullies and dry stream beds and ranging from 750-950 m, run from east to west and dominate the landscape.

The reserve supports a population of resident wild elephant, tiger, leopard, sloth bear, garu, blue bull and wild dog. Other common animals are sambar, chital, hog deer, barking deer, langur, rhesus macaques, striped hyena, ratel, palm civet and jungle cat.

There are nearly 300 recorded species of bird in the reserve. Giant hornbill, one of the endangered species, is found in certain forest patches. Peafowl, red jungle fowl, flycatchers and woodpeckers are a few of the other common birds found in the reserve.

The reserve's office and its entrance is located just off the main road (Tribhuvan Highway) at the village of Amlekganj, south of Hetauda.

Tharu villages

an insight into this unique culture

Tharus are the Terai's dominant ethnic group. Organized tours of a traditional Tharu village are a popular diversion for visitors to Chitwan. These tours were first conducted by one of the larger lodges for visiting groups with many others subsequently joining the bandwagon, often using bullock carts as a traditional mode of transportation. While the villagers may benefit financially from such tours, some people find the idea of organized gawking at people going about their daily lives in and around their houses too embarrassing to be educational. Local operators offer half- and full-day tours.

The historical domination of the Tharus, Chitwan's indigenous ethnic group, changed following the malaria eradication programme of the 1950s when mass migration brought other ethnic groups – notably Bahuns, Chepangs, Chhetris and Tamungs – from throughout Nepal into Chitwan and the surrounding areas.

Hiring a cycle also allows you to explore the villages and fields of areas surrounding the park. The roads are quiet and you can get a real insight into the everyday lives of these friendly people.

Cultural programmes

Programmes of music and dance by Tharus and some of the Terai's other indigenous ethnic groups are performed most evenings in season and occasionally during off-peak seasons in several of Sauraha's lodges. These are often lively and entertaining.

Ask in your lodge or hotel for details. Some performances charge an admission fee, others are free if you eat in the restaurant.

Central
Terai

Nepal's Central Terai is a bustling chaos of everyday life. Main roads from east to west converge with the India–Kathmandu highway. Lorries, decorated so ornately that drivers can hardly see through their windscreens, ply up and down, packed buses and minibuses weave in between and the towns are packed with people, passengers, hawkers and stall holders.

Yet turn off any of the main roads and within a few hundred metres you are driving on dust roads through pretty villages, many still built of the traditional mud brick and thatch, with livestock and chickens roaming their yards. Lush fields show why the Terai is such an attraction, why the ingenuous Tharu people, born with a natural resilience to malaria, now share the area with peoples drawn from their hard existences in the hills and from the plains of northern India.

Many of these peoples share much common history and ancestory with those of North India and it was this region that lead the protests against the new constitution in 2015, which they believed gave too much power to the mountain communities of northern Nepal.

Devghat

Devghat is a popular place for Hindus to go to die. It's where that the Kali Gandaki and Trisuli rivers merge, their confluence creating the Narayani river, one of the main tributaries of the Ganges. A third sacred river is also said to merge in here, creating a *tribani*, a very holy place because of the imagery of the trident of Vishnu.

Many older Nepalis come here to live out their last days, knowing that to die here will help them on their quest to escape the endless cycles of reincarnation. If they cannot make it in life many request for their ashes to be scattered here, including the late King Mahendra.

Situated in the forests at the very edge of the foothills, it is a tranquil spot, with hundreds of shrines left by pilgrims. Around the confluence itself there are several ashrams, a sacred cave and numerous small temples. There are usually sadhus here as well as resident gurus. It used to be the home of Crazy Baba, a guru famous for cutting off his own arm when instructed to do so in a dream. His pain was probably eased by the large marijuana joint that he usually held in his remaining hand.

Essential Debghat

Finding your feet

If you are travelling in your own vehicle from Kathmandu or Pokhara, cross the suspension bridge you reach after emerging from the narrow gorge from Mugling. It is a few kilometres after the bridge. There are buses to Devghat from the bus station in Narayangarh.

★ Tansen

Spread out on a Churia hillside at 1371 m, Tansen is something of a rough diamond. Picturesque though not especially pretty, it is one of the most typically Nepali towns where Hindu temples, Buddhist shrines and even a mosque coexist easily in a timeless urban setting surrounded by hills and valleys. If you are travelling from Pokhara to the Terai, and especially Lumbini, it's a pleasant place to break the journey.

Tansen is the administrative headquarters of the district of Palpa. It is itself often referred to as **Palpa**, and its people as Palpalis. Until the late 18th century it was the capital of the Sen Kingdom, one of the many autonomous regions which made up Nepal before its political unification under the Gorkhas. Indeed, Palpa is renowned for being the last kingdom to fall to the Gorkhas, not relinquishing its independence until 1806. Even then it required deceitful means to lure King Mahadutta Sen to Kathmandu where he was arrested, imprisoned and subsequently executed.

The town lies on a small, oval-shaped plateau and centres around a former Rana palace, now the seat of local bureaucracy. The surrounding cobbled streets are the focus for the town's commercial activity, notably the production and sale of *dhaka* cloth. Of woven cotton or muslin, this cloth is characterized by jagged, linear designs originally made famous by weavers in Dhaka (or Dacca), Bangladesh. Principally red, black and white, the cloth is used to make saris as well as *topis* (*Palpali topi*), the hat that is an integral part of the national dress for men. The town is also known for its *Palpali koruwa*, a brass water jug.

Forested slopes to the north lead to **Srinagar Hill** from where there are excellent views in all directions. One of the finest views is of the **Mardiphant Valley** to the north. See it first thing on a winter morning when it is draped in a thick silvery layer of mist. There are also a couple of excellent walks from Tansen.

Birendra Phulbari

The southwest corner of the Tundhikhel is marked by a statue of King Birendra, complete with painted black jacket, *topi* and spectacles. The statue stands on a marble lotus plinth in the shade of a large tree. The surrounding garden (*phulbari*, 'flower garden') contains more than 150 varieties of rose.

Amar Narayan Mandir

This fine three-storeyed Vaishnavite temple was built by Amar Singh Thapa in 1807 and is the oldest and best known of Tansen's temples. Surrounded by a broad stone wall ('the great wall of Tansen'), the roofs are tiled and are supported by struts beautifully carved with images of various deities. There is also some magnificent woodwork on the ground floor. The shrine houses an image of Mahadev and to one side is a natural spring. Daily worship takes place in the early morning and evening.

Immediately to the southwest is another, smaller temple, the **Shankar Mandir**. It is in a sad state of disrepair, with numerous tufts of grass growing from its single roof, but it also has some finely carved woodwork and must have looked beautiful once.

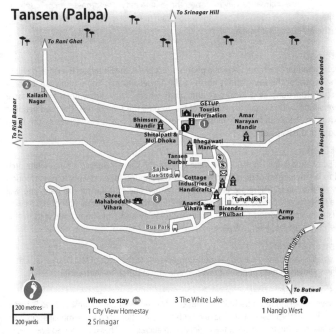

Tansen (Palpa)

To Srinagar Hill
To Rani Ghat
To Gorbanda
Kailash Nagar
To Ridi Bazaar (17 km)
GETUP Tourist Information
Bhimsen Mandir
Amar Narayan Mandir
Shitalpati & Mul Dhoka
Bhagawati Mandir
To Hospital
Tansen Durbar
Sajha Bus Stop
Cottage Industries & Handicrafts
Shree Mahaboddhi Vihara
Tundhikhel
Ananda Vihara
Birendra Phulbari
Army Camp
To Pokhara
Bus Park
Siddhartha Highway
To Butwal

N

200 metres
200 yards

Where to stay
1 City View Homestay
2 Srinagar

3 The White Lake

Restaurants
1 Nanglo West

GEOGRAPHY
The Terai

The Terai runs along the northern margin of the Gangetic Plain. Formerly a malarial region covered for millennia by dense forest, it is this, combined with relatively high rainfall and humidity, that has created such rich agricultural land. With the eradication of malaria and the subsequent deforestation that took place from the 1950s it has become an overflow area from the increasingly congested hills.

The southernmost 15-km-wide strip contains the best agricultural land, backing on to a marshy region, while to the north the Terai reaches as far as the first slopes of the Bhabhar and Churia (or Siwalik) range of hills. Some descriptions refer to this as the 'Outer Terai', and include the Churia hills, with their broad valleys that extend up to the Mahabharat mountains, as defining characteristics of an 'Inner Terai'. The word Terai itself, however, implies plains or flat areas of land.

The start of the hills effectively marks the point at which the Indian landmass joined with the central Asian plate more than 100 million years ago, pushing north and creating the Himalayan ranges from about 35 million years ago. The latest mountain-building period, responsible for the Churias, began less than five million years ago and still continues.

There is something of an enduring fascination in contemplating the abruptness with which the plains give way to slopes, the joining of two landmasses so precisely demarcated along 2500 km, from the Karakoram of Pakistan to the Kuron Range of northern Burma (Myanmar).

Shitalpati

Built by Khadgar Shamsher Rana as a pilgrims' rest place, the Shitalpati is a white pavilion in the centre of the roundabout north of the Tansen Durbar. The originally octagonal structure functions as a local meeting point where men and women sit in casual conversation, with a cigarette or glass of tea, to pass the time of day. The road heading north from Shitalpati leads to Tansen's largest mosque which also serves as the main mosque in the Palpa district.

Mul Dhoka

Mul Dhoka (or Baggi Dhoka) is the main gate to the Tansen Durbar, a huge white arch said to be the largest of its kind in Nepal and big enough for elephants to pass through with their mounts. There are lion pillars on either side and, facing the gate, you will see a fantastically carved window on the building to the left, a reminder of the Newari craftsmanship imported from the Kathmandu Valley and which has flourished in this region since the late Middle Ages.

Bhimsen Mandir

This small two-storeyed pagoda temple immediately to the west of Mul Dhoka has a tiled roof with an attractive copper engraved *torana* above the shrine entrance.

Tansen Durbar

This severe-looking red-brick building was constructed by Pratap Shamsher Jung Bahadur Rana in 1927 as the local seat of Rana rule. With the restoration of effective monarchy in 1951, the palace became the centre of the regional bureaucracy and has remained so ever since.

Bhagawati Mandir

Just to the north of the Durbar, this small temple was built by Ujir Singh Thapa in 1814 to commemorate the Nepali victory over the invading British forces. The event is celebrated with a festival every August when a procession parades its deities through the town. It was badly damaged in the 1934 earthquake and several renovations have left it smaller than its original size.

Buddhist sites

Tansen has several Buddhist shrines and monasteries. The best known is the **Ananda Vihara**, near the bus park. It is the oldest monastery in western Nepal, its main *chaitya* having been built by Sunder Sakya in 1806. It contains images of the 'Panch Buddha' (five Buddhas) and two more of the Buddha himself, though all are later additions.

The **Shree Mahaboddhi Vihara** is a modern Buddhist monastery where occasional meditation courses are held. The **Mahachaitya Vihara**, at Taskar Tole in the northwest of town, was built just before the Second World War and has a number of bronze statues and other Buddhist objets d'art.

Listings Tansen *map page 267.*

Tourist information

GETUP information service
North of the town centre.
This small tourist office provides leaflets and can help with local information, including walking routes, maps, finding guides and visits to local coffee plantations.

Where to stay

$$ Hotel Srinagar
Srinagar Hill, T075-520045,
www.hotelsrinagar.com.
Located on the slopes of Srinagar Hill, Hotel Srinagar gives you a good 20-min head start if climbing to the top for dawn. The en suite rooms are comfortable rooms and have a great view over the mountains, town and the surrounding countryside. Decent restaurant.

$ City View Homestay
North of the town centre, T075-520563.
This tiny homestay is run by the manager of the GETUP information service next door. Clean and basic, it has great views of town from the rooftop and is an atmospheric and friendly base for your stay.

$ Hotel The White Lake
Near the bus stop, T075-520291.
Go for the rooms in the new wing which are a decent size, clean and have fine views. There is a good restaurant and terrace, also with great views.

Restaurants

Most people eat in their hotels as restaurants tend to be small, local eateries offering *dhal bhat* with various options.

$$ Nanglo West
Neat the tourist office, T075-520184,
www.nanglo.com.np. Open 1000-2030.
Excellent Newari food, as well as a variety of other Nepali dishes and plenty of Western favourites, including steaks. The best place in town for a meal out.

Transport

The bus stand is located to the south of town. Buses leave for **Pokhara** in the morning, 5 hrs, US$3.20. Services to **Kathmandu** take 11 hrs, US$6.50.

For the **Terai** you should head to **Butwal** and change there. There are regular services throughout the day, taking 2½ hrs, US$1.

Srinagar Hill

Looming some 200 m above Tansen to the north, you can reach the top of Srinagar Hill in 45 minutes. The walk takes you through a delightful, fragrant pine forest. From the top there are panoramic views over the Kali Gandaki Valley to the Himalaya, including both peaks of Machapuchare. On a good

> **Tip...**
> For details of these routes, maps and the option of hiring a guide, go to the **GETUP** office in town first, as some of the routes are quite tricky to follow.

day you can see the entire Annapurna range and as far as Dhaulagiri. The best time to view is November to February. The way up is signposted from Shitalpati. Alternatively, follow the ridge up from the Hotel Srinagar. There is also a motorable road to the top. The Srinagar Jatra festival is held in August.

Rani Ghat

This is probably the best walk from Tansen if you are staying here for any length of time. Rani ('Queen') Ghat is the site of the magnificent skeleton of a palace built in 1896 by Khadgar Shamsher Rana (also responsible for Tansen's Shitalpati) for his wife, Tej Kumari. Khadgar was 'exiled' from Kathmandu following an unsuccessful attempt at a political coup. Although overgrown with weeds and trees, it requires little imagination to visualize the palace in its former isolated splendour, its grand colonnaded porch and terraced gardens playing host only to Khadgar's wistful thoughts of what might have been. Built on a broad spur of rock on the bank of the Kali Gandaki river, work aimed at renovating the palace was started in 1996 but doesn't seem to have progressed far.

It is a walk of about three hours there and four hours back, so allow a full day. The path leaves Tansen at Kailash Nagar where there is a signboard with a map of the route. The walk is fairly straightforward, but after about 1 km the path branches; if in doubt, ask any local for Rani Ghat. You pass through several tiny hamlets and terraced farmland before entering a narrow, forested valley with a crystal-clear stream. The trail is distinct, though steep and uneven at times. You can't see the palace itself until you get to the large steel suspension bridge crossing the river. There are a couple of tea stalls and snack shops at Rani Ghat, but it is advisable to bring enough water and a substantial packed lunch with you.

Ghorabanda-Khorbari

This small village lies on the Siddhartha Highway about 3 km north of the Tansen junction. Its 'Kumal' potters are the main suppliers of pots, water vessels and other earthenware goods to the area. Because the pots need to be 'sun dried', all pottery activity is confined to the dry, winter months. Little English is spoken here. The village also has good views across the valley. To get there it is best to hire a car, though there is also a cross-country walking route passing close to the hospital.

Chandi Bhanjyang

A hilltop viewpoint with what is locally considered to be a better Himalayan vista than the one from Srinagar Hill.

Ridi Bazaar

Ridi is venerated by Hindus for its sacred location at the confluence of the Kali Gandaki and Ridi Khola rivers, 17 km west of Tansen. The area is also rich in saligrams, the fossilized ammonites dating back more than 100 million years to a warmer geological age when the region was under water and before the Himalayan uplift began. Saligrams are regarded as religiously significant by Vaishnavite Hindus.

The town's **Rishikesh Mandir** is believed to have been established by the great Palpa king, Mani Mukunda Sen, though the present structure was built in the early 19th century. The temple is one of Nepal's more important pilgrimage sites. According to local legend, the temple idol (Rishikeshab) was found in a river and has developed from youth to adulthood since it was installed. Major festivals are held in the month of Magh (January-February), including Ridi's most important festival of **Magh Sankranti**, which involves fasting and bathing in the river; and in Bhadra (August-September).

Buses leave Tansen's bus park in the morning only. En route, 9 km from Tansen, is **Bhairabsthan**, with its **Kala** ('black') **Bhairab Mandir** known for having the largest *trisul* (Vishnu's trident) in Asia.

★ Lumbini

the birthplace of Buddha

Buddhist scriptures describe how the Great Maya (deified as Maya Devi), the Buddha's mother, dreamt of a white elephant representing the reincarnation of Buddha into her womb and experienced a pregnancy free from all "fatigues, depressions and fancies". When the time came for her to give birth, "she set her heart on going to Lumbini, a delightful grove with trees of every kind, like the grove of Citraratha in Indra's Paradise".

The birth of the Buddha, Gautama Siddhartha, in Lumbini in about 563 BC (sources differ) is the single best-known event in the history of the Terai, and has had a significant impact on the culture not only of Nepal but on much of Asia and the world's one billion Buddhists. The Chinese traveller Fa-Hien described the ruins at Lumbini in the fourth century AD, and his compatriot Hiuen Tsang visited the site two centuries later. The ancient Ashokan pillar was not discovered until 1895 by the German archaeologist Alois Führer.

The restoration of Lumbini which began in 1895 with Alois Führer received a huge boost in 1967 when the then UN Secretary General, U Thant from Burma (Myanmar), visited Lumbini and inaugurated the Lumbini Development Project. It wasn't until the 1970s that the Nepalese Government decided to develop the area, for reasons, one suspects, that were more financially than spiritually enlightened.

With UN backing, a religious park was established and Buddhist nations were invited to open their own temples and monasteries inside it. Some 13 countries, including Korea, Japan, India and the USA, contributed to the formulation of a Master Plan under Professor Kenzo Tange, a Japanese architect. The objectives of the plan included development and restoration of the Sacred Garden, the creation of a monastic zone and of the 'Lumbini Village', which was to provide accommodation and facilities for visitors as well as a Visitor Centre. It became a UNESCO World Heritage Site in 1997.

Pipeline plans have become a pipeline reality with the construction of a museum and research centre, a 420-seat auditorium and a library, all dedicated to advancing Buddhist learning and practice. All have been built in the same unusual and unmistakable style, like huge concrete tubes stacked beside and on top of each other; unique but to some not very enlightened.

Today Lumbini is an unexpectedly tranquil site where ground-level archaeological excavations coexist with modern places of worship. There are several entrances, the main gate being to the southeast, conveniently close to the Sacred Garden.

① Lumbini master plan

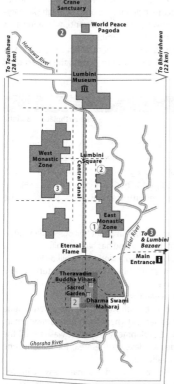

N

500 metres

500 yards

Sights ◯
1 Burmese Lokamani Gula Pagoda

2 Royal Thai Monastery
3 Zhang Hua monastery

Where to stay 🛏
1 Buddha Maya Gorden
2 Lumbini Hotel Kasai
3 Lumbini Village Lodge

Sacred Garden
Open dawn to dusk, US$1.80.

This small complex lies at the southern end of Lumbini. It marks the spot where the Buddha is reputed to have been born and contains all the area's important historical monuments and archaeological finds.

Maya Devi Mandir Sections of the Maya Devi Mandir are believed to date as far back as the third or fourth century BC, though much of the structure consists of later additions. The temple contains a stone bas relief illustrating the Buddha's nativity. It is thought to date from the Malla period, and shows Maya, the largest of the figures, clutching the branch of a tree with the baby Gautama Siddhartha standing at her feet, right arm raised and a halo around his head. Three attendants assist Maya, while groups of celestial beings observe from afar. The original carving is very worn and was removed to a nearby protected location, but a 1950s marble replica by the Nepali sculptor Chandra Man Maskey is the focus of devotees' worship.

The temple was gradually being destroyed by the roots of a large peepal tree, beneath which the Buddha was believed to have been born and, in the early 1990s, archaeologists began disassembling the building brick by brick and relocating it. The archaeologists believed that the temple had been built on top of a still more important site. Excavations continued with great care until 1996 when the experts' predictions were vindicated in the most

➡ Lumbini maps
1 Lumbini master plan, page 272
2 The Sacred Garden, page 273

significant of the finds. At a depth of some 5 m and three layers below the original temple, they discovered a series of rooms and a stone slab which is now believed to mark the exact location at which the Buddha was born.

The peepul tree, which was cut down, was almost certainly not the original that may have survived into the sixth or seventh century AD. Another large peepul tree remains nearby and is honoured by proxy with a number of garlands and prayer flags.

Ashokan Pillar Now enclosed by metal railings and bound by metal rings following damage caused by lightning, the Ashokan Pillar has a circumference of 2.78 m and stands 7.79 m tall, though a large section is below ground. It was erected by the greatest of the Mauryan emperors, Ashoka, in 249 BC, "in the 20th year of his reign", when he visited Lumbini. The inscription is in the Brahmi script and Prakrit language and declares that he made the village "free of taxes and a recipient of wealth".

The pillar is Nepal's oldest known monument. As well as marking the extent of his Mauryan Empire, Ashoka's inscribed edicts are of unique historical value as they are amongst the earliest written sources in a region where history and culture were either transmitted orally or were recorded on materials that were unable to withstand the rigours of the climate.

The Pushkarni This is the pool in which Maya Devi is believed to have bathed prior to giving birth and where the infant Buddha was given his first bath. Terraced steps lead down to the water. It was excavated in 1933. Despite its present rectangular shape, it is thought that the original pool was round or oblong.

② The Sacred Garden

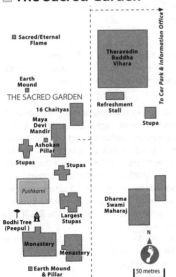

The ground-level archaeological ruins to the southeast are of monasteries built between the second century BC and the fourth century AD. The ruins to the immediate west of these date one century further back. The rectangular plinth in the northeast corner of the garden formed the base of a set of 16 small stupas or *chaityas*, probably dating from the eighth or ninth century AD.

Set apart at the periphery of the garden is a recent and incongruous addition: a marble column erected to commemorate the visit of the then King Mahendra in 1956. On the northern side of the garden is the eternal flame, established as a symbol of peace by Crown Prince Gyanendra Bir Bikram Shah in 1986. The stupa-like mounds to the north and south are simply the grassed-over piles of earth from the excavations.

→ **Lumbini maps**

Theravadin Buddha Vihara

Opposite the Sacred Garden, this modern monastery was constructed by the Government of Nepal. The open-arched shrine contains a large bronze image of the Buddha. This is flanked by two smaller images: to the right as you face the shrine is another bronze from Burma (Myanmar), while the marble statue to your left is from Thailand. The walls of the main hall have paintings of the wheel of life as well as depictions of scenes from the Buddha's life. In the neighbouring courtyard are two *chaityas*, one of which is sacred to the memory of **Dharmlok Mahasthavir** (died 1967), a leading campaigner for the restoration of Lumbini. Visitors are allowed into the shrine room, a very peaceful place.

Dharma Swami Maharaj

Near the Theravadin Monastery, this Tibetan Mahayana Vihara was built in 1968 by either (sources differ) the Raja of Mustang or by the well-known teacher Chogya Trichen Rinpoche. Popular with Tibetan pilgrims, it has a central image of the Buddha along with numerous smaller representations and other Buddhist artwork. It is home to between 30 and 50 monks.

Lumbini Museum

T071-580318, Wed-Mon 1000-1600.

Located to the north of the zone, the museum tells the life of Buddha, not just his birth at Lumbini but with photos and artefacts from other important sites and regions he visited.

World Peace Pagoda

Open dawn-dusk.

To the north of the Lumbini area, this 41-m-high pagoda was completed in 2001 and makes an impressive sight with its dazzling white and gleaming gold. It contains a golden Buddha.

Lumbini Crane Sanctuary

Free.

With its forests and peaceful setting, Lumbini is a great spot for birdwatchers, with over 200 species recorded. This small reserve, near the Peace Pagoda is a sanctuary for the Sarus crane, the world's tallest flying bird, as well as a host of other waders.

The monastic zones

To the north of the Sacred Garden, on either side of a central canal that cuts the site north to south, are two monastic zones where a variety of temples and monasteries have been built by different countries. To the west lie those from the Mahayana sect and the east are those who follow the Theravada philosophy. It has created a living map of Buddhism, with all the main sects and styles of worship represented, letting you see the different architectural styles and ways of worship of the same religion in different countries.

You can visit most of the temples and monasteries, many offering courses to teach Buddhism or, you get the feeling, their own version of it. Worth visiting are the **Burmese Lokamani Gula Pagoda**, based on the Shwedagon Temple in Yangon, the **Royal Thai Monastery** and the **Chinese Zhong Hua Monastery**.

The best way to get around is by bike. The roads are flat and quiet and you can cover the large area quickly and easily and can explore the areas away from the main sights. Bikes can be rented from most hotels or in Lumbini village.

Tourist information

Tourist Information Office
Main gate to the south east of the site.
Open 0600-1800.

Where to stay

There is a good selection of hotels and guesthouses in and around Lumbini. As most visitors are Buddhist pilgrims, many places cater for the Japanese and Asian markets and for tour groups.

The majority of budget hotels are in Lumbini Bazaar, the village near the main entrance, while the more expensive hotels are mainly to the north of the site or within their own grounds.

$$ Lumbini Hotel Kasai
In the north of the religious zone,
near the Shantu Stupa, T071-404036,
www.lumbinihotelkasai.com.
Good-quality hotel with 28 en suite rooms and a fine restaurant serving organic food.

$$$ Buddha Maya Garden
Located to the southeast of the site,
T071-580220, www.ktmgh.com.

A pleasant resort set in nice grounds about 5 mins' walk from the sites. Good-sized rooms and a decent restaurant. Part of the **Kathmandu Guest House Group**.

$ Lumbini Village Lodge
T071-580432
This budget lodge offers large, clean rooms, with en suite facilities and a pleasant central courtyard shaded by a large tree. You can hire bikes from here and the owner will arrange tours of the site and nearby attractions.

Restaurants

Most people eat in their hotels and the food is generally good. There are places to eat in the small village of Lumbini Bazaar, or you can go to one of the hotels.

Transport

Bus
There are a couple of tourist bus services to **Kathmandu**, US$7.50-11, 8-9 hrs. There is also a public morning bus that takes a little longer but costs a little less.
    Local buses run frequently to **Bhairawa** (US$0.50, 1 hr). A taxi will cost US$10.

Around Lumbini

outlying monuments and sites

There are a few possible excursions from the Lumbini area to places of historical interest. To visit any of these, it is best to hire a jeep from Bhairahawa or Lumbini Bazar.

Leaving Lumbini to the west you reach **Taulihawa**, a busy little market town, after 21 km. The remains of an early *pokhari* and of four mounds with possible religious significance were discovered at **Kudan**, 2 km southwest of Taulihawa. Another 3 km to the southwest is the village of **Gotihawa**, where you can see the broken remains of an Ashokan pillar and a large stupa made of bricks believed to date from the third or fourth century BC.
    Some 3 km to the north of Taulihawa is **Tilaurakot**, a small village containing the ruins of a fort, a monastery and a stupa, which were possibly part of the ancient town of **Kapilvastu**. Archaeological investigations have shown Kapilvastu to have been a walled city which may have had a well developed culture. It is thought to have been the capital of the Sakya Kingdom, from whose royal lineage Gautauma Siddhartha was born and where

he lived before embarking upon his search for enlightenment. Just north of Tilaurakot at **Chatradei** are ruins of a medieval settlement where pottery, Sakya coins and other artefacts have been found.

Archaeologists have discovered other major sites at **Niglihawa** (or Niglisagar), further north. These include two pillars related to Ashoka. The first is not thought to have been placed by Ashoka himself and predates the other and Lumbini's famous pillar by six years. '*Om mani padme hum*' is inscribed in the Devanagri script the pillar bears the image of two peacocks. The other has an inscription in Ashoka's more familiar Brahmi script and Prakrit language and refers to a second enlargement of the Kanaka Muni stupa at the emperor's behest. Another 4 km to the north, in the **Sagarhawa forest**, are the ruins of a Sakya tank, first uncovered by Alois Führer.

Everest &
the Khumbu

superb mountain scenery in the land of the Sherpas

Mention Nepal to most people and the first thing they think of is Mount Everest. At 8848 m, it is the world's highest mountain and it sits on the country's northern border with Tibet.

To Nepalis it is known as Sagarmatha and to Tibetans it's Chomolungma, the 'Holy Mother'. To the local peoples it is a sacred peak and for most keen walkers, the trek to Everest Base Camp is a life-long ambition.

Since it was first recorded by the outside world in the 1840s, it has held a fascination magnified by the fact that it was located in a forbidden kingdom. Early attempts to climb it via Tibet, one of which led to the disappearance of Mallory and Irvine in 1924, were followed by millions through newspaper dispatches and magazine reports. When it was finally climbed in 1953 it was headline news worldwide.

The approach to the mountain is through the Khumbu, the homeland of the Sherpa people, an area steeped in their culture and Buddhist beliefs. Its spectacular scenery varies from steep-sided valleys with seemingly endless terraces tumbling down to roaring rivers, to glaciers and high-altitude meadows. Prayer flags proliferate, mani stones litter the trails and the traditional squat village houses merge this traditional life with the lodges and restaurants for passing trekkers.

Best for
Climbing ▪ Culture ▪ Trekking ▪ Yeti

Footprint
picks

★ **Lukla airport**, page 282
One of the most amazing landings and take-offs you will
ever experience.

★ **Thame**, page 287
Unspoilt walking through pretty forests and peaks.

★ **Everest Base Camp**, page 292
The most famous trekking destination in the world.

★ **Tengboche Monastery**, page 292
The Sherpa's most holy place in the shadow of Everest.

★ **Gokyo Lakes**, page 294
Great views of Everest and spectacular mountain scenery.

Essential Everest and the Khumbu

Finding your feet

Most people who visit the Khumbu fly into the small mountain airstrip at Lukla. The biggest challenge is the weather, as visibility has to be good for flights to operate. To trek in you leave the Kathmandu Valley via Dhulikhel on the Tibet road, before turning east to the road head at Shivalaya. From here, it is a six-day walk to reach Lukla. There are other airstrips, such as Phaplu, that can be used to allow different approaches to the Khumbu.

Getting around

The whole region is covered by an extensive networks of trails and paths, used for

centuries by Tibetan traders who brought their goods through the Khumbu to trade with the lowlands further south. Everything is done on foot, although you do meet trading caravans of mules or *dzows* (a yak-buffalo cross) bringing goods in and out of the mountains. Happily, plans for a cable-car to bring trekkers up the steep climb to Namche Bazaar have been scrapped.

When to go

Weather conditions can change very rapidly at high altitude, particularly as a result of unforeseen changes in the western jet stream. The region's climate is dominated by the mountains that encircle the valleys. They deflect much of the wind coming off

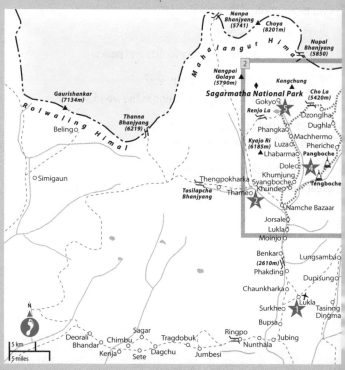

the Tibetan High Plateau and act as a wall against the rain-bearing monsoon clouds brought in from the Bay of Bengal.

Heavy frosts are common in Namche Bazaar from late October onwards and gradually the ground freezes to a depth of around 500 mm. There is light snow in autumn, while December, January and February are the coldest months with heavy falls of snow occurring after December. From January to March, the weather is fairly settled with periods of clear weather lasting for up to three weeks at a time. These are broken by short stormy periods lasting a few days.

Between November and March, the average daily temperature is only a few degrees above freezing. At night it can fall to -15°C at Namche Bazaar and below -20°C beyond Lobuche. These temperatures rise steadily from March onwards until the onset of the monsoon. This is a period of little rain and increasing heat and haziness.

The monsoon arrives in mid-June. Rain clouds form rapidly to cover the peaks and fill the valleys by midday. Light mist turns into heavy rain by nightfall and, at higher altitudes, this turns to snow. Visibility is poor and clinging mists can hang around in valleys for weeks. From mid-September the clouds and rain withdraw. Some 75% of the annual rainfall of 1000 mm comes during the monsoon. The peaks receive most of their snow at this time too, and the snow line comes down to 5500 m.

Time required

The great unknown is the Lukla flight. Most visitors suffer no delays but when bad weather does set in flights can be cancelled for several days at a time, which creates huge backlogs. Always allow a spare day or two at the end if you have an international flight connection. The other factor to bear in mind is the altitude. All treks in the Everest area and many in the Khumbu involve high altitude. Acclimatization is vital so when walking times seem short that doesn't mean that because you are fit you can go further faster. Your body needs time to acclimatize which is why the itineraries are structured as they are (see page 448).

Makalu Barun National Park

Footprint
picks

1 **Lukla airport**, page 282
2 **Thame**, page 287
3 **Everest Base Camp**, page 292
4 **Tengboche Monastery**, page 292
5 **Gokyo Lakes**, page 294

Lukla is the first stop for many trekkers visiting the Everest region. A flight into the Tenzing-Hillary Airport is the exciting arrival point, a tiny patch of tarmac jutting out into the Dudh Kosi Valley. It sits at a 10% angle, with the planes landing uphill and taking off down the slope. Before being surfaced it used to be known as "the ski jump" as fully laden planes would fall off its end in order to pick up enough speed to start climbing. Happily this is no longer necessary.

Lukla

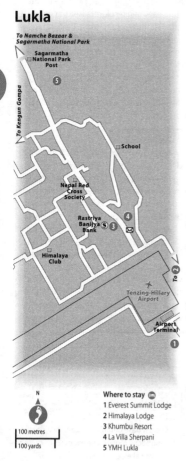

Where to stay 🏠
1 Everest Summit Lodge
2 Himalaya Lodge
3 Khumbu Resort
4 La Villa Sherpani
5 YMH Lukla

Flights are still dependent on the weather, however, and if low cloud sets in it's not unusual for them to be cancelled for several days. You should always make sure you have a couple of buffer days in Kathmandu if connecting to your international flight. Sometimes Lukla seems to be bursting at the seams with stranded trekkers but the airlines put on extra flights as soon as the weather improves to clear the waiting list.

The airport has revolutionized the village. Before its construction, Lukla was just another small community. Now, as the trailhead for Everest, it is packed with lodges, shops, bars and equipment stores, all there to cater to trekkers and mountaineers. Gone are the days when you slept on the floor around the fire. These days the lodges offer en suite rooms and Wi-Fi.

The village is basically arranged along the one cobbled street that runs through it and the small alleys that run off this. At its northern end is a gateway that marks the end of the village and the start of the Everest trail.

There is not a great deal to do in Lukla and most people only stay for a night at the start or finish of their trek. There is the small **Kengun Gompa** below the village and a market on Thursday mornings. There is also a good hospital.

If you do get stranded, there are some pleasant walks, from a short climb to a Buddha statue to longer excursions to nearby Sherpa villages. A walk to the village of Bom gives great views back over the airstrip.

Essential Lukla

Finding your feet

There are two ways to Lukla; you fly or walk. Flights to the airport operate daily in good weather. There are several operators but the most frequent service is offered by **Tara Air**. A one-way flight costs US$165 for foreigners. Because of the size and nature of the airstrip all flights are operated by STOL (Short Take-off and Landing) aircraft, meaning that they seat only about 18 passengers.

When flying out of Lukla you should reconfirm your flight the day before, between 1500 and 1600. During the high season there can be over 70 flights per day so waiting lists can grow quickly – the record is over 7000.

Tip...
Flights do not operate in bad weather so never try to connect directly through to an international flight.

Walking to Lukla is a great way to start your trek so long as you have the time. Most people start at the small village of Shivalaya, where the road from Kathmandu ends. It takes about six days to Lukla but be warned, it's a fairly demanding trek. It crosses several valleys rather than following them, meaning a lot of ascent and descent. The countryside is very rewarding, however, with forests, villages and steep terracing and, unlike the trails higher up, it is much less crowded.

A slightly shorter walk-in is if you fly to **Phaplu** and walk the three days to Lukla. Flights here are operated by **Tara Air**, US$136. Another alternative is to fly to **Lamidanda**, further south, and walk for five days.

Listings Lukla map page 282.

Where to stay

There are plenty of lodges in Lukla, ranging from smart en suite properties to the basic teahouse. Lukla escaped the 2015 earthquakes largely undamaged but quite a few lodges close in the quieter periods when their owners head to Kathmandu.

$$$ Everest Summit Lodge
www.everestlodges.com.
17 comfortable rooms with en suites, good restaurant with varied menu and a small bar for relaxing in post-trek. Convenient location near the airstrip and a lovely garden. Part of a small group with 4 other lodges higher up the Khumbu.

$$$ YMH Lukla (Yeti Mountain Home)
www.yetimountainhome.com.
Situated about 15 mins from the airstrip, this excellent lodge has 20 rooms with en suite bathrooms decorated in local style. It even offers electric blankets. They have a good restaurant using home-grown produce with great views over the valley. Part of a small group with 6 good lodges in the Khumbu.

$$ Himalaya Lodge
www.himalayalodge.com.
Built in 1978 the Himalaya claims to have been the first proper lodge in Lukla. It offers a wide range of rooms and good-value prices including en suite deluxe. Pleasant grounds with views of the airstrip about 10 mins' walk away.

$ Khumbu Resort
T038-550005, www.khumburesort.com.
This large lodge, situated in the middle of the village, has fairly basic rooms but is clean and functional. It also offers great coffee.

$ La Villa Sherpani
T038-550105.
Go for one of the newer rooms and you get a comfortable en suite. It has a nice garden, complete with its own stupa, to relax in.

The majority of people eat in their lodges, most of which have decent restaurants offering similar menus ranging from traditional to a variety of Western dishes. There are plenty of cafés and bars to choose from as all lodges on the main street are open to non-residents. You can also get a great cup of coffee in Lukla.

Namche Bazaar

the capital city of the Sherpas

The town of Namche Bazaar, a two-day walk from Lukla and the main settlement of the Sherpa people in the Khumbu region, sits in a natural amphitheatre with views out over the Bhote Kosi Valley. It has grown enormously over the last 30 years from a local trading settlement to the centre of trekking in Sagarmartha National Park. Its neat, cobbled streets are lined by lodges and restaurants, connected by steep alleys and steps as the town tumbles down the hillside.

There are echoes of a past life, with a vibrant Saturday morning market still attracting many locals to barter, buy and socialize. The goods these days no longer come over the Nangpa La with Tibetan traders but up from the lowlands. Trekking now drives the economy and every year new lodges and restaurants open, built using the traditional stone and timber frames that give the town such character. (Although the stone roofs have been replaced by corrugated-iron sheets).

It's a pleasant place to stay for a couple of nights, which is a good thing as it is a vital acclimatization stage on most treks going higher. There are several things to do and walks that can be undertaken.

Essential Namche Bazaar

Finding your feet

Most visitors fly into Lukla and trek the two days to Namche. Because of the altitude, it is necessary to stay for two nights to get acclimatized. There is also a small helicopter landing area above Namche at **Syangboche** used by visitors to the **Everest View Hotel**. As it is at an altitude of 3770 m, it is not used much in trekking itineraries as it is too high to start the acclimatization process.

Sagarmatha National Park Visitor Centre
Sun-Fri 0800-1600, free.

Located above the eastern side of Namche village Sagarmatha National Park Visitor Centre is in nearby Chhorkhung. From outside the centre you get great views, perhaps your first, of **Everest** (8848 m) as well as of **Nuptse** (7861 m) and the picturesque **Ama Dablan** (6856 m.)

The centre itself has seen better days and could do with a coat of paint, but it has guides to the flora and fauna you can hope to see within the national park as well as information on the local Sherpa culture.

Namche Gompa

The town's main monastery is only 100 years old but feels older. It is an atmospheric place with plenty of colourful murals and a large statue of the Rinpoche. There is worship in the mornings and late afternoon, and the monotone Buddhist chanting is mesmerizing. Look out for the large prayer wheels nearby.

Namche Gonda Museum
Open 0800-1300, 14-17, US$1.

Next to the *gompa* is a museum about the Sherpas and their way of life. It's fairly small but is an interesting insight into the local culture.

Sherpa Culture Museum
www.sherpa-culture.com.np, open 0900-1700, US$1.

This interesting museum is also towards Chhorkhung and has been set up by Lhakpa Sonam Sherpa, a local man who lost his hearing to meningitis when young but has gone on to have a great career in tourism and as a photographer. The museum covers the Sherpas and their culture, has information on all the local summiteers of Everest and photo displays of colourful local festivals and events. You can buy copies of his photos, including some amazing mountain views.

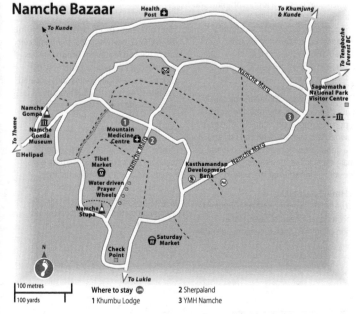

Namche Bazaar

100 metres
100 yards

| Where to stay | 2 Sherpaland |
| 1 Khumbu Lodge | 3 YMH Namche |

ON THE ROAD

Sherpa customs

The following few hints on social behaviour will help you to appreciate Sherpa culture and to avoid local faux pas.

- Out of courtesy to Sherpas, don't attempt to climb Khumbi-yul-lha, the mountain directly behind Khunde and Khumjung, as this is the sacred abode of the deity that protects the Khumbu region.
- The name of a dead person should not be mentioned to his close relatives or in his house as this may attract his reincarnated spirit.
- Many Sherpas do not allow whistling in their homes for the same reason.

- Do not write a Sherpa's name in red ink, as this symbolizes death and is used for inscriptions at funeral ceremonies.
- If you offer food or drink to a Sherpa and it is politely refused, you should offer it twice more. Traditional Sherpa hospitality requires that you offer something three times.
- The Sherpa word for 'thank you' is *tuche*.

Listings Namche Bazaar *map page 285.*

Where to stay

Namche has plenty of lodges offering good rooms with en suite facilities, and very few got damaged in the 2015 earthquake. Some do close out of season or when business is slow. The standard of lodge has risen dramatically over the last 20 years.

$ Khumbu Lodge
T038-540144, www.khumbulodge.com.
With its green roof, Khumbu, the oldest lodge in Namche, sits right in the heart of the town. The rooms are clean and tidy and there is a good restaurant with a varied menu. Its main claim to fame was having the ex-US President Jimmy Carter stay here in 1985.

$ Hotel Sherpaland
T038-540107, www.hotelsherpaland.com.
Located in the heart of town, Hotel Sherpaland has 22 en suite rooms, all nicely

decorated with Tibetan-style touches. it has a good restaurant and, amongst other things, can arrange a yak ride for you.

$$$ YMH Namche (Yeti Mountain Home)
T01-400 0711, www.yetimountainhome.com.
Part of the **Yeti Mountain Group** that has several lodges throughout Khumbu, this option has 20 en suite rooms and is located just above the main town. It has a good restaurant and nice lounge with fireplace.

Restaurants

Most people eat in their lodges and the menus all offer a good variety of Nepali, Indian and continental food. You can even get a pizza in some places. There are several cafés in town offering reasonable coffee and tasty cakes and pastries. There are also several bars.

★ Thame

This is a beautiful walk with far fewer trekkers than on the Base Camp Trail. It makes a good acclimatization walk for those going higher, and offers excellent mountain views as it wanders in and out of forest on the side of the canyon of the **Theshyo Khola**. This trail is also followed by trekkers doing the **Three Passes** and is one of the longer day trips from Namche, just under 10 km each way. Of course, you don't have to go the whole way; there are a few small lodges en route where you can stop for a drink and return if you want.

Thame is a traditional village that has escaped the crowds trekking to Everest and has one of the older monasteries in the region. Although the village did get damaged in the 2015 earthquake, there are still lodges open and the locals are grateful for the custom. The village is famous for being the home of **Apa Sherpa** who has climbed Everest over 20 times.

Khunde and Khumjung

These two villages lie above Namche and make a great acclimatization walk for those trekking higher. They are quite traditional compared to Namche, mainly because they lie off the main Everest trekking route. **Khumjung** is the regional centre, managing much of the upper Khumbu and with nearly 2000 inhabitants and a school built by the Sir Edmund Hillary Trust. It has a monastery with a scalp said to be from a Yeti, and is an interesting place for a visit. **Khunde** is smaller and has a hospital built by the Hillary Trust in 1966.

The valley lies at between 3800 and 4000 m, with **Mount Khumbila** rising over it. There are great views of **Ama Dablin** (6812 m), a beautiful peak whose name translates as 'mother's necklace' because of a hanging glacier high on the peak.

Head northwest from Namche towards Thame and after about 30 minutes look for a trail heading off right to Syangboche. It's about an hour from here to Khunde, uphill much of the way. As you arrive there is a gateway and stupa complete with Buddha eye. Continue down the valley to the village of Khumjung. From here you can either follow the main trail back to Namche or climb to **Everest View Hotel** (see below). The trails are easy to follow but if you get lost the locals are always happy to point you the right way.

Everest View Hotel

Probably the most popular of the day walks, it is a long half day or a 'lazy' full day and a good acclimatization walk for those trekking higher. It starts with a 450-m climb up the slope behind Namche and then heads north along a long ridge to the **Everest View Hotel**. Once there you can enjoy a drink (the most expensive in the Khumbu) and a rest on the terrace behind the hotel with a superb panorama of Everest, Ama Dablam and the upper Khumbu.

The hotel was designed by Japanese architect **Yoshinobu Kumagaya** and opened in 1971. There is a small helicopter landing area nearby where guests can land, although the altitude makes this a potentially risky arrival point. (The hotel has oxygen in the rooms for guests unaccustomed to the altitude.) If you are not going on to Base Camp this is a good spot to get a view of Everest.

Sagarmatha National Park

Sagarmatha National Park was established in 1976 to preserve the environment around the world's highest mountain. Visitors must abide by a few simple rules, the most important being that they must not use firewood for cooking or heating and should dispose of their rubbish carefully. In 1979, it was declared a UNESCO World Heritage Site and in 2002 an additional 275 sq km were added as a buffer zone. It adjoins the Qomolangma National Nature Preserve in Tibet and the Makalu Barun National Park in the east, protecting a vast swathe of the High Himalaya.

Vegetation in the park varies from pine and hemlock forests at lower altitudes, to fir, juniper, birch and rhododendron woods at mid-elevations, scrub and alpine plant communities higher up and bare rock and snow above the tree line. The famed bloom of rhododendrons occurs during the spring (April and May) although many of the flowers are at their most colourful during the monsoon season (June to August).

The park is populated by approximately 3000 of the famed Sherpa people, originating from Tibet in the 15th-16th centuries. Their lives are interwoven with the teaching of Buddhism. The main settlements are Namche Bazaar, Khumjung, Khunde, Thame, Thyangboche, Pangboche, Dingboche and Phortse. There are also temporary settlements in the upper valleys where the Sherpas graze their livestock during the summer season.

Wildlife

In terms of animal conservation, the park has proved an outstanding success and the numbers of many creatures have increased. It has the largest population of Himalayan tahr and the similar serow and ghoral. The sure-footed tahr, the size of an American mountain goat, can be seen on seemingly unscalable hillsides. Snow leopards also live here but are rarely seen, as do red pandas, wolves and musk deer.

The park provides a habitat for at least 118 species of bird. The most common are the Impeyen pheasant (the national bird of Nepal), blood pheasant, cheer pheasant, jungle crow, the red-billed and yellow-billed chough and snow pigeon. Also seen are the Himalayan griffon, lammergier and snow pheasant.

Essentials Sagarmatha National Park

Finding your feet

The park entrance is near Monjo, a short day's walk from Lukla. At the gate you must either show your park entrance ticket or buy one (see below). You must also log your TIMS trekking card so there is a record of your route and plans. It takes about three hours from here, including a long climb at the end, to reach Namche Bazaar.

Park information

Sagarmartha National Park Office, Namche Bazaar, T038-540114, www.sagarmatha

nationalpark.gov.np. Entrance fee US$27.50 (US$14 if you pay in advance in Kathmandu).

Emergencies

The **Himalayan Rescue Association** has a clinic at Pheriche (on the Base Camp Route) to assist visitors with altitude sickness. There are also clinics at Machhermo and Gokyo run by the IPPG. All three facilities have foreign doctors and give talks on altitude sickness and what symptoms to look out for.

There is a hospital in Khunde, located above Namche Bazaar. Namche Bazaar has a small hospital/clinic, a dentist and a pharmacy.

ON THE ROAD
The legend of the Yeti

He is hairy, has big feet, is of large humanoid appearance, consumes an omnivorous diet and smells of garlic and rotten eggs. He is also extremely elusive. But the Yeti, or Abominable Snowman, features strongly in Sherpa mythology in which he is endowed with various supernatural qualities including the capacity to become invisible.

The Yeti is often held responsible for sporadic vicious attacks on yaks, an occupation which has not endeared him to yak herders. He apparently kills by grabbing the unfortunate yak by the horns and using them to twist its neck. In 1974, a village girl was reportedly assaulted by a Yeti in Machhermo, two days' walk north of Namche Bazaar towards Gokyo. The local police confirmed the attack, but failed to apprehend the suspect. It was this kind of antisocial behaviour, combined with his decidedly malodorous aspect, which led to the epithet 'abominable' being bestowed upon this abstruse creature. The word 'yeti', meanwhile, seems to have entered the English language in the 1920s and is thought to derive from the Tibetan *me t'om k'ang mi*, meaning 'man/bear snowfield man'.

The existence of an Abominable Snowman was first suggested to the world in 1898 by a Major L Wassell who discovered a series of large and inexplicable footprints in Sikkim. There have been numerous subsequent reported sightings either of the creature himself or of his 'footprints', notably by Eric Shipton in 1951. Yet he has continued to thwart all efforts to locate him or verify his existence. Footprints in the snow are written off as those of another animal which have been enlarged by the warmth of the sun, while an analysis of a Yeti skull from a Khumbu monastery revealed it to be that of a humble Himalayan serow, a goat-like antelope.

Studies of various relics and remains have suggested that there may well be something behind the legend. DNA analysis has shown similarities with the modern polar bear: perhaps an undiscovered and rare species of bear adapted to the harsh, upper climate of the Himalaya and (explaining its more aggressive nature) rearing up and walking on two legs. Until one is found, the legend goes on.

Trekking in the
Everest Region

The Everest Base Camp trek is the oldest established trek in Nepal, first being walked by a group of three intrepid American ladies in 1965.

The classic trek to Everest Base Camp from Shivalaya takes around three weeks. You move from the predominantly Hindu Middle Hills to the Tibetan Buddhist High Himalaya. Mountaineering expeditions enjoyed the trek as a way of getting fit as well as acclimatizing. Indeed, the successful

2 Trekking the Upper Khumbu

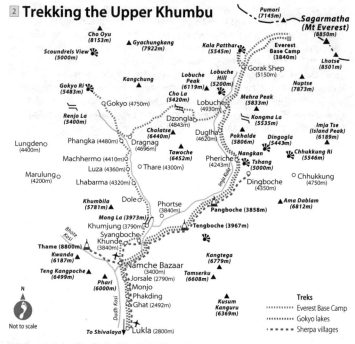

Pumori (7145m)
Sagarmatha (Mt Everest) (8850m)
Cho Oyu (8153m)
Gyachungkang (7922m)
Kala Patthar (5545m)
Everest Base Camp (3840m)
Scoundrels View (5000m)
Lhotse (8501m)
Gorak Shep (5150m)
Lobuche Peak (6119m)
Lobuche Hill (5200m)
Gokyo Ri (5483m)
Kangchung
Cho La (5420m)
Lobuche (4930m)
Mehra Peak (5833m)
Nuptse (7873m)
Gokyo (4750m)
Renjo La (5400m)
Dzonglha (4843m)
Kongma La (5535m)
Imja Tse (Island Peak) (6189m)
Cholatse (6440m)
Duglha (4620m)
Pokhalde (5806m)
Dingogla (5443m)
Lungdeno (4400m)
Phangka (4480m)
Dragnag (4696m)
Tawoche (6452m)
Pheriche (4243m)
Nangkan
Chhukkung Ri (5546m)
Machhermo (4410m)
Tshang (5000m)
Marulung (4200m)
Luza (4360m)
Thare (4300m)
Dingboche (4350m)
Chhukkung (4750m)
Lhabarma (4320m)
Dole
Phortse (3840m)
Ama Dablam (6812m)
Khumbila (5781m)
Mong La (3973m)
Pangboche (3858m)
Khumjung (3790m)
Syangboche
Tengboche (3967m)
Bhote Kosi
Khunde (3840m)
Thame (8800m)
Kangtega (6779m)
Kwanda (6187m)
Namche Bazaar (3400m)
Teng Kangpoche (6499m)
Tamserku (6608m)
Phari (6000m)
Jorsale (2790m)
Monjo
Phakding
Kusum Kanguru (6369m)
Ghat (2492m)
Dudh Kosi
Imja Kola
N
Not to scale
To Shivalaya
Lukla (2800m)

Treks
••••••••• Everest Base Camp
••••••••• Gokyo lakes
- - - - - Sherpa villages

1953 expedition walked all the way from Bhaktapur in the Kathmandu Valley as there were no roads beyond there.

Tip...
Yak attacks do occur! Give these creatures a wide berth and if you are passing them on the trail, always go around them on the upslope side.

Most trekkers fly to and from Lukla but a great itinerary, if you have the time, is to walk in and fly out. Delays at Lukla are common, so allow a few extra days for flexibility. Because of its popularity, the trail and the Sagarmatha region are well served with lodges and restaurants, although these do get more basic the higher you go.

It can get extremely cold north of Namche Bazaar, so appropriate clothing is necessary. You can hire down jackets in Namche Bazaar for around US$2.30 per day; this saves carrying them from Kathmandu.

You need to be fit. A couple of walks in the park will not prepare you. The effects of altitude, not the sickness just the extra effort required to walk, should not be

Tip...
Downhill walks can be tough on the knees and ankles: a stick or knee support can help. Begin walking early in the morning, as showers can develop from early afternoon.

underestimated. Don't hurry. The walking days can be quite short because of altitude gain requiring an overnight stop, so take your time.

TREKKING ITINERARIES

★ Everest Base Camp

The Base Camp route follows the trails used by the 1953 British Everest Expedition. In those days it was a little-visited valley, famous as the site of the ★ **Tengboche Monastery**, one of the Sherpa's most holy sites. As you climb you slowly leave the villages and steeply terraced fields behind, walking through high-altitude grazing before climbing onto the Khumbu ice flow for the last few hours to Base Camp. Most visitors also take time to climb **Kala Patthar**, a viewpoint to the west of the glacier which gives great views of Everest and its flanking peaks. You cannot see Everest from Base Camp.

Walking in from Shivalaya

Days 19 days   **Highest point** 5560 m   **Trek type** Camping and teahouse

Days	Itinerary	Altitude	Duration
Day 01	Drive to Shivalaya	1790 m	9 hours
Day 02	Shivalaya to Bhandar	2190 m	5 hours
Day 03	Bhandar to Sete	3000 m	6 hours
Day 04	Sete to Junbesi	2700 m	6 hours
Day 05	Junbesi to Nunthala	2194 m	7 hours
Day 06	Nunthala to Bupsa	2730 m	5 hours
Day 07	Bupsa to Phakding	2610 m	7 hours
Day 08	Phakding to Namche	3440 m	6 hours
Day 09	Acclimatization day	3440 m	
Day 10	Namche to Deboche	3710 m	5 hours
Day 11	Deboche to Dingboche	4410 m	5 hours
Day 12	Acclimatization day	4410 m	
Day 13	Dingboche to Lobuche	4910 m	5 hours
Day 14	Kala Patthar (5550 m)	4910 m	7 hours
Day 15	Lobuche to Pangboche	3930 m	6 hours
Day 16	Pangboche to Namche	3440 m	7 hours
Day 17	Namche to Phakding	2610 m	5 hours
Day 18	Phakding to Lukla	2840 m	3 hours
Day 19	Fly back to Kathmandu	1400 m	

Flying to Lukla

Days 16 days   **Highest point** 5360 m (Everest Base Camp)   **Trek type** Camping or lodge

Days	Itinerary	Altitude	Duration
Day 01	Fly to Lukla and trek to Monjo	2835 m	6 hours
Day 02	Monjo to Namche	3440 m	4 hours
Day 03	Acclimatization day	3440 m	
Day 04	Namche to Khumjung	3780 m	4 hours
Day 05	Khumjung to Deboche	3710 m	4 hours
Day 06	Deboche to Pangboche	3930 m	3 hours
Day 07	Pangboche to Dingboche	4410 m	4 hours
Day 08	Acclimatization day	4410 m	
Day 09	Dingboche to Lobuche	4910 m	5 hours
Day 10	Spare day at Lobuche*	4910 m	
Day 11	Base Camp, back to Lobuche	4910 m	10 hours
Day 12	Lobuche to Pangboche	3930 m	6 hours
Day 13	Pangboche to Mongla Danda	3800 m	7 hours
Day 14	Mongla Danda to Monjo	2835 m	5 hours
Day 15	Monjo to Lukla	2840 m	6 hours
Day 16	Fly back to Kathmandu	1400 m	

* Option: Early morning climb of Kala Patar, overnight at Goral Shep (5164 m).
Next day to Base Camp (if route is open) and return to Lobuche.

TREKKING ITINERARIES

★ Gokyo Lakes

Many consider this to be the ultimate mountain trek and if you are fit enough it's worth thinking about. You visit Everest Base Camp before crossing the Chola Pass into the Gokyo Valley. With its three main lakes, supposedly created by the trident of Shiva, it is a sacred place for both Hindus and Buddhists, and in August up to 500 holy men will come here to bathe in the waters, the highest lake system in the world.

Cho Oyu, Everest, Lhotse and Makalu are clearly visible from Gokyo Ri above Gokyo Lake. One of the most remarkable features is the views of the tremendous ice ridge between Cho Oyu and Gyachung. There are also magnificent views of the Ngozumpa Glacier – the largest in Nepal's Himalaya.

This also makes a good, shorter stand-alone trek without visiting Base Camp or crossing the Chola.

Days 18 days **Highest point** 5550 m **Trek type** Camping and teahouse

Days	Itinerary	Altitude	Duration
Day 01	Fly to Lukla and trek to Monjo	2840 m	6 hours
Day 02	Monjo to Namche	3440 m	4 hours
Day 03	Acclimatization day	3440 m	
Day 04	Namche to Debuche	3710 m	5 hours
Day 05	Debuche to Dingboche	4410 m	5 hours
Day 06	Acclimatization day	4410 m	
Day 07	Dingboche to Lobuche	4910 m	5 hours
Day 08	Kala Patthar (5550 m), Gorak Shep	5160 m	7 hours
Day 09	Base Camp, back to Lobuche	4910 m	9 hours
Day 10	Lobuche to Dzongla	4800 m	4 hours
Day 11	Dzongla to Dragnag (Cho La Pass 5420 m)	4700 m	9 hours
Day 12	Dragnag to Gokyo	4750 m	4 hours
Day 13	Hike to Gokyo Ri, camp at Machherma	4400 m	8 hours
Day 14	Machherma to Mongla Danda	3800 m	6 hours
Day 15	Mongla to Namche	3440 m	4 hours
Day 16	Namche to Phakding	2600 m	4 hours
Day 17	Phakding to Lukla	2840 m	3 hours
Day 18	Fly to Kathmandu	1400 m	

TREKKING ITINERARIES
Sherpa Villages Trek

The opportunity to walk in the Khumbu, experience the Sherpa culture, see Everest but avoid the higher altitudes and tougher days. You still need to be fit but as the itinerary is shorter, with two optional walk days, your stamina does not get sapped so much. There are also good-quality lodges for the nights.

Days 9 days   **Highest point** 3860 m   **Trek type** Lodge

Days	Itinerary	Altitude	Duration
Day 01	Fly to Lukla, trek to Phakding	2610 m	3 hours
Day 02	Phakding to Namche	3440 m	6 hours
Day 03	Acclimatization – walk to Thame	3440 m	
Day 04	Namche to Tengboche	3860 m	5 hours
Day 05	Day walk to Dingboche	3860 m	
Day 06	Tengboche to Namche via Khumjung	3440 m	7 hours
Day 07	Namche to Phakding	2610 m	5 hours
Day 08	Phakding to Lukla	2804 m	3 hours
Day 09	Fly to Kathmandu		

Kanchenjunga
& eastern Nepal
remote mountains, tea estates and vast landscapes

The east of Nepal offers some of the finest trekking in the country. Stunning views of some of the Himalaya's highest peaks combine with diverse flora and fauna and picturesque villages to make it a rewarding and unspoilt destination.

Easier to access and get around than the west, it's perfect for those who wish to leave behind the crowded main trails while still seeing huge peaks. On many of the routes there are lodges and teahouses, meaning only the longer, high-altitude sections entail camping.

The most famous mountains are Kanchenjunga, situated on Nepal's eastern border with Assam in India, and Makalu. Both are conservation areas and offer wonderful, uncrowded trekking similar to the Everest and Annapurna trails of 30 years ago. If you want something a little easier, then the Milke Danda ridge has superb views of the mountains and countryside. You can even walk into the Khumbu and Everest from here, following much less-frequented trails that those from Shivalaya.

Eastern Nepal is not just about mountains, however. The sacred Hindu town of Janakpur, with its Janaki Mandir, lies in the Terai, as does the Koshi Tappu Wildlife Reserve, famous for its amazing birdlife and wild buffalo. It's also the centre of Nepal's tea and coffee plantations, the most famous being those at Ilam on the Sikkim border.

Best for
Landscapes ▪ Tea ▪ Trekking ▪ Villages

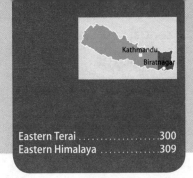

Kathmandu
Biratnagar

Footprint picks

★ **Janakpur**, page 302

One of Hinduism's most sacred sites, a blur of colour.

★ **Koshi Tappu**, page 305

A magnet for migrating waterfowl and a twitchers' delight.

★ **Ilam**, page 308

Rolling tea plantations encircle this sleepy town.

★ **Kanchenjunga**, page 310

The world's third highest peak surrounded by pristine wilderness.

★ **Makalu**, page 313

A little-visited area of high valleys, roaring rivers and glaciers.

Essential Kanchenjunga and eastern Nepal

Finding your feet

Getting to east Nepal is comparatively straightforward. There are flights to the area's biggest town Biratnagar, as well as Janakpur and Taplejung up in the hills. Road access is also good: a turning off the Arniko Highway at Dhulikhel winds its way down to the Mahendra Highway, the great east–west road. Access to the mountains has also improved and, although journey times are long, the services are reliable. Roads reach as far as Taplejung for Kanchenjunga and Num for Makalu.

Getting around

All Terai towns are well served by road and Janakpur is unique in that it has Nepal's only short stretch of railway. In the mountains, like everywhere else in Nepal, there are few roads and the only way in is to trek after either a flight to one of the remote airstrips or a long, slow and bumpy bus ride.

When to go

The general Nepal weather holds true for east Nepal, with October/November and March/April being the most popular trekking times. December and January should be avoided in the High Himalaya but the lower foothill treks can be very pleasant at this time with lovely, clear views. The tea plantations come alive in April and May when the tea is harvested by the many pickers, a process that continues until the plants stop sprouting as the cold of winter starts. The monsoon in eastern Nepal tends to be wetter than the west, experiencing the full force as it moves its way up from India. If you go during this time expect hot temperatures and lots of rain.

Time required

A couple of days is enough to see the sights of the Terai, which then leaves the hills. If you want to spend time at the tea plantations, then a minimum of two nights is needed to get there and explore the area. In the mountains, it depends on what you decide to do, with treks varying from a few days on the Milke Danda to over three weeks if you want the reach the base camp of one of the 8000-m peaks.

Weather Biratnagar

January	February	March	April	May	June
14°C	18°C	19°C	16°C	20°C	24°C
0°C	2°C	1°C	8°C	4°C	1°C
11mm	11mm	17mm	44mm	122mm	268mm

July	August	September	October	November	December
20°C	25°C	23°C	20°C	20°C	18°C
2°C	2°C	1°C	1°C	0°C	1°C
440mm	290mm	247mm	84mm	9mm	5mm

TIBET

Kangchungtse
Makalu II
(7129m)
Pethangtse ▲
▲ ★ 5
Makalu
(8463m)
Sherpani Col ▲ Peak 3
(7129m)
Pyramid Peak ▲ Peak 4
(7168m) ▲ ▲
Peak 6 Keke La
Peak 7 Ghungru La

Janak Himal

Nupchu Dangu Nepal
(6690m) ▲ (3665m) ▲ Peak
Sharpu I ▲ Rantang ▲ (7168m)
(6553m) ▲ Kanchenjunga
Sharpu II (8586m) ★ 4
(6236m)
▲ Kabure
Khumbhakana
(Jannu)
(7710m)

♦ *Makalu Barun
National
Park*

*Kanchenjunga
Conservation
Area*

Runbaun ○
○ Num

○ Chichila

○ Khandbari

Tumlingtar ✈
(3900m)
Baneshwor

Bhojpur

Tamaphok

○ Taplejung

○ Amarpur

INDIA

Pakribas ○ Parewadin ○

Rani
Gaun ○ Bharapa
○ Phidim

Aangsharang ○ ○ Embung

Dhankuta ○

Mahabharat ○

★ 3
Dharan ○ Ilam ○ Suryogaya
Goduk ○

Budhabare ○

★ 2
*Koshi Tappu
Wildlife
Reserve*
Itahari ○ Belbari ○ Damak ○ Kankai ○ Kakarbhitta
Bintamode
Bhokraha ○ Duhabi ○ ○ Gauradaha
Bhaluwa Itahara ○
Biratnagar ○ Rangeli ○

INDIA

*Makalu Barun
National
Park* ♦ *Kanchenjunga
Conservation
Area*

○ Taplejung

*Koshi
Tappu
Wildlife
Reserve*
★ Janakpur Itahari
Kakarbhitta

N

20 km
20 miles

Footprint picks

Eastern
Terai

The eastern Terai is similar in topography to the western areas, the Mahabharat Hills running between the main Himalayan range and the hot, lowlands of the Indian plains. It borders Bihar, West Bengal and Sikkim and has the Mahendra Highway running east–west across it. It finishes at Kakarbhitta where you can continue into Sikkim and the famous hill station of Darjeeling.

The landscape is lusher, however, than in the west, with a more tropical feel that is reflected in the lifestyle of the population. You could be in India, and in some areas you rarely hear Nepali spoken, replaced by a dialect from Northern India.

It is also the most industrial area of Nepal and has few towns that offer much to the visitor. Most tourists are travelling through en route to the hills and High Himalaya trekking, but there are a couple of exceptions. These include the holy Hindu city of Janakpur, the wildlife reserve at Koshi Tappu and, heading north into the hills, the small town of Ilam.

Biratnagar is Nepal's second largest city and foremost industrial town. It lies 23 km south of Itahari on the Mahendra Highway and is the district headquarters of Morang.

In its layout, the town bears remarkable similarity with Nepalgunj in the western Terai, though there is a marginally better selection of accommodation available here. The city has two long north- to south-running principal roads between which are its main bazaar and commercial areas along with most of its hotels.

The airport is 3 km north of the centre, while 6 km to the south is the village of **Rani Sikiyahi** and the Indian border. There are a few small temples and shrines, but nothing stands out as worth travelling to see. It serves as a transit town if you're travelling elsewhere in eastern Nepal.

Essential Biratnagar

Getting around

Biratnagar has no auto-rickshaws, though there are plenty of cycle-rickshaws. For longer distances there is a taxi rank at Mahendra Chowk. The taxis have no meters, so you'll need to negotiate the fare. You can save a lot of time and aggravation by asking your hotel for an idea of the right fare, or ask them to book it for you.

Listings Biratnagar

Where to stay

$ Eastern Star
T021-471626.
26 spacious rooms all with bath and TV, some with a/c. In a good location and with a decent Indian restaurant.

$ Hotel Panchali
T021-472520, www.hotelpanchali.com.np.
Built in 2013 this modern hotel has clean, functional rooms with en suite bathrooms. There is a restaurant and small roof terrace. Convenient for the bus station.

$ Hotel Xenial
T021-472950.
Comfortable rooms in pleasant grounds. There is a good Indian restaurant and free transfers to/from the airport.

Transport

Air
The airport is on the Dharan Rd, 3 km north of the Main Bazaar area. A taxi from the centre will cost around US$5.50 and a rickshaw about US$1.40.

There are daily flights to/from **Kathmandu** operated by **Yeti** and **Buddha** airlines, 40 mins, US$155-200. There are also seasonal, weekly flights to various airstrips in the hills including **Tumlingtar**, **Thamkharka** and **Lamidanda**. Always book in advance and accept that flights are subject to cancellation depending on weather conditions.

Bus
The bus park is on Dharan Rd, south of Mahendra Chowk. There are regular day and night buses to **Kathmandu**, 12-15 hrs, ranging from normal to deluxe services, US$9-14. There are also buses to Pokhara, 12 hrs, US$10.50 and Janakpur, 6 hrs, US$3.50.

Local buses serve all local towns, including **Hile**, 3-4 hrs, US$2.70, and **Dharan**, 1½ hrs, US$0.75.

Arriving in Janakpur from Kathmandu is rather like leaving Nepal for India. It is certainly one of the Terai's more interesting places and is ideally suited for a short stay to break the numbing journey between Kathmandu and Kakarbhitta. The town is a feast of temples: there are more than 100, dominated by the spectacular Janaki Mandir. It also has a sizeable Muslim minority, mostly long-term migrants from Bihar, and a small mosque (*masjid*) stands beside the Janaki Mandir. Economically it relies mainly on agriculture although there is some light industry.

Aside from its religious role, Janakpur has the distinction of being the focus of Nepal's only railway line. This is essentially no more than a short, narrow-gauge extension of a line in North Bihar and is currently being upgraded.

Essentials Janakpur

Getting around

Janakpur, 25 km south of the Mahentra Highway, is a small town and, as cars are banned from its centre, it is easy to explore on foot. There are numerous small temples and shrines, lots of ponds and tanks and hundreds of pilgrim hostels which, if you come during the festivals, are crammed with sadhus. Make for the old quarter beside the Janaki Mandir to really get the Indian feel of the town.

There are no taxis in Janakpur. Rickshaws are available for longer journeys. Remember to haggle. The ride to the airport (2-3 km) should cost about US$1.50-2.50; the shorter ride to the bus station about US$1.30.

When to go

Temperatures peak in May when they reach over 40°C and humidity is high. June to September is the monsoon. The cooler winter months, between November and February, are best, when temperatures average 20-30°C. Most people plan their trips around the festivals (see page 304).

Its contemporary significance is derived from its role as an important centre in the religious and historical geography of Nepal, and the town is often referred to as Janakpurdham, the suffix added in deference to its sacredness. Hindu pilgrims come from all over Nepal and India to worship at the town's many temples, shrines and *pokharis*, and during the main Hindu festivals Janakpur is said to attract more than double its own population in visitors.

The town takes its name from King Janak, ruler of the ancient and prosperous kingdom of Mithila who, the epic *Ramayana* records, found the baby Sita lying in a field at what is now Sitamadhi village just outside Janakpur.

Janaki Mandir

Known locally as Naulakha, this temple dedicated to Sita houses a large image of Sita said to have been found in a river near Ayodhya. It is built of white marble and its design resembles a Mughal fort, with an arched main gate and windows and octagonal parapets set into the towers on both sides.

It is said to have been built on the spot where King Janak found the infant Sita in a field. The temple was commissioned by Brishbhana Kunwar, the Maharani of the princely state of Tikamgarh in present-day Madhya Pradesh, central India. Construction was completed in 1911. The huge building contains 60 rooms and dominates the centre of Janakpur. Regular *puja* worship takes place in the early morning and in the late afternoon, especially evocative at the latter when candles flicker and hymns are chanted.

Boys are brought here to undergo the ritual of *chewar*, the first shaving of the head – look out for the dancers who are hired to perform at the ceremonies.

Non-Hindu visitors are not allowed into the shrine room, but can walk around the outer courtyard where you can see the magnificent marble tracery and other artwork.

There is a small **museum** ① US$0.15, telling the story of Rama and Sita inside the temple complex, as well as displaying some Maithili paintings.

Vivaha Mandap
Open 0500-2100, US$0.05.

The name of this modern addition to the Janaki Mandir complex means 'marriage pavilion'. It has a pagoda roof and, unusually, glass walls. The large images of Rama and Sita sit on a raised platform inside and commemorate their fabled wedding in full colour.

Janakpur

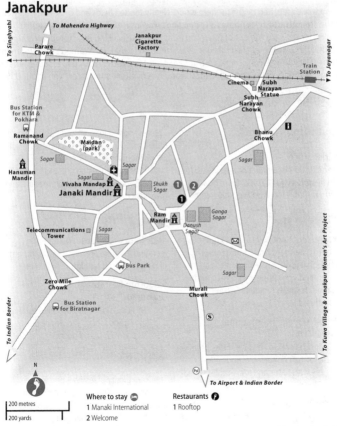

To Mahendra Highway
To Singhyahi
Parare Chowk
Janakpur Cigarette Factory
To Jayanagar
Train Station
To Jayanagar
Cinema
Subh Narayan Statue
Subh Narayan Chowk
Bus Station for KTM & Pokhara
Ramanand Chowk
Maidan (park)
Bhanu Chowk
Hanuman Mandir
Sagar
Sagar
Sagar
Sagar
Shukh Sagar ❶ ❷
Vivaha Mandap
Janaki Mandir
❶
Ram Mandir
Ganga Sagar
Danush Sagar
Telecommunications Tower
Sagar
Bus Park
Sagar
Zero Mile Chowk
Bus Station for Biratnagar
Murali Chowk
To Kuwa Village & Janakpur Women's Art Project
Ⓢ
Pol
To Airport & Indian Border
To Indian Border
N
200 metres
200 yards

Where to stay 🛏
1 Manaki International
2 Welcome

Restaurants 🍴
1 Rooftop

Ram Mandir

Janakpur's oldest temple, this was built in 1882 by Amar Singh Thapa, who was also responsible for Tansen's Amar Narayan Mandir. It lies at the heart of the old part of Janakpur, 200 m southeast of the Janaki Mandir. A shrine stands in the centre of the courtyard. Non-Hindu visitors are allowed in, but shoes and leather items should be removed and left outside. Just to the east is **Danush Sagar**, one of the town's holiest *pokharis* where pilgrims take a ritual cleansing bath before *puja*.

Old Quarter

To the south and east of the Janaki Mandir and centred around the Ram Mandir is the old town, an interesting mixture of shops, stalls and the sacred. To its east lies the **Ganga Sagar**, a large *pokhari*, considered the holiest of Janakpur's many ponds. On its western side is a dharamsala and ghat, now used mostly for washing.

Around Janakpur

There is some lovely countryside around Janakpur and some charming villages, many seemingly untouched by the modern world. Neatly tended fields and groves of fruit trees nestle around mud-brick houses and buildings. The local economy is entirely agricultural. A rickshaw can take you out of town and from there the walking is easy and fascinating.

Kuwa, one of the nearest villages, is home to the **Janakpur Women's Development Centre** ① www.jwdonline.com, Sun-Thu 1000-1700. Here you can buy paper souvenirs and fabrics, all profits going to helping local women. A rickshaw should cost you about US$2.

Listings Janakpur *map page 303.*

Tourist information

Tourist office
Station Rd east of Bhanu Chowk, close to the railway station, T041-20755. Sun-Thu 1000-1600, Fri 1000-1500. Nov-Jan 1000-1400.

Where to stay

Janakpur does not have a wide choice of tourist-standard accommodation. Although it is usually sufficient to cater for demand, rooms are very scarce during the main festivals when it is essential to book ahead.

$ Hotel Manaki International
T041-521540.
Unexciting rooms in need of a little attention, but clean and comfortable. Rooms are available with baths and a/c. Good, central location and friendly staff.

$ Hotel Welcome
T041-520646, www.nepalhotelwelcome.com.

The best option in town and one of the oldest, Hotel Welcome has a new wing with 39 a/c rooms to add to the 20+ it already had. It has a good restaurant and the staff can help you organize your sightseeing and give advice on bus schedules.

Restaurants

Aside from streetside food and hotel restaurants, there are very few restaurants of note in central Janakpur.

$ Rooftop Restaurant
Open 0930-2130.
You can sit outside at this upstairs restaurant and enjoy good Indian and Nepali dishes, washed down by a cold beer.

Festivals

There are plenty of festivals and lots of worshipping going on most of the time, meaning you can get a feel for how sacred the city is to Hindus whenever you visit.

During these main festivals the town can get really crowded.

Feb/Mar **Parikrama** is held at full moon, with tens of thousands of pilgrims walk the 8 km around the town, many prostrating themselves as they go.

Mar/Apr **Ram Navami** is celebrated after the full moon with 9 days and nights of music, drama, dance and other pageants. It is in honour of Ram's birthday and is a popular time for Sadhus to visit.

Oct/Nov **Dasain**, Nepal's largest national festival, is relatively small here, but is celebrated over 10 days, with goats being sacrificed at some temples on the last 2 days.

Nov **Lakshmi Puja** is the highlight of Diwali and is marked with thousands of small candles and lights being illuminated throughout the area, music all day and all night, and firecrackers (despite being officially banned by the local government). At dawn on the 3rd day women bathe in the sacred ponds and give offerings to the sun god Surya.

Nov/Dec Hundreds of thousands of pilgrims visit the temple for **Vivah Panchomi** ('marriage over 5 days'), the town's major annual festival, when the marriage of Sita and Rama is celebrated with numerous reenactments. An image of Rama is brought to the Janaki Mandir in a big procession and leaves the following day with that of Sita. It is held on the 5th day after the full moon and is a popular time for weddings.

Transport

Air
The airport is 2 km south of the town's main intersection. There is a daily flight to/from **Kathmandu** with **Buddha** and **Yeti Airlines**. The flight time is 30 mins.

Bus
There are buses throughout the day of varying standards of service to **Kathmandu** plus departures to **Pokhara**, **Biratnagar** and **Kakarbhitta**.

Train
The railway attracts attention because it is unique in Nepal, but it's not an especially comfortable or adventurous journey, and is used mainly by commuters. It is currently out of service as the track is being upgraded, with a scheduled reopening date later in 2017. It runs 27 km southeast to **Jayanagar** in India, and 19 km northwest to **Singhyahi**. There is a further stretch of disused and now broken track to Bijalpura in the hills.

★ Koshi Tappu Wildlife Reserve

a birdwatcher's paradise

Koshi Tappu (*tappu*, 'island') is the easternmost and the smallest of the Terai's national parks and wildlife reserves. It covers 175 sq km of the Sapt Koshi flood plain, immediately northeast of the Koshi Barrage, where the Sapt Koshi and Trijuga Khola rivers converge.

Comprising mainly grasslands and wetlands, Koshi Tappu is an internationally important area for wildfowl and waders. Flocks of duck number in the thousands, if not tens of thousands, and there are 17 globally endangered species, such as the red-necked falcon and Bengal florican.

Wildlife
The reserve does not contain any tigers or rhinos but was established to protect the endangered arna, a long-horned water buffalo in its last existing habitat. It also has nilgai (blue bulls), spotted and hog deer, monkeys, jackals wild boar and various other small mammals. Wild elephants occasionally pass through the reserve.

Essential Koshi Tappu Wildlife Reserve

Getting around

Walking is the most popular way of visiting the reserve. Guides will cost about US$18-23 for the day. Not only will they take you to the best locations, they also have eyes like hawks for spotting birds. Most of the lodges have resident ornithologists to take their walks, usually included in the price.

Park information

Pay your entry fee of US$9 per day at the reserve headquarters (T985-205 5405, open 0600-1800) at Kushaha on the eastern side of the reserve. To get there turn north off the Mahendra Highway at the village of Jamuha and drive for a couple of kilometres. There is also a small museum.

When to go

October to March is the coolest time to visit, before the heat and humidity of pre-monsoon and before the rains and flooding of the monsoon itself. It's possible to see the Himalayan peaks during this cool period.

The best time to spot winter migrants is during December and January. Late migratory species pass through in March. These are the best times to visit as temperatures are at their coolest and there is the most variety of fauna. Local villagers cut grasses for thatch during January, so animal spotting is easier after this.

Gangetic dolphins, darker-skinned relatives of the more familiar silver-skinned bottle-nosed dolphin, are occasionally seen jumping in the rivers, best spotted from the bridge at the Koshi barrage. The endangered gharial crocodile inhabits the area in small numbers which have been boosted by the re-introduction of more from the Chitwan breeding centre. The marsh mugger crocodile is more common, as are turtles. The waters are well stocked with over 200 species of fish, an important food source for the villages around the reserve's boundaries.

Above all, Koshi Tappu is known for its birdlife, with about 500 species including 20 species of duck, ibis, stork, swamp partridge, heron, egret, Bengal florican, red-necked falcon and many other exotic and migratory waterfowl not found elsewhere in Nepal. In the winter it's an important stopover for 165 migratory species.

Flora and environment

The vegetation is a combination of scrub grassland (kharpater) and deciduous riverine forest. The landscape changes dramatically with the seasons. It is at its best during the monsoon when the river swells to become a wide and powerful torrent heading south and feeding into the Ganges. Much of the flood plain is submerged to depths of up to 3 m.

In the dry months leading up to the monsoon, meanwhile, the flow is radically reduced and numerous sandy islands appear. The plains are flat and exposed to the strong winds which are a prominent feature of Terai weather at certain times of year. Prolonged vigorous gusts often whip up water from the river to create oblique screens of mist to give the area a spectacularly wild appearance.

Many of the small villages around Koshi Tappu, notably in the western flood plains, rely on fishing in the rivers for their livelihood, and fish (eg kaddi macha) forms an important part of the local diet. They are given fishing permits to allow them to do this, as well as cut grasses during January for use as thatch.

Game viewing

Birdwatching This is by far the most popular activity. Guided walks are usually made in the early morning and in the late afternoon. The variety and quantity of species is amazing. Visitors can spot over 150 species in one day. If you are staying in one of the lodges (see below) there will be a trained ornithologist to guide you and help identify your sightings. Several of the camps and lodges have viewing hides in their grounds, enabling you spot as you relax.

Boat trips You can choose between a canoe, raft or wooden *dunga* for river trips in the reserve. This peaceful way of exploring is perfect for both game and bird viewing, letting you enjoy the sounds of the reserve as well as the sights. Any of the lodges and camps can arrange a trip for you. The best time is late afternoon when the animals come to drink after the heat of the day.

Game-drives Some lodges offer jeep safaris, a good way of seeing more of the landscape and terrain. Walking and boat trips give more of a feel for the reseve, however, and – as animals are not the priority here – allow you to hear the birds.

Listings Koshi Tappu Wildlife Reserve

Where to stay

The lodges tend to offer full board, with all activities and guiding included. A few small lodges offer rooms but, once the activities are included, they don't necessarily work out more economical.

$$$$ Koshi Camp
T985-100 3677.
This pleasant camp on the eastern side of the park is about 6 km from reserve HQ and offers 11 large luxury, natural-colour safari tents with spacious dining and a bar. Run by a group of local naturalists it is very active in bird conservation and popular with international birdwatchers.

$$$$ Koshi Tappu Birdwatching Camp
T980-736 8484, www.koshitappu.net.
Situated right next to reserve HQ, this small camp has 10 safari tents, nicely situated on a small island, plus a few rooms in local-style cottages. Bathrooms are shared, but there's a good restaurant, a full range of activities and transfers can be arranged. Price includes all activities.

$$$$ Koshi Tappu Wildlife Resort & Camp
T01-422 6130, www.koshitappu.com.
Situated in the northeast corner of the reserve near the village of Prakashpur, the camp provides accommodation in 12 comfortable tents. It has a restaurant and bar. Activities including boat rides and guided walks with its own in-house guides. It has nice grounds with a hide and was the first camp to open in 1993. Price includes guides and activities.

Transport

Most people arrive at Koshi Tappu on an organized package, staying at a lodge with transfers and all game viewing included. If you are travelling independently, the best option is to fly to **Biratnagar** and take a taxi to the reserve, US$28-37. If you take the bus you must travel to **Laukahi**, then either connect to a local bus or get a lodge to collect you.

the centre of Nepal's fledgling tea industry

Ilam is an attractive, uncongested hill town concentrated along its main cobbled street in an almost Dickensian fashion. Long brick terraces with balconies overhanging a succession of small shops and eateries line the street as it climbs from west to east. The town square, a casual meeting place with a central statue of King Birendra atop a lotus, lies at the northeast end of town. Situated in the Churia Hills, it is some 90 km by road from Kakarbhitta, and is both central to, and synonymous with, Nepal's tea industry. Summer temperatures rise to around 30°C in May and dip to about 5°C in January. Annual rainfall is approximately 1600 mm.

The town is surrounded by tea gardens which extend like a broad belt of green carpet through the Churias of eastern Nepal and into India. The Ilam district is essentially an extension of the Darjeeling tea-growing area and is virtually identical in climate, soil and topography. There are also pockets of cardamom (*Elattaria cardamomum*) cultivation.

Ilam sees few Western visitors, but there is a genuine feeling of warmth (as well as an opportunity for locals to practise their English) for those that do make the trip. Although there are no Himalayan views, there are numerous opportunities for walks, especially through the quietly picturesque tea gardens.

With the upgrading of the road to Taplejung, the starting point of several excellent Kanchenjunga treks, it's now possible to start or finish in Ilam. It's a long journey, taking up to seven hours by jeep.

Listings Ilam

Where to stay

Ilam is not over blessed with places to stay, most are very basic.

$ Chiyabari Cottage
T027-520149.
A basic option but in a lovely location with great views out over the plantations and hills.

$ Green View
T027-520616, www.hotelgreenview.com.np.
A pleasant hotel that is in town but also with views of a tea plantation. Friendly

hosts and with good-sized rooms, some with private bathrooms.

Transport

Bus and jeep
Jeeps leave regularly to/from **Birtamod**, about 3 hrs, US$3.20. Buses are a bit cheaper but slower. The road is twisty and bumpy. Buses to **Kathmandu** from Ilam it take 18 hrs. Jeeps north to **Taplejung** take 7 hrs and cost US$7.30.

Eastern
Himalaya

Nepal's eastern Himalaya offer some of the country's finest mountain landscapes of towering peaks, raging rivers, deep valleys and untouched nature. In Kanchenjunga and Makalu it possesses two of the most impressive peaks, surrounded by vast areas of wilderness and remote, traditional villages.

Some people are deterred from trekking in this region because of the distance and expense of getting there from Kathmandu. But those that do make it this far will find an environmentally and culturally diverse region, still relatively unvisited by Westerners, that allows an insight into traditional community living and offers attractive trails not littered with previous trekkers' garbage.

Just below the looming crown of Kanchenjunga (8586 m), the Kanchenjunga Conservation Area covers a huge 2035 sq km. The area is made up of alpine grasslands, rocky outcrops, dense temperate and subtropical forests, and low river valleys. Higher up it gets more rugged, and over 60% of the park is estimated to be covered in rock, ice and snow.

The conservation area is situated in the Taplejung District and is bordered by the Tibet Autonomous Region of China in the north, Sikkim in India in the east and Nepal's Sankhuwasabha District to the west.

Wildlife

Kanchenjunga Conservation Area harbours a rich diversity of wildlife, including the endangered snow leopard, Himalayan black bear, musk deer and red panda. Other animals in the area include the blue sheep and many others. In a survey undertaken in spring 2016 some 29 snow leopards were recorded living here, making it one of their most important habitats in the world.

Impheyan pheasant, red-billed blue magpie and the shy drongo are some of the many birds found in the region.

Essential Kanchenjunga Conservation Area

Finding your feet

Ideally you would fly direct to Suketar, a couple of hours' walk from the regional centre of Taplejung, which tends to give its name to the airstrip. Flights are meant to operate once a week with **Tara Air** but can be erratic. If you are camping you may well bypass the town and head straight off (it is no great loss).

You need a TIMS card and a trekking permit to visit Kanchenjunga, US$10 per person per week. Note, however, that these can only be applied for by a registered trekking agency for groups of two trekkers or more. You will also need to pay your entrance fee to the conservation area, US$28. The agency will obtain this for you before you leave Kathmandu.

Park information

The area headquarters in Taplejung was established in 2016 when a long-running

Tip...

You will be asked for your permit and entrance fee receipt as various places on the treks so keep them to hand.

project with the World Wildlife Fund ended. Based here are two rangers and one conservation officer, whose focus has been to help the local community achieve more sustainable agriculture and grazing, as well as to boost the development of trekking.

When to go

The trekking seasons are similar to those of other High Himalaya treks: October and November are best for clear views and April to mid-June are best for the amazing flora. Winters are cold with heavy snowfall, so high passes and routes are not possible. The area bears the full brunt of the monsoon between June and September.

TREKKING ITINERARIES

Kanchenjunga Base Camp Trek

The valleys in eastern Nepal run south out of the Himalaya, meaning lots of ascents and descents as you cross them to reach Kanchenjunga. Its worth the effort. The scale of the mountains is breathtaking, the landscape's beautiful and you are rewarded with visits to Kanchenjunga's two main base camps and views of its picturesque companion, the mountain of Jannu.

Days 25 days **Highest point** 5400 m **Trek type** Camping only

Days	Itinerary	Altitude	Duration
Day 01	Fly Kathmandu/Biratnagar. Drive to Ilam	1200 m	7 hours
Day 02	Tharpu	1200 m	6 hours
Day 03	Dadagaon school	1500 m	6 hours
Day 04	Khebang	1740 m	8 hours
Day 05	Yamphuddin	1990 m	8 hours
Day 06	Lapche danda	2700 m	5 hours
Day 07	Torangdin	2800 m	4 hours
Day 08	Cheram	3980 m	5 hours
Day 09	Ramche	4580 m	5 hours
Day 10	Visit South BC (5400 m) and return to Cheram	3980 m	5 hours
Day 11	Sele La high camp	4440 m	9 hours
Day 12	Cross Sele la (4290 m) to Ghunsa	3795 m	5 hours
Day 13	Rest day at Ghunsa	3795 m	
Day 14	Kambachen	3960 m	6 hours
Day 15	Lhonak	4785 m	5 hours
Day 16	Pangpema (North BC 4940 m), return to Lhonak	4785 m	7 hours
Day 17	Kambachen	3960 m	4 hours
Day 18	Phale	3140 m	7 hours
Day 19	Thyangyam	2405 m	7 hours
Day 20	Sekathum	1650 m	7 hours
Day 21	Chirwa	1240 m	5 hours
Day 22	Mitlung	1140 m	6 hours
Day 23	Taplejung	1840 m	5 hours
Day 24	Drive to Ilam	1200 m	6 hours
Day 25	Drive to Biratnagar for flight to Kathmandu	1400 m	

Flora and landscape

The lowlands are full of tropical hardwoods. Further up, these get replaced by oaks and pine, and higher still the vegetation includes larch, fir and juniper up to the tree line.

The conservation area is home to 15 of Nepal's 28 endemic flowering plants. Almost all the 30 kinds of rhododendron species are found here. You can also look for 69 of Nepal's 250 orchid species.

Fact...
In spring, the area has an excellent display of flowering rhododendrons, orchids, lilies, primulas and many other flowers.

ON THE ROAD

The yak

Nothing quite characterizes the Tibetan-dominated, higher reaches of the Himalaya like the yak. Indeed, with its appearance at altitudes of 3000-6000 m, you know that you have arrived in the heart of the mountains. The animal has been closely associated with Tibetan groups since antiquity and its use as a pack animal – carrying loads rather than passengers – and has contributed to the wealth and livelihood of nomadic herders as well as traditional farming communities. It also forms an important part of the diet, providing meat, milk, butter, curd and cheese, all high in protein. Its hide, meanwhile, is used for footwear, and its coat for clothing. Even its dung is used, dried and them burnt on the fire for fuel.

The yak (*Bos grunniens* – literally, 'grunting ox') is a member of the bovine family and has the same number of chromosomes as the common dairy cow. The word *yak* comes from the Tibetan *gyag* and is in fact the male of the species, while the female is known as a *nak* by Sherpas and *dri* by the Bhotias. It has been successfully cross-bred with the domestic cow to produce the *dzo*, a strong ploughing animal which is also renowned for the richness of its milk.

The yak is well adapted to its lofty habitat. Its long, coarse outer coat covers a fine undercoat which together provide warmth against the extremes of high-altitude temperatures. The skin is thick and has very few sweat glands to further conserve heat by reducing perspiration, although this can become a liability at lower elevations. Its lungs are larger than those of other bovines and its blood contains up to four times as many red blood cells, enabling the maximum utilization of available oxygen.

Its digestive system has become highly efficient at metabolizing low-quality fodder, while its tongue and short teeth allow it to graze off the short grass and other scarce vegetation of high altitudes. Curiously, one of the main causes of yak mortality is insufficient food intake resulting from worn-out teeth. A yak's normal life span rarely exceeds 20 years.

If you meet a train of yaks lumbering down a mountain trail be sure to stand on the mountain side. Their loads swing from side to side and can easily knock the unsuspecting trekker off the trail to the river below. Also, check before you start crossing a suspension bridge – yaks don't like the bounce and sway and tend to speed up as they cross – not a good thing to meet face to face when halfway across.

People and culture

As the original settlers of the Upper Tamur Valley, the Limbu are the dominant ethnic group in the lower regions. Here the cultivation of cardamom is an important source of income.

The Sherpa/Lama people live in the higher regions, where they arrived from Tibet more than 400 years ago. These Sherpas have a distinct culture and different traditions from those in the Solu Khumbu district in the Everest region.

In total, approximately 5000 people live in the conservation area from 13 distinct ethnic groups. Other main groups include Rais, Chhetris and Brahmins.

Where to stay

There are some basic teahouses and lodges available on some of the routes, usually at the lower altitudes. Higher up there are none. They cater for local porters as much as for trekkers, so the standards are very low compared to the main routes. They are also closed over the winter and should not be replied on. Most people come with a trekking agency, and these supply camping equipment, porters, food and guides. Camping also gives you the flexibility to stay in some beautiful locations.

Transport

Air

The Suketar airstrip, which is near **Taplejung**, has just reopened after being surfaced for the first time. It is the best starting point for many of the treks. **Tara Air** currently flies from Kathmandu on Fri, about 50 mins, US$279.

Bus and jeep

You can reach the conservation area by bus through **Dharan** (the road finishes at **Basantpur**). There is also a jeep road from **Ilam** to Taplejung, a bumpy journey that will take you 7-8 hrs, about US$7.40.

★ Makalu-Barun National Park and Conservation Area

stunning high-altitude landscapes

High in the heart of the eastern Himalaya, seven valleys radiate from Mt Makalu, the world's fifth-highest peak. These valleys, especially the Barun Valley, contain some of the last remaining pristine forest and alpine meadows in the country. It offers excellent trekking, either as a destination in its own right or as a route into or from the Khumbu.

From the bottom of the Arun Valley, just 435 m above sea level, the Himalaya rise to the snow-covered summit of Makalu, 8463 m, over a distance of just 40 km. With such a variety of altitudes and climates, the national park contains some of the richest and most diverse habitats for plants and animals in Nepal.

The park and conservation area were established in 1992 as Nepal's eighth national park and the first to include from its inception an adjacent inhabited conservation area as a buffer zone. This new park management approach encourages local people to become involved in protecting the forests and natural resources upon which their lives depend, and in turn conserve their own cultural heritage.

Living in the lower reaches of the park are communities of Rai, Sherpa and Shingsawa villagers, surviving through subsistence farming. Though economically poor and geographically isolated, they have retained a strong cultural heritage that is fascinating to witness.

Traditional ways of resource management, such as community-controlled grazing and forest guardianship, are being strengthened, and low-level technologies have been introduced where appropriate. The aim is to improve local living standards through better infrastructure and education, as well as income-generating activities, while protecting and maintaining the environment and cultures.

Covering 2330 sq km Makalu-Barun is a vital component of the greater Mount Everest ecosystem and includes Nepal's 1148-sq-km Sagarmatha National Park to the west and the 35,000 sq km of Tibet's Comolangma Nature Preserve to the north.

Wildlife

The snow leopard is present in the park but is elusive. Also found here are the endangered red panda, Himalayan black bear and the clouded leopard. Other mammals include ghoral, tahr, wild boar, barking deer, Himalayan marmot and weasel, common langur monkey and the serow.

The park has over 400 species of bird, including the spotted wren babbler and the olive ground warbler, two of Nepal's rarest birds.

The Arun river that roars through the park has around 84 varieties of fish.

Flora and landscape

The incredibly steep topography and heavy monsoon rains (1-4 m per year) of the eastern Himalaya include a diverse range of bioclimatic zones and nurture a veritable storehouse of medicinal plants.

Alpine pastures above 4000 m contain dwarf rhododendron and juniper, aromatic herbs and delicate wildflowers, including 47 different varieties of orchid. Subalpine forests of fir, birch and rhododendron, and temperate stands of oak, maple and magnolia thrive at 2000-4000 m. Luxuriant orchids drape the chestnut and pine forests of the subtropical zone (1000-2000 m) and sal forests reach their northernmost limit within Nepal along the banks of the Arun (below 1000 m).

Essential Makalu-Barun National Park and Conservation Area

Finding your feet

Most of the Makalu-Barun National Park is remote wilderness, with just a few small settlements and seasonal herding in high pastures. Apart from the occasional climbing expedition, few foreigners have visited the area.

The inaccessible lower Barun Valley, a glacier-fed tributary to the Arun river, and its tributary the Saldima, flow through the most pristine area in the park and have now been designated as a Strict Nature Reserve, the first in Nepal. The whole area is closed to visitors, protected in an undisturbed state for scientific study and environmental monitoring.

Park information

The park entrance fee, US$27.50, can be paid in advance in Kathmandu or at the small checkpoint at Bung. There are no additional trekking permits required other than a TIMS card.

When to go

Late September to November are peak trekking periods here, with generally clear days and good views. The winters are cold and heavy snowfall makes the upper trails impassable. Spring brings warmer temperatures and the flora is at its best from April to early June. The monsoon months tend to be very wet making approach jeep roads and some trails all but impassable. Leeches abound at this time.

Fact...

It's now possible to trek from Kanchenjunga to Makalu via a high-level route that is part of the Great Himalayan Trail – a footpath that stretches the length of the country. It involves high passes and requires a good level of fitness. It is a camping trek.

TREKKING ITINERARIES
Makalu Base Camp Trek

Makalu is one of the most distinctive of the 8000-m peaks, a hump-sided pyramid of rock and ice. Unlike Everest it is not hidden behind other mountains nor visited by thousands of people every year. A trek to its Base Camp, at the top of the Barun Valley, lets you explore this little-visited area of wilderness.

Days 18 days   **Highest point** 4900 m   **Trek type** Camping

Days	Itinerary	Altitude	Durataion
Day 01	Fly to Tumlingtar and drive to Chichila	1850 m	3 hours
Day 02	Trek to Num	1505 m	6 hours
Day 03	Sedua	1460 m	6 hours
Day 04	Tashigaon	2200 m	4 hours
Day 05	Kauma Kharka	3470 m	7 hours
Day 06	Shipton La–Mumbuk	3500 m	7 hours
Day 07	Nehe Kharka	3670 m	5 hours
Day 08	Extra day or hike to Langmale Kharka	3670 m	
Day 09	Sherson	4700 m	6 hours
Day 10	Makalu Base Camp	4900 m	4 hours
Day 11	Rest day or day hike	4900 m	
Day 12	Rest day or day hike	4900 m	
Day 13	Tematan Kharka	3500 m	6 hours
Day 14	Sano Pokhari	4100 m	7 hours
Day 15	Sedua	1460 m	6 hours
Day 16	Chichila	1850 m	7 hours
Day 17	Tumlingtar	460 m	4 hours
Day 18	Fly Tumlingtar–Kathmandu	1400 m	

People and culture

Some 32,000 people live in the conservation area, coming from a mixture of cultural backgrounds. The majority in the lower valleys belong to various tribes of Rais and practice an ancient religion which reinforces harmony with nature. A handful of other hill tribes including Gurung, Tamang, Magar, Newar, Brahmins, Chhetris and occupational castes also live in the lower elevations.

Shingsawas and Sherpas are both Bhotia people originally from Tibet, and they live at the higher elevations and carry on Buddhist traditions.

These people live in isolated villages much as they have for centuries. As farmers, herders and seasonal traders, their livelihoods depend heavily upon forest resources for animal fodder, fuel, food, housing materials, fertilizers, medicine and other creative uses, such as clothing spun from *allo* (nettles), paper made form *lokta* (daphne bark) and countless items made from bamboo including furniture, containers, baskets, musical instruments, raincoats and aqueducts.

Milke Danda Trek

This not-too-strenuous trek starts in Tumlingtar. You trek along the Milke Danda, a high forested ridge between the Arun and Tamur valleys, with excellent views of both Kanchenjunga and Makalu. The area is renowned for its flowers, especially for its rhododendron forests which bloom in the spring. A good level of fitness is still required.

Listings Makalu-Barun National Park and Conservation Area

Where to stay

If you are trekking between Tumlingtar and Lukla, along the traditional east–west trade route that has been used for centuries, there are small lodges and local teahouses in most villages. Do not expect the same standards as those of the Everest region. These are much more basic, many with dormitory-style accommodation in smoky rooms. The local food is tasty after a long day's walk.

The Makalu Base Camp trek (see page 315) also has teahouses, though these are even more basic than the Lukla route ones and are only open during the main walking seasons of Oct, Nov and Apr.

Always check ahead, asking in each village where the next available accommodation is.

Camping is a good option, with official campsites as well as the option of staying next to teahouses in the small villages and hamlets.

$ Urubashi Resort
Tumlingtar, T029-575033.
Urubashi Resort has the best rooms and a decent restaurant, although it's not the most atmospheric of places. If you push on to Num, heading towards Makalu in the Arun Valley, you might need to change jeeps in Khandbari. If you have to overnight here, the **Aarati ($)** is the pick of the bunch.

Transport

Air
The most common starting/finishing point is the airstrip at Tumlingtar. Both **Buddha Air** and **Yeti Airlines** currently have daily flights from **Kathmandu**, US$145. Check before you travel as this can change with the season and demand.

Bus
The long, bumpy journey from **Kathmandu** adds a few extra days to your trip and is not great preparation for a tough trek. A bus from **Dharan** to Tumlingtar takes 10 hrs, or a jeep/bus combo is quicker at 7 hrs.

If you are heading to Makalu Base Camp you can go further than Tumlingtar, with a road going all the way to **Num** via **Khandbari**, some 4 hrs further north by jeep.

Rara & western Nepal

a little-visited and pristine area of wilderness and cultures

If you want to get far from the beaten tourist routes and experience Nepal as it must have felt to the first travellers in the 1950s and 60s, then the western region of Nepal is worth considering.

Even though its Terai contains national parks that offer some of the best game and bird viewing in the country, the west tends to be overlooked for several reasons. Firstly, it's hard to get to and the infrastructure is less developed than in other regions. Flights are necessary which makes travelling there unpredictable and pricey. And then there's the scenery which doesn't offer the draw of any big names, such as Everest or Annapurna. The Himalaya have arced north into Tibet, leaving mountains that are small by Nepalese standards, a mere 6000-7000 m high. And finally, there is the question of access. Several regions still require special permits as they enter sensitive political and cultural zones which in some cases can add a fairly hefty fee to your visit.

But as a reward your travels will be little affected by tourism. Mountain kingdoms, such as Dolpo and Humla, will offer insights into Tibetan culture as well as desolate, harsh landscapes as they sit high in the rain shadow of the Himalaya.

Best for
Adventure ▪ Culture ▪ Unspoilt beauty

Footprint
picks

★ **Bardia National Park**, page 327
Best tiger viewing in Nepal, far from the crowds.

★ **Karnali river**, page 332
A thrilling descent of one of the world's best rafting rivers.

★ **Rara Lake**, page 336
Nepal's largest lake set in a stunning landscape of forest and meadows.

★ **Dolpo**, page 338
This remote area is an untouched insight into Tibetan culture.

★ **Shey Phoksundo National Park**, page 341
Nepal's biggest park and an area of pristine wilderness that's home to
snow leopards.

★ **Khaptad National Park**, page 342
Meadows, grassland and forest with an abundance of flowers and birdlife.

★ **Humla**, page 345
A high-altitude, remote valley in the very far west.

Essential Rara and western Nepal

Finding your feet

Visiting the Terai region, most people fly to Nepalgunj, a one-hour flight from Kathmandu. Jumla is the starting point for many trips to the western mountains, with daily flights from Nepalgunj. These are susceptible to the weather and often get cancelled. There are other small airstrips that can be used for specific treks, Juphal for Dolpo, for example. It is possible to travel by bus to Jumla but the road is very slow and it is not recommended unless you have plenty of time to spare and a lot of patience.

Getting around

The great east–west highway runs across the western Terai but turn off this and the roads soon become unsurfaced. Roads, or jeep tracks as they should be called, are slowly penetrating the mountains of the west, but they are very slow and don't reach into the Tibetan-influenced valleys on the northern border. To get here, and to most of the trekking destinations, you need to walk. If you are a good rider you can hire ponies, a popular way for the locals to travel, but this is expensive.

Tourist facilities

Compared to the rest of Nepal, tourist facilities are very limited, with only basic lodges and teahouses available. Many visitors choose to camp which is more expensive but makes the trip more enjoyable and more of an adventure.

When to go

The mountains in the north of the region are best visited in May, June or September. Temperatures are at their best and, being in the rain shadow of the hills, you'll be protected from the rains. It gets very cold in the winter months. The lower mountains, around Rara Lake, are best between October and April, while the coldest temperatures are in December and January. Bardia and the Terai can be visited year-round, but it does get very hot and humid between June and September.

Time required

Visiting the west of Nepal is not advised if you're on a tight schedule. Flights are often cancelled, meaning you need a couple of slack days within your itinerary and after your trip. Logistics are complicated, with few lodges and restaurants, making camping the best option in many places. Because of the effort and costs involved, most visitors stay for at least a couple of weeks to make the trip worthwhile.

Western
Terai

Travel in the western Terai brings its own particular rewards. The magnificent Seti, Karnali and Bheri rivers all flow through the region from their High Himalaya origins before going on to join the Ganges system in India. If you have time, the Sukla Phanta and Bardia national parks cover a combined area of more than 1100 sq km, as yet unspoilt by commercial exploitation, providing a protected habitat for a wide range of birds and other wildlife including a number of endangered species such as the tiger, pygmy hog and swamp deer.

Neither park yet features prominently on the main tourist trail and, although individual budget travellers may find access a bit challenging, organized tours are available from Kathmandu. It is possible that Bardia might undergo more development for tourism but until it does, both parks remain sanctuaries undamaged by the modern world and allowing an almost undisturbed appreciation of a natural wilderness.

Nepalgunj is an important regional centre, the hub of a fairly extensive bus and air network, one of Nepal's border crossings to India and, in effect, capital of western Nepal. It is not an especially attractive town and offers little of tourist interest. Most visitors only transit through to Bardia National Park or connect to a flight up into the mountains.

The town spreads out from two, long north–south roads, 11 km south of the Mahendra Highway and a few kilometres north of the Indian border. Its centre is dominated by a bazaar area of narrow lanes and side streets, at its busiest early in the morning when fruit, vegetables, meat, textiles and other essentials are haggled over. It's an interesting place to wander for an hour or so, a bazaar totally geared to the town's inhabitant rather than tourists.

Like many of the larger Terai towns, Nepalgunj has a significant Muslim population, the result of long-established patterns of migration between the Terai and the Indian states of Uttar Pradesh and Bihar. This is reflected in the number of mosques in the town. It is also the centre for expats working in the western areas.

Sights

The **Bagheshwari Mandir**, slightly to the south of the main bazaar area, is the largest of the town's temples. A modern, three-storeyed concrete structure of lurid pink, it is dedicated to Kali, the goddess of destruction. A small Shiva linga shrine stands in the courtyard. To the west is a large *pokhari* where a walkway leads to a central shrine also containing an image of Shiva. The **Janaki Mandir** comprises the two traffic islands on either side of **Tribhuvan Chowk**, whose shrines attract worship from passers-by. Some 400 m south of Tribhuvan Chowk and next to the main *tonga* stop is the small **Hanuman Mandir**.

There are several **mosques** dotted around town, the largest just north of BP Chowk. Friday is the main day of worship for Muslims.

Essential Nepalgunj

Getting there

Air

Nepalgunj is the main hub for air travel in western Nepal. The airport is located about 6 km north of town. A taxi to/from the airport is about US$6.

There are daily flights to Kathmandu, taking about an hour. **Buddha Air**, T081-525745, www.buddhaair.com, and **Yeti Airlines**, T081-52655, www.yetiairlines.com, both fly the route. A one-way ticket costs US$180.

There are flights to Jumla, Dolpo and Simikot from here, all of which are dependent on the weather and prone to cancellation. There are also less frequent flights to Rara.

Bus

The bus station is about 1 km northeast of the bazaar. There are services to both Pokhara and Kathmandu, both trips taking approximately 12 hours. Most leave in the early morning. Buses to Bardia head to Thakurdwara and take three hours.

Getting around

Nepalgunj is one of the few Terai town where *tongas*, horse-drawn passenger carts, are an important form of local transport. They run on set routes and the main stop is 400 m south of Tribhuvan Chowk. There are also taxis, tempos and cycle-rickshaws. A taxi to/from the airport is about US$6.

Where to stay

Should you need to stay in Nepalgunj, accommodation is limited.

Nepalgunj

To ①③① & Airport
Main Bus Park
(Long Distance)

Local,
Mahendranagar &
Thakurdwara Buses

Tank

Ⓢ Ⓢ
Birendra
Ⓢ Chowk

Annapurna
Supermarket

Bagheshwari
Mandir

BP Chowk

Shrine

Tank

Nepalgunj
Industrial
Estate

Janaki
Mandir

Tribhuvan
Chowk

Rani
Pokhari

Janaki
Mandir

Hanuman
Mandir

Tonga Stop

Ⓢ Nepal Bank

N

Not to scale

Surkhet Rd

Where to stay 🛏
1 Siddhartha
2 Sneha
3 Traveller's Village

Restaurants 🍴
1 Candy's Place

$$ Hotel Sneha
A couple of kilometres south of the bazaar, T081-520487.
This mid-range hotel has reasonable rooms set in a pleasant garden with pool. The garden is the main attraction.

$$ Siddhartha Hotel
Near the airport, T081-521200.
This modern hotel is the most convenient if waiting for a flight. There are 50 rooms, gardens to sit in, a pool and a rooftop terrace restaurant with views of the airport.

$ Traveller's Village
2 km northeast of Birendra Chowk, T081-550329.
A very comfortable and clean guesthouse, popular with expats and often full, so do ring ahead.

Restaurants

Nepalgunj is not renowned for its culinary excellence. Most people eat at the hotel restaurants which tend to offer Nepali and Indian dishes.

$$ Candy's Place
T081-550329.
This is the best (and only) option for steak. They also serve burgers, roast chicken, beer and wines. Just what you need after a couple of weeks of *dal bhat*.

Kipling meets African savannah

The most westerly and least visited of Nepal's major wildlife reserves, Sukla Phanta covers an area of 355 sq km. Almost 30% of this total area is grassland, making it unlike any other park in South Asia; in fact, it has been likened to the savannahs of sub-Saharan Africa. Formerly open forest, it was first given protected status as a royal hunting reserve in the 1960s, then re-designated a wildlife reserve in 1973. The 'extension area' to the east and northeast of the original reserve was subsequently incorporated to bring it to its current size.

The reserve's name probably derives from the colour of the flowering grasses: *sukila* is a Nepali and Tharu word for white, while *phanta* is the Tharu term for grassland usually occurring in sal forest. It was first mentioned in Western literature in the early 20th century by Baden-Powell in his *Indian Memoirs*. The Mahakali River flows to the west of the reserve and is flanked by swamp land.

The park provides a natural habitat for over 500 species of bird, reptile and mammal, including what is thought to be the world's largest population of swamp deer.

Essential Sukla Phanta Wildlife Reserve

Finding your feet

The reserve's remote location makes it awkward to get to independently, but also ensures that it remains almost completely undeveloped. The main entrance and reserve office are about 4 km south of the Mahendra Highway (the junction to it is 2 km west of Bhimdatta (Mahendranagar), past the airstrip).

Getting around

Walking is not allowed inside the reserve. Sukla Phanta is not well geared up for independent visitors, although the park office can assist with information and guides.

Reserve information

It is possible to visit the reserve both independently or on a tour. The reserve office is at the park entrance and is open daily 0600-dusk. You must pay your US$9 permit fee here and hire a guide if you don't have one (a guide is compulsory inside the park – the office can provide information). There is a vehicle charge of US$18.

When to go

The best time to visit is November to February after the tall grasses have been burnt off and before the temperatures start rising. The months of December and January are fairly cold and misty with temperatures ranging from 10-12°C. These rise gradually to 22-25°C in February and March. In the pre-monsoon period (April-June) the temperatures range from 30-32°C and sometimes reach over 42°C with increasing humidity. During the monsoon the tracks inside the park become impassable and it is impossible to visit.

Tip...

Beautiful Rani Tal in the centre of the park is a popular watering hole and the nearby lookout tower provides a superb vantage point.

Wildlife

Sukla Phanta shares its fauna with the Bardia National Park to the east and with the forests of Uttar Pradesh extending as far west as Corbett National Park. It lies on the migratory trail between Nepal and

India of numerous species of bird as well as several of the larger mammals, including elephants and tigers. The open expanse of grassland increases the confidence of deer and other animals wary of predators, resulting in a high degree of visibility and excellent sighting opportunities.

The reserve itself has elephants, rhino (translocated from Chitwan) and, attracted by an ample supply of prey, a small tiger population, estimated at a maximum of 20 individuals. Most are migratory, passing between parks and reserves.

A smaller number of leopards are found, but these are generally even more elusive than the tiger. Various species of deer, notably the endangered swamp deer and also the spotted, barking and hog deer, abound, with possible sightings of several hundred at one time. Deer mostly inhabit swampy areas by rivers, but are also found at the forest margins.

Monkeys, especially the common langur (black face, hands and feet, silvery coat and long tail) and the rhesus macaque (reddish face and red-brown body) constitute the reserve's largest population of mammals.

Reptiles include the gharial, and marsh mugger crocodiles are present in the marshy areas around Rani Tal and along the Mahakali River. Otters are common in swampy areas and along river banks where they hunt for fish, including the large catfish, with speed and great agility.

Most prominent is the reserve's stunning array of birdlife, the most diverse of any park in Nepal. The forest, grassland and riverine environments attract almost 500 species, both resident and migratory.

Flora and environment

About 65% of the reserve consists of sal-dominated forest, almost 30% is phanta grassland, and the remainder is swamp and water. Many kinds of waterfowl live in the wetland zones, such as Rani Tal and Sikari Tal (lakes).

The reserve's extensive open grasslands are famous for the largest herds of swamp deer in the world and for rare grassland birds such as the Bengal florican.

The phanta grasslands comprise three main types of grass: *dhaddi*, a broad-leafed variety growing up to 2 m and extensively used by Tharu communities for thatching; *siru*, growing up to 60 cm; and elephant grass (*Typha elephantina*) which can grow up to 6 m.

The frequent comparisons with sub-Saharan savannah are not misplaced, as Sukla Phanta also experiences the seasonal fires characteristic of savannah ecology. Far from damaging the environment, as is often perceived, these fires are crucial to its cyclical regeneration.

The tall, straight-growing and broad-leafed sal tree is predominant, but there are a number of other varieties, some flowering. The 'flame of the forest' tree produces attractive, deep red flowers in March and April.

Game-viewing

Jeep safaris are the only way to explore the reserve, as walking is banned and elephant rides are no longer an option. With the network of tracks jeeps are a good way to explore the different terrains and with the open grasslands it does have the feel of an African safari.

There are two viewing towers to the south of the reserve, the first in the Sukla Phanta area of grassland, to help you spot the large herds of deer, and the second overlooking Rani Lake. Try to get here early when the birdlife is at its noisiest; dawn chorus is impressive.

To complete the Kipling *Jungle Book* feel, you might discover the overgrown walls of the Singpal Fort, the fabled ruined palace of an old Tharu King.

Listings Sukla Phanta Wildlife Reserve

Where to stay

Accommodation near the park is limited, so some travellers choose to stay in Bhimdatta (Mahendranagar) and make a day trip by jeep.

$$ Hotel Opera
Bhimdatta (Mahendranagar), T099-522101, www.hoteloperanepal.com.
The pick of the bunch of the Mahendranagar accommodation, Hotel Opera offers decent rooms in a quiet location. The restaurant is also probably the best available.

$$ Shuklaphanta Jungle Cottage
Near Park HQ, T099-524693.
Nestling in the buffer zone, the Shuklaphanta Jungle Cottage has pleasant a/c rooms arranged in a peaceful garden. The restaurant serves a limited menu but uses good, organic ingredients. You can arrange guides and jeeps through the lodge and even undertake an overnight camping trip.

$$ Shuklaphanta Wildlife Camp
About 500 m from the park gate, T974-106 0150
This tented camp run by the local guide association offers transfers to/from the airport and full guided activities.

Transport

Air
The nearest airport is Dhangadhi which has daily flights to **Kathmandu**.

Bus
Buses run to/from **Kathmandu** (16 hrs), **Pokhara** (14 hrs) and **Nepalgunj** (4 hrs).

Jeep
A jeep in **Bhimdatta** (**Mahendranagar**) will cost about US$46 to hire for the day for a game drive.

★ Bardia National Park

pristine jungle, no crowds and tigers

Covering an area of 968 sq km, Bardia is the largest of the Terai's national parks. It has more than 30 species of mammal, over 400 species of bird and several reptiles. It is said to be the best place in South Asia for tiger sightings and many visitors prefer it to Chitwan.

Originally set aside in 1968 as a Royal Hunting Reserve, the area became a wildlife reserve in 1982 and a national park in 1986. The main objectives of the park are to conserve a representative ecosystem of the mid-western Terai, particularly that of the tiger and its prey species. During the Maoist insurgency of the 2000s Bardia suffered terribly from poaching, and the one-horned rhino that had successfully been reintroduced from Chitwan was all but eradicated once more. More have since been transferred, the latest in March 2016, and their population is growing again under the protective eye of the army.

Essential Bardia National Park

Finding your feet

The main entrance at is at Thakurdwara, a small village about 3½ hours northwest of Nepalgunj. The park is bordered to the west by the Geruwa River, a major tributary of the Karnali, and extends into the forested slopes of the Churia Hills to the north and east. The Mahendra Highway joins the boundary from the south, passing through the park's 'buffer zone' before veering north to cross the Karnali Bridge at Chisapani. The Babai River runs an east–west course through the park. To the east of Bardia lies the adjoining Banke National Park.

Getting around

Most visitors explore Bardia by 4WD jeep. An extensive network of tracks criss-crosses the park and a game drive is the best way of seeing lots of animals and birds in a short space of time. The best way to see a tiger is to park near a known river crossing, turn off the engine and wait for the tiger to come to you.

Walking is another popular way to explore and this must be done with a qualified guide. Viewing platforms in strategic places give good views of open areas of grassland and river beds. The rhinos are often seen in the rivers, eating the thick weed that grows on the riverbed. Being on foot allows you to see and hear the jungle animals that would otherwise have hidden from the jeep. You can also come face to face with a tiger or rhino. Always listen to your guide's instructions and remember his safety briefing given before you start. (See page 331.)

Park information

Park headquarters, at the park entrance at Thakurdwara, T084-429719, is open dawn until dusk and sells park permits costing US$9.
Tharu Museum (Tue-Sat 1200-1500, US$0.45, or free if you've visited the Crocodile Breeding Centre), located near the park HQ, has displays on the culture and beliefs of the indigenous Tharu people. You can also arrange to see Tharu dancing or a Tharu cultural tour to nearby villages through your lodge.
Elephant Breeding Centre (dawn-dusk US$0.45), south of park HQ, will allow you to get pretty close to the elephants. But you'll need to visit in the morning or late afternoon as the elephants are working in the park during the day, so there is little to see.

When to go

The best times to visit are between October and early April when weather is warm and dry. Grasses are cut in late January/February meaning that visibility is much better in the surrounding forests for game-viewing. From April onwards the temperatures rise, peaking at around 45°C in May and pre-monsoon thunderstorms continue until late September. During this time most roads and rivers become impassable and most lodges remain closed. Leeches are present in numbers and the Khaura River, between the park entrance and the main area of the park, is also often too high to cross, further restricting visits.

Flora and environment

Numerous small rivers and streams, tributaries of both the Karnali and Geruwa rivers, flow through the western areas of the park. In the months preceding the monsoon, many dry up or are reduced to minor trickles around large gravel islands.

About 70% of the park is forested, the rest being a mix of grasslands, savannah and riverine forest. Riverine forest includes flowering trees such as the silk cotton tree with its delightful scarlet blossoms from March. Nearly 850 different flora species have been recorded.

Wildlife

Along with the adjoining 550 sq km of Banke National Park, Bardia offers a haven to several of South Asia's most endangered animals.

It is home to a healthy population of around 40 tigers, a marked increase after the Maoist years when poaching was rife. It also has over 30 one-horned rhino and a small population of wild elephants.

There are five species of deer. The reddish-brown barking deer (*Muntiacus muntjac*) is concentrated in the park's northeast forested slopes, though it is also regularly seen in the lowland riverine forest. The hog deer (*Axis porcinus*) is a smaller relative of the spotted deer, and is usually found in pairs or small groups. The sambar deer (*Cervus unicolor*) is the largest of South Asia's deer and an adult buck can weigh over 300 kg. It is found in small groups on the forested slopes and along riverine forest margins. The attractive and immensely graceful spotted deer (*Axis axis*), or chital, has a reddish-brown coat with white spots. It has relatively small antlers and is the park's only deer found in large herds. It inhabits grassland, forest margins and riverine areas. The endangered swamp deer

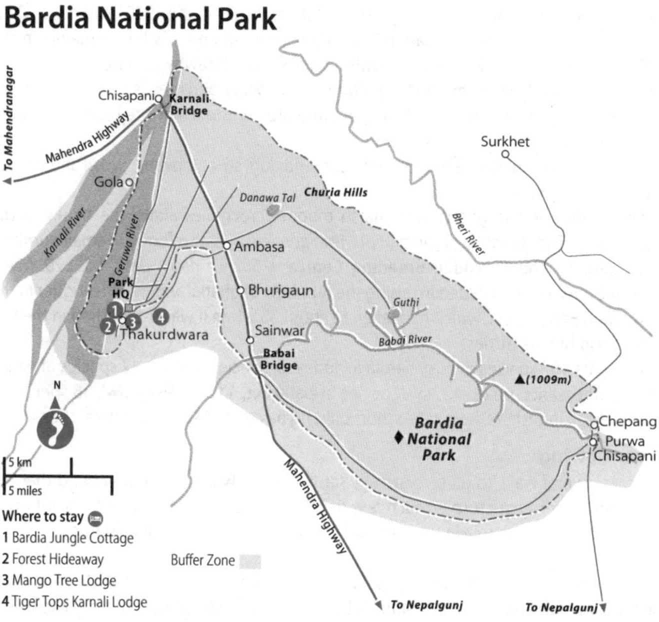

Bardia National Park

Where to stay
1 Bardia Jungle Cottage
2 Forest Hideaway
3 Mango Tree Lodge
4 Tiger Tops Karnali Lodge

(*Cervus duvauceli*), often prey to the tiger, can be found in small to medium groups, usually in the riverine forest margins.

The nilgai (*Boselaphus tragocamelus*), or blue bull, is in fact a large antelope standing 1.4 m at the shoulder and 2 m long. It inhabits the forest margins and grassland, and may be seen individually or in small groups. Numbers of the smaller black buck (*Antilope cervicapra*), 80 cm tall and 1.2 m long, reduced dramatically in the 1990s and early 2000s due to poaching, but the population is slowly recovering and it is found mainly in the southeast area of the park. The doe is without antlers and is tawny coloured.

Monkeys, notably the common langur (*Presbytis entellus*) and rhesus macaque (*Macaca mulatta*), occupy trees throughout the park and are an important prey species of both tiger and leopard.

Other mammals include leopard, wild boar, wild dog, striped hyena, jackal and various species of mongoose.

Reptiles include the gharial and marsh mugger crocodiles along the banks of the Geruwa River. The gangetic dolphin (*Platanista gangetica*) is also found in small numbers in the Geruwa. The **Crocodile Breeding Centre** ⓘ *Sun-Fri dawn-dusk, US$1.20, free if visiting the park*, has succeeded in raising the numbers of gharial and marsh mugger in the Geruwa and Babai rivers, which had fallen to about 35 when it was established in the late 1970s. It also breeds turtles.

Among its 407 species of bird, Bardia includes six species of stork, 12 species of eagle, vultures, pheasants, peacocks, five species of parakeet, 13 species of owl, 16 species of woodpecker, kingfishers, bee-eaters, hornbills, mynas and 20 species of flycatcher.

Game-viewing

There are several ways to game watch in Bardia but it's worth bearing in mind that the park's tourism infrastructure is much less developed than at Chitwan. The advantage is that there are fewer people in the park and you'll get a true feeling of wilderness.

Jeep safaris These are the most popular way to visit the park, either at dawn or dusk when the animals are most active and visible. It's also possible to do a full-day excursion,

ON THE ROAD

In case of attack

The worst thing that happens to most visitors to the jungle is a mosquito bite but what do you do if you are on a walking safari and come face to face with a dangerous animal? First and foremost, follow the advice of your guide who will know the terrain, the animal and how to react to it much better than you.

Rhinos Rhinos can run faster than you and, being big and heavy, can run straight through undergrowth you will have to dodge. The general advice is to climb a tree big enough not to be pushed over (and that can take your weight). Rhinos have bad eyesight but a keen sense of smell so hiding is not the best option. If there are no big trees nearby, run in a zigzag and drop an item of clothing. The rhino will hopefully stop and attack this, giving you time to find that elusive tree.

Sloth bears Keep together as a group, making yourselves look larger and potentially too dangerous for the bear to fight. Your guide/s will then hit the ground, imitating a large animal stamping the ground, to scare it off.

Tigers/leopards Don't run even though you will want to. They are predators used to running down scared prey. Keep eye contact and slowly walk away. The big cats are normally shy and will only attack to protect young or if they feel threatened. They won't recognize you as a normal meal so their instinct will be caution.

---

bringing a packed lunch; this lets you get further into the park. There are about 300 km of driveable routes and going by jeep lets you reach place like the **Guthi Valley** to the east, a popular watering hole for rhinos and elephants.

The disadvantage of being in a vehicle is that some of the animals hear you coming and disappear into the jungle before you get there. It also prevents you from hearing the forest sounds of bird and animal calls. Most jeep safaris get around this by driving you to places known to be good for sightings and stopping, letting you get out of the vehicle. You then walk short distances to viewpoints over riverbeds or to watchtowers where you can game-watch in silence before moving on. On day trips you may stay in the same spot for an hour or so, hoping that the animals will come to you.

Walking safaris Going on foot (the 'jungle walk') with a guide is considered by many to be the most exciting way to see the park. With a good and experienced guide, it can be a superb adventure that allows you to get right into the park with minimum disturbance.

Tip...
Lightweight walking boots or trainers are best for walking in the park as undergrowth can be thick.

Soon after you enter through the main gate you have to cross the Khaura River to get to the main area of the park. The bottom is stony and extremely uncomfortable with bare feet, so bring waterproof sandals to change into.

Walking is particularly good for seeing and hearing birds. Animal sightings are also good as you have access to the viewing platforms, and the trails often follow river banks with clear views out over the river beds. You should always follow the advice of your guides and be aware that there are dangerous animals living where you are.

Tiger attacks and rhino and elephant charges are rare but not unknown (see boxes on pages 330 and 331).

Rafting

It is possible to combine a visit to Bardia with a rafting trip down the Karnali River. These usually finish at Chisapani. They tend to be half- or full-day trips and are more floating that white-knuckle adrenalin rides. They are a great way to see game as you silently drift downstream looking for animals that have come to drink. In the months prior to the monsoon the water levels can be too low for some stretches to be navigable. After monsoon, the water level is higher and the flow faster, making animal spotting more difficult.

Listings Bardia National Park *map page 329.*

Where to stay

With only a few exceptions, all Bardia's accommodation is at Thakurdwara. The lodges inside the park were closed in 2011 when their leases were not renewed.

$$$ Tiger Tops Karnali Lodge
2 km from Thakurdwara, just outside the park, T01-4361500, www.tigertops.com.
16 comfortable rooms in thatched cottages and a new wing of deluxe doubles offering excellent facilities. The restaurant and bar are in a lovely thatched building constructed around a large fireplace. It's on the edge of the community forest and has qualified guides, as well as jeeps and rafts and a full range of jungle activities on offer.

$ Bardia Jungle Cottage
The closest lodge to the park entrance, T084-402014, www.bardiajunglecottage.com.np.
A range of rooms, most with bath (hot water available), a restaurant that does good, large Nepali meals, a bar and attractive grounds. It's run as a family concern by Bardia's most experienced guide and former ranger, the unassuming Premi Khadka, who can arrange all activities for you.

$ Forest Hideaway
Near the park gate, T01-4225973, www.foresthideaway.com.
With a range of standard and deluxe rooms, plus several safari tents, this atmospheric resort is set in nice gardens. All activities can

be arranged for you, including transfers to/from Ambasa.

$ Mango Tree Lodge
5 mins from the park entrance, T084-402008, www.mangotreelodge.com.
This eco-lodge has thatched cottages with Tharu-style interiors. Set in pleasant grounds and with an excellent restaurant (supplied by its own organic gardens), it's one of the most comfortable options and there's a full range of activities on offer.

Restaurants

There are no separate restaurants, but all lodges do their own food.

What to do

Cycle hire
Cycling is not permitted inside the park, but there are some pleasant trips through traditional Tharu villages in the surrounding countryside on quiet, if bumpy, roads. Basic cycles are available from most lodges.

Elephant rides
Elephant rides used to be a popular way of touring the park but are no longer available. The national park elephants are now used for anti-poaching purposes and general park maintenance, while **Tiger Tops Karnali Lodge** no longer keeps elephants for this purpose. The 2 elephants they have left

are an old matriarch too old to work and a younger female to keep her company.

Fishing
The Karnali, Geruwa and Babai rivers all offer good fishing opportunities, especially for mahseer. Once caught, the fish should be returned to the river. Permits are required, available from the park office. In theory, you can fish all year round, but the best time is after the monsoon when the rivers are high. Ask your lodge for best places to fish and to arrange transport.

Transport

Air
The nearest airport is at Nepalgunj (see page 323). The 1-hr flight from Kathmandu has stunning views of the Himalaya as far east as Dhaulagiri and you can clearly see the twin peaks of Machapuchare. The best seats are on the left-hand side for flights to Kathmandu and on the right-hand side on flight from the capital. If you are on a package tour, your lodge will meet you and provide transport from and to Nepalgunj.

Bus
Although there are no long-distance buses direct to Thakurdwara, all buses running between Nepalgunj and Mahendranagar stop at **Ambasa**, a small village on the Mahendra Highway, 10 km southeast of the Chisapani bridge. From here, you can catch a local bus or take a jeep to **Thakurdwara** (11 km, 45 mins). **Note** The road to Thakurdwara fords a couple of small rivers. During the monsoon, these can become too high to cross, thus effectively isolating Thakurdwara.

From Bardia, local buses to **Nepalgunj** via Ambasa leave daily. Buses to **Kathmandu** and **Pokhara** leave regularly from Nepalgunj.

Western Himalaya

As the main Himalaya sweep westwards they slowly swing northwards into Tibet, leaving the west of Nepal with a wide swathe of foothills and upland plateaux. There are no famous mountains (Api Himal is the main peak in the far west) and the area is little visited by Western trekkers. That doesn't mean it's an unexplored wilderness. The area is packed with villages and has an extensive network of trails that criss-crosses the region, allowing trade and travel for the local population and a wealth of opportunities for the intrepid traveller.

What it lacks in 8000-m peaks it makes up for in variety of terrain and diversity of cultures. The northern regions of Dolpo and Humla are in the rainshadow of the Himalaya, a huge area of dry, upland desert and arid valleys. These areas have more in common with Tibet than Nepal, inhabited by Buddhist peoples who, for contact with the outside world, have always looked north rather than south. To the south of these areas are pine forests, lakes, high plateaux and pasture: alpine beauty on an epic scale. The area has a different feel to the rest of Nepal. Until Jumla was captured by Bahadur Shah in 1788, the people of western Nepal had very little reliance on or contact with Kathmandu.

It is a hard and expensive area to access, with flights required to get into the mountains and a very sparse trekking infrastructure. Those who make the effort will see a Nepal rarely glimpsed on the main trekking routes, unchanged by the outside world and existing as it has done for centuries.

Visitors tend to fly to western Nepal and the most popular arrival point is Jumla. This small town, sitting on the banks of the Tila Khola at 2375 m, is famous for its production of red rice, which, ironically, is all exported with white rice from the plains being flown in for local consumption.

Compared to other towns in the region, Jumla is the height of sophistication for travellers, although local facilities lag far behind those in other trekking areas. You can pick up a limited selection of food supplies at the bazaar.

Listings Jumla

Tourist information

Rural Community Development Service
T87-520227.
Can help with finding guides and porters. Otherwise ask in your hotel.

Where to stay

$ Kanjirowa Hotel
T974-1111 733.
A newly built stone hotel is probably the pick of the available options, with comfortable rooms and a decent restaurant.

Transport

Air
Jumla's airport is about 10 mins from the town. In good weather there are daily flights from **Nepalgunj**, 35-40 mins.

Road
Driving to/from Jumla is possible depending on road and weather conditions. It normally takes about 2 days to/from **Nepalgunj** but is a long, tiring and very bumpy journey.

beautiful lake set in alpine scenery

Set in one of the most isolated regions of western Nepal, this small national park (106 sq km) contains the country's largest lake (10.8 sq km) and is renowned for its beauty. It was established in 1967 to protect the landscape of Lake Rara and to protect a representative example of flora and fauna of the Humla-Jumla region. The lake is in a deep basin at an altitude of 2990 m and has a maximum depth of 167 m. It drains to the Mugu Karnali River via the Nija Khola.

The lakeside pasture in the south gives way to the steep slopes of **Gurchi Lekh**, its crest culminating at **Chuchemara** in a horse-shoe-shaped opening to the south drained by the Jiun River. On the west, river valleys cut through a ridge which forms the natural boundary to the park.

Wildlife

A small portion of the park serves as an ideal habitat for the endangered musk deer. Other species found in the park are the Himalayan black bear, leopard, musk deer, goral, jackal, Himalayan tahr, yellow-throated marten, wild dog, wild boar, common langur, rhesus macaque and common otter.

The resident birds and migrant waterfowl are also of interest to park visitors. Coot are plentiful in the lake, many staying year-round. Great-crested grebe, black-necked grebe, red-crested pochard, mallard, common teal, merganser and gulls are seen during winter.

Essential Lake Rara

Finding your feet

Park headquarters is about 32 km north of Jumla near the village of Bhulbule. Most of the park including Lake Rara lies in Mugu District, with a small area in Jumla District of Karnali Zone.

Getting around

Trekking is the only way to explore the national park and it is necessary to bring your own camping equipment, food and fuel for cooking. There are no settlements inside the park and therefore no lodges. Residents of two villages, Rara and Chhapru, were moved out in 1976 and resettled in Bardia District. Villages around the park are Jyari, Pina, Topla, Tuma, Ruma and Murma.

Park information

A special permit is required costing US$70 for the first week and US$15 per additional day.

You will need to show it at the park HQ at Bhulbule, as well as your US$27.50 entrance ticket to the national park and TIMS card.

When to go

The best time to visit is October to November or March to early June. The winter is quite severe with ground frost occurring from October. From December to March there is snowfall with the temperatures dropping to below freezing point. High passes tend to be closed by heavy snowfall during this period. April brings the warmer weather and monsoon season is June to August, although western Nepal gets a lot less rain than the rest of the country being in the rain shadow of the main Himalaya and trekking can be very pleasant.

TREKKING ITINERARIES

Lake Rara

Perhaps the most famous of western Nepal's treks, the Lake Rara area is renowned for its beauty. Pine forests and meadows surround its clear waters and, with few visitors, it feels like pristine wilderness.

Days 10 days   **Highest point** 3271 m   **Trek type** Camping

Days	Itinerary	Altitude	Duration
Day 01	Fly to Jumla, trek to Patmara	2910 m	5 hours
Day 02	Bumra	2830 m	6 hours
Day 03	Pina	2430 m	6 hours
Day 04	Rara Lake	3040 m	6 hours
Day 05	Rest day in Lake Rara	3040 m	6 hours
Day 06	Gorusingha	3271 m	6 hours
Day 07	Sinja	2490 m	5 hours
Day 08	Jaljala Chaur	2987 m	5 hours
Day 09	Jumla	2370 m	5 hours
Day 10	Fly Jumla to Nepalgunj		

Other common birds in the park are snow cock, chukor partridge, Impeyan pheasant, kalij pheasant and blood pheasant.

Flora and the environment

The park contains mainly coniferous forest. The area around the lake is dominated by blue pine up to 3200 m; rhododendron, black juniper, west Himalayan spruce, oak and Himalayan cypress are other species. Above this elevation the vegetation is replaced by a mixed coniferous forest of pine, spruce and fir. At about 3350 m pine and spruce give way to fir, oak and birch forest. Other deciduous tree species found in the park are Indian horse-chestnut, walnut and Himalayan poplar.

Chuchemara Peak (4048 m) on the southern side of the lake presents a magnificent backdrop with the gleaming blue water within a basin of well forested hills. Other summits are **Ruma Kand** (3731 m) and **Malika Kand** (3444 m) to the north of the lake. From these peaks one can enjoy the view of the lake and peaks to the south and the beautiful Mugu Karnali river valley to the north.

Listings Lake Rara

Where to stay

Many of the overnight stops do not have teahouses or lodges so you'll need to bring camping equipment. You will also need to carry much of your food as supplies on the trek are unreliable. Many people organize the treks through an operator in Kathmandu or before departure as supplies

in Jumla and porters can be in short supply and expensive if arranged locally.

Transport

Most people fly to **Jumla** and trek from here (see Itineraries, page 344). There are a couple of routes, both travelling through beautiful, unspoilt scenery as you approach the park itself. It's also sometimes possible to fly to **Talcha**, near the small regional centre of **Gamgadhi**, which is only a few hours' walk from the lake itself. **Tara Air** and **Nepal Airlines** occasionally fly to Talcha from **Nepalgunj**. There is now a very rough road following the Jumla–Rara approach route. It's likely to be closed for much of the year.

★ Dolpo

remote, little-visited Buddhist ex-kingdom

Overlooked for centuries because of its bleak geography, Dolpo became part of Nepal 200 years ago when the Gurkhas gained control of the region. Ties of blood and religion made the district a natural refuge for Tibetans who fled the Communist Chinese takeover of Tibet in 1959.

Because of its isolation, few people visit Dolpo, something that has protected its unique character and fragile culture. In 2014 only 1000 trekkers visited Lower Dolpo and fewer than 500 made it to Upper Dolpo.

Within Dolpo's ring of massive mountains live a people economically and culturally different from much of the rest of Nepal. North of the main east–west line of the Himalaya, Dolpo sits in their rain shadow and has much in common with Ladakh, Zanskar, Lahul and Spiti in India, and with Mustang, its eastern Nepali neighbour. Thousand-year-old Buddhist monasteries dot the Shey and Ban Tshang valleys. The principal religion in Dolpo is Tibetan Buddhism.

Geographically it is part of the Tibetan plateau with its subsistence economy, based on livestock and barley cultivation, wrested from the steep mountainsides at altitudes up to 4000 m.

Two groups of ethnic Tibetans make up Dolpo's sparse population. The **Rungba**, or 'valley farmers', whose yellow village houses belong to the monks, while those painted white belong to the lay population. The **Drok** are nomadic yak herders. Interestingly, Drok girls mix grease and black root extract to use as a sunblock on their faces at high altitudes.

There are several trekking routes to follow, offering stunning, unspoilt scenery and a rich culture. It may be difficult and expensive to get to, but those who make the effort rarely regret it.

Essential Dolpo

Permits

Depending on your route, there are various trekking permits you will require. Firstly everybody will need a TIMS card and if you are entering the Shey Phoksumdo National Park you will need to pay the US$27.50 entrance fee.

If you are sticking to the outer Dolpo area, including most routes to Dho, Tarap and Phoksumdo Lake, the permit is US$10 per week. This is a wonderful and often underrated trek area. If, however, you are heading to inner Dolpo things get more expensive. The current fee is US$500 for 10 days, plus an additional US$50 per day for every additional day.

It's advisable to trek with a specialist agency who can sort out the logistics as well as permits and guides. These areas are remote and little visited and a local guide will not only make the trip easier and more enjoyable but also help you get much more out of the experience.

TREKKING ITINERARIES
Inner Dolpo

Dolpo conjures up visions of mysterious monasteries, snow leopards and blue sheep. Peter Matthiessen's *The Snow Leopard* and David Snellgrove's *Himalayan Pilgrimage* have contributed to the mystique and attraction of Dolpo; this trek takes you into the extraordinary landscape and culture. Camping is necessary due to the remoteness of the area and lack of infrastructure. It is highly recommended for those with limited time but determined to see something of Dolpo.

Days 15 days   **Highest point** 5309 m (Numa La)   **Trek type** Camping

Days	Itinerary	Altitude	Duration
Day 01	Fly to Juphal, trek to Dunai	2140 m	3 hours
Day 02	Tarakot	2540 m	7 hours
Day 03	Laina	3370 m	8 hours
Day 04	Nawarpani	3475 m	8 hours
Day 05	Dho	3964 m	9 hours
Day 06	Rest at Dho	3964 m	
Day 07	Numala BC	4440 m	6 hours
Day 08	Numa La pass (5309 m) to Danigar BC	4512 m	8 hours
Day 09	Baga La pass (5169 m) to Yak Kharka	3860 m	7 hours
Day 10	Phoksundo	3641 m	5 hours
Day 11	Rest day	3641 m	
Day 12	Chepka	2838 m	8 hours
Day 13	Sulighat	2282 m	8 hours
Day 14	Juphal	2475 m	4 hours
Day 15	Fly to Nepalgunj		

TREKKING ITINERARIES

Lower Dolpo via Beni

This is the route that Peter Matthiessen took in his superb book *The Snow Leopard*. It takes you through some amazing landscapes, from the lush foothills into the arid terrain of Dolpo and its unique culture. You will see very few, if any, trekkers and the locals you encounter still have a natural curiosity that has been lost in the more popular walking areas. It's an insight into cultures as yet unchanged by the outside world.

Days 24 days   **Highest point** 5200 m (Baga La)   **Trek type** Camping

Tented trek

Days	Itinerary	Altitude	Duration
01	Drive Kathmandu to Beni	1000 m	10 hours
02	Dharapani	1540 m	6 hours
03	Lumsum	1900 m	6 hours
04	Jalja La (3350 m) to Rivercamp	3100 m	5 hours
05	Dhorpatan 2900 m to Forest Camp	3050 m	7 hours
06	Forest Camp to Thankur	3250 m	8 hours
07	Thankur to Tadopani	2100 m	7 hours
08	Tadopani to Dhule	3335 m	5 hours
09	Dhule to Seng Khola		7 hours
10	Seng Khola to Purbang	4050 m	5 hours
11	Purbang to Sahartara/Tarakot	2980 m	7 hours
12	Tarakot (rest day)	2980 m	
13	Sahartara to Lahini	3250 m	7 hours
14	Lahini to Toltol	3525 m	7 hours
15	Toltol to Dho	4080 m	6 hours
16	Rest day in Dho	4080 m	
17	Dho to Tok Khyu	4200 m	3 hours
18	Numa La (5190 m) to Baga La BC	4450 m	7 hours
19	Baga La (5200 m) to Yak Karka	3860 m	7 hours
20	Phoksumdo Valley Camp	3700 m	2 hours
21	Phoksumdo to Reji to Sepka	3150 m	6 hours
22	Sepka to Sulighat of Dunai	2150 m	5 hours
23	Sulighat/Dunai to Juphal	2350 m	4 hours
24	Fly to Nepalgunj		

vast area of protected high-altitude

Shey Phoksundo National Park covers large swathes of the Dolpo and Mugu Districts. Created in 1984, it is the largest national park in the country, protecting an area of 3555 sq km. The main objectives of the park are to preserve the unique trans-Himalayan ecosystem with its typical Tibetan flora and fauna and to protect endangered species such as the snow leopard and musk deer.

Much of the park lies north of the Great Himalayan Range with Kanjiroba Himal lying at the southern edge of the trans-Himalayan region of the Tibetan plateau. The high Dolpo plateau in the northeast of the park is drained by the Langu (Namlang) river. The southern catchment of the park is drained by the Jugdula and Suligad rivers, which flow south and drain into the Bheri river.

Nepal's second largest lake, Phoksundo, considered by many to be its most beautiful, lies at 3000 m in the upper reaches of Suligad. The lake is drained by a waterfall of nearly 150 m, making it the highest in the country.

People and culture

The peoples' lifestyle and culture are still strongly reminiscent of Tibet. Local inhabitants believe in the Buddhist religion but the community of Phoksundo area practices Bon, a pre-Buddhist religion. Almost all villages have their own communal gompas. There are

Essential Shey Phoksundo National Park

Finding your feet

The easiest and shortest route to reach the park is to fly from Nepalgunj to Juphal airstrip in Dolpo. From there it is an easy one-day walk to reach the park guard post at Suligad and three days' walk to reach park HQ at Sumduwa. Alternate routes include overland by road from Pokhara to Beni. Trek from here on the Peter Matthiessen *Snow Leopard* route via Dhopatan towards Dho Tarap.

Getting around

There are several settlements in the park, totalling an approximate population of 2000. Everywhere is reached on foot although the locals do ride small ponies, and yaks are used in the caravans that trade across the region.

Park information

There is a park guard post at Suligad and park HQ is in the village of Sumduwa. You will need a TIMS card and then pay the park entrance fee of US$27.50. You also need to have the correct trekking permit, depending on the route you are following.

When to go

Spring season (mid-April to mid-June) usually has fine weather although high passes will still have some snow underfoot. Being located behind the main Himalayan range, the park is little affected by monsoon rain from June until September and weather usually remains clear. However, getting to Jumla by air can be affected by the monsoon rains that are falling in Kathmandu and Nepalgunj. The alpine flowers are at their best during these months. Post-monsoon (October) the temperatures start dropping, making the higher altitudes and passes very cold. In winter temperatures drop below freezing. Occasional heavy snowfall in mid-winter closes the trails for several days.

good examples of these in the villages of Phoksumdo Lake and Tarap. The local economy is heavily based on subsistence agriculture, mainly potatoes, buckwheat, mustard, beans and some barley. Animals provide food and wool for weaving clothes. The local people trade with Tibet, exchanging grain for salt and wool.

Wildlife
The park provides prime habitat for snow leopard and blue sheep. The blue sheep are mainly concentrated around Shey Gomba and Dolpo. Other common animals found in the park include goral, Himalayan tahr, serow, leopard, wolf, jackal, Himalayan black bear, Himalayan weasel, Himalayan mouse hare, yellow-throated marten and langur and rhesus monkeys.

The park is equally rich in birds. Most commonly seen are Impeyan pheasant (danphe), blood pheasant, cheer pheasant, red- and yellow-billed choughs, raven jungle crow, show partridge and many others.

Flora and landscape
The southern river valleys along Suligad contain luxuriant forests mainly comprising blue pine, spruce, cypress, poplar, deodar, fir and birch. The Jugdula river valley, on the other hand, consists mostly of *Quercus* species. The trans-Himalayan area has a near-desert-type vegetation comprising mainly dwarf juniper and caragana shrubs.

Listings Shey Phoksundo National Park

Where to stay
There are very few teahouses in the region and those that there are are very basic so camping is a must. It is also very difficult to get supplies so you will need to bring these with you.

Transport
Porters to carry camping equipment and supplies can be hired on arrival at Jumla airport, but it can take time. It's advisable to use a reputable ground handler in Kathmandu or Pokhara who can arrange everything prior to arrival.

★ Khaptad National Park
the remotest and least-visited of Nepal's parks

Located in the far west of Nepal, Khapad National Park is rarely visited. It is an area of pristine wilderness perfect for the traveller who really wants to get off the beaten track and have a wilderness adventure. (In 2014 the official figures show that it was visited by only 47 foreign visitors.) Khaptad was declared a national park in 1985 and consists of 225 sq km of forest and grassland, and lies on a plateau (altitude about 3000 m) where the districts of Bajhang, Bajura, Doti and Achham meet. A buffer zone of 216 sq km was created around the park in 2006.

Among Nepalis, Khaptad is best known as a holy site and is closely associated with a revered ascetic who lived here for many years and was known simply as the 'Khaptad Swami'. It is believed that he convinced the king to create the national park here (see box, page 344).

ON THE ROAD

Bheeg

The bheeg is a flower that a resembles white rose and grows in several parts of Khaptad National Park. It is said to be so poisonous that a single sniff from close up can be lethal. Symptoms of poisoning are believed to begin with joint pain, lethargy, nausea and vomiting. Some people carry lemons and chillies with them as an antidote when walking through the area, though it is interesting to remember that strings of lemons and chillies are also widely used elsewhere to ward off evil spirits.

Wildlife and flora

Much of the park is upland moorland, with a small lake in its northeast corner, and the forests comprise a mixture of tall fir, yew, rhododendron and oak along with dense stands of bamboo and numerous shrubs; it represents one of the last remaining such areas in the Lower Himalaya.

Eighteen species of mammal have been recorded in the area including leopard, Himalayan black bear, wild dog, wild boar, musk and barking deer, kasturi goats, yellow-throated marten, rhesus monkey and langur monkey. There are also wolves and jackals.

It is estimated that about 567 species of plant, including four endemics, representing 11% of Nepal's flowering plants, are found in Khaptad. There are no less than 224 species of medicinal herb.

The park also offers excellent birdwatching, with 270 species of bird, most commonly several varieties of Impheyan pheasant, peregrine falcon, partridges, bulbuls, cuckoos and eagles.

Essential Khaptad National Park

Finding your feet

Getting to the park involves one or two flights followed by a long, bumpy road transfer. An operator in Kathmandu will be able to handle the logistics.

Getting around

Inside the park you walk and camp, bringing with you your food and cooking fuel.

Park information

The park entrance is in the tiny village of Jhigrana. The entry fee is US$9. There is little infrastructure so all visitors to Khaptad should be self-sufficient in food and supplies, and be accompanied by a guide. It is recommended you go with an organized trekking company; book in Kathmandu or before arrival in Nepal.

When to go

The best time to visit is from March to October. The monsoon is relatively weak in western Nepal and the area is at its warmest, with many plants in flower. Early autumn and spring offer the best visibility. If you are visiting in the autumn, there are several festivals that are worth catching (see below). Winters are harsh: snow makes travel to and through most areas impractical and the wind makes it very cold.

Khaptad Swami

The origins and background of Khaptad Swami, who died in 1996 at the grand old alleged age of 110, are shrouded in mystery. Some speculate that he was a doctor from India who renounced his worldly life in favour of a purely spiritual existence in a remote part of the holy Himalaya. In any event, he never divulged either his name or anything of his own life to anyone – not even to King Birendra who went to consult him on three occasions.

He was undoubtedly a learned and widely read man who also had a good command of English. He lived in a cave on the eastern side of the park and pilgrims travelled from far and wide to see him and receive his counsel and blessings. It is said that Khaptad Swami was instrumental in persuading the king to give national park status to Khaptad.

About 1 km from the Swami's cave is the small Bhagawan Shankar Mandir with a dharamsala. Nearby is a small pond, or *pokhari*, whose water is said to be lethally contaminated by the bheeg (see page 343) and other toxic flowers growing around it. Fencing now surrounds the pond.

A tranquil meditation zone has been set aside at the core of the park encompassing the religious sites and ashram of Khapatad Swami.

Listings Khaptad National Park

Where to stay

There are a few basic lodges and teahouses on the approach to the park but none inside. You must camp and be fully self-sufficient in food, equipment and fuel for both cooking and heating.

Festivals

Sep/Oct **Khaptad Mela** attracts several thousand pilgrims from throughout western Nepal for whom this pilgrimage is believed to be especially meritorious. Celebrations include the pouring of milk over the linga of the Bhagawan Shankar Mandir and, reminiscent of Diwali, the lighting of ghee lamps at night.

Transport

It takes 2-3 days to get to the park from the nearest road head or airport, through untouched landscapes and villages that add to the remoteness of the experience.

Air

The nearest airport is at **Dipayal** which has flights to/from **Nepalgunj**. From here you have to trek to **Jhigrana**, the park HQ, and then on to **Chorpani** (3 hrs).

Bus

You can get a bus from the **Terai** up to the village of Silgari. From here it is a 4-hr walk along a clear trail to the park office at Jhigrana.

Humla is the ultimate final frontier when it comes to trekking in Nepal. Situated in the very far northwest of Nepal, it borders Tibet and is Tibetan in its culture. Despite covering an area of over 5650 sq km it has a population of only 50,858 (2011). The access point is the airport at Simikot, a route flown by Tara Airways (US$96 one way) from Nepalgunj. From here it is a five-day walk to the Tibetan border at Hilsa, the access point for a visit to Mount Kailash, the most sacred mountain in the Buddhist faith. The Nyin and Limi valleys are also fascinating areas to visit.

Camping is essential and, if crossing the border, a Chinese group visa must have been obtained in advance by a recognized trekking agency in Kathmandu or Pokhara. For those who make the effort (and accept the expense) the reward is a wonderful insight into an unchanged corner of Nepal, its unique culture and pristine landscapes.

Background

History

South Asia: settlement and early history

The first village communities in South Asia grew up on the arid western fringes of the Indus Plains 10,000 years ago. Over the following generations successive waves of settlers – sometimes bringing goods for trade, sometimes armies to conquer territory and sometimes nothing more than domesticated animals and families in search of land to cultivate and peace to live – moved across the mighty Indus and into India. They left an indelible mark on the landscape and culture of all the countries of modern South Asia.

First Settlers

Recent research suggests ever earlier dates for the first settlements. A site at Mehrgarh, where the Indus Plains met the dry Baluchistan Hills, has revealed evidence of agricultural settlement as early as 8500 BC. By 3500 BC agriculture had spread throughout the Indus Plains and in the 1000 years that followed, there were independent settled villages well to the east of the Indus. By 1500 BC the entire Indus Valley civilization had disintegrated. The causes remain uncertain: the violent arrival of new waves of Aryan immigrants, increasing desertification of the already semi-arid landscape, a shift in the course of the Indus and internal political decay have all been suggested as instrumental in its downfall. Whatever the causes, some features of Indus Valley culture were carried on by succeeding generations.

Vedic period

From this time, the northern region of the subcontinent entered what has been called the Vedic period. Aryan settlers from the northwest moved further and further east towards the Ganges Valley. Grouped into tribes, conflict was common. Even at this stage it is possible to see the development of classes of rulers (*rajas*) and priests (*brahmins*). In one battle of this period a confederacy of tribes known as the Bharatas defeated another grouping of 10 tribes. They gave their name to the region east of the Indus which is the official name for India today: Bharat. The centre of population and culture shifted east from the banks of the Indus to the land between the rivers Yamuna and Ganges. This region, known as the *doab* (pronounced *doe-ahb*, literally 'two waters'), became the heart of emerging Aryan culture which, from 1500 BC onwards, laid the literary and religious foundations of what ultimately became Hinduism.

The first fruit of this development was the Rig Veda from around 1300 BC. The later Vedas show that the Indo-Aryans developed a clear sense of the *doab* as 'their' territory. Modern Delhi lies just to the south of this region central both in the development of history and myth in South Asia. Later texts extended the core region from the Himalaya in the north to the Vindhyans in the south and to the Bay of Bengal in the east. Beyond this core region lay the land of mixed peoples and then of barbarians, beyond the pale of Aryan society. In the central valleys of 'Nepal', meanwhile, there ruled a series of obscure dynasties called Gopala, Mahishapala and Kirati. A fierce, war-like people possibly of middle-eastern origin, the Kiratis are thought to have moved towards the Kathmandu Valley from the east and established a dynasty lasting over 28 generations.

The *Mahabharata* records one of the first Kirati kings, Yalumbar, as having been killed in the great battle. Elsewhere, small kingdoms were ruled over by clans whose society was becoming increasingly hierarchical. In around 563 BC the Buddha, Gautama Siddhartha, was born in Lumbini, in the northern Gangetic Plains.

Licchavi Dynasty

By the fifth century BC, there were a number of dispersed political units in the Ganges Plains region and political authority had become localized. One such unit, the Licchavi clan, probably originated from the area of what are now the Indian states of Uttar Pradesh and Bihar. They began to move north and by around 400 BC had succeeded in replacing the Kirantis as rulers of the Kathmandu Valley, where they remained as the first dynasty of Indian plains origin until the late ninth century AD. To the south, the Maurya Dynasty established a hegemony in the Ganges Valley from 321 BC and brought the previously independent territorial states together under one administration. The greatest of its emperors, Ashoka who came to the throne in about 272 BC, conquered Kalinga (modern Orissa) but remorse at the destruction that this had entailed led to his religious conversion. Although it is widely said that he embraced Buddhism, it was more the peaceful Buddhist philosophy of *dharma* which motivated him. Many of his edicts were inscribed on stone or on specially erected pillars and these, which include several in and around Lumbini, provide the earliest written historical records of the region.

The greatest of the Licchavi rulers was King Manadeva I who reigned from about AD 464 to 505. Inscriptions from his reign constitute the earliest specifically Nepali written historical records and include one at Changu Narayan which chronicles his success in expanding and consolidating Licchavi power beyond the Kathmandu Valley. The Licchavi era was noted for its tolerance of the growth of Buddhism and other non-Hindu religions.

The next major event was the ascension of King Amshuvarma to the throne in AD 609. Though himself not a Licchavi, he had married the daughter and only child of the Licchavi king Shivadeva and gained the throne upon his death. By this time, the main trade route between India and China was already well established and Amshuvarman did much to strengthen cultural and political relations with Tibet and China. In AD 644 the first official Chinese envoy arrived in Kathmandu, a visit which was reciprocated by a Nepali envoy in AD 647. Amshuvarman's daughter, Bhrikuti, married the heir to the Tibetan throne and it was through her that Buddhism was introduced into Tibet. She has passed into Buddhist legend and its peculiarly Himalayan pantheon as one of the Tantric Taras. Amshuvarman also ushered in what is known as Nepal's golden period, a time in which the arts, architecture and culture flourished. He also introduced major administrative innovations, including the classification of religious and secular institutions and the first proper system of coinage. His philosophy further resulted in a number of social reforms. The king's palace, at Deopatan near present-day Pashupatinath, was renowned for its decoration and splendour. A descendant of the Licchavis, Narendradeva, regained the throne in AD 679 and further strengthened ties with Tibet.

The reign of King Raghavadeva began in AD 879 and marked the inauguration of the Nepalese Era. In the west, he defeated the invading army of King Jayapida Vinayaditya of Kashmir. The following two centuries were characterized largely by political instability, by increased conflict between rival clans and periodic warfare with Tibet, but included the reign of King Gunakamadeva during which the city of Kathmandu was founded. It also marked the introduction of Vajrayana Tantric Buddhism into Nepal.

The post-Licchavi transitional period ended with the early hegemony of the Malla family in the Kathmandu Valley. The first important king, Arideva Malla, established his capital in Bhaktapur. Arideva was succeeded by Abhayadeva. Following his reign, the valley was divided between his two sons, Anandadeva who ruled from Bhaktapur and Jayadeva who made Kathmandu his base and included Patan under his authority.

In western Nepal, meanwhile, a steady immigration of Hindu Rajputs (refugees from the Indian kingdom of Rajputana) and Khasas was taking place from the ninth century through to the 14th. It was a movement which was to shape the future course of Nepali history in ways unimaginable to those early migrants. The Rajputs were warriors and they settled and assimilated with the numerous kingdoms (*rajyas*) in the region, including the Baishi Rajya ('22 kingdoms') of the Karnali area and the Chaubishi Rajya ('24 kingdoms') in the Gandaki region.

To the south of the valley, King Nanyadeva had founded the Karnot Dynasty in 1097 which was based in Makwanpur (Simraungarh). The dynasty extended over six reigns, but disintegrated under civil unrest and later came under the control of the Sen Dynasty. The only Muslim invasion of Nepal to have reached the Kathmandu Valley occurred in 1346 when the ruler of Bengal, Sultan Shamsuddin Ilyas, launched his unsuccessful bid to wrest control from the Mallas.

Returning to events in the Kathmandu Valley, the most distinguished of the early Mallas was King Sthithi Malla (reigned 1372-1395) who, along with his son Jyotir Malla, introduced numerous social reforms including the first major codification of caste laws. The reign of King Yaksha Malla, 1428-1482, was the last in which all 'Nepal' (the Kathmandu Valley and surrounding areas) was under a single monarch. It was marked also by the expansion of the Malla territory north into what is now Tibet, though from west to east it stretched barely 80 km. While the monarch maintained his position, effective administrative power was exerted by an increasingly strong and hereditary nobility. The foundations for the eventual fall of the Mallas were laid by Yaksha who, for reasons unknown, allowed his kingdom to be divided between his three sons, with Ratnabe coming king of Kathmandu and Patan, Raya of Bhaktapur and Rana of Banepa. The administrative nobility, however, retained all but nominal control of Kathmandu, Patan and Banepa. Petty rivalry increasingly came to characterize relations between the individual kingdoms. A result, however, was the assertion of individual identities through the blossoming of art, architecture and culture which each encouraged.

Paradoxically, it was through this combination of often small-minded competition and immense pride that agricultural economies flourished, that systems for the distribution of drinking water were established and that the magnificent palaces and temple were constructed. King Lakshmi Narasimha Malla started the building of Kathmandu's Kasthamandap, considered by some to have been the world's oldest extant wooden building before its destruction in the 2015 earthquake. His reign also witnessed a major increase in trade with Tibet, which was heavily promoted by one of the king's wealthiest ministers, Bhima Malla. Lakshmi Narasimha's son, Pratapa Malla, was noted for his vision and religious tolerance, even allowing Jesuit missionaries to settle in Kathmandu. King Jayaprakash Malla came to power in 1732. His was a difficult reign which faced numerous attempts to usurp his power, including one from his brother Rajyaprakash and another from his wife.

While the Mallas squabbled among themselves, however, something altogether more threatening to their collective security was developing beyond their borders. As the cities of Kathmandu, Patan and Bhaktapur vied for the greatest palaces and the finest temples, so the successors to the early Rajput migrants in the west sought new land for cultivation, new forests for timber and new opportunities for trade. And between the Rajput *rajya* and the valley's Malla kingdoms lay the small state of Gorkha.

Unification of Nepal

Prithvi Narayan Shah was crowned king of Gorkha in 1742, aged 22. He was the 10th of the Shah Dynasty which had been founded in the 15th century by Dravya Shah. Prithvi inherited a kingdom that could not compete with its neighbours in either the fertility of its land or in its wealth. His vision of controlling the riches of the Kathmandu Valley and its fertile soils provided the initial motivation for a military campaign against the valley and by way of incentive he promised a part of that land to all who fought with him. His first strategy, employed between 1744 and 1754, was to block the established trade route to Tibet which deprived Kathmandu, by then the strongest of the valley's cities, of its Tibetan income which had until then paid for the upkeep of its mainly mercenary army. The Malla king resorted to 'plundering' the treasures of his own temples to pay the soldiers' wages, a move so unpopular that he was deposed. Somewhat optimistically, Prithvi attempted to take Kirtipur in 1757 but his forces' reliance on bows and arrows resulted inevitably in failure. Maintaining his hold on the Tibetan trade route, from 1754 Prithvi turned his attention to the south, intending to cut off links with India and imposing an economic stranglehold on the valley. This strategy involved taking the fortified town of Makwanpur in 1762, capital of the Sen Kingdom which corresponds approximately to the modern district of Palpa.

The Sens turned to India for help and specifically to the Nawab of Bengal, Mir Kasim. The Nawab sent his army which was roundly defeated by the Gorkhalis, who had by now developed into an effective, well-disciplined fighting unit. Victory also brought Prithvi prized spoils in the form of a large quantity of muskets which could be usefully employed in renewed attacks against the Mallas' walled defences. In 1766, he again laid siege to Kirtipur and, after a few weeks, succeeded in taking the town.

In desperation, the Mallas turned to the British in India who responded to the plight of their trading partners by sending an army of 1000 men. But the British force was unprepared. It left with minimal supplies which the Mallas were of course unable to supplement, because of the Gorkhalis' hold on all routes. It was also completely unprepared for the malarial jungle of the Terai, so that by the time the weary army reached the Churia Hills they were emphatically crushed by the Gorkhalis. More muskets were recovered and Prithvi went on to take Kathmandu with ease in September 1768. Patan followed in October of that year, with Bhaktapur the last to fall in November of the following year. With control of the Kathmandu Valley, it required little to add the rest of eastern Nepal which was completed in 1774.

Prithvi Narayan Shah was a ruthless leader who established a strong though wise system of administration. His government was a military meritocracy, but it depended on strong leadership. He even introduced appraisal schemes in which everyone was subject to an annual review. But he was aware also of the growing British presence in India and his mistrust of foreigners for fear of possible alliances which might threaten the kingdom led to the expulsion of Christian missionaries from Nepal and to the imposition of heavy restrictions of foreign trade. Recognizing the country as akin to a "ram between two boulders", he built upon the friendship with Tibet, ensuring that no foreigners would be allowed to enter from the north. Having united Nepal politically for the first time, he now ruled over a nation as diverse in its ethnic composition as in its geography, but according to Ludwig Stiller (1993), his system "provided a basis for union, not uniformity" – a considerable achievement by the standards of any age.

Prithvi died in 1775 at his fort at Nuwakot, perched on the rim of the Kathmandu Valley overlooking the kingdom he had created. He was succeeded by his son, Pratap Singh Shah who died in 1777, leaving his 16-month-old son, Rana Bahadur Shah, as King of Nepal. The country was now in the hands of two competing regents: Rajendra Lakshmi, Rana Bahadur's mother and Bahadur Shah, Prithvi's second son. Ironically, within three years of Prithvi's death the seemingly brilliant system of government he introduced was held hostage by that requirement of strong leadership which he himself had so embodied.

Despite these conflicts, the Gorkhalis continued to expand their territory to the west under the command of Bahadur Shah. Conquests included the Chaubishi and Baishi *rajyas*. Bahadur Shah maintained his father's policy of promising and allocating land from the newly captured territories to his men, but he soon found that the system demanded ever more land and revenue if it were not to collapse. An ill-advised war with Tibet in 1792 led to a humiliating Gorkhali defeat, then to Bahadur's imprisonment in 1797. He died in prison later that year.

In the meantime, Rana Bahadur Shah had begun to rule in his own name, but his reign ended when in desperation he abdicated at the request of his dying wife in 1799 and his son Girban Juddha, aged just 18 months, became king. This led to further factionalism and intrigue in Kathmandu and, ultimately, to Rana Bahadur's flight to India. Following discussions with the British East India Company and the signing of a Treaty of Friendship in 1801, Nepal agreed to accept a British resident in Kathmandu in exchange for assurances that the former king would be prevented from returning to Nepal. Now impoverished, however, Nepal could not keep to the financial obligations of the treaty. The British resident thus returned to India and in 1804 Rana Bahadur returned to Kathmandu to become 'adviser' to his son, the king. His own adviser, Bhimsen Thapa, was to play a major role in Nepali politics over the next three decades.

In 1806, Rana Bahadur unilaterally assumed the title of Mukhtiyar ('Chief Minister'). He was assassinated later that year by opposing factions fearing his return to the throne. An alert Bhimsen Thappa immediately charged his political opponents with the murder and had them put to death, thereby clearing the way for his own assumption of effective power. Under his control, the Nepali armies further extended their territories to the west which reached the maximum extent with the capture of Kangra in 1809. Meanwhile, Rajendra Bikram Shah was born as successor to the throne in 1816.

Anglo-Nepali War

Concerned by what was seen as Nepali land-grabbing, the British Governor General in India fired a diplomatic warning across Bhimsen's bows. He recognized, crucially, that the Terai lands constituted the key to Nepali wealth and were thus absolutely central to its ability to finance an army. Further discussions concerning the ownership of several Terai villages resulted in the British taking possession of these villages in 1814. Finding no resistance, the British military presence was removed that summer. Bhimsen concluded he had to act decisively and sent his troops in to retake the area. The British waited until the monsoon was over to retaliate. In the first attack, near Dehra Dun, their leader Major General Rollo Gillespie was killed, but they eventually took the village. To the east, further attacks were mounted through Butwal, along the Bagmati Valley and near Janakpur.

In May 1815, the Nepali forces surrendered. The resultant Treaty of Sagauli reduced Nepal's territory by roughly one-third, depriving them of most of the previous Terai gains and re-establishing the position of the British resident in Kathmandu. The British, meanwhile, had been so impressed by the fighting qualities of their opponents that they established the so-called Gurkha Brigade which has continued to be an integral part of the British army until now.

There followed a period of stagnation. Bhimsen continued as de facto leader of the country with the support of the regent queen, Tripura Sundari. Following her death in 1832, King Rajendra Bikram asserted his right to power with the help of Queen Samrajya Lakshmi and the influential Pande family. Together, they mounted a campaign against Bhimsen Thappa which succeeded in removing him in 1837. He died in prison in 1839. The intense rivalry which had become established soon after the death of Prithvi Narayan Shah, continued to influence political developments. Rajendra Bikram was a weak king and could do little to combat the increasing dominance of Queen Rajya Lakshmi after the death of his mother, Samrajya Lakshmi. Rajya Lakshmi desperately wanted her own son to become heir apparent in place of the legitimate heir, Surendra. But when her plan was opposed by the prime minister, General Mathbar Singh Thappa, she arranged for Jung Bahadur Kanwar Rana to have him assassinated in 1845.

Kot Massacre

The following months were imbued with political intrigue, mutual mistrust and an ineffective administration. Rajya Lakshmi was represented in government by General Gagan Singh Bhandari, while Jung Bahadur had been promoted to the rank of general as reward for removing Mathbar Singh Thappa. Jung Bahadur's influence grew in Kathmandu and he made sure that he was aware of every development to affect the political situation.

On 14 September 1846, as evening fell over Kathmandu and its people prepared to settle down for the night, General Gagan Singh Bhandari was murdered. Devastated, the queen arranged for a full meeting of council at the army fort – the Kot – that very night. The meeting took place in a heated atmosphere. While Jung Bahadur's soldiers stood guard outside, accusations and insults were exchanged. Who was responsible for the murder? Confusion and anger reigned. Then someone accused Jung Bahadur of complicity, whereupon fighting and shooting began. The prime minister, Fatte Jung Shah, was one of the first to die; next was one of his close aids, then others. When the guns at last stopped, over 30 of the country's most influential people lay dead. The queen almost immediately appointed Jung Bahadur prime minister, a position which was to remain Nepal's most powerful for the next century.

At a stroke, Nepal's leading nobility and its political elite had been removed. Their families were either expelled or left the country voluntarily. The internal feuding which had so characterized the previous five decades largely disappeared and the country was once more under strong leadership. Jung Bahadur recognized the might of the British Empire in India and concluded that the most pragmatic foreign policy was one of friendship and isolation. Contact with the British, once established, was kept to a minimum. Internally Jung Bahadur maintained the monarchy, but demoted it to non-executive ceremonial status, while he had himself made Maharaja. The powers of the Maharaja were absolute, with the king and prime minister obliged to carry out his instructions. The position was made hereditary.

In 1857, Jung Bahadur led some 8000 Nepali troops against the Indian *sepoys* who were mutineering against British rule in India. As ever, his decision was entirely politically motivated. He saw that the *sepoys* were not going to overcome the greater might of the imperial forces, so it was a simple matter of backing the winner for the future interest of Nepal. In return, the British continued to respect the territorial sovereignty of Nepal.

By the time of his death in 1877, Jung Bahadur Rana had instituted several social reforms, including a revision of the penal code and the establishment of a new tax system. He also introduced a system of land ownership closely related to the *zamindari* system of India, which increased the importance of the administrative classes. But by placing members of his own wider family in positions of responsibility, he also ensured that nepotism became firmly entrenched in the social fabric. Inevitably, this led to inefficiency and corruption as established hallmarks of Nepal during his later years and, indeed, throughout the remaining period of Rana rule. These qualities, moreover, were not entirely alien to him and by the end of his life he had amassed a considerable personal fortune.

Jung Bahadur was succeeded as prime minister by the army's Commander-in-Chief, Ranoddip Singh. Ranoddip persuaded the nominal monarch, King Surendra, to grant him also the title of Maharajah of Kaskiand Lamjung, in which capacity he ruled – ineffectively – until his assassination by Bir Shamsher, Jung Bahadur's nephew, in 1885. By hook or more usually by crook, the Shamsher wing of the family remained in power for the remainder of the Rana period. Bir Shamsher introduced further tax reforms intended to increase government revenues from the Terai landowners. The government, of course, was Shamsher. It was also thoroughly corrupt, overwhelmed by often unnecessary administrative burdens and quite out of touch with the greater needs of the country.

Although Bir can claim credit for a number of public works, his preoccupation was the accumulation both of wealth and of self-promotion. The former was easily serviced by the system, while the British contributed to the latter by awarding him a knighthood. In turn, members of the Shamsher family increasingly invested their ill-gained wealth in the Calcutta market, but failed to invest at all in the development of Nepal's agricultural economy from which their wealth was gleaned.

Bir was succeeded by Dev Shamsher in 1901. Although Dev began his prime ministership with a number of social innovations which threatened to bring a degree of equity to the country, he was overthrown by his younger brother, Chandra Shamsher, after just three months in power.

Suspicion exists that he was assisted in the coup by the British who, under Viceroy Curzon, were demonstrating an increasing and – for some – disturbing interest in Nepal. Chandra was quickly recognized by the British. At home, he soon started construction of his palace, the Singha Durbar which when completed was the biggest palace in Asia. He later encouraged trade with India, building bridges to improve communications and laying the foundation for Nepal's first and only stretch of railway, around Janakpur. His term is also remembered for the abolition of *sati*, the introduction of electricity to Kathmandu and the revision of the civil administration including the first attempts at proper forest management. With the outbreak of war in Europe in 1914, Chandra offered military assistance to the British and more than 100,000 Nepalis served in the British army. The British in return pledged an annual payment of Rs 1 million (Indian) in perpetuity and in 1923 signed the Treaty of Friendship which again assured Nepal its independence.

In 1929 Chandra died and was succeeded by his brother, Bhim Shamsher. His term was marked by the beginnings of civil disquiet and increasing unease with Rana rule. Bhim died in 1932 and Juddha Shamsher became prime minister. Barely 16 months later, the great earthquake of 1934 rocked Nepal. Juddha, who had been on holiday in west Nepal, returned to the devastated capital and organized a remarkably successful rebuilding operation. But this could not prevent the rumours which began circulating in 1939, rumours designed to de-stabilize his position, rumours which expressed growing widespread dissatisfaction with the Ranas, rumours of a plot to overthrow the regime. In October 1940, 56 members of the Nepal Praja Parishad (Nepal People's Council) were arrested for plotting against the government. Many more were implicated, including the nominal king, Tribhuvan. Four were eventually executed, including at least one whose innocence was indisputable.

The Ranas' clock was ticking ever more loudly. The aftermath of the 1934 earthquake had placed additional burdens on the national exchequer, Nepali men were again away from the fields in their thousands fighting in the Second World War and a century of Rana rule had left the country desperately impoverished. In late 1945 Juddha resigned, handing over the reins of power to his reluctant nephew, Padma Shamsher. He inherited all Juddha's unresolved problems and more. As the head of a family which had traditionally supported the British in India, Padma was faced with an India about to become independent, while on his northern borders was the newly communist China.

Furthermore, the Ranas had become hopelessly divided. Padma did not have the strength to enforce his social reforms. On 15 August 1947, the day of Indian independence, Padma ordered the release from jail of BP Koirala, leader of the Nepali National Congress freedom movement. From India Jawaharlal Nehru was encouraging the Ranas towards democracy and Padma's new Constitution of Nepal was approved in 1948. This allowed the freedom of speech which was widely used to berate the Ranas. Padma resigned in 1948 and was succeeded by Mohan Shamsher.

One of Mohan's first acts was to ban the Nepali National Congress. He ordered the arrest of anyone involved in anti-Rana activities. Another plot to overthrow the regime was uncovered in 1950 and was found to implicate King Tribhuvan. Tribhuvan fled with his family to India, escaping the control of the Ranas by driving into the Indian Embassy in Kathmandu, supposedly en route to a hunting trip.

Following immense Indian diplomatic pressure, Tribhuvan returned to Kathmandu the following February as king and de facto ruler of Nepal. He initially headed a coalition government of Mohan Shamsher's Ranas and the Nepali Congress, but this had collapsed by the end of the year leaving Congress in government and MP Koirala as prime minister.

Though politically momentous, little actually changed for the common man with the restoration of the monarchy. A bicameral parliamentary system of government was adopted, but patronage remained fundamental to securing position and nepotism remained strongly entrenched. King Tribhuvan died in 1955 and his son Mahendra assumed the throne. Following calls for greater democracy, King Mahendra approved a new constitution in 1959. It embraced numerous democratic ideals, but crucially allowed the king to suspend the constitution and impose a State of Emergency. That same year, the Nepali Congress Party won the general election with a two-thirds' majority. Congress used its position as the governing party to strengthen its own nationwide support, much as its namesake in India had done. In November 1959, King Mahendra used his constitutional powers to suspend the constitution, declare an Emergency and arrest many leading members of the Nepali Congress.

In 1962, the king established a new form of government known as the *panchayat* system, which was supposedly better fitted to Nepali conditions. A *panchayat* is a traditional village council. This model was intended to be 'partyless' and political parties were banned. Instead there was a five-tiered structure headed by the king himself and followed by the prime minister, a council of ministers and regional councils. The 'Panchayat Democracy' remained in place until 1980, though characterized by inflexibility and the continuing importance of patronage.

King Mahendra died in 1972 and was succeeded by his son, King Birendra Bikram Bir Shah Dev. The new king soon recognized that the country was lagging behind in its development efforts as well as economically. The old guard was changed as Birendra brought in educated, younger people to push the country forward. This achieved considerable success in administrative reorganization, but had little effect on the country's economy. Realizing that the key to further development lay in political reform, the king called for a national referendum to choose between continuing with the *panchayat* system or reverting to a multi-party system. The outcome was extremely close, but resulted in the maintenance of the status quo. Officially, political parties remained banned but their existence was tolerated.

From late 1989, the major parties (including the increasingly powerful Communists) joined to campaign against the *panchayat* system. Strikes and frequently violent mass demonstrations followed in which several people were killed. However, the movement succeeded and on 18 April 1990 a joint-party interim government headed by KP Bhattarai was appointed to prepare for elections and draw up a new constitution.

Following the announcement of the new constitution on 9 November 1990 in which the king was given powers to act unilaterally only in limited exceptional circumstances, the general election was held on 12 May 1991. The Nepali Congress Party emerged as the clear winners, securing 110 of the 205 seats, with the Communist Party of Nepal (United Marxist-Leninist – CPN-UML) forming the main opposition with 69 seats. KP Bhattarai, the former interim Prime Minister, lost his seat and GP Koirala became prime minister.

National politics remained unstable when no party achieved an overall majority in the November 1994 general election and after 10 months of minority rule under Prime Minister Man Mohan Adhikari, the CPN-UML were ousted by a coalition headed by Sher Bahadur Deuba of Congress in September 1995. Deuba's government lasted just 17 months, being defeated in a confidence motion in March 1997. The leader of the tiny Rashtriya Prajatantra Party, Lokendra Bahadur Chand, was then sworn in as prime minister with the support of the CPN-UML. The coalition stumbled through the next two years, surviving internal divisions and widespread accusations of corruption and inefficiency which served to further undermine public confidence in the country's political system. The coalition fell in early 1999.

The Maoist uprising and the fall of the monarchy

In some remote areas of northwest Nepal, centred on Rolpa and Rukum, insurgents of the Nepal Communist (Maoist) Party began a violent campaign in early 1996 hoping to destabilize the present democracy and to abolish the monarchy. They called it a 'People's War' and by mid-1999 the campaign had spread to the central western areas of the country, including the Gorkha region, bringing further violence and sporadic armed confrontation with police.

The fight was financed by robbing banks and demanding protection money from businesses. It was spent on building schools and health centres, land was seized and redistributed to the poor and programmes started to help the lower castes and various minorities. After the perceived indifference of central government and the king it was a popular message. Within five years they controlled a quarter of the country and had influence in another 25%.

The legal, political wing of the Maoists has benefited from the growing disillusionment with Nepal's governing parties in the late 1990s to increase its popular support in rural areas particularly. In 2001 it came to a head when Maoist leader Pushpa Kamal Dahal issued his demands for peace: a Constitutional Assembly with seats for the Maoists and the abolition of the Monarchy. Prime Minister Girija Prasad Koirala responded by getting his government to set up a dedicated police force with special powers to combat the rebels. Crucially it didn't deploy the army which, on paper at least, was loyal to the king.

The whole situation changed dramatically on the 1 June 2001. The Crown Prince Dipendra, upset that he wasn't being allowed to marry the commoner he wanted to, went on the rampage through the palace, drunk, high on drugs and armed with a gun. By the end of it King Birendra, Queen Aishwatya and seven other members of the family were dead. He then turned the gun on himself. For two days he survived in hospital, in theory the king. After he died his uncle Gyanendra came to the throne.

It was a disaster for the monarchy, not just for those murdered but also for its future. Gyanendra was very unpopular, seen as hard-line and dogmatic. His son Paras, who became the crown prince, was despised by most, perceived as arrogant and egotistical. Rioting erupted in Kathmandu and, amid political uncertainty, the 11th government in as many years was sworn in on July 2001 under the leadership of Sher Bahadur Deuba. It was not strong, seeming more interested in internal power building within the Congress Party than ruling.

In November of that year the Maoists got what they'd been hoping for, an event to unify the country against the existing system. As predicted by many, King Gyanendra declared a state of emergency. With the powers thus assumed, he suspended civil liberties and started imprisoning anyone who spoke out against him. Thousands were taken. He also mobilized the army, using them to search for and pursue Maoists rebels, destroying their infrastructure and killing or imprisoning without trial anyone suspected of collaborating.

The situation was spiralling out of control. In response the Maoists started to target dams and hydroelectric plants, telecommunication and other vital services. By 2004 an estimated 15,000 Nepalese were dead and the country was at a stalemate. Despite managing to seriously disrupt supplies to Kathmandu, once blockading it for over a week, the Maoists didn't have the strength to capture the capital. The army was too strong to be defeated in the Kathmandu Valley but in the hills it could not cope with such a mobile enemy, so couldn't drive it back.

In the meantime, the economy was in tatters, the tourism industry had collapsed and many NGOs had pulled out because of the dangers. Still the politicians did nothing as weak and indecisive governments failed and fell and the king kept actively interfering.

Something was needed to break this deadlock and the trigger was provided, predictably enough, by the determined Gyanendra. In February 2005 he seized power and declared martial law in an effort to re-establish the monarchy as the supreme power in the country. By doing so he did the impossible by successfully uniting all the political parties who'd spent the last decade bickering amongst themselves. They formed the Seven Party Alliance (SPA) and signed an understanding with the Maoist leaders. In exchange for backing the Maoist demands for a Constituent Assembly and dropping support of the monarchy, the Maoists agreed a ceasefire.

The autumn of 2005 and the start of 2006 was marked by riots, strikes and protests, countered by a ferocious government response of arrests and heavy-handed attempts to disperse crowds. General strikes were not uncommon nor were curfews. It became known as the Democracy Movement, or Lokantra Andolan, and culminated in April when hundreds of thousand protested daily on the streets of Kathmandu, refusing to disperse and too numerous for the army to control.

Gyanendra realized he was losing so, in a desperate attempt to retain his position, he called on the SPA to select a new prime minister. On 24 April parliament was reinstated under Girija Prasad Koirala. The king had lost control and for the first time in nearly two decades, things started moving quickly. The Maoist leader Comrade Prachanda arrived in Kathmandu in June after years of being in hiding. The 1990 constitution was scrapped, Nepal was declared to no longer be a kingdom and the king's powers were drastically reduced. Elections were called for the creation of the first Constituent Assembly. As a result, in November 2006 the Maoists signed the Comprehensive Peace Accord. They agreed to surrender their weapons under UN supervision and send their fighters to UN-monitored areas.

Modern Nepal

Republic of Nepal

In April 2008 the Maoists won a decisive victory in the elections, winning over one-third of the 600 seats. This was twice as many as Congress or the established Communist Party (CPN-UML). The following month Nepal officially became a republic and Gyanendra was given three days to leave the Royal Palace. Comrade Prachanda became the first Prime Minister of the Federal Democratic Republic of Nepal, using his proper name of Pushpa Kamal Dahal. It proved a false dawn.

The unity of the parties forged when fighting a common enemy soon fractured, meaning that the assembly descended into petty squabbles and in-fighting rather than drafting a new constitution. Ethnic tensions boiled to the surface, further fracturing the unity as everybody sought to gain an advantage as the country moved through this enormous transition.

It was during this period that the Madheshi Andolan or Movement for Madhesh, first came to prominence, campaigning for the rights of the ethnically Indian peoples (Madheshis) of the Terai. The most radical wanted independence and bomb blasts and protests were relatively commonplace in the main Terai towns. Other movements represented the growing numbers of disillusioned young people, educated but unable to find jobs. The economy shows few signs of recovering, not helped by the global downturn and the dilapidated state of the country's infrastructure. In August 2008 the collapse of the Koshi Dam killed thousands downstream in Nepal and India and was a further crippling blow to the country's electricity generation. Power cuts in Kathmandu often ran to 20 hours a day. The only glimmer of hope came from tourism, with numbers of visitors ballooning to over half a million.

The government finally resigned in May 2009 but as so often in Nepali politics not because of national issues but because of political posturing. The Maoists wanted a greater say on the shape of the new constitution and on integrating Maoists into government and the army and were prepared to sacrifice political stability to achieve

Official name Federal Democratic Republic of Nepal
Official language Nepali
Official religion Hinduism
National flag Double pennant of crimson with blue border on peaks; white moon with rays of light in the centre of the top peak; white quarter sun, recumbent, in centre of bottom peak
National anthem Sayaun Thunga Phulka (Made of hundreds of flowers)
Area 147,181 sq km
Population 29,860,000 (2014)
Life expectancy 67.98 (2012)

their end. In the following elections a 22-party coalition – basically everyone other than the Maoists – formed a government under Madhav Nepal.

The Maoists, unhappy not to have been re-elected, organized vast protests on the streets, called general strikes and blockaded Kathmandu. It was political chaos as 16 attempts to elect a new prime minister were blocked and the deadline to write a new constitution expired. The country was barely functioning as its natural resources were plundered and many of the young left the country to take any jobs they could find overseas.

Finally in August 2011 the parties agreed to elect the Maoist co-leader Baburam Bhattarai as prime minister. Perceived as the Maoist leader with the most integrity, he was also an accomplished academic with a PhD. In October 2011 he successfully negotiated and signed the Seven-Point Pact with the opposition parties. It was agreed that 6500 Maoists would be taken into the Nepalese Army, others paid off with generous settlements and in return confiscated property and land would be returned. A Truth and Reconciliation Committee would be established to look into crimes by both sides. While not popular with hard-line Maoists, it was by now evident that Nepalis hadn't the stomach for any more fighting and that a compromise settlement had been reached.

Still it wasn't settled. In May 2012, another deadline to agree the new constitution was missed and the Supreme Court suspended the Truth and Reconciliation Commission over concerns it would give amnesty to many of the worst offenders from the times of the troubles. In the November 2013 election there was no outright winner and then, in February 2014, after further elections, Sushil Koirala of the Nepali Congress became prime minister. He'd had a long and varied political career, had spent 16 years in exile in India and nearly three years in prison for involvement in a plane hijacking. In November 2014, he made an important leap forward as Nepal and India signed a US\$1 billion agreement to build a huge new hydroelectric plant on the Arun River, a crucial step to relieve Nepal's crippling power shortage.

New constitution and border blockade

Finally, on 20 September 2015, the new constitution was passed into law. It was described by Pushpa Kamal Dahal as "a victory for the dreams of the thousands of martyrs and disappeared fighters." Sadly not everybody agreed. The Madhesi groups in the Terai felt they had been marginalized by the mountain regions and the belief that those of Indian descent were being discriminated against through the new citizenship laws. These stated that a child would not be automatically Nepali if only the mother was from Nepal.

Honouring an earlier pledge, Koirala resigned after the constitution was passed and, despite being ill with cancer, ran for re-election. He lost and the new prime minister, Khadga Prasad Sharma Oli of the CPN-UML, was voted to power just in time to face the escalating Madhesi protests. The border crossings to India were blocked by activists, with the supposed support of India keen to reinforce its own influence in Nepal. A four-month blockade started, leading to acute shortages of fuel, medicine and other essential items and hampering the relief efforts after the devastating 2015 earthquakes.

One consequence of the blockade that will have major consequences was the development of the relationship between Nepal and China. In January 2016 the Chinese gave one million litres of fuel to the Nepalese, transporting it across the Tibetan plateau to the border crossing at Zhangmu. From here it was transported by small tanker along the Araniko Highway to Kathmandu.

While not a realistic long-term option, it showed the Nepalese the importance of not being reliant on one country (India is currently responsible for over 60% of its imports). There is talk of road improvements and even a railway and pipeline link to Tibet and China.

Economy

The economy of Nepal is overwhelmingly agricultural. Around 73% of the population is employed in subsistence food production which accounts for about 34% of the country's gross domestic product (GDP). These figures have been declining since the 1990s as more young people leave the land and move to the cities.

Since the 1980s there has been a steady increase in small-scale manufacturing concentrated mainly in the Terai towns, accounting for about 15% of GDP. This is mainly the production of garments. Hand-woven carpets also represent an important export, an industry boosted by the influx of Tibetan refugees since the 1950s.

The country is heavily dependent on wages earned by Nepali foreign workers, particularly in the Gulf states, who send their salaries back to their families in Nepal. Foreign aid is also a large part of the country's annual budget, the main donors being the UK, the USA, Germany and Japan.

Resources

The known deposits of coal, iron ore, pyrites, limestone and mica are too small to be mined commercially. The country's river systems offer tremendous potential for further hydroelectric development, but the Himalayan valleys present a costly and dangerous environment for large-scale development. Potential investors are also deterred in partnership schemes by the instability and corruption of the government.

Tourism

Since the 1960s tourism has grown into one of Nepal's most important industries. It accounts for around 15% of the country's total foreign exchange earnings and about 4% of its GDP. Approximately nine out of every 10 tourists enter the country through Kathmandu's Tribhuvan Airport. Indians form by far the largest number of visitors, while Germans lead the way of the other nationalities, followed by the British, Americans, Japanese and French. The most popular month to visit is October, while July is the least popular.

Although tourism in Nepal has come a very long way since the country first opened its doors to the outside world in 1952, there remains immense potential for it to grow still further. While there is significant government backing for the industry inside the country, little seems to have been done to promote it abroad with the government relying instead on individual and corporate entrepreneurship. The effects of tourism are widely discussed. While Nepal's economy has undoubtedly benefited, it is believed that a substantial proportion of earnings again leaves the country to pay for imports or for investment abroad.

The impact of tourism is highly localized, both economically and culturally. The Kathmandu Valley is the focus for most visitors. The landscape of Kathmandu itself has changed dramatically over the last 30 years, with substantial sections now completely dominated by tourist hotels, restaurants and shops which contrast sharply with traditional architecture. Pokhara, too, is now largely geared towards tourism. Chitwan National Park has led the way in 'jungle tourism' and its consistently large numbers of visitors have probably contributed to its success in wildlife conservation. In the mountains, the Annapurna and Everest regions in particular now have many Western-standard hotels and lodges.

While some people consider these places as examples of progress and development, others concentrate on the less positive impacts. They point particularly to increasing economic disparities and to the effects on the environment. Trekkers, for instance, are said to consume five times as much firewood per capita as local people, while the huge quantities of garbage they leave are devastating the natural beauty of the environment. Another major criticism is to do with the impact of increased exposure to Western culture on traditional local cultures.

But probably the greatest dilemma is that of Nepal's reliance on the income from tourism. It is a fragile dependence which is constantly subject to factors beyond the control of the industry. The 2015 earthquakes, the 2015-2016 border blockade, the avalanche near Annapurna in 2014 and the deaths on Everest in 2014 and 2015 all let to a serious downturn in tourism numbers.

However, tourism is still a success story and, as the infrastructure and facilities improve, it will open the country to more sustainable tourism and higher-yielding visitors whose money will stay in the country.

People

The distribution of ethnic groups reflects for the most part the geography of the country. The majority of Nepal's population (some 80%) are of Indo-Aryan stock, with the remainder of Tibetan origin. The latter include not only the Tibetan and Bhotia inhabitants of north Nepal (such as the Sherpas, the Dolpowas and the Lopas of Mustang), but also the related inhabitants of the central belt: Newars, Tamangs, Rais, Limbus, Sunwars, Magars and Gurung peoples.

The four main divisions of caste in Hindu Nepal are known respectively as: Bahun, Chhetri, Vaishya and Shudra. The family names of some Hindu castes may reflect locality as well as occupation. In Newari society, for example, potters are often called Kumar (or Kumali), while the Chippas are masons and the Bares, goldsmiths or jewellers. Non-Newari Bahun (ie Brahmin) family names common in east Nepal include Gotame, Sharma, Regmi, Nepal, Acharya, Upadhaya, Aryal, Bhandari, Adhikari and Paudel; those from west Nepal include Pant, Joshi, Bista, Bhatta, Pandey, Lohini and Upreti. Chhetri (ie Kshatriya) family names include that of the royal family, Shah, in addition to Thakuri, Singh, Pal, Malla, Chand, Kalyal and Pande.

Peoples of the Terai and Churia Hills

The Terai people are sometimes collectively referred to as Madeshis. The region is dominated by Tharus who number about 1.7 million (2011).

Tharus are dark-skinned and and are ethnically related to the Sakya clan into which the Buddha, Gautama Siddhartha, was born. They are mostly agricultural by occupation. Their language is also known as Tharu, though there are several dialects which have been influenced by, from west to east, Hindi, Urdu, Maithili, Bhojpuri and Bengali. Tharu religion combines elements of Hinduism, Buddhism and Animism.

The Tharus are believed to be descended from the original inhabitants of the Terai and are distributed along the length of it, but there is a strong affinity with the people of Uttar Pradesh and Bihar. The Indian classics suggest that the central region south of the Himalaya already had close cultural contact with the plains of India at least 2500 years ago.

For many years they were the only people capable of living in the malaria-infested Terai. The illness didn't seem to affect them, and research has shown that that, before its eradication from the area, Tharus were seven times less likely to die from malaria than other ethnic groups. Research has also shown that this is down to genetics as well as diet and lifestyle.

Bahuns and **Chhetris** predominate in the western and eastern Churias and **Gurungs** in the mid-western hills. Smaller populations of **Danuwars**, **Majhis** and **Darais** live in the eastern Churias and the central and eastern Terai. The Majhis are largely fishermen by occupation, with the Danuwars and Darais being farmers. Their language is of Sanskritic origin, but distinct from Tharu. They practise a form of Hinduism. The agricultural **Rajbanshi** communities of the eastern Terai speak a language influenced by the people of northern Bihar and Assam.

The eradication of malaria and the fertility and availability of land led to an extraordinary rate of migration during the latter part of the 20th century. This has brought together ethnic groups from throughout Nepal and from some parts of India. In addition to the movement of people from both the south and the north, the last century has also witnessed a drift of population from the west to the east. Recent Indian migrants are distributed throughout the Terai. Each has brought its own traditions and customs, influenced by religion and environment, to make the Terai something of a cultural melting pot. Ethnic identities, however, together with traditional social structures are maintained. The vast majority of marriages are still arranged strictly according to caste principles: marriage between castes and between ethnic groups is rare.

The Nepali language is as widely understood as Hindi, but a number of regional languages and dialects reflecting the Terai's many different ethnic groups are predominant among local communities. Dialects derived from Sanskrit and related to Hindi are spoken on both sides of the Terai border. Awadhi is the main dialect spoken in Nepalgunj and the western Terai as well as in Uttar Pradesh, while Urdu is also understood in Nepalgunj with its significant minority of Muslims. Bhojpuri is another local language both of Uttar Pradesh and of the central Terai area, while Maithili is spoken in the central and eastern Terai as well as in the neighbouring Indian state of Bihar. English is generally only spoken as a second or third language in larger towns and cities, rarely in villages. With the rise of satellite TV and radio local dialects are becoming increasingly rare as the young aspire to life further afield.

The role of the Terai as the country's main food-producing region and the reliance of Terai cultivators on a good harvest bestows special significance to festivals celebrating or associated with the harvest. The two most important of these festivals are **Dasain**, celebrated over 15 days in October, and the five days of **Tihar** (or **Diwali**) usually in early November. The dates of both are determined according to the position of the moon. The full moon marks the final day of Dasain, while Tihar begins with the 13th day of the waning moon. Both are joyous occasions, propitiating respectively the Mother-Goddess Durga in the triumph of good over evil, of light over dark, and Laxmi, Goddess of Wealth.

Peoples of the middle zone

The **Newars** are of Mongolian origin and are the dominant ethnic group of the Kathmandu Valley and surrounding central areas of Nepal. Despite their geographical origins, the majority are now Hindus following received Hindu customs, although communities of Newari Buddhists do remain. They represent perhaps the greatest synchronism of the Tibetan and Indian traditions of any of Nepal's ethnic groups and also incorporate aspects of Animism. The Newari language has been influenced by both the Tibeto-Burmese and Indo-European families.

Traditionally Nepal's leading traders, Newars once organized trains of basket-carrying porters over the trans-Himalayan passes to Tibet. They are also remarkable craftsmen and developed the unique building style that successfully blends influences from India, China and Tibet, with carved wood beams and pagoda-like temple roofs.

Tamangs dominate the area around and to the east of the Kathmandu Valley, numbering over one million. Ethnically Tibetan-Mongolian, their language is of the Tibeto-Burmese family. Tamang religion is a form of Buddhism with strands of Bon, Tantrism and Hinduism.

Rais and **Limbus** together make up the **Kirantis**, also a Tibetan-Mongolian people who were perhaps the first ethnic group to have settled permanently in Nepal. There are over 550,000 Rais and around 300,000 Limbus, the former concentrated in and around Dhankuta in the east Terai/Churia Hills and the latter in the far east. Both groups have contributed to the Gurkha regiments of the British and Indian armies in significant numbers. They speak a language derived from the old Kiranti, while Kiranti religion is a mixture of Animism, Buddhism and Shaivite Hinduism.

In the higher parts of the central hills, the **Gurung** population is a little under 500,000. Religion again combines Lamaist Buddhism with aspects of Hinduism. The Gurung economy is both sedentary agriculture and seasonal nomadic pastoralism, though many have served in Gurkha regiments.

The **Magars** are one of the largest ethnic groups of the middle zone, totalling over two million, as well as having been one the main recruiting groups for the British Gurkhas.

They include the **Thakalis** who are conspicuous in Pokhara and in the Annapurna region as owners of tourist hotels and lodges. They originate from the Kali Gandaki Gorge and, like many Nepali groups, have been subject to both Hindu and Buddhist influences. Adept entrepreneurs, they have cashed in on the trekking boom and have established little hotels all along the Annapurna Circuit and have also extended their influence to other parts of the country. They are only about 15,000 in number. Before Nepal was opened up to tourism, their economy was dominated by subsistence farming and, in the Kali Gandaki area, by salt trading.

The **Magars** originate in the western and central areas of Nepal, though are found in scattered communities throughout the country. They may be of either Hindu or Buddhist faith. Traditionally hill farmers inhabiting the lower slopes, they are also known for their fighting abilities and many have been recruited into Gurkha regiments of the British and Indian armies. There is thought to be a strong cultural bond between Magars and Gurungs.

Peoples of the Higher Himalaya

Ethnically, these people are almost entirely of Tibetan origin. Many **Tibetans** have moved south into Nepal since the Chinese occupation of their homeland from the 1950s. Some have assimilated with the indigenous **Bhotia** (from Bhot – 'Tibet') populations, while others have settled around Pokhara and Kathmandu.

The **Dolpowas**, people of Dolpo, number only a couple of thousand and are concentrated to the north of Jomsom and Kagbeni. They supplement their cultivation (potatoes, barley and wheat) of the relatively infertile land of four valleys with animal husbandry, speak a dialect of Tibetan and follow Lamaist Buddhism.

Lopas live in Lo Manthang, the capital of the high and arid region of Mustang, once an independent state. Of Tibetan ethnicity, they follow Tibetan Buddhism and number about 6000 with an economy that has traditionally been characterized also by long-distance trade.

The **Sherpas** live in the Solu Khumbu region of glacial valleys at the southern approaches to Everest. Their name tells of their origin (*Sha* – east, *pa* – people) and has come to be almost synonymous with the great peak that dominates their country. They emigrated from Tibet around 600 years ago. Earlier they were traders and porters, carrying butter, meat, rice, sugar, paper and dye from India, and salt, wool, jewellery, Chinese silk and porcelain from Tibet and beyond. The closure of the border following the 1962 border war between India and China undermined their economy. Fortunately, with the arrival of mountaineering expeditions and trekkers, the Sherpas found their load-carrying skills, both on normal treks and in high altitudes, in great demand.

The Khumbu region has provided a valuable contingent of able-bodied, hardy and seemingly fearless Sherpa porters and guides. Over the last 100 years they have built up a mountaineering reputation as the elite of Himalayan porters. Early expeditions took Sherpas from Darjeeling to climb in far-flung places in the Himalaya. They were often referred to as 'Tigers', but they were rarely accorded the recognition of their full worth. Tenzing Norgay, the best-known Sherpa guide for his involvement with the first Western expedition to reach the summit of Everest, received the British civilian award for bravery, while John Hunt, the expedition leader, was elevated to the peerage and Edmund Hillary was knighted. This led to the first ever Sherpa strike on Everest in 2014 after an avalanche in the Khumbu ice flow killed 16 Sherpas.

Sunwars and **Jirels** are related groups, small in number, and are found in the area around and to the east of Jiri, the place that gives the Jirels their name. Their religion is significantly influenced by Hinduism, but has distinct practices and deities.

The **Bhotia** live in the northern parts of Bhutan, Sikkim, Nepal and along the Indo-Tibetan border in Garhwal, Kumaon and Himachal Pradesh. Tibetan Buddhism plays an important part in shaping Bhotia society. The monastery is at the centre of the social environment, and the prayer flags, prayer wheels and chortens are a vital part of daily life.

Bhotia groups combine the same activity as the Sherpas: subsistence agriculture, animal husbandry and trade, the last two complementing the first because the altitude at which they live only permits one cropping season per year. The crops grown are hardy: wheat, barley, buckwheat and potatoes. The livestock includes sheep, goats and yaks (*Bos grummans*). Yaks provide many essentials of daily life, the cows producing one litre of rich milk daily.

The **Baragaunle** – the name means '12 village people' – are also ethnically Tibetan and live in the Muktinath Valley and follow a form of Lamaistic Buddhism that also incorporates elements of Animism.

The **Limipas** are a small group living in the Limi Valley in the northwest of Nepal.

The **Manangis**, also known also as Manangpa or Nyeshang, live in the Manang region and along the northern stretches of the Marshyangdi River. They are perhaps the wealthiest of any Bhotia groups thanks to a still extant 18th-century decree by Rana Bahadur Shah which gave them trading privileges with Tibet and which has today been adapted to the trade of luxury items from Hong Kong and China, many of which find their way to Kathmandu.

Culture

Art and architecture

As in many other Asian countries, there is a great deal of overlap between art and architecture in Nepal and both are, by tradition, characteristically religious. Early Nepali art and architecture is also that of northern India or southern Tibet; only with the establishment of the Licchavi Dynasty in the Kathmandu Valley did it begin to demonstrate distinctive characteristics.

Stone sculpture

From the fifth century AD, there emerged a tradition of stone sculpture, a much-favoured form of artistic expression influenced by ideas and skills brought from India, notably those of the Gupta and the Pala schools. These were adopted by both Hindus and Buddhists, though differences between the two remained more iconographical than stylistic.

The classic period of Licchavi sculpture lasted from the fifth to the eighth centuries and was largely dominated by Hindu representations of Vishnu in his various forms and of Umamaheshwar and by Buddhist sculptures of the Avalokiteshvaras, Vajrapani and Padmapani. The first-known Vishnu sculpture from the valley, that known as the Vishnu Vikranta Murti from the year AD 567, portrayed the god wearing tassels from his waist, a model which was subsequently widely reproduced both in Nepal and India. The sculpture of human and animal forms was notable for its sensitivity and naturalism and Licchavi sculpture was distinctive also for its use of a polished and lustred finish.

Its geographical separation from the heart of artistic activity to the south meant that Nepal was generally slow in adopting new techniques or forms. Sculpture continued to be strongly based on the classical Licchavi model. The period from the end of the ninth to the 14th centuries is regarded as the 'post-classical era' and was characterized, as the name seems to suggest, more by insipid reproduction than by the vitality of earlier work.

The Bengali Pala school influenced the form of sculpture from the east in around the 11th century and is marked by its purity of style. This resulted in the development of some regional distinctiveness, notable, for example, in the increased ornamentation of figures and the use of a lotus pedestal. The growth of Tantrism and its associated pantheon during this period also provided sculptors with plentiful opportunities for diversification.

The concurrent growth in the popularity of bronze as a medium, however, led to a period of innovative stagnation until the 17th century when some of Nepal's finest stone sculpture was created in the three cities of the Kathmandu Valley. Bhaktapur's Durbar Square in particular was noted for its superb statuary commissioned by King Bhupatindra Malla, though sadly much was destroyed in the devastating earthquake of 1934.

Bronze work

The origins of bronze art in Nepal are largely due to its popularity in Tibet to where much was exported. In style and development, however, it owes much once again to Bengali Pala influences from the 11th century and for the next 150 years or so images notable for their precision and fineness of detail were produced. Most is Buddhist created by Buddhist artisans in Patan.

From the early 16th century, the art of hollow casting and repoussé (images produced in relief by hammering from the reverse), became more widespread and figures are noted for the increase in their clothing. Much tantric bronze art dates from this period. Later 17th-century sculpture is characterized by composite production and the addition of a 'scarf' to many images. Into the 18th century, sculpture becomes distinctive by the acquisition of a 'halo' or *torana* and noticeably longer earlobes of many deities and higher mortals.

Painting and art

Nepali painting began in earnest from the early 11th century and consisted of miniature wooden-cased palm-leaf illustrations of Mahayana Buddhist themes. These have been described as replicating the linear grace of the Buddhist wall paintings at Ajanta and Ellora, dating from the centuries either side of the birth of Christ. These usually accompanied Buddhist texts, though did not always correspond to the text they illustrated, fulfilling instead a 'magical, protective function'.

The development of painting in Nepal is once again attributable to the influence of the Palas of eastern India thanks to whom the art was continued even after the destruction of most of the Indian paintings by the invading Muslim forces in the late 12th century. From the 14th century, the art of the *paubha* (or *pata* in Sanskrit; *thangka* in Tibetan), began to predominate. Also representing religious (often highly metaphysical) themes, they were painted instead on cloth, either cotton or silk. Nepali *paubhas* were subject to the influences of both Tibetan and Mughal-Rajput art.

There are two broad divisions of the *paubha*. The *mandala* may be thought of as painted diagrams representing the deity to whom it is dedicated, at the centre of the artist's conception of the cosmos. Often complex arrangements of circles and other geometric shapes are also typical and adhere to a prescribed rather than random formula. Rather less esoteric, meanwhile, the *pata* is usually symmetrical, with the deity at the centre of the picture surrounded by lesser divinities. Nepali painting of this and later periods was characterized by little use being made of colour and shade to produce form, with figures which were usually portrayed two dimensionally from the front and colour employed primarily to occupy otherwise empty spaces between the lines.

Royal architecture and planning

The finest examples of palace architecture are found in the three cities of the Kathmandu Valley. The peak of architectural activity here occurred between the late 17th and 19th centuries, a time when Malla rule of the valley was characterized by increasing rivalry among the family's various branches. The respective rulers of Kathmandu, Patan and Bhaktapur competed with one another for the grandest buildings as symbols of their importance.

The royal palace was typically the city's focal point (or *layaku*) to which and from which all roads led. To reflect what was perceived as a divine legitimacy to rule, the Palace (Durbar) Square became a concentration of temples dedicated to numerous deities, often ornately decorated. The palace area would be surrounded by defensive walls with gateways providing access. Malla palaces characteristically comprised an original three-storeyed structure around a central courtyard (chowk) which was subsequently augmented by other buildings by later kings. The result was a complex of courtyards of varying sizes, usually containing a shrine or temple. The entrance and exterior often displayed the superb craftsmanship for which the valley's architecture is renowned. The Golden Gate of Bhaktapur (1754) is one of Nepal's most astounding pieces of art, a product of the cultural blend of Newari and Tibetan styles.

For a time from the late 19th century, European styles were introduced by the aristocratic Ranas who had begun to travel overseas. The best-known example is the new wing of the Hanuman Dhoka Palace, at the heart of Kathmandu's Durbar Square which, although badly damaged in the 2015 earthquake, still illustrates this trend.

Temple architecture

The principles of religious building were laid down in the Sastras, sets of rules compiled by priests. Every aspect of Hindu and Buddhist religious building is identified with conceptions of the structure of the universe. This applies as much to the process of building – the timing of which must be undertaken at astrologically propitious times – as to the formal layout of the buildings. The cardinal directions of north, south, east and west are the basic fix on which buildings are planned. The east–west axis is nearly always a fundamental building axis. George Michell suggests that in addition to the cardinal directions, number is also critical to the design of the religious building. The key to the ultimate scale of the building is derived from the measurements of the sanctuary at its heart.

Indian-style temples were nearly always built to a clear and universal design, which had built into it philosophical understandings of the universe. This cosmology of an infinite number of universes isolated from each other in space, proceeds by imagining various possibilities as to its nature. Its centre is seen as dominated by Mount Meru, which keeps Earth and Heaven apart. Continents, rivers and oceans occupy concentric rings around the mountain, while the stars encircle the mountain in another plane.

Nepali pagoda

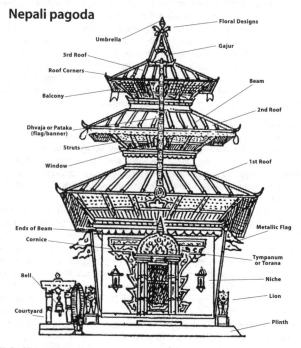

Floral Designs
Umbrella
Gajur
3rd Roof
Roof Corners
Beam
Balcony
2nd Roof
Dhvaja or Pataka (flag/banner)
Struts
Window
1st Roof
Ends of Beam
Metallic Flag
Cornice
Tympanum or Torana
Bell
Niche
Lion
Courtyard
Plinth

By means of the mandala diagram, the Sastras show plans of Jambudvipa, the continent where humans live, organized in concentric rings and entered at the cardinal points. Such a geometric scheme could then be subdivided into almost limitless small compartments, each of which could be designated as having special properties or be devoted to a particular deity. The centre of the mandala would be the seat of the major god. The mandala thus provided the ground rules for the building of stupas and temples across the subcontinent and provided the key to the symbolic meaning attached to every aspect of religious buildings.

Nepali architecture

Nepali architects and artists travelled widely. They helped to build the great stupa at Borobodur in Java around AD 800 and went to China as court architects in the 11th century. The towering tiers of pagoda roofs, supported by elaborately carved beams and struts characteristic of the cities of the valley, are a unique synthesis of exotic building styles. The five-storeyed Nyatapola Mandir in Bhaktapur is one of the country's most magnificent. In the late 13th century Kathmandu was a crossroads for Indian and Chinese architectural styles.

Arniko, a Newar architect and craftsman from the 13th century (after whom the highway between Kathmandu and Lhasa is named) was invited to Tibet as an advisor. From here, he joined the court of the Ming Emperor of China before returning to the valley where he introduced the multi-tiered pagoda style which, interestingly, had its origins in the Buddhist stupa. The word 'pagoda' actually developed from the Persian word *butkada* (*but* – 'idol', *kada* – 'temple' or 'dwelling'). Other Newari artists travelled abroad, many to Tibet where their skills were prized. While Bhaktapur artists tended to concentrate on wood as a building and decorative medium, Patan became the centre of metallurgy.

The other main form of Hindu temple architecture is the Shikhara (or Nagara) style which came from India. It is characterized by a tower or spire, either cone-shaped or rectangular. The idol is usually contained within the sanctum below, which may be surrounded by porticos. One of Nepal's finest examples is Patan's Krishna Mandir, built in 1636 by King Siddi Narasimha Malla. Shikhara temples are invariably built of brick or stone in contrast to the wood used mostly in the construction of pagodas. The focal point of the temple lies in the sanctuary, the home of the presiding deity known as the womb-chamber (*garbhagriha*). In large temples, a series of doorways leading through a succession of buildings allowed the worshipper to move towards the final encounter with the deity itself and to obtain *darshan* – a sight of the god. Both Buddhist and Hindu worship encourages the worshipper to walk clockwise around the shrine, performing *pradakshina*.

Buddhist architecture

Buddhist architecture is largely characterized by its stupas and viharas. The earliest extant examples are found in and around Lumbini and were constructed by the emperor and Buddhist convert Ashoka in the third century BC. His supposed visit to the Kathmandu Valley and the stupas named after him in Patan are, in all probability, just a legend. The great stupas of Swayambhunath and Bodhnath are Nepal's finest and most impressive. Swayambhunath probably formed the model for most subsequent stupa construction. In particular, the form of its *finial* (the ornate emblem at the top of the stupa), was widely copied and became standard from the medieval period onwards. The dome of the Bodhnath stupa is Nepal's largest. Viharas (or *baha*), Buddhist monasteries, have two distinct characteristics: a large open courtyard and an image placed opposite the main entrance.

Wood carving

The unique wood carvings in the royal palaces of Kathmandu, Patan and Bhaktapur reveal a mixture of Buddhist, Hindu and early Animist influences. So profuse is the ornamentation of the temples and palaces in the Kathmandu Valley that it is said that a true Newari cannot let a piece of wood lie without first decorating it. They developed confidence in a variety of media. The magnificent wood carvings in Bhaktapur show an ability to use highly ornamented dark wood against a background of red brick.

This age of brilliance passed with the decline of the Mallas in the 18th century. The Rana regime appears to have been little interested in Newari art and even tried to suppress it. The Shah Dynasty encouraged an artistic revival since the 1950s and assistance to restore monuments was received from Germany (especially in Bhaktapur), Japan and international agencies such as UNESCO. Much of this is ongoing after the 2015 earthquake.

Music

Nepal has a long tradition of both classical and folk music which have been shaped by Indian as well as Tibetan influences. In common with much of that of India, Nepali classical music can trace its origins back to the metrical hymns and chants of the Vedas, in which the production of sound according to strict rules was understood to be vital to the continuing order of the universe. Over more than 3000 years of development, through a range of regional schools, Nepal's musical tradition has been handed on almost entirely by ear. The chants of the Rig Veda developed into songs in the Sama Veda and music found expression in every sphere of life, closely reflecting the cycle of seasons and the rhythm of work.

Over the centuries, the original three notes, which were sung strictly in descending order, were extended to five then seven and developed to allow freedom to move up and down the scale. The scale increased to 12 with the addition of flats and sharps and finally to 22 with the further subdivision of semitones. Indian books of musical rules go back to the third century AD. Most compositions have devotional texts, though they encompass a wide range of emotions and themes and many are designed to be sung for specific events or in certain seasons. Although the term *sangita* is now widely used to describe music, it originally referred to music intertwined with dance and drama.

Reflecting the close association of music and religion, many Shaivite Nepalis believe that the original five ragas were revealed by Shiva, with another added by Parvati. The development of Tantrism was also influential and helped give the otherwise very Indian tradition of classical music a distinct Nepali flavour. The essential structure of a melody is known as a *raga* which usually has five to seven notes and can have as many as nine or even 12 in mixed *ragas*. The music is improvised by the performer within certain governing rules and although theoretically thousands of *ragas* are possible, because of the need to be aesthetically pleasing only a few hundred exist of which only about 100 are commonly performed.

Ragas have become associated with particular moods and specific times of the day or year. Another distinctive feature of Nepali classical music is the wider use of wind and percussion instruments, in contrast to the more commonly heard stringed instruments south of the border. These include various types of flute as well as the *madal* and *damphu*, both types of drum, although of course the *saranghi* and sitar are also popular.

While classical music is often localized, folk music exists and thrives throughout the country. It embraces a broad range of regional variations which reflect the country's enormous cultural, ethnic and environmental diversity. Many are specific to seasons, with planting or harvesting having a particularly wide stock of traditional songs and dances. Small groups of itinerant minstrels include the Damais and the Gaines.

Dance

Traditionally, music has been inseparable from dance and there is the same broad division between folk and classical forms. Classical dance is once again largely North Indian in character and the subject of much of it is based on religion and myth. Both the *Mahabharata* and *Ramayana* are widely interpreted in dance. There is an extensive grammar of movement and technique, especially in respect of hand gestures. The rules for classical Indian dance were laid down in the *Natya shastra* in the second century BC and this still forms the basis for some modern dance forms. There are three essential aspects of the dance itself: *nritta* (pure dance), *nrittya* (emotional expression) and *natya* (drama). The religious influence in dance was exemplified too by the tradition of temple dancers (*devadasis*), girls and women who were ostensibly dedicated to the deity of major temples to perform before them.

Literature

Although extensive, very little Nepali literature has been translated into English or any other Western language making it almost inaccessible to Western readers. With the exception of religious texts and sycophantic eulogies of royalty or aristocracy, a literary tradition does not truly begin until after the Gorkha conquest in the 18th century and the resultant unification of Nepal and spread of the Nepali language. Publication of printed books began in the early 20th century in Kathmandu. Local printers are making more Nepali works available in translation but they are often hard to locate outside the country. **Pilgrims** bookshop in Thamel is a good place to start a search for translated Nepalese classics.

Probably the most important figure in Nepali literature is **Bhanu Bhakta Acharya** (1814-1868). Often known affectionately as Bhanu, his statue stands in many a Nepali town. He is best known for his poetic rendering of the *Ramayana*. Other poets of the 19th century include **Rajibalochan Joshi** and **Patanjali Gajured**. The Rana regime did little to encourage the growth of Nepali literature. They established a system of censorship under the Gorkha Bhasa Prakashini Samity, which was strictly enforced. In 1918 one **Krishna Lal**, the author of a book enthrallingly titled *Makaiko Kheti* (Cultivation of Maize), was imprisoned for failing to have it approved by the censor before publication. Although several histories of Nepal were published, they invariably demonstrated both bias and inexhaustible sycophancy. Though less pronounced, this tradition has been successfully maintained by some writers into the post-Rana era.

The influence of Indian and Western literature began to assert itself in Nepal from the early 20th century. Forms of writing new to Nepal, such as modern dramas, short stories and novels, were introduced. Of the major 20th-century writers, Professor T Riccardi considers **Bal Krishna Sara** and **Lakshmi Prasad Devkota** to be the most outstanding, saying of the latter that he has "influenced the course of Nepali literature perhaps more than any other figure" since Bhanu Bhakta Acahrya.

Religion

It is impossible to write briefly about religion in Nepal without greatly over-simplifying. About 81% of Nepalis are Hindu and around 9% are Buddhist. Muslims constitute a little over 4% of the population, while the remainder is made up of Kiratist (local Animist beliefs), Christians and others.

Both Hinduism and Buddhism have influenced and been influenced by the other to a high degree in their practices, with adherents of either readily accepting many of the tenets of the other. Thus, if you ask a Nepali his religion, he may reply Hindu – but Buddhist too. Both have also been influenced by forms of Animism, an ancient spiritualist religion originating in Tibet.

Hinduism

It has always been easier to define Hinduism by what it is not rather than by what it is. Indeed, the name Hinduism was given by foreigners to the peoples of the subcontinent who did not profess the other major faiths such as Islam or Christianity, but adhered to a system of beliefs and social and cultural norms indigenous to the subcontinent. The term was accepted by Hindus themselves, because there was no alternative word which could satisfactorily embrace its broad concept. The name already implies territoriality. Of those components common to all religions, which also include faith and 'escape', the element of belonging is perhaps most strongly embedded in Hinduism. In many religions, this sense is both expressed and specifically reinforced by rites of passage, such as Christian baptism and confirmation, or the assumption of the Hajji title by Muslims who have made the trip to Mecca. These all imply movement resulting in changes of status. There are few such processes in Hinduism; it is impossible, for example, for someone born into one caste to ascend to another. Rather, Hinduism is characterized as much by its culture, society and hierarchical social structure as by the beliefs through which they have been shaped. At the broadest level, therefore, a person is a Hindu because he is born into Hindu society and this becomes as much a defining characteristic as, say, his height or shoe size. Accordingly, someone born into this society but who professes no religious faith is still a Hindu.

Hinduism has no definitive creed, set of practices, canon or uniformity of worship, but embraces a wide spectrum of philosophies and approaches to a common pantheon of deities. Some Hindu scholars and philosophers talk of Hinduism as one religious and cultural tradition, in which the enormous variety of belief and practice can ultimately be interpreted as interwoven in a common view of the world. Yet, there is no Hindu organization, like a church, with the authority to define belief or to establish official practice. There are spiritual leaders and philosophers who are widely revered and there is an enormous range of literature which is treated as sacred. Despite the many thousands of gods, goddesses and lesser divinities which give it the outward appearance of a polytheistic faith, it is in essence monotheistic with these multifarious deities seen as personified attributes of a single, supreme God. On a very different scale, the Christian trinity of Father, Son and Holy Spirit as three persons in one Godhead may help in conceptualization.

BACKGROUND
The four stages of life

It is widely believed that an ideal life has four stages: that of the student (*brambhachari*), the householder (*grihast*), the forest dweller (*banaprasta*) and the wandering dependent or beggar (*sannyasi*). These stages represent the phases through which an individual learns of life's goals and of the means of achieving them, in which he 'carries out his duties and raises sons' and then retires to meditate alone; and then finally when he gives up all possessions and depends on the gifts of others. It is an ideal pattern which some still try to follow. One of the most striking sights is that of the saffron-clad sadhu, or wandering beggar, seeking gifts of food and money to support himself in the final stage of his life.

There may have been sadhus even before the Aryans arrived. Today, most of these wanderers, who have cast off all the moral requirements of their surrounding cultures, are devotees of popular Hindu beliefs. Most give up material possessions, carrying only a strip of cloth, a staff (*danda*), a crutch to support the chin during meditation (*achal*), prayer beads, a fan to ward off evil spirits, a water pot, a drinking vessel (which may be a human skull) and a begging bowl. You may well see one, almost naked, covered only in ashes, on a Kathmandu street or at Pashupatinath.

The age in which we live is seen by Hindu philosophers as a dark age, the *kaliyuga*. The most important behaviour enjoined by Hindus for this period was that of fulfilling the obligations of the householder. However, each of the stages is still recognized as a valid pattern for individuals.

Origins

There are virtually no accurate records of dates in the development of Hinduism, a "defect" considered by the eminent Sanskrit scholar, AA Macdonell, to have "darkened the whole course of Sanskrit literature". Unlike the Messianic Christianity or the prophetic religions of Judaism and Islam, Hinduism does not date from a specific historical event but is characterized by continuing evolution and development of beliefs and practices. Its earliest origins probably date to pre-Dravidian Animism (ie the belief that natural phenomena and objects have souls and the worship thereof) and Totemism (ie tribal veneration of objects or symbols). The influence of both is still in evidence among a few (especially tribal) communities. The worship of a mother-goddess is noted in the region's earliest known major settlements, the Indus Valley Civilization (in modern Pakistan), from around 2300 BC, along with that of the bull and other animals. Artefacts from Harappa and Mohenjo Daro also suggest that phallus worship was common and that the peepul tree was already associated with religion, all of which feature prominently in later Hinduism. In northern India, these early practices developed into Vedism (or Brahminism) from around 1000 BC under the influence of the Aryans, an Indo-European people probably from the region around modern Iran, who first arrived in the subcontinent about 500 years earlier.

The following outlines the early development of Hinduism through its literature.

Vedas

The Vedic Age lasted from 1200-800 BC and was a period of immense growth and change. Aryan society was military and pastoral in character, but contained an important priestly class (the Brahmans) who were effectively the prototype Brahmins. The word *vedic*

BACKGROUND

The caste system

Socially, the most important contribution of the Vedic age was the development of the four-stage caste system. (The word 'caste' was given by the Portuguese in the 15th century and means 'breed' or 'race'.) The Rig Veda records how the original single caste, the **Hamsa**, was divided as a result of the continuing moral decline of man through the ages. In descending hierarchical order, the **Brahmins** represent the unsullied Hamsa and were seen as coming from the mouth of Brahma, while the **Kshatriyas** are the warrior class coming from Brahma's arms, the **Vaishyas**, the mercantile and professional class, coming from Brahma's thighs, and the **Shudras**, the working class, who came from Brahma's feet. A fifth class is considered to be outside the caste system, and known variously as **outcastes**, **untouchables**, **Panchama** and **Harijans**. 'Untouchable' refers to ritual pollution suffered upon contact by a caste member, while 'Panchama' means 'fifth'. The term 'Harijan' was first coined by Gandhi in the early 1930s and means 'a person of Hari (Vishnu)', or 'a child of God'. They were left with the jobs which were regarded as impure, usually associated with the dead (animal or human) or with excrement.

Those of the top three castes are considered to be *dvija*, or 'twice born', a reference to the additional 'spiritual birth' that takes place with the ceremony of the 'sacred thread'. The exact origins of the system are unclear. Some theories maintain that it was initially based on the obvious criterion of skin colour, or Varna (the Aryans were fair skinned), while others point to differences in religious practice and traditions among communities, or simply to a meritorial division of society by occupation. There are, in addition, several thousand sub-castes – including over 1800 subdivisions of Brahmins. In theory, interaction between members of different castes is strictly regulated. There should be no intermarriage, for example, nor should those of one caste share food with lower castes lest they become polluted. In practice, a rather more pragmatic approach is often adopted: pollution may be ritually cleansed and some communities have a more liberal interpretation of marriage rules.

In 1962, a law was passed making it illegal to discriminate against castes, making all castes equal in the eyes of the law. Despite an acknowledgement of equality of all people before the law in the 1967 Constitution of Nepal, reiterated in the 2015 Constitution, the caste system itself was not actually abolished and it continues to play an important role in the structure and organization of Nepali society.

means 'known' and was the language in which the four vedas ('books of knowledge') were composed: the Rig, Yajur, Sama and Atharva vedas. Believed to be of divine origin, these were not in fact books, but were handed down orally through generations; indeed, the first written records were put down about 1000 BC, although we do not have extant originals. The vedas were largely comprised of hymns, usually chanted during rituals.

The **Rig Veda** is the earliest and most important and that from which the others take their cue. Its composition, thought to have occurred mainly in the Punjab region, began from 1500 BC and probably attained its final form in around 900 BC or later, although some sources date it much earlier on astronomical assumptions, possibly as far back as 5000 BC. It consists of over 1000 sacrificial hymns, chants and allusions to legends, divided either into eight 'octaves' (*ashtaka*) or 10 'circles' (*mandala*). It includes the earliest references to Vishnu (here a minor divinity), Indra (previously the major Aryan god of war, but here merely the god of rain), Rudra (later to become Shiva) and to Agni, the god of fire who retains enormous contemporary relevance. Important consideration is given to the origins of the universe, though no unanimous conclusion is reached.

Among its later hymns, the *Purusha shukta* ('Hymn of the Primeval Man'), is of great significance and postulates that the eponymous 'man' (or god) survived his sacrifice-by-dismemberment at the beginning of time and created the universe and the four social classes, the first reference to a caste system. For the casual reader, however, the Rig Veda is undoubtedly hard work, with an understanding of much of its content requiring wider knowledge of other texts. In purely spiritual content it is also limited, with many of its prayers considered by Bhandarkar (1940) to be "saturated with selfish, sordid aims", while Walker (1968) maintains that it "contains a mass of dry, stereotyped hymnology".

The concept of sacrifice assumed importance from around 900 BC, its practice being seen as propitiating the gods and ensuring boons in the next life by repeating that first sacrifice of Purusha with all its associations with creation and regeneration.

The **Yajur Veda** was composed between around 700 and 300 BC probably further east along the Gangetic plains, reflecting the early movement of peoples into this area of high fertility. It is based on the Rig Veda though is more concerned with instructing Brahmin priests in the performance of the sacrificial ritual (*yaja*, 'sacrifice'). It also emphasized the increasing power of the priestly class and reflected the influence which they exerted (and, to a degree, still do), on society. Somewhat fancifully, one might think, the Yajur Veda also asserts that even the gods were in some ways subservient to the will of the Brahmins.

Composed at around the same time, the **Sama Veda** is a collection of over 1500 verses, mostly metrical and largely detailing the correct tunes, melodies and intonations to be performed in the sacrificial ritual. Specifically, many deal with sacrifices to Soma, god of the moon and of sacrifice.

The **Atharva Veda** again deals with sacrificial practice and promotes the role of the priest. But it also contains an important magical and ayurvedic formulary. There are herbal prescriptions for the cure of, for example, jaundice, fevers and leprosy along with accompanying incantations, as well as charms and spells to be intoned for, inter alia, the loss of another man's virility and the recovery of one's own.

Brahmanas

Strictly speaking, the Brahmanas belong to the late Vedas but are considered as a body of their own. They consist of a series of procedures and often highly elaborate rituals to be performed by Brahmin priests and have been alluded to as the 'Hindu Talmud'. They place particular emphasis on sacrifice and caste, thereby seeking to further underline the authority and power of the priestly class. The first dates from around 600 BC. Their spiritual relevance has been dismissed – often in delightfully sharp criticism – by scholars: in 1867 Max Muller compared them to "the twaddle of idiots", while Ghosh (1951) considers them "an arid desert of puerile speculations on religious ceremonies marking the lowest ebb of Vedic culture".

Upanishads

In complete contrast to the above, the Upanishads are a series of often beautiful spiritual treatises composed over a very long period: the earliest date from around 700 BC while the latest were not composed until the late medieval period. The word Upanishad means 'sitting near' which refers to the manner of their dissemination, ie in talks given by sages to groups of followers or interested listeners. That enlightened scholar and interpreter of Sanskrit literature, Juan Mascaro, offers the comparison of Jesus' Sermon on the Mount. By their spirituality, the Upanishads also contrast strongly with the Vedas which were more concerned with practice than devotion.

The Upanishads brought a fundamental change in the direction and form of Hindu thought and practice, a reaction against external religion. They also provided the inspiration for Vedanta, a range of philosophical systems which marked the conclusion of Vedic literature and systemized the teachings of the Upanishads. Whilst acknowledging the values enshrined in the Vedas, the Upanishads play down the roles of sacrifice and Brahmin ritual, instead placing greater emphasis on the unity of the individual soul. The **Svetasvatara Upanishad**, for example, asks: "Of what use is the Rig Veda to one who does not know the Spirit from whom the Rig Veda comes?" With the development of an Upanishadic tradition, mysticism became a cornerstone of the Hindu religion for the first time. There are over 100 Upanishads which differ in particulars and doctrine. The language of many is highly metaphysical, even rarefied, though the 19th-century German philosopher, Schopenhauer, declared "Sie ist der Trost meines Lebens gewesen und wird der meines Sterbens sein" (They have been the solace of my life and will be that of my death).

The Upanishads represent some of the most important Hindu texts. The earlier ones are much concerned with the relation of the individual with the Supreme and tend to express themselves indirectly, often through allegorical dialogue, as in this oft-quoted story from the Chandogya Upanishad (6. 12-14):

"Bring me a fruit from this banyan tree." "Here it is, father." "Break it." "It is broken, Sir." "What do you see in it?" "Very small seeds, Sir." "Break one of them, my son." "It is broken, Sir." "What do you see in it?" "Nothing at all, Sir." Then his father spoke to him: "My son, from the very essence in the seed which you cannot see comes in truth this vast banyan tree. Believe me, my son, an invisible and subtle essence is the Spirit of the whole universe. That is reality. You are that." "Explain more to me, father." "So be it, my son. Place this salt in water and come to me tomorrow morning." In the morning his father said to him: "Bring me the salt you put in the water last night." The boy looked into the water but could not find it, for it had dissolved. His father then said: "Taste the water from this side. How is it?" "It is salt." "Taste it from the middle. How is it?" "It is salt." "Taste it from that side. How is it?" "It is salt." "Look for the salt and come again to me." The son did so, saying: "I can not see the salt. I only see water." "In the same way, my son, you can not see the Spirit. But in truth he is here. An invisible and subtle essence is the Spirit of the whole universe. That is reality. That is truth. You are that." (The Upanishads, trans Juan Mascaro, Penguin: 1965.)

Om

The Upanishads also propagated the use of the word Om in contemplation. Consisting of just 12 verses, the **Mandukya Upanishad** is one of the shortest and speaks exclusively of this 'eternal word', dividing it into three distinct sounds: 'a', 'u' and 'm'. The first, it says, represents 'waking consciousness', the second 'dreaming consciousness' and the third 'sleeping consciousness'. Put together, they represent 'supreme consciousness'. The later Maitri Upanishad also devotes itself to contemplation and union, describing Om as the 'sound of Brahman', the intonation of which is followed by 'the silence of joy'.

The two great Hindu epics

Mahabharata This epic poem of approximately 100,000 stanzas (including an appendix of a mere 16,375 verses), is the world's longest. It was compiled over a period probably starting around 300 BC or before and, following centuries of inflation, was completed by around AD 500. It centres around the ancient battle between the families **Pandava** (representing incarnate deities) and **Kaurava** (incarnate demons). The historical events, originally a secular story that was transformed into a religious narrative by Brahmins, is traditionally held to have taken place at the beginning of the Kali era (about 3000 BC), but archaeological evidence suggests a date of around 800 BC. The subject matter is seen as an expression of the gradual trend away from Brahmin domination of religion and towards one with wider relevance, in this case that of the Kshatriya (warrior) class. The process of inflation led to the inclusion of very many extraneous episodes and to the existence of no single definitive version. The numerous renditions vary both geographically and in their often-contradictory interpretations of the same incident.

The *Mahabharata* is especially significant for its 'introduction' of Krishna, a god unknown to the Vedas, who appears as an incarnation of Vishnu. Krishna is perhaps Hinduism's most popular god. In his youth, legend relates his particular liking for milk and butter which he obtained in the course of regular illicit forays and for the *gopis*, or cow-girls (including Radha), with whom he made himself especially popular. His prodigious adulthood is noted, inter alia, by 16,108 wives and 180,008 sons.

It is important to note that Krishna's narrative, recorded also in the Puranas, is considered amoral in relation to accepted human behavioural norms. That is, a deity is not bound by mortal morality and although Krishna is to be worshipped, his relations with the *gopis* are not meant to be followed.

The **Bhagavad Gita**, the best known of the *Mahabharata*'s many philosophical teachings, is also one of the most influential Hindu texts. It takes the form largely of Krishna's didactic address to Arjuna, one of the five Pandava brothers, as they waited for the great battle of the *Mahabharata* to commence. Arjuna is questioning the morality of the forthcoming battle and whether it is right to pursue even a just cause if it involves destruction. Krishna replies that man should be "concerned with the deed, not with its results" and speaks of duty and devotion to dharma. He says that it is better to do one's own duty imperfectly (or that of one's own caste) than to do the duty of another well. As a Kshatriya, Arjuna should therefore undertake his warrior duty without sensual attachment and with his mind cast upon the 'highest soul'. The underlying themes are concerned with 'right' and 'wrong' actions irrespective of the result (though not advocating the end as justification of the means); with adherence to the caste system; with the merit of work; with respect for one's dharma; and with devotion to a supreme and personal God.

Krishna

The Gita is widely regarded as having been derived of the Upanishads, especially in respect of the stress it places on the transcendent reality of God. Though criticized by some as spiritually disappointing, excessive in its digressions and even promoting a 'cult of murder', it exerted great influence on the later development of Hindu systems of philosophy.

Ramayana Although reciting events which predated those of the *Mahabharata* by around 150 years, the *Ramayana* was compiled later, probably between around 350 BC and AD 250. Like the *Mahabharata*, the original *Ramayana* was secular in character and was composed in Prakrit, possibly by Buddhists. It was only later translated (and liberally augmented) by Brahmins into the Sanskrit and transformed into a religious work replete with symbolism. It consists of 24,000 stanzas which are divided into seven books. In contrast to Krishna, Rama is portrayed in a more kingly fashion. He is responsible and slightly remote, yet still loving and approachable: the ideal king and lover.

The first book deals with the boyhood of Rama (who many centuries later became worshipped as an incarnation of Vishnu), the second with his marriage to Sita (daughter of King Janak – see also Janakpur, page 302). The third describes how Sita was abducted by the demon Ravana (the original Prakrit version had Ravana as the non-demonic king of Ceylon, or Lanka). In the fourth book, Rama resides with the monkey king with whose help a bridge is constructed in the fifth book for Rama to cross to Lanka. The sixth book details Rama's battle with Ravana and the death of the latter, the recovery of Sita and their return to Ayodhya. The final book describes Rama's jealousy, the banishment of Sita into the forest and the birth of her sons, then the reunion of Rama and Sita followed by her return to the earth from which she came.

Ravana

Medieval Hinduism

From the early second millennium AD, Hinduism began to crystalize particularly into two main sects devoted to Shiva (Shaivites) and to Vishnu (Vishnuvites). This was part of a process which had been continuing for several centuries previously. Within both there are numerous sub-divisions.

One of the most important developments of the medieval period was the emergence of a devotional form of Hinduism known as *bhakti*. A sequence of ideas leading to this movement are found in both the Puranas and Upanishads.

Puranas

The Puranas are a series of 18 principal writings (in verse) comprised of religious instructions and legends compiled between the sixth and 16th centuries AD. The word means 'ancient' and each contains interpretations on the creation of the universe, its history, destruction and recreation, on the lineage of gods and saints, on ancestral rules and traditions and on the divine legends. All are in the form of dialogue and, like the Upanishads, they stress the transcendent and personal nature of God. Historically, they are of great importance as sources of mythological chronology as well as for their reflections on regional architectural and artistic developments. They are divided equally in praise of Vishnu, Shiva and Brahma and reflect overlapping qualities of, respectively, purity (*sattva*), gloom (*tamas*) and passion (*raja*).

The **Vishnu Puranas** speak of Vishnu as creator and sustainer of the world; stress the doctrine of *bhakti*; describe the youth of Krishna; explain the rites and processes of death; advocate astrology and worship of the sun; and explain the creation of the world. The **Shiva Puranas** contains discussions on the attributes of Shiva and on the philosophy of

Sexual imagery in Hinduism

Visitors to many of Nepal's Hindu temples will have seen often elaborately carved portrayals of the sexual acts and other 'erotic' scenes. These largely symbolize the traditionally fundamental role of creation and re-creation in Hinduism, a theme which has persisted since its early development.

Evidence of linga worship has been found in seals of the Indus Valley Civilization, probably reflecting the importance these agricultural communities placed on the role of divinity in fertility and the successful cultivation of crops on which, of course, life depended. Frequently lurid details of the sexual act are recorded in the *Yajur Veda*, while the woman is elevated to a position of sanctity by both the Brahmanas and the Upanishads, bringing the act of copulation within the realms of the sacred.

The role of sex in Hinduism receives its fullest exposition in Tantrism. Here it is seen not so much for its procreative qualities nor necessarily for its sensual aspect, but as a means for attaining the highest spiritual experience. The act becomes a ritual, preceded by meditation and believed to lead ultimately to salvation. The distinct subject of eroticism, meanwhile, is concerned with the purely sensual and is extensively set forth in many Hindu religious texts, the best known being the *Kama Sutra*, written in the fifth century AD by Vatsayana (according to legend, a lifelong celibate!).

Siva, in the form of Kamadera at Deopatan

This and other treatises propounded etiquette and postures to be adopted during sex. It is these, expressing the deeper religious significance, that are represented in temple art. It is also useful that the Newari goddess of lightning was believed to be very shy. By having erotic images carved on temple roof struts it was believed that she was too embarrassed to strike them.

linga worship, as well as historical chronologies, cosmology and medicine. The first of the **Brahma Puranas** is dedicated to Surya, the sun-god. Others are noted for assuming the marriage of Krishna and Radha (in the **Bhagavata Purana**) in addition to advocating the cult of the mother-goddess.

Together, these 18 Puranas are referred to as the **Mahapuranas** to distinguish them from the many other Upapuranas, minor works often compiled much later.

Tantras

Tantrism carries popular and not altogether erroneous, notions of debauchery. Although some believe it developed from remnants of a pre-Aryan culture, its precise origins are unknown. It was an esoteric cult which held particular sway from the latter part of the first millennium AD to the medieval period. It probably originated in China and some of its philosophies are common to Hindus and Buddhists. A moderate form of Tantrism has significantly influenced approaches to both Hinduism and Buddhism in Nepal. Hindu tantrics believe its principles, enshrined in the Tantras, to have been revealed by Shiva, and much of tantric scripture consists of dialogues between Shiva and his consort, Parvati. Indeed, Parvati is herself an expression of the shakti ('energy') aspect of Shiva. Although Shakti is strongly identified with Tantrism (and usually specifically with Shiva), its own origins are also unclear. Evidence of devotion to a 'mother-goddess' is found in some pre-Aryan cults. The concept includes notions of unity through the dual aspect of divinity, with the incarnate form of Shakti variously perceived as personifying fertility, motherhood, virginity, sexuality and conjugality as well as merciless terror (eg Kali and Durga). More than one of these qualities may be present in a single goddess. In temples, the Shakti is often represented as the yoni in association with the linga of Shiva.

Though notable for its reactions against the caste system and for the equality it granted to both sexes, Tantrism is much concerned with superstitious magic or occultism and their associated rituals. The emphasis placed on the 'terrible' aspects of deities (eg Shiva in the form of Bhairab, whose name means 'terror'), is also characteristic. Taken as a whole, however, its higher principles of transcendental philosophy and meditation are considered by some to be compromised by its extremities, such as necrophilia, sexual-demonic worship and other perversions embraced in the name of mysticism. Tantric writings contain, according to Walker (1968), "the loftiest philosophical speculation side by side with the grossest obscenities; the most rarefied metaphysics with the wildest superstition", while Chattopadhyaya (1959) described them as "the most revolting and horrible that human depravity could think of".

Bhakti

Although it also features in Shaivism, bhakti is a strand of Hinduism strongly associated with Vishnu, probably because Vishnu is seen as the most approachable of the Hindu trinity. The word means 'attachment' and is used to describe both ardent devotion to God and the bhakti movement that emerged in the medieval period. This stressed an intensely emotional, caring relationship between God and the individual, with God having an accessible, loving personality. In many ways, it also represents the closest that Hinduism comes to classical Christian spirituality. There are also parallels with Islamic Sufism. The 'way of bhakti' is known as bhakti-marga.

There are two main approaches to bhakti: **sagun-bhakti**, which emphasizes devotion to gods that have attributes and characteristics; and **nirgun-bhakti** which perceives an abstract, wholly spiritual God. Rama and Krishna feature strongly in bhakti literature. The poet **Tulsidas** (1532-1623) is perhaps the greatest of all Rama-bhakti writers. He is chiefly remembered for his enormously popular *Ramacharitamanasa*, a re-writing of the *Ramayana* characterized by themes of spiritual purity and morality which is often referred to as the 'Bible of Northern India'. He typified the Rama-bhakti beliefs of one supreme God, of the sinful unworthiness of man and that God became incarnate in the person of Rama to remove sin from the world. The story is often presented in dramatic form, making it accessible to the majority. The influence of Tulsidas has been considerable, leading Snell (1989) to assert that he "presents not only an ideal model for Hindu society but also a devotional theology firmly based on orthodox Hinduism". Expressions of **Krishna-bhakti**, meanwhile, take their cue from the stories of Krishna and the *gopis*. A central theme is the portrayal of Krishna as the lover, variously perceived as a friend (as with Arjuna and Krishna), as a child or parent, or with the longing of a lover (as exemplified by that of Radha and other gopis to Krishna).

Modern Hinduism

A number of ideas run like a thread through modern intellectual and popular Hinduism. According to the great Indian philosopher and former president of India, South Radhakrishnan, religion for the Hindu "is not an idea but a power, not an intellectual proposition but a life conviction. Religion is consciousness of ultimate reality, not a theory about God".

That reverence does not necessarily carry with it a belief in the doctrines enshrined in the text. Thus, the Vedas are still regarded as sacred by most Hindus, but virtually no modern Hindu either shares the beliefs of the Vedic writers or their practices, such as sacrifice, which died out 1500 years ago. Not all Hindu groups believe in a single supreme God. In view of these characteristics, many authorities argue that it is misleading to think of Hinduism as a religion at all.

Be that as it may, the evidence of the living importance of Hinduism is visible throughout most of Nepal. Hindu philosophy and practice in Nepal has also touched and been touched by Buddhism and other minority religions particularly in terms of social institutions such as caste.

Aspects of Hindu practice

Darshana One of Hinduism's recurring themes is 'vision', 'sight' or 'view' – *darshana*. Applied to the different philosophical systems themselves, such as yoga or vedanta, '*darshana*' is also used to describe the sight of the deity that worshippers hope to gain when they visit a temple or shrine. Equally it may apply to the religious insight gained through meditation or prayer.

Four human goals Many Hindus also accept that there are four major human goals: material prosperity (*artha*), the satisfaction of desires (*kamaand*), performing the duties laid down according to your position in life (*dharma*). Beyond these is the goal of achieving liberation from the endless cycle of rebirths into which everyone is locked (*moksha*). It is to the search for liberation that the major schools of Indian philosophy have devoted most attention. Together with dharma, it is basic to Hindu thought.

Dharma The *Mahabharata* lists 10 embodiments of dharma: good name, truth, self-control, cleanliness of mind and body, simplicity, endurance, resoluteness of character, giving and sharing, austerity and continence. In Dharmic thinking these are inseparable from five patterns of behaviour: non-violence, an attitude of equality, peace and tranquillity, lack of aggression and cruelty and absence of envy. Dharma represents the order inherent in human life. It is essentially secular rather than religious, for it does not depend on any revelation or command of God.

Karma The idea of karma, 'the effect of former actions', is central to achieving liberation. As C Rajagopalachari, a leading Tamil philosopher put it: "Every act has its appointed effect, whether the act be thought, word or deed. If water is exposed to the sun, it cannot avoid being dried up. The effect automatically follows. It is the same with everything. The cause holds the effect, so to say, in its womb. If we reflect deeply and objectively, the entire world will be found to obey unalterable laws. That is the doctrine of karma".

Rebirth The belief in the transmigration of souls (*samsara*) in a never-ending cycle of rebirth has been the most distinctive and important contribution to Hindu culture in

BACKGROUND
Good or bad karma

According to karma, every person, animal or god has a being or self which has existed forever. Every action, except those that are done without any consideration of the results, leaves an indelible mark on that self. This is carried forward into the next life and the overall character of the imprint on each person's 'self' determines three features of the next life. It controls the nature of his next birth (animal, human or god) and the kind of family he will be born into if human. It determines the length of the next life. Finally, it controls the good or bad experiences that the self will experience. However, it does not imply a fatalistic belief that the nature of action in this life is unimportant. Rather, it suggests that the path followed by the individual in the present life is vital to the nature of its next life and, ultimately, to the chance of gaining release from this world.

South Asia. The earliest reference to the belief is found in one of the Upanishads, around the seventh century BC, at about the same time as the doctrine of karma made its first appearance. By the late Upanishads it was universally accepted and in Buddhism and Jainism there is never any questioning of the belief.

Ahimsa AL Basham pointed out that belief in transmigration must have encouraged a further distinctive doctrine, that of non-violence or non-injury: *ahimsa*. Buddhism and Jainism campaigned particularly vigorously against the existing practice of animal sacrifice. The belief in rebirth meant that all living things and creatures of spirit – people, gods, devils, animals, even worms – possessed the same essential soul. One inscription which has been found in several places threatens that anyone who interferes with the rights of Brahmins to land given them by the king will "suffer rebirth for 80,000 years as a worm in dung". Belief in the cycle of rebirth was essential to give such a threat any weight.

It is common to talk of six major schools of Hindu philosophy. The best known are yoga and vedanta.

Yoga Yoga is concerned with systems of meditation that can ultimately lead to release from the cycle of rebirth. It can be traced back as a system of thought to at least the third century AD. It is just one part of the wider system known as Vedanta, literally the final parts of the Vedantic literature, the Upanishads. The basic texts also include the **Brahmasutra** of Badrayana, written about the first century AD and the most important of all, the **Bhagavad Gita**, which is a part of the epic *Mahabharata*.

Vedanta There are many interpretations of these basic texts. Three major schools of Vedanta are particularly important:

Advaita Vedanta: According to this school there is no division between the cosmic force or principle, Brahman and the individual self (which is also sometimes referred to as soul). The fact that we appear to see different and separate individuals is simply a result of ignorance. This is termed *maya*, sometimes translated as illusion, but Vedanta philosophy does not suggest that the world in which we live is an illusion. Rather it argues that it is only our limited understanding which prevents us seeing the full and real unity of self and Brahmin.

Shankaracharya, who lived in the seventh century AD and is the best known Advaitin Hindu philosopher, argued that there was no individual self or soul separate from the creative force of the universe, or Brahman, and that it was impossible to achieve liberation, or *moksha*, through any kind of action, including meditation and devotional worship. He saw these as signs of remaining on a lower level and of being unprepared for true liberation.

Vishishtadvaita: Shankaracharya's beliefs were repudiated by the school of Vedanta associated with the 12th-century philosopher, Ramanuja. He transformed the idea of God from an impersonal force to a personal God. His school of philosophy, known as Vishishtadvaita, views both the self and the world as real but only as part of the whole. In contrast to Shankaracharya's view, devotion is of central importance to achieving liberation and service to the Lord becomes the highest goal of life.

Dvaita Vedanta The 14th-century philosopher, **Madhva**, believed that Brahman, the self and the world are completely distinct. Worship of God is a key means of achieving liberation.

Worship

The abstractions of philosophy do not mean much for the millions of Hindus living across South Asia today, nor have they in the past. South Radhakrishnan puts a common Hindu view very briefly: "It does not matter what conception of God we adopt so long as we keep up a perpetual search after truth".

The Sacred in Nature Some Hindus believe in one all-powerful God who created all the lesser gods and the universe. The Hindu gods include many whose origins lie in the Vedic deities of the early Aryans. These were often associated with the forces of nature and Hindus have revered many natural objects. Mountain tops, trees, rocks and above all rivers, are regarded as sites of special religious significance. The **Khaptad National Park** in west Nepal serves as one such example. They all have their own guardian spirits. You can see the signs of the continuing lively belief in these gods and demons wherever you travel in Nepal.

Reflecting the historical dynamism of Hinduism, its gods have constantly undergone changes. Rudra (the Roarer), the great Vedic god of destruction, became Shiva, one of the two most worshipped deities of Hinduism. At times, other gods disappeared, but the creative spirit of Hindus constantly led to new names being given to forces to be worshipped, because, as Basham says, "the universe for the simple Hindu, despite its vastness, is not cold and impersonal and though it is subject to rigid laws, these laws find room for the soul of man. The world is the expression of ultimate divinity; it is eternally informed by God, who can be met face to face in all things".

Pilgrimage Most Hindus regard it as particularly beneficial to worship at places where God has been revealed. They will go great distances on pilgrimage, not just to the most famous sites such as Pashupatinath, but to temples, hill tops and rivers across Nepal. Many pilgrims come from throughout India, often on a whistle-stop tour of Nepal's holy sites, often including a stop at the holy city of Varanasi in the Indian state of Bihar.

Puja For most Hindus today, worship (often referred to as 'performing puja'), is an integral part of their faith. The great majority of Hindu homes will have a shrine to one of the gods of the Hindu pantheon. Individuals and families will often visit shrines or temples and on special occasions will travel long distances to particularly holy places such as Pashupatinath. Such sites may have temples dedicated to a major deity but will always have numerous other shrines in the vicinity dedicated to other favourite gods.

Acts of devotion are often aimed at the granting of favours and the meeting of urgent needs for this life – good health, finding a suitable wife or husband, the birth of a son, prosperity and good fortune. In this respect the popular devotion of simple pilgrims of all faiths in South Asia is remarkably similar when they visit shrines whether Hindu or Buddhist or those of other faiths.

Performing puja involves making an offering to God and darshana – having a view of the deity. Although there are devotional movements among Hindus in which singing and praying is practised in groups, Hindu worship is generally an act performed by individuals. Thus, Hindu temples may be little more than a shrine in the middle of a street, housing an image of the deity which will be tended by a priest and visited at special times when a darshan of the resident god can be obtained. When it has been consecrated, the image, if exactly made, becomes a channel for the godhead to work.

Images The image of the deity may be in one of many forms. Temples may be dedicated to Vishnu or Shiva, for example, or to any one of their other representatives. Parvati, the wife of Shiva and Lakshmi, the wife of Vishnu, are the focus of many temple shrines. The image of the deity becomes the object of worship and the centre of the temple's rituals. These often follow through the cycle of day and night, as well as yearly lifecycles. The priests may wake the deity from sleep, bathe, clothe and feed it. Gifts of money will usually be made and in some temples there is a charge levied for taking up positions in front of the deity in order to obtain a darshan at the appropriate times.

Festivals Every temple has its special festivals. Some draw Hindus from all over Nepal and India. Others are village and family events. See page 21.

Hindu sects

Three gods are seen as all-powerful: Brahma, Vishnu and Shiva. Their functions and character are not readily separated. While Brahma is regarded as the ultimate source of creation, Shiva also has a creative role alongside his function as destroyer. Vishnu, in contrast, is seen as the preserver or protector of the universe. There are very few images of Brahma; Vishnu and Shiva are far more widely represented and have come to be seen as the most powerful and important. Their followers are referred to as Vaishnavites and Shaivites respectively and numerically they form the two largest sects in South Asia.

Deities

Brahma Popularly, Brahma is interpreted as the creator in a trinity alongside Vishnu as preserver and Shiva as destroyer. In the literal sense, the name Brahma is the masculine and personalized form of the neuter word Brahman.

In the early Vedic writing, Brahman represented the universal and impersonal principle which governed the universe. Gradually as Vedic philosophy moved towards a monotheistic interpretation of the universe and its origins, this impersonal power was increasingly personalized. In the Upanishads, Brahman was seen as a universal and elemental creative spirit. Brahma, described in the early myths as having been born from a golden egg and then to have created the Earth, assumed the identity of the earlier Vedic deity Prajapati and became identified as the creator.

Some of the early Brahma myths were later taken over by the Vishnu cult. For example, in one story Brahma was believed to have rescued the earth from a flood by taking the form of a fish or a tortoise and in another he became a boar, raising the earth above the flood waters on his tusk. All these images were later associated with Vishnu.

By the fourth and fifth centuries AD, the height of the classical period of Hinduism, Brahma was seen as one of the trinity of gods – the Trimurti– in which Vishnu, Shiva and Brahma represented three forms of the unmanifested supreme being. It is from Brahma that Hindu cosmology takes its structure. The basic cycle through which the whole cosmos passes is described as one day in the life of Brahma – the *kalpa*. It equals 4320 million years, with an equally long night. One year of Brahma's life – a cosmic year – lasts 360 days and nights. The universe is expected to last for 100 years of Brahma's life, who is currently believed to be 51 years old.

By the sixth century AD, Brahma worship had effectively ceased – before the great period of temple building, which accounts for the fact that there are remarkably few temples dedicated to Brahma, the most famous one being at Pushkar in the Indian state of Rajasthan. Nonetheless, images of Brahma are found in many temples. Characteristically, he is shown with four faces, a fifth having been destroyed by Shiva's third eye. In his four arms he holds a variety of objects, usually including a copy of the Vedas, a sceptre and a water jug or a bow. He is accompanied by the goose, symbolizing knowledge.

Sarasvati The 'active power' of Brahma, popularly seen as his consort, Sarasvati has survived into the modern Hindu world as a far more important figure than Brahma himself. In popular worship, Sarasvati represents the goddess of education and learning. The development of her identity represented the rebirth of the concept of a mother goddess, which had featured strongly in the Indus Valley Civilization over 1000 years before and which may have been continued in popular ideas through the worship of female spirits. It is possible that her origins are associated with the now dry River Sarasvati in Rajasthan, but unlike Brahma she plays an important part in modern Hindu worship. Normally shown as white coloured and riding on a swan, she usually carries a book and is often shown playing a *vina*. She may have many arms and heads, representing her role as patron of all the sciences and arts. She has an honoured place in schools, colleges and universities.

Vishnu Vishnu is seen as the god with the human face. From the second century AD a new and passionate devotional worship of Vishnu's incarnation as Krishna developed in South India. By AD 1000 Vaishnavism had spread across this region and it became closely associated with the devotional form of Hinduism preached by Ramanuja. Rebirth and reincarnation were already long established by the time Ramanuja's followers spread the worship of Vishnu and his 10 successive incarnations in animal and human form. For Vaishnavites, God took these different forms in order to save the world from impending disaster. See page 386.

Vishnu

Rama and Krishna By far the most influential incarnations of Vishnu are those in which he was believed to take recognizable human form, especially as Rama (twice) and Krishna. As the Prince of Ayodhya, history and myth blend, for Rama was probably a chief who lived in the eighth or seventh century BC – perhaps 300 years

Vishnu's ten incarnations

Vishnu is believed to have descended in ten different forms, or avatars, in order to restore cosmic order:

Matsya (fish) Vishnu took the form of a fish to rescue Manu (the first man), his family and the Vedas from a flood.

Kurma (tortoise) Vishnu became a tortoise to rescue all the treasures lost in the flood, including the divine nectar (Amrita) with which the gods preserved their youth. The gods put Mount Kailasa on the tortoise's back and when he reached the bottom of the ocean they twisted the divine snake round the mountain. They then churned the ocean with the mountain by pulling the snake.

Varaha (boar) Vishnu appeared again to raise the earth from the ocean's floor where it had been thrown by a demon, Hiranyaksa. The story probably developed from a non-Aryan cult of a sacred pig.

Narasimha (half-man, half lion) Having persuaded Brahma to promise that he could not be killed either by day or night, by god, man or beast, the demon Hiranyakasipu then terrorized everybody. When the gods pleaded for help, Vishnu appeared at sunset, when it was neither day nor night, in the form of a half-man and half-lion and killed the demon.

Vamana (dwarf) Bali, a demon, achieved supernatural power by asceticism. To protect the world Vishnu appeared before him in the form of a dwarf and asked him a favour. Bali granted Vishnu as much land as he could cover in three

strides. Vishnu then became a giant, covering the earth in three strides. He left only hell to the demon.

Parasurama (Rama with the axe) Vishnu was incarnated as the son of a Brahmin, Jamadagni as Parasurama and killed the wicked king for robbing his father. The king's sons then killed Jamadagni and in revenge Parasurama destroyed all male *kshatriyas*, 21 times in succession.

Rama (Prince of Ayodhya) As told in the *Ramayana*, Vishnu came in the form of Rama to rescue the world from the dark demon, Ravana. His wife Sita is the model of patient faithfulness while Hanuman is the monkey-faced god and Rama's helper.

Krishna (Charioteer of Arjuna, many forms) Krishna meets almost every human need, from the mischievous child, the playful boy, the amorous youth to the Divine.

The Buddha Probably incorporated into the Hindu pantheon in order to discredit the Buddhists, dominant in some parts of India until the sixth century AD. An early Hindu interpretation suggests that Vishnu took incarnation as Buddha to show compassion for animals and to end sacrifice.

Kalki (riding on a horse) Vishnu's arrival will accompany the final destruction of this present age, Kaliyuga, judging the wicked and rewarding the good.

after King David ruled in Israel and the start of the Iron Age in central Europe, or at about the same time as the Greeks began to develop city states.

In the earliest stories about Rama he was not regarded as divine. Although he is now seen as an earlier incarnation of Vishnu than Krishna, he was added to the pantheon very late, probably after the Muslim invasions of the 12th century AD. The story has also become part of the cultures of Southeast Asia.

Rama (or Ram – pronounced with a long 'a' as in arm) is a powerful figure in contemporary Hinduism, particularly in India where his supposed birthplace at Ayodhya has become a focus of fierce disputes between Hindus and Muslims. Some Hindus identified Ram's birthplace as a site occupied by a mosque. One of India's leading historians, Romila Thapar, has argued that there is no historical evidence for this view, but it has taken widespread hold. The mosque was destroyed on 6 December 1992 during a huge and politically charged demonstration. After years of arguments the Indian Supreme Court ruled in 2010 that one-third of the site should be given to the various religious groups claiming it – the Sunni Muslims and two Hindu movements.

Krishna is worshipped extremely widely as perhaps the most human of the gods. His advice on the battlefield of the *Mahabharata* is one of the major sources of guidance for the rules of daily living for many Hindus today.

Hanuman The faithful monkey assistant of Rama in his search for Sita, Hanuman is widely worshipped throughout Hindu South Asia. The *Ramayana* tells how he went at the head of his monkey army in search of the abducted Sita across India and finally into the demon Ravana's forest home of Lanka. He used his powers to jump the sea channel separating India from Sri Lanka and managed after a series of heroic and magical feats to find and rescue his master's wife. Whatever form he is shown in, he remains almost instantly recognizable and is often painted red.

Shiva Shiva is interpreted as both creator and destroyer, the power through whom the universe evolves. He lives on Mount Kailasa with his wife Parvati and two sons, the elephant-headed Ganesh and the six-headed Kartikkeya. Shiva is always accompanied by his 'vehicle', the bull (Nandi). They form a model of sorts for family life.

Shiva is often seen as rather more remote than Vishnu, but he is also widely portrayed in sculpture and art, most famously as the Natraj, or Nataranjan, dancing in a circle of cosmic fire. He is also shown as an ascetic, sitting among the mountain peaks around Mount Kailasa, accompanied by his wife Parvati and meditating on the nature of the universe.

More widely than either of these forms, Shiva is represented in Shaivite temples by the lingam, or phallic symbol, a symbol of energy, fertility and potency. This has become the most important form of the cult of Shiva. Professor Wendy O'Flaherty suggests that the worship of the linga of Shiva can be traced back to the pre-Vedic societies of the Indus Valley Civilization (c 2000 BC), but that it first appears in Hindu iconography in the second century BC.

From that time, a wide variety of myths appeared to explain the origin of Linga worship. The myths surrounding the 12 *jyoti linga* (linga of light) found at centres like Ujjain in India go back to the second century BC and were clearly developed in order to explain and justify linga worship. O'Flaherty has translated this story of competition between the gods, in which Shiva (in the form of Rudra) terrorizes the other gods into worshipping him with a devotion to the linga.

Ganesh

Ganesh Ganesh is one of Hinduism's most popular gods. He is seen as the great clearer of obstacles. Shown at gateways and on door lintels with his elephant head and pot belly, his image is revered across Nepal. Meetings, functions and special family gatherings will often start with prayers to Ganesh and any new venture from the opening of a building to the inauguration of a company will often not be deemed complete without a Ganesh puja. Successive kings of Nepal have paid homage at a shrine to Ganesh in Kathmandu's Durbar Square as one of their first acts following the coronation.

Shakti, the Mother Goddess One of the best-known cults is that of Shakti, a female divinity also worshipped in the form of Durga. The worship of female goddesses developed into the widely practised form of devotional worship which became known as Tantrism. Goddesses such as Kali became the focus of worship which often involved practices that flew in the face of wider Hindu moral and legal codes. Animal and even human sacrifices and ritual sexual intercourse were part of tantric belief and practice, the evidence for which may still be seen in the art and sculpture of some major temples in Nepal and India. Tantric practice affected both Hinduism and Buddhism from the eighth century AD and was further influenced by the development of tantric Buddhism in Tibet from the 10th century.

Durga

Marriage, which is still generally arranged, continues to be dictated almost entirely by caste rules. It is usually seen as an alliance between two families. Great efforts are made to match caste, social status and economic position, although the rules which govern eligibility vary from region to region. In some groups, marriage between even first cousins is common, while among others marriage between any branch of the same clan is strictly forbidden.

Kali, Mother Goddess

Buddhism

Although followed by about 10% of the country's population, Buddhism is dominant in the northern, mountainous regions of Nepal and is conspicuously represented also in the middle zone. The number of Buddhists expanded greatly following the Chinese takeover of Tibet when many thousands of Tibetans sought refuge in Nepal. The area around the Bodhnath stupa, east of Kathmandu, now has a majority Tibetan population, as does that of Swayambhunath. Though notoriously difficult to define succinctly, very generally it consists of a set of existential philosophies followed on a path towards 'enlightenment'. The question of whether it is, or is not or has ever been a religion is largely one of semantics, depending on the definition of 'religion'. Buddhism neither recognizes nor explicitly denies the existence of a supreme God in the traditional sense, but contains many of the hallmarks of traditional religious practice. It is characterized by, among other things, the assumption of suffering as an integral condition of human existence, systems of ethics and moral precepts and self-sufficiency in the adherent. Although India was the original home of Buddhism, today it is practised largely on the margins of the subcontinent.

There are three main schools (or 'Ways') of Buddhism: **Hinayana**, **Mahayana** and **Vajrayana**. Mahayana Buddhism is dominant in the northern regions of Buddhist Asia (with tantric Vajrayana especially important in Nepal), while Hinayana predominates in the southern regions, notably in Sri Lanka.

Buddhism evolved from the teachings of Siddhartha Gautama of the Shakya clan (known as the Buddha, the 'Awakened/Enlightened One'), who lived in northern India in the sixth or fifth centuries BC. The Buddha's teachings are rooted in a compelling existential observation: that despite all persons' efforts to find happiness and avoid pain, their lives are filled with suffering and dissatisfaction. However, the Buddha did not stop there. He recognized the causes of suffering to be the dissonant mental states – delusion, attachment, aversion, pride and envy and realized that it is possible to free oneself permanently from such sufferings through a rigorous and well-structured training in ethics, meditation and insight, which leads to a profound understanding of the way things really are, that is, enlightenment.

The Buddha was born a prince and had known great opulence, but had also experienced great deprivations when he renounced his life of luxury to seek salvation through ascetic practice. He concluded that both sensual indulgence and physical deprivations are hindrances to spiritual evolution. He taught the **Middle Way**, a salvific path which was initially interpreted to mean isolation from the normal distractions of daily life, by living in communities devoted to the pursuit of spiritual liberation, which were disciplined but did not involve extreme deprivation. These communities, consisting of both monks and nuns, preserved and put into practice the Buddhist teachings. Initially the teachings were preserved through oral transmission, but by the first century BC were increasingly committed to written form. Unlike other of the world's leading religious traditions, Buddhism does not rely on a single literary source (eg the Bible, Koran or Talmud), but on a vast, rich, sophisticated literary corpus. The preservation of Buddhism brought literacy to hundreds of millions in Asia.

Buddhism's path to salvation depends largely on the individual's own efforts. Its emphasis on self-reliance and non-violence appealed to the merchant class in India and thus it spread along trade routes – north through Central Asia, into China and then into the Far East, Korea and Japan. It also spread south to Sri Lanka and Southeast Asia:

Burma, Thailand, Indo-China and Indonesia. Later, Nepal and Tibet embraced Buddhism at the zenith of its development in India and it was this tradition which eventually came to permeate Mongolia, Manchuria and Kalmukya. In recent decades, Buddhism has also found adherents in the West.

A Buddhist is one who takes refuge in the Three Precious Jewels (Triratna: Buddha, Dharma (his teachings) and Sangha (the monastic community). Beyond this, Buddhism has evolved remarkably different practices to bring about liberation, its teachings having been interpreted and reinterpreted by commentators in each new generation and in each cultural milieu. For its followers, the brilliance of Buddhism lies in its universality – its compelling existential appeal and, crucially, its efficacy. Historically, it has appealed to peasants and to kings, to philosophers and to the illiterate, to prostitutes and to murderers and to those already close to sainthood. And though it was not its intention, Buddhism has transformed the cultures in its path, imbuing them with ideals of universal compassion and profound insight.

The Buddha

Siddhartha Gautama, who came to be given the title of the Buddha, was born a prince into the Kshatriya (warrior) caste in the gardens of Lumbini near the Sakya capital of Kapilavastu about 563 BC. Some accounts suggest that his father received an 'annunciation' prior to Siddhartha's birth, others that his mother, Maya (deified as Maya-devi) dreamt of her conception by a white elephant, representing the eternal Buddha, holding a silver lotus in its trunk. Maya died soon after giving birth. He was married to Yasodhara at the age of 16 with whom he had a son, Rahula. Following several years contemplating the nature of human existence, he left home at the age of 29. This incident, known as the Mahabhinishkramana ('the Great Renunciation') occurred after he awoke in the middle of the night feeling "like a man who has been told his house is on fire". He looked upon his sleeping wife and child, resisting the temptation to bid them a final farewell.

He exchanged his clothes with those of a beggar and wandered as an ascetic, studying with various gurus all of whom failed to satisfy his search for the truth. Neither did his life of often extreme material deprivation lead him any closer. After about six years he went to Bodh Gaya where he meditated beneath the Bo (peepul) tree, resolving not to leave until he had attained enlightenment. Here he was tempted by the demon, Mara and his daughters with all the desires of the world. Resisting these temptations, he remained in his 'trance' supposedly for one full day and night and received enlightenment (*bodhi*, or *sambodhi* – 'full enlightenment'). This, which occurred sometime between 533 and 528 BC, took the form of a vision in which he saw an endless cycle of birth and death – the destiny of all men – followed by the enlightenment.

These scenes are common motifs of Buddhist art. The next landmark was the preaching of his first sermon Dharma Chakra Pravartana ('Setting into Motion the wheel of the Law'), to his first five disciples in the deer park at Sarnath near Benares (modern Varanasi). Other sermons followed during the course of his many travels, including the 'Fire Sermon' at Uruvela as a result of which his audience of fire-worshippers converted. The number of disciples increased as did their accounts of the Buddha's miraculous powers which he derided.

Later, the Buddha returned to Kapilavastu where he met his family for the first time since he had left. His son, Rahula, joined his father. The disciple, Ananda, to whom the Buddha is recorded as speaking in scriptures ('the most intimate'), was his cousin. Another cousin named Devadutta, meanwhile, nourished a lifelong hatred of the

The Buddha preached Four Noble Truths: that life is painful; that suffering is caused by ignorance and desire; that beyond the suffering of life there is a state which cannot be described but which he termed nirvana; and that nirvana can be reached by following an eight-fold path.

The concept of nirvana is often understood in the West in an entirely negative sense – that of 'non-being'. The word has the rough meaning of 'blow out' or 'extinguish', meaning to blow out the flames of greed, lust and desire. In a more positive sense, it has been described by one Buddhist scholar as "the state of absolute illumination, supreme bliss, infinite love and compassion, unshakeable serenity, and unrestricted spiritual freedom". The essential elements of the eight-fold path are the perfection of wisdom, morality and meditation.

Buddha and on three occasions tried to have him killed. The assassins sent on the first occasion confounded Devadutta by converting to Buddhism. Next, a giant rock was rolled down from Vulture Peak but broke into two pieces, both missing their target. The final attempt is perhaps the best known: a wild elephant was released to trample the Buddha to death but declined to do so, reportedly preferring to listen to the Buddha preach a sermon. Thereafter, Devadutta gave up and is believed to have converted to the Buddhist faith on his deathbed.

By the time he died, the Buddha had established a small though expanding band of monks and nuns known as the Sanghaand had followers across North India. The all-male Sanghawas divided into *sramana* (ascetics), *bhikku* (mendicants), *upasaka* (lay disciples) and *sravaka* (laymen). The nuns were known as the *bhikkuni*, which came to include Yasodhara, the Buddha's wife. The Buddha was initially somewhat wary about the potential distractions that might result from the presence of women, wisely advising Ananda: "Do not see them, Ananda. If you have to see them, abstain from speech, Ananda. And if you have to speak to them, keep wide awake, Ananda". Following his death (referred to as the *parinirvana* – 'final extinction'), his body was cremated and the ashes, regarded as precious relics, were divided up among the peoples to whom he had preached. Some have been discovered as far west as Peshawar in the northwest Frontier of Pakistan and at Piprawa close to his birthplace.

After the Buddha's death Soon after the Buddha's death, factions began to emerge among his followers. Within a year of his death, the First Council of the Sanghawas convened with the aim of, if not codifying, then interpreting and systemizing his teachings to a general concensus. Another was held in around 390 BC which marked a schism between two major sects, the **Mahasanghikas** (who followed what became known as the Mahayanaway) and the orthodox **Sthaviras**. A **Third Council** was convened at Patiliputra (modern Patna) 48 years later, where the first Buddhist canon was agreed upon. By this time the faith had seen the conversion of the great Mauryan Emperor Ashoka which had resulted from the dismay he felt at the devastation and destruction caused by his victory over the Kalingas in modern Orissa. It is said that Ceylon (Sri Lanka) was converted to Buddhism by Mahendra, Ashoka's son. This council also resulted in the expulsion of 'heretics' who were seen as having failed in their monastic duty and discipline. The final **Fourth Council** was held in Kashmir in AD 120, the 'minutes' of which were supposedly recorded on red copper sheets, then buried. This is significant for the fact that it decreed the Buddha's divinity and published a series of Buddhist scriptures in Sanskrit. By this time there were almost 20 major Buddhist sects, though the principal branches had now crystallized into the Mahayana and Hinayana approaches. A tantric form of Buddhism, known as Vajrayana, emerged from the mid-fourth century AD.

Buddhism's decline in India The decline of Buddhism in India probably stemmed as much from the growing similarity in the practice of Hinduism and Buddhism as from direct attacks on it. Mahayana Buddhism, with its reverence for bodhisattvas and its devotional character, was more and more difficult to distinguish from the revivalist Hinduism characteristic of several parts of North India from the seventh to the 12th centuries AD. In South India, the Chola Empire contributed to the final extinction of Buddhism in the southern peninsula, while the Muslim conquest of northern India dealt the final death blow, being accompanied by the large-scale slaughter of monks and the destruction of monasteries. Without their institutional support, Buddhism in India gradually faded away, retreating to the regions peripheral to mainland India. By this time, however, it was already well established in Tibet where it continued to grow under the influence of migrating Indian Buddhism and through indigenous cultivation. The greater part of Nepali Buddhism remains Tibetan in character.

The Buddha in Dhyanmudra – meditation

India still has many sites of great significance for Buddhists around the world. Some say that the Buddha himself spoke of four places his followers should visit: **Lumbini**, the Buddha's birthplace in the central Terai near the present border with India; **Bodh Gaya**, where he attained his 'full enlightenment', is about 80 km south of the modern Indian city of Patna; the deer park at **Sarnath**, where he preached his first sermon and set in motion the Wheel of the Law, is just outside Varanasi; and **Kushinagara**, where he died at the age of 80, is 50 km east of Gorakhpur. In addition, there are remarkable monuments, sculptures and works of art, from Gandhara in modern Pakistan to Sanchi and Ajanta in central India.

The Buddha in Bhumisparcamudra – calling the earth goddess to witness

The three yana

The *yana* are the three principal 'ways' or 'vehicles' of Buddhism, with their distinctive points of emphasis. The use of the word 'vehicle' derives from its conception as a vessel upon which people are carried across the ocean of this world to nirvana. A primary distinction is made between the sutra texts which emphasize the gradual or casual approach to enlightenment and the tantras with their emphasis on the immediate or resultant approach.

Hinayana The Hinayana ('Little Way' or 'Lesser Vehicle'), insists on a monastic way of life as the only path to achieving nirvana. Divided into many schools, the only surviving Hinayana tradition is the Theraveda Buddhism (from *thera*, meaning wise man or sage), which was that taken to Sri Lanka by Ashoka's son, Mahendra (or Mahinda). It became the state religion under King Dutthagamenu in the first century AD and uses the sutra, vinaya and abhidharma texts. Hinayana holds that doubts and defilements are eliminated by renunciation.

Mahayana In contrast to the Hinayana schools, the followers of the Mahayana school ('Great Way/Vehicle') believed in the possibility of salvation for all. They practised a far more devotional form of meditation and new figures came to play a prominent part in their beliefs and their worship – the bodhisattvas, 'saints' who were predestined to reach the state of enlightenment through thousands of rebirths. They aspired to Buddhahood not for their own sake, however, but for the sake of all living things and were believed to have returned to lead others to salvation. The Buddha is believed to have passed through numerous existences in preparation for his final mission. These additions probably represent the Hindu influence, with some considering its propositions as tending much towards hyperbole. One of the most notable Mahayana philosophers was the saint, Nagarjuna. Mahayana Buddhism became dominant over most of South Asia and its influence is widespread in Buddhist art.

The development of Mahayana is thought to parallel that of early Christianity and to have been influenced by it. The concept of **bodhisattva**, the increasing emphasis on compassion (a divergence from older Buddhism) and a preoccupation with future spiritual states all have their corollaries in the Christian ethos. Furthermore, similarities have been noted between some of the respective scriptures which seem likely to have been influenced by the existence of established trading routes which linked the areas of their composition, notably between the eastern regions of the Roman Empire and southern and northwestern India. The Buddhist Perfection of Wisdom, for example, is referred to as 'sealed with seven seals' and is shown to a bodhisattva named 'Ever weeping' who later sacrificed himself to attain the perfection of wisdom. The Bible's book of Revelations, meanwhile, has St John weeping bitterly as there is no one to break its seals but the sacrificial lamb.

Vajrayana The 'Diamond' or 'Indestructible' way is related to the Mahayana tradition, though resembles magic and yoga in some of its beliefs. The ideal of the Vajrayana Buddhist is to be "so fully in harmony with the cosmos as to be able to manipulate the cosmic forces within and outside himself". It had developed in the north of India by the seventh century AD, matching the parallel growth of Hindu Tantrism. Its adherents are concentrated in the northern regions, including Nepal. Its texts are the esoteric teachings of the Tantras which were transmitted by accomplished masters such as Manjushrimitra, Indrabhuti and Padmasambhava.

Lamaism and Tibetan Buddhism

Lamaism is the name sometimes used to describe Tibetan and Mongolian Buddhism. It is largely a Mahayana form which has included elements of pre-existing Bon shamanism.

Much of the Buddhist Nepal, particularly in the higher Himalayan regions, is either characterized or strongly influenced by Lamaism. Among all the Buddhist countries of Asia, the highest developments of Indian Buddhism were preserved in Tibet. This was due partly to geographical proximity, partly to temporal considerations and partly to the aptitude which the Tibetans themselves displayed for the diversity of Indian Buddhist traditions. The sparse population, the slow measured pace of daily life and an almost anarchical disdain for political involvement have encouraged the spiritual cultivation of Buddhism to such an extent that it came to permeate the entire culture.

All schools of Buddhism in Tibet maintain the monastic tradition of the *vinaya*, the graduated spiritual practices and philosophical systems based on the sutras and their commentaries, the *shastras* and the esoteric meditative practices associated with the Tantras. Different schools developed in different periods of Tibetan history, each derived from distinctive lineages or transmissions of Indian Buddhism.

The oldest, the Nyingmapa, are associated with the early dissemination of Buddhism. The Sakyapa and the Kagyupa, along with the Kadampa, appeared in the 11th century on the basis of later developments in Indian Buddhism. The Gelukpa originated in Tibet during the 14th century, but can claim descent from the others, particularly the Kadumpa and the Sakyapa. Each of these schools has had its great teachers and personalities over the centuries. Each has held political power at one time or another and each continues to exert influence in different regions.

Nyingmapa The Nyingmapa school maintains the teachings introduced into Tibet by Shantaraksita, Padmasambhava, Vimalamitra and their contemporaries during the eighth century. The entire range of the Buddhist teachings are graded by the Nyingmapa according to nine hierarchical vehicles, starting from the exoteric sutras of the Lesser Vehicle and the Greater Vehicle and continuing through the classes of Outer Tantras to those of the Inner Tantras. It is the Inner Tantras, known as Mahayoga, Anuyoga and Atiyoga which are the teachings of the Nyingmapa par excellence.

Kadampa When the Bengali master **Atisha** (982-1054) reintroduced the teachings of the gradual path of the enlightenment into Tibet in 1042, he transmitted the doctrines of his teacher Dahrmakirti of Sumatra, which focussed on the cultivation of compassion and the propitiation of the deities Tara, Avalokiteshwar, Acala and Shakyamuni Buddha. During the early 15th century, this tradition was absorbed within the indigenous Gelukpa school.

Kagyupa The Kagyupa school maintains the lineages of the Indian masters Tilopa, Naropa and Maitripa, which emphasize the perfection stage of meditation (Sampannakrama) and the practice of the Great Seal (Mahamudra). These were introduced here by Marpa Lotsawa (1012-1096) and Zhang Tselpa (1122-1193). Marpa had four main disciples including the renowned yogin Milarepa (1040-1123), who passed many years in retreat in the mountain caves of Labchi and adjacent Himalayan valleys. Milarepa is one of a select group of Tibetan masters revered for their attainment of enlightenment or Buddhahood within a single lifetime.

Atisha

Sakyapa The Sakyapa tradition represents a unique synthesis of early eighth-century Buddhism and the later diffusion of the 11th century. The members of the Khon family had been adherents of Buddhism since the time of Khon Luiwangpo Sungwa, a student of Padmasambhava. Then, in 1073, his descendent, Khon Gyelpo, who had received teachings of the new tradition from Drokmi Lotsawa, founded the Gorum temple at Sakya. His tradition therefore came to emphasize the ancient teachings on Vajrakila, as well as the new teachings on Heajra, Chakrasamvara and the esoteric instruction known as the Path and its Fruit.

Tsongkhapa

Other important sub-schools of Sakya also developed from the early 15th century. Among them, Ngor was founded in 1429 by Ngorchen Kunga Zangpo, Nalendra in 1435 by Rongton Sheja Kunzik and Derge Lhundrupteng in 1448 by Tangtong Gyelpo.

Gelukpa The Gelukpa school maintains the teachings and lineage of Je Tsongkhapa (1357-1419), who established a uniquely indigenous tradition on the basis of his Sakyapa and Kadampa background. He instituted the Great Prayer Festival at Lhasa and propagated his important treatises on the sutra and tantra traditions in and around the Tibetan capital. Some of his students became the prime teachers in the new Gelukpa order, including Khedrup Je who was retrospectively recognized as Panchen Lama I. Another was Dalai Lama I Gendun Drupa.

The successive emanations of the Dalai and Panchen Lamas enhanced the prestige of the Gelukpa school, which swiftly gained allegiances from the Mongol forces of the northeast. Following the civil wars of the 17th century, many Kagyu monasteries were converted to the Gelukpa tradition and the regent Sangye Gyatso compiled his Yellow Beryl (Vaidurya Serpohistory) of the Gelukpa tradition.

Buddhist literature

The whole corpus of Buddhist literature, including scriptures and commentaries, is to put it mildly, immense. Put together, it represents a record of the continuing Buddhist traditions which, not unlike those of the main Christian denominations, have constantly evolved, though there is no Buddhist equivalent to the Bible. In the centuries following the Buddha's death, scriptures were transmitted orally from generation to generation. They only came to be written down from around the first century BC, while the period from the end of the first century AD is to around AD 400 is considered by many to be the 'golden era' of Buddhist literature, a time when the creative impulse was at its strongest.

The earliest scriptures are in Pali and are those used by the Thereveda Buddhists. These are known as the Tripitaka ('three baskets') and were probably completed in Sri Lanka around the beginning of the first century BC. They comprise the Vinaya, a canon of monastic rules; the Sutta, with guidance mainly for non-monastic Buddhists, along with a miscellany of accounts of the Buddha's life, sermons, poetry and a succinct 'confession of faith' (I put my faith in Buddha, Dharma, Sangha; and the Abhidhamma, a more in-depth exposition of Buddhist philosophy). These are among the principle scriptures used today by Theraveda Buddhist of Sri Lanka and much of Southeast Asia.

Mahayana literature was largely composed in Sanskrit and is later in origin, dating from the second century AD to the sixth century. Most is in sutra form, a combination of the Buddha's sermons along with discourses usually presented as dialogue. Principal Sutras include the **Saddharma pundarika** (the Lotus Sutra) and the Perfection of Wisdom Sutra. These encouraged belief in the worship of certain divine forms, including the bodhisattvas, as well as a devotional approach akin to Hindu bhakti. The Vajrachedika ('Diamond Sutra') is largely concerned with the concept of *sunyata* ('voidness' or 'emptiness') expounded by Nagarjuna and others.

Calendars

Two solar calendars (the Nepali and Gregorian) are in common use, and three lunar calendars (the Nepali, Newari and Tibetan). The latter affects the Buddhist festival dates, the full moon being especially auspicious. Eclipses are often thought to be a bad omen. For festivals, see page 21.

Nepali Calendar

Also known as **Bikram Samvat** (BS, or BE for Bikram Era), this is the official calendar and is followed by the government in its administration. Your official travel documents will also be dated according to this calendar. It is 57 years ahead of the Western (Gregorian) calendar, with new year beginning in mid-April (the month of Baisakh). Thus, from mid-April 2017 it is the year 2074 BS/BE; 2018 is 2075 BS/BE; 2019 is 2076 BS/BE; 2020 is 2077 BS/BE, and so on.

Both Nepali and Gregorian years have 365 days, but the former has 12 months lasting from 29 to 32 days. The Nepali financial year begins in mid-July. This calendar is named after King Bikram Aditya, who reigned in Ujjain (modern day Madhya Pradesh) in India. It was first followed by the Licchavis, becoming fully established during the Malla era.

Newari Calendar

This regional calendar is called **Newari Samvat** (abbreviated to NS) and is used only by the Newars of the Kathmandu Valley. It is 879 years behind the Gregorian calendar. It was introduced by the Mallas with new year falling in mid-November. Thus, from mid-November 2016, it is 1137 NS; 2017 is 1138 NS; 2018 is 1139 NS; 2019 is 1140 NS, and so on.

Tibetan Calendar

This is a lunar calendar which is calculated each year by astrologers. It is based on a cycle of 60 years, each of which is named after one of 12 animals and one of five elements in combination. A calendar year normally contains 12 months, but the addition of an extra intercalary month for astrologers is not uncommon.

In general, the Tibetan lunar month is about two months behind the Western calendar. In order to work out how major events in the Tibetan calendar correspond to dates in the Western calendar, it is necessary to wait until late autumn or winter when the following year's calendar is prepared. The 10th day of every month is dedicated to Padmasambhava who introduced the highest Buddhist teachings from India in the eighth century.

The 25th day of each month is a Dakini Day, associated with the female deities who are agents of Buddha-activity. The 29th day of every month is dedicated to the wrathful doctrinal protector deities, while the 15th and 30th are associated with the Buddha, and the eighth day with the Medicine Buddha.

Kali Era

This calendar is largely associated with religious observances and festivals and is not generally used for administrative purposes. It is based on lunar and solar criteria and is rather complicated, but runs roughly as follows: lunar months are divided into two fortnights (*paksha*), comprising the bright half (*shukla paksha*) and the dark half (*krishan paksha*).

Several Hindu festivals take their name from one of the 14 days of the *paksha*, which are: Pratipada (1), Dwitya (2), Tritya (3), Chaturthi (4), Panchami (5), Shasthi (6), Saptami (7), Astami (8), Nabami (9), Dashami (10), Ekadashi (11), Dwadashi (12), Trayodashi (13) and Chaturdahi (14).

The lunar months are: Magh (January-February), Phalgun (February-March), Chaitra (March-April), Baisakh (April-May), Jyestha (May-June), Asadh (June-July), Shravan (July-August), Bhadra (August-September), Ashwin (September-October), Kartik (October-November), Marga (November-December) and Paush (December-January).

Eternity is divided into three units, the smallest being an 'age' (*yuga*), of which there are four: Krita, Treta, Dwarpar and Kali (the present *yuga*, which began in February 3102 BC, and lasts around 432,000 solar years). Together, these form one 'great age' (*maha yuga*). Finally, 1000 *maha yuga* make one *kalpa* which lasts some 4,320,000,000 solar years. One *kalpa* is considered to be one day in the life of Brahma. Brahma is the creator, one of the supreme trinity of Hindu gods.

Land &
environment

Nowhere else on Earth has a greater diversity of landscapes within as small an area as Nepal. In a north–south cross-section of less than 200 km are the subtropical plains of the Terai, the temperate Himalayan 'foothills' of the Churia and Mahabharat ranges and the High Himalayan peaks themselves. More than half of the country is higher than 3000 m above sea level, around a quarter is at elevations of about 3000 m and less than one-fifth is below 300 m.

Geology and environment

The Terai

The Terai constitutes the northern belt of the Gangetic Plains. Sloping gently from west to east, it comprises less than 20% of the total land surface and is Nepal's most densely populated region. Dotted across its breadth are a few towns and cities, mostly minor commercial and light industrial centres. But more important are the thousands of villages, traditional farming communities cultivating the country's most fertile stretch of land and producing most of its agricultural output: the Terai has over 1 million ha under paddy. The region shares much with the neighbouring Indian states of Uttar Pradesh, Bihar and West Bengal and the border is far more political in character than cultural.

The Terai was formed around 40 million years ago, during the Eocene period. Many of the rocks which form the Indian Peninsula were formed alongside their then neighbours in South Africa, Australia and Antarctica. Then, as the great plates on which the earth's southern continents stood broke up, the Indian Plate started its dramatic shift northwards, eventually colliding with the Asian plate. That collision is still reverberating and as the Indian Plate continues to get pushed under the Tibetan Plateau so the Himalaya continue to rise.

The process of plate tectonics is still continuing, rendering this boundary region between the two land masses seismically unstable and resulting in major earthquakes like those of April and May 2015. Beneath its uniformly flat surface are a series of geological troughs and ridges, a sort of subterranean mountain range. The many major rivers flowing through the Terai deposit clay and sandy or calcareous silts which contribute to the high fertility of its soils and allow the cultivation of 1.4 million ha of land (most under paddy) by over 1 million individual farm holdings.

Throughout all but the most recent part of its history, the Terai was almost entirely forested and was a zone where malaria was endemic. This belt also provided a natural barrier for the Kathmandu Valley and elsewhere against invading forces. This changed only in the second half of the 20th century, when a deliberate programme of deforestation was initiated with the aims of eradicating malaria and creating new lands for settlement. The result has been massive migration from the hills together with urbanization on an unprecedented scale.

The forest, meanwhile, has been denuded beyond recognition: less than 20% now remains and gives an idea of what there once was. It is dominated by the deciduous sal

(*Shorea robusta*), a straight and tall-growing tree that reaches heights of 30 m and more. It is used as a main source of building material. There are also stands of teak (*Tectona grandis*), concentrated in the west, whose timber is highly sought after for building as well as in the production of furniture. Both trees have a good resistance to fire which has helped to mitigate the increasing dominance of man and his attempts to transform more land for agricultural use. Restrictions have been placed belatedly on the commercial exploitation of timber. These, however, are notoriously difficult to enforce with the appeal of additional income combined with local power structures and political allegiances often ensuring that a blind eye is turned to illegal logging operations.

Middle zone

This region of Himalayan foothills forms a buffer zone between the Gangetic Plains to the south and the High Himalaya proper to the north. The term 'foothills' is something of a euphemism, as many of its 'hills' are much higher than Ben Nevis, the highest peak in the UK. Immediately north of the Terai are the forested **Churia Hills** (known in India as the Siwaliks and by geologists as the Sub-Himalaya). The suddenness with which the flat expanse of Terai gives way to the hills and the contrast between the two can be quite dramatic. The Churias are comprised of relatively recent metamorphic rocks, including limestone and, at their northern extent, are characterized by the many doons (valleys). Known also as the Inner Terai, these are often river valleys which can be highly fertile. Elsewhere, the Churias are extensively terraced for cultivation, but soils are generally poorer which limits cropping seasons.

The Churia Hills belt has provided researchers with crucial information on the process of Himalayan orogeny. It is rich in the fossils of both fauna and flora. By boring deep into the ground and extracting a vertical sample of rock, scientists have been able to establish the sequence of geological, environmental and climatic changes by analyzing the sediments.

To the north of the Churias is the **Mahabharat Lekh** ('Great Indian Range'), the narrow southern band of what geologists know as the **Lesser Himalaya**. Peak elevations increase to heights of up to 2600 m and rocks consists entirely of metamorphosed varieties, with quartzites especially evident. Slopes are also forested, sometimes heavily with evergreen oaks and firs, while in areas of higher rainfall the rhododendron (Nepal's national flower) flourishes. Formerly under water, much of this region has major lacustrine deposits. The broader Pahar zone extends from the Mahabharat Lekh to the High Himalaya. This region includes both the Kathmandu and Pokhara valleys, while elevations range from less than 1000 m above sea level to 4000 m and higher. The many river valleys in this belt allow often intensive cultivation of land, with slopes also cultivated with intricate terraces. At lower elevations (eg along the Arun Valley in East Nepal), forests are characteristically subtropical, while with an increase in altitude they become moist temperate, consisting largely of pine, spruce, cedars, firs and the attractive rhododendron whose white, purple or typically deep red flowers blossom from late March to early May. Deodars (*Cedrus deodora*) are particularly conspicuous in the west of Nepal.

High Himalaya

The High Himalaya mark the zone of maximum uplift resulting from the northward movement of the Indian land mass into the Central Asian plate. The range stretches some 2500 km from northwest to southeast and is around 400 km at its widest and is the world's highest as well as youngest mountain range. Eight of the world's 10 highest peaks are in Nepal, including, of course, **Everest** (8848 m). Its geology is complex, but consists

ON THE ROAD

Mount Everest

For 13 years after it was found to be the highest mountain in the world, Peak XV had no European name. In 1865, the then Surveyor General of India suggested that it be named after his predecessor, Sir George Everest (1790-1866), the man responsible for the Great Trigonometrical Survey, completed in 1841, which ultimately determined its height. Everest himself, though honoured, was privately unhappy, as it was official policy that mountains be given their local vernacular name. However, an exception was made and the name stuck. It is known as **Sagarmatha** in Nepal and **Chomolungma** in Tibet.

Early expeditions in the 1920s, including the mysterious disappearance of Mallory and Irvine in 1924, all attempted Everest from the Tibetan side as Nepal was closed to foreigners. It wasn't climbed until Nepal opened its borders, and in 1953 **Tenzing Norgay** and **Edmund Hillary** finally stood on its summit as part of a British Expedition, led by **Colonel John Hunt**. The Swiss Expedition of the previous year had failed only a few hundred metres short of the summit.

Since then, Everest has been climbed many times and by many routes. The route taken by Hunt's 1953 expedition is the 'Ordinary Route', disparagingly called the 'Yak Route' by Sherpas. Following his achievement on Annapurna's Southern Face, **Chris Bonnington** led two expeditions to tackle Everest's southwest face and succeeded in 1975. The Americans traversed it in 1963. In 1970, **Yuichiro Muira** tried to ski down the Lhotse Face from the South Col, but spent most of the time airborne and out of control, ending unconscious on the edge of a crevasse. **Rheinhold Messner** climbed without oxygen and then solo. In April 1988, two teams of Japanese climbers met on the top, having scaled the north and south faces. And there, to record the event, was a television crew.

Peter Hillary followed in his father's footsteps and stood on the summit in 1990. Then, in April 1993, the team that first climbed Everest trekked to the Base Camp for a 40th anniversary re-union: they found 1500 other climbers waiting their turn to climb to the top of the world. These days, commercial climbs offer the opportunity for anyone with climbing knowledge (and a lot of cash) to climb the mountain. A record number of 633 ascents were recorded in 2007. In spring 2016 over 450 climbers made it to the top, 209 of them on the same day. There were five deaths from altitude and frostbite.

So much activity on the mountain does bring the risk of a major incident. In 1996 eight guides and clients died when caught high on the mountain in a storm after queues for the summit had delayed their ascents and, in 2014, 16 Sherpas were killed by an avalanche while establishing the route for their clients. In 2008 a helicopter 'landed' on the summit, placing its skid bar on the snow. How long until the ultimate day trip is possible?

of highly metamorphosed rocks dating from the Tertiary and all other major periods. A series of massifs are separated from one another by deep gorges: separating Dhaulagiri from the Annapurnas, the 6000-m-deep **Kali Gandaki** is the deepest in the world. The mountains are still rising at up to 15 mm a year. The entire region is subject to intense geological activity. Satellite imagery reveals deep fault zones throughout the range and

ON THE ROAD

Tenzing Norgay

Tenzing Norgay (c 1914-1986) is remembered as the quintessential Himalayan mountain guide. Brought up in the Khumbu he moved to Darjeeling in his late teens looking for climbing work on mountaineering trips in Tibet. His career started as the companion and guide of the Italian Tibetologist, Guiseppe Tucci.

He was part of three British expeditions to the mountain from the Tibetan side in the 1930s, as well as an unsuccessful Canadian attempt in 1947.

His experience and expertise was recognized by the Swiss in 1952 when their Everest Expedition, for the first time allowed to approach the mountain through Nepal, recruited him as a full expedition member rather than as a Sherpa guide. He and Raymond Lambert turned back just before the southern summit at 8595 m.

In 1953 he was once more recruited by the British for their expedition and he was paired with the New Zealander Edmund Hillary. They were the second summit team and, when the first failed, he finally reached the summit of Everest at 1130 on 29 May 1953.

Unable to write, he dictated his biography to Malcolm Barnes. He became an honorary Indian and, as Director of the Himalayan Mountaineering Institute in Darjeeling, he was an inspiration to thousands. Without Tenzing and his Sherpas, it is doubtful that the 1953 expedition or many others afterwards, would have been successful.

between 1870 and 2016 there have been over 60 major earthquakes (measuring over six on the Richter scale), to have occurred here and along fault lines of the Tibetan Plateau.

Tibetan Plateau

This region covers an area as large as Western Europe, with elevations ranging from the low-lying southern gorges at 1700 m to the massive 8000-m Himalayan peaks. Most of the Tibetan Plateau is considered to have formed the bed of the Neotethys Ocean which disappeared some 210-250 million years ago, with the meeting of the two land masses. This collision, believed to have taken place some 2012 km south of the Indus-Brahmaputra watershed, finally formed the plateau around 66 million years ago, following a long period of orogeny in the northern areas of Tibet between about 570 and 245 million years ago. The massive plateau, subject to widespread volcanicity, continues to extend upwards and outwards under its own weight, as the Indian subcontinental plate moves ever northwards at a speed of about 6.1 cm per year.

Origins of Uplift

Only 100 million years ago, the Indian peninsula was still attached to the great land mass in the southern hemisphere called Pangaea, or Gondwanaland, of which South America, South Africa, Antarctica and the Indian subcontinent were part. It included some of the world's oldest rocks, such as crystalline granites and gneisses (metamorphic rocks, often layered and with high crystalline content), which today make up a large part of India south of the Ganges plains. Towards the end of the Palaeozoic era, ie from about 160 million years ago, Gondwanaland began to separate. This process of plate tectonics (that is, the movement of 'plates' of the earth's crust), resulted in the northward drift through the great Tethys Sea of four major land masses which became South America, Africa, the Indian peninsula and Australia. The South Asian plate was eventually subducted beneath the great Central Asian Plate around 55 million years ago, creating a concertina-like folding and faulting of the area of impact – the Himalaya – and causing the uplift of the Tibetan Plateau.

The first ranges of the Himalaya to begin the mountain building process were probably the Karakoram in modern Pakistan. The central core of the Himalayan ranges did not begin to rise until about 35 million years ago, followed by further major movements between 25 and 5 million years ago. The latest mountain building period, responsible for the Siwaliks, began less than 5 million years ago and is still continuing. The rocks of the central core of the Himalaya were formed under the intense pressure and heat of the mountain building process. Before that, the present Himalayan region and what is now the Tibetan High Plateau had lain under the sea.

Rivers

Nepal's rivers descend further and faster than any other rivers in the world. As a result, many have cut sheer-sided valleys thousands of metres deep, creating enormously unstable hillsides. Any external action – an earthquake, severe rainfall, the construction of a road – can trigger catastrophic earth and rock slides which sometimes form natural dams that create large lakes, only to burst open and flood the valleys downstream.

The country's three main river systems – the Kosi, Gandaki and Karnali – originate in glaciers and go on to form part of the Ganges river system. A few rise in Tibet, but all ultimately flow into the Ganges. In their lower courses, they are subject to severe flooding. The Kathmandu Valley is drained by the Bagmati River which rises to the north near Tare Bir (2732 m) and leaves the valley through the Chobhar Gorge. By Nepali standards, it is not a great river.

The Himalayan region has many glaciers. As the west is very dry, the biggest are in the east. The Mahalangur and Khumbarkarna ranges have the largest, while the east Himalaya are also the source of the major Kanchenjunga, Yalung, Nuptse and Langtang glaciers. The Khumbu glacier, running off Everest from the Western Cwm is the world's highest, starting at over 7600 m.

Climate

The climate of Nepal reflects its topography. The Terai and Churia Hills experience a subtropical monsoonal climate in common with the rest of the northern Gangetic Plains. Peak temperatures in summer rise to above 40°C, while winter night temperatures drop to just above freezing. The middle zone of the Mahabharat and Pahar regions are temperate, with a climate similar to that of Central Europe. Summer peak temperatures can reach just below 40°C, while the winter regularly experiences temperatures below zero, with snow common in the higher areas. Neither the cities of the Kathmandu Valley nor Pokhara have snow, though the surrounding hills do. The climate of the High Himalaya is alpine.

The monsoon extends across the whole country from June to September, when over 75% of the annual rainfall occurs. The influence of the monsoon and the amount of rainfall decreases from east to west and from south to north. Beyond the High Himalaya and into Tibet, it is arid and cold. If you do the classic three-week Annapurna Circuit trek, you will go from the subtropical lushness south of the mountains to this stark arid beauty of the north.

The post-monsoon period of October-November is characterized by settled weather, clear skies, little rain and moderate to high temperatures. As winter approaches it gets cooler, especially at night. Temperatures drop further in winter. At lower altitudes it is dry and often very dusty. Higher up it is extremely cold at night. See also, page 17.

Vegetation

The natural vegetation reflects altitude and climate, but has been severely modified by man since the latter part of the 20th century.

Several hundreds of Nepal's plants and herbs have been used for centuries as ayurvedic treatments and are increasingly exported worldwide as acceptance of their medicinal value becomes more widespread. The first definitive writings on their therapeutic uses are contained in the Hindu Ayur Veda (*ayur* – 'life' or 'vital power'; *veda* – 'knowledge'), written between 2500 BC and 600 BC.

The Terai

The most significant form of vegetation in the Terai is its band of deciduous forest. Formerly completely forested and a malarial zone, much of the region's tree cover has been removed since the 1950s to make way for settlement and cultivation. The **sal** (*Shorea robusta*) is the Terai's dominant tree, though stands of **teak** (*Tectona grandis*) are also found. There have been efforts at reforestation which, though isolated, are portentous for the future. A few areas have also witnessed the introduction of 'community forest' schemes in which local communities have a stake in new plantations.

A savannah environment of phanta grassland is found in the far west (Sukla Phanta Wildlife Reserve) as well as smaller areas in the mid-west and elsewhere. Riverine forest, including sissoo and acacia, extend along the floodplains of the main rivers. The **silk cotton tree** (*Bombax ceiba*) is conspicuous and grows up to 25 m in height. The bark is light coloured, often grey and usually bears conical pines. In big trees there are noticeable buttresses at the bottom of the trunk. It has wide-spreading branches and, though deciduous, keeps its leaves for most of the year. The flowers appear when the tree is leafless and have rather flashy red, curling petals up to 12 cm long forming a cup shape, from the middle of which the stamens all appear in a bunch. The fruit pod produces the fine silky cotton which gives it its name.

The Terai's national parks have succeeded in maintaining pockets of the region's natural biodiversity as well as the habitats of endangered fauna. Cultivation is largely of rice, though wheat, corn, millet and vegetables also feature prominently. **Rice** (*Oryza sativa*) is a grass of which there are many hundreds of varieties with different colours, growing seasons and other characteristics.

The Terai also supports a number of fruit trees, the bewildering produce of which you will see in many a town market. The **mango** (*Mangifera indica*) is a fairly high tree growing up to 15 m or higher with spreading branches forming a rounded canopy. You will often see it along roadsides (much of the Bhairahawa–Lumbini stretch is a true mango avenue). The distinctively shaped fruit is delicious.

From a distance, the **jackfruit** (*Artocarpus heterophyllus*) tree looks similar to the mango. It is a large evergreen of the mulberry family with dark green leathery leaves, some of which may fall in cold weather. The bark is warty and dark brown in appearance. Its huge fruit, which can be as much as 90 cm long, 40 cm thick and weigh more than 30 kg, grows from a short stem directly off the trunk and branches. The immature fruit is used as a vegetable. The skin is thick and rough, almost prickly. The fruit itself is an acquired taste and some find the smell of the ripe fruit unpleasant.

The **banana** plant (the *Musaceae* family) is not in fact a tree but a gigantic herb arising from an underground stem. The very large leaves grow directly off the trunk and the plant can grow higher than 7 m. The leaves are often tattered and the fruiting stem bears a large purple flower (also used in cooking), which yields up to 100 fruit bunched up the stem.

The **papaya** (*Carica papaya*) has a slender, palm-like trunk up to 8 m tall, though it is usually much shorter. The large hand-shaped leaves come off in one, two or three stages, with one always at the top. Only the female tree bears fruit (immature fruits are also used as vegetables) which hang down from near the base of the branches.

The **leechitree** (*Litchi chinensis*) is a native of China which has spread down through Nepal and into India. A member of the **soapberry** (*Sapindus*) family, it bears small round fruit containing a black stone, sweet, white, jelly-like flesh and has a brittle pink or red shell.

The **guava** (*Psidium guajava*) is a small tree with spherical to pear-shaped fruit.

The **pineapple** (*Ananas comosus*) is a bromeliaceous plant whose familiar fruit develops from a head of flowers close to the ground and has a crown of spiky leaves.

The **cashew** (*Anacardium*) tree is related to the mango and pistachio. Usually less than 7 m in height, it has bright green, shiny rounded leaves. The rather thick foliage casts a dense shadow. The nut is suspended from a fleshy fruit called a cashew apple.

The **tamarind** (*Tamarindus indica*) is an evergreen with feathery leaves and small yellow and red flowers which grow in clusters. It has a short straight trunk and a spreading crown. The bark is often thickened with scar tissue which gives it an irregular appearance. The noticeable fruit pods are long, curved and swollen at intervals down their length. It has a slightly bitter pungent taste. It is widely used in South Indian cooking and is a vital ingredient in Worcester sauce.

The **coconut palm** (*Cocus nucifera*) is common throughout the Terai, with its tall (15-25 m), slender, unbranched trunk, feathery leaves and large green fruit, so different from the brown fibre-covered inner nut which makes its way to Europe.

The **eucalyptus** (*Eucalyptus grandis*) was introduced into the subcontinent from Australia in the 19th century. It provides both shade and firewood. There are several forms of eucalyptus, but all can be readily recognized by their characteristic thin long leaves and brown or grey bark. The leaves and fruit of the tree often have a pleasant fresh smell, especially after rain.

The **banyan tree** (*Ficus benghalensis*) is featured widely in Eastern literature. Curiously, its seeds germinate in cracks in walls and in crevices in the bark of other trees. In a wall the growing roots will split the wall apart as can be seen in many old temples. As it grows more roots appear from the branches until the original host tree is surrounded by a cage-like structure which eventually strangles it. So a single banyan appears to have multiple 'trunks', which are in fact roots.

Related to the banyan and growing in similar conditions is the **peepul tree** (*Ficus religiosa*). This tree is particularly associated with holy Hindu sites and is frequently found in or by a temple or shrine. In some instances, shrines have actually been built beneath the original peepul tree. It also cracks open walls and strangles other trees with its roots. It has a smooth grey bark and can easily be distinguished from the banyan by the absence of aerial roots and by the leaves which are large, rather leathery and heart shaped, the point of the leaf tapering into a pronounced 'tail'. It bears abundant figs which are about 1 cm across.

Churia Hills

The Churia Hills bring the first indications of changes in vegetation type. Population settlement is thinner here, so although there is a considerable amount of terraced cultivation, a reasonable proportion of the slopes remain wooded. At lower levels, sal is again prominent. In the far east, there is widespread tea cultivation. Tea gardens stretch from the Indian border near Darjeeling to west of Ilam, producing an attractive carpet-like landscape of deep green. Cardamom is also grown here in commercial quantities.

With the increase in height, between 1000 and 2000 m sal gives way to extensive stands of wet hill, coniferous forest including **pine** (notably the *Pinus roxburghi*) along with **chestnut** (*Castanopis indica*), **spruce** and **evergreen oak** (*Quercus lamellosa*). Significant stands of deodars are restricted to the far west of Nepal.

Bougainvillea is widely distributed. It is a dense bush or a climber with oval leaves and rather long spines. The flowers often cover the whole bush and can be a variety of striking colours, including pinkish-purple, orange, yellow and white. If you look carefully at one of the flowers, you will see that the brightly coloured part is not formed by the petals, which are quite small and undistinguished, but by large bracts at the base of the flower.

Continuing up into the Mahabharat Lekh and Pahar zones above 2000 m, **rhododendrons** are common. These trees, with their gnarled stems and twisted branches, flower profusely from late March and are Nepal's 'national flower'. They thrive in a wet climate and are found in dense tracts in east Nepal particularly along the upper stretches of the Arun and Tamur valleys. With the exception of this area, the rhododendron is rarely found in isolation. **Poplars** (eg *Populas ciliata*) which extend east into Bhutan and **larches** (*Larix* species) as well as **juniper** are also well represented in much of the eastern part of the country. All these species are water-demanding, so distribution diminishes with decreasing longitude.

In contrast to the very low and often bone dry under storey of Terai sal forest, that of the wetter areas is full with numerous species of fungi and mosses which give the forest a characteristically fresh and heady smell. **Bamboo** (the *Bambusa*, *Phyllostachys* and *Dendrocalamus* species) is strictly speaking a grass and is another common component of forest undergrowth, though there are occasional solitary stands of enormous varieties whose stems are so strong that they are used as building materials. It is conspicuous in the lower Annapurna regions. Various **cypress** (*Cupressus* species) trees are found in the west, including the indigenous Himalayan cypress.

Rhododendron cover continues above 3000 m but alpine forest starts becomes dominant. These elevations are characterized also by fairly extensive stands of birch, pine and juniper. The tree line (ie the highest altitude at which trees grow) lies at just below 5000 m. Again reflecting precipitation patterns, rhododendrons can flourish up to this elevation in the east, while shrubbery dominates in the west. These elevations support various grasses, with patches of grassland extending 500 m or more above the treeline. From April, the seemingly hostile climate gives way to an array of flowering plants. These include species of gentian, primroses (some of the first to blossom), roses of the genus *Potentilla* and buttercups.

Since the 1970s there has been a welcome increase in awareness of the importance of Nepal's flora and fauna which has led to the establishment of numerous protected areas. There are now 10 national parks, three wildlife reserves, six conservation areas and one hunting reserve. Over 23% of Nepal is now protected within them.

The flora and fauna of national parks are protected and should not be removed: penalties may be enforced. All visitors are required to be self-sufficient in cooking materials; the use of firewood is prohibited and rubbish should be burned, buried or carried out.

An entrance fee is payable by each visitor. Be sure to keep the receipt, as you may be required to show it. Full details of exploring individual parks are included in the relevant section of the guide. The visitor figures are from the Nepal Tourism Statistics for 2014, compiled by the Department of National Parks and Wildlife Conservation.

Bardia National Park (1) *2014 foreign visitors: 14,197.*

Situated in southwest Nepal, it lies on the east banks of the Karnali River. It is the Terai's largest national park and covers an area of 968 sq km. It consists of almost untouched Terai forest ('jungle') of sal, rivers and riverine forest and small areas of savannah-like phanta grassland. The diverse environment supports an equally diverse fauna.

It is said to be the best place in Nepal for tiger sightings. It has small herds of wild elephants, five species of deer, crocodiles and a few rarely seen Gangetic dolphins. The rhinoceros was re-introduced from Chitwan in the 1980s and numbers increased significantly until the Maoist uprising which led to poaching in the absence of the army to protect the park. The rhinos were all but wiped out, as were the elephants. They are being reintroduced and four more rhino were brought from Chitwan in March 2016, creating a healthy and growing population.

Banke National Park (2)

This park was only established in 2010 and sits alongside Bardia National Park. Its 550 sq km, when added to Bardia, form the Tiger Conservation Unit Banke-Bardia. This is linked, via wildlife corridors, to Suhelwa and Katerniaghat wildlife sanctuaries in India.

National Parks

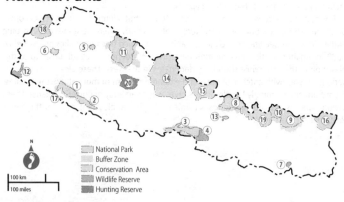

National Park
Buffer Zone
Conservation Area
Wildlife Reserve
Hunting Reserve

100 km
100 miles

Around Banke is a buffer zone, an area of 344 sq km that is inhabited but has wildlife and environmental controls on it.

The national park is home to eight eco-systems, from sal forest to flood plains and parts of the Churia Hills. Over 124 plant species, 34 mammals and more than 300 types of bird have been recorded. At the last census there were seven tigers known to be living in the reserve. There are also striped hyena and four-horned antelope.

Chitwan National Park (3) *2014 foreign visitors: 173,425.*

Nepal's first and most visited national park lies within easy reach to the southwest of Kathmandu. Originally the hunting grounds of the Rana Prime Ministers, it initially became a rhino sanctuary set near the Rapti River as early as 1963. The national park itself was created in 1973 and became a UNESCO World Heritage Site in 1984.

It covers an area of 932 sq km, consisting of areas of the Churia Hills, ox-bow lakes, and the flood plains of Rapti, Reu and Narayani rivers. The Churia Hills rise gradually eastwards from 150 m to over 800 m. The lower but most rugged Someshwor Hills occupy most of the western portion of the park. The park boundaries have been delineated by the Narayani and Rapti rivers in the north and west, and the Reu River and Someshwor Hills in the south and southwest. It shares its eastern border with Parsa Wildlife Reserve.

Some 70% of the park is tropical or subtropical forest, with smaller areas of riverine forest and grasslands. It is home to 43 species of mammal including the tiger, common leopard, one-horned rhino, elephant and sloth bear. It also has over 450 species of bird and 45 reptiles, including the gharial crocodile.

Parsa Wildlife Reserve (4) *2014 foreign visitors: 376.*

Established in 1984 this reserve covers 499 sq km, adjoining Chitwan to the east. The Churia Hills, ranging from 750 m to 950 m and which run east–west, form the dominant landscape of the reserve. The soil is primarily composed of gravel and conglomerates which make it very susceptible to erosion and very porous with water from the hills running underground and surfacing at a distance of about 15 km from the hills' base.

The flora and fauna is very similar to its neighbour Chitwan, with sal forests being dominant. It has good populations of tigers and leopards, and a wild elephant population.

Rara National Park (5) *2014 foreign visitors: 181.*

With an area of just 106 sq km, Rara, created in 1967, is Nepal's smallest national park. It centres around Lake Rara (also known as Mahendra Tal) which, at 10.8 sq km, is Nepal's largest lake. The park lies at altitudes of 3000 m plus. It's renowned for its almost alpine scenic beauty, with Chuchemara Peak (4048 m) lying to its south and Ruma Kand (3731 m) to the north. The Karnali River begins its long journey to the Ganges to the east of the lake.

The park is made up of mainly coniferous forest, with forests of blue pine dominating around the lake. Rhododendron, spruce, black juniper and Himalayan cypress are also found in the park. The summer months are also very good for wild flowers, with hundreds of varieties on display.

Amongst the mammals living ibn the park are musk deer, Himalayan black bears, leopards, jackals, wolves, wild dogs and otters. The birdlife is varied, being especially good for waterfowl, both resident and migratory.

Khaptad National Park (6) *2014 foreign visitors: 47.*

Created in 1984 Khaptad covers the relatively small area of 225 sq km in western Nepal. It encloses an area of mid-mountain terrain, mostly around 3000 m in altitude, that comprises an upland plateau of grassland and some forest. There are also stands of bamboo at the lower elevations and a wide variety of herbs used in local traditional medicines.

The most common animals are leopards, Himalayan yellow-throated marten, black bears, wolves, jackals and a range of grazers. The birdlife includes several pheasants and birds of prey, and the park is excellent for butterflies.

It also contains two important Hindu religious sites at Tribeni and Sahashra Linga and the ashram of Khaptad Swami, a Hindu sage and holy man who died in 1996.

It is one of Nepal's most remote parks, with several days' walk required to access it whether you approach by plane or road. There are no trekking facilities or accommodation inside the park.

Koshi Tappu Wildlife Reserve (7) *2014 foreign visitors: 7349.*

The reserve lies along 175 sq km of flood plains of the mighty Sapt Koshi River in southeast Nepal. The word *tappu* means 'island'. It was created in 1976 and during the monsoon the river floods, resulting in a dramatic change of appearance. The reserve can be flooded to a depth between 10 and 300 cm. There are now flood barriers and gates to stop the river changing its course too dramatically year on year as used to happen.

Vegetation consists mainly of tall khar-pater grassland along with riverine and deciduous forest.

It is especially known for its birdlife with nearly 500 recorded species, including seasonal migrants. Ibis, stork, duck and other waterbirds thrive. Its home to 17 globally endangered species.

Itinerant mammals include deer, wild boar and blue bull, while there is also a small population of wild buffalo.

Langtang National Park (8) *2014 foreign visitors: 12,552.*

Situated north of Kathmandu this is one of Nepal's major trekking regions, although it was badly affected by the 2015 earthquakes. There were about 45 villages and hamlets in the park and some were completely destroyed with a high loss of life. Trekking is possible but check locally before proceeding.

The park was established in 1971 and formalized in 1976, the first national park in the Himalayan region. It covers 1710 sq km of mountainous terrain and includes the sacred Gosainkund Lake. The park covers the upper catchment areas of the Trisuli and Sun Kosi rivers and its highest point is Langtang Lirung (7234 m).

The most popular areas to visit are the Langtang Valley, for its mix of culture and mountain scenery, and the Gosainkundu area of high-altitude lakes, a popular Hindu pilgrimage destination.

Tamangs are the dominant peoples in the southern areas, while Bhotias and ethnic Tibetans live in the north.

Vegetation ranges from that of the temperate region to alpine and you'll see rhododendron, oak and deciduous forest.

Common animals include various deer, monkeys and wild boar at lower elevations, with musk deer, red pandas and the elusive snow leopard inhabiting the higher reaches.

Makalu-Barun National Park and Conservation Area (9) *2014 foreign visitors: 1083.*

This park was established in 1992, Nepal's eighth national park and the first to be created with an adjacent conservation area. This was a new management approach, encouraging the local inhabitants to be involved in the protection of their forests, natural resources and way of life. In return they benefit from the development of infrastructure, education, health care and income generation.

The park covers some 2330 sq km and, together with the Sagarmatha National Park and the Comolangma Nature Reserve in Tibet, forms an area of more than 38,000 sq km protecting the Everest ecosytem.

Most of the Makalu-Barun National Park is remote wildness, with just two small settlements and seasonal herding in the high pastures. Previously, few foreigners had visited the area except for the occasional climbing and trekking expeditions needing permits and camping equipment. Now it's possible to trek to Makalu Base Camp.

The lower Barun Valley and its tributary the Saldima have been designated as Nepal's first Strict Nature Reserve. This means it cannot be visited except for scientific research or monitoring.

The park has 400 species of bird, including the spotted wren babbler and the olive ground warbler. These two species had never been seen in Nepal before.

There are many wild animals including the endangered red panda, Himalayan black bear and the clouded leopard. Other wildlife found in the park are: ghoral, tahr, wild boar, barking deer, Himalayan marmot and weasel, common langur monkey and the serow.

The Arun River rushing through the park has around 84 varieties of fish, including salmon.

The surrounding conservation area is home to approximately 32,000 people of various ethnic groups. The majority belong to various tribes of Rais and practice an ancient religion which reinforces harmony with nature. Shingsawas and Sherpas, both groups originally from Tibet, live at higher elevations and maintain a Buddhist culture. A handful of other hill tribes, including Gurung, Tamang, Magar, Newar, Brahmins and Chhetris, live in the lower elevations.

Sagarmatha National Park (10) *2014 foreign visitors: 35,157.*
Sagarmatha is the Sherpa name for Mount Everest and the national park covers an area of 1148 sq km. The area, known as the Khumbu, was given protected status in 1976 and is now also a UNESCO World Heritage Site. It is the homeland of the Sherpa people, who originated in Tibet and moved here in the 1500s. Their main settlements are at Namche Bazaar, Khumjung and Khunde and there is evidence of their Buddhist beliefs everywhere.

Much of the park area lies above 3000 m, a rugged terrain of glaciers, steep ice faces and deep gorges. At lower elevations, pine and hemlock forests dominate. With an increase in altitude, rhododendron is again widespread, with juniper, birch and scrub higher up. The rhododendrons are in flower in March and April.

Mammals include the Himalayan tahr and black bear, musk deer and, if you are very lucky, the Yeti There are over 118 bird species recorded and you are likely to see the lammergeyer vulture, Himalayan griffon and other birds of prey. Nepal's national bird, the impeyan pheasant, is found here.

Shey Phoksumdo National Park (11) *2014 foreign visitors: 417.*
This is Nepal's largest national park, created in 1984 and covering an area of 3555 sq km. It borders Tibet to the north and straddles the districts of Dolpa and Mugu. Shey Phoksumdo takes its name from the Shey Monastery and Phoksumdo Lake. It includes the Kanjiroba Himal range, with numerous peaks above 6000 m. It was created to protect a trans-Himalaya ecosystem with Tibetan-type flora and fauna as the park lies north of the Great Himalayan range.

The northern area of the park includes the high-altitude Dolpa plateau, with a similar arid mountainous topography as Mustang. The southern area includes river valleys with thick forest of willow, walnut and pine. Higher elevations have scrub and extensive juniper. Phoksundo Lake is drained by a 150-m tall waterfall, the highest in Nepal.

The park is an important habitat for the snow leopard and the blue sheep, as well as leopard, Himalayan black bears and wolves. There is a small local community within the park, mostly Buddhists but with some worshippers of Bon, a pre-Buddhist religion. It is protected to its south and east by a buffer zone.

Sukla Phanta Wildlife Reserve (12) *2014 foreign visitors: 984.*

Located in the far southwest of the country, this is a unique reserve of 305 sq km. The name comes from the Tharu words for 'white' (*sukla*) and a particular form of savannah-like 'grassland' (*phanta*). Combined with the Terai's sal-dominated forest, it contains a diverse range of environments and wildlife. At its centre is the Rani Tal, a small lake which attracts a wide variety of terrestrial and aquatic birdlife, some migratory. The reserve is also renowned for a large population of swamp deer and lies on a migratory trail of tigers and wild elephants. Although it is visited by few tourists, good accommodation is available near the reserve and Sukla Phanta remains something of an undiscovered gem in Nepal's natural heritage.

Shivapura Nagarjun National Park (13) *2014 foreign visitors: 180,464.*

Shivapura lies on the northern rim of the Kathmandu Valley and covers an area of some 192 sq km. It is named after its highest point, Shivapuri Peak (2732 m) It was originally protected in the late 1970s to safeguard an important water catchment area for the city of Kathmandu. This protected status was upgraded to that of national park in 2002.

Lying on the transition zone between subtropical and temperate there is a good variety of flora within the park. It contains both Himalayan subtropical forest as well as Eastern Himalayan broadleaf. Over 2100 floral species have been recorded, including patches of rhododendron forest on northern slopes.

Leopards, jungle cats, golden jackals and over 20 other species of mammal live in the park. And 318 species of bird have been recorded, including the Eurasian eagle owl.

Being so close to Kathmandu, it is a popular hiking destination, with a reasonable network of trails. There are also some religious sites within the park which can be visited. It is a popular place for day walks and weekend picnics.

Annapurna Conservation Area (14) *2014 foreign visitors: 129,966.*

Originally established in 1985 and formalized in 1992, the Annapurna Consevation Area covers a mountainous region of over 7629 sq km in central Nepal. It is Nepal's most popular trekking destination, containing the world's deepest river gorge (Kali Gandaki River) as well as some of its highest mountains, including Annapurna I (8091 m) and the magnificent Macchapuchare (6997 m).

It is the diversity of culture and terrain that make the area such a draw. From the lush, terraced fields and villages of the foothills to the stark stone houses and monasteries of the upper valleys, the Hindu culture to its south and the Buddhist cultures of the north.

Within its boundary is a population of some 120,000 people from 10 main ethnic groups, including Newars and the Hindu castes of the lower regions, Gurungs, Magars, Thakalis and Manangis in addition to the Lopas and ethnic Tibetans of Mustang. The aim of ACAP (Annapurna Conservation Area Project) is conservation, integrated development and the promotion of environmentally sensitive trekking.

Vegetation types range from lowland chestnut forest to oak and coniferous forest of the middle elevations and juniper and scrubland to the tree line. There are broad tracts of rhododendron forest and more than 40 species of orchid. It is also home to nearly 100 species of mammal, including the snow leopard and blue sheep, and 478 species of bird.

Manaslu Conservation Area (15) *2014 foreign visitors: 3764.*

Bordering the Annapurna Conservation Area to the west and Tibetan Plateau to the north and the east, the Manaslu Conservation Area covers 1663 sq km. Established in 1998 it is in the Gorkha District of Central Nepal and has an altitude range of between 1200 m and 8163 m.

With such a large altitude range, the flora varies accordingly, from rhododendron forests to pine to high-altitude meadow. There are 11 types of forest and up to 2000 species of wild flower and plants. In the valleys there are plenty of villages, mostly inhabited by Gurungs, with terraced hillsides.

The area has 33 indigenous mammals, from the snow leopard to the Himalayan Tahr. Over 115 bird species have been recorded, including the large birds of prey.

Manaslu is becoming increasingly popular as an alternative to the Annapurna Circuit, although some of the villages were badly hit by the 2015 earthquake with many lodges badly damaged. Most have reopened and in need of custom. Check locally on current status.

Kanchenjunga Conservation Area (16) *2014 foreign visitors: 777.*

Created in 1997, this 2035 sq km area lies in the far northeast corner of Nepal, bordering both the Qomolangma Reserve in Tibet and the Kanchenjunga Biosphere Reserve in Sikkim.

The lower areas are inhabited by the Limbu, while the Sherpa people live at the higher altitudes. Their Buddhist culture can be seen in the prayer walls and flags that proliferate. It's estimated that 5000 people live in the area, from 13 different ethnic groups.

The area is made up of alpine grasslands, rocky outcrops, dense temperate and subtropical forests, and low river valleys. It also contains Kanchenjunga (8586 m) with its high-altitude valleys and glaciers. It is estimated that over 60% of the conservation area is a landscape of rock, snow and ice, making it one of the most dramatic mountain areas in Nepal.

The lowlands contain various species of tropical hardwood, changing to oak and pine as altitude increases, with larch, juniper and fir growing just below the tree line. It is an excellent destination for lovers of rhododendrons and orchids, with 23 types of rhododendron identified.

Animals include the snow leopard, musk deer, red panda and blue sheep. It is also home to the Impheyan pheasant and the shy drongo.

Blackbuck Conservation Area (17)

This tiny reserve in mid-western Nepal, also known as Krishnasaar Conservation Area, was established in 2009 to help conserve the endangered blackbuck antelope. Only 16 sq km in size, it contains the most northerly herd in the world, numbering just over 200 individuals.

Api Nampa Conservation Area (18)

Covering 1903 sq km, this conservation area in the very far northwest of Nepal is named after two peaks within its boundaries: Mount Api (7132 m) and Nampa (6757 m). To its west lies India and to its north is Tibet. It is within the Mount Kailash Sacred Landscape, one of Tibetan Buddhism's most holy places. Due to its remote location, it is little visited.

The conservation area was established in 2010 to protect the landscape, its bio-diversity and the cultural heritage of the area. Over 50,000 people live within it, from the Bhote, Kami, Damai, Sarki and Chhetri ethnic groups. The Byash people are still nomadic, moving between high-altitude grassland in the summer and the valleys during the winter.

The central area is a plateau of grasslands intermixed with oak, coniferous forest and riverine deciduous temperate forest. The vegetation includes sal, fir, hemlock, oak and juniper. It is home to the snow leopard, clouded leopard and musk deer.

Gaurishankar Conservation Area (19)

This conservation area was established in 2010 with the purpose of connecting the Langtang and Sagarmatha national parks. It covers 2179 sq km and includes the Rolwaling Area. It contains several glacial lakes, including Tso Rolpa, and over 2.5% of its area is covered by glaciers.

Over 55,000 people live in the conservation area, mainly the Tamang, Sherpa and Chhettri peoples. It also contains the Kalinchowk Bhagwati shrine, a famous pilgrimage destination for Hindus.

Gaurishankar is rich in biodiversity, with 16 varieties of forest identified. It is home to a recorded 34 species of mammal, including the red panda, and 235 species of bird.

Dhorpatan Hunting Reserve (20) *2014 foreign visitors: 89.*

The country's only hunting reserve, Dhorpatan was formally created in 1987 and covers an area of some 1325 sq km to the south of Dhaulagiri (8167 m) in mid-west Nepal.

Hunting is strictly regulated with permits issued in certain seasons by the Department of National Parks and Wildlife Conservation in Kathmandu. The hunters' principal target is the blue sheep, whose numbers have increased to nuisance levels for local communities. Species of goat, bears and wild game birds are also hunted.

The reserve is characterized by alpine, sub-alpine and high-temperate vegetation. Common plant species include fir, pine, birch, rhododendron, hemlock, oak, juniper and spruce. As well as the hunted species, it is home to populations of leopard, Himalayan thar, musk deer, red panda and wolves.

The reserve itself has numerous villages to its south, east and west whose inhabitants depend on access to the reserve for their firewood, grazing and fodder. It's estimated that nearly 100,000 head of livestock enter the reserve every February for summer grazing.

Flora and fauna

Large mammals

The widest variety of wildlife is once again found in the Terai, although the steady destruction of forests and wooded areas both in the Terai and further north has removed the natural habitat of some larger mammals. The best places for watching the wildlife are the Terai's national parks, especially Bardia and Chitwan.

Asiatic elephants (*Elephas maximus*) The greatest concentrations of the Asiatic elephant living in the wild are found in the Royal Bardia National Park which lies on a traditional elephant migratory route from the western Terai into India (including the Corbett National Park). Numbers were badly affected during the Maoist uprising of the 2000s when the army had to withdraw from many parks and poaching became endemic. It is estimated that there are 100-170 wild elephants in Nepal, mostly migratory. The animals come down to water in the evening, either in family groups or in herds of individuals. Elephants are also frequently domesticated and are used as beasts of burden.

Buffalo (*Bubalus bubalis*) Very few buffalo remain in the wild, though a small herd is found in and around the Koshi Tappu Wildlife Reserve in the eastern Terai. When domesticated it is known as the water buffalo, a solid beast standing some 170 cm at the shoulder. The black coat and wide-spreading, curved horns are common to both sexes. It is often seen immersed in water or large, muddy puddles which it uses to keep cool.

Indian rhinoceros (*Rhinoceris unicornis*) The Indian rhinoceros was formerly widely distributed through the Terai but, like its African relative, it is now an endangered species (though numbers have increased since the 1980s). This thick-skinned perisodactyl has a single horn (the African rhino has two) of up to 60 cm, stands 170 cm at the shoulder and has a total body length of around 3 m and a tail of around 60 cm.

Leopard (*Panthera pardus*) Another endangered species, the leopard or panther is also found in Nepal, but is even more elusive than the tiger. Although it shares many of the tiger's prey species, it is generally found away from tiger habitats both in the drier lowland areas and in the hills. There are two types, the rare clouded leopard and the common leopard. Common leopards are found throughout the country, even sometimes in the suburbs of Kathmandu.

Snow leopard (*Panthera uncia*) The fabled snow leopard lives in the High Himalaya. It is long haired with a creamy-grey coat and rose-like spots. It feeds on small mammals, has a smaller head than the *pardus* and is even more elusive.

Tiger (*Panthera tigris*) The best known of Nepal's mammals is, of course, the tiger. Once widely prevalent throughout the Terai, the tiger is a land-demanding creature and the destruction of forest has reduced numbers drastically and placed unprecedented pressures on those that remain. It has been designated an 'endangered species'. Populations have been further reduced by poachers lured by the high sums they can earn for a tiger skin or for parts of its anatomy which are prized as natural remedies or treatments especially in Southeast and East Asia. Tigers are not community animals, preferring to hunt singly or in pairs and living in small family groups. Naturally shy, they hunt largely by night and from early evening and may be seen along or near riverbanks stalking their prey, of which deer form a major part.

Red panda (*Ailurus fulgens*) The lesser panda lives in the Himalayan forests and bears little outward resemblance to the more familiar black and white giant pandas. A reddish-brown animal with a horizontally striped tail, it is related to the raccoon and is considered by some experts to be its original ancestor. It is around 60 cm long with a tail of 50 cm.

Sloth bear (*Melursus ursinus*) The sloth bear stands about 75 cm at the shoulder and can be seen in thinly wooded areas of scrub and rock. It is unkempt looking with a shaggy black coat and a yellowish V-shaped mark on the chest. The hairless eyelids and long dull grey snout give it a mangy look. It has a distinctively long and pendulous lower lip.

Monkeys
One of the most frequent sightings are monkeys, which inhabit both forested and urban areas from the Terai as far north as the Pahar zone. They are a commonly found beside roads and in temple complexes around the Kathmandu Valley.

Common langur (*Presbytis entellus*) The most widespread of monkey species is the common langur, a long-tailed monkey with a silver-grey body and black face, hands and feet. It is around 75 cm long with a tail of 95 cm, which it is often seen to use as a means of suspension.

Rhesus monkey (*Macaca mulatta*) The rhesus monkey is also widely distributed. You see them at many of Kathmandu's main temples and at sites across the country, where they have learnt that pilgrims and tourists mean food. Don't carry any in your bag or they will find it. They have even been known to steal phones in the knowledge that people will swap them for food.

Deer
Barking (*Muntiacus muntjak*) The barking deer, or muntjac, 60 cm at the shoulder, is a small, shy deer which is most often glimpsed in pairs darting for cover. It is brown with darker legs. It has white underparts, a white chest and white under the tail. The stag carries a small pair of antlers which arise from bony, hair-covered protuberances and has one short tine just above the brow. The main part of the antler is only about 10-12 cm long and curves inwards slightly. Their startlingly staccato 'bark' is heard more often than they are seen.

  Muntjak were introduced into the UK in the 1800s by country estates wanting exotic animals to roam their parklands. They are now common in many areas of the country.

Musk (*Moschus moschiferus*) The musk deer is found in small numbers in the middle ranges of Nepal. It is hornless and is the country's smallest deer, standing just 50 cm at the shoulder. Poaching has reduced numbers alarmingly. It is sought for its scent which is used in perfumery and consists of a secretion in a glandular sac beneath the skin of the abdomen of the male.

Sambar (*Cervus unicolor*) Standing at 150 cm at the shoulder is the magnificent sambar. It has a noticeably shaggy coat which varies in colour from brown with a yellow or grey tinge, through to dark, almost black, in older stags. The females tend to be somewhat lighter in colour. The coat of the stag is thickened around the neck to form a mane. The mature stags carry large, three-tined antlers. Immature males carry one to three tines depending on age. The sambar is a forest-dwelling deer, often also found on wooded hillsides. They do not form large herds, but live in groups of up to 10, or sometimes as solitary individuals.

Spotted (*Axis axis*) The attractive spotted, or chittal, deer is quite small, standing only 90 cm at the shoulder. The bright rufous coat, spotted with white, is unmistakable. The stags carry antlers with three 'spikes', or tines, on each. Chital occur in herds of 20 or so in grassy areas and are often seen near rivers.

Swamp (*Rucervus duvaucelii*) Herds of swamp deer are found principally in the Sukla Phanta Wildlife Reserve, in the southwest corner of Nepal.

Antelope
Black buck (*Antilope cervicapra*) The black buck is found mainly in the Bardia area. It is a dark brown antelope with two single-stemmed twisting antlers up to 60 cm long and stands 80 cm high at the shoulder.

Blue bull (*Boselaphus tragocamelus*) The blue bull or nilgai is a large antelope standing 140 cm at the shoulder. The male has short horns and is a blue-grey colour, while the female is hornless and is mid-brown in colour.

Other mammals

Canines There are small numbers of canines, including the **wild dog** (*Cuon alpinus*), a reddish-brown hunting dog with a black-tipped tail and muzzle. It is present in small numbers, but may be seen individually or in pairs. The **golden jackal** (*Canis aureus*), related to the wolf, is mainly nocturnal and rarely observed. In some areas, though, you can hear its long howl at night. The **striped hyena** (*Hyaena hyaena*) is also rarely seen. It is tawny coloured with black stripes. Much of its strength lies in its jaws and front portion. It usually scavenges and hunts in forest margins.

Common mongoose The common mongoose (*Herpestes edwardsi*) is an inhabitant of scrub and open jungle, but you can also see it in gardens and fields. It is well known as a killer of snakes (including cobra and venomous varieties), but will also take rats, mice, fowl and birds' eggs. The ferret-like mongoose is tawny with a grey, grizzled tinge. It is about 90 cm in length, of which almost half is the tail which always has a pale tip.

Marten The marten (*Martes flavigula*) resembles the mongoose, is also carnivorous and shares its habitational zones, but is shorter and lives in trees. It has a long, dark brown glossy coat and a bushy tail.

Wild boar The wild boar (*Sus scrofa*) is easily identified by its sparse hair on a mainly black body and pig-like head. The hair thickens down the spine to form a sort of mane or crest. A well-grown male stands 90 cm at the shoulder and has sharp tusks, which are absent in the female. The young are striped. They are commonly seen in grass and light bush especially in the Terai's two main national parks and near water where it often causes great destruction of crops.

Others There are numerous squirrels inhabiting not just wilder places but just about every town and village in the lowlands and temperate regions. The five-striped **palm squirrel** (*Funambulus pennanti*) is about 30 cm in length, about half of which is tail.

Look out also for the 'flying fox' (*Pteropus giganteus*) which has a massive wing span of 120 cm. These are actually fruit-eating bats and are found in concentrations in the middle zones. The road between Kantipath and Lazimpath, on the western side of Kathmandu's Royal Palace, used to be lined with trees full of these hanging bats but they were cut down in the 1990s as the bats were considered a health hazard. They roost in large, sometimes huge, noisy colonies in tree tops, often in the middle of towns or villages, where they look like folded umbrellas hanging from the trees. In the evening, they can be seen leaving the roost with slow measured wing beats.

Reptiles and amphibians

Most reptiles inhabit the warmer regions of the Terai.

Crocodiles Most impressive are the crocodiles which, previously hunted almost out of existence, have increased in number due entirely to the efforts of breeding centres, notably at Chitwan and Bardia.

Gharial The gharial, or gavial is native to the Indian subcontinent and grows up to 6 m in length. Its distribution is similar to that of the marsh mugger and it is listed as an endangered species. It is famous for its slender snout used for hunting fish, its primary diet.

Marsh mugger (*Crocodilus palustrus*) The marsh mugger grows up to 3-4 m in length and is found mostly along the rivers in or near Chitwan and Bardia. It feeds on animals coming to drink from the river.

Snakes You will occasionally see snakes slithering through the undergrowth of a forest region or near water. They include the venomous **kraits** and the **Indian cobra** (*Naja naja*) which grows up to 180 cm in length and is distinguished by its ability to flatten its neck to a hood-like form when disturbed. The **common python** (*Python molorus*) is an endangered species which can be 6 m or more long. It is a boa constrictor which kills its prey by coiling around it and squeezing it to death. **Vipers** (eg the *Vipera berus*), along with **coral snakes** (eg the *Micrurus fulvius*) are also common in the Terai. **Water snakes** are found around rivers and lakes, including Pokhara's Phewa Tal. There are very few venomous snakes in the middle and higher mountains.

Others There are **turtles** and many species of **frog**, including the hyla and other tree frogs. You will almost certainly encounter a **lizard** of some kind. In the forested areas, **skinks** are common. The number of amphibians has declined markedly in the Terai with the indiscriminate use of anti-mosquito DDT.

Insects and invertebrates

These are most prevalent in the Terai, where their buzzing and warbling is particularly noticeable at night. Especially beautiful at night is the **firefly** (or glow worm), a nocturnal beetle of the family *Lampyridae*. Its light is produced by a special organ at the rear of the male abdomen. You will also see various species of predacious *mantis*, including the 'praying mantis' so-called because it holds its forelegs in a raised, prayer-like position in preparation for its prey.

Butterflies are found at all elevations up to the tree line. In the mountains they are most conspicuous in late spring, in the middle regions (including Kathmandu and Pokhara) from April to September and from March to November in the Terai. If you are interested in butterflies then a visit to the Natural History Museum and its collection in Pokhara is recommended.

There are about 100 species of **mosquito** (the *Culicideae* family) of which around one-third are carriers of malaria. These are known as anopheline (*Anopheles genus*) mosquitoes. They are about 6 mm long and are dipterous creatures, characterized by one pair of membranous wings towards the front. Anopheline mosquitoes are distinguished from other species by their slanting, head-down position when resting, while the non-harmful species tend to remain horizontal. The transmission of malaria is achieved by the infected female which injects thousands of microscopic sporozoites through its saliva in a single bite. The mosquito thrives in wet and moist conditions, eg swamp land. Until it was shown to be the actual cause of the disease, the term 'malaria' was coined by 18th-century European colonialists to describe the fever then believed to have been caused by stale, unwholesome air (*mal* and *air*).

Another unpleasant (though less harmful) invertebrate is the **leech** (eg the *Hirudo medicinalis*). It is a parasitic worm which can grow up to 15 cm long. It thrives in moist conditions and feeds by attaching itself to the host and sucking blood until it is full, when it drops off. It has the courtesy to inject a local anaesthetic so that the host may donate blood with minimum discomfort. It is most active between May and October.

Birds
Nepal is also home to a huge range of birdlife. The best places for birdwatching are Sukla Phanta and Koshi Tappu.

To date, 876 species of bird have been recorded in Nepal. Of these 35 are globally threatened species, 19 are near-threatened species and 15 are restricted-range species. The **spiny babbler** is the only recognized endemic bird.

As many as 130 breeding and wintering species (15% of Nepal's birds) are considered nationally threatened. Habitat loss is the main threat; hunting, illegal trade and poisoning are the other threats.

Bee eaters (*Meropidae* family) Often seen scavenging along the ground or putting their head down holes in search of insects. The little **green bee eater** (*Merops orientalis*) is common in open countryside and is usually seen in pairs, perching on posts and dead branches. The green of its plumage contrasts with the blue throat and chestnut top of the head.

Birds of prey The **lammergeier** (*Ger*, 'lamb vulture'; *Gypaetus barbatus*) which is distributed from the mountains of southern Europe through to China is the region's largest bird of prey. It is dark brown with a distinctive 'moustache' of black feather drooping from below the beak. It has a wingspan of up to 3 m which allows it to soar effortlessly through the air. It is usually found in the lower mountains at elevations of up to 4000 m.

The **brahminy kite** (*Haliastur indus*) is a familiar scavenger and is seen around water. It has a chestnut plumage with a white head and breast.

The **pariah kite** (*Milvus migrans*), also known as the dark or black kite, measures around 65 cm. This is a brown bird with a fairly long tail which looks either forked when the tail is closed or slightly concave at the end when spread.

Flycatchers Of the many types of flycatcher, the **paradise flycatcher** (*Terpsiphone paradisi*) is especially conspicuous, seen flitting from its perch in pursuit of insects in woodland and open spaces. The head is a shiny metallic black with a noticeable crest which contrasts with the white of the underparts. The wings and tail can be either white or chestnut. The male has particularly long tail feathers and distinctly blue eyes.

Hornbills There are a few species of hornbill, including the **Malabar pied hornbill** (*Anthrococerus malabricus*). This is a large heavy-looking bird, 90 cm long, seen in small noisy flocks often in fruiting trees. The plumage is black and white and the long tail has white edges. The massive bill is mainly yellow and carries a black and yellow protuberance (known as a casque) along the top. It makes a spectacular sight in flight.

Kingfishers (*Alcedinidae* family) There are also several species of kingfisher, usually brightly coloured with long tail, a large crested head and a substantial beak. At 27 cm, the **white-breasted kingfisher** (*Halcyon smyrnensis*) is frequently found away from water and is readily seen as it perches on wires and posts. The rich chestnut of its body plumage contrasts with the brilliant blue of its wing feathers, particularly noticeable when it swoops down to gather its prey. The red bill and white front make it unmistakable as well as supremely beautiful.

Parrots/parakeets Especially beautiful and numerous are parrots, including many species of parakeet, which are endemic throughout the Terai and as far north as the Pahar zone. The rose-ringed parakeet (*Psittacula krameri*) is around 40 cm long. Its long tail is noticeable both in flight and when the bird is perched. Females lack the red collar. They can be very destructive to crops, but are attractive birds which are frequently kept as pets.

Common sightings The all **black drongo** (*Dicrurus adsimilis*) is around 30 cm long and is almost invariably seen perched swallow-like on telegraph wires or bare branches. Its distinctively forked tail makes it easy to identify. The related **racquet-tailed drongo** (*Dicrurus paradiseus*) is also recognized by its distinctive tail which ends in long streamers with broadened tips. The head bears a tufted crest. As well as its unique appearance in flight, it has the habit of sitting on conspicuous perches, which makes it easy to identify.

Another common sight is the **egret** of which there are several species. Particularly common are the **little egret** (*Egretta garzetta*), which is over 60 cm long, and the **cattle egret** (*Bubulucus ibis*), which is 50 cm long. In the non-breeding season, both birds are white, but can be readily distinguished by their different coloured bills: yellowish in the cattle egret, but all black in the little egret. In addition, the legs of the little egret are black with yellow toes, but this is not always easy to see. The little egret is a taller more elegant looking bird, while the cattle egret often has a hunched appearance. In the breeding season the cattle egret develops golden or buffish plumes on its head and back.

The **painted stork** (*Ibis leucocephalus*) stands 1 m tall. It is also mainly white, but has a pinkish tinge on the back, greenish black marks on the wings and a broken black band on the lower chest. The bare yellow face and yellow down-curved bill are conspicuous.

The **common mynah** (*Acridotheres tristis*) is about 22 cm long. It is mostly black, but look for the white under the tail and the bare yellow skin around the eye, the yellow bill and legs and, in flight, the large white wing patch.

The **magpie robin** (*Copsychus saularis*) is 20 cm long. In the male, the wings, head and upper parts are mainly black, but with a noticeable white wing bar. Below, it is white. The long white and black tail is often held cocked up. The female's colour pattern is similar, but the black is greyish. It is a delightful songster and has a trim and lively appearance.

The **red-vented bulbul** (*Pyconotus cafer*) is another songbird (often mentioned in Persian literature and perhaps mistaken for a nightingale) and is widespread in the lower regions. A mainly brown bird, it can be identified by the slight crest and a bright red patch under the tail.

The **spotted dove** (*Streptopelia chinensis*) is an attractive, 30-cm-long bird found in woodland and open spaces. It can be identified by the speckled appearance of its back and by the wide half collar of white spots on a black background. The head and under parts are pink.

The **house crow** (*Corvus splendens*) is really quite smart looking with a grey body and black tail, wings, face and throat. It is common in every mid- and lowland town in South Asia, where it makes a vivacious contribution to the dawn chorus.

Books

Ferguson, Robert *Sacred Mountain.*
Historical drama set in the Khumbu
and Tibet, as an ex-Gurkha officer seeks
redemption from wartime memories.
Hertzog, Maurice *Annapurna I.* Dramatic
account of the exploration of Dhaulagiri and
Annapurna and the first ascent of an 8000-m
peak at a dreadful physical cost.
Matthiessen, Peter *The Snow Leopard.*
A beautifully written account of a 1973
journey to the remote Dolpo area in search
of the snow leopard.

Morris, James *Coronation Everest.* The
account of the successful 1953 Everest
expedition told by the Times correspondent
who accompanied them onto the mountain.
Peissel, Michel *Tiger for Breakfast.*
A biography of Boris Lissanevitch, owner
of the first hotel in Kathmandu when it
opened to the World in the 1950s, giving
a fascinating insight into Nepali society.
Whelpton, John *A History of Nepal.*
Comprehensive account of Nepal's long
and turbulent history, including the Royal
Massacre of 2001.

Practicalities

Getting there

The only international airport is **Tribhuvan International Airport** in Kathmandu (www.tiairport.com.np). In 2016 work started on a new airport in Pokhara but this is not due for completion for several years. When completed it will be able to handle regional international flights. **Bhairawa Airport** in the Terai is currently being upgraded, mainly to handle Asian tourists coming to visit Lumbini. It is due to open in spring 2018.

Nepal Airlines is the state carrier but, like all Nepalese airlines, is banned from flying to the EU. It is a fairly basic operation with a chequered safety record. It owns an **Airbus 320**, a couple of ageing Boeings and has aspirations to buy a wide-bodied 330.

Prices can differ considerably from day to day during peak periods so if your dates are flexible search before and after. All airlines have seat sales and special offers so again prices can vary greatly.

From Europe

The only direct flight from Europe to Kathmandu is operated by **Turkish Airlines** from Istanbul. The majority of visitors fly via the Middle East or India. Most European and Indian airlines fly to Delhi or Mumbai, from where there are several Indian and Nepalese carriers offering connecting flights to Kathmandu.

Those offering connecting flights all the way to Kathmandu are **Air India** (www.airindia.com) and **Jet Airways** (www.jetairways.com). **British Airways** (www.BA.com) and **Virgin** (www.virgin-atlantic.com) fly to Delhi where you must change carriers. Via the Middle East are **Qatar Airlines** (www.qatarairways.com), **Etihad** (www.etihadairways.com) and **Emirates**/flyDubai (www.emirates.com).

From North America

From the east coast it is generally better to fly via Europe and/or the Middle East. **Turkish Airlines** have flights to Nepal, connecting in Istanbul. **Emirates** have direct flights to Dubai, connecting to **flyDubai** (www.flydubai.com) for Kathmandu. **Air India** fly non-stop from New York to Delhi and connect on to Kathmandu.

From the west coast it's best to travel with the Asian carriers, connecting in their home country. These include **Singapore Airlines/Silk Air** (www.singaporeair.com), **Thai** (www.thaiairways.com), **Malaysian** (www.malaysiaairlines.com) and **Cathay Pacific/DragonAir** (www.cathaypacific.com).

From Australia and New Zealand

Air Asia (www.airasia.com) fly from Australia to Kathmandu, via Kuala Lumpar. The Asian carriers, such as **Singapore Airlines**, **Thai**, **Malaysian** and **Cathay Pacific/Dragon/Air** (www.cathaypacific.com) all fly to Kathmandu via their home bases. It's also possible to fly to Delhi on **Qantas** or **Air New Zealand**, via a connection in Asia and then on with a local carrier. Unless you have loyalty points to use up, this is a long option.

From South Africa

Flights via the Middle East with **Emirates** or **Qatar**, or via Delhi on **Jet Airways** are the best options.

Packing for Nepal

You may like to take some of the following items with you from home: sunglasses designed for intense sunlight; earplugs for sleeping on aeroplanes and in noisy hotels; high-factor sun cream with moisturising cream; insect repellent containing Deet for preference; lightweight permethrin-impregnated mosquito net; travel sickness tablets; tampons; condoms; water sterilizing tablets; sachets of rehydration salts plus anti-diarrhoea preparations; painkillers such as Paracetamol or Aspirin.

First-aid kit: take a small pack containing a few sterile syringes and needles and disposable gloves. The risk of catching hepatitis etc from a dirty needle used for injection is now negligible in Nepal, but some may be reassured by carrying their own supplies – available from camping shops and airport shops.

Airport information

The approach to Kathmandu airport is a picturesque one requiring some good old-fashioned visual navigation, with the valley rim rising on either side as you descend towards the city. You approach over Patan, from a southerly direction. Diversions (and, consequently, delays) are not uncommon in poor visibility but much less frequent than 20 years ago.

Tribhuvan Airport is situated to the east of the city and has separate domestic and international terminals. A new domestic terminal was built a couple of years ago but seems to be only currently used to queue in as you pass security into the old terminal. It is due to come into service in the coming months.

When you arrive at the international terminal you walk to immigration. If you have a visa you go straight to the immigration kiosks. If not, you need to first pay your visa fee at the bank counter and then present this receipt with your visa application.

Once through go down the stairs to baggage reclaim, being security checked as you enter for some bizarre reason. Sometimes they try to collect your customs declaration form here – don't give it in otherwise you may be asked for it again when you go through customs with your luggage.

Baggage reclaim usually takes some time. Ensure you keep your baggage ticket receipts as these will be checked against your bags as you pass through customs. Just after this is the taxi counter, a small tourist information kiosk and several banks for changing money. You then leave the building to a sea of guides and drivers with meet-and-greet boards.

Pre-paid taxi booths at both terminals charge the airport taxi syndicate rate of Rs 800 (US$7.50) into central Thamel. An ordinary taxi will charge about Rs 500 (US$4.50) and takes about 20 minutes. Drivers tout for business as you leave the terminal. You will need to haggle and look at the car before agreeing the fare to ensure it is a proper taxi and appears roadworthy.

Departure On departure there is a comfortable lounge, with several decent shops, a small duty-free and cafés. You can pay to sit in the executive lounge if you have a long wait. It costs US$25 and offers complimentary food and drinks.

Baggage allowance

Check with your airline as different companies have different policies. Some have a weight allowance, varying between 20 and 30 kg, while others allow two pieces. Remember that internal flights, especially to a mountain strip, have less baggage, usually 12 or 15 kg and you will need to have a soft bag to be squashed into odd-shaped holds.

Airport tax

Airport and departure taxes are gathered in your ticket price so there are no taxes that need to be paid in cash at the airport.

Road

India

There are six official border crossing points between India and Nepal. All are in the southern Terai region, either directly on or near the Mahendra Highway, the main east–west road through Nepal. All have bus and some air connections with Kathmandu.

Some travel agencies in Kathmandu, Pokhara and Nepal's border towns offer inclusive through ticketing to destinations in India. While many of these deals are genuine and trouble-free, others require you to collect the ticket for your journey from another travel agency in one of the border towns or/and again at an intermediate town in India. There are two main drawbacks to this system. First, the more people are involved in such a transaction, the greater the potential for 'mistakes' to occur; and, second, you may not actually end up with the routing, time or class of travel that you thought you had paid for. The best way to avoid hassle is by booking through a good and reliable travel agent; give them as much notice as possible. Ask around and check reviews.

Tibet

You can visit Tibet only as part of an organized group tour with a recognized tour operator, and not independently. The tour operator will make all visa and travel arrangements. Prices vary seasonally and according to what is included.

After the earthquakes of 2015 the border crossing at Kodari was closed, initially because the road was blocked by landslides and the border villages had suffered damage. However, permits were not issued for overland travel by the Tibetan Tourism Agency even when the damage was repaired. Currently there are no land-crossings open, apart from a few remote passes where permits have been issued to climbing groups. The only connection between Nepal and Tibet for Westerners is by air. There are daily flights between Kathmandu and Lhasa.

BORDER CROSSINGS

India–Nepal

Sunauli (Belahiya)

Sunauli lies at the southern end of the Siddhartha Highway which runs to Pokhara, via Butwal and Tansen. Nearby is Lumbini, the birthplace of the Buddha and an important Buddhist pilgrimage site with archaeological ruins. Sunauli (Belahiya) is an unattractive place and it is better to stay in either Bhairahawa (4 km to the north) or in Butwal (40 minutes by bus), both of which have a range of better (though still not great) accommodation.

There are frequent buses from the border to Pokhara (eight hours), Chitwan National Park (four hours) and Kathmandu (eight hours). The nearest airport is north of Bhairahawa which has flights to Kathmandu. Gorakhpur is the nearest Indian city and there are several buses throughout the day. Varanasi is a bus journey of about nine hours.

Bhimdatta (Mahendranagar)

In the far southwest of the country, Mahendranagar has road connections with Delhi. The stretch of the Mahendra Highway from Mahendranagar to Nepalgunj is in bad condition and an extremely bumpy ride. Heading east from Mahendranagar, you can break the long journey to Kathmandu with a stay at Bardia National Park, some five hours by bus from the border. Alternatively, the excellent and little-visited Sukla Phanta Wildlife Reserve is minutes from Mahendranagar.

The nearest airport is Dhangadhi which has daily flights to Kathmandu. Yeti Airlines, Buddha Air and Nepal Airlines all offer services.

Nepalgunj

Effectively a regional capital for southwest and west Nepal Nepalgunj is a few kilometres south of the Mahendra Highway. There is an airport with frequent flights to Kathmandu and it is the hub of flights to western Nepal with flights to many of the more remote and mountainous destinations, including Jumla. It is an easy three-hour bus journey to the Bardia National Park, while buses to both Kathmandu and Pokhara take around 14 hours. South of the border, there are road and rail links with Delhi as well as Lucknow, Kanpur, Faizabad (for Ayodhya) and Gorakhpur.

At the southern end of the Tribhuvan Highway, the first major road to be constructed in Nepal, Birgunj is a convenient crossing point for the Chitwan National Park, a four-hour bus journey away. The majority of buses to Kathmandu take the longer route via Narayanghat and Mugling, because of the poor condition of the Tribhuvan Highway. The journey time to both Kathmandu and Pokhara is around eight hours. The nearest airport is in Simara which is about 20 km from Birgunj and it takes about 30 minutes to reach Kathmandu by air.

Across the border is Raxaul Bazaar which is the terminus of a narrow-gauge railway line. Patna is a six-hour bus journey away and is a busy railway junction with frequent connections to Delhi and Kolkata. It also has a foreign tourist ticket quota where you can usually get a reservation to most destinations quite quickly.

Kakarbhitta

Kakarbhitta is in the far southeast of Nepal, a long bus journey to Kathmandu (18-20 hours), so you might think about stopping overnight en route. You can get to the attractive hill station of Ilam, the centre of Nepal's tea-growing region, in around five hours. Alternatively, break the journey at Janakpur, the Terai's most important Hindu town. The nearest major airport is at Biratnagar (three to six hours by bus), which has frequent flights to Kathmandu and also to the mountain villages of Tumlingtar and Taplejung.

On the Indian side, Siliguri, a short bus or auto-rickshaw ride away, is the departure point for buses and jeeps heading up to Darjeeling and buses to Kolkata (12 uncomfortable hours away). Trains to Kolkata (14 hours) leave from the neighbouring town of New Jalpaiguri. The nearest airport is at Bagdogra, between Siliguri and the border, which has regular flights to Kolkata and Delhi.

Dhangadhi

This is a little-used crossing in the western Terai, useful if travelling to/from Lucknow. There are flights from here to Kathmandu with Yeti Airlines, Buddha Air and Nepal Airlines.

Getting around

Kathmandu is the hub for most of Nepal's domestic aviation, though there are regional hubs at **Nepalgunj** (serving the more remote destinations in West Nepal) and **Biratnagar** (for East Nepal). It is the quickest way of travelling around a country not designed for roads. A one-hour flight can save many hours of travel, but there are disadvantages. Many flights are dependent on the weather and visibility, and cancellations are fairly common. **Lukla**, the airstrip at the start of Everest treks,

Tip...
There are some truly spectacular routings with stunning views of the Himalaya. Consider which side of the aircraft is likely to have the best views and ask for that side on check-in or (if there is no seat allocation) try to be among the first to board. This applies also to flights to/from the Terai.

once had a backlog of several thousand passengers waiting for 18-seater planes to arrive. You should certainly never fly back to Kathmandu for an international connection without leaving a buffer day or two.

Nepal also has a chequered safety record, and not only because of the terrain, making it more risky than other countries. There have been several crashes in recent years caused, or contributed to by, mechanical failures or pilot errors. There have been 10 crashes since 2008, the most recent in February 2016 when a flight en route to Muktinath crashed in the Annapurnas. When choosing which airline to use, check reviews and airline safety websites and find out which airlines the largest overseas tour operators use as they will have carried out safety audits as part of their duty of care. The vast majority of flights operate to schedule and the local pilots are experienced in difficult conditions.

Nepal Airlines Corporation (NAC), the national carrier, has a small domestic operation but is notoriously unreliable so most operators use the private airlines instead. There are now several of these on many of the routes. **Yeti Airlines** (www.yetiairlines.com) and **Buddha Air** (www.buddhaair.com) have the largest networks.

Officially, you have to check in for domestic flights one hour before departure. Longer is recommended on flights which may be drastically overbooked (for example Lukla and Jumla) and where there is a chance that your reservation will not be honoured. On other routes, you will find people arriving just a few minutes before departure.

Tip...
Most of the airlines offer early morning mountain flights, a circuit to/from Kathmandu that takes you along the Himalaya to Everest and back. If you want to see the world's highest mountain but are trekking elsewhere you get amazing views and don't worry about your seat allocation – they make sure both sides get equal time gazing at the Himalaya.

Security checks involve x-ray and physical checks of each passenger and their luggage. Carry any knives or other potential weapons only in your checked baggage.

At less busy airports, a claxon is sounded a few minutes before arrival of the inbound aircraft. This is to advise people of the imminent arrival so that goats, buffaloes and other grazing livestock may be removed from the runway in time.

Helicopters

Helicopters are adaptable and can fly to many places unreachable by fixed-wing aircraft. They are used for mountain rescue as well as for cargo and passenger flights. There are a number of private helicopter operators including **Shree Air** (www.Shreeair.com, T01-422 2948) and **Dynasty Aviation** (www.airdynastyheli.com, T01-447 7560). They operate 'mountain flights' from Kathmandu and Pokhara and also a morning visit to the Everest Base Camp area or the Langtang Valley. Most work mainly on a charter basis and are also involved in medical evacuation work from the mountains. Private charters can be arranged quite rapidly. Ask around at good travel agents, for example on Durbar Marg or in Thamel in Kathmandu, or contact the charter company directly.

Rail

There is no rail network in Nepal, the only small stretch of track being a narrow-gauge line that runs for a few kilometres from the Terai town of Janakpur to the Indian border. This is currently closed as it undergoes repair and 'upgrade' work.

Road

In 1951 there were fewer than 100 cars in Kathmandu and no road to link the city with the outside world. The vehicles that were there had all been dismantled and carried through the hills by porters. The first road, the **Raj Path**, was completed in 1958 and since then the road network has slowly expanded. The sheer scale of Nepal's mountainous terrain is hard to grasp, so that even its main roads look like tiny ribbons winding their way along precipitous valleys. Many roads, even the highways, get blocked every monsoon by mud and rock slides and the 2015 earthquakes caused significant damage to roads. Most are now repaired or cleared.

There is also the traffic. Nepal's winding roads are packed with vehicles, many in a state of disrepair that's hard to comprehend. From trucks and tankers shuttling endless loads from India, to buses and minibuses trying to arrive before their competitors, a road journey is as much of an adventure as a trek into the mountains. The Kathmandu Valley has an estimated 700,000 vehicles using less than 1000 km of surfaced road.

Tourist buses, minibuses and cars used by reputable tour operators are maintained to a high standard, driven by chauffeurs who appreciate that their passengers will not be used to, or happy with, usual Nepalese road techniques. A journey with a good driver lets you really appreciate the skill of the road engineers and the landscapes they have conquered.

Bus

Bus travel is extremely cheap by Western standards, and buses link Kathmandu with most parts of the country. As with domestic aviation, Kathmandu is the main centre of operations while Nepalgunj and Biratnagar serve as important regional hubs. A long bus journey in Nepal invariably demands physical and mental endurance especially if you are tall, as all buses are built for a smaller physique than that of the Western traveller. There is compensation, however: you will travel through many areas of stupendous natural beauty and get to meet some fascinating and friendly people.

Tourist bus Normally run by the larger travel agencies, these buses serve the popular tourist destinations and link **Kathmandu**, **Pokhara** and **Chitwan**. You buy a ticket, get

Major routes

Mahendra Highway

This, Nepal's most important road, runs the length of the Terai from Bhimdatta (Mahendranagar) in the west to Kakarbhitta in the east. A number of major junction towns have developed out of erstwhile villages along the highway: **Butwal** (at the junction of the Siddhartha Highway, with Sunauli and Lumbini to the south and Tansen and Pokhara to the north), **Narayanghat** (with a direct and much-used link to Mugling on the Prithvi Highway), **Hetauda** (at the junction with the Tribhuvan Highway, with Birgunj to the south and the Prithvi Highway and nearby Kathmandu to the north), and **Itahari** (with Biratnagar to the south and Dharan and Dhankuta to the north).

Most of the Mahendra Highway is in reasonable condition although some stretches in the more rural areas are in a poor state of repair. Perhaps its most attractive stretch is in the west of Nepal, where it follows a smooth, well-surfaced section through the **Bardia National Park** where you can see deer, wild peacocks and other animals foraging along the roadside and in the forest margins. For much of its long course, the highway runs through or beside the Terai's ever-diminishing forested belt, which consists largely of sal (*Shorea robusta*) trees. Now and then, monkeys make an appearance from the forest. The highway runs north of the **Chitwan National Park**, through Narayanghat to Hetauda where it joins the **Tribhuvan Highway**. The two roads combine briefly before the Mahendra Highway continues its eastward course from Amlekhgunj, by the entrance to the **Parsa Wildlife Reserve**. It crosses the mighty Sapt Kosi River west of Biratnagar before heading to Kakarbhitta and leaving Nepal for Siliguri.

Prithvi Highway

Probably the road most travelled by visitors to Nepal, the Prithvi Highway links **Kathmandu** with **Pokhara**. It is in fair condition for most of the way, though the stretch that climbs in/out of the Kathmandu Valley is very winding and slow. Soon after leaving the Kathmandu the road meets the Tribhuvan Highway at Naubise. It follows the Trisuli River as far as the junction town of Mugling, midway between Kathmandu and Pokhara. Thereafter, it follows the Marshyangdi river before that river turns north to its source high in the Annapurnas. The scenery along most of the Prithvi Highway is quite superb, with picturesque river valleys and hillsides, and snow-capped mountains forming a spectacular horizon.

The journey from Kathmandu to Pokhara takes between five and seven hours and there are places to stop for lunch along the way. (See page 192.)

a reserved seat and normally a meal is included at a reasonable restaurant to break the journey. They are more expensive than public buses (albeit still good value) but are more comfortable, reliable and have a good safety record. They are an excellent alternative to expensive flights.

Operators include **Greenline** (www.greenline.com.np) and **Golden Travels** (T01-422 0036). Bookings can be made either direct or through travel agents in the three destinations.

Siddhartha Highway

This road links **Pokhara** with **Sunauli** (**Belahiya**) on the Indian border, and is a highway in both senses of the word. But for the short stretch between Sunauli (Belahiya) and Butwal, the road is in dreadful condition. It snakes its way, often precariously, through the Mahabharat and Churia Hills. At times the road is little more than a single lane carved into the hillside, with numerous blind corners. Overtaking along these stretches should be impossible, but is still attempted and usually accomplished by impatient local drivers. There are, nevertheless, some fine views. The highway passes Tansen, an important and attractive hill town, before descending to the Terai which it meets at Butwal. From here, it is an easy 40-minute ride to the border. Nearby is **Lumbini**, the birthplace of the Buddha. Most buses between the border and Pokhara take the much longer (and safer) route via Narayanghat and Mugling; the journey time is the same as along the Siddhartha Highway.

Tribhuvan Highway (the Raj Path)

This was the first highway to be constructed in Nepal, and was the first direct motorable route from India to Kathmandu. It is narrow, constantly undulating and shows its age. It is only 32 km as the crow flies from Naubise, on the Prithvi Highway, to Hetauda, the town on the Terai where is emerges, but the twisting Tribhuvan Highway makes it an astonishing 107 km. Because there are few buses that take this route (preferring instead to go via Mugling and Narayanghat), it is the highway that fewest Western visitors will experience. It is known, however, for the village of **Daman** which has probably the finest panoramic view of the Himalaya extending (on a good day) from Dhaulagiri in the west to Everest in the east. For those with a little more time it is an interesting, if slow, road to take in one direction to/from the Terai.

Arniko Highway (Tibet Road)

This follows an ancient trade route and runs from Kathmandu leaving the valley through Dhulikhel before veering north to Kodari and the Tibetan border. It used to lead to the only official land crossing point for foreigners between Nepal and Tibet but this crossing has been closed since the 2015 earthquakes and is yet to be reopened. Beyond Bansbari, regular landslides cause major delays during the monsoon. In the 2016 monsoon 21 houses in the village of Tatopani, near Kodari, were washed into the river and the road badly damaged.

Those people driving to the trailhead for Everest and the Khumbu follow the Arniko Highway before turning off eastwards at Khadichaur on the Bhote Khosi River. It also offers access to the adventure travel resorts **Borderlands** and the **Last Resort**, great places to escape to from Kathmandu for some outdoor activities.

Public bus There is little regulation over the condition of public buses and many are poorly maintained. Combine this with poor roads and low standards of driver training and the result is serious accidents and frequent breakdowns. Accidents at night are more frequent so whenever possible travel during the day. Never travel on a bus you are not happy with.

Tip...
Only use public buses if there is no other option.

ON THE BUSES

Getting comfortable

Seating arrangements are 2x2 (that is, 2 seats either side of the aisle), 2x3 or 3x3. If there is a choice, ask for a 2x2 bus. You can request your seat at the time of booking. Public buses can get very cramped and very hot. They do, however, offer a cheap way of getting around. Watch out for the very front seats. There may be more legroom but in the event of a crash the survival rate is low as safety belts are not usually available. Don't sit on the metal casing beside the gear stick, as it gets very hot, or on the seats above wheels. Also avoid the back row which often does not recline.

Most buses have audio systems which, when operational, are wont to play Hindi film music very loudly. Some have TVs, so you get to see the film as well and a few even offer Wi-Fi. But don't get your hopes up about streaming a film as you travel. You are usually lucky just to logon. You may think about bringing some ear plugs for when you want to rest. Also bring an inflatable sitting or head cushion.

Public buses are usually full to overflowing, with room for baggage (and more passengers) on the roof. Make sure that your luggage is padlocked to the roof rack so it doesn't bounce (or get thrown) off. It is illegal to ride on the roof and the conductors are reluctant to let Westerners do so in case they get stopped and fined. It's best not to anyway as large potholes and low cables are real risks that cause the death every year of some roof sitters.

Buses don't usually depart until full (as in packed) and will make regular stops en route to pick up more passengers. It can get very cramped, very hot and noisy if the stereo is working. It does, however, offer a very cheap way of getting around.

Tip...
Day buses are a safer option than night buses.

Deluxe bus For a little more you can reserve a seat, have a thin curtain to keep the sun off and maybe even get air conditioning. These are a halfway house between the public and tourist services and an acceptable way of getting from A to B, especially if there are no tourist services available. Watch out if a bus is advertised as a 'non-stop express'. Distances are often excessive for a driver to undertake in one go, especially given the trying conditions that demand total concentration and, as all buses travel at top speed, the time taken is never very different.

Microbus These small minibuses ply the same routes as the long-distance buses but pride themselves on being quicker, mainly because they stop less frequently and overtake other vehicles in places they really shouldn't. They charge slightly more than a local bus, are not much more comfortable and are involved in more accidents, usually caused by the driving and the vehicle being overloaded.

They are also used in Kathmandu and other towns and are a useful way of getting around town, so long as you can work out where they are going from the shouts of the conductor.

Car

Most hotels and travel agencies can get you a car and driver for the day. The cost varies on where you wish to travel, but starts from around US$40-50 per day. Although more expensive than taking the bus, it is safer and does allow you to do much more, as you will be dropped off and picked up at your destination, not a bus stop, and not have to wait for connections. Many of the drivers speak reasonable English and know how to get from A to B by the quickest route.

If you only have a day or two in Kathmandu or Pokhara to explore, a car is a great option to maximize your time. You can also hire a car for overnight trips and journeys from Kathmandu to Pokhara and back, allowing you to divert and stop whenever you wish.

A cheaper option is to 'charter' a taxi for the day, negotiating a daily rate rather than using the meter. Most drivers are very happy to do this but check that their permit covers the places you wish to visit as some are restricted to the city.

Fuel Nepal has no natural reserves of its own and all its petrol, diesel, kerosene and gas is transported in from India. It costs just over a US$1 per litre and there are plenty of petrol stations around.

After a dispute over a new constitution in September 2015 the Indian border was blockaded for nearly six months, leading to acute fuel shortages and dramatic price rises as the black market tried to keep up with demand. The Nepali and Chinese governments are now looking at potential ways for Nepal to buy fuel from China in future but the logistics of delivery through the Himalaya are likely to prevent it becoming a viable alternative. There is even talk of a pipeline.

Car hire Several car-hire companies have offices in Kathmandu and offer a range of vehicles from small saloons to 4WDs but it's not possible to hire one unless you have a Nepali or Indian passport. This is no great loss. To the newly arrived visitor it can seem that the only rule of the road is that there are no rules. It takes up to eight policemen to control just one junction in Kathmandu. Hiring a car with driver will save you time as there are not many signposts and those that there are will be in Nepalese.

Cycling/mountain biking

When embarking on a long bike trip, make sure that you have enough water with you, as safe drinking water is not widely available. One benefit of the 2015 fuel blockage was the boom in the import of bicycles, wanted by the locals to commute to work on. This has greatly improved availability.

Cycle hire There are several good places in Kathmandu and Pokhara where you can hire anything from a good mountain or road bike to a heavy, old boneshaker. Cycling is undoubtedly one of the best ways of exploring the countryside but Kathmandu is busy, bustling and polluted so not so much fun. Most places within the Kathmandu Valley are accessible by bike (though there are a few steep climbs and descents and the traffic is heavy on many routes leaving town) and a day trip allows you to build up a healthy appetite for dinner in one of the capital's many excellent restaurants. There are off-road routes you can follow, avoiding the worst of the busy roads. A guide or good map from one of the bookshops in Thamel is useful but locals are happy to point you in the right direction. From Pokhara, there are some good routes into the surrounding village areas and to the valley's other lakes.

Some of the cycle hire shops also offer guided rides, from day trips to excursion of several days. This is worth looking into as a local guide will be able to get you off the busy roads.

Cycle hire is also available in the Terai, though less so. The Terai countryside is mainly a combination of forest and wide open farmland scattered liberally with traditional villages. The land is largely flat, so cycling is easy and is by far the best way to get an insight into the traditional life that characterizes the rural areas of the Gangetic Plains. The hotels and lodges at Chitwan usually have bikes to rent. Always check the condition of the bike (for example gears, brakes, tyres, pump) before you hire it. Lock the bike securely when you leave it anywhere.

Taxi

Taxis are widely available in Kathmandu and Pokhara, less so elsewhere. Most are relatively modern Indian or Japanese cars. They are often small models so it can be a bit of a squeeze if you are tall. All licensed taxis should use their meter (always set in Nepali, not Indian, rupees), though you will often have to negotiate a rate. If you have a rough idea of what the fare should be, but less of an idea of the exact route, it may be better to settle the price before leaving so that you don't end up on an unscheduled sightseeing tour and an excessively high meter fare. Most taxi drivers don't speak much English but do have a good knowledge of the main sights, hotels and the necessary vocabulary to haggle.

Rickshaw There are two types of rickshaw: the three-wheeler, electric 'auto-rickshaw' (like the Thai tuk-tuk), and the cycle-rickshaw. The auto-rickshaw is found in Kathmandu, with petrol ones in Pokhara and all the major Terai towns. They can seat up to three passengers (or more if you don't mind wedging in). You can hire them as you would a taxi. Although most have meters, the drivers are often unwilling to use them and you usually have to bargain the price before setting off. Fares are around half those of a taxi and they are a good way of getting around town, often squeezing through impossibly narrow gaps in the traffic. Electric auto-rickshaws, especially in Kathmandu, run on specific routes like local buses and fares are fixed at just a few rupees. They usually won't leave before the vehicle is full.

The cycle-rickshaw is a curious though useful contraption for travelling short distances. The tricycle seats two (small to medium-sized) people. Although not especially comfortable, they are an interesting way to tour a town or city. A two-hour sightseeing ride should cost around US$2.75, while local rates are about US$0.23 per kilometre. If you decide you want a go, and successfully persuade your driver to let you try, be warned: they are hard to steer, especially when going fast!

Tonga Only Nepalgunj, in southwest Nepal, has *tongas*. These are horse-drawn carts that run on fixed routes, including to and from the border. Sadly, *tonga* travel is not quite as romantic as it sounds: it is slow and, because of the number of people crammed onto the platform, really quite uncomfortable.

Walking

With its incredible terrain, walking has always been the way to get around Nepal. The old trade routes to Tibet are often stone trails and steps worn smooth by centuries of feet and hooves. A vast network of trails, linking village to village, summer pasture to valley has evolved over the centuries to create the bedrock on which all modern trekking is planned. These days, as rough jeep roads push into the mountains you are more likely to hear an engine than you were 20 years ago but in many areas you can still walk for days without seeing a road.

Local customs

Cleanliness and modesty are appreciated even in informal situations. Nudity is not appreciated and causes widespread offence. Displays of intimacy between a man and a woman are not considered suitable in public. Though Nepali men and women rarely hold hands in public, you will sometimes see men holding hands. This is an accepted expression of friendship without other significance. It is not traditionally acceptable for women to shake hands with men. Do not photograph women without permission.

Great warmth and hospitality will be experienced by most travellers, but with it comes an open curiosity about personal matters. Don't be surprised if total strangers on a bus or elsewhere ask details about your job, income and family circumstances.

Local customs and social behaviour

Many customs are concerned with cleanliness and appearance. Use your right hand for giving, taking, eating or shaking hands, as the left hand is considered to be unclean. The feet are also considered unclean. It is thought to be rude and disrespectful for someone to put their feet up on a chair or table, for example, or to kick someone else even in jest. It is not considered proper to step over someone else. Shoes are customarily removed before entering a room or someone's house.

The greeting when meeting or departing used universally by Hindus throughout South Asia is the palms joined together as in prayer usually accompanied by the word *Namaste*, which translates as 'I salute all the divine qualities in you'. 'Thank you' (*Dhanyabad*) is often expressed by a smile and a slight sideways-and-upwards movement of the head. Generally, verbal expressions of thanks are neither expected nor proffered.

To give something respectfully, the item is usually offered with the right hand while the left hand touches the forearm or elbow, and the head is slightly bowed. You may see this, for example, when a waiter hands you your restaurant bill.

Nepali culture has many other dos and don'ts, some of which are specific to a certain caste, community or religion. In the main tourist centres, people have become accustomed to the different habits of Westerners, but any demonstration of Nepali customs by visitors is invariably appreciated. Kesar Lall's interesting and entertaining booklet, *Nepalese Customs and Manners*, is available inexpensively in Kathmandu and is full of local proverbs, superstitions and social observations.

In some households, only the cook is permitted to enter the kitchen. Food is considered by some castes to have been ritually 'contaminated' upon contact with a person of a lower caste, which includes Westerners who are outside the caste system. Some castes will not eat in the presence of lower castes: this is a social norm and is not meant to be offensive.

Beef is generally not eaten by Nepalis and the slaughter of cattle is illegal. Until the 1980s you received a longer prison sentence for running over a cow than a human.

When drinking, many Nepalis will not allow the rim of the glass or bottle to touch their lips. The impressive pouring of water into the mouth, down the throat and into the stomach in a single action without appearing to swallow does not come naturally to most Westerners. To try, start by pouring a small amount and gradually increase.

Many Nepalis are highly superstitious and hold a firm belief in astrology, in omens and spirits. These are deeply held beliefs which it is both impolite and unwise to ridicule. Numbers are often considered auspicious. The number three, for example, is thought to be unlucky. When a payment is made, or money given as a wedding present, the amount will often end in one and will never be an even number. Handing someone a red chilli or putting it on another's plate is believed to result in an argument. The crow is considered a bad omen – you will occasionally see dead crows hung outside a house to ward off misfortune. The spirits of the dead are believed to play an active role in the world. The souls of one's ancestors may be honoured in rituals and food prepared and left out for them.

It is worth underlining the importance of proper dress, especially when trekking outside the more popular routes. Nepalis do not consider it decent for men to walk bare top. Women are not thought to be properly dressed if they wear skirts above the knee, low cut or revealing tops. Take care also when you are washing and bathing. If you are in the vicinity of local people, don't bathe topless or in the nude. At best, people will be highly shocked.

Visiting religious sites

Although non-leather footwear may be permitted in some temples, it will be appreciated if shoes are removed as a matter of course before entering a temple. Other leather items of clothing (for example watch straps, handbags and belts), should also be removed. Some people (including Nepali and Indian Hindus) keep their watch in a pocket while inside the temple, though this should be done discreetly.

Non-Hindus are generally not permitted into the inner sanctum of Hindu temples and occasionally not even into the temple itself. Look for signs or ask.

Special rules apply to visiting Buddhist shrines. Walk clockwise around the stupa (or deity) and on the left-hand side in monasteries. Many Buddhist monasteries are open to all; you may even visit the resident lama (priest). Offering boxes are provided for those who wish to make donations (money will be used for the upkeep of the temple or monastery). Do not hand directly to priests or monks since they may be forbidden to touch money. It is not customary to shake hands with a priest or monk – a '*Namaste*' will suffice as a greeting.

If visiting one of Nepal's few mosques, women should be covered from head to ankle. Mosques may be closed to non-Muslims shortly before prayers.

Rafting essentials

The physical demands of rafting are not for everyone, but aficionados maintain that once the bug takes root, it's there for life. There are various levels of difficulty – or ease – according to the stretch of river and the season, and you certainly don't have to be an expert, or indeed to have had any previous experience of rafting, to be able to enjoy and take competent part in an organized, lower-grade run. What is required is moderate physical fitness and some affinity for water.

Best rafting seasons
Nepal's most popular rafting season extends from mid-October through to the end of November, when the climate is ideal and generally stable and rivers have their best range of flows. March until the end of May or early June is also good. The winter can be a pleasant time for shorter rafting trips at lower elevations and it will usually be possible to find reputable rafting companies that offer such trips.

Preparations
Most rafting companies are based in Kathmandu and some have offices in Pokhara; all can be contacted and researched before arrival. Some of the main companies now have their own base set up along the banks of the Trishuli itself. Instead of having to transport all equipment to and from the river every time there is a trip, the bases provide camping, stores, food and drink. Leading the development has been **Himalayan Encounters** (see page 96), a river-running company with a base (**The Big Fig**) at the Trishuli Centre.

Prices vary dramatically, but are considerably cheaper than their equivalents in the West. They start at about US$50 and rise to US$150 or more per day. At the bottom end, equipment and transport are likely to be basic and the food can be monotonous. The price will also depend on the logistics required for the river you are rafting. A river a short drive from Kathmandu will be less expensive than a remote one in the far west that involves several days of travelling.

Since 1989 the **Nepal Association of Rafting Agencies** (NARA, www.raftingassociation. org.np) has promoted rafting and good practice. There is plenty of information on their website as well as a list of its members. These members should take safety seriously and their trips should generally include all permits, private transport to and from the river, professional, qualified and trained guides, good hygienic food, and modern rafts and safety equipment.

When booking a trip, find out what is and what is not included in the package. Additionally, find out what will be expected of you during the trip: for example who does the paddling, carrying, fetching and cooking? You can book through a rafting operator or an agent representing the operator. While entirely legitimate, the agents' talents may be more conspicuous in the sell than in knowledge of what exactly they are selling.

Insurance
Make sure your insurance policy specifically covers rafting in Nepal. There may be an additional premium to pay.

Equipment
All the reputable companies should provide safety equipment. In addition to the safety aspects, the difference in price is reflected in the non-essential desirables which create the distinction between an experience and a really enjoyable experience.

Alloy or hardened plastic paddles are lighter and easier to use than the traditional wooden varieties. Check the types of tents that will be used. Will you spend a night at a lodge? What is the standard and what is included? What are the cooking arrangements? Will the kitchen be constructed above sand level and will there be a separate eating tent? In recognition of the appetite generated by a day on the river, some leading operators make a considerable effort in their catering, bringing fresh vegetables and meat, fruit juices, porridge and even honey and Marmite.

Personal equipment is best kept to a minimum. Check whether your operator provides sleeping bags. A set of dry clothes for the evening (and a fleece in winter), a camera and a pair of strong canvass shoes or sandals are useful. The operator you travel with will advise on what is required. Don't forget water-resistant sun screen; it's easy to burn on the water.

Rafting and the environment

It is important to adhere to the Code of Practice outlined on page 456 so that in the future other people too will be able to enjoy the rivers and their magnificent surroundings. Check that kerosene will be used for cooking, or only as much driftwood as is needed and only if it is surplus to local people's requirements.

Safety

NARA has pushed for the establishment of operating standards but it remains a voluntary code of practice. While the company you go with should have its own safety equipment, training and procedures, there are a number of things that you can do to make your trip as safe as possible. There are some 55 NARA-registered companies offering their services.

In selecting an operator, ask about the types of rafts used and their age. Self-bailing rafts are essential particularly on the more testing rivers. They operate by having a system of manufactured holes below an inflated floor through which a ton of water will drain in about 45 seconds. The raft should also be equipped with a first-aid kit and throw lines, cylindrical sacks attached to the raft and containing a brightly coloured coiled rope.

The quality of life-jacket is important; check its condition and make. Exposure to the sun deteriorates the outer shell. Helmets should have approval for the type of rafting they are being utilized for. You can ask the operator to see a sample helmet; in the past some operators used poor quality, motorcycle-type helmets which, in an emergency, are more likely to sink than to float.

The quality and experience of accompanying guides is crucial. Ideally the guide leading the trip should have 10 years' constant river experience including five years' training and at least five trips on the river being rafted. Training includes competence in first-aid and in cardiac-pulmonary resuscitation (CPR). For a three-raft trip, the top rafting companies would normally employ one guide on each raft and perhaps three manning the safety raft. A reasonable level of spoken English will also help with communication. Nepal has over 20 of the world's top rafting guides, most of whom will be working with the leading operators.

The number of rafts on a trip is another important consideration. An accompanying safety raft is there to help in an emergency. A raft can also carry much of the equipment avoiding overload in the others. Many companies use experienced safety kayakers as well as they are more able than a raft to reach a stranded person in difficult parts of a river.

Trekking essentials

Good preparation, especially if you are trekking independently, goes a long way to ensuring that your trek is safe and enjoyable. The following is an overview of things to do and to think about before setting off. For more detailed discussions, consult a specialist trekking guide or operator.

Ways of trekking

There are essentially five options: an escorted trek organized from overseas; a locally organized trek with guides and/or porters; an independent lodge trek; a community trek; and a backpacking camping trek.

Escorted treks organized overseas

A company with local knowledge and expertise organizes a trip and sells it. All necessary permits, reservations, some or all camping equipment or lodge accommodation, food, planning, decision-making based on progress and weather conditions, liaison with porters, lodge owners, etc are all taken care of. The company will also arrange to meet you upon arrival, transfer you upon departure, organize any sightseeing and the necessary transfers for internal flights, etc.

This is a good, safe introduction to the country. You will be able to get to places which, as an individual you might not reach, and without the expense of having to completely kit yourself out. You should read and follow any advice in the preparatory material you are sent, as your enjoyment will greatly depend on it. This applies particularly to recommendations concerning physical fitness.

An escorted trek involves going with a group. If you are willing to trade some of your independence for careful, efficient organization and to make the effort to ensure the group works well together, the experience can be very rewarding. Ideally, there should be no more than 15 trekkers in a group; preferably fewer. Before booking check the itinerary (is it too demanding, or not adventurous enough?) and what exactly is provided.

Locally organized treks

Trekking companies in Kathmandu and Pokhara will also organize treks, doing permit applications and reservations, providing all Sherpas, porters, cooks, food and equipment (if required). They offer the main itineraries but, as you will be travelling as a private group, you will have more flexibility to change/shorten/lengthen your trek. This method is recommended for groups wanting to follow a specific itinerary and requiring greater control than would be offered on escorted group treks.

It's easy to find, research and contact local specialists online in advance of your visit, meaning everything can be arranged by the time you arrive. Ensure your operator has a government permit, is a member of a reputable trade association and look at the online reviews before committing. Also check what is included, such as hotel nights in Kathmandu and sightseeing in the valley. Many of these operators are extremely experienced and actually handle the groups for the Western tour operators.

Independent lodge trek

Also known as 'teahouse trekking'. Less expensive, these require little equipment, but facilities can be basic in the more remote areas. You carry clothes and personal equipment in your backpack, or employ a porter to carry them for you, and for food and shelter you rely on lodges and teahouses. These are usually owned and run by local villages where, for a few hundred rupees a night, you get a basic room with communal facilities, or in the larger, more sophisticated (and expensive) inns, a room and private shower. The food is simple – usually *dal-bhad-tarkari* (lentils, rice and vegetable curry) which, although repetitive, is healthy and can be tasty. On the popular treks to Everest and in the Annapurna region, such delicacies as apple pie, carrot cake and pancakes are available, and can be washed down with soft drinks or beer.

This approach brings you into closer contact with local people, the limiting factor being the routes where accommodation is available.

Luxury lodge trek

In the more popular trekking areas of the Annapurnas and Everest there are small chains of luxury lodges that you can trek between. Your baggage is carried by porters between the properties, leaving you to walk with just a day pack, usually lead by a local guide. Some people stay in the same lodge for a few nights, doing day walks to local cultural attractions or viewpoints. The trekking tends to be gentle and the accommodation of a high standard considering your location.

Community trekking/homestay

A comparatively new way of trekking is to do a community trek, whereby you walk from village to village on a pre-established route sleeping every night in the house of a local villager. This is a great way to get a real insight into the lives of the people although the facilities can be basic so it's important to get full details before you go. This style of trekking is still in its infancy and facilities are still limited in many areas. The Lamjung area is a good area to consider for such a trek.

Independent camping trek

Many people arrive in Nepal each year with a pack and some personal equipment, buy some food and set off trekking, carrying their own gear and choosing their own campsites or places to stay. Of all the regions in the Himalaya, Nepal caters for this group best. There are some outstandingly beautiful treks, though they are often not the 'wilderness' sometimes conjured up. Many areas outside the Kathmandu Valley are quite densely populated even if they are remote, with many farming communities connected by traditional trails that can make excellent trekking routes to follow.

You cannot be too much of a free spirit – you still need a trekking permit and TIMS card recording your proposed route. You also need to bring your own fuel and food if within a national park and camp in defined places only. Supplies of fuel are scarce and flat ground for camping rare. It is not always easy to find isolated and 'private' campsites, especially during the crop-growing season, and when you do, you will need to pay the landowner.

Insurance

This is really important. Travel insurance is not available in Nepal, so get a policy before leaving home. Make sure that it includes trekking – some policies explicitly exclude Himalayan trekking, but you can usually pay extra to have it included. For further information, see page 452.

Fees and permits

National park and conservation area fees

Your visa to enter Nepal effectively allows you to travel throughout the Terai and the Kathmandu and Pokhara valleys. An additional fee is payable for all national parks and conservation areas. These are usually included in the price on organized itineraries and are taken care of by the operator.

For **Sagarmartha** (Everest), **Makalu Barun**, **Rara**, **Shey-Phoksundo** and **Langtang** you can pay the fee at the park/reserve entrance or in advance from the **National Parks Office** (T01-422 4406, www.dnpwc.gov.np, Sunday-Friday 0900-1400). The fee is currently Rs 3000 (US$27) per park.

For the **Annapurna** and **Manaslu** you pay the Annapurna Conservation Area Project (ACAP) (T01-422 2406, www.ntnc.org.np, 0900-1600). In Pokhara they are based at the **Nepal Tourist Board Office** at Damside (T061-463376, 0100-1700). The permit costs Rs 2000 (US$18) and you will need two photos. If you buy the permit at a checkpoint you will be charged Rs 4000 (US$37).

Trekking permits for restricted areas

The main treks in the Annapurna, Everest and Langtang areas do not require special permits. Other areas do and the fees for them vary greatly. To get one you must be travelling in a group (although that group can be only two people). It must be applied for by a trekking agency. This is to ensure that independent trekkers don't visit without the necessary equipment or regard for the cultures and people.

For **Kanchenjunga** and **Lower Dolpo** the permit costs US$50 for the first week, then US$7 per day.

For **Manaslu** it's US$70 for the first week, then US$10 per day.

For **Upper Mustang** and **Upper Dolpo** it's US$100 for the first 10 days, then US$50 per day.

Equipment and clothing

Good quality equipment can be bought or hired from a variety of trekking shops in Kathmandu and, to a lesser extent, in Pokhara. On the Everest trek, Namche Bazaar and Lukla also have shops selling clothing and equipment. The daily hire charges are usually quite small, but a larger deposit may be required.

Backpacks If you intend carrying all of your gear it is worth spending money on a good, ergonomically designed rucksack, preferably one that has padded contours, a light (for example aluminium) internal frame and comfortable waist bands that allow the weight of the load to be shifted from the shoulders. A separate day pack is essential. Other things to consider include: is the backpack lockable? Is it waterproof? Is it sufficiently hardy for your trek? Or, if you are going on a fully organized escorted trek, do you really need that up-to-the-minute super-expensive backpack?

Clothing Clothing requirements depend on the season and altitude you will be travelling in, so plan ahead. Operators will advise on what to bring.

Loose, light cotton trousers or long shorts/skirts are good for low-altitude treks. For colder, higher-altitude treks, take a combination of thermal underwear, warm woollen sweaters, warm fleece and a down or synthetic jacket. Water- and windproof jacket and trousers to go over other clothes are also good in extreme conditions.

Take good socks, gloves and a hat or balaclava. Daytime temperatures can get quite hot, so bring light, loose-fitting cotton clothing. A wide-brimmed hat is also useful.

Footwear should be comfortable as well as providing adequate ankle support. Again, what you take will depend on where you are trekking. Good-quality trainers are quite adequate for many of the lower-level treks. Make sure they provide suitable shock absorption and that the soles have good grip. If you are wearing boots, you could take a spare pair of trainers; they are good for fording streams and for changing into after several days' hard walking.

Boots are a must on the higher and more challenging treks. It is essential that they are worn in before you set off. They should come over the ankle (particularly important on a downhill walk), provide good grip and shock absorption, and be waterproof. Specialist footwear is required for treks on snow and with technical elements.

Flashlight/torch A head torch is ideal, leaving your hands free and always pointing where you are looking. A separate small lamp is useful to set up/suspend in your room or tent to provide some general light.

Food and cooking equipment Unless you are trekking well away from the main trekking routes there is no need to carry all your food as lodges and teahouses are available to sell you a snack or meal. On the most popular routes the menus will include pizza and chips; in more remote places you will always be able to get a *dhal bhat*. You only need to take snacks like muesli bars and nuts to give yourself a boost on any hard days. If you are trekking with an operator, all practicalities, including food, will be taken care of.

If you do need to get your own supplies, there are numerous shops in Kathmandu and Pokhara selling a range of packed and tinned foods suitable for taking on a trek. In Kathmandu, supermarkets stock imported foods, including pasta, tea, coffee, biscuits, muesli, chocolate and sachets of vitamin-enriched powdered drinks (check expiry dates). Prices in Pokhara can be higher than in Kathmandu.

The use of firewood is banned in national parks. If you plan to trek in remote areas away from villages you will need to take a kerosene stove with you or your group. National park officials may check to see that you have your own cooking equipment with you when you enter. Kerosene is sporadically available in the mountains, but may be impure so take sufficient supplies with you. You can hire jerry cans from shops in Kathmandu and Pokhara. You could also take a strainer (fine gauze mesh) for sifting out impurities. The MSR stove is lightweight and has been recommended for its efficiency. Make sure that you also take spare parts for the stove. If problems occur, start by ensuring that the pump is always properly oiled and that the vaporizing jet holes are clear.

Medical kit Take a small medical kit which might include water purification tablets, oral rehydration salts/solution, plasters (including blister plasters), bandages, antiseptic cream, anti-diarrhoea medicine and painkillers.

Before you leave for Nepal, you might think about asking your doctor for advice on treatment/prevention of altitude sickness. Just remember, taking your time is key. There is no way around that. For further information, see page 448.

Sunglasses are essential, especially if you are trekking above the snow-line. Make sure that they are of the type that absorb both ultraviolet and visible light. If you wear contact lenses bring a spare pair. Disposable lenses have been recommended, especially in places like the Kali Gandaki where wind and dusk can be an issue.

Women should carry extra tampons or sanitary towels. Imported brands are available in Kathmandu's supermarkets, but are less common along the trekking routes. High altitude can affect the menstrual cycle and cause irregular periods.

Tents and sleeping bags If you are going to be trekking/climbing away from villages then a good-quality tent providing high levels of insulation as well as protection from high winds (for example domed or tunnel) is crucial. On an organized trek these will be provided by your tour.

A good sleeping bag is also vital. A fleece sleeping bag liner can be used inside the main sleeping bag for warmth and comfort, and may also suffice for sleeping at lower, warmer altitudes. A thick foam or inflatable under mat is lightweight; it helps considerably with insulation and is a lot more comfortable than the hard ground.

Trekking poles Many people now use one or two collapsible trekking poles to help with balance and taking the strain off their knees when descending. They are inexpensive and readily available in Nepal.

Money

Your expenses while on the trek should be relatively low. Indeed, there is little to spend your money on other than food and accommodation. Credit cards are accepted in main towns and villages and at some of the larger and more expensive properties. Otherwise you need to take cash. You should carry some low denomination notes when walking and visiting small refreshment stands, but otherwise Rs 500 and Rs 1000 will be fine in the main villages. See also Money, page 453.

Books and maps

Books There is no shortage of trekking guides and travelogues, available both in Nepal (bookshops in Thamel and Pokhara) and in Europe and the USA. Note that route descriptions may have been accurate at the time the trek was researched, but topography changes with season (is the river a raging torrent or a mere trickle of water?) and routes change through, for example, access to a new and better trailhead, established paths being washed away, the construction or destruction of bridges and so on.

Maps There is a wide range of trekking maps available in Kathmandu. You can also buy them online before you go. Because of their popularity, the Annapurna and Everest regions have the best cartographic coverage but decent maps exist of all trekking routes.

The Austrian **Schneider** (or **Research Scheme Nepal Himalaya**) series are printed in colour and are widely considered to be the best, but they are also the most expensive. There are Schneider titles (1:50,000) covering the region from Kathmandu to far eastern Nepal, including Everest and Kanchenjunga. There is also a 1:100,000 map of Helambu and Langtang, but this is not as accurate as those of the eastern regions.

The Nepali-produced **Mandala** (or **Latest Trekking Map**) series of maps are much cheaper and the most popular with trekkers. Some are full colour, others are blue dyeline. This series is widely acknowledged to be of variable accuracy, though is usually sufficient for most trekkers. Most trekking regions are covered, scales from 1:50,000 to 1:200,000. Other locally produced maps include the colour **Nepal and the Himalayan Map House** series.

Communications These have improved enormously in the last 10 years. There are landline connections and mobile signals in many areas of the hills and most lodges and cafés will boasts about their Wi-Fi speeds. They are often slow but good enough to contact the outside world. In remote areas there are police and army posts with access to satellite phones in the case of an emergency. If you are travelling to remote regions it's possible to hire one for emergencies.

Daily routine On an organized camping trek, you will probably be woken at around 0600, have a light breakfast, start walking at around 0730, stop for a cooked midday meal at around 1100, start again a couple of hours later and arrive in camp at around 1500-1600. You will have supper in the early evening and usually everyone is tucked up in bed by 2100.

Lodge treks have more flexibility but the routine tends to start and finish early, with big breakfasts and supper and a picnic or snack lunch.

On the main routes there are plenty of teahouses and lodges where you can stop and buy a cold or hot drink and snack throughout the day, should you need refreshment or a rest.

Guides and porters On an organized trek your guide and porters will be arranged by your tour operator, with full accountability. If you are doing your own thing then guides and porters can be hired in Kathmandu or Pokhara through trekking companies, equipment shops, hotels, restaurants and elsewhere.

It is best to talk to recently returned trekkers who can make recommendations (or give warning). Also check the noticeboards around Thamel for referrals and suggestions. On the main routes you don't necessarily need a guide, especially if you have trekked before, but having one can make things a lot smoother en route. The ability to communicate easily is also an important consideration, so try to find a guide with a reasonable knowledge of English. If you do not want to use a guide then consider hiring a local porter. This will not only lighten your load but will also provide much-needed employment.

During the peak trekking seasons (October-November and March-April) the demand for trekking personnel is at its highest, so it pays to begin making enquiries as early as possible if you want the best crew. Some people have found that guides and porters from the mountainous ethnic groups are the most reliable. Sherpas, the ethnic group from the Everest and Solu Khumbu region, have long been regarded as the quintessential Himalayan guides. The Sirdar, or head guide, generally does no carrying. Tamangs and Gurungs in the Pokhara area are also generally reliable.

The guide will contribute to many of the decisions to be taken during a trek, such as where to camp/sleep and which route to follow. It is not unknown for these judgements to be influenced by considerations extraneous to the requirements of your trekking party. It is worth agreeing on routes and the location of overnight stops before you start.

If you are planning to trek to high/cold areas you will have to provide your porters with clothing and equipment for snow and cold weather, as well as insurance. This includes footwear, warm clothes and protective glasses or goggles. If you are camping out, remember to provide shelter, food and cooking equipment for all personnel.

You are also responsible for the costs of porters' and guides' transport throughout the trek as well as on the return. The individual duties and system of wages for porters and guides can seem rather complicated and reflect the hierarchical structure of Nepali society. Rates will vary according to their experience and linguistic abilities, the law of

Himalayan code of conduct

By following these simple guidelines, you can help preserve the unique environment and ancient cultures of the Himalaya.

- Limit deforestation – make no open fires and discourage others from doing so on your behalf. Where water is heated by scarce firewood, use as little as possible. When possible, choose accommodation that uses kerosene or fuel-efficient wood stoves.
- Do not pick flowers or collect local seeds.
- Remove litter, burn or bury paper and carry out all non-degradable litter.
- Graffiti are permanent examples of environmental pollution.
- Keep local water clean and avoid using pollutants such as detergents in or near streams or springs.
- If no toilet facilities are available, make sure you are at least 30 m away from water sources, and bury or cover waste.
- Plants should be left to flourish in their natural environment – taking cuttings, seeds and roots is illegal in many parts of the Himalaya.
- Help your guides and porters to follow conservation measures.
- As a guest, respect local traditions, protect local cultures, maintain local pride.
- When taking photographs, respect privacy – ask permission and use restraint.
- Respect holy places – preserve what you have come to see, never touch or remove religious objects.
- Shoes should be removed when visiting temples.

- Giving to children encourages begging. A donation to a project, health centre or school is a more constructive way to help.
- You will be accepted and welcomed if you follow local customs. Use only your right hand for eating and greeting. Do not share cutlery or cups, etc. It is polite to use both hands when giving or receiving gifts.
- Respect local etiquette. See page 433.
- Remember when you're shopping that the bargains you buy may only be possible because of the low income of others.
- When buying souvenirs, ensure they are not encouraging poaching or deforestation by being made from rare or endangered materials.
- Try to spend your money so that it goes directly into the micro-economy of the areas you are visiting.
- Visitors who value local traditions encourage local pride and maintain local cultures.
- Learn a few words of the local languages, such as Hello and Thank you (see Useful words and phrases, page 459).
- Please help local people gain a realistic view of life in Western countries.
- Try to spend your money so that it goes directly into the micro-economy of the areas you are visiting.
- The Himalaya may change you – please do not change them.

supply and demand (that is where and when you hire) and what else is included, for example food, clothing, etc.

Tipping has become routine and is expected if you are trekking with porters and other Nepali personnel. It is advisable to decide on the approximate amount your group will tip before leaving, remembering that there is a hierarchy among porters, cooks, Sherpas, guides, etc and making allowance for performance. Set aside in advance your own share of the overall tip according to how much each person will receive.

Police checkpoints These are dotted along all trekking routes and elsewhere. Your TIMs card, trekking permit (if applicable), park entrance receipt, etc may be checked, and you will probably be asked to enter your name in a register. If you are on an organized trek your guide will usually deal with things. Don't avoid the checkpoints, as this may raise suspicion.

Terrain The footpath is the principal line of communication between villages. Especially in the main trekking regions, paths tend to be very good, well graded and in good condition, but without many flat stretches. Most large rivers are crossed by steel suspension bridges, although some smaller wood and log ones exist on more out-of-the-way trails. Before you start to cross, look over to the far bank to ensure a yak or mule caravan is not approaching. You don't want to meet them halfway.

Sherpas and guides rarely give you a distance when asked how far to the next camp or lodge. Instead they give a time as 1 km descending will be much quicker than 1 km climbing.

Environment

Energy and fuel Trekking is just one of the factors contributing to deforestation in the Himalaya, but it is significant. It's difficult to measure exactly either the rate at which forests are being denuded or how quickly they are regenerating. It is certain, though, that the former is happening on a disturbingly large scale whereas the latter takes generations. Much deforestation, moreover, is concentrated in areas which include several trekking routes.

The use of firewood is banned in all national parks and trekkers have to use liquid fuel stoves. The same is encouraged elsewhere. If you do use wood, keep it to a minimum. For example, cook at the same time for all members of the group; restrict the amount of hot water for washing and cleaning; use chemicals to purify drinking water instead of boiling it. If you have a choice, stay at a lodge with solar energy or one that uses kerosene for cooking, and order your food at the same time as others.

Rubbish Rubbish is an eyesore as well as a pollutant and there is nobody coming to clear up after you. Plastic bottles and wrappers have become a major issue. Increasingly, groups are employing an extra porter to carry out all the rubbish generated on the trek. Alternatively, you can separate the biodegradable waste and burn and bury it. The rest can be carried out.

Toilets Use proper toilets whenever possible. If none are available find a suitably discreet spot a good distance from a river or water source (at least 30 m). This will avoid the gradual seepage of excrement into other people's supply of drinking water. Dig a hole in which to bury the waste matter (bring a small plastic trowel) and cover it up. Alternatively, burn the toilet paper or, when the ground is hard, cover everything with rocks. Some groups use one large plastic bag in which to collect all toilet paper, packed individually, for burning later; it's only embarrassing to start with.

Natural resources The people are friendly and welcoming but their natural resources are limited. Make sure that your visit doesn't exploit their hospitality or put a strain on their reserves. The prices they charge are reasonable and if you think you can get it

TREKKING
Safety checklist for trekkers

The vast majority of trekkers in Nepal have a trouble-free trek, often the highlight of their trip. Just follow some basic rules to ensure that should the worst happen, you are prepared.

- Make sure your insurance covers air evacuation, including helicopter evacuation from the mountain in Nepal. Have the contact details with you and with someone you can contact easily or who is travelling with you.
- Make sure people know where you are, through the TIM scheme, your embassy and family. If you do go missing, it helps when the search party knows where to start looking. Keep someone updated, by email or text as to where you are.
- Go with a friend. Nearly all casualties in the mountains were trekking alone.

If you slip and fall from a trail no one knows where you are.
- On high passes and more dangerous sections, trek as a group. If a trekker gets injured or suffers from mountain sickness, someone needs to get help while another person remains with the casualty.
- Make sure you have the correct equipment for all eventualities. If it's a sunny morning, it doesn't mean it won't be snowing in the afternoon. Blisters hurt and can form at any time depending on the trail and your socks. Have a small medical kit with you to deal with any small problems.

cheaper go and find it rather than negotiating too hard. A few rupees saved for you means nothing but makes a tangible difference to them.

Safety and security

Trekking in Nepal is generally as safe as you want it to be. Of course, there are occasional natural occurrences which do present significant dangers, but these are a consequence of the environment through which you are travelling.

The **Trekkers' Information Management System (TIMS)** makes all trekkers log their personal information and proposed itineraries into a central database run by the **Nepal Tourism Board (NTB)** and **Trekking Agencies' Association of Nepal (TAAN)**. If a problem or a disappearance does occur, TIMS provides details of where people may be, saving time in search operations. A TIMS card costs Rs 1000 (US$9) for a member of a group and Rs 2000 (US$18) for independent trekkers. It is a compulsory scheme. See also Safety, page 454.

Essentials A-Z

Accident and emergency

Police: T100; **Police emergency**
(Kathmandu): T01-4228435; **Tourist police**
(Kathmandu): T01-4226359/4226403.
Otherwise you ring the hospitals for an
ambulance (see page 451).

Bargaining

There are 'fixed price' shops (for example
supermarkets and the more expensive stores
on and around Kathmandu's New Rd). But
bargaining is the norm.

Before making a purchase – especially
an expensive one – it is worth doing a
little research. Shop around, as prices vary
enormously from one shop to the next.

Remember to bargain with a smile.
Outrage and anger will not bring the price
down. If the vendor is asking too much and
won't come down to a price you are happy
with, leave. Also remember that to a villager
selling bananas a few rupees is his livelihood.

Children

Children of all ages are widely welcomed
and warmly greeted. In the big hotels,
you'll have no difficulty in obtaining safe
baby foods. Western varieties of baby
food are also available in Kathmandu and
Pokhara supermarkets but not reliably
elsewhere. You can also buy Western
disposable nappies here, though they are
expensive, as well as Indian brands which
are considerably cheaper.

Both Kathmandu and Pokhara have a
wide range of excellent restaurants where
it will normally be perfectly safe for a child
to eat, many offering pizzas, burgers and
sandwiches as well as local dishes. Bring
along some anti-bacterial hand gel which
can be applied just before they eat. It's
advisable to avoid salads and unwashed fruit.

Most mountain lodges also offer good,
simple food, as do the jungle lodges in the
national parks. There are also plenty of shops
offering crisps, biscuits ('Coconut Crunchies'
are particularly moreish), chocolate bars and
soft drinks. Some of the crisp flavours can be
spicy so go for plain ones.

Extra care must be taken to protect
children from the sun and heat. Use creams
and hats, and avoid being out in the
middle of the day when it can get very hot.
Remember that it's a near tropical sun that
burns quickly and this is exacerbated if you
are at altitude. Cool showers or baths help if
the children get too hot. Dehydration can be
counteracted with plenty of drinking water.
See also Health, page 448.

The biggest hotels provide baby sitters but
you need to give them advance warning.

With proper preparation, there is no
reason to avoid trekking with young
children, though it is better to go on an
organized trek with back-up. Choose a
popular route (eg in the Annapurnas)
where there are decent facilities. Many
Nepali women carry their children in a type
of backpack which you can buy locally.
Porters can carry younger children on trek
in special carriers or in standard porters'
doko or baskets. Your tour operator will
be able to provide details and costs.

Customs and duty free

Upon arrival, you have to complete and
hand in a customs declaration form. Tourists
bags are very rarely searched, the main duty
of customs at the airport seems to be to
ensure that passengers are leaving with
their own luggage.

Tourists are permitted to bring in
personal effects free of duty. Other duty
free allowances include 250 cigarettes or
50 cigars and distilled liquor up to 1.15 litre.

The following items for personal use may be imported free of duty, but must be re-exported when you leave: 1 pair of binoculars, 1 video camera, 1 still camera, 1 sleeping bag and 1 walking stick.

The import and export of narcotic drugs (processed or in their natural state), arms and ammunition is illegal. The export of antiques and artefacts is subject to tight control. Any item over 100 years old (or appearing so to a Customs' official), including precious and semi-precious stones, must have a certificate obtained from the **Department of Archaeology** in Kathmandu (Ram Shah Path, T213 701/2) before it may leave the country.

Similar controls apply to gold, silver, wild animals and any part of their anatomy or any product made from them. These restrictions may be strictly enforced by thorough baggage checks at Kathmandu airport and other departure points.

Disabled travellers

Nepal is a difficult, though certainly not impossible, country for disabled travellers. Travelling alone is not recommended if you have walking difficulties, as there are probably just too many uneven surfaces and slopes to climb and descend. With an able-bodied companion, however, there is much that Nepal has to offer and, depending on the disability, there is no reason why you can't enjoy several activities such as jeep safaris, sightseeing in Kathmandu and viewing the mountains from Pokhara.

Basic wheelchairs are available on arrival at Kathmandu airport, which also has a lift. The airports at Pokhara, Bharatpur (for Chitwan) and Nepalgunj (for Bardia) are all ground level. Boarding any of the smaller aircraft will pose a few problems, but there will always be people willing to help. When flying, request the pilot to radio ahead so that a wheelchair or other assistance will be ready on arrival. You can also ask your hotel to send a vehicle to meet you.

Hotels are not particularly well geared up for disabled guests, though many of Kathmandu's better hotels have lifts and ramps. There are even fewer facilities in Pokhara, but there are plenty of decent hotels with accessible ground-floor rooms. At Chitwan, several of the private lodges can cater for disabled travellers. The helpful and professionally run **Tiger Tops** lodges, both at Chitwan and Bardia, have all ground-level accommodation in comfortable rooms with attached bathroom and a ground-level restaurant and bar. They also have jeep tours through the jungle.

Some travel companies specialize in exciting holidays, tailor-made for individuals depending on their level of ability. **Global Access, Disabled Travel Network** (www. globalaccessnews.com/index.htm) provides travel information for 'disabled adventurers' and includes a number of reviews and tips from members of the public.

Drugs

Narcotic drugs are illegal in Nepal. Do not use them. Some drugs, especially cannabis and its derivatives, are widely and openly available and the musty stench of a burning joint is seldom far from innocent nostrils in the main tourist areas. Cannabis plants (*Cannabis sativa*) grow wild in fields, gardens, along the roadside and elsewhere in several parts of the country, although much has been eradicated from the main urban areas.

Drug laws have been tightened in recent years and sniffer dogs are a common site at airports and at some road blocks as you travel the main highways. Westerners can expect harsh penalties, including lengthy imprisonment. Never be lulled into taking drugs across an international border. Awareness of the conditions prevailing in Nepal's jails should act as a strong deterrent.

Electricity

220v/50 cycles. Most plugs have 3 round pins, some 2 round pins. Best to bring your own adapter; otherwise you can buy one in Kathmandu or Pokhara.

Nepal suffers from a shortage of electricity, a nonsense considering its potential with hydroelectric power. Load shedding – scheduled black outs – are common and more frequent when the water levels are lowest in the spring. Hotels have lists of when these will occur so you can plan your charging accordingly. It can be for as much as 18 hours a day. Major hotels and restaurants have generator back-up to provide electricity during these periods.

Embassies and consulates

For information on visas and immigration, see page 456. For a list of Nepal's embassies and consulates worldwide see www.mofa.gov.np.

Several international embassies send out an automated welcome text when you arrive in Kathmandu giving their contact details. If you are planning to visit the more remote areas or stay for a longer period of time it's a good idea to register with your embassy with details of your visit.

Health

Before you travel

See your GP at least 6 weeks before your departure for general advice on travel risks, malaria and vaccinations. Contact a specialist travel clinic if your own doctor is unfamiliar with health in the region.

Take out medical insurance. Make sure it covers all eventualities especially repatriation to your home country by plane. If you are going to be trekking, it should also cover emergency evacuation by helicopter to Pokhara or Kathmandu.

Get a dental check (especially if you are going to be away for more than a month), know your own blood group and if you suffer a long-term condition such as diabetes or epilepsy make sure someone knows or that you have a **Medic Alert** bracelet/necklace with this information on it.

If you wear glasses or contact lenses, bring your prescription with you to Nepal. Optical costs are considerably lower in South Asia than in the West, and some people even have a 2nd pair made up for their future use.

If you are on regular medication, make sure you have enough to cover the period of your travel. Remember that it is risky to buy medicinal tablets abroad because the doses may differ and Nepal has a huge trade in counterfeit drugs.

Vaccinations and antimalarials

Confirm that your primary courses and boosters are up to date. Vaccination against the following diseases are worth considering when consulting your doctor or travel clinic: diphtheria; hepatitis A; tetanus; typhoid. You may also consider vaccinating against cholera; hepatitis B; Japanese encephalitis; rabies. You may be asked for a yellow fever certificate if you have been travelling in a country affected by the disease immediately before travelling to Nepal.

Specialist advice should be taken on the current practice for the prevention of malaria. Antimalarial tablets are not usually advised for travel to Nepal although they can be considered for travellers who may be at higher risk and who are travelling to certain areas, such as the low-lying Terai districts bordering India. All travellers should avoid mosquito bites by covering up with clothing such as long sleeves and long trousers especially after sunset, using insect repellents on exposed skin and, when necessary, sleeping under a mosquito net.

A-Z of health risks
Altitude sickness

Altitude sickness can creep up on you as just a mild headache with nausea or lethargy during your visit to the Himalaya. The more serious disease is caused by fluid collecting in the brain in the enclosed space of the skull and can lead to coma and death. There is also a lung disease version with breathlessness and fluid infiltration of the lungs. The best cure is to descend as soon as possible. Preventative measures include getting acclimatized and not reaching the highest levels on your first few days of arrival. Try to avoid flying directly into the cities of highest altitude.

Some climbers like to take treatment drugs as protective measures but this can lead to macho idiocy and death. The peaks are still there and so are the trails, whether it takes you a bit longer than someone else does not matter as long as you come back down alive.

Remember that the Himalaya and other mountain ranges are very high, very cold, very remote and potentially very dangerous. Mountain rescue is extremely difficult and medical services may be poor (see page 451).

To prevent the condition: on arrival at places over 3000 m have a few hours' rest in a chair and avoid alcohol, cigarettes and heavy food. If the symptoms are severe and prolonged, it is best to descend to a lower altitude and to re-ascend slowly or in stages. In no circumstances should ascent above 3000 m be rushed. As a general rule 2 nights should be spent at each point with a gain of 600-700 m. In the Everest area, for example, this means 2 nights at Namche Bazaar and 2 nights at Dingboche or Pangboche when approaching Everest Base Camp. During rest days it's fine to trek higher during the day; it's the sleeping altitude that is important. These night stops are crucial in allowing the body time to adjust.

The **Himalayan Rescue Association**, www.himalayanrescue.org, has a good pamphlet on mountain sickness and information on their website.

Bites and stings

These are mostly more of a nuisance than a serious hazard. Use a mosquito net to avoid getting bitten. Use insecticide in your room and repellents, which are effective against a wide range of pests, on your clothes, ankles and wrists.

If you are bitten or stung, itching may be relieved by cool baths, antihistamine tablets (take care with alcohol or driving) or mild corticosteroid creams, eg hydrocortisone (never use if there's any hint of infection). Bites which become infected should be treated with a local antiseptic or antibiotic cream, as should any infected sores or scratches.

Diarrhoea and intestinal upsets

With most people suffering no more than a stomach upset during their travels in Nepal, a sensible balance of caution and pragmatism should overcome any inclination towards dietary paranoia – a condition which itself can be as debilitating as the occasional bout of diarrhoea. Travellers' diarrhoea and vomiting is due, most of the time, to food poisoning, usually passed on by the insanitary habits of food handlers. As a general rule the cleaner your surroundings and the smarter the restaurant, the less likely you are to suffer.

The standard advice for diarrhoea prevention is to be careful with water and ice for drinking. If you have any doubts about where the water came from then boil it or filter and treat it. There are many filter/treatment devices now available on the market. Food can also transmit disease. Be wary of salads (what were they washed in, who handled them), re-heated foods or food that has been left out in the sun having been cooked earlier in the day. There is a simple adage that says wash it, peel it, boil it or forget it. Also, be wary of unpasteurized dairy products. These can transmit a range of diseases from brucellosis (fevers and constipation), to listeria (meningitis) and tuberculosis of the gut (constipation, fevers and weight loss).

The key treatment with all diarrhoea is rehydration. Try to keep hydrated by taking the right mixture of salt and water. This is available as Oral Rehydration Salts (ORS) in ready-made sachets or can be made up by adding a teaspoon of sugar and a half teaspoon of salt to a litre of clean water. You can also use flat carbonated drinks. Drink at least 1 large cup of this drink for each loose stool. Drugs such as Imodium and Lomotil are designed to plug up your bowels rather than cure diarrhoea, and are best avoided unless you have an unavoidable long coach/train journey or are on a trek; generally it's better to let the nasties work their way out of your system as nature intended. Antibiotics – obtained by private prescription in the UK – can be a useful for some forms of travellers' diarrhoea. If it persists beyond 2 weeks, with blood or pain, seek medical attention. One good preventative is taking probiotics which are available over the counter.

Paradoxically, constipation is also common, probably induced by dietary change, inadequate fluid intake in hot places and long bus journeys. Simple laxatives are useful in the short term and bulky foods and plenty of fruit are also useful.

Heat and cold
Full acclimatization to high heat takes up to 2 weeks. During this period it is normal to feel a bit apathetic, especially if the relative humidity is high. Drink plenty of water, use salt on your food and avoid extreme exertion. Tepid showers are more cooling than hot or cold ones. Large hats do not cool you down, but do prevent sunburn (see below). Remember that, especially in the highlands, there can be a large and sudden drop in temperature between sun and shade and between night and day, so dress accordingly. Warm jackets or woollens are essential after dark at high altitude. Loose cotton is still the best material when the weather is hot.

Hepatitis
This means inflammation of the liver. The most obvious symptom is a yellowing of your skin or the whites of your eyes. However, prior to this all that you may notice is itching and tiredness. There are vaccines for hepatitis A and B; the latter spread through blood and unprotected sexual intercourse. Unfortunately there is no vaccine for

hepatitis C or the increasing alphabetical list of other hepatitis viruses.

Malaria
See Vaccinations and antimalarials, page 448.

Rabies
Remember that rabies is endemic throughout Nepal, so avoid dogs that are behaving strangely. If you are bitten by a domestic or wild animal, do not leave things to chance: scrub the wound with soap and water and/or disinfectant, try to at least determine the animal's ownership, and seek medical assistance at once. The course of treatment depends on whether you have already been vaccinated against rabies. If you have (this is worthwhile if you are spending lengths of time in remote areas of developing countries) then some further doses of vaccine are all that is required. If not already vaccinated then anti-rabies serum may be required in addition. It is important to finish the course of treatment whether the animal survives or not.

STDs
In Nepal the instances of STDs and HIV is increasing and heterosexual transmission is the most common cause. Unprotected sex can spread HIV, hepatitis B and C, gonorrhoea (green discharge), chlamydia (nothing to see but may cause painful urination and later female infertility), painful recurrent herpes, syphilis and warts, just to name a few. You can cut down the risk by using condoms, a Femidom or avoiding sex altogether. Condoms can be bought in supermarkets in Kathmandu and all main towns.

Sunburn
Watch out for sunburn at high altitude. The ultraviolet rays are extremely powerful. Protect yourself with high-factor sun screen and don't forget to wear a hat. The air is also excessively dry and you might find that your skin dries out and the inside of your nose becomes crusted. Use a moisturiser for

the skin and some Vaseline wiped into the nostrils. Some people find contact lenses irritate because of the dry air.

Ticks and leeches

It is only if you are walking through pasture and forest that **ticks** can become an issue. They attach themselves usually to the lower parts of the body often after walking in areas where cattle have grazed. They swell up as they start to suck blood. The important thing is to remove them gently, so that they do not leave their head parts in your skin because this can cause a nasty allergic reaction later. Do not use petrol, Vaseline, lighted matches etc to remove the tick, but, with a pair of tweezers remove it gently by gripping it at the attached (head) end and rock it out in very much the same way that a tooth is extracted.

Trekkers should beware of **leeches**, especially during the monsoon. They sway on the ground and on twigs and bushes waiting for a passer-by and get in boots when you are walking. They feed on blood, but their bite contains an anaesthetic so you may not feel them. They drop off when they are full leaving you with blood soaked boots and legs.

Don't try pulling one off, as the head will get left behind and cause infection. Pour some salt, or hold a lighted match near it, which will encourage its rapid departure. Before starting off in the morning it may help to spray socks and bootlaces with an insect repellent. There are no adverse long-term affects of a leach bite unless it becomes infected, so keep them clean.

Medical services

Medicines are available from pharmacies located in most towns and do not require prescriptions. Most doctors are based in Kathmandu and the other main urban centres and your embassy may be able to provide a list of recommended medical and dental practitioners. Most insurance companies will also have guidance on clinics and hospitals. In remote areas facilities are very limited, so bring a basic medical kit with you.

Kathmandu and Pokhara

Nepal International Clinic (T01-443 4642) and the **CIWEC** clinic (T01-442 4111) are both used by expats and have good standards. **CIWEC** now has rooms and operates as a well-equipped hospital. It also has a clinic in Pokhara (T061-463082).

Grande International Hospital (T01-515 9266, www.grandehospital.com), situated in northern Kathmandu, opened in 2010 and is Thai-owned, offering comprehensive medical care.

Norvic Hospital (T01-425 8554, www. norvichospital.com), also in Kathmandu, is a modern hospital with 200 beds, specializing in cardiology but offering most medical services at international prices.

Both the above hospitals have international liaison officers, who will coordinate any treatment with your insurance company back home and assist with any travel arrangements.

Trekking centres

There are clinics, manned during the main trekking seasons by Western staff, near Everest, Gokyo and Manang on the Annapurna Circuit, to advise and treat altitude sickness as well as other problems trekkers might be experiencing.

When you return home

If you have had attacks of diarrhoea it is worth having a stool specimen tested in case you have picked up amoebas. Report any untoward symptoms and tell the doctor exactly where you have been and, if you know, what the likelihood of disease is to which you were exposed.

Further information

MASTA (Medical Advisory Service to Travellers Abroad), masta-travel-health.com.

Fit for Travel, fitfirtravel.scot.nhs.uk.
CIWEC Clinic, ciwec-clinic.com.

Insurance

Always have good insurance and check your policy to ensure it covers the activities you will be doing on your trip. It should also cover helicopter evacuation from the mountains in an emergency and repatriation to your home country as well as medical expenses.

Make sure you have the emergency contact numbers written somewhere so the insurance company can be contacted quickly in an emergency. Remember, it might not be you looking for the details so leave them somewhere obvious like inside your passport.

Leave a copy of the policy and any important telephone numbers with a family member at home and make sure that they know what to do with it in case of emergency. It is well worth shopping around and comparing policies and prices well in advance. Policies directed at young people and students do not necessarily offer the best value.

Internet

Most hotels in the main cities and towns have Wi-Fi. Some still charge if you want it in your room but offer it free in public areas. Cafés and restaurants all claim to offer it free but if you are stopping to specifically check your email, logon first to check it works before ordering your coffee.

There is also Wi-Fi on the more popular trekking routes, although speeds are slow, and on some deluxe buses which usually drive considerably faster than they download.

Language

See also Useful words and phrases, page 459.

Nepali is the official national language of Nepal. It is one of the Indo-Aryan family of languages brought from Central Asia by the Aryans from around 1500 BC. In addition, there are over 30 other languages spoken in different parts of the country and many more regional dialects. English is spoken in Kathmandu, Pokhara and other tourist destinations, including the main trekking routes. Indeed, most signs on these are in English and most guides speak reasonable English.

According to the 2011 census, Nepali is spoken as a mother tongue by 45% of the population. It is followed in importance by Maithili, Bhojpuri and Tharu. Other important regional languages include Abadhi, Gurung, Hindi, Limbu, Magar, Newari, Rai/Kiranti, Sherpa, Tamang and Urdu. Minor languages recorded in the census include Kumhale, which has just over 1500 speakers.

LGBT travellers

Nepal does not criminalize same-sex relationships, a right enshrined in a 2007 Supreme Court judgement. It's an easy, generally non-judgemental place to travel, and the Nepalese are accepting of gay couples, although you will attract attention if you are overly affectionate in public. For more information and advice try the **Blue Diamond Society**, www.bds.org.np, Nepal's first gay organization.

Media

Newspapers

Nepal has many national, regional and local Nepali-language newspapers and 4 main national English-language dailies: *The Kathmandu Post*, *The Himalayan Times*, *República* and *The Rising Nepal*. All are published in Kathmandu and are available in Pokhara and other nearby towns later the same day. All include local, national and international news as well as sport. They all have websites which carry their latest editions and which are free to visit. *The New York Times* is published with *República* and is excellent value at Rs 25. Other foreign newspapers, including the *International New*

York Times, are widely available in Kathmandu and also from a couple of shops along Lakeside, Pokhara. It's also possible to visit the websites of all major news organizations and newspapers, such as the BBC. Nepal does not have internet censorship.

Radio
In Kathmandu the BBC World Service can be found on FM 103 MHZ.

Money

US$1 = Rs 109; €1 = Rs 117; £1 = Rs 136 (Jan 2017).

Currency
The rupee is divided into 100 paisa. Notes come in denominations of Rs 1000, 500, 100, 50, 20, 10 and 5. Coins exist in denominations of Rs 1 and 10 paisa, although most tourists will not usually encounter the lower-value coins. Notes of higher denomination are sometimes difficult to change outside the main towns and on trekking routes. Major international currencies are readily accepted and many hotels and travel agents can only accept foreign currency or payment by international credit card when billing overseas customers.

Currency exchange
There are plenty of official money changers in Kathmandu and Pokhara who will exchange cash. Shop around for the best rate, displayed on boards outside and if you are exchanging a large amount, ask for a better rate.

ATMs, traveller's cheques and credit cards
Don't forget to notify your bank of your dates of travel to Nepal otherwise it might well block transactions as potentially fraudulent.

Major credit/debit cards are accepted in the main tourist centres as well as most smaller towns. You can even use them in some of the trekking lodges, although sometimes getting a connection can be slow. Payment by credit card sometimes incurs a 3-6% commission, especially for flights.

There are plenty of ATMs in all the main cities, although not many from banks you will recognize. It will say on the machine which cards are accepted; these always includes Visa and MasterCard. American Express is not much used or accepted. You get charged a fee for every withdrawal. Avoid the machines that have a low maximum withdrawal. Some give you the chance to fix the exchange rate at the time of the transaction or leave the rate until it reaches your bank.

Don't use ATMs during the power-sharing blackouts as the links to the bank can be down and that will results in your transaction being rejected. Try to use ATMs that are attached to a branch of the bank. Many ATMs are in small kiosks and should your card be retained there is nowhere to go to get it back.

Traveller's cheques can still be exchanged in a few places but are getting increasingly rare, and are generally not recommended.

Currency regulations
There are no restrictions on the amount of foreign currency that can be brought into Nepal but if you are bringing more than US$2000 in cash it needs to be declared upon arrival. Changing Nepalese rupees back into foreign currency requires receipts showing proof of exchange and is limited to 10% of the total originally exchanged. You are supposed to change foreign currency at banks or authorized money changers only and, as there is no black market these days, it is sensible to do so.

Cost of living
The cost of living is low by Western standards. The top-of-the-range hotels and the best restaurants are cheaper than their equivalent in the West. Budget accommodation in Kathmandu and Pokhara is plentiful. These budget options are often

excellent value and prices can be negotiable, especially during off-peak season.

The quality of food in the major tourist centres is better than elsewhere, but then prices are also rather higher. A main course in one of central Kathmandu's tourist restaurants would cost in the region of US$5-9, although you can eat local food much cheaper. Outside the Kathmandu Valley and Pokhara, the price of food reduces dramatically, but with it the choice which is usually limited to *dal-bhad-tarkari* (lentils, rice and vegetables) or a variation thereon, and a typical Nepali meal here might cost US$2.

Opening hours

Banks Sun-Fri 0930-1600, Sat morning only.
Embassies Mon-Fri 0900-1300, 1400-1700, Fri 0900-1200.
Government offices Mon-Thu 0900-1600, Fri morning only.
Museums Usually closed Tue. Opening hours depend on the season so check with your hotel.
Shops Open all day, closing in the early evening.

Photography

There are abundant photographic opportunities throughout Nepal and a camera is a must. Many Nepalis like being photographed, particularly if you have a polaroid and can give them a copy. Sensitivity and discretion are required at all times. If in any doubt, ask. Avoid intruding on private activities. Most festivals allow photography. Participants sometimes go into a trance and may act unpredictably. It is safest to avoid taking photographs under such circumstances.

Postal services

Nepal's postal system is slow, particularly if you are posting or receiving air mail outside Kathmandu. To Europe, North America,

Australia and New Zealand, air mail letters often take around 2 weeks to arrive.

There are 2 main ways to send parcels. You can post them at the **Foreign Post Office** (in GPOs; next to the GPO in Kathmandu). This can be a tiresome chore, as you have to leave the parcel open for inspection, fill out a customs declaration form, pay tax where applicable, have the parcel wrapped, then weighed before you pay. By international standards, rates are extremely reasonable whether you send it by air or sea. Alternatively, you can spend more and send it through a reputable private freight company or courier. There are plenty of these in Kathmandu and a couple in Pokhara, including **DHL** and **FEDEX**.

Most carpet shops and large souvenir outlets offer a courier service, meaning you do not have to lug your items home as hand luggage or stagger across town to the GPO. This is more expensive but if you have limited time is well worth considering. As a rule the items are well wrapped and eventually turn up at your home in one piece.

Public holidays

There are so many holidays and festivals in Nepal, all based on the various calendars, that's it all but impossible to give a definitive list. See Festivals, page 21 for a guide and check locally when you arrive.

Safety

Probably the greatest risk to your safety comes from the hazards inherent in adventure activities, such as rafting and trekking. Violent crime against foreigners is extremely rare but does occur, especially in places where tourists undertake day walks by themselves in countryside near the cities. Always walk with friends or as a group.

Road accidents account for a healthy percentage of injuries for tourists. Don't travel on the cheapest bus to save a few rupees. See page 429. Don't travel on the roof. It's illegal, dangerous and after the first few kilometres not much fun. Tourist buses offer a much safer journey (see page 427). If you are travelling as a family or group, consider renting a car (with driver) which gives you more freedom as well as security. Microbuses are to be avoided on longer routes.

Police and crime

Crime rates, although low by international standards, are increasing in some areas. Take care in the main tourist centres where pickpocketing is not unheard of. Be careful with any major purchase and make sure that expensive 'silk' carpets, gold and precious stones are in fact authentic. Travellers have been conned into parting with huge sums for items of little value.

It is advisable to make all your travel arrangements (particularly for combination bus/train journeys to India) with a good and reputable agency or, in the case of rafting or trekking trips, book directly with the operator instead of an agent wherever possible.

Senior travellers

Nepal is a great place to travel as an older person. If you want to get into the mountains you need to be fit but there are plenty of viewpoints and the mountain flights that can give you breathtaking views if you are not so agile. Hotels in Kathmandu, Pokhara and Chitwan especially have excellent facilities and the cost of private transport – a driver with car – is an inexpensive and hassle-free way of getting around. The Nepalese are also very respectful of the older generations, often calling you Uncle or Auntie and doing their utmost to be courteous and helpful.

Smoking

Smoking is not allowed in public places after legislation passed in 2011. This includes airports, hotels, restaurants, government buildings and other public places. Anyone caught doing so could be fined up to US$9 on the spot although this is rarely enforced.

Taxes

All hotel and restaurant bills have 13% VAT added to the price that they advertise and most tourist establishments also have a 10% service charge. Check your bill – there is no need to tip again if this is already added.

Telephone

The dialling code for Nepal is 977. The code for Kathmandu is 01 and for Pokhara 06 (drop the '0' if dialling internationally). Making calls is straightforward, although reverse charge calls can only be made to the US, UK, Canada and Japan.

Most international networks have roaming agreements with Nepalese operators – you will receive a welcome text when you turn your phone on at Kathmandu airport telling you who it is with and the costs involved.

Ncell, www.ncell.com.np, is the best network from which to buy a SIM card for your stay. You just need to bring your passport and a photo to one of their offices (including one at the airport) and choose from the packages available. These vary from basic call/text to 3G and data packages. Their coverage is surprisingly good given the terrain – expect to get texts at Everest Base Camp. The other large network is **Nepal Telecom**, www.ntc.net.np (also available at the airport).

Time

GMT + 5¾ hrs.

Tipping

Most hotels and restaurants add a 10% service charge to their bills; there is no need to tip above this. If you are in a taxi paying by the meter a small tip of 10% is appropriate if the journey is satisfactory. If you have negotiated the fare, no tip should be added.

If you are on a tour its usual to tip your guide and driver. Likewise on a trek you would be expected to tip your sherpas and porters. Your tour operator will advise on the correct rates and ratios between the different staff, as it will depend on the length of trek and its difficulty.

Toilets

Toilets in the main tourist centres will be Western. Outside these areas the squat toilet rules. Toilet paper is usually placed in the small bin by the toilet, not down the toilet itself. If there is no paper, a small tap or bucket of water is strategically placed beside you; this is to clean yourself with. Traditionally you use your left hand.

Toilets in the remote areas can be very basic so watch your footing. If caught short on the trail, make sure the spot you choose is away from water sources and dig a small hole.

There are public toilets at strategic spots on the highways. You pay a few rupees to use them, with the options of 'Urination' or 'Defecation' normally painted on a pricelist on a wall. The latter is more expensive, although they are unlikely to check.

Tourist information

The **Nepal Tourist Board**, T01-425 6909, www.welcomenepal.com, has a useful website with various guides you can download or request. They have a small branch at the airport. Their main office is the **Tourist Service Centre**, Brikuti Mandap to the east of the Tundikhel, on the corner of Durbar and Pradarshanti Margs, Kathmandu. It is open Sun-Fri 1000-1300, 1400-1700. There is also a 24-hr tourist hotline: T01-422 5709. They don't provide many handouts, but do have some maps, posters and leaflets and are very helpful. You can also get TIMS cards and national park entrance tickets from the same building.

Tour operators

There are hundreds of tour and trekking operators in Nepal. It can be hard to choose. Check that they are accredited by local trade associations, such as the **Trekking Agents Association of Nepal** (TAAN) and the **Himalayan Mountaineering Association** (**NMA**). You can also check recent reviews on the internet.
Ace the Himalaya, T01-442 3719, www.acethehimalaya.com.
Summit Trekking, T01-552 5408, www.summit-trekking.com.
Footloose in the Himalaya, T0985-105 2795, www.footlooseinthehimalaya.com.

Trekking permits

See Trekking essentials, page 439.

Visas and immigration

Visas are required by all nationalities except Indians. They are available from Nepalese embassies and consulates abroad, at official border crossings with India (Bhimdatta [Mahendranagar], Nepalgunj, Sunauli [Belahiya], Birgunj and Kakarbhitta), Tibet (Kodari, but currently closed) and on arrival at Tribhuvan Airport, Kathmandu.

Visa regulations can be rather complicated and are subject to change without notice, so it is advisable to check the current rules with a Nepalese embassy or consulate before travelling.

The chief advantage in obtaining a visa in advance lies in the time and potential hassle saved on arrival, although the system in Kathmandu is reasonably straightforward: fill in the form, pay the visa fee at the bank and proceed through immigration. Even better, fill the form out before departure or on the plane and head straight to the bank to pay your fee. This is often the longest queue. You can also now apply online at **www.online.nepalimmigration.gov.np/ tourist-visa**. This gives you a confirmation number on a print-out which you hand to the immigration official upon arrival. In truth it just saves you having to fill out the form on the plane as you still need to pay your visa fee when you arrive. (When you go onto the visa application area of the website make sure you click the 'Tourist Visa' link in the red navigation bar at the top. Otherwise it defaults to a marriage visa!)

Each application should be accompanied by a passport-size photograph. At Kathmandu airport you can pay the visa fees in other currencies, although the exchange rates used on arrival are not favourable. At land crossings only US dollars are accepted. Visa costs are currently: US$25 (single entry, up to 15 days); US$40 (single entry, up to 30 days); US$100 (single entry, up to 90 days). Multiple-entry visas cost an additional US$20.

Visa validity

A maximum of 120 days may be spent in Nepal on a tourist visa in a year (January-December), although 150 days are allowed if you can show reasonable grounds. Entry must be made within 6 months of the date of issue. A visa is officially only valid for the Terai region, the Kathmandu and Pokhara valleys, and most of the towns linked by the country's main roads. It is not valid for any other areas, including trekking and rafting routes. If you are going on a rafting trip and the start point involves travel through an area not covered by the visa, you'll need the appropriate trekking permit from the Kathmandu or Pokhara Immigration Offices, along with any national park entry fee receipt (also available at the park entrance). **Note** If you overstay your visa you may be prevented from boarding your flight and will have to apply for an extension, as well as being liable for a fine of twice the extension fee.

Visa extensions

Tourist visas can be extended at the **Kathmandu and Pokhara Immigration Offices** (www.nepalimmigration.gov.np) and require a passport photo. Beyond 1 month, extensions cost US$2 per day up to 90 days, then from 90 days to 150 days this increases to US$3 per day. Usually, visas cannot be extended further than 3 months, after which at least 1 month must be spent outside Nepal before re-entry is permitted. Extending your visa to 150 days' continuous stay can only be done at the Kathmandu Immigration Office (not in Pokhara) and you have to show 'reasonable reasons' for wanting the extension.

Weights and measures

The metric system.

Women travellers

In general, Nepal is remarkably safe for women travelling alone, particularly in the main tourist areas of the Kathmandu Valley, Pokhara and Chitwan National Park.

It is not advisable, however, for women (or indeed for men) to trek alone (see Trekking, page 445). Travel in some of the Terai towns close to the Indian border can pose potential problems of harassment for unaccompanied women. It is always better to be both courteous and wise and not to invite unwanted attention by wearing revealing or tight-fitting clothes. In more remote rural areas you are advised to follow the basic dress code (see page 433).

Footnotes

Useful words and phrases

There are more than 30 recognized mother tongues spoken throughout Nepal. Nepali is the offical national language and is spoken as a first language by over nine million people, with at least another five million speaking it as a second or third language, making it the most widely spoken of the country's languages. Although Nepali is widely understood in the mountainous regions of Nepal, it is quite distinct from those regions' principal languages which are of the **Tibeto-Burmese** linguistic family.

Learning Nepali

If you are staying in Nepal for any length of time, and especially if you are trekking along any of the less popular routes, some knowledge of Nepali can help you in both practical ways and in being welcomed by local people who will appreciate the effort you have made. Nepali is often considered to be one of the easier of South Asia's languages to learn. There are several short language courses on offer in Kathmandu and, to a lesser extent, in Pokhara. Keep an eye on the notice boards around Thamel; courses are also advertised by the numerous leafleteers in the city centre.

Pronunciation

The pronunciation of vowels alone is fairly straightforward, while aspirated, retroflex and dental consonants often require more practice. Remember that you don't have to have a perfect command of all of the nuances of the language to make yourself understood! All the vowel sounds also have nasal forms.

Vowels

a a short 'u' sound, as in *until*
aa a long 'ar' sound, as in *cart*
ai a diphthong, as in *bail*
au a diphthong, as in *now*

e a long 'eh' sound, like the first *e* in *premier*
i a long or short 'ee' sound, as in *deem*
o a long 'or' sound, as in *mould*
u a long or short 'oo' sound, as in *hoot*

Consonants

Among the many different consonant sounds, there are three in particular to look out for. **Aspirated** consonants are articulated with an imaginary 'h', as if the sound is made while exhaling. In Romanized transliteration, the letter *h* after the consonant is usually used to indicate aspiration. It is most common in the following consonants: **b**; **chh** (in which the *ch* is aspirated, eg *Chhetrapati*); **d**; **g**; **k**; **p** (pronunciation varies from a very airy *p* to an *f* sound, eg *Phewa Tal*); **t** (aspiration results in a gentle dental sound between *t* and *d*, as in *Thamel*, but not as in the English word *the*).

  Dental consonants are expressed with the tip of the tongue at the teeth. They comprise aspirated and non-aspirated **d** and **t**, and also **n**. These same letters are also subject to **retroflex** expression, the main difference being that the tongue is arched further back to the roof of the mouth while speaking.

Tips on speaking and grammar

Generally, the **verb** comes at the end of a phrase and sentences are usually constructed according to **subject object verb**. Unlike most European languages, **prepositions** are placed *after* the noun (eg *the preposition the noun after is placed*). The appropriate use of the familiar and honorific **forms of address** often causes difficulty. Put simply, the honorific form is used when addressing elders or superiors, whilst the familiar form is for children or friends. The **tone** in which you speak conveys far more of the meaning of what you are saying than in European languages.

Pronouns

I *Ma*	**She** (hon) *Wahaa*
You (fam) *Timi*	**We** *Haami*
You (hon) *Tapaai*	**They** (fam) *Uniharu*
He (fam) *U*	**They** (hon) *Wahaaharu*
He (hon) *Wahaa*	
She (fam) *Tini*	**Key**: fam = familiar; hon = honorific

Verbs

A verb infinitive usually ends with the suffix *-nu*. As in any language, it gets a bit complicated when you start to conjugate verbs. Start by removing the suffix. Two of the first important verbs to learn (both meaning 'to be') are **Hunu** and **Chhanu**. The first is used to state condition, as in, *'I am a tourist'*.

Ma **hu**	*U/Tini* **ho**
Timi **hau**	*Haami* **hau**
Tapaai **hunuhunchha**	*Uniharu* **hun**

The other is used to state position, eg in response to 'where *are* you?'

Ma **chhu**	*U/Tini* **chha**
Timi **chhas**	*Haami* **chhau**
Tapaai **hunuhuncha**	*Uniharu* **chhan**

These same endings are used also for other verbs in the **simple present** tense. For example, the verb *jaanu* ('to go') is conjugated as follows: *jaanchhu, jaanchhas, jaanuhunchha, jaanchha, jaanchau, jaanchhan*. The **present progressive** tense is a little different and uses the stem *jaadai* to indicate process (*jaadai chhu*, 'I am going'): *jaadai chhu, jaadai chhas, jaadai hunuhuncha, jaadai chha, jaadai chhau, jaadai chhan*. The **negative form** is expressed by the additional suffix **na** (or a variation thereof) which usually also changes the verb ending. The negative form of the present progressive tense of *jaanu*, as above, is: *jaadai chaina, jaadai cchainas, jaadai hunuhuna, jaadai chhaina, jaadai chhainu, jaadai chhainan*. This, too, can get rather complicated, but if you remember to put *na* at the end of the verb, you can usually make yourself understood.

Meeting and greeting

Excuse me *Hajur* (also used for 'Pardon me?', with appropriate intonation) The expressions *O, Daaju* ('O, Brother') or *O, Didi* ('O, Sister') are widely used as a less formal way of saying 'Excuse me' or for attracting someone's attention.)

Hello/Goodbye *Namaste* (said with hands together) *Namaskar* is used in very formal or respectful contexts.

How are you? *Sanchai chha?*; more familiarly *Kasto chha?*

Fine/I am well/It's going OK *Thik chha.* To follow this with an inquiry as to the questioner's health ('and you?'): *tapaailaai ni?*.

Thank you *Dhanyabad.* This is not said routinely and is usually implied and substituted by a slight sideways nod of the head. It is not considered rude not to say thank you.

I'm sorry *Maph garnus*

You're a good boy/girl *Timi raamro keta/keti ho*

What's your name? *Tapaaiko naam ke ho?*

My name is Sudeshna *Mero naam Sudeshna ho*

Speak more slowly (please) *Bistarai bolnus*

How old are you? *Tapaai kati barsha hunu bhayo?*

I'm ... years old ... *barsha bhaye*

Are you married? *Tapaaiko biya bhayo?*

Yes, I'm married *Mero ta bhayo*

No, I'm not married *bhaiko chhaina*

How many sons do you have? *chhori kati chhan?*

And daughters? *chhora ni?*

See you again *Pheri betaunla*

Commands

In common with many of the languages of South Asia, the imperative is used in a quite different way than in most European languages. Once again, it is the tone of voice that is as important as the actual words and the word 'please' is implied though not spoken. In practice, this can seem somewhat abrupt at first, but it's not (necessarily), nor is it impolite.

Be quiet *chup laaga* (fam); *chup laagnus* (hon)

Come in *bhitra aau* (fam); *bhitra aaunus* (hon)

Come quickly *yahaa aau* (fam); *yahaa auunus* (hon)

Give (it to me) *malaai deu* (fam); *malaai dinus* (hon)

Go (away) *jau* (fam); *jaanus* (hon)

Hurry up *chhito*

Leave it *chhoda* (fam); *chhodnus* (hon)

Put *raakha* (fam); *raakhnus* (hon)

Put it there *tyahaa lyau* (fam); *tyahaa lyaununus* (hon)

Sit down *basha* (fam); *bashnus* (hon)

Shopping

Bargaining is the norm when shopping. Using a few words of Nepali can increase your chances of a fair deal.

Do you have ...? *... paainchha?; ... chha?*

How much (is it)? *Kati rupiya?*

How many/much for ... rupees? *... rupiya kati?*

That's expensive (is it made of gold?) *Mahango bhayo (sonar chha?)*

Will you accept ... rupees? *... rupiya maa dine?*

No (I won't accept) *Na dine*

Then will you accept ... rupees? *... rupiya ni?*

Take it *linos*

How much in total? *jamaa kati bhayo?*

I have no change *Masanga khudra chhaina*

See you again *Ma aunechhu*

Food and lodging

Do you have a room available? *baas paainchha?*

How much is the room? *suteko kati linu hunchha?*

Do you have food? *khaana paainchha?*

Yes (there is food) *paainchha*

It will take time to prepare *samaya laagchha*
Mmm, delicious! *Mmm, mitho!*
I'm hungry *bhok laagyo*
I'm thirsty *tirkhaa laagyo*
How much is the food? *khaanako kati honi?*

When and where

what's the time? *kati bajyo?*
... o'clock *... bajyo*
quarter past one *sawaa ek bajyo*
half past one *saadhe ek bajyo*
quarter to one *paune ek baje*
about one o'clock *ek bajetira*
where are you going? *tapaai kahaa jaadai hunuhunchha?*
I'm going to ... *Ma ... jaadai chhu*
where is the ...? *... kahaa chha?*
where does this bus go to? *yo bus kahaa jaanchha?*

when does this bus leave? *yo bus kati baje jaanchha?*
how long does it take? *kati samaya laagchha?*
how far is ...? *... kati taadhaa chha?*
where is ...? *... kahaa chha?*
to the right *daya tira*
to the left *baya tira*
straight ahead *sidaa tira*

Sickness

help! *guhaa!*
I have diarrhoea *Malaai dishaa paani laagyo*
I have a headache *Malaai taauko dukhchha*
I have a fever *Malaai jwaro aikochha*
what's wrong? *ke bhayo?*
where is a hospital? *haaspital kahaa chha?*
call a doctor (please) *daktar bolaidinus*

Glossary

A

acharya religious teacher

agarbathi incense

Agni Vedic fire divinity, intermediary between the gods and men

ahimsa non-harming, non-violence

ambulatory processional path

amrita ambrosia, drink of immortality

Ananda Buddha's chief disciple

Ananta huge snake on whose coil Vishnu rests

Andhaka demon killed by Shiva

Annapurna goddess of abundance; one aspect of Devi

apsara heavenly nymph figure

arati Hindu worship with lamps

architrave horizontal beam across posts or gateways

Ardhanarisvara Shiva represented as half-male, half-female

Arjuna hero of the *Mahabharata* to whom Krishna delivered the Bhagavad Gita

Aruna charioteer of Surya

Aryans lit 'noble' (Sanskrit); prehistoric peoples who settled in Persia and North India

asana a seat or throne

ashram hermitage or retreat

Ashta Matrika the 8 mother-goddesses who attended Shiva or Skanda

astanah threshold

atman philosophical concept of universal soul or spirit

Avalokiteshwar Lord who looks down; Bodhisattva, the compassionate

avatara 'descent'; incarnation of divinity, usually Vishnu's

B

bada cubical portion of a temple up to the roof or spire

bagh garden

Bahadur title, meaning 'the brave'

baksheesh tip

bandh closed, strike

bas-relief carving of low projection

bhadra flat face of the shikhara (tower)

Bhadrakali tantric goddess and consort of Bhairab

Bhagavad Gita 'song of the lord'; section of the Mahabharata in which Krishna preaches a sermon to Arjuna explaining the Hindu ways of knowledge, duty and devotion

Bhairab the fearful tantric aspect of Shiva

bhang cannabis (bhang lassi)

bhatti tea house or inn, especially of the Thakalis

bhavan building or house

Bhima Pandava hero of the *Mahabharata*, famous for his strength

Bhimsen deity worshipped for his strength and courage

bidi tobacco leaf rolled into small cigarette

bodhisattva enlightened one; destined to become a buddha but remaining in the world to relieve suffering

Bon pre-Buddhist religion of the Tibetan Himalaya, incorporating animism and sorcery

bhumi 'earth'; refers to a horizontal moulding of a shikhara

bo-tree *Ficus religiosa*, a large spreading tree

Brahma universal self-existing power; Creator in the Hindu trinity

Brahmachari religious student, accepting rigorous discipline imposed for a short period, including absolute chastity

Brahman (Brahmin) highest Hindu caste of priests

Brahmanism ancient Indian religion, precursor of modern Hinduism and Buddhism

Buddha the enlightened one; Gautama Siddhartha, the founder of Buddhism who is worshipped as a god by certain sects

C

capital upper part of a column or pilaster

caryatid sculptured human female figure used as a support for columns

cella small chamber, compartment for the image of a deity

chaam Himalayan Buddhist masked dance

chakra sacred Buddhist Wheel of Law; also Vishnu's discus

chamfer bevelled surface, obtained by cutting away a corner

Chamunda terrifying form of Durga

Chandra moon; a planetary deity

chatta ceremonial umbrella on stupa (Buddhist)

chauki recessed space between pillars; also entrance to a porch

chhatra honorific umbrella; a pavilion (Buddhist)

Chhetri Hindu warrior caste (Kshatriya), second in status to Brahmins

chiya Nepali tea, brewed together with milk, sugar and spices

chokhang Tibetan Buddhist prayer hall

chorten Himalayan Buddhist relic shrine or memorial stupa

chowk open space or courtyard

circumambulation clock wise movement around a stupa or shrine

cornice horizontal band at the top of a wall

crore 10 million

cupola small dome

curvilinear gently curving shape, generally of a tower

cusp projecting point between small sections of an arch

D

dacoit bandit

dais raised platform

dakini sorceress

darshan(a) sight of the deity

Dattatreya synchronistic deity; an incarnation of Vishnu, a teacher of Shiva, or a cousin of the Buddha

daulat khana treasury

deval memorial pavilion built to mark royal funeral pyre

devala temple or shrine (Buddhist or Hindu)

Devi goddess; later, the supreme goddess; Shiva's consort, Parvati

dharma moral and religious duty

dharmachakra wheel of 'moral' law (Buddhist)

dhobi washerman

dhyana meditation

dikpala guardian of one of the cardinal directions (N, S, E or W)

doon valley

drum circular wall on which the dome rests

durbar palace, a royal gathering

Durga principal goddess of the shakti cult; riding on a tiger and armed with the weapons of all the gods, she slays the demon Mahisha

dzong Tibetan lamasery or monastery

E

eave overhang that shelters a porch or verandah

ek the number 1, a symbol of unity

epigraph carved inscription

F

fenestration with windows or openings

filigree ornamental work or delicate tracery

finial emblem at the summit of a stupa, tower, dome or at the end of a parapet; generally in the form of a tier of umbrella-like motifs, or a pot

foliation ornamental design derived from foliage

frieze horizontal band of figures or decorative designs

G

gable end of an angled roof

gaddi throne

Ganesh popular elephant-headed son of Shiva and Parvati, the god of good fortune and remover of obstacles

gandharvas celestial musicians of Indra

ganja cannabis

gaon village

Garuda half-human, half-eagle mythical 'vehicle' of Vishnu

Gauri 'Fair One'; Parvati; Gaurishankar – Shiva with Parvati

ghat landing place; steps by a river (burning ghat, washing ghat)

ghazal Urdu lyric poetry, often sung

godown warehouse

gompa Tibetan Buddhist monastery

Gopala cowherd; a name of Krishna

Gopis cowherd girls, milkmaids who played with Krishna

Gorakhnath historically, an 11th-century yogi who founded a Shaivite cult; an incarnation of Shiva

gumpha monastery, cave temple

guru teacher or spiritual leader

H

haat market, usually weekly especially in eastern Nepal

Hanuman monkey hero of the *Ramayana*; devotee of Rama; bringer of success to armies

Hara (Hara Siddhi) Shiva Hari Vishnu

Harihara, Vishnu-Shiva as a single deity

harmika the finial of a stupa in the form of a pedestal where the shaft of the honorific umbrella was set

hippogryph fabulous griffin-like creature with body of a horse

hiti a water channel or spring; a bath or tank with water spouts

I

icon statue or image of worship in a temple

impeyan a species of pheasant, Nepal's national bird

Indra king of the gods, god of rain; guardian of the East

Ishvara Lord Shiva

J

Jagadambi lit 'mother of the world'; Parvati

Jagannath lit 'lord of the world'; Krishna

Jamuna goddess who rides a tortoise

Janaka father of Sita in the *Ramayana*; mythical founder of Janakpur

jangha broad band of sculpture on the outside of a temple wall

jarokha balcony

jawab 'answer'; a building which duplicates another to provide symmetry

jaya stambha victory tower

jhankri shaman, or sorcerer

-jee honorary suffix added to male names out of reverence and/or politeness

Jyotirlinga luminous energy of Shiva manifested at 12 holy places; miraculously formed lingams having special significance

K

Kailasa Shiva's heaven

kalasha pot-like finial of a tower

Kali lit 'black'; terrifying form of the goddess Durga, wearing a necklace of skulls/heads

kalyan mandapa hall with columns, used for the symbolic marriage ceremony of the temple deity

karma present consequences of past lives; impurity resulting from past misdeeds

kata ceremonial scarf presented to high Tibetan Buddhist figures

Kartik son of Shiva, god of war; also known as Skanda

khola river or stream

khukuri traditional curved knife, best known as the weapon of Gurkha soldiers

kirti-stambha 'pillar of flame'; free standing pillar in front of a temple

kot fort

kothi house

Krishna 8th incarnation of Vishnu; the mischievous child, the cowherd (Gopala) playing with the gopis; the charioteer of Arjuna in the Mahabharat epic

Kumari virgin; Durga; living goddess in the Kathmandu Valley

kumbha a vase-like motif

kumbhayog auspicious time for washing away sins

kund well, pool or small lake

kutcha raw; crude; unpaved

kwabgah bedroom; lit 'palace of dreams'

L

la mountain pass

lakh 100,000

Lakshmi goddess of wealth and good fortune; associated with the lotus; consort of Vishnu

lama spiritual mentor

lathi bamboo stick with metal bindings, used by police

lattice screen of cross laths; perforated

linga(m) Shiva as the phallic emblem

Lokeshwar 'lord of the world'; Avalokiteshwar to Buddhists, and Shiva to Hindus

lungi wrapped-around loin cloth worn by men, often checked

M

Macchendra(nath) the guardian deity of the Kathmandu Valley, guarantor of rain and plenty; worshipped as the Rato (red) Macchendranath in Patan, and the Seto (white) Macchendranath in Bhaktapur

maha great

Mahabharata story of the great Bharatas; ancient Sanskrit epic about the battle between the Pandavas and the Kauravas

Mahabodhi great enlightenment of the Buddha

Mahadeva lit 'great lord'; Shiva

mahal palace, grand building

mahamandapam large enclosed hall in front of main shrine

maharaja 'great king'

maharani 'great queen'

Mahayana the 'greater vehicle' from Buddhism

mahseer large freshwater fish

Maitreya the future Buddha

makara crocodile-shaped mythical creature symbolizing the River Ganges

mandala geometric diagram symbolizing the structure of the universe, the basis of a temple plan; orders deities into pantheons

mandapa columned hall preceding the sanctuary of a temple

mandir temple

mani stones with sacred inscriptions at Buddhist sites (eg 'mani wall')

Manjushri legendary Buddhist patron of the Kathmandu Valley; god of learning; destroyer of falsehood and ignorance

mantra sacred chant for meditation by Hindus and Buddhists

Mara temptor who sent his daughters (and soldiers) to disturb the Buddha's meditation

marg wide roadway

masala spices

masjid mosque; lit 'palace of prostration'

math Hindu monastery

maya illusion

medallion circle or part-circle framing a figure or decorative motif

mela festival or fair

Meru axial mountain supporting the heavens

Mohammed 'the praised'; The Prophet, founder of Islam

moksha lit 'release'; salvation, enlightenment

monolith single block of stone shaped into a pillar or monument

moonstone the semi-circular stone step before a shrine (also chandrasila)

mukha mandapa hall for shrine

N

Naga snake deity; associated with fertility and protection

nal staircase

nal mandapa porch over a staircase

Namaste traditional greeting said with joined palms

Nandi a bull, Shiva's vehicle and a symbol of fertility

nandi mandapa portico or pavilion erected over the sacred bull

Narayana Vishnu as the creator of life

nata mandapa (nat mandir; nritya sala) dancing hall in a temple

Nataraj Shiva, lord of the cosmic dance, often portrayed dancing in a circle of fire

nath suffix to indicate divinity, or place

natya the art of dance

navagraha nine planets; represented usually on the lintel or architrave of the front door of a temple

navaranga central hall of temple

nirvana enlightenment; lit 'extinguished'

niwas small palace
nritya pure dance

O

obelisk tapering and usually monolithic shaft of stone with pyramidal axis
oriel projecting window

P

pada foot or base
padam dance which tells a story
padma lotus, moulding having the curves of the lotus petal (padmasana – lotus throne)
pagoda tall structure in several storeys
pahar hill
Pali ancient language derived from Sanskrit
panchayat 'council of five'; a government system of elected councils at local and regional levels; the system of national government introduced by King Mahendra in 1962
pandit teacher or wise man sometimes used as a title; a Sanskrit scholar
parapet wall extending above the roof
Parinirvana the Buddha's state prior to nirvana, shown usually as a reclining figure
Parvati daughter of the mountain; Shiva's consort, sometimes serene, sometimes fearful
pashmina a fine mountain goat's wool found mainly in NW India
Pashupati(nath) lit 'lord of the beasts'; Shiva; one of the principal deities of Nepal
paubha Newari word for thangka
pendant hanging, generally refers to a motif depicted upside down
peristyle range of columns surrounding a courtyard or temple
pilaster ornamental small column with capital and bracket
pinjra lattice work
pithasthana place of pilgrimage
pokhari pool, bathing tank
portico space enclosed between columns
pradakshina patha processional passage or ambulatory
pralaya the end of the world
prasad consecrated temple food offerings

puja ritual offerings to the gods; worship
punya merit earned through actions and religious devotion (Buddhist)
pukka solidly built, reliable; lit 'ripe' or 'finished'
Puranas Sanskrit sacred poems; lit 'the old'

R

Radha Krishna's favourite consort
raja ruler, king
rajbari palaces of a small kingdom
Rajput dynasties of west and central India
Rama 7th incarnation of Vishnu; hero of the *Ramayana* epic
rana warrior
ranga mandapa painted hall or theatre
rani queen
rath temple chariot; sometimes also refers to temple model
rekha curvilinear portion of a spire or shikhara
Rig Veda oldest and most sacred of the Vedas
Rimpoche blessed incarnation; abbot of a Tibetan Buddhist monastery
rishi 'seer'; inspired poet, philosopher or wise man

S

sabha columned hall (sabha madapa – assembly hall)
sadhu ascetic; religious mendicant, holy man
sal hardwood tree (*Shorea robusta*)
samadhi funerary memorial, like a temple but enshrining an image of the deceased
samsara eternal transmigration of souls
sangarama monastery
Sangha ascetic monastic order founded by the Buddha
sankha a shell, emblem of Vishnu
sanyasi wandering ascetic; final stage in the ideal life of a Hindu man
Saraswati wife of Brahma and goddess of knowledge; usually seated on a swan holding a veena
sarod Indian stringed musical instrument

Sati wife of Shiva who destroyed herself by fire; the act of self immolation on a husband's funeral pyre

satyagraha 'truth force'; passive resistance

serow a wild Himalayan antelope

Shaiva the cult of Shiva (Shaivite)

Shakti energy; female divinity often associated with Shiva; also a name of the cult

shaligram stone containing fossils worshipped as Vishnu

shaman animist priest, village doctor

Shankar Shiva

shastras ancient texts setting norms of conduct for temple architecture, use of images and worship

shikhara curved temple tower or spire

Shitala Mai a former ogress who became a protector of children; worshipped at Swayambhunath

Shiva the destroyer among Hindu gods; often worshipped as a lingam or phallic symbol

Shiva Ratri lit 'Shiva's night'; festival dedicated to Shiva

sindur vermillion powder often combined with mustard oil used in temple ritual; applied in the hair parting by some women to indicate married status

singh (sinha) lion; also Rajput caste name adopted by Sikhs

sirdar a guide, usually a Sherpa, who leads trekking groups

Sita Rama's wife, heroine of the *Ramayana* epic; worshipped by Hindus especially in Janakpur, her legendary birthplace

Skanda the Hindu god of war

soma sacred drink mentioned in the Vedas

soma sutra spout to carry away oblations in the shrine of a temple

sridhara pillar with an octagonal shaft and square base

stambha free-standing column or pillar, often with lamps or banners

stupa principal votive monument in a Buddhist religious complex; hemispherical funerary mound

stylobate base or sub-structure on which a colonnade is placed

Sudra the lowest of the Hindu castes

superstructure tower rising above sanctuary or gateway, roof above a hall

Surya the sun god

Swami Hindu holy man

swastika auspicious Hindu/Buddhist emblem

T

tahr wild mountain goat

tandava dance of Shiva

Tara historically the Nepali Princess Bhrikuti, now worshipped by tantric Buddhists and Hindus in Nepal particularly

terracotta burnt clay used as a building material and for pottery

thana police jurisdiction; police station

thangka traditional Tibetan religious painting on cloth, often silk (Nep – paubha)

tika (tilak) vermillion powder applied by Hindus to the forehead as a symbol of the divine; auspicious mark on the forehead

tole street

torana gateway with two posts linked by architraves

Trimurti the highest trinity of Hindu gods, Brahma, Vishnu and Shiva

trishul(a) trident, emblem of Shiva

tympanum triangular space within the cornices of a pediment

U

Uma Shiva's consort in one of her many forms

Upanishads ancient Sanskrit philosophical texts

V

vahana mandapa hall in which the vahanas or temple vehicles are stored

Vaishya the 'middle class' caste of merchants and farmers

Valmiki sage, author of the *Ramayana* epic

Vamana dwarf incarnation of Vishnu

Varaha boar incarnation of Vishnu

varna 'colour'; possible basis for social division of Hindus by caste

Veda (Vedic) oldest known Hindu religious texts

vedi altar, also a wall or screen

vihara Buddhist monastery with cells opening off a central court

vilas house or pleasure palace

vimana towered sanctuary containing the cell in which the temple deity is enshrined

Vishnu a principal Hindu deity; creator and preserver of the universal order; appears in 10 incarnations ('dashavatara')

W

wallah suffix often with an occupational name, eg rickshaw-wallah

Y

yagasala hall where the sacred fire is maintained and worshipped; place of sacrifice

yajna major ceremonial sacrifice

Yaksha semi-divine being, associated with nature in folk religion

Yama god of death, judge of the living; guardian of the south

yantra magical diagram used in meditation

yashti stick, pole or shaft (Buddhist)

Yogini mystical goddess

yoni a hole in a stone, symbolizing the vagina or the female principle

Index

Entries in bold refer to maps

L

FOOTPRINT

Features

About the author

Robert Ferguson first travelled to Nepal in 1984, aged 18, with a huge rucksack and tiny budget. He got a board and lodging job with a local trekking agency that finished with a trek around the Annapurna Circuit. He was hooked. He returned in his early 20s as a mountain guide, based in Kathmandu and leading groups around the Annapurnas, the Everest region and Kanchenjunga. He also climbed two of Nepal's trekking peaks.

For five years he ran his own trekking agency and also worked as the Operations Manager for a leading UK tour operator, running their Nepal trekking and cultural programmes. Being an Archaeology graduate from Durham University his passion for history and culture has led him to explore the Kathmandu Valley and beyond, visiting its many cultural gems.

The highlights of many trips there over the years are his honeymoon, which involved driving from Lhasa to Kathmandu, and a recent visit with his wife and teenage daughters, trekking in the Annapurnas, rafting and tiger watching in the Terai.

Robert lives in North Norfolk from where he runs a luxury tour operator and writes. He returns regularly to Nepal to explore new areas and visit old friends.

Acknowledgements

A guide is never the work of one or two individuals but a wide collaboration of many people. Primary amongst these is Robin Marston. It's not often you get to work with someone who helped shape the tourism of a country. Many of the areas visited and trails used by today's travellers were pioneered by Robin and his colleagues at Mountain Travel and Himalayan River Exploration. His suggestions, contacts, proofing and general background knowledge were a huge help in writing the guide, as was his trusty 4x4 in getting up some tracks I thought were going to defeat us. A thank you also to Wendy Marston for sharing her knowledge of the artisans and craftsmen of the Kathmandu Valley, the result of many years working with them on various stunning design projects.

An old friend from my younger trekking days Karma Sherpa Lama and his company Footloose in the Himalaya helped me with my logistics, supplying itineraries and he personally reacquainted me with the best restaurants in Kathmandu. A thank you also to Summit Trekking and Ace the Himalaya for helping ensure that trekking information and itineraries are current after the 2015 earthquake.

A thank you to Joe Parry and Andrew Tatton for accompanying me on a couple of my fact-finding trips, their assistance and support was much appreciated and allowed for much more ground to be covered than if I'd been travelling on my own.

On the Nepal side a final thank you to all the drivers, guides, hotel proprietors, restaurant owners and other people who were always so patient to answer my questions and to point me in the right direction.

As with any later edition of a guide I must thank the previous authors and contributors for creating the bedrock upon which this edition has be constructed. Some sections, such as the background on religion, carries a level of knowledge and expertise I could not have come near to replicating. I like to think that the old and new have fused seamlessly to create the best edition yet. And not forgetting the Footprint staff who get presented with a vast manuscript that they must make into an attractive and accessible book. How Felicity, Kevin and Emma manage it, I'll never know.

Credits

Footprint credits
Editor: Felicity Laughton
Production and layout: Emma Bryers
Maps: Kevin Feeney
Colour section: Angus Dawson

Publisher: Felicity Laughton
Marketing: Kirsty Holmes
Advertising and content partnerships: Debbie Wylde

Photography credits

Front cover: Curioso/Shutterstock.com
Back cover top: Nicram Sabod/Shutterstock.com
Back cover bottom: Pikoso.kz/Shutterstock.com
Inside front cover: Steve Davey.

Colour section
Page 1: Steve Davey. **Page 2**: lzf/Shutterstock.com. **Page 4**: Alexander Mazurkevich/Shutterstock.com, MOROZ NATALIYA/Shutterstock.com **Page 5**: Steve Davey, Arturo Cano Miño/Superstock.com. **Page 6**: natalia_maroz/Shutterstock.com, Hakat/Shutterstock.com. **Page 7**: Alexander Mazurkevich/Shutterstock.com, Zzvet/Shutterstock.com. **Page 8**: Hakat/Shutterstock.com. **Page 9**: Lucio Braga/Shutterstock.com, Utopia_88/Shutterstock.com. **Page 10**: Steve Davey. **Page 11**: Steve Davey. **Page 12**: Steve Davey, Alex Treadway/Superstock.com. **Page 13**: Steve Davey. **Page 14**: Efimova Anna/Shutterstock.com, Vladimir Zhoga/Shutterstock.com. **Page 15**: Tomas 1962/Shutterstock.com. **Page 16**: Steve Davey.

Duotones
Page 38: evenfh/Shutterstock.com.
Page 98: Skreidzeleu/Shutterstock.com.
Page 124: CRSHELARE/Shutterstock.com.
Page 148: Belozorova Elena/Shutterstock.com.
Page 192: Muslianshah Masrie/Shutterstock.com.
Page 216: chariya chaisu/Shutterstock.com.
Page 246: Steve Weisberg/Shutterstock.com.
Page 278: Vadim Petrakov/Shutterstock.com.
Page 296: JNShea/Shutterstock.com.
Page 318: Daniel Prudek/Shutterstock.com.

Publishing information
Footprint Nepal
3rd edition
© Footprint Handbooks Ltd
March 2017

ISBN: 978 1 911082 11 8
CIP DATA: A catalogue record for this book is available from the British Library

® Footprint Handbooks and the Footprint mark are a registered trademark of Footprint Handbooks Ltd

Published by Footprint
5 Riverside Court
Lower Bristol Road
Bath BA2 3DZ, UK
T +44 (0)1225 469141
footprinttravelguides.com

Distributed in the USA by
National Book Network, Inc.

Printed in Serbia by Grafostil

Every effort has been made to ensure that the facts in this guidebook are accurate. However, travellers should still obtain advice from consulates, airlines, etc about travel and visa requirements before travelling. The authors and publishers cannot accept responsibility for any loss, injury or inconvenience however caused.